RHETORICAL STYLE

Rhetorical Style

THE USES OF LANGUAGE IN PERSUASION

Jeanne Fahnestock

OXFORD
UNIVERSITY PRESS

OXFORD
UNIVERSITY PRESS

Oxford University Press, Inc., publishes works that further
Oxford University's objective of excellence
in research, scholarship, and education.

Oxford   New York
Auckland   Cape Town   Dar es Salaam   Hong Kong   Karachi
Kuala Lumpur   Madrid   Melbourne   Mexico City   Nairobi
New Delhi   Shanghai   Taipei   Toronto

With offices in
Argentina   Austria   Brazil   Chile   Czech Republic   France   Greece
Guatemala   Hungary   Italy   Japan   Poland   Portugal   Singapore
South Korea   Switzerland   Thailand   Turkey   Ukraine   Vietnam

Copyright © 2011 by Oxford University Press, Inc.

Published by Oxford University Press, Inc.
198 Madison Avenue, New York, New York 10016

www.oup.com

Oxford is a registered trademark of Oxford University Press

Library of Congress Cataloging-in-Publication Data
Fahnestock, Jeanne
Rhetorical style : the uses of language in persuasion / Jeanne Fahnestock.
p.   cm.
Includes bibliographical references and index.
ISBN 978-0-19-976412-9 (hardcover : alk. paper)—ISBN 978-0-19-976411-2 (pbk. : alk. paper)
1. Persuasion (Rhetoric)   2. English language—Rhetoric.   3. English language—Style.   I. Title.
P301.5.P47F34 2011
808'.042—dc22   2010053171

Printed in the United States of America
on acid-free paper

To Stephen

Table of Contents

Introduction 3

    Style in the Rhetorical Tradition 6

    Schools of Language Analysis 9

    Rhetorical Stylistics and Literary Stylistics 12

    Plan of the Book 13

    Source of Examples 16

    What This Book Is Not—and Is 17

    Notes 19

PART ONE | WORD CHOICE

1. Language of Origin 23

    The Historical Layers of English 23

    The Old English Core 24

    The Norman French Contribution 25

    The Language of Learning from Latin and Greek 27

    Incorporations from World Contact 29

    An American Vocabulary 30

    Homonyms and Synonyms from Different Origins 31

    Clarity and Sincerity: When Core Words Dominate 32

    Elevation and Panache: Featuring French Borrowings 33

    Formality and Erudition: Words from Latin and Greek 34

    Analyses with Word Origins 35

    Summary 39

    Notes 40

2. *New Words and Changing Uses* 42

    From Nonce Constructions to Wider Use 42

      1. Foreign Borrowings 43

      2. Compounds 44

        Free versus Bound Morphemes 45

      3. Adding Prefixes and Suffixes 45

        Prefixes that Change Meaning 45

        Suffixes that Change Use 46

        Derivational Families 46

      4. Clipping 47

      5. Blends 47

      6. Conversions 48

      7. Catachresis 49

      8. Acronyms 50

      9. Proper Names to Common Nouns 50

      10. Analogy 50

      11. Fabrication 51

      12. Onomatopoeia 51

      13. Taboo Deformation 52

      14. Doubling 52

    Loss and Migration 53

    Junk: A Case Study 54

    Accumulating Senses 57

    Summary 58

    Notes 59

3. *Categories of Word Choice* 61

    Lexical Field 62

    Level of Generality 63

    Abstract versus Concrete Diction 64

    Levels of Generality in Argument 66

    Ad Hoc Levels of Generality 68

    Functional Categories 70

    Taking a Census of Parts of Speech 70

    Modern Rhetoricians on Word Choice: Burke and Weaver 75

    Summary 76

    Notes 77

4. *Language Varieties* 79

    Low, Middle, and High 80

    Geographical and Social Varieties of English 81

Regiolects and Sociolects 82

Idiolects 83

Registers: Occupation, Avocation, Discipline 83

Genre and Register 85

Shifting and Mixing Language Varieties 86

Language Varieties and Humor 88

Spoken versus Written Style 90

Familiar Language 91

Prepared Phrases, Clichés, and Idioms 92

Maxims and Proverbs 94

Allusions 95

Summary 96

Notes 97

5. *Tropes* 100

Synecdoche 101

Metonymy 102

Antonomasia 103

Metaphor 104

Extended Metaphor and Allegory 107

Simile 109

Full Analogies 110

Irony 111

Irony in Written Texts 112

Irony and Intention 114

The Persuasive Effects of Irony 115

Intolerable Irony 116

Hyperbole and Litotes 117

The Amphiboly and Paradox 118

Paralepsis/Praeteritio: Denying while Saying 119

Grice's Maxims and the Detection of Other Meanings 120

Analysis: Women Drivers 121

Summary 122

Notes 123

6. *Figures of Word Choice* 127

Schemes of Words 127

Agnominatio 127

Metaplasms: Altering a Single Word 129

Polyptoton 130

Spreading Concepts through Polyptoton 132

Etymological Arguments 132

Ploce 133

Antanaclasis (Puns) 134

The Presence of the Word 135

Figures of Sound 136

Figures of Word Selection 137

Synonyms (Synonymia) 137

    Synonyms and Conceptual Drift 138

    Euphemism 139

Correctio 139

Emphasis (Significatio) 140

Summary 141

Notes 142

PART II | SENTENCES

7. *Sentence Basics: Predication* 147

    Active versus Stative Predication 148

    Subject Choices 149

        1. Humans 149

        2. Rhetorical Participants 150

        3. Things 150

        4. Abstractions 151

        5. Concepts 152

        6. Slot Fillers 152

    Analyzing Subject Choices 152

    Verb Choices 154

        1. Tense 154

        2. Aspect 156

        3. Mood 156

        4. Negation 157

        5. Modality 158

        6. Active versus Passive Voice 159

            In Defense of the Passive 160

        7. Semantic Categories 162

    Analyzing Verb Choices 163

    Subject/Verb Analysis 164

    The North Pole 164

    A Trend at New Trier 166

    Nominal versus Verbal Style 168

    Nominalizations 169

    Personification (*Personae Fictio*) 170

Personification in Science 171

Multiplying Subjects and Verbs 172

Summary 174

Notes 175

8. *Sentence Construction: Modification* 178

Adverb Clauses 179

Adjective Clauses 180

Noun Clauses 182

The Consequences of Clause Types: Kennedy's Options 182

Modifying with Phrases 183

Phrases Built on Verbs 184

  Participial Phrases 184

  Infinitive Phrases 186

Phrases Built on Nouns 187

  Appositives 187

  Absolute Phrases 188

  Resumptive Modifiers 188

  Summative Modifiers 189

Prepositional Phrases 189

Single-Word Modifiers 190

An Epithetical Style 191

Multiplying and Embedding Modifiers 192

Amount of Modification 194

Minimal Modification 194

Heavily Modified Styles 195

Analyzing Modification 196

The Ubiquitous Saddam 197

"To the People of Ireland" 198

Summary 199

Notes 200

9. *Sentence Architecture* 203

Emphasis 203

Emphasis by Position 205

Emphasis by Sentence Role 206

Emphasis from Inversions 207

Combining Sources of Emphasis 208

Placement of Modifiers: Branching Left, Right, and in the Middle 208

Loose and Periodic Sentences 210

Periodic Sentences 210

Loose Sentences 211
A Periodic Style 212
A Loose Style 213
Composition 214
Iconic Form 215
Absence in Words, Presence in Syntax 217
The Default Form/Meaning Relationship 219
Summary 220
Notes 221

10. *Figures of Argument* 223
    Parallelism 224
    In Syllables (Isocolon) 224
    In Stress Patterns 225
    In Grammatical Structure (Parison) 225
    From Repetition 226
    Uses of Parallelism in Argument 226
        Comparison 226
    Induction 227
        Eduction 228
    Strategic Repetition 230
    Antithesis: Argument from Opposites 231
    Antimetabole: Argument from Inversion 233
    Definition as a Figure 235
    Summary 237
    Notes 237

11. *Series* 239
    Definition of a Series 240
    Series and Categorization 241
    Bracketing 242
    Series and Order 243
    Item Length and Order 245
    Gradatio 246
    Series and Conjunctions 246
    The Overall Length of Series 248
    Opening Up or Shutting Down 249
    Summary 250
    Notes 251

12. *Prosody and Punctuation* 253
    Speech and Writing 254

Prosody 255

Prosody into Punctuation 257

Printing and Punctuation 259

Punctuation and Meaning 264

Figured Prosody 266

Passage Prosody 267

Variety in Sentence Length 269

Summary 271

Notes 272

PART III | INTERACTIVE DIMENSION

13. *Speaker and Audience Construction* 277

Pronouns 279

Uses of I 280

Uses of You 281

I to *You*: Genres of Fictional Address 283

Uses of We 284

The Objective Voice 286

Changing Footing: Managing the Interactive Dimension 287

Pronoun Analysis: Lincoln's First Inaugural 288

Disidentification 290

Figures of Speaker/Audience Construction 291

Calling on: Apostrophe 291

Partitioning the Audience 293

Purging the Audience 295

Frankness of Speech: Licentia 296

Figuring Speech Acts 297

Asking and Answering Questions 298

Rogatio and Formal Arguments 301

Summary 302

Notes 303

14. *Incorporating Other Voices* 306

Direct Speech 307

The Stylization of Direct Speech 309

Indirect Speech 311

Ambiguous Zones in Indirect Speech 311

Reporting Speech Acts 314

Representing Thoughts 315

Texts as Speakers and "Text Acts" 315

Invented Speakers 316

Double Voicing and Heteroglossia 319

Multivoicing: The Blogger's Specialty 321

Summary 322

Notes 323

15. *Situation and Occasion* 325

Immediate Deixis 325

Thematizing Deixis 327

Immediate Deixis in Written Texts 328

Occasion 329

Constructing Situations and Occasions 331

Exigence in Written Texts 332

The Burkean Scene 333

Imaginary Deixis 334

Demonstratio *and* Descriptio 335

Description and Emotion 336

Ekphrasis: The Stand-Alone Description 337

Summary 339

Notes 340

PART IV | PASSAGE CONSTRUCTION

16. *Coherence* 345

Signs of Cohesion 346

Given/New or Topic/Comment Patterns 348

Interrupting the Topic String 351

Schemas and Coherence 352

Interclause Meaning Relations 355

Inferred Relations 357

Signaled Relations 359

Combining Sources of Coherence 360

Summary 362

Appendix: Interclause Meaning Relations 363

Notes 370

17. *Passage Patterns* 372

Compositional Units in the Rhetorical Tradition 373

Syllogism and Enthymeme 374

Progymnasmatic Patterns 378

Comparison in Different Grain Sizes 379

Paragraphs 381

Parataxis and Hypotaxis 382

Metadiscourse: Figures of Discourse Management 384

Summary 386

Notes 387

18. *Amplification* 390

Quintilian's Methods of Amplification 391

Analysis with Quintilian's Methods 393

Copia and Presence: *Multa de Multis* 394

Erasmian Methods for Copia 396

Epicheireme 399

Diminishing 402

Amplification and the Sublime 404

The Last Paragraph of *On the Origin of Species* 405

On Darwin's Word Choices 407

On Darwin's Sentence Architecture 408

On Darwin's Passage Construction 410

On Darwin's Amplification and Interaction with Readers 411

Summary 414

Notes 415

References 419

Index 435

RHETORICAL STYLE

INTRODUCTION

IN 1984, AN archivist for the U.S. Congress discovered a text that had been missing for forty-three years: the "podium" copy of the speech President Franklin D. Roosevelt delivered on December 8, 1941, asking Congress to declare war on Japan. Roosevelt had evidently left this copy behind in the House of Representatives, and it had been duly filed away. This typed version of the President's address contains four corrections in his handwriting, and during the actual delivery, Roosevelt made several more changes. These continuing adjustments to the exact wording of his text represent the last stages of a process of revision that began the preceding day, shortly after news of the attack on Pearl Harbor, when Roosevelt dictated the first version to his typist Grace Tully, complete with punctuation marks, and then began to work over the language. Below are the opening sentences of that dictated first draft with the changes that Roosevelt made by hand.[1]

infamy –

Yesterday, December 7, 1941, – a date which will live in ~~world history~~, ₍ₐ₎

suddenly

the United States of America was ~~simultaneously~~ and deliberately attacked by

~~without warning~~

naval and air forces of the Empire of Japan. ₍ₐ₎

at the solicitation of Japan

The United States was at the moment at peace with that nation and ₍ₐ₎ was

still in
~~continuing the~~ conversations with its Government and its Emperor looking toward the maintenance of peace in the Pacific. Indeed, one hour after Japanese air
Oahu
squadrons had commenced bombing in ~~Hawaii and the Philippines~~, the Japanese Ambassador to the United States and his colleague delivered to the Secretary of
recent American   While
State a formal reply to a ~~former~~ message, ~~from the secretary.~~ This reply
stated   it seemed useless to continue the existing
~~contained a statement~~ that diplomatic negotiations ~~must be considered at an end~~
it   or   war or
~~but~~ contained no threat ~~and no~~ hint of an armed attack.
It will be recorded that the distance~~s of Manila, and especially~~ of Hawaii,
s   was
from Japan make it obvious that the~~se~~ attack~~s were~~ deliberately planned many
or even weeks
days ago.

How can the language of both FDR's original phrasing and his changes be described? And what further principles of analysis can account for his stylistic decisions and his second thoughts? Any description of his language will depend on what the describer is prepared to notice, and any explanation of the features noticed will depend on the analyst's preferences for what counts as a satisfactory explanatory rationale. One obvious rationale would consider Roosevelt's language based on his purpose. Roosevelt wants Congress to pass a declaration of war (or actually acknowledge a state of war), and he has to give them reasons for doing so. At the same time, in a speech broadcast live on radio, he is addressing the entire nation, and he must also secure their support for war and for the coming sacrifices. His text is a means to accomplish these goals. It is, in the ancient and enduring sense of the word, *rhetorical*, constructed to have an impact on the attitudes, beliefs, and actions of its audiences. And while justifying a declaration of war after an attack may seem an easy goal given the circumstances, nevertheless an argument had to be made explicitly and war had to be declared formally.

Roosevelt's opening strategy for accomplishing his purpose is, first, to amplify the treachery of the enemy, a common move in deliberative speeches calling for war. His language choices in the passage above can be assessed against that particular strategy. It is therefore not surprising that he opens by citing what is on everyone's mind, the attack of the day before, and his choice of passive voice in his first sentence correctly makes the United States, while filling the role of grammatical subject, nevertheless the recipient and victim, while Japan is the agent: *the United States…was…attacked…by…the forces of the Empire of Japan* (Jasinski 2001, 13). Of all the options for naming the target, Roosevelt did not at this point choose *Pearl Harbor* or *Oahu* or *Hawaii*; he named the entire nation collectively and formally—*the United States of America*—since, collectively and formally, a unified nation had to respond.

The opening words of Roosevelt's first sentence locate the attack in time in a series of renamings ordered by their expanding perspective (Stelzner 1993, 111). The first word, *Yesterday*, places the crucial event in terms of the present moment for Roosevelt and his listeners; it happened on their *yesterday*. The second identifying phrase gives the precise date of the attack, *December 7, 1941*, widening the temporal location to a calendar address that will not change when it is no longer yesterday. The third appositive identifies this *date* in a new and still wider frame of reference. Here Roosevelt's first and most stunning revision occurs in naming this final location: his replacing *world history* with *infamy*. A word that came into English from Norman French, *infamie* (originally meaning "dishonor" or "ill repute") carries the military and even chivalric associations of many such French-sourced terms, and it arguably has greater force than a more familiar alternative like Old English *shame* or a less familiar one like the Latin *perfidy*.[2] The term also fits well in its grammatical place in the sentence as the third and final in the series of locations. In the first version, the attack is lodged in the storehouse of *world history*. As a destination, *world history* does serve Roosevelt's argument as a standard of evaluation: this attack ranks with other similar acts of treachery significant enough to be recorded in world history, and this ranking justifies a declaration of war in response. The revision to *infamy* replaces this standard with a vaguer but much more powerful one, a qualitative measure of heinousness transposed into a place, like a reserved spot in Dante's hell where acts of evil live forever. To highlight this new standard, Roosevelt, ever mindful of prosodic effects, also changed the punctuation around this third appositive, replacing the commas with dashes to remind himself to set this third phrase off from the rest of the sentence. In speaking, these slightly longer pauses before and after emphasize an internal sentence element that might not otherwise receive emphasis from its mid-sentence position. Altogether, in his opening phrases, Roosevelt amplifies the attack with a series whose items increase in length and significance, precisely the method of heightening recommended by Quintilian two thousand years ago (see chapter 18).

Many of Roosevelt's other changes in this opening follow from his second thoughts about citing the attack on the Philippines along with the attack on Hawaii. The air assault on the Philippines occurred several hours after the attack on Pearl Harbor (causing a subsequent controversy about lack of preparation), and Roosevelt first paired them as attacks on U.S. territories and forces. But he later made a significant decision, perhaps as more military intelligence came in, to argue by partitioning events differently, isolating the attack on *Oahu* from all the others that occurred that day; in a subsequent draft, these are all mentioned in a dramatic listing of Japan's multiple targets (see below, p. 227). In his actual delivery, Roosevelt added the identifying epithet *the American Island of* before *Oahu*, an identification that is both geographical and patriotic. Roosevelt's strategy of heightening this one much more devastating attack—the one earlier, first reported, and closer to home—fixes his audiences on the single event they were already aware of and neither divides their attention nor complicates their outrage. Amplification through quantity will come later in the speech. Having made the decision to focus, Roosevelt crosses out a *simultaneously* that no longer applies, though he still wants the cadence of the multisyllabic double adverbs and wisely chooses *suddenly* instead. He also needs to change the two calculations of distance, from Manila and Hawaii, to one, and the multiple attacks become *the attack* planned not only days but *even weeks* ago.

Much more could be said about Roosevelt's language in relation to his argument. His many constitutive choices deserve mention, such as his use of static linking verb constructions in the second sentence or the agentless *it seemed* in the fourth. But to focus only on changes, his crossing out of *without warning* removes the redundancy with *suddenly*, and it also preserves the end-of-sentence emphasis on the first mention of the enemy, notably named more formally with the longer and more significant sounding epithetical name, *the Empire of Japan* (changed again in delivery). Also, because the first paragraph grounds treachery in hypocrisy, Roosevelt must tell a complicated story of peace negotiations initiated by an enemy intent on war and of diplomatic memos exchanged while an attack was underway. To simplify, he removes the confusing and too alliterative *formal reply to a former message from*, dropping in *American* in the process. And he wisely changes the entire architecture of the last sentence of the first paragraph, from a single independent clause with parallel verbs (*this reply contained a statement... but contained no threat*) to a sentence with an opening adverbial clause delivering the qualifications, followed by the main clause carrying the main point about what the message did not contain, *no threat or hint of war or armed attack*, a phrasing that balances symmetrical doubles around the preposition *of*. This prosodically satisfying final phrase also delivers an *a fortiori* argument, defined in rhetorical manuals as a comparison argument from the lesser or the greater. Since the second item in each pair is the lesser of the two, the construction is understood as furthering the case for the enemy's duplicity by pointing out that they did not indicate their true intent or even some lesser version of it: they did not threaten "or even" *hint* at war "or even" at *armed attack*. Without a glimpse of this underlying argument, there is otherwise no explanation for the downstep in each pair.

Style in the Rhetorical Tradition

The brief and partial comments offered here on how Roosevelt's revisions to his words, sentences, and sounds construct his argument derive primarily from the body of rhetorical thinking on persuasion and language that is the product of over two thousand years of reflection in the west. Beginning in Greece in the fourth and fifth centuries BCE, producers and then commentators identified and codified features of language that might enhance its power over audiences. Early landmarks in attention to effective style include the display orations of the sophists Gorgias and Isocrates and the observations on language in the third book of Aristotle's *Rhetoric*. Advice on effective expression (*lexis* in

Greek, *elocutio* in Latin) eventually became one of the canons or parts of the rhetorical curriculum, following behind *invention* (the discovery of content and especially of lines of argument), *judgment* (the selection of content appropriate for the situation), and *arrangement* (the ordering of the selected parts for the audience and situation) and preceding *memory* (the internalization of a text for recall) and *delivery* (the management of voice and body). But of all the parts of rhetoric, style is arguably the most implicated in the others, since linguistic choice is the point of realization for the rhetorical precepts and theories belonging to the other canons.

Before students turned to the study of rhetoric, they first had to achieve fluency in reading and composing. From antiquity to the seventeenth century, that meant mastery of either Latin or Greek or both, a second and third language for many students. (Greek was the language of advanced rhetorical training for Romans.) In the classical system of education, language competence was acquired under the *grammaticus*, the professional teacher of higher literacy who introduced his pupils to the parts of speech, to declensions and inflections, to constitutive and preferential rules of sentence formation, and to a "starter set" of the figures of speech. The medium for this instruction was the close reading of the great epics, the *Iliad, Odyssey,* and *Aeneid.* Young boys pored over these texts. They parsed every word by its part of speech and grammatical role. They learned etymologies and the histories of words, which were coined or archaic, and what each offered compared to possible synonyms. They identified the meter required by the line as well as every figural device. The basics of language taught at this level were codified in grammars such as those surviving from late antiquity by Donatus and Priscian. In many ways, the grammarians' descriptive view of language, largely a product of curricular consolidation by Hellenistic scholars, postdates the rhetorician's purpose-driven view. But their program of tuition in linguistic fluency and cultural literacy preceded and supported and continued into further rhetorical studies (Cribiore 2001). Advice about style in the rhetorical tradition builds on a mastery of language basics while preparing the student for life as an active citizen.

The rhetorical tradition in the West offers hundreds of texts defining, listing, grouping, and exemplifying strategic language choices, choices always tied to the rhetor's developing arguments, self-presentation, and audience appeals. In different eras, the rhetorical canon of style has expanded (notably in the sixteenth century) or contracted (notably in the early twentieth century), but it has never disappeared. Most of its recommendations have been remarkably enduring and *trans*lingual, and devices identified in the Latin *Rhetorica ad Herennium* of 80 BCE can easily be identified in contemporary discourse. Though virtually every text in the rhetorical tradition has had its say on style, the key texts from antiquity include Aristotle's *Rhetoric* (fourth century BCE), Cicero's treatises on the art and the *Rhetorica ad Herennium* (first century BCE), and Quintilian's *Institutio Oratoria* (first century CE). The stylistic constructs, categories, and devices first recorded in these works have been repeated, refracted, and enriched in a host of texts in every succeeding century, from the style manuals of late antiquity to those of the twentieth century.

A high point, even to some extent a new beginning, occurred in the early modern recovery of ancient rhetoric, when attention to style was spurred by the humanists' desire for phil-ological accuracy and Ciceronian eloquence. This fifteenth- and sixteenth-century revival of rhetoric accommodated newly found and improved classical sources and eventually adapted their advice to contemporary European languages. Early modern texts devoted to style, and especially to the figures of speech, are also important sources for the rhetor-ical study of style, including Erasmus's *De Copia* (1512–1530), Susenbrotus's *Epitome Troporum ac Schematum* (1541), Melanchthon's *Elementorum Rhetorices* (1542), and, among English accommodations, Peacham's *The Garden of Eloquence* (1593) and Hoskins' *Directions for Speech and Style* (ca. 1600). The eighteenth century also offers penetrating treatments of persuasive language, from the Italian jurist and philosopher Giambattista Vico (ca. 1740) to the rhetoricians of the Scottish Enlightenment, including George Campbell (1776) and Hugh Blair (1783). These are particularly rich sources, but no age has been without its commentators on style; even the second half of the twentieth century saw the monumental *La nouvelle rhétorique/The New Rhetoric* (1958/1969) of Chaïm Perelman and Lucie Olbrechts-Tyteca renew the argument/language connection. Each new text across the centuries has selected or deleted from the common stock, offering intriguing revisions and changes in emphasis, as well as fresh examples and applications that keep the tradition current and always relevant.

The main benefit of such a rhetorically inflected stylistics is its connection with advice on persuasion and with argument analysis. Rhetorical theory presents a rich array of methods for understanding actual arguments, spoken or written—from the genres of persuasion and taxonomy of issues to the special and common lines of argument or *topoi*, and from the overall arrangement of a case and the potential parts of a full oration to its management in small-scale units or moves. All this theoretical superstructure, codified from actual practice, was put at the service of the individual case and the constraints of time, place, and persons. Rhetoricians, furthermore, always took into account the inex-plicitness of real-world arguments and the audience's role in filling in and filling out.

This book offers methods of language analysis derived from the rhetorical tradition. It uses the descriptive categories standard in rhetorical treatments of style involving still familiar matters of word choice and sentence construction, since rhetoric's treatment of language informs much of what is still taught about language. But rhetoric's attention to style also identifies structures below the sentence level (e.g., repeated phrases or minor switches in word order), as well as multisentence structures that emerge across passages, the most neglected level of analysis. These features are then linked to the argumentative moves they can perform. In other words, rhetorical stylistics provides a point for making choices, or observations of others' choices, in the first place. To offer an example: seman-ticists (and dialecticians long before them) traditionally describe differences in levels of generality in the lexicon: *bird* is more general than *robin, family member* than *mother, commodity* than *wheat.* But what function is served in switching between "abstract" and less abstract or "concrete" terms in a particular text? One answer merely restates the device: to change the scope of reference. Another answer is found in the observations of the second-century BCE rhetorician Hermagoras of Temnos, reported by Cicero (1942, 357) and Quintilian (1921, II 399–401). They note that propositions for argument can be general (labeled a *thesis* in Greek) or particular (labeled a *hypothesis,* literally a lower thesis). This difference yields issues or questions at different levels of generality such as, to adapt one of Quintilian's examples, "Should a citizen participate in government?" versus "Should you take a position as Commissioner of Sewers in this administration?" Quintilian, and Erasmus following him fifteen hundred years later, noted that the more comprehensive *thesis* includes the *hypothesis* and that arguing for the former can help as support for the latter, the particular *hypothesis* usually being the point in contention. Obviously, switches in the level of generality of word choice often mark the places where an arguer pursues the *thesis/hypothesis* strategy (see chapter 3).

A stylistics drawn from the rhetorical tradition also adds to the vocabulary of language analysis. Here the richest source of descriptive concepts comes from the figures of speech. Lists of such devices appear as early as the first century BCE, and catalogues of the figures expanded dramatically in the early modern period. Analysts, however, are rarely grateful for new terms, and impatience with the lexicon of rhetorical stylistics in all its polysyllabic Greek and Latin splendor has been particularly sharp. But if a terminology helps to bring useful distinctions to attention, it is certainly worth keeping. This text includes many figures of speech that arguably do make useful distinctions; some of these are well known, others not. But the figures are introduced and explained in a somewhat novel way. They are dispersed throughout the book, and chapters or digressions on the figures follow accounts of unmarked or default language features. There is, for example, a well-known set of methods in English for forming a new word or altering its function by adding an affix to a root. When two or three such derivatives or inflections are deployed in a single sentence or short passage (e.g., *the gift that keeps on giving*), they constitute the figural move identified in antiquity as *polyptoton,* a device noted since Aristotle as the linguistic signature of a particular line of argument (see chapter 6). So the tongue-twisting labels for the figures are often worth retaining, as are many other insights into functional style that can be found in rhetorical manuals. The guiding motive for this book is that all this material, this heritage, is too valuable and interesting to ignore.

Schools of Language Analysis

Despite the rich and enduring legacy of rhetorical approaches to style, many if not most scholars who analyze language today do not in fact consciously draw on the rhetorical tradition. With the exception of some self-declared rhetorical scholars, most language-conscious academics are more likely to identify with linguistic approaches to language study or to consult linguistics and its subdisciplines for methods of language analysis. If asked to date the origins of their discipline, most linguists would probably pick a point in time in the last two hundred years. Some might point to the great philologists of the eighteenth and nineteenth centuries who traced the histories of the European languages, reconstructed Indo-European, and decoded ancient languages. Others might cite Ferdinand de Saussure, who in the early twentieth century dissociated the study of the system of language, *langue*, from its use, *parole*, and identified the former as the true object of scientific study. Linguists are not likely, at any rate, to graft their discipline directly onto the older rhetorical tradition. This discontinuity is justified, since linguistics, in many of its various schools, has as its goal an account of "language in general," of invariant constitutive features in and across languages, of language acquisition by children and second language learners, and, more recently, of language in the mind, the sign and medium of cognition.

There are, however, branches of linguistics that overlap with the functional approach to style found in rhetoric. The subdisciplines of pragmatics, discourse analysis, and sociolinguistics are all ultimately concerned with language in use, and hence they inevitably identify communicative features. Pragmaticists, for instance, who focus primarily on spoken discourse in nonscripted settings, have developed an elaborate taxonomy of the turn-taking rituals used in spontaneous conversational exchanges. Discourse analysts, who may work with spoken or written texts, describe the consistent features of practical genres as well as devices of passage construction. Sociolinguists compile language features characteristic of groups, whether defined by region, race, occupation, or interactive setting. All these disciplines grew up without any connection to the centuries-long tradition of rhetoric. Sociolinguistics has worked in tandem with anthropology; pragmatics and discourse analysis were animated in part by the speech act theory of the natural language philosophers J. L. Austin and John Searle, who brought to attention the performative dimension of language, the actions accomplished by speakers through their words.

Though they share with rhetoric an interest in "language in use," sociolinguistics, discourse analysis, and pragmatics have as their starting point a general notion of interactive discourse and not the more specific rhetorical notion of planned discourse intended as persuasive with specific audiences in specific settings. One of their preferred objects of analysis is spontaneous, "naturally" occurring conversation, caught on tape or video. They have therefore largely ignored the rhetorical taxonomy of genres and rhetoric's focus on argumentation. But despite their dissimilarities in origin and purpose, these disciplines offer insights that can add substantially to rhetorical stylistics. They begin from a fresh perspective and intersect "the plane of study" from a new angle. So, for example, while ancient Latin grammarians like Donatus and Priscian did require the identification of all the constituents of a sentence, including the subject and verb, the attention to whether the subject is also an *agent,* that is an active *doer* of the action named by the verb, is a recent emphasis used in text analysis by contemporary grammarians and discourse analysts. The linguistics originating from M. A. K. Halliday, which promotes such "transitivity analysis," is only one of the approaches to language developed in the twentieth century that offer rhetorical scholars an enriched view of the persuasive potential of ordinary language.

Paul Hopper (2007) notes a growing convergence between the discourse disciplines and the rhetorical tradition. A recent anthology edited by Barbara Johnstone and Christopher Eisenhart offers applications of linguistic methods to informal genres, to "rhetoric on the street" and online (2008, 4). Other scholars, whose point of departure is their interest in argumentation, have turned the tools of linguistics and discourse analysis on argumentative language.[3] The pragma-dialectical school of Franz van Eemeren and his collaborators in the Netherlands (Rob Grootendorst, Peter Houtlosser, Francisca Snoeck Henkemans, and Bart Garssen) has perhaps pushed the farthest in this endeavor. From their focus on discussions that aim at resolving differences, they have aggressively pursued a complete system of explanation for dialogic and monologic argument that includes linguistic analysis (van Eemeren et al., 1996) and, more recently, an incorporation of the rhetorical tradition (van Eemeren and Houtlosser, 2002). Among contemporary French scholars, the linguists Jean-Claude Anscombre and Oswald Ducrot have developed a fine-scale analysis of argumentative language, especially of the single-word *operators* and *connectors* that can give any sliver of text an edge of "argumentativity" (1983). At the University of Leiden, an interdisciplinary group including Arie Verhagen, Maarten van Leeuwen, J. C. de Jong, and Suzanne Fagel, is uniting linguistic, literary, and rhetorical approaches to language under the rubric of stylistics. Still another movement applying discourse analysis to argumentative texts is pursued at the University of Tel Aviv by the research group ADARR (Analyse du discours, Argumentation et Rhétorique) led by Ruth Amossy along with Roselyne Koren, which examines the particularities of persuasive prose, its markers and distinctive features, using the methods of discourse analysis and linguistics. Finally, scholars with a focused interest in political discourse take an approach known as critical discourse analysis (e.g., van Dijk, Fairclough, Chilton). Their goal is ideological critique informed by the methods of discourse analysis.

Still another linguistic subfield rich in possibilities for intersection with the rhetorical tradition is corpus linguistics. This branch of study uses large searchable databases of oral and written texts, such as the 1.5-million-word British National Corpus (BNC) and the 3.5-million-word Corpus of Contemporary American English (COCA). These storehouses of sampled usage provide evidence of the dominance of fixed phrases (suprasegmentals) in actual usage, and, in recent theorizing, of the radical linearity of language.

Another emerging orientation is "cognitive linguistics," a confederation of approaches that emphasize the mental processes underlying language features, including rationales based on the physical and "embodied" determinants of the conceptual systems realized in a language. Descriptive cognitive approaches link up with the discipline that will eventually underwrite all the others, namely psycholinguistics or, as it is sometimes called more recently, neurolinguistics. Researchers in this field seek an understanding of how language is produced and interpreted in the physical brain, and to that end they conduct controlled experiments on selected subjects with various prompts and, increasingly, with neural imaging of the brain during language processing. Results from this field have, for example, shown the extensive involvement of different areas of the brain in ordinary comprehension, overturning earlier claims for extreme localization. The insights of the ancient rhetoricians on how, for example, sound patterns like *isocolon* (phrases of equal length) can have attention-riveting effects underpinning the acceptance of content, should someday receive explanations in terms of the brain's physical processing of these segments. Every week, intriguing new research is reported, though the uses of such "ultimate" explanations for those forming or analyzing arguments may be limited.

RHETORICAL STYLISTICS AND LITERARY STYLISTICS

There is one other very active enterprise of language analysis that needs to be distinguished from rhetorical stylistics. In contrast to rhetoricians who focus on texts that influence the attitudes and actions of their audiences, those who study literature attend to texts (fiction, poetry, drama) prized ultimately for their aesthetic value and uniqueness. Though most current scholars in fact read literary texts for their political and ideological import, as representations of times and people, most would still grant literary works a special status. The study of this special status in terms of language goes by the name *stylistics*, minus any modifier. This stylistics, a *literary stylistics*, identifies the signature language manipulations of the literary artist. Stylistics informed by linguistics, for some the functional-systemic linguistics of M. A. K. Halliday, is energetically pursued in Great Britain and Australia, as evidenced by the continuing stream of publications (e.g., Turner 1973; Bradford 1997; Verdonk 2002; Simpson 2004).[4] One of the most influential of these works has been Leech and Short's *Style in Fiction* (1981/2007), a text which introduces the linguistic study of literary style with penetrating illustrative analyses. The premise driving these studies is the distinction between "literary" and "ordinary" usage, though of course some concept of the typical has to underwrite any project of discovering the unique. In pursuit of the ordinary as foil to the extraordinary, literary stylisticians often build on or even offer their own observations on how language "works" in general.

Though for centuries the analysis of literary texts served rhetorical training, rhetorical and literary stylistics now differ in their goals and methods. While a rhetorical stylistics can be, and often is, deployed to identify the unique features of a text or rhetorical artist, its goal is not the discovery of uniqueness per se. Its theoretical aim is rather the identification of functional features in language that have a predictable potential no matter who uses them, so that given similar purposes, it is likely that authors will choose similar functional structures. Nothing illustrates the difference between the literary and the rhetorical study of style more than the fate of the figures of speech in these two dispensations. The figures, especially the tropes and especially metaphor, have monopolized attention and have been adopted as virtual markers of the literary. Yet they were defined and illustrated in great detail in rhetorical manuals for over two thousand years for their practical quality of epitomizing arguments and having persuasive effects on audiences. Their telos was their communicative power.

Just as discourse analysts have turned their methods on argumentation, some practitioners of literary stylistics have generalized their discipline to apply to nonliterary texts. One notable extender has been Walter Nash, who glossed the rhetorical tradition in *Rhetoric: The Wit of Persuasion* (1989) and investigated nonliterary texts in *Designs in Prose* (1980) and, with Ronald Carter, in *Seeing Through Language* (1991). *Linguistic Criticism* (1996) and *Language in the News* (1991), by another critic known for applying linguistics to literature, Roger Fowler, feature deft insights into functional prose that, but for the absence of argument awareness, are model rhetorical analyses.

This book pays selective attention to works from the many schools of language analysis cited here, but it in no way attempts to combine in representative or equal fashion all the potential methods from these newer disciplines of language study with the methods of language analysis in the rhetorical tradition. With persuasive texts as the goal, rhetorical critics since antiquity have commented on the effectiveness of language choices. But their final purpose was to train people to use language persuasively, and commenting on how others used language effectively or ineffectively was only a means to that end.[5] So nowhere in the rhetorical corpus is there attention to patterns of word choice as revelations of an author's "mind style" (see Leech and Short 1981) or "ideology" (see Fairclough 2003). Although they were deeply aware of the assumptions and attitudes implicated by language choices, rhetoricians did not consider the language a code nor themselves decoders. Therefore, some of the methods of analysis discussed in this book—finding patterns in word origins or significant distributions in functional categories, etc.—do not appear in the rhetorical tradition as the first-order goals they are in contemporary linguistic or literary criticism.

The primary allegiance in this work is to the rhetorical tradition. Scholars from other fields will find only some of their methods used or referenced. The complementarity or outright overlap between these newer disciplines and a traditional rhetorical approach is significant. Those who know the rhetorical tradition in depth and detail may find the discoveries from the new language disciplines less than new, while proponents of the new disciplines may be put off by the layers of terminology and the historical distance of much in the rhetorical tradition. But there is something to gain from rapprochement in full awareness that rhetoricians and linguists, discourse analysts and literary stylisticians, have somewhat different objects of study and different goals.

Plan of the Book

This work is divided into four sections, covering word choice issues, sentence forms, the "interactive" dimension in texts, and finally passage construction. This order is not derived from the five rhetorical canons overall, which begin at the big end of the wedge with matters of "invention" generating content. In fact the plan of this book reverses the path that people typically follow when composing texts, a path that usually begins with the writer or speaker's awareness of context, purpose, and selection of genre; the selection of genre determines the individual compositional "chunks" or sections, those sections constrain the individual sentences, and those sentences in turn predispose composers to certain word choices. A kind of weak determinism transfers down the chain.

The reverse word-to-passage order is followed here for two reasons. First and most important, these four divisions correspond to the "levels" of analysis traditionally used in discussions of style per se in the rhetorical tradition, and their order corresponds to the order followed in rhetorical treatises that feature lengthy treatments of style, for example, the third book of Aristotle's *Rhetoric*, the eighth and ninth books of Quintilian's *Institutio Oratoria*, Erasmus's *De Copia*, and the eighteenth-century manuals in English produced by Blair and Campbell. All these treatises begin by commenting on principles of word choice and figures of substitution (tropes) before moving on to sentence forms and schemes, matters of managing rhetor/audience interactions, and issues involving the composition of longer passages. The notion of distinct "levels" is of course problematic, suggesting incorrectly that words are chosen in isolation from their sentence roles or that sentence forms vary without passage constraints. But this division has always been a convenient way to organize rhetorical advice and devices. Second, at the same time that this four-part division carves rhetorical stylistics at its joints, it reflects contemporary habits of language analysis, which tend to focus primarily on the material covered in part I, that is, on word choice issues. Indeed when scholars are confronted with a "language of" study, it is usually a study of individual words or of patterns in word choice. So this text begins at a familiar point.

Part I opens with a brief historical overview of English as a way of explaining the persuasive resources of the English lexicon, especially its size and range of synonyms, allowing choices from an older core vocabulary associated with directness and sincerity and later additions that provide the slight elevation of borrowings through Old French or that achieve "rational distance" with terms taken directly from classical languages, primarily Latin. Statistical profiles of texts in terms of word choices, now often visualized in "word clouds," can be meaningful, but it is usually more revealing to look at strategic choices, at critical places in an argument where the rhetor switches to a core or a French-sourced or a Latinate term. The second chapter covers the dynamics of the lexicon, the constant formation of new words and the constant changing of meanings or senses deformed in usage. Viewed as products of persuasion, methods of word formation can be arguments in themselves, a possibility noted in figures of speech that involve morphing of these forms.

Just as anglers need hooks, critics need categories to snag words for special attention. Chapter 3 covers traditional methods of categorizing words, by fields, levels, and functional categories (parts of speech). The lexical categories of rhetorical theorists like Kenneth Burke or Richard Weaver offer ways of categorizing word choice that connect directly to audience effects. The methods used by socio linguists and pragmaticists to characterize language varieties are covered in chapter 4. Here the useful notion of register is put to persuasive work in a *register shift*, a deliberate switch in the level or social/ occupational overtone of a word choice to express an attitude. This chapter also makes a rhetorical defense of familiar language or *fixed expressions*, the "stringiness" of language that corpus linguistics has recently put on view. Denigrated by style mavens, this "ordinary" language is a powerful vehicle for persuading audiences to accept new ideas.

Chapters 5 and 6 review the traditional figures of word choice, both the tropes, classically defined as substitutions for predictable usage, and the less familiar word schemes, which amount to gaming with word similarities. In the chapter on tropes, the *rhetorical metaphor* is preferred to the *conceptual metaphor* that now dominates discussion. A rhetorical metaphor will not turn up multiple hits in a Google search. Also contested in the chapter on tropes are looser, current definitions of irony that bleed through the distinctions clearly made in the older manuals.

Part II takes up phrases and sentences, the *commata, cola,* and *periodi* of the rhetoricians. While "language of" studies frequently discuss word choice, with special attention to metaphors or patterns defining lexical fields, sentence parts, types, and patterns are rarely noticed. Attention at this level is left to the specialists. The chapters in this section aim to facilitate sentence analysis. Chapter 7 focuses on predication, the subject and verb choices that construct the rhetorical world, who and what exist and how they are or act. Chapter 8 looks at the modification that hangs on the predication, first by reviewing the scale of possibilities, from clauses and phrases to single words. The samples analyzed then demonstrate how the type, number, and placement of modifiers can carry on an argument in genres that are not explicitly persuasive. With the main predication and added modification in place, chapter 9 looks at the resulting "architecture" of the sentence. Key words and phrases can occupy positions of emphasis, while loose versus periodic forms alternate for effect. Sentences can even exhibit "iconicity" when their form encodes their meaning. The figures of speech known as schemes (e.g., *antithesis, antimetabole*) can in fact be defined as prepared iconic forms, sentence patterns waiting for content to deliver predictable lines of argument. These are covered in chapter 10, and the special case of series, lists embedded in sentences, is covered in chapter 11. The final chapter in this section on sentences covers the prosody, or sound contour, of sentences and passages. It traces the two sources of the punctuation that shapes sentence prosody, from manuscript marks for oral performance to signs of grammatical structure, and then takes the issue of prosody to the passage level, where sentence variety in openings, type, and length can create special sound effects reinforcing an argument.

Rhetorical discourse by definition, as discourse that is sourced, situated, and addressed, has a prominent "interactive" dimension. **Part III** reviews the techniques for giving presence to this dimension in spoken or written texts. Chapter 13 covers the basics of pronoun choice for managing the "footing" between rhetor and audience, and it then reviews the figures of speech that stretch the possibilities, such as calling on fictional listeners or singling out individuals for direct address. The full range of interactive questions, beyond the "rhetorical question," is also reviewed. Next, chapter 14 concentrates on how other speakers can be given a voice in a text. Here the methods for analyzing incorporated speech developed by Leech and Short are the primary source, though these too have their rhetorical analogues. Chapter 15 looks at the ways that time and place become marked as occasion and setting in arguments. Given the importance of *kairos*, of seizing the opportune moment in rhetorical planning, this dimension has special persuasive potential. While linguists have identified the *deictic* features in discourse that refer to physically present people and objects, this chapter also looks at the extended description, a pedagogical genre in the rhetorical tradition, as *imaginary deixis*, the skillful transport of rhetor and audience to a scene from the past or future, described in a way that will influence attitudes and beliefs.

Since antiquity, rhetorical manuals have focused on the overall construction of persuasive cases in extended texts, but under the rubric of "composition" they have also provided a great deal of advice on units of composition composed of several sentences. **Part IV** ventures beyond the sentence boundary to comment on these often invisible units of passage construction. Chapter 16 begins with a review of the techniques for signaling the perception of coherence between sentences in sequence, a topic thoroughly investigated by linguists and discourse analysts in terms of topic/comment organization, schema theory, and interclausal semantic relations. How a coherent string of sentences can then become a functional unit, contributing to a longer passage, is discussed in chapter 17, which reviews the advice provided in the rhetorical tradition for generic, multisentence units of argument like the enthymeme, epicheireme, or extended comparison. The contrary tendencies of parataxis and hypotaxis, first noted by Aristotle, are also discussed here as passage builders. Finally, chapter 18 reprises what is arguably the single most important goal in rhetorical stylistics, the goal of amplification, of endowing an element with conceptual importance by making it salient in a text and prominent in perception. Rhetoricians have provided ample advice for achieving amplification, both through devices of highlighting and through tactics of *copia,* which involve expanding the amount of text devoted to an item in order to preoccupy the audience's attention. Furthermore, amplification is linked historically to effects of the *sublime,* to not only persuading audiences but overwhelming them. How this transcendence can be achieved is the subject of a final detailed analysis of the last paragraph of Darwin's *Origin of Species,* an analysis that also functions to review many of the methods of word, sentence, interaction, and passage construction in rhetorical stylistics.

Given its length and coverage in its four parts, this book is more easily dipped into, consulted, or sampled in sections than read straight through. It offers an overview of the basics of language analysis and pushes further into the special devices taught in the rhetorical tradition. Each part could be treated more deeply. Overall the book celebrates the incredible power and richness of rhetorically crafted language.

SOURCE OF EXAMPLES

The language patterns and devices discussed in this book are illustrated for the most part by sentences and passages taken from actual texts, with a bias toward more recent sources. Real examples are preferred here to demonstrate the continuing use of devices that might otherwise seem far-fetched, and to support the enduring nature of rhetorical style, of language torqued in predictable ways because of what it has to do. The use of snatches from actual texts is adhered to even in the case of defining grammatical features, though, for convenience, in some explanations and brief definitions, illustrative examples are invented. The overwhelming majority of the texts used were composed in English, though many of the devices discussed come from works written in Greek or Latin. The applicability of these devices to other Indo-European languages is often obvious.

Many of the illustrations come from the canon of American oratory reaching back to the eighteenth century. Most readers of English are likely to be familiar with these speeches, or at least with the speakers, so a minimum of contextualizing information is provided. In most cases only small sections are cited, and these citations and references are never intended as definitive rhetorical analyses. They are merely illustrations drawn from one aspect of the artistry of a Lincoln or Franklin Roosevelt or Martin Luther King Jr. Other illustrations come from common, functional prose genres, from nonfiction works (particularly on history and science), and from journalism. (Since examples come from both spoken and written texts, to generalize across these modes, the somewhat unfamiliar term *rhetor* is often used to refer to either a speaker or writer.) The inclusion of examples published in major monthlies like *Harper's* will probably surprise no one, but the use of newspaper reports to illustrate "rhetorical style" might. While everyone acknowledges that editorials and op-ed pieces are species of rhetorical argumentation, the news itself is usually considered merely informative or "expository." But news articles can be viewed as arguments. They argue directly for the existence or occurrence of the events and trends that they report and indirectly for certain viewpoints. They deploy the evidence of witnesses, experts, and firsthand observation to convince readers of the factuality of their stories. And they also inevitably, by their inclusions, omissions, and language choices, induce readers to have certain attitudes toward the content reported. Their methods may be less obvious than those of the explicit arguer, but their language is no less artful.

What This Book Is Not—and Is

Books on language and style abound, so it might also be useful to explain up front what this book is not and what it does not attempt. Though this book pays some attention to the history of English and to older language conventions, it is not a history of the language or of English style, of which many full and partial histories are available.

And though it offers some overview of sentence elements and uses traditional terminology, this book is emphatically not a grammar. It offers no systematic description of the English language according to any school, nor are the grammatical terms employed used with allegiance to any particular grammatical system. Furthermore, it stays with conventional terms like *word* over more precise but less familiar terms such as *lexeme*, and like *direct* or *indirect object* of a verb rather than its *argument*, to avoid a confusing competition with the usual sense of *argument* in common usage and in rhetorical manuals.

This book has language analysis and not language production as its goal, so it is not a "how to" manual. Unlike the many rhetorical treatises it draws from, it offers no direct advice on text construction. Instead, it provides templates or probes for examining language. Patterns defined analytically are, however, always susceptible to use as models, and some readers may try to incorporate some of the constructions identified. (If that were to happen, the author would be delighted.)

This book is also not a jeremiad complaining about current usage or recommending improved language practices. Works with these purposes have had an important place in the language awareness of most centuries, and in the last century, criticism motivating reform has ranged from the general semanticists' call for language purified of vagueness and prejudice, to Orwell's indictment of political jargon, to the present horror at the rapid spread of IM acronyms and Twitter compression. There are "defenses" of some language practices in this text as well as critical observations on certain usages, especially in newspaper prose, and on how individual writers and speakers might have done things differently and presumably "better" given their context and purpose. But this book offers no social critique based on language habits nor any path to salvation through better language practices. Bias of course is inevitable, but many oxen will probably be gored.

Finally, by way of a traditional preface, a word on what this book is: the product of years of teaching and conversation about style with many brilliant students and colleagues who share the same intense interest in language and the rhetorical tradition. I am especially indebted to the students who used early versions of these chapters, who drew my attention to what they found murky or valuable and who offered new examples. Among students I thank Sonya Brown, Heather Brown, Jonathan Buehl, Martin Camper, Barbara Cooper, Stanley Dambrowski, Liz Driver, Lindsay Dunne, William Fitzgerald, Judy Fowler, Tom Geary, Naria Gigante, Wendy Hayden, Jeanine Hurley, Aletha Hendrickson, Sandra Hill, Mark Hoffmann, Adam Lloyd, Alisse Portnoy, Marjolaine Tin Nyo, Elisa Warford, and James Wynn for teaching me so much about rhetoric in so many different settings. Among colleagues at home I thank John Auchard, Linda Coleman, Lea Chartock, Jane Donawerth, Robert Gaines, Michael Israel, Jim Klumpp, Shirley Logan, Linda Macri, Michael Marcuse, Michele Mason, Leigh Ryan, and Vessela Valiavitcharska. And among colleagues at large, I thank especially Alan Gross (who gave valuable advice on early versions of chapters) and Michael Leff (role model to all rhetorical stylisticians, whose death in 2010 is irreparable), as well as Linda Bensel-Meyers, Carol Berkenkotter, Don Bialostosky, Davida Charney, Nancy Christiansen, Richard Graff, Keith Grant-Davie, Martha Kolln, Sara Newman, Art Walzer, and Sue Wells. I am grateful for the continuing friendship of Marie Secor, whose skills of language analysis are matchless. I owe a special thanks to Franz van Eemeren and his colleagues in Amsterdam for encouraging a rhetorical approach to argumentative style. I also had the privilege of learning about coherence from Joe Williams, and I have benefited enormously from the comments and corrections of Randy Allen Harris, who could improve on every part of this work. Finally, I want to thank the professionals at

Oxford University Press for easing the path from manuscript to book: Peter Ohlin, Brian Hurley, Natalie Johnson, Allison Finkel, Harikrishnan Niranjana, and especially Steve Dodson, who caught many of my errors and offered useful suggestions.

NOTES

1. The original typed draft with Roosevelt's changes, plus a third draft with a suggested addition from his aid Harry Hopkins, are housed in the Franklin Delano Roosevelt Presidential Library in Hyde Park, New York. Facsimiles of Roosevelt's versions, from which the passage in this text is taken, are available at *www.archives.gov* and as links in the article "FDR's 'Day of Infamy' Speech: Crafting a Call to Arms" (2001). In a line-by-line stylistic analysis of this speech, Hermann G. Stelzner, who consulted the early drafts in the library, concluded, "Changes from draft to draft are not extensive. Grace Tully, Roosevelt's secretary, indicates that the address was delivered in almost the identical form in which it was originally dictated to her by the President" (Stelzner 107, n17).

2. Once *infamy* appeared in Roosevelt's speech and became part of the description by which the speech is remembered, its profile of usage changed. After December 8, 1941, for English speakers in the United States, similar uses of *infamy* carry associations with this single usage.

3. Another instance of this approach to persuasive language through "scientific" methods is the work of the Swedish psychologist, Rolf Sandell (1977). Sandell attempted a statistical and experimental approach to identify features of language that might make a difference in the acceptability of advertisements. The results are somewhat compromised by the absence in his experimental protocols of features identified a priori as potentially persuasive.

4. Linguistic approaches to literature were popular in the United States in the 1960s and into the '70s. Ohmann used transformational grammar to analyze Faulkner (in Freeman 1971), and Stanley Fish used the linearity of syntax to characterize "affective stylistics," exemplifying this approach with the response of readers to seventeenth-century prose (1982). The older, computational stylistics of Louis Milic (1967) and others builds on the notion that there are unique personal differences in habits of language use. Linguistic approaches to literature lost favor in the United States in the late '70s and '80s, displaced by structuralism and deconstruction. They have had a revival in the last twenty years, especially in the new approach calling itself *cognitive poetics*, an offshoot of *cognitive linguistics*.

5. Given their interest in production over analysis, the rhetorical manuals have their direct descendents in the communication and composition scholars whose primary teaching commitment is to arts of speaking and writing. Among the latter group were many scholars who worked largely in the '60s and '70s, including Francis and Bonniejean Christensen, Richard A. Larson, Richard Braddock, and Mina Shaugnessy. Much of their work focused on language issues in composing, on phrasing, sentence types, sentence combining, and paragraph structure. They have been succeeded by many works of practical stylistics, notably from scholar/teachers like Joseph Williams (1989) and Martha Kolln (1998) who combine linguistic and rhetorical insights to give advice for improving style. There has been recent attention to teaching writing through style in Paul Butler's *Out of Style* (2008), in the "writing about writing" movement (Downs and Wardle 2007), and in two works that appeared after this MS was written: Holcomb and Killingsworth's *Performing Prose: The Study and Practice of Style in Composition* (2010) and Stanley Fish's *How to Write a Sentence: And How to Read One* (2011).

Word Choice

LANGUAGE OF ORIGIN

With *hatred/malice/antipathy* toward none, with *love/charity/compassion* for all, with *strength/firmness/fixity* in the right as *God/the Lord/the Deity* gives us to *see/perceive/discriminate* the right, let us strive on to *end/finish/complete* the work we are in, to *bind up/dress/cauterize* the nation's *wounds/injuries/lacerations*, to care for him who shall have *borne/endured/tolerated* the battle and for his widow and his *child/orphan/progeny*, to do all which may *earn/achieve/produce* and cherish a *fair/just/impartial* and *lasting/enduring/sustainable* peace among ourselves and with all *lands/nations/territories*.

ABRAHAM LINCOLN,
Second Inaugural, March 4, 1865

THIS "UNWRITING" OF the famous conclusion to Lincoln's Second Inaugural Address offers two alternatives along with Lincoln's original word choice. Each option comes from one of the three major layers of English vocabulary:—the Anglo-Saxon core, the French additions initiated by the Normans, and the direct borrowings from Latin or Greek. Lincoln had even more choices than those listed, and indeed almost every word in his speech, beyond the articles, pronouns, and prepositions, could have been replaced by other more or less synonymous words and phrases. Those familiar with the original no doubt will judge that Lincoln's choices were unerringly the best possible. As it turns out, he chose predominantly from the Anglo-Saxon or Old English core and frequently from the slightly more formal French layer (*malice, charity, firmness, finish, orphan, achieve, nations*). But he avoided words borrowed directly from Latin or Greek (Cmiel 1990, 116–18).[1]

The Historical Layers of English

Every contemporary speaker and writer of English constantly makes such choices among synonyms, whether consciously or not. The sheer number of alternatives available illustrates one special feature of the English language: the size of its lexicon. On the basis of entries in the *Oxford English Dictionary* (OED), David Crystal estimates that English users can access half a million words and perhaps another half million technical words (1988, 37; for larger claims, see Crystal 2004, 119). The size of this potential vocabulary does not mean that any one speaker of English has a larger working vocabulary than the speaker of any other language. But English does offer an astonishing range of synonyms and near synonyms, allowing precision and nuance in word choice. The reasons for this variety are largely matters of historical accident, and detailed accounts can be found in scholarly histories of the language.[2] The following offers a brief sketch of the influences that have created contemporary English with its wealth of synonyms. An awareness of the historical layers of English is necessary grounding for a "first approximation" of the rhetor's options in word choice.

THE OLD ENGLISH CORE

The standard history of English, told again and again from the Venerable Bede to Jonathan Swift to PBS's Robert MacNeil, is a story of invasion, conquest, and displacement. In this familiar account, the population inhabiting what is now England in the first century BCE had been there for centuries and spoke a Celtic language. After they were conquered by the Romans between 44 BCE and 50 CE, a hybrid civilization thrived until the legions withdrew in the fifth century CE, leaving the Romanized Celts vulnerable to invaders. Those from northern Germany and Denmark colonized different parts of the island and pushed the surviving Celts to the west, to Cornwall, Wales, and Ireland, where the languages still spoken belong to the Celtic subfamily of Indo-European languages.

This standard account has been challenged recently by Stephen Oppenheimer (2007) and others on the basis of DNA evidence. In the competing narrative, the British Isles, depopulated by the Ice Age, were repopulated circa 16,000 BCE by people coming up the coast of western Europe. This population, whose genetic imprint, according to Oppenheimer, still dominates throughout the British Isles, was subsequently invaded by Celtic and then by Germanic speakers, and at the time of the Roman invasions, the population in the south of England presumably already spoke a Germanic language. In this account, the Anglo-Saxon invasions of the fifth and sixth centuries were only a later migration of a small group from the same language family.[3]

The competing narratives differ fundamentally on when speakers of Germanic languages first colonized southeastern England. But neither version alters the surviving documentary evidence that by 600 CE the written language of the people settled in England was the Germanic variant sometimes called Anglo-Saxon and referred to by linguists and lexicographers as Old English (OE). This is the language of the Beowulf saga, Caedmon's Hymn, Bede's *History*, and other literary, historical, legal, and religious works surviving in a corpus of some three million words. Its orthography includes special letters for the *th* sounds, and, unlike later forms of English, it is an *inflected* language: the grammatical roles of words are signaled by their case endings. But it is filled with words current English users can still recognize fifteen hundred years later: *freond (friend), aefter (after), full, hand, claene (clean), inn, land, lust, norþ (north), baec (back), tear, slaep (sleep), weorþ (worth), biernan (burn), lif (life), deaþ (death)*. Old English also has many words of Greek and Latin origin, some brought in when its speakers adopted Christianity and along with it the Greek and Latin words for religious objects and ideas: for example, *priest, altar, relic, shrine, alms, disciple, epistle, chalice, hymn.* But *God, heaven,* and *hell* were native to Old English, as were *fiend* and *doom.* The English term for the third person of the Trinity, the *Holy Ghost,* comes from the Old English term for *spirit,* namely *gast* (in German, *Geist*). Hence the Latin *Spiritus Sanctus* became the Old English *Halig Gast.*

From the eighth century on, the Old English–speaking population fell victim to invasions from the Vikings of Scandinavia. Within fifty years of their successful raids on the east coast of what is now England, these "Danes" had conquered half the country, settled in substantial numbers, and also converted to Christianity. During the following years of cultural blending, hundreds of words entered Old English from Scandinavian, including many basic terms like *they, dirt, hit, flat, egg, give, are, get, leg, raise, want, die* and most words beginning with *sc* or *sk,* such as *scare, sky, skirt, scrap, skill, skin.*[4] Combining the lexicon of Old English and the additions from Old Norse forms what can be called the **core** vocabulary in contemporary English, the oldest layer in the language and the source of its simplest and most frequently used words.[5]

THE NORMAN FRENCH CONTRIBUTION

Relatives of the Nordic people who invaded England in the eighth and ninth centuries also conquered and colonized the north of France. Within two centuries of settlement, these "Normans" (i.e., Northmen) had adopted the culture and language of the Romanized Gauls, and in the late eleventh century they successfully invaded England, seized administrative control, both civil and ecclesiastical, of the country, and maintained that control by their military presence in a string of fortified castles built across the country. The government and the courts conducted business in French for the next three hundred years. But the Normans did not really colonize England in large numbers (Williams 1975, 84). Instead, a French-speaking minority ruled the English-speaking majority, creating a social stratification reinforced by language difference.

The influence of Norman French on English after 1066 was significant but selective. Estimates of borrowings run as high as ten thousand words, but many of these additions cluster in areas of meaning that represent aspects of life controlled by the Normans. For example, since the Normans took over the law courts, many current English words associated with legal proceedings derive from Old French: for example, *felony, attorney, inquest, jury, plaintiff, sue, plea, verdict, warrant, bailiff, bail, crime, depose, fine, perjury.* Some technical legal terms retain their obvious French origins, like *voir dire* and *remand.* The Normans also controlled the civil administration, as indicated by words like *mayor, minister, parliament, court, chancellor, sovereign, tax, revenue,* and *government* itself. And of course they maintained this control through military domination, as demonstrated in French words like *soldier, lieutenant, army, enemy, garrison, guard, retreat,* and *battle.*

French military and aristocratic culture is especially evident in the curious language of heraldry, itself a word of Anglo-Norman origin.

At the same time that they controlled the government, the military, and the courts, the Norman French commanded the best of the available goods. So, not surprisingly, many words for fine clothing and food came into English from French. In an often-quoted passage from the first chapter of *Ivanhoe*, Sir Walter Scott pointed out the telling differences in origin between "Saxon" words for farm animals versus "Norman" words for the meat from those animals: *swine* is Old English but *pork* Old French, *calf* is Old English but *veal* comes from Old French, and the same pattern persists with *ox* or *cow* versus *beef*, *sheep* and *lamb* versus *mutton*, *hind* and *stag* versus *venison*, *chicken* and *hen* versus *poultry*. It is easy to distinguish producers from consumers in these clusters based on origins.

In the centuries of Norman cultural dominance, 1100–1400, French words sometimes pushed out existing Old English terms; *people* (from OFr *pueple*), for example, replaced OE *leod*. But often, outside the special contexts mentioned above, English core words and French borrowings coexisted and eventually acquired slightly different meanings and usage domains. Most English speakers would easily separate pairs like *strength/vigor, hearty/cordial, house/mansion, wish/desire* (in each case the OE word is given first).

After three hundred years, English, enriched by Norman French, once again became the "official" language. The Norman ruling class had been cut off from its French connection after the Hundred Years War, and many had intermarried with the English. In 1362 Parliament conducted business in English again, instead of French, and by 1415 Henry V revived English in official documents. Chaucer (1340–1400), who commanded French and Latin as well, chose to write *The Canterbury Tales* in English. The English of roughly 1100 to 1500 with its French additions, called Middle English (ME), was a simpler language than Old English. Nouns lost their case endings except for the genitive -*s* (the priest's book), resulting in a greater use of prepositional phrases to compensate. Word order therefore counted more than inflection in determining the functions of words, and the basic order of the English sentence, noun phrase + verb + noun phrase, was established (Mueller 1984, 7). Verbs still retained endings according to person, which they have since lost (e.g., *say/sayest/sayeth*, first, second, and third person singular respectively); infinitives with *to* came into use; and French spellings for English sounds were adopted: *qu* for *cw* and *th* for thorn (þ) and eth (ð).

French, of course, is a vernacular offshoot of Latin, and stylistic analyses that pay attention to word origins often distinguish only the core English vocabulary from all later infusions, whether derived directly from Latin or indirectly through a Romance language like French. But given the historical accidents that produced modern English, the borrowings from French deserve special attention because of their quantity, their clustering in certain areas of meaning, and their special connotations when they exist as synonyms with core words. Furthermore, English rhetoricians beginning in the eighteenth century, newly aware of the history of their language and perhaps influenced by then-popular French rhetorics (Fenelon, Rollin, Massillon), emphasized the French-derived layer in English. In his *Lectures on Rhetoric and Belles Lettres*, delivered in 1762, Adam Smith described English as formed from the "French and the Saxon" (11), and Hugh Blair, in a work of the same title first published in 1783, described English as a combination including a distinct French source: "the English which was spoken afterwards [after the Norman Conquest], and continues to be spoken now, is a mixture of the antient [sic] Saxon, and this Norman French, together with such new and foreign words as commerce and learning have, in progress of time, gradually introduced" (2005, 92).

In that "progress of time" French has continued to be a dominant source in English for words describing luxury items, for *haute couture* and *haute cuisine*. Many of these "fancy French words" in contemporary English were borrowed centuries later, not in the Norman period. The current association of French terms with fine food and fashion, strenuously cultivated by advertisers, is more a product of France's European influence during and since the Enlightenment, the source and sign of a continuing presumption of French refinement in arguments for cultural excellence. But many words from the older Norman French layer, in addition to these more recent borrowings, still carry an aura of dignity and elevation.

THE LANGUAGE OF LEARNING FROM LATIN AND GREEK

In Norman-controlled England, while the workers were speaking English and their rulers speaking French, the clergy, the scholars, and other officials were reading, writing, and often speaking Latin. All over Europe, England included, Latin remained the language of learning from antiquity through the seventeenth and even into the nineteenth centuries. In the universities, like Oxford, that began to appear in the twelfth century, all texts were read and all lectures and disputations were held in Latin. For native speakers of English or French, or indeed of any European vernacular, entry into the social and ecclesiastical elite of the learned required years of Latin instruction. Over the centuries, the Latin used in the church and schools evolved, as does any language in use. Thus medieval scholarly and ecclesiastical Latin and early modern Neo-Latin differ from classical Latin.

Because of its constant presence as the alternate language of learning and Christian worship, Latin has always been a source of borrowed words in English. But in the fifteenth through seventeenth centuries, Latin borrowings increased as Europeans improved their access to and understanding of classical Latin texts and began to acquire classical Greek, which became the second language of the ablest scholars. All the university disciplines studied in Europe—theology, medicine, law, astronomy, mathematics, philosophy, logic, and rhetoric—were studied in Latin and derived their key terms from either Latin or Greek. So, inevitably, when scholars began to write on these subjects in their native languages, they incorporated words from Latin and Greek for the concepts and entities they were used to reading and writing about in those languages. The extent of this borrowing is on display in the so-called "Tree of Porphyry," the scheme for organizing the world of "substances" derived from Porphyry of Tyre and repeated in dialectical treatises for centuries. Here is the version, in Latin, from Philip Melanchthon's *Erotemata Dialectices* in 1547 (1963b, 530):

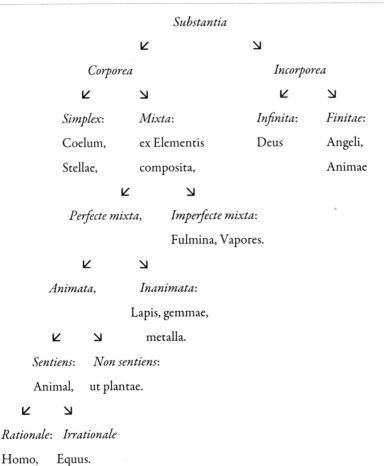

Substantia

Corporea   *Incorporea*

Simplex: *Mixta*:   *Infinita*:   *Finitae*:

Coelum,   ex Elementis   Deus   Angeli,

Stellae,   composita,   Animae

Perfecte mixta,   *Imperfecte mixta*:

Fulmina, Vapores.

Animata,   *Inanimata*:

Lapis, gemmae,

metalla.

Sentiens: *Non sentiens*:

Animal,   ut plantae.

Rationale: *Irrationale*

Homo,   Equus.

No knowledge of Latin is needed for the English speaker to recognize words that were borrowed directly and that still carry the same meanings: *substance, corporeal, incorporeal, composite, infinite, finite, animate, inanimate, animal, sentient.* (Other Latin words in this passage came into English from Latin through French: *simple, mixed, perfect, imperfect, rational; plant,* however, came into Old English from Latin much earlier.)

Modern English owes the majority of its vocabulary, some two-thirds of its words (though not its most frequently used words), to borrowings directly from Latin, or from other Latin-derived vernaculars, especially French, Spanish, and Italian. But just as French words cluster in those areas of meaning that reflect the Norman cultural presence in England, so deliberate Latin and Greek borrowings cluster in the academic disciplines and in areas of meaning covered in formal documents that once would have been written in Latin. Many of these learned borrowings have become indispensable for any communication not about everyday objects and topics. Among the words adapted from Latin and Greek in the early modern period are such now common words as *fact, explain, exist, necessitate, crisis, contradict, appropriate, relaxation, external, scheme, system, conspicuous, obstruction, habitual, expensive.* But the direct borrowings still create a Latin and to some extent Greek layer in English that constitutes its vocabulary of learning. The correlation holds fairly well: the more formal, abstract, and academic the text, the more Latinate the vocabulary. The informal spoken language is filled with words derived from Germanic, Scandinavian, and sometimes French; the formal written language has proportionately more Latin and Greek words, a distribution that has marked consequences for the vocabulary of persuasion.

Periodically, language reformers, from Jonathan Swift to George Orwell, have called for purging English of its classical and foreign borrowings and restoring its pure or native vocabulary. Even as early as the sixteenth century, some English scholars objected to the heavy incorporation of "inkhorn" terms from Latin and Greek. In an attempt to restore an "Anglo-Saxon" vocabulary, one Elizabethan scholar, Ralph Lever, wanting to avoid Latin terms when writing a treatise on logic, renamed his subject *witcraft* from native English words (*wit* + *craft*), and proposed replacing the Latin and Greek lexicon of logic with other English equivalents: a *proposition* would be a *saying*, a *definition* a *saywhat*, an *affirmation* a *yeasay*, a *negation* a *naysay*, and a *conclusion* an *endsay* (Howell 1956, 61). Needless to say, generations of English users have found the Latin derivatives used in the study of logic clear enough. There can be a distinct advantage in having a vocabulary dedicated to a particular subject, without overlapping more common words that carry multiple associations. (See Crystal 2003, 125, and Cmiel 1990, 114 on reform movements.)

INCORPORATIONS FROM WORLD CONTACT

English speakers from the British Isles have always taken in words from the many cultures they have had contact with, through trade or colonization, and the pace of these borrowings quickened in the sixteenth century. On ships of exploration and commerce, English speakers encountered not only new cultures with new languages, but also sailors from other European maritime powers—especially the Spanish, the Portuguese, and the Dutch—who had acquired new words in their voyaging and coined useful nautical terms. The lexicon of older foreign borrowings into English comes then either directly from the original language or from the language of another maritime power. By these contacts over centuries, English picked up words, as it picked up goods and knowledge, from virtually every culture on the globe: *clamp, yacht, cruise* (Dutch); *mahogany* (Spanish/Mayan); *caravan* (Persian); *tea* (Dutch/Malay); *teak* (Portuguese/Malay); *zero* (Italian/Arabic); *pundit, guru* (Hindi); *curry, pariah* (Tamil); *kangaroo* (Guugu Yimidhirr, an Australian Aboriginal language); *coffee* (Turkish/Arabic), *kiosk, turban* (Turkish/Persian).

In part as a response to the flood of new words, the French, Spanish, and Italians established academies centuries ago to pass judgment on admissible language and good usage. Still in business in the twenty-first century, the French *Académie's* language police forbid the official, published use of many foreign words, especially Americanisms, in place of French terms. English-speaking countries have never been either so organized or so resistant. As a result, English is a great stew of foreign borrowings, and the lid is still off the pot. (See the section on foreign borrowings in "New Word Formation.") And English is now out of the hands of native English speakers; as a lingua franca, often used as a medium of communication between speakers of different languages, it exists in a variety of "world Englishes."

AN AMERICAN VOCABULARY

English landed in North America in the early seventeenth century as the language of immigrants in Virginia and Massachusetts, and by the time of the Revolution (1790 census), nine out of ten of the colonists were English speakers. But the English of the colonies began to diverge from the English of England from the moment the first immigrants encountered plants, animals, geographical features, and indigenous peoples they had never known before. When confronting new things unnamed in their own language, people can either adapt a word from their own vocabulary or adopt a word from a language that has named it already. English speakers in North America did both, stretching their word *robin* to refer to a different species of bird and narrowing their word *corn*, meaning any grain, to refer to *maize*. They also borrowed many words from Native American languages: *raccoon, skunk, squash* (the vegetable), *hickory, pecan, chipmunk, moose, terrapin*. The process of borrowing from Amerindian languages, sometimes through the French fur trappers, continued into the nineteenth century for terms naming items in Native American culture: *wigwam, teepee, squaw, moccasin, tomahawk, pemmican*.

Africans sold into slavery in the Americas to some extent maintained their own languages. English words traceable to African languages include *banana, tote, banjo, juke,* and *yam*. In Sierra Leone and on the slave ships and in the slave markets, a hybrid English developed for communication from the seventeenth century, one that some scholars describe as the source of Caribbean English and of African American Vernacular English (AAVE) in the United States (see Dillard 1973; Labov 1973). Growing out of distinct social and regional experiences (e.g., the Gullah spoken on the islands off South Carolina), AAVE is better described as an independent dialect that has continually fed into other varieties of English.

The English spoken in the United States has also been heavily influenced by contact with Spanish speakers from Florida to Texas to California. Their cattle-rearing culture in the arid Southwest provided regional terms that became general in the late nineteenth century: *mesa, corral, ranch, lariat, lasso, stampede, sombrero, plaza, tornado, arroyo*. Spanish New World food terms (*chocolate, tomato,* themselves taken from the indigenous Nahuatl) and cooking terms (*barbecue, enchilada, tortilla*) were adopted as eagerly as the cuisine. The process of borrowing from Spanish speakers is increasing with the increasing presence of Hispanics in the United States.

Homonyms and Synonyms from Different Origins

The notion of a *word* stands for a form/meaning pairing. In a deliberately designed language, every form/meaning pair would be unique. But English has many identical forms, words that are spelled (*homographs*) and/or pronounced (*homophones*) the same way, though their meanings differ. Many of these *homonyms* have come into English from different languages, and most dictionaries consider identical forms derived from different sources to be separate lexical items, really separate words, requiring separate entries.

match[1] = one like another, from OE *gemaecca* = companion or mate
match[2] = small piece of wood with ignitable tip, from OFr *mesche* = lamp wick.

Given its chaotic origins, English has accumulated a large number of such indistinguishable word forms with distinguishable meanings.[6] They pose few problems in understanding, since context usually clarifies which homonym makes sense, though these identical forms do provide sources for meaningful wordplay that persuaders can exploit (see chapter 6).

But while homonyms are often curiosities, synonyms, different forms with close or identical meanings, are the fuel of rhetorical power in English. The layering of languages that produced the English lexicon—the Germanic core, the French additions, and the Latin and Greek incorporations—gives its users an especially rich repertoire of synonyms roughly equivalent in meaning but different in other communicative dimensions (see Gramley and Pätzold 2004, 29).

OE core	French	Latin/Greek
scare	*frighten*	*terrify*
kind	*generous*	*magnanimous*
hate	*loathing*	*antipathy*
food	*viands*	*comestibles*
anger	*rage*	*consternation*
apart	*asunder*	*divided*
thin	*gaunt*	*emaciated*

English users would be able to distinguish among these options on the basis of shaded meanings and typical context of use. Most users would agree that *to terrify* is worse than *to frighten* or that *anger* is more intense than *consternation*. Many larger sets of synonyms from multiple origins exist, like the series *phoney* (Gaelic), *fake* (nineteenth century coinage from an OE root), *false* (OFr), *artificial* (OFr), *simulated* (L). Most contemporary English users would give these words the common denotation of *not genuine* or *not real*. But these words are hardly equivalent, and each has acquired special senses and usage restrictions. Contemporary English users would readily produce the pairs *false teeth*, *fake fur*, *artificial sweetener*, and *simulated pearls*, but they would rarely haphazardly substitute one of these adjectives for another, as in *fake teeth*, *false pearls*, *simulated sweetener*.

The familiar pairs are established collocations, fellow travelers in usage. A language user's sense of where a word can be used and where it cannot comes from exposure to actual usage. Rhetors can either unobtrusively match this sense, using the familiar collocation (e.g., *artificial sweetener*), or they can tweak expectation for effect (e.g., *fake sweetener*).

Clarity and Sincerity: When Core Words Dominate

The simplest English words and the words in widest use tend to be the oldest, the core words from Old English and Old Norse in use before 1000 CE. According to a statistical analysis of current British English, ninety-eight of the hundred most frequently used words come from this indispensable functional core—a predictable proportion, since these most frequent words include the basics like *the, is, in,* and other determiners, prepositions, and conjunctions (Crystal 2006, 54; the two not of Germanic origin are *people* and *use*). Words from this oldest layer also include terms for everyday, material reality—*bread, milk, water, sun, moon, sky, house*—and for the simplest actions, *see, run, look, fall.* Any grammar school reader, like the one sampled in the following passage, shows that the earliest words taught and learned are words from this core vocabulary.

The Wood Lot

"Look out!" shouted Lucy. Then she stood speechless. She couldn't tell Mark what to look out for, but he knew. Dropping his ax, he sprang back from the tree he had been cutting and slipped a little on the softening March snow. It was a fortunate slip. It carried him out of the way of the second tree that came crashing to earth just where he had been standing. (Coatsworth and O'Donnell 1949, 5)

Of the fifty-four nonrepeated words in this passage, forty-two come from the core OE vocabulary, including words for simple actions (*stand/look/drop*) and things (*ax/tree/snow*), as well as the tense, modality, and negation markers in the verb phrases (*had been/could not*) and the relational words (*but/that/where/what/to/of*) that shape the syntax. Of the nine words that do not come from OE or ON (e.g., *shout* is from Old Norse), *March, fortunate, carry,* and *second* are French additions, *slip* comes from Middle Dutch, and both *cut* and *crash* first appear in Middle English but probably have older sources. So even these nine have been in the language for a very long time, and, with the possible exception of the two names, *Mark* and *Lucy*, none of the words in this text came in directly from Latin.

A passage in which the core vocabulary dominates so noticeably will strike most English users as simple and straightforward. This effect occurs because core words, the oldest in the language, are also the oldest in the experience of native speakers; they are the first heard, the first spoken, the first read, the first written. They are associated with simple messages, and often with immediate, familial, and physical contexts. They have the force of familiarity and truthfulness. Hence texts perceived as clear and even sincere will tend to feature words from the Old English core of the language. Martin Luther King Jr., for example, toward the end of his "I have a dream" speech, used the following phrase, which, as he noted, came from an old spiritual:

Free at last! Free at last!
Thank God Almighty, free at last!

All these words come from Old English. Had King selected words from the French layer of the language at this point, he might have said, *Liberated finally* or from the Latin layer, *Emancipated ultimately!*[7] A speaker might deliver such phrases with the same vocal intensity, but only the original, in core words taken from the "lifeworld," communicates the force and sincerity of King's passion.

Elevation and Panache: Featuring French Borrowings

The different persuasive effects of choosing frequently from the French layer of English are vividly on display in the following passage from a full-page advertisement that appeared in the *National Enquirer* for a special-edition Barbie Doll.

> Autumn Glory Barbie
> She captures forever the majesty of autumn, with its vibrant colors and regal hues. Introducing Autumn Glory Barbie, from the Enchanted Seasons Collection. A stunning tribute to the colors of fall.
> Barbie doll shimmers in hues of copper and auburn. Adorned with fall leaves and accented with hints of purple and gold, her gown flows around her like an autumn breeze. Her long auburn hair and dark wine hat add the final touch to this autumn portrait.
> Complete with Certificate of Authenticity, you can acquire this Collector Edition doll only through direct subscription for five easy payments of $15.80.
> Autumn Glory Barbie doll, from the Enchanted Seasons Collection. A doll you will cherish like autumn itself. (September 10, 1996, 15)

Many of the nouns and adjectives in this text came into English from Old French. Not surprisingly, they are the words that convey the aura of elegance and beauty that is really on sale here. The two key words that give this Barbie her special label, *autumn* and *glory*, are both French borrowings, as are the two words that describe her type: she belongs in the *Enchanted Seasons* Collection. French-derived *autumn* exists in the language side by side with its OE synonym, *fall*, also used in the ad (*colors of fall, fall leaves*), but *autumn* carries associations of spectacle that the more common *fall* does not, simply because it is a less frequent word used in special contexts.

Other words from French in this passage carry notions of royalty typically associated with fashion, for example, *majesty* and *regal*; and from Old French also come the words to describe the response to this special Barbie's effect: she is *stunning*, she *captures*, and you will *cherish* her. And the French lexicon for fashion provides the terms for her *gown*: it is *adorned* and *accented,* and her hat adds a *final touch.* Another dominant word in this passage, *color*, came into Middle English from French, where it replaced an older and more general word, OE *heo*, which became *hue.* This term, which in ME meant one's general complexion or appearance, is now a less familiar and more specialized word for color choices in paints, dyes, etc. Surprisingly, the actual color lexicon in this passage—*copper, purple, gold, wine*—comes from OE. The greater age of these terms, pressed into descriptive service in this passage, stems from the fact that they derive from commodities traded in antiquity; *purple*, for example, comes ultimately from the Greek name for the mollusk from which purple dye was derived. The only color term from French is *auburn,* which has no single OE equivalent. Its use adds to the dominant *au* and *ah* sounds in the passage from the French-derived words: *autumn, auburn, adorned,* and *around.* Even the more legalistic words from French, *authenticity* and *acquire,* carry on the assonance. Paradoxically, the two defining words in this text, the species term *Barbie* and the genus term *doll,* cannot be glamorized. *Barbie* is a diminutive for *Barbara*, a name derived from the Latin feminine form of *barbarus*, the source of *barbarian.* And *doll* is a word of no traceable pedigree; it appears in English in the sixteenth century and is thought to be a corruption of the name *Dorothea.* It takes significant swathing in the lexicon of elegance from French-derived words to make this *Barbie Doll,* formed from a few cents worth of fabric and plastic, command a price of $75.[8]

Formality and Erudition: Words from Latin and Greek

In remarks that he made at a political dinner in 1966, President Lyndon Johnson defended his increasingly unpopular buildup in Vietnam by declaring his personal dedication to peace. Using core words to convey sincerity, he declared, "I want the killing to stop" (Windt 1983, 91). Two years later, on the very different occasion of a televised address to the nation, the president used words from a different level of the language: "I am taking the first step to deescalate the conflict. We are reducing—substantially reducing—the present level of hostilities" (Windt 1983, 100). Here, key choices are Latin derivatives that express the high seriousness of a formal policy announcement on a grave matter. The layer of classical borrowings in English is not only indispensable for formal and impersonal discourse, it is also the language of the scholarly disciplines. This layer is on display in the following passage from the twenty-seventh edition of *Gray's Anatomy*.

Cerebral Cortex.—Each hemisphere presents a convex superior and lateral surface (*facies convexa cerebri*), a flat medial surface (*facies medialis cerebri*), and an irregular inferior or basal surface (*basis cerebri*). A distinct medial or superior margin separates the lateral and medial surfaces; a more rounded lateral margin separates the lateral and inferior surfaces. The anterior end is the frontal pole, the posterior end the occipital pole, and the anterior end of the laterally protruding temporal lobe is the temporal pole. The surface of the hemisphere is marked by numerous irregular grooves, the fissures and sulci, with intervening rounded eminences, the convolutions or gyri. At first glance they appear quite irregular, but they can, with study, be fitted into a basic plan. The two hemispheres of the same brain differ from each other and they differ in turn from every other brain. (Gray 1959, 882).

The lexicon here is dominated by Greek and Latin terms because the knowledge conveyed has accumulated for centuries, beginning in the Greek texts of Hippocrates and the Greek and Latin texts of Galen. Indeed, medicine was taught exclusively in Latin well into the nineteenth century, and it still retains its classically derived vocabulary. This particular passage describes the gross anatomy of the cerebral cortex, the outer rind of the brain as it is typically visualized. The presence of Latin and Greek terms is so ubiquitous here, even to the point of untranslated Latin phrases in parentheses, that it makes more sense to notice the words that do not come from those two languages. The few words taken from the core vocabulary (other than the pronouns, prepositions, and articles) provide the ultimate referent (*brain*, that thing in the head), the indispensable verbs (*is, mark, can, be*), the orienting words (*end, flat* [ON]), and the comparing terms (*more, two, each, same, in turn*). Notably, the last sentence switches primarily to core words, and to the uninitiated,this sentence probably seems the clearest and most direct in the passage.

Analyses with Word Origins

While Old English provides the language of simplicity and sincerity and French adds words for elegance and order, Latin and Greek provide the special terms of scholarly and formal English. They are the source languages for technical vocabularies (as anatomy above) and, in general, of the lexicon of what can be called **rational distance**, in part because these words are not in everyday informal use. This quality of detachment dominates in the language of academics, as the following opening from a scholarly article appearing in the journal *Nature* demonstrates.

The existence of cooperation and social order among genetically unrelated individuals is a fundamental problem in the behavioural sciences. The prevailing approaches in biology and economics view cooperation exclusively as self-interested behaviour— unrelated individuals cooperate only if they face economic rewards or sanctions rendering cooperation a self-interested choice. Whether economic incentives are perceived as just or legitimate does not matter in these theories. Fairness-based altruism is, however, a powerful source of human cooperation. Here we show experimentally that the prevailing self-interest approach has serious shortcomings because it overlooks negative effects of sanctions on human altruism. (Fehr and Rockenbach 2003, 137)

There are two ways to analyze word choice in a passage such as this one based on language of origin: either by calculating the proportion from the different layers or by examining the pedigrees of the rhetor's most frequently used words. There are ninety-nine different words in this passage; of these, thirty-eight come directly from the core vocabulary. Five of the remaining sixty-one derive ultimately from Old English words, but *shortcomings, overlooks,* and any compound with *self* are later coinages from simpler roots.[9] The other fifty-six words, all the subjects, verbs, and important modifiers, came into English either directly from Latin and Greek or from Latin via French. A formal style then can be defined quantitatively as a style in which either a high percentage of total words (approximately 56% in this passage) or an even higher percentage of important words (totaling almost 100% of the nouns, verbs, and adjectives in this passage) are not part of the core vocabulary. Words that entered Middle English from French do contribute significantly to the formality of this passage, but the higher the proportion of words incorporated directly from Latin and Greek, the more learned and specialized.

However, another way to analyze word choice by origin in this passage is to consider only the words that are most critical to the content, the "key" words that are likely to appear in an abstract of the article or a list of words for retrieval purposes. What is the most important word in the section quoted? Language analysts often select the most frequent word (outside of functional words) as the most important, and in this passage it is *cooperation,* which appears in four out of the five sentences, while the verb form *cooperate* appears once. The passage sets the problem of explaining how or why cooperation should exist. *Cooperation* is a borrowing directly from Latin. It creates a general activity, unified into a single abstract term that can be contemplated all at once, as something that needs to be explained.

This passage from the science journal *Nature* could not have been written, and arguably not even conceptualized, but for the great range of abstract concepts, the rational distance, made available in the language by the addition of learned borrowings and coinages from Latin and Greek. It is not that core English does not have the resources to express the same ideas; cooperation, for example, could be expressed in OE cognates: to *cooperate* is to *get along with* or *to work with* (as usual, phrasal verbs). But the state of "getting along with" or of "working together" ("getting-along-ness," "working togetherness") is harder to express in the core vocabulary than it is in the ready-made abstraction *cooperation* (which itself, in the core vocabulary of Latin, literally means "working with").

Instead of the brute-force quantitative methods just described, a rhetorical stylistics can use selective analysis, choosing keywords on the basis of their strategic use. In other words, with an awareness of the type of argument being pursued in a text, analysts can make other selections of key words. From this perspective, the selection of words from the different historical layers of English, with their different connotations and uses, constitutes an important persuasive resource; the particular choices at key points can support or subvert an argument.

An example of the usefulness of this method of "language of origin" awareness in rhetorical analysis comes from a *New Yorker* eulogy of the actress Audrey Hepburn written by John Lahr. A eulogy is of course an epideictic speech in praise, and, as one might expect in a piece celebrating someone so fashionable, words from French, old and recent, abound: *sensational, fine, elegantly, royalty, charm, gorgeous, delight, manners, aristocratic, privilege, gaiety, piquant, gamine.* But Lahr's specific epideictic thesis depicts Hepburn as someone who offered a rare combination of European sophistication with character traits that made her acceptable to "democratic America." He sums up in the final paragraph:

> What the camera caught behind the gaiety was the sweetness of a personality that seemed to move through the world without being tainted by it. Hepburn offered us a sense of wholeness, not hype. She radiated a freshness—what Truman Capote in his description of Holly Golightly [the character Hepburn played in *Breakfast at Tiffany's*] called "an almost breakfast-cereal air of health"...(Lahr, 1993, 72)

Noticeably, when Lahr celebrates Hepburn's internal qualities, the reality behind the glamorous appearance that, according to his argument, endeared her to American audiences, he selects terms that come from the core vocabulary, both in root and suffix: *sweetness, wholeness,* and *freshness,* core qualities in core terms.

The persuasive effects of differences in word choice based on origins can be subtle. The following brief argument comes from a science news story reporting the claim that wild populations of chimpanzees exhibit different "cultures." This argument depends on readers perceiving distinctions in the chimps' reported behavior; it depends, in other words, on a *topos* or argument from contrast. How does the language support this goal?

[1] [a]Some chimpanzees greedily slurp ants off a stick as if it were a wriggling lollipop, [b]while others daintily pluck them one by one.

[2] [a]Some chimps mop their brows with leaves; [b]others demurely raise their arms while companions groom them.

[3] Researchers now agree that the variety of behavior exhibited by mankind's closest relative can be summed up in a single word: culture. (Verrengia, 1999)

The term *chimpanzee* itself, the subject of all the attention, comes from the Portuguese, who in turn took it from an African language, Kongo: *ci-mpenzi.* The functional and structural words in this passage come, of course, from Old English: *some, off, as, if, it, were, while, others, one, by, their, with, now, that, the, can, be, up.* None of the words reporting chimpanzee behavior in this popular account is a learned borrowing from Latin. The majority of the key words in sentences 1 and 2 also come from Old English or from cognate languages like Dutch or Middle Low German. These core words provide the basic categories of observation, the language of sense description: *arm, brow, ant, stick, leaf.* However, a few significant words come from French, and they are not randomly distributed. Each of the sets of observations reported in the first and second sentences breaks into two parts containing examples that are meant to be in contrast. These groups are marked in the passage by *a*'s and *b*'s: for instance, the slurping chimps versus the plucking ones, or the brow-mopping chimps versus the ones grooming with raised arms. Only the *b* groups have words derived from French, words that came into English primarily between 1100 and 1300 and that describe polite manners: *daintily* (which once meant excellently) and *demurely.* Not surprisingly, these help to create the impression of refined groups contrasted with uncouth ones (part of the significant anthropomorphizing going on in this argument). The very possibility of contrasting types of behavior is essential to the argument in this text: if chimps exhibit different learned behaviors, they have different cultures.

The third sentence of the article sums up or generalizes from the observations reported in the first two. Significantly, only one word in this sentence comes straight through from OE, and that is the word *word*; only two others come ultimately from OE roots, *behavior* and *mankind*, but these were not in use until Middle English. All the rest—*researchers, agree, variety, exhibited, closest, relative, summed, single,* and *culture*—came into English via Old French (and ultimately from Latin).[10] In other words, the explanatory and summative, or generalizing and abstracting, vocabulary comes from a different level in the language, not from the core words. However, significantly, this interpretive vocabulary is not derived directly from classical languages and so is not, in fact, as abstract or general as it could be, since this piece appeared in a newspaper. A more scholarly vocabulary of interpreting and generalizing would come from direct Latin or Greek borrowings.

The examples offered above show how selection from different layers in the language can serve an argument, in these cases arguments that characterize and evaluate. Difference in word choice according to origins can also deliver the arguer's projected ethos or character, always a rhetorically salient dimension of a text. An arguer can also switch from one layer of the language to another to convey different degrees of intensity or commitment to a claim. An example of this practice, which amounts to an internal translation from one level to another, comes from a scholarly article about plagiarism written in part in the first person:

> I ask myself what I am to do, as a WPA [Writing Program Adminstrator], given my beliefs about the roles that our construction of plagiarism play in reproducing and naturalizing social hierarchy and its constituent discourses—including, in this case, the constituent discourse of compulsory heterosexuality and binary gender.

I don't like cheating. I'm mad when I discover that a paper has been ghostwritten. I don't think teachers should look the other way. (Howard 2000, 487)

This passage moves in and then out of formal, Latinate diction. After the word *roles* (from OFr), the author's language comes from an academic register of abstract terms and therefore abstract ideas. Latin borrowings and coinages include *construction, reproducing, constituent, discourse, sexuality, binary,* and the most important word, *plagiarism* (from L *plagiarius,* meaning kidnapper). Latin-derived *constituent* is used in the unusual sense of *constituting* and not the more common meaning of *a part of. Compulsory, naturalize, gender,* and *social* come from Latin via French. Both *hierarchy* and *hetero* in *heterosexuality* come from Greek.

However, in the first line of the quoted passage and in its second paragraph, words from the core Old English vocabulary dominate. While *cheating* (cognate with the legal term *escheat*), *discover,* and *paper* come from Old French, the remaining words making up the common phrases come from the core: *I don't like, I'm mad, I don't think teachers should look the other way.* Most interesting in this section is the synonym for plagiarism, *ghostwritten,* which is in fact a compound formed in the German manner from two OE roots.

There is, then, in this passage a marked difference in effect that depends on the language of origin. Where the author expresses her personal reactions, her gut feelings, the words come from the core vocabulary of sincerity. Where her points reflect the common idiom of her discipline and its ways of naming and defining, Latin scholarly terms dominate. But it might be more correct to put this point in the reverse way: readers take some phrases as the expression of sincere feelings *because* the core vocabulary dominates, and they count other parts as learned, analytical, and abstract because they feature Latinate diction.

Summary

Every language offers its users certain "affordances," certain options and constraints, because of both its fixed constitutive forms and its historically contingent features. With its composite lexicon, English offers its users a rich array of choices and synonyms that tend to cluster, as this chapter argues, in three levels: the Anglo-Saxon core, the French additions beginning with the Normans, and the direct borrowings from Latin and Greek. These levels stand proxy for environments of usage. Given the typical contexts for words from these origins, English users associate words from these different levels with differences in persuasive appeals: the familiar, the elevated, the erudite. Rhetorical analysts can use this linguistic resource in two ways when analyzing a text: they can calculate proportions of words from the varying origins quantitatively to assess the overall level, or they can examine subsets or individual words judged important according to some criterion of selection. It is especially useful in this profiling to combine facts about language strata with argument analysis, noting the origins of terms that are critical in defining, characterizing, or evaluating. Also worth attention is the way a rhetor or text moves in and out of different layers of the lexicon, now aiming at a summative overview in distancing Latinate diction, now elevating with words interlaced from French, now using closer, look-you-in-the-eye core words, the oldest, simplest, and often strongest in the English language.

NOTES

1. In his discussion of Lincoln's oratory, Kenneth Cmiel emphasizes Lincoln's "Saxon eloquence" (1990, 116). He also notes that Lincoln replaced Latin words with Anglo-Saxon equivalents in his First Inaugural and that he often achieved a "dignified nobility," particularly in the passage cited from the Second Inaugural (117). But Cmiel does not identify the source of this dignity in Lincoln's occasional choice of words from the lexical layer of Norman French origin.

2. The many available histories of the English language include Albert C. Baugh and Thomas Cable, *A History of the English Language,* 5th ed. New York: Prentice Hall, 2001; Barbara Strang, *A History of English,* London: Methuen, 1970; Joseph M. Williams, *Origins of the English Language: A Social and Linguistic History,* New York: Macmillan, 1975; David Crystal, *The Stories of English,* New York: Overlook Press, 2004; Lynda Mugglestone, ed., *The Oxford History of English,* New York: Oxford University Press USA, 2006; Richard Hogg and David Denison, *A History of the English Language,* Cambridge: Cambridge University Press, 2006; Seth Lerer, *Inventing English: A Portable History of the Language,* New York: Columbia University Press, 2007; and Charles Barber, Joan C. Beal, and Philip A. Shaw, *The English Language: A Historical Introduction,* 2nd ed. Cambridge: Cambridge University Press, 2009.

3. Whatever the merits of this account, it does have the political benefit of genetically unifying the inhabitants of the British Isles, a benefit that Tony Blair drew on in his speech to the Irish Parliament (1998): "We experienced and absorbed the same waves of invasions: Celts, Vikings, Normans—all left their distinctive mark on our countries."

4. On the chronology of assimilating Old Norse into Old English, see Crystal 2004, 65–77. Crystal points out that ON words, which obviously entered the spoken language first, do not actually appear in documents until centuries later (73).

5. When words are rank-ordered according to their frequency in a given corpus, their distribution follows the statistical pattern known as Zipf's law. Thus the most common word (*the*) appears twice as often as the next most common (*of*) and so on, with proportionally diminishing occurrences down the ranks.

6. Other homonyms exist because one word has acquired quite distinct, albeit plausibly derived, meanings over time.

brogue[1] = a heavy shoe of untanned leather formerly worn in Scotland and Ireland. From Irish and Scottish Gaelic *broc* = shoe

brogue[2] = a strong dialectical accent, especially a strong Irish accent (probably from the brogues worn by Irish peasants).

7. The precise Latin term for freeing someone from slavery was *manumission*. A directly Latin-derived variant of King's phrase might be *manumitted terminally*. The prevalent Latinate choice was, however, *emancipated*.

8. In 1846, in the seventh edition of his *Elements of Rhetoric*, Richard Whately, a British clergyman, firmly associated French terms with sham elegance: "It is worthy of notice, that a Style composed chiefly of the words of French origin, while it is less intelligible to the lowest classes, is

characteristic of those who in cultivation of taste are below the highest. As in dress, furniture, deportment, &c., so also in language, the dread of vulgarity constantly besetting those who are half-conscious that they are in danger of it, drives them into the extreme of affected finery" (262).

9. The words in this passage can be separated into the following categories based on language of origin:

Latin and Greek: *existence, cooperation, genetically* (Greek), *unrelated, fundamental, biology* (Greek), *economics* (Greek), *exclusively, incentives, theories* (Greek)

French: *social, order, individual, problem, science, prevailing, approach, rewards, face, view, interested, altruism* (a late borrowing directly from French but coined from a Latin root), *sanction, rendering, choice, perceived, just, legitimate, matter, bas(ed), source, human, experiment(al)(ly), serious, negative, effects*

Old English: *the, of, and, among, is, a, in, as only, if, or, whether, are, does, not, these, however, here, we, show, that, has, because, it, on, self, behavioural* (ultimately from OE *behaven*), *fair(ness), short(comings), over(looks). They* is from Norse.

10. The identification of origins of the key words (nouns, verbs, adjectives, adverbs) produces the following profile, sentence by sentence:

First sentence: *(a)* **greedily** (from *greedy,* OE *graedig*); **slurp** (from Dutch *slurpen*); **ant** (from OE *aemete*); **stick** (from OE *sticca*); **wriggling** (*wriggle* from MLGer *wrigglen*); **lollipop** (source unknown; perhaps from *lolly* = tongue);

(b) **daintily** (from *dainty,* from OFr *deintie* from L. *dignus* = worthy); **pluck** (from OE *pluccian*).

Second sentence: *(a)* **mop** (from ME *mappe,* perhaps from OFr dial. = napkin from L *mappa* = cloth, towel); **brow** (from OE *bru*); **leaves**/leaf (from OE *leaf*);

(b) **demurely**/demure (probably from OFr *mur, meur* = mature, serious); **raise** (from ON *reisa*); **arm** (from OE *earm*); **companion** (from OFr *compaignon*); **groom** (from ME *grom* = boy, servant, perhaps from OE *growan* = to grow).

Third sentence: **researchers** (*research* from MF *recercher* from OF *re* + *cercher* = to search); **agree** (from MF *agreer* from L *ad* + *gratum*); **variety** (from MF or L; MF *varieté* from L *varietatis*); **behavior** (from *behave,* ME *behaven* = *be* + *haven* from OE); **exhibited**/exhibit (ME *exhibiten* from L *exhibitus,* past participle of *exhibere* = to present); **mankind** (from ME *mankind* from OE *man* and OE *cyn* = kin); **closest** (*close* from MF *clos* from L *clauses,* past part. of *claudere* = to close); **relative** (from MF *relatif* or LL *relativus*); **summed up** (phrasal verb *to sum up; sum* from OFr *summer* from ML *summare*); **single** (from MF from L *singulus*); **word** (from OE *wort*); **culture** (from MF from L *culturus*).

Once upon a time, governments were made to conform to the popular will by the mechanism of elections. This is now passé: politicians are striving to replace elective democracy with a new, pre-emptive version. In pre-emptive democracy, politicians employ the wizards of opinion polls and focus groups to tell them what the people want, and then deliver promptly. It is a system fitting for the modern age. Food is fast, credit is immediate, manufacturing is just-in-time. So why not instamocracy?

LEXINGTON, 1996

2

NEW WORDS AND CHANGING USES

THE AUTHOR OF this paragraph rummaged around in the language to find words with just the right associations for the key notions in his argument. "Lexington" used the durable but unassimilated French word *passé* for things out of fashion and adopted the adjective *pre-emptive*, created from the verb *pre-empt* and usually collocating with a term of art from warfare (e.g., *pre-emptive strike*) to modify *democracy*. The term *wizard* may be used with a nod to its newer sense as a program subroutine and the triple-word compound *just-in-time* to suggest the business practice of reducing inventory and speeding up production. Finally the author coined a new term by clipping the last letters off *instant* and the first letters off *democracy* and smashing the resulting morphemes together to form *instamocracy*.

From Nonce Constructions to Wider Use

An invented word like *instamocracy* is always intentional, and hence such coinages are stylistic and rhetorical "hot spots." They indicate where the rhetor found the existing language wanting in a word with the just the right denotation and connotation and so invented a *nonce word* to fill a unique need. A dictionary entry in itself, a *nonce word* is a "word occurring, invented, or used just for a particular occasion" (*American Heritage Dictionary*). Writers and speakers often invent new terms or *neologisms* to express a precise sense with just the appropriate nuance they want to convey. In some genres, such pyrotechnics with the language are the norm, and the presence of coined or morphed words becomes a persuasive dimension in itself.

> Are they slam-grass? Or y'all-ternative? These are trick questions. As the Bad Livers' aptly titled fifth full-length implies, Austinites Danny Barnes and Mark Rubin are simple, hard working, post-post-Dustbowl balladeers who put the country back in alt-country. Perhaps they're the Abbott & Costello (the lanky Barnes and the stout Rubin, respectively) of the Americana scene, but the Livers' vast charms remain intact as they infuse folk forms with ingenuity and verve. (Woodlief 1999)

Here the author, pressured to describe a new musical style derived from older styles, creates a new compound, *slam-grass*, from the genre labels *slam dancing* and *bluegrass*. He takes the established clipping *alt* from *alternative*, once a term for more experimental musical styles, morphs it into the Southern U.S. version of the second person plural, *y'all*, and puts that back on the remaining *ternative* with a hyphen to create *y'all-ternative*.

Such wordplay appeals to those who value new trends, so, not surprisingly, new words spangle the genres which review and hence sell new music, clothing, accessories, lifestyles, and theories. In fact, the creation of a new word can be taken as an implicit argument for newness on the assumption that the just-now-named object, perception, or concept is new because the language is. These nonce constructions are, however, also a means of language expansion. While most special nonce creations disappear after a single, original use, some become widely used if they fill a need. It is not likely, for example, that *Abe-apalooza* (a blend of *Abe* + *lollapalooza*), coined to describe President Obama's Lincoln-themed inauguration, will be around two hundred years from now (though urbandictionary.com gives a spurious stability to these one-off coinages). But *gerrymander*, compounded in 1812 from a governor's name and the last two syllables of *salamander*, is still in use. Appreciating how new words enter the language for the moment or for the duration, requires reviewing the sources of language expansion. Some of these sources reveal the structural basics (morphology) of English word forms; all the methods highlight the ingenuity of language users.

I. FOREIGN BORROWINGS

The history of English already illustrates how a language can grow by taking in words from other languages. The core language, Old English, acquired new words through successive borrowings or impositions from Scandinavian, Norman French, Latin, Greek, and any other language that English speakers came in contact with, producing the extensive vocabulary that English has today. Generally, words enter a language when the things they denote enter people's lives. The new words typically represent new referents, so, not surprisingly, foreign borrowings loom large among words for cultural borrowings (*tae kwon do, salsa dancing*) or adopted foods (*focaccia, quesadilla, dim sum*).

Foreign "loanwords" differ in their rhetorical effects, however, depending on whether they assimilate or not. Some retain their foreignness in the host language; they are frequently italicized to indicate that they are snatched from another tongue, and hence their borrowed status is marked. They can keep their foreign aura even when they have been in use for decades or centuries: for example, *coup d'état* (the French word for overthrowing a government) or *Weltanschauung* (the German word for worldview or outlook on life). In older English prose, the use of foreign words usually indicated that the writer knew another language and drew on it selectively for precision and some display of erudition. So the use of unassimilated foreign borrowings can be the sign of a multilingual rhetor or of a special register. Other foreign words assimilate; depending on a publication's style sheet, they cease to appear in italics (e.g., "angst" from German; "safari" from Swahili). Fairly recent borrowings will sometimes be seen in either form (e.g., *paparazzi* from Italian). When foreign borrowings lose their marked profile, they can lose their rhetorical punch. Furthermore, the ultimate meaning of a foreign borrowing depends on the host culture's ability to comprehend the new term. In the post-9/11 United States, for example, audiences learned of *madrassas* (or *madrassahs* or *madrasahs*) as schools of religious instruction or of anti-Western indoctrination. The instability in the English phonetic spelling shows the recency of this incorporation and matches a certain instability in meaning. Such foreign borrowings are often defined by the ambient argument.

2. COMPOUNDS

Languages also grow when users yoke existing words together to create compounds. Compounding is common in German, where more complex or abstract words are formed by combining simpler roots, for example, *Schadenfreude* = joy at another's pain. English allows the same combining of separate words into compounds with new meanings, often joining different parts of speech in the process: nouns with nouns (*toothache, hatband*), adjectives with nouns (*gentleman, whitecap*), verbs with nouns (*runway, brainwash*).

Compounds come in three varieties according to spelling conventions. First, words may occur together so frequently (usually an adjective and a noun) that they are considered a single lexical item and given their own entries in a dictionary: for example, *open house, open admissions, open sesame*. Second, two words may be combined through hyphenation. This compounding is frequently used to create adjectives: for example, *open-air, open-minded, open-ended*. Third, two words may simply be fused into a single word, though the two so combined will still be distinguishable: for example, *openhearted, openhanded*. The first category, compounds from collocation, is an important source of terms in politics and contemporary commentary: for example, *special interests, political correctness, road rage, peace process.*[1]

Free versus Bound Morphemes

In most compounds, the original two words are obvious, and each element can be used on its own. "Words" that are meaningful on their own ("strings of letters" would be more appropriate here) are called *free morphemes*. The word *lamp*, for example, has meaning by itself and contributes this meaning in compounds like *lamp-stand*, *lampshade*, and *lamp-light*. There are, however, some unusual morphemes that exist in a particular meaning only in combinations. These are *bound morphemes*, and many frequently used prefixes and suffixes belong in this class (see below). The morpheme *gate*, for example, meaning *scandal*, is a bound morpheme that acquired a special argumentative use in the late twentieth century. In 1973, President Nixon was involved in a complex scandal that became known collectively as *Watergate*, the name of the office/hotel complex where the initiating event occurred. Since the early '70s, the term *gate* has appeared in combination with other nouns, usually to indicate a scandal that involves a president. For Reagan it was *Irangate*; for Clinton it was *Monicagate* or *Troopergate*. These compounds usually emerge in print journalism, and they last about as long as interest in the story. But they have the rhetorical effect of assimilating the current scandal to the original one that led to the resignation of a president. In 2009, the morpheme appeared in an extra-presidential context in *climategate*, the label for a scandal involving e-mails among climate scientists. The morpheme *gate* obviously has a special meaning in these compounds, something like *high profile scandal*, that it has never acquired on its own (though uses like, "What will this president's *gate* be?" are always possible). Otherwise, *gate* as a free morpheme still means the "door" in a fence or barrier.

3. ADDING PREFIXES AND SUFFIXES

Recruiting words into new uses is often achieved by simply adding prefixes or suffixes to a root. The same root can even acquire several layers of affixes at both ends. The routine use of such before-or-after *affixes* creates large **derivational families** of words, and these families of related terms in turn can become a significant resource in argument (see chapter 6 on *polyptoton*). As a rough first principle for sorting out the results of these additions, prefixes can be said to alter meaning and suffixes to alter use.

Prefixes that Change Meaning

English offers a host of prefixes that add predictable meanings to the words they preface; they can be thought of as bound morphemes. Many of these come from Latin and Greek words, especially prepositions, and the meanings they add are derived from their meanings in these languages. Prefix + root combinations like the following, sometimes hyphenated and sometimes not, could almost be considered compounds: **co-** (meaning *with*): *copilot, codependent, coeval*; **hyper-** (meaning *above* or *beyond* and hence *exceedingly*): *hyperventilate, hyperactive, hypermedia, hypercorrect*; **multi-** (meaning *many*): *multitasking, multimedia, multiplex, multiparty*.[2]

The set of meaningful prefixes is not closed in English. New prefixes, or new bound morphemes, can be pressed into service. Decades ago the prefix *e-* created a host of words that have become part of the semantic field of computers or the internet: *e*-mail, *e*-commerce, *e*-dating. The prefixes *bio* (meaning *biological in origin*, e.g. *biofuels*) and *nano* (meaning *extremely small* or *molecular-scale,* e.g., *nanotechnology*) are recent additions, often used to suggest "green" (environmentally friendly) or innovative technologies and hence to sell a host of products and policies. So too the little *i* introduced by Apple in the *i*Pod spread to other products and beyond (e.g., *i*Phone, *i*Tunes, *i*Pad). These new prefixes lend their essence to the trailing term, often with persuasive consequences.

Suffixes that Change Use

English has a small number of *inflectional suffixes* indicating, for example, possession (the girl's/girls' book) or the comparative and superlative forms of adjectives (smart*er*, smart*est*).[3] Other suffixes can move a word or root into a different functional class. **Adverbs**, for example, are created by adding *ly* to an adjective: for example, beautiful → beautiful*ly;* quick → quick*ly*. **Adjectives** can be created by a wide variety of possible suffixes added to nouns and verbs: for example, *-ous* (pore → por*ous*); *-ate* (sense → sens*ate*); *-able* or *-ible* (discuss → discuss*able*); *-esque* (usually to a proper name: Truman→ Truman*esque*).[4]

Many routine suffixes also exist to create **nouns** or to modify existing nouns in predictable ways. Adding *-er, -or, -ant, -eer* to almost any verb creates an agent that performs or fulfills the activity named by the verb: strain→strain*er*; create → creat*or*; claim → claim*ant*; profit→ profit*eer*. The suffix *–ist* also names the doer of an action, but it tends to be added to other nouns, not to verbs: piano → pian*ist*; bigamy → bigam*ist*. The ability to create agents gives language users significant labeling power.

Another important class of suffixes from the perspective of argument creates abstract nouns. Adding *–ing* to a verb can form gerunds, abstract nouns naming the activity achieved by the verb: melt → melt*ing,* sing → sing*ing,* pray → pray*ing*. Adding *-ation, -tion,* or *-sion* to a verb forms a noun that names the result of that verb: starve → starv*ation*, devote → devo*tion*, provide → provi*sion*. Some suffixes, around since Old English, create abstract nouns meaning the "state of," "quality of," or "condition of": *-hood*, added to nouns (state → state*hood*, brother → brother*hood*), and *-ness*, added to adjectives (sweet → sweet*ness*, tender → tender*ness*). Important Latin suffixes creating abstract nouns include *-ty, -ism, -ology, -tude,* and *-cy*. Finally, suffixes added to adjectives or nouns can create **verbs**: *-en* (cheap → cheap*en*), *-fy* (beauty → beautify), *-ize*(capital → capital*ize*), *-ate* (orchestra → orchestr*ate*)—another rich resource for spreading a concept into new functions.

Derivational Families

With affixes for forming different parts of speech from the same root, families of words come into existence with related meanings in different sentence roles: for example, *The* **lover** *loves the* **loved** *one* **lovingly**. Here the same root is seen in a noun, verb, adjective, and adverb. (The ending on the verb *loves* is an inflectional ending, indicating third person, and not a derivational ending.) Suffixes also have the power to form words at higher and higher levels of abstraction: *contain* → *container* → *containerize* → *container-ization*. The first word in this series comes from a Latin verb, itself a compound from *con/com* + *tenere* = together + hold. Adding –*er* produces the noun for the "thing that contains"; in English, this word tends to denote an object like a bin or box or bag that holds other objects. Adding -*ize* to this noun creates a new verb that means the act of putting things in such containers. In contemporary usage, this word has specialized to mean the practice of putting merchandise into larger containers more easily loaded on and unloaded from ships and trains. Adding -*ation* to this verb creates the new abstract noun *container-ization*, the action or state or condition of containerizing things. The whole process can now be talked about under a single label. President Nixon used this method of abstraction by suffixation in his 1969 speech explaining changing U.S. policy in the war in Vietnam: "In the previous administration, we Americanized the war in Vietnam. In this administration, we are Vietnamizing the search for peace" (Safire 1997, 915). Going one step further, Nixon called this policy *Vietnamization* (915), suggesting an orderly, planned process. The potential rhetorical payoff from these routine methods of word formation is discussed below in the section on "Schemes of Words" in chapter 6.

4. CLIPPING

Both combining words into compounds or adding prefixes and suffixes create longer words. But new words can also be formed by taking parts off of existing ones to create shorter coinages. This process is called clipping. Identifying a clip often requires historical knowledge about which form of a word was available in the language first.[5] The following are some well-known examples.

fax ← *facsimile*   *porn* or *a porno* ← *pornography*   *ap* ← *application*
dis ← *disrespect*   *detox* ← *detoxification*   *hyper* ← *hyperactive*

As this group suggests, most clips come into the language informally, in spoken discourse, since speakers naturally tend to shorten multisyllabic words and delete endings, especially when they use a word frequently. When these shortcuts are used, they also indicate that the speaker is taking a certain license with a word; hence clipping often indicates familiarity and sometimes an edge of disrespect, as in shortening *professor* to *prof.*

5. BLENDS

A celebrity magazine refers to the duo of Brad Pitt and Angelina Jolie as *Brangelina,* a single name for the fused couple (with perhaps the dominance of Jolie shining through). This new term is a blend, made from parts of existing words melded together. Blends, sometimes called *portmanteau words*, can be thought of as compounds of clips, but the separate words may no longer be recognizable. Below are some common blends and the probable pair of words that were combined to create them:

chunnel = channel + tunnel   *televangelist* = television + evangelist

infomercial = information + commercial   *globesity* = global + obesity

emoticon = emotion + icon   *shockumentary* = shock + documentary

Blends are rhetorically potent; they visibly and phonetically combine terms to create new entities fusing their referents. A case in point is Indian Minister of Commerce and Industry Jairam Ramesh's coinage *Chindia*, a blend that combines *China* and *India* to epitomize his argument for the combined power of these giant economies in bordering nations (Ramesh 2006). Obviously, blends like *Chindia* require some cooperation from the words involved; they should ideally share a syllable or result in a pronounceable combination of phonemes. President's names, frequent sites for word coinage, either lend themselves to combinations (*Reagonomics, Obamamentum*) or they do not (Eisenhower, Roosevelt). Because of their radical and playful melding of roots, blends tend to occur in informal genres as they signal creative new combinations, like Joe Klein's *pajamahadeen* (pajama + mujahadeen) for the bloggers who detected a forged letter on George Bush's military service. Over time, blends can lose their novelty and their evocation of the blended words; they become as staid as *brunch* (= breakfast + lunch).

6. CONVERSIONS

In the mass-circulation women's magazine *Family Circle*, a contributor wrote, "Usually I lame out on a Valentine's gift for my husband." Further down on the same page, another contributor lamented that when it came to sunscreen, "I don't always have time to do a full slather" (Inner Circle 2009, 15). These easily found examples illustrate the common process of conversion, pressing a term from one part of speech into service in another. In the first case the adjective *lame*, meaning, colloquially, *pathetic* (not the verb meaning *to cripple*), is used as in a phrasal verb, *to lame out* (perhaps with a nod to the older *to flame out*), and in the second case the verb *slather*, to spread on thickly, is used as a noun, *a full slather*. Normally, English uses suffixes to change a word from one part of speech or "word class" to another (see the sample suffixes above). But English also allows speakers simply to begin using a word with no alteration in form as a different part of speech. The most frequent migration occurs when nouns become verbs. A *bonus*, for example, is a noun meaning an extra gift or benefit. But an enterprising ad writer, describing a special offer, promised that if the prospective customer bought the product, the manufacturer would "*bonus you*" with an extra item. The noun becomes a transitive verb, the action of giving someone a gift as a bonus. This conversion does not seem to have caught on, but recruiting the noun *text* to the verb *to text* is now indispensable in the era of instant messaging (*I just texted him*). The dictionary demonstrates that conversions often become established; many entries for a single lexical item have two parts, one for the noun and one for the verb form (e.g., *ride* is well established as a noun and verb, but *go* is noticeable when used as a noun: *There's no go in him*).

Adjectives and nouns can also change places without any added endings: *He is creative* (adjective); *You need a creative to do that* (noun). Indeed, any word can become a noun by putting an article in front of it (*a/the*), and this process can work in reverse. Nouns easily become adjectives: the *tape* recorder, a *New England* accent. The item *paper* can in fact fill in for three parts of speech—verb, noun, and adjective—without changing form: *Paper your walls with a paper that has a paper surface*. David Crystal shows that in British English *round*, without alteration, can function in five word classes, as a noun, verb, adjective, adverb, and preposition (2003, 207).

7. CATACHRESIS

Listed among the tropes in rhetorical style manuals, *catachresis* is the borrowing of an available word to designate something that lacks a label. The mechanism of new word formation here often involves *metaphor*, lifting a word out of one context and inserting it into another. But the *Rhetorica ad Herennium*, Quintilian, and other classical sources distinguish replacing an available word with another (e.g., calling a *warrior* a *lion*) from filling a void with a borrowed word. A metaphor substitutes for another word and may invite attention to itself as a replacement, a marked alternative. A catachresis cannot also invoke another word because there is no other word. When speakers or writers want to name the unnamed, they can coin an entirely new word, as Michael Faraday did when he used Greek roots, at the suggestion of William Whewell, to invent the words *anode* and *cathode* for parts of his electrolysis apparatus. But it is also possible to just borrow a word from another semantic field and carry it over to a new one. If the new word sticks and the context for its use arises frequently, the borrowed sense will simply become an additional meaning of the word.

A case in point is the word *spam*. For language users in the twenty-first century, *spam* means *unwanted e-mail* or *junk e-mail* (see "Loss and Migration" below for the history of *junk* itself). Originally *spam* was a trade name for a kind of canned lunch meat that was popular during World War II when meat was rationed. It is listed in the dictionary as a proper noun, *Spam*. To the chagrin of Hormel, the company that makes canned spam (still available, and quite tasty fried), the word was adopted (or stolen) to refer to unsolicited e-mail. In this new sense, it has migrated to other parts of speech and taken on other forms: *to spam, spamming, spammers*. Taking a word for a food product and applying it to cyberspace excess is certainly a case of borrowing from an alien semantic field, but despite its catachrestic origins, its current use is not metaphorical. Most users of the word in its computer context (as the author has informally determined) have no idea of its origins. The language is filled with such catachrestic borrowings, which can lose their original meaning as their new context expands.

8. ACRONYMS

Acronyms are words formed from the first letters of strings of words. This method of word creation is expanding, thanks to the substantial number of technical terms and titles that have entered relatively wide usage. Accurate but lengthy labels are often too ponderous to repeat fully, so after a first usage they are shortened to initials. When the acronyms become common, that is, more familiar to more people, they are used alone: *DNA* = deoxyribonucleic acid; *MRI* = magnetic resonance imaging; *WMD* = weapons of mass destruction. If the acronym happens to form a pronounceable word, it will be treated as one, even when all caps are used to mark the fact that it is an acronym: *NATO* = North Atlantic Treatise Organization, *nimby* = not in my backyard.[6] When the acronym does not cooperate, it remains a set of separately articulated letters: *FBI, CIA*. Because of their frequent source in new technologies and new organizations, acronyms carry the rhetorical freight of expertise and authority. The expanding lexicon of instant messaging has also spawned new acronyms for prepared phrases that would be too tedious to *thumb* in: *imho* (in my humble opinion); *lol* (laugh out loud), *btw* (by the way), and keypad creations using the rebus principle, like *b*4, *gr*8.

9. PROPER NAMES TO COMMON NOUNS

The proper names of people and products can migrate into the language as common nouns and occasionally as other parts of speech. Manufacturers may file lawsuits when their product names are used by others for profit, but there can be advantages when the name of a particular brand becomes the generic name of a product. That has happened with Kleenex, Coke, and most successfully with Xerox, a proprietary name pressed into service as a noun (a *Xerox* = a photocopy), a verb (*to Xerox* = to photocopy), and even an adjective (*Xeroxed* copy). In this manner, the names of people and countries are the sources of common words like the following: *lynch, limousine, bowdlerize, diesel, chauvinism, sandwich, saxophone, watt, sadism, bikini, china, duffel, boycott, platonic.*

Proper names can be easily turned into adjectives for nonce usage, depending on which suffix sounds best: *Reaganesque, Clintonesque, Carter-like, Nixonian*. A proper noun can also be turned into an abstract noun standing for the essential properties of a person, a usage that was separately marked in figure manuals: "He is a *Malfoy*," "She is a *Mata Hari*." Urbandictionary.com is studded with such fugitive proper name abstractions.

10. ANALOGY

In this method, a new word is formed according to the model of another word that is close in meaning. The terms *prequel* and *interquel*, for example, were formed by analogy with *sequel* and the appropriate prefixes. *Masculism* as a critical perspective was formed off *feminism, pax Americana* from *pax Romana,* and *earjacking* from *carjacking* (itself a blend from car + hijacking, *hijacking* itself a backformation and derivational alteration of *highjacker,* which has a further history).

Martin Luther King Jr. used analogical word formation when he spoke on behalf of striking sanitation workers in Memphis in 1968. Following the success of the *sit-in* in the civil rights movement, he called for a *bank-in movement* and an *insurance-in*. He wanted African Americans to take their money out of white-owned businesses and patronize only black-owned banks and insurance agencies. In naming these very different activities, King reached through analogy for the connotations, the cultural capital, of the *sit-in* (King 1968).

In the last ten years, the term *genomics* has gained currency. It stands for the study of the *genome*, the entire complement of genes in an organism. Scientists who wished to study the entire collection of proteins in a cell subsequently called their discipline *proteomics* and their object of study *the proteome*. Such coinages are not trivial. They bring an object of knowledge into existence, and as such they have persuasive value. In this case also, the similarity in naming between *proteomics* and *genomics* suggests equal importance and hence equal funding rights.

11. FABRICATION

Advertisers with a new product to sell know the importance of a clever name in persuading buyers. They have two possible avenues for name formation. They can create a product name from existing words with persuasive connotations (*Mr. Clean, Crest, Close-Up, Tide*), or they can fabricate an entirely new word as a name (*Pantene*, a shampoo; *Tyvek*, a building material; *Lycra*, a synthetic fabric). Car models often have names fabricated to sound euphonious: *Camry, Elantra, Cantera*. A large number of product names, it should be noted, fall in both these categories. They are compounds or blends or morphed forms echoing meaningful single words: Amtrak's fastest train, for example, is named the *Acela*, a word suggesting speed as in *accelerate*; a brand of the sweetener sucralose was named *Splenda,* with hopeful associations.

A few common words with no known etymology are thought to have come into the language as complete fabrications: for example, *fribble, taffy*. One of these is *kluge/kludge*, referring to a patched-together system or clumsy piece of software. This word, and the many invented product names like those listed above, raise again the interesting question of whether individual morphemes have broad meanings related to their sound. Would a combination including a *sh* or *an*, combined in the fabrication *Shangri-la* (the mythical kingdom in James Hilton's *Lost Horizons*), ever sound as awkward as a combination with the *kl* and *ug* of *kluge*?

12. ONOMATOPOEIA

Giambattista Vico, an eighteenth-century jurist and rhetorician, clarified the meaning of *onomatopoeia*: "it is not a trope, but it is that activity by which the most fitting terms are formed having been fashioned after the sounds themselves" (Vico 1996, 151). Several word classes can be explained from this mimicry. The interjections, for example, originate in the expressive syllables of human emotion: *Ah or Ahh, Oh, Huh? Ugh! Eh? Yeck!* (but evidently not the conventional and somewhat archaic *Alas,* which is now used to express feigned regret). Other words are meant to imitate sounds in naming them: *whiz, whirr, clang, clatter, clink, honk, rumble, boom, bang, squeak, swish*—and for animals, *growl, woof, meow, moo, baa, cluck, neigh, snort, grunt, hee-haw,* and the ever popular but never heard *cock-a-doodle-do.*

These "sound words" name the sound as nouns, but they can also be used as verbs to describe the action of making the sound ("The cows *mooed* in the fields") or as adjectives ("the *mooing* cows"). In short, some terms of onomatopoeic origin have become full-fledged words taking regular endings. Others remain oddities, used not simply to refer to sounds but to represent the experience of the sound (*varoom, clickety-clack, rat-tat-tat, kaboom*). Some of these are one-time creations for sound effects in a particular text, such as Jon Krakauer's "THWOCK-THWOCK-THWOCK-THWOCK" to invoke the sound of a helicopter (Krakauer 1997, 276) or Tom Wolfe's *Ggghhzzzzzzzzhhhhhhggggggzzzzzzzeeeeong,* the sound of Junior Johnson's souped-up car running a roadblock (Wolfe 1965, 123).

13. TABOO DEFORMATION

Among the remaining methods of generating new words is **taboo deformation**. This process "deforms" or creates a sound-alike word as a polite replacement for a word that might offend. *Darn it* is the gentler form of *Damn it; Gee whiz* avoids taking Jesus' name in vain; *goldarned* spares the speaker from swearing *God-damned.* The number of replacement terms for parts of the body and their functions is large, but many of these are not used as polite substitutes. They signal familiar, colloquial, informal, and even vulgar registers instead and hence can quite clearly communicate attitudes and value judgments. The contemporary tolerance for profanity and the naming of parts in public seems to have eliminated the need for taboo deformation, but even radio jocks have been heard to use the acronym *mf.* A speaker's, and less frequently a writer's, use of profanity and vulgarity is a marked rhetorical resource inviting inferences about their edginess, honesty, etc. Such flirting with profanity is a matter of register, discussed below. But in general, a language is rhetorically impoverished, without the resource of certain effects, if it has no boundary-defining taboo deformations.

14. DOUBLING

Yet another source of new words is the practice of **doubling** or **reduplication**. A *goody-goody* is more than just good, and to *pooh-pooh* is to dismiss utterly; as usual, repetition means intensification. More common than just repeating is changing a vowel or the initial consonant in the second half of a double, as Jon Krakauer did when he described crossing ice crevasses on unstable ladders as *herky-jerky* (Krakauer 1997, 83). This doubling with variation has produced many now established terms, including *riff-raff, mishmash, criss-*

cross, shilly-shally, roly-poly, sing-song, willy-nilly, itsy-bitsy, hurdy-gurdy. Edward Sapir observed that this method of word formation was "all but universal," and he described such doubles as often "contemptuous in psychological tone" (Sapir 1949, 76). The tendency, revealed in this method of word invention, to generate a second word form on the basis of phonetic similarity helps to explain the persuasive effects of the rhetorical scheme *agnominatio* described below.

Loss and Migration

Francis Bacon wrote *The Proficience and Advancement of Learning* (1605) in English, but the twenty-first-century reader of a sentence like the following might wonder: "The second method of doctrine was introduced for expedite use and assurance sake; discovering the more subtile forms of sophisms and illaqueations with their redargutions, which is that which is termed *elenches*" (Bacon 1952, 60). Not only does this passage use familiar words in odd ways (e.g., *discovering . . . forms*), but several of its words have dropped from use entirely. Bacon was writing when English had many more borrowings directly from Latin than it has now. A similar decoding challenge faces anyone encountering older technical terms. In one of the first texts to describe objects seen through a microscope (a fairly recent coinage itself in the seventeenth century), Robert Hooke examined the "Beard of a wilde Oat." He described it as "wreath'd like a With," and noted that if it were dipped in "well rectify'd spirit of Wine" it would untwist itself, and then "upon the avolation of the spirit" retwist itself (Hooke 1665, 147). The reader encountering passages like these from Bacon and Hooke has no choice but to consult a historical dictionary that lists *archaic* or *obsolete* words and records the lost meanings of still familiar words.[7]

While the processes of word formation and the rhetorical pressures for nonce terms constantly add new words to English, the language also changes as words disappear, lose meanings, or acquire new ones. This constant process of meaning change, "semantic progression," or "drift" resembles "genetic drift," as though the language were an organism with an inherent property to mutate at a fixed rate over time. Actually, of course, it is only a convenience to speak of *words* changing meaning. As has often been pointed out, words themselves mean nothing; people mean things with words. It is speakers and writers who abandon or invent words or begin to use existing words in new ways as they adapt them to changing contexts and novel purposes. But typical usage masks this obvious fact; sounds and marks are instead endowed with meaning in themselves, and the typical question is "What does that word mean?" not "What do you mean by that word?" Since language users are the source of meaning, efficiency in communication would seem to favor unchanging meanings. But in fact, over decades and centuries, as any good historical dictionary will demonstrate, even what a lexical item denotes can change dramatically.

Junk: A Case Study

The process of meaning migration will strike anyone who reads older texts and comes upon a familiar word used in an unfamiliar way. Going through a single extended example of meaning shifts for a single form will illustrate the paths of change and the care needed in historical recovery. The following passage comes from *The Voyage of the Beagle*, Charles Darwin's account of his journey as a gentleman naturalist on board a surveying ship. Darwin's travel narrative includes many passages on the animals he encountered in South America and the Pacific Islands. In this excerpt, he describes a crab discovered on Keeling Island:

> I have before alluded to a crab which lives on the cocoa-nuts [sic]: it is very common on all parts of the dry land, and grows to a monstrous size: it is closely allied or identical with the Birgos latro. The front pair of legs terminate in very strong and heavy pincers, and the last pair are fitted with others weaker and much narrower. It would at first be thought quite impossible for a crab to open a strong cocoa-nut covered with the husk; but Mr. Liesk assures me that he has repeatedly seen this effected. [...] These crabs inhabit deep burrows, which they hollow out beneath the roots of trees; and where they accumulate surprising quantities of the picked fibres of the cocoa-nut husk, on which they rest as on a bed. The Malays sometimes take advantage of this, and collect the fibrous mass to use as junk. (1845, 462–63).

A twenty-first-century reader is likely to find the last word in this passage confusing. Why would anyone deliberately collect coconut fibers to use as *junk?* To today's readers, *junk* is something to get rid of. The usage in this context does not fit the current definition. What did Darwin mean?

The *Oxford English Dictionary* (OED), the basic resource for historical meanings, lists four separate entries for the noun *junk*. In the first, labeled obsolete, *junk*, brought in through Old French, refers to a *rush*, a reedy plant that grows in marshes whose stems are used for making baskets, etc. The latest passage cited with *junk* in this sense dates from 1526. However, the word *junk* meaning reeds or rushes was retained by surgeons, who used *junk* or reeds to make stiff bandages and splints. In this specialized context, according to OED citations, the word was still in use in medical texts in the nineteenth century.

A completely separate entry lists *junk* in use from the fifteenth century as a nautical term of "obscure origin" referring to old rope or cable, a commodity with many uses on board a ship. (*The American Heritage Dictionary* lists a usage in this sense from 1353.) From referring to old rope on ships, the word was generalized in meaning, according to further senses listed under this entry in the OED, to stand for any object discarded but still potentially useful. This extension, a case of metonymy, perhaps came about because there were once shops in ports that sold this old rope as well as other discarded nautical items, a surmise noted in a "Word History" note for *junk* in the *American Heritage Dictionary* and based on the early appearance of the compound *junk shop*. This broader meaning of *junk* as potentially reusable material is now listed in many dictionaries as its first (because most widely used) meaning, and subsequent senses show even further generalization. Users extended the term to nonobjects, so that now even ideas, comments, proposals, and just about anything can be labeled *junk* in informal contexts. This spread shows in the many compounds using *junk*, some of recent coinage like *junk mail, junk bonds,* and even *junk DNA*. By conversion, the term was also pressed into service as a verb, *to junk*.

The meaning migration of *junk* did not stop with the uses listed so far. The OED records a use as *slang* and *origin U.S.* under the second entry: *junk* referring to narcotics and especially to heroin. This meaning left its first textual tracks in the early twentieth century, but no doubt it had been in use for decades. This extension in meaning may have come about through a metaphorical borrowing, since *junk* was extended in the eighteenth century from old rope to salted meat carried on long voyages, which no doubt looked about as appetizing as old rope. But it is more likely that the extension to *heroin* came through metonymy, *heroin* and *junk* as old rope or other nautical discards coming in on the same ships and perhaps being sold in same dockside shops. *Junk* meaning heroin may itself now be less widely known than the term derived from it by adding a suffix, *junkie*, a narcotics user and dealer. This term has in turn been extended to label anyone who is avid consumer (e.g., *fast food junkie*).

Of the remaining two OED entries, the least common is *junk*[4], a regional term designating a seam in a bed of slate, a term of art among slate miners in southwestern England with scant textual trace. More important for the usage in question is *junk*[3], a type of sailing vessel common in the South China Sea. This *junk* entered English from the Portuguese *junco* or the Dutch *jonk*, versions of the Javanese and Malay word for these boats, *djong*. It might seem that this word would be related to *junk* signifying old rope, but that meaning was established before Europeans had direct contact with its users. It may, however, not be too far-fetched to think of heroin acquiring the label *junk*, again by metonymy, from the sailing *junks* that often carried heroin in Southeast Asia, rather than from *junk* as old rope.[8]

But which of these meanings covers Darwin's use in the passage from *The Voyage of the Beagle?* At that point on his journey, Darwin had been aboard a sailing vessel for several years. He had certainly seen his share of old cable and other nautical discards. He was in the Indian Ocean, southwest of the Malay Archipelago, and Darwin describes Malays as the transplanted residents on Keeling Island, collecting coconut husk fibers from crab burrows as a fresh material *to use as junk*. Were they using the fibers to make rope? To press into some other service? There is another intriguing possibility. Darwin had studied medicine at Edinburgh for two years and was likely familiar with the specialist meaning of *junk* surviving in the nineteenth-century lexicon of surgery.[9] Were the Malays using the coconut husks to stiffen bandages? Was Darwin likely to have observed this practice? His usage remains problematic.

English offers many examples of words, like *junk*, whose usage has migrated far from an original meaning. The paths of such meaning migration invite codification. (1) The process of expanding or generalizing the meaning is typical, as in the extension of *junk* from "old rope" to "anything discarded." (2) The reverse process can happen as well: meanings can narrow as usage becomes specialized. The word *meat*, for instance, now refers exclusively to consumable animal flesh. Some people even distinguish meat from chicken and fish. But *meat* was the Old English word for food, any food. Hence the old phrase "meat and drink" refers to "food and drink," not just to a beverage plus a slab of animal protein. (3) By conversion, users also press words into service as other parts of speech: the noun *junk* became the verb *to junk*. (4) Finally, certain "borrowed" uses of words can permanently add to or alter a word's meaning. Presumably, *junk* came to label heroin because it already labeled the nautical items traded and sold nearby, a case of metonymy, extending to something physically associated. In a case of analogical extension, the term *icebreaker*, originally the name of a ship that can force a passage through surface ice, was borrowed to label any activity that facilitates social interaction. This figural meaning is now listed in dictionaries as an established meaning of *icebreaker*, and in fact the borrowed sense is probably now more widely used than the original.

When a word like *junk* is encountered in a context where the current meaning does not fit, the problem is actually a blessing. Analysts know they have to search for a plausible historical sense. Much more difficult cases occur when a term can be understood in a passage under a current meaning, though that meaning is actually less likely than a meaning now lost. Such cases are always matters of interpretive argument. The term *race* is an example. In its contemporary meaning, it typically refers to broad groupings separating blacks, whites, and Asians; people asked how many races there are will usually answer three. But in the nineteenth century, this term also referred to what would now be called an *ethnic group*. Hence there were several European *races* according to nineteenth-century physical anthropologists, including the Nordic, Alpine, and Mediterranean. A reader encountering the term *race* in a nineteenth-century text may be misled.

Stories of meaning migration like those given above are the stuff of feature writing. People enjoy discovering that *bureau*, now the ubiquitous term for government offices, once designated the cloth covering a dresser, or that the word *decimate*, which now means roughly "to devastate," once very precisely meant "to kill one in ten." People sometimes believe that the older meaning of a word is the correct meaning, and later meanings are mistakes. This common assumption can be invoked in arguments where the sense of a word is at stake. But from a rhetorical and linguistic perspective, the "correct" meaning of a word is the meaning that language users will recognize and accept in a particular context.

Accumulating Senses

In the examples given above, words have changed by shedding meanings and acquiring new ones over time. *Junk* is no longer used to describe rushes or old rope, and *bureau* no longer refers to the cloth covering a desk. In another standard process of language change, users tweak available words into new contexts, and as a result words simply acquire new senses, nuances, and associations without losing any older ones. The oldest core words often carry such multiple senses, since they have been pressed into ever widening service for centuries. Take for example the verb *keep*, from the Old English *cepan* = to seize. The *American Heritage Dictionary* lists the following glut of senses for *keep* as a transitive verb:

> 1. To retain possession of. 2. To have as a supply. 3. To support (a family, for example). 4. To put customarily; to store. 5.a. To supply with room and board for a charge. b. To raise: *keep chickens*. 6. To maintain for use or service. 7. To manage, tend, or have charge of. 8. To preserve (food). 9. To cause to continue in a state or course of action. 10.a. To maintain records in: *keep a diary*. b. To enter (data) in a book. 11.a. To detain: *kept after school*. b. To restrain. c. To prevent or deter. d. To refrain from divulging. e. To save; reserve. 12. To maintain: *keep late hours*. 13. To adhere to; fulfill. 14. To celebrate; observe.

All these senses seem clustered around the same basic meaning of *retaining*. Alternatively, the variety of uses acquired by *keep* as a transitive verb really amount to a catalog of the kinds of objects that this verb can be paired with. People can *keep records, keep goldfish, keep a secret, keep milk in their refrigerators,* and *keep loved ones in their memories,* though these different uses do not convey quite the same kind of *keeping*. Furthermore, as an intransitive verb used in sentences without taking an object, *keep* has still another set of meanings:

> 1. To remain in a state or condition; stay.
> 2. To continue to do: *keep guessing*. [Here *keep* functions like an insistent or iterative *is* as used in the progressive; consider *is asking* versus *keeps asking*.]
> 3. To remain fresh or unspoiled.

These senses seem clustered around the notion of *remaining,* the result of *retaining.* Michael Stubbs cites the fact that the most frequent uses of the lexeme *keep,* as revealed by corpus data, occur in phrases like *kept locked* [i.e., remaining locked], not what people might think of as the primary meaning (2007, 129). And, not surprisingly for a word that has been around for so long, *keep* appears in many phrasal verbs (*keep at, keep down, keep off, keep to, keep up*) and in many idioms (*for keeps, keep an eye out, keep company, keep one's chin up, keep pace, keep time, keep to oneself*). No doubt new senses of this verb, transitive and intransitive, will arise in new contexts.

Words (*lexemes*) like *keep*, where related senses have accumulated, and homonyms like *match* (see above, 31), where distinct meanings coexist, can be described as *polysemous* (from the Greek words *poly* = many and *sema* = sign). A polysemous form can have many shaded or even distinct meanings, but English users rarely have problems distinguishing senses or meanings in context. They readily separate the *bank* of a river from a *bank* deposit; a *course* taken in school, the *course* of a *ship,* and the *course* of a meal; the *scale* of a fish, a *scale* on the piano, and a *scale* at a Weight Watchers' meeting. But in rhetorical stylistics, such polysemous word forms become a rich resource for the rhetorical figure *antanaclasis,* commonly called the pun (see above, 134).

Summary

Aristotle briefly suggested that new words should be used sparingly (Roberts, 168); Quintilian, who recognized compounds, derivations, analogical formations, and foreign borrowings, was more tolerant, though he noted other teachers who banned coinages for orators (1921, III, 227–31). For oral discourse, where the premium is on immediate clarity, the advice to minimize coinages remains sound. Early modern rhetoricians continued the same warnings; Erasmus approved of new coinages and using words in new ways, "if only they are interspersed in moderation" (Erasmus 1963, 23). But in contemporary English, at the service of a culture driven by fads and an economy fueled by innovation, new words abound, and they are persuasive in themselves as signs of new items, ideas, and ideologies. To invent a word is taken prima facie as a sign of invention. Furthermore, the methods of coinage available in English add a unique dimension to a new word: those formed with affixes join a family of similar terms; those borrowed from a foreign language carry foreignness until they assimilate; those coined analogically force comparisons with a model; those clipped from a longer word suggest the user's familiarity or even control.

At the same time that new words flood in, old ones trickle out, the pace of loss having slowed recently thanks to the storage and retrieval media now available. But ready access to older texts invites misreading and requires sensitivity from rhetorical analysts to avoid imputing current senses to previous uses. Again, rhetorical treatises marked this problem of construing the meanings of unstable terms in older texts as an argumentative issue. The *Rhetorica ad Herennium* ([Cicero] 1981, 81–87) and Cicero's *De Inventione* (1976, 285–313) note interpretive conflicts over ambiguities and "the letter versus the spirit," over what a term might have meant precisely at the time of its use, and what the author might have generally intended given the terms available. Rhetors have every reason to force this issue, pushing the envelope and stretching current words into new contexts where they might not quite mean what they have meant before.

NOTES

1. An excellent source of political terms and phrases, their origins and meanings, is William Safire's *Political Dictionary* (2008). These temporarily important terms and collocations come into the language by all the means listed in this chapter.

2. Other prefixes from Latin and Greek with fixed meanings include the following: *a/an- anti- ante- bi- de- dis- equi- ex- for/fore- hyper- hypo- in/im- mega- mis- mono- multi- non- post- pro- pre- semi- sub- super/supra- un-*.
Some suffixes also change a word's meaning in set ways, like *let* meaning small (as in *booklet, leaflet*) or the now avoided *ess* meaning a female version (*stewardess, poetess, actress*) and *ette* (related to *let*), suggesting a female or smaller version: *majorette, kitchenette*.

3. The inflectional endings in English, beyond those indicating possession and degrees in adjectives, include indicators of the third person singular of regular verbs (she laugh*s*) and the past tense or past participle (laugh*ed*), the *ing* of the present participle and progressive aspect (is laugh*ing*), and the endings marking plurals (hat*s*, child*ren*).

4. Other adjective-producing suffixes include *-ly* (friend → friend*ly*), *-like* (lady → lady*like*), *-ful* (dread → dread*ful*), and *-ish* (freak → freak*ish*). These function-changing suffixes come into English from different languages: *like, ful, and ish* from OE *ous* and *able* from Latin. But English happily mixes language of origin in affixes and roots. The easiest way to form adjectives, however, is to add *-ed* and *-ing* to verbs, creating past and present participles: *-ed* (overcook → overcook*ed*: *The overcooked vegetables remained on the plate*), *-ing* (lose → los*ing*: *The losing team also received a trophy*).

5. Describing how one part of speech can be created from another by adding a suffix, or one meaning can be derived from another with a prefix, does not mean that historically the root came into being before the form with an affix. In fact, a word can come into existence with an affix and can then be "back-formed" into a simplified "root." The process of back-formation can be distinguished from clipping, since in back-formation an affix, or supposed affix, is removed; the result is sometimes a word with a different meaning and different sentence functions, for example, *edit* back-formed from *editor*. Recognizing a back-formation also requires historical evidence of the earlier form.

6. A few acronyms have entered the language as ordinary words. *Awol* is one; a soldier who is *awol* is "away without leave." *Snafu* originated in World War II as a way of facetiously characterizing military operations: "situation normal, all f****d up." *Fob* is another, meaning "fresh off the boat."

7. The most widely used of these compendia is the *Oxford English Dictionary*, first compiled in the late nineteenth and early twentieth centuries and kept up to date with supplements. It is conveniently available and easily searchable online. It is, however, primarily a record of British usage, and although it quotes sentences demonstrating usage from sources, its sources are obviously skewed to written texts and further to literary over functional texts (Crystal 2004, 154, 289). For American English, the best historical dictionary sampling usage is *Webster's Third New International*, now a half-century old but also available online. Students of texts written from the late eighteenth century on have the option of consulting contemporary dictionaries, such as Noah Webster's first dictionary in 1828. Many specialized dictionaries are also available recording regional, spoken, and technical varieties of English.

8. The story of *junk* continues. In the last few years, *junk* has been pressed into service as yet another term for male genitalia. And informants told the author in 2007 that in the Washington, D.C., area they have heard "That *junks* is nice/sweet" (Halim Mahjid) or "That *junks* is crucial" (Michael Alan Blair). In the context of use, the denotation, they report, is often to music and the connotation is entirely positive.

9. See for example, Wharton's *Minor Surgery and Bandaging*, 1893, 300–1. The term "junk bags" appears, without explanation, referring to stiff bandages or splints on broken legs.

3

CATEGORIES OF

WORD CHOICE

Your Honor stands between the past and the future. You may hang these boys; you may hang them by the neck until they are dead. But in doing it you will turn your face toward the past. In doing it you are making it harder for every other boy who in ignorance and darkness must grope his way through the mazes which only childhood knows. In doing it you will make it harder for unborn children. You may save them and make it easier for every child that some time may stand where these boys stand. You will make it easier for every human being with an aspiration and a vision and a hope and a fate. I am pleading for the future; I am pleading for a time when hatred and cruelty will not control the hearts of men. When we can learn by reason and judgment and understanding and faith that all life is worth saving, and that mercy is the highest attribute of man.
Clarence Darrow, closing argument, ILLINOIS V. NATHAN LEOPOLD AND RICHARD LOEB

WHAT WORDS IN this passage are worth noticing? And why are they worth noticing? Any description or explanation of how words are used in a text has to rely on principles for selecting and categorizing those words. Such principles can be applied to generate an interpretation or evaluation. or an interpretation or evaluation may drive the selection in the first place, since some language data will fit one interpretive regime better than others. Some may fit none at all, at least a priori, but will simply add to the pile of descriptive data that can be accumulated about the words in a text. It would, for example, be fairly easy to categorize all the words in a text according to what letter of the alphabet they begin with, but it is not yet obvious (alliterative schemes notwithstanding) what could be said about the language used based on the frequencies of words beginning with *b* or *k*, etc.

Some principles of categorization have been introduced already. The overall word choice in a text or passage, or a selected set of terms, or even a single word can be described according to the language of origin (chapter 1) or with attention to new coinages or to lost or changing meanings (chapter 2). The next chapter (chapter 4) will take up other principles of selection based on social dimensions of word usage such as register or dialect. But other categorizing schemes are possible and are in fact in wide use. These methods include considering the lexical or semantic field of the words chosen, looking at the level of generality in the wording, and simply taking a census of the parts of speech to see what patterns, if any, emerge from the results. Individual rhetorical theorists have also introduced various categories of word choice. Those derived from Kenneth Burke, a self-styled *logologist* or student of words, have been especially influential in rhetorical analysis and in political criticism using rhetorical analysis.

Lexical Field

What other words come to mind when someone says *chair*? In the late nineteenth century, Francis Galton introduced word association tests as a way to explore the organization of the mental lexicon. He posited that using words as conceptual prompts would retrieve related words and even reveal an individual's thought patterns, though he never disclosed the results of his own evidently disturbing lexical probing. Since Galton, psychologists have used such tests to uncover predictable patterns in word associations. So, for example, George Miller reports that of one thousand people prompted with *chair*, 191 answered *table*, 127 *seat*, 107 *sit*, 83 *furniture*, 56 *sitting*, 49 *wood*, and many responded with a type of chair: 38 *stool*, 32 *rocker* or *rocking*, and so on (1991, 157). When adjectives or adverbs are prompts in such association tests, *antonyms* are frequent responses (e.g., *hot* retrieving *cold*). Such results suggest that the mental lexicon, the vocabulary in the heads of most people using the same language, has words grouped into fuzzy sets with meanings related in predictable ways. These areas of meaning, or lexical-conceptual fields, can be defined broadly (e.g., terms related to *religion*) or more narrowly (e.g., terms related to *prayer*).[1] Roget's *Thesaurus* offers a familiar instantiation of this principle in its synopsis of categories. Of course, not all the words in a text will belong to a definable semantic field; the function words (conjunctions, prepositions, etc.) are the same no matter what the subject, and a large part of English vocabulary is occupied by very general words difficult to assign. But many of the nouns and verbs will belong to a given conceptual area of the language. They would be retrieved in tests for associations and would be discovered to collocate in analyses of large databases of a language (see below). Their grouping into a lexical field depends, ultimately, on a neighborliness that can be statistically described.

The role of semantic or lexical fields in textual analysis is so basic as to be virtually invisible. If a reader or listener makes a decision about the subject of a text, it will usually be made on the basis of the dominant semantic field in that text; if the text features words like *track, engine, station,* it is probably about trains or traveling by rail. A title can direct the selection of a dominant lexical field in the wording, but ultimately the terms have to be there. Decisions about subject matter according to patterns in word choice have been made visible in the social science practice of **content analysis**, where the text is dissolved into clustered lists of words with related meanings. Analysts will be particularly aware of interwoven semantic fields when a text with a topic expressed in one semantic field consistently features terms from another, or when rhetors seem to avoid a given semantic field or even abandon it and adopt allegory. In such analyses, the semantic categories employed are usually ad hoc creations of the critic rather than those identified by philosophically inclined semanticists seeking a finite set of the high-level concepts in a language.

The kind of basic analysis that involves lexical fields can be illustrated with the following paragraph from one of President Carter's speeches advocating the treaty that turned over control of the Panama Canal to the government of Panama (a formulation of the issue that is in itself an argument).

> What we [the United States] want is the permanent right to use the canal—and we can defend this right through the treaties—through real cooperation with Panama. The citizens of Panama and their government have already shown their support of the new partnership, and a protocol to the neutrality treaty will be signed by other nations, thereby showing their strong approval. (Windt 1983, 250)

The words "on topic" here come from what could be called the lexical or semantic field of *government* (*right, defend, treaty/treaties, citizens, government, protocol, neutrality, nations*) and specific terms for this case (*Panama, canal*). At the same time there is another obvious clutch of general terms that have to do with good social relations: *cooperation, support, partnership, approval.* Carter amplifies three of these terms with positive intensifiers: *real cooperation, new partnership, strong support.* Carter's speech was an attempt to sell the treaty before the Senate began debate on its approval. The terms from the government and case-specific lexical fields are the givens of the topic; Carter had to use these or he would have been talking about something else. Those from the second field of positive social relations are terms that he has interspersed to bring the evaluation of the treaty to the positive side. In a sense, irrespective of the actual claims he makes or the premises he supplies, his word choices argue for him.

Level of Generality

The words available in a language, or in a lexical field, can also be grouped or matched according to other principles of categorization (synonymy, antonymy, etc.). One of these principles is level of generality, relating terms as though they were organized into a Linnaean system of classification. The more general a word, the higher it is in the system and the more potential referents it has; the less general, the fewer it has. So a word like *furniture* sits above a more particular word like *chair,* which in turn is more general than a term like *recliner.* Terms higher in the hierarchy are **hypernyms**; terms lower are **hyponyms** (Lyons 1995, 125). In the following schematic, *chair* is a hyponym of furniture and a hypernym of *rocker.*

Furniture

    ↙   ↙   ↘   ↘

chair   table   sofa   chest of drawers

    ↙ ↘

rocker recliner

The large database WordNet, the result of on ongoing research project at Princeton, organizes thousands of English terms according to these and other relations.[2]

Words on different levels are not used in the same ways. For example, words higher in generality do not typically have *ostensive* or pointing functions: e.g., not *What a nice furniture*. Instead, English has a set of words used most often in this pointing function (*bird, chair, house*, etc.). Furthermore, one term in a hierarchy will often be used more frequently than others; it will serve as the **prototype** for its area of meaning (Rosch 1973). In rhetorical terms, a prototype is the member of a group most likely to occur to an audience as a representative of that group. For example, in the United States the prototypical bird is a robin, a status perhaps earned as much by its frequency in texts as in nature.

ABSTRACT VERSUS CONCRETE DICTION

Levels of generality presumably correlate with the associations aroused by words in readers' or listeners' minds. Which word, for example, would provoke a mental image more quickly, *implement* or *shovel*? Or to put this question another way, which of these terms would be easier to draw? *Implement* labels any member of a large category of tools or devices, but *shovel*, from Old English, refers to an object familiar to most English users; it may even evoke kinesthetic memories in anyone who has ever dug a hole or *shoveled* snow. Many writers about language label words that can be used to refer to physical objects and actions or to immediate sense impressions (*loud, velvety*) **concrete** words. Conversely, words higher in the lexical hierarchy that refer to general qualities, broad categories, or relationships are called **abstract**. Once again, from the perspective of language of origin, most concrete words in English come from the Old English core vocabulary and most abstract words come into the language from Latin via French or from Latin or Greek directly. However, the terms *abstract* and *concrete* are not so much distinct categories as they are the ends of a scale. Terms can be more or less concrete or abstract (Perelman and Olbrechts-Tyteca 1969, 147).

The notion of levels of abstraction in the language was emphasized by the general semantics movement for language reform that began in the 1930s. Language critics associated with the movement popularized the notion that the more abstract a word, the higher in a hierarchy, the less meaningful it is, on the premise that such words sit far away from particular, real-world referents. One of the most influential works to come out of this movement was S. I. Hayakawa's *Language in Thought and Action*, still in print. The following list illustrating a hierarchy of words from the concrete to the more abstract is adapted from a similar diagram in Hayakawa (1978, 155). It features terms that could be used in different contexts to ultimately refer to a single dog.

> ***Marco*** This is the name given to the individual dog, a mass of hair, bone, and enthusiasm for tennis balls. The individual dog is immediately available to the human senses.
>
> > ***golden retriever*** Marco could also be referred to by breed, the standardized set of physical qualities for categorizing dogs.
> >
> > ***dog*** This term groups Marco with all other dogs, including poodles, Yorkshire terriers, and mastiffs, which are quite different physically.
> >
> > ***pet*** Marco could also be placed in this larger category, which includes not only dogs but also cats, goldfish, and hamsters, the kinds of animal sold in a pet shop.
> >
> > ***animal*** This category, larger than the preceding one, includes all living things that are not plants or unicellular organisms. In some contexts, it is a term that excludes human beings; in others, it includes them.
> >
> > ***organism*** This category includes everything that lives (animals, plants, bacteria, perhaps even viruses) and that has replicative capacity based on DNA or RNA.
>
> (*Dog* and *pet* are from Old English and Old Irish respectively. *Animal* comes from Latin and *organism* from Latin via French.)

The crusading general semanticists believed, with some justice, that misunderstandings could be caused by the language itself when abstract category terms, especially labels for groups of people, were used to refer to entities in a way that discounted their uniqueness. To counter this danger, they recommended adding subscripts to general labels for entities persisting over time, e.g., Congress$_{1996}$ or the United Nations$_{2002}$. But all abstract language is not dangerous because some abstract terms are misused. It is, at any rate, impossible to think, speak, or write without terms that sit above the level of referring to immediate physical objects and experiences.

Nevertheless, popular style manuals often advise writers to use predominantly concrete words because such words are presumably more vivid (literally, seeable) and therefore make a stronger impression. This strain of advice certainly appears in the rhetorical tradition. In *The Philosophy of Rhetoric* (1776), for example, Campbell observes, "Nothing can contribute more to enliven the expression, than that all the words employed be as particular and determinate in their signification as will suit with the nature and scope of the discourse" (286), though he later also concedes that "individuating the object" is not always preferable (290). In the twentieth century, however, this advice tends to come without hedging. The invasively influential *Elements of Style* by Strunk and White gives the directive "Prefer the specific to the general, the definite to the vague, the concrete to the abstract," and justifies this advice as follows:

If those who have studied the art of writing are in accord on any one point, it is on this: the surest way to arouse and hold the attention of the reader is by being specific, definite, and concrete. The greatest writers—Homer, Dante, Shakespeare—are effective largely because they deal in particulars and report the details that matter. Their words call up pictures. (1979, 21)

As Strunk and White's examples make obvious, they derive their standard from literary language. Their generalization is doubtful and their evaluative criteria are questionable (not to mention self-violating, since a phrase like *specific, definite, and concrete* is not). First, as dialecticians noted centuries ago, so-called concrete words can be used as abstract category labels—consider *my little red sand shovel* versus *the shovel in Neolithic times*—but the difference in reference is substantial. As this example suggests, Strunk and White neglect the qualities imposed on language based on the situation of use (author, audience, context). Furthermore, even *my little red sand shovel* "abstracts" as a step into language away from the physical. Nor are concrete terms, when they do have immediate physical referents, inevitably clear; any uninitiated person reading a magazine for a special sport or hobby—knitting, surfing, stamp collecting, archery—will quickly discover how concrete terms can fail to communicate a vivid experience.

Finally, abstract language can be as rhetorically appropriate and effective as concrete language, particularly when it expresses large ideas that are meant to hold across individual cases. There would be no philosophy, ethics, science, or political and social theory without it. Some of the greatest documents in U.S. history derive their force from their use of generalized, Latinate language:

We the People of the United States, in Order to form a more perfect Union, establish Justice, insure domestic Tranquility, provide for the common defense, promote the general Welfare, and secure the Blessings of Liberty to ourselves and our Posterity, do ordain and establish this Constitution for the United States of America. (*The Preamble to the Constitution*)

Rhetorical effectiveness in English is not reducible to concrete rather than abstract, or for that matter, to core versus Latinate diction. There are occasions that call for simplicity and physical referents, and others that call for noble abstraction and large ideas.

LEVELS OF GENERALITY IN ARGUMENT

A more important issue for rhetorical stylistics than general "effectiveness" is how terms at different levels of generality function in arguments. Classical and early modern dialectic and rhetoric did pay attention to category and level distinctions among terms, but less under style than under the "locus" or line of argument concerning *genus*. An agreed-on genus classification, placing a hyponym in a category in standard definition form, can be used as a premise (e.g., "*Since Hockessin is an incorporated township*, residents can elect a mayor"). Claims can also concern which genus, that is which hypernym, is the correct category for an item, and arguments can then depend on convincing an audience to place a subject in an appropriate genus or to change the genus. So, for example, David Zarefsky, subordinating one general term under an even more general one, made a convincing case that the correct genus term for *argument* is *practice,* and specifically a *practice of justifying* rather than, for example, a *confrontation* or a *written* or *spoken text* (van Eemeren et al. 1996, 191). Many arguments hinge on such categorizations or recategorizations relating hyponyms and hypernyms.

Another argumentative strategy well defined in the rhetorical tradition literally demands a shift in the level of diction. Since antiquity, rhetors have been advised to distinguish between a *thesis* or indefinite claim (*infinitae questiones* or *propositum* in Latin) and a *hypothesis*, an under-thesis or definite claim (*finitae questiones*). Cicero offers an early description of this distinction in the *Topica* (1976, 443) and the *De Partitione Oratoria* (1942, 357), and Quintilian elaborates: "*Indefinite* questions [points at issue] are those which may be maintained or impugned without reference to persons, time or place and the like," while "*Definite* questions involve facts, persons, time and the like" (1921, I 399). Quintilian illustrated this difference with the examples "Should a man marry?" versus "Should Cato marry?"—questions which survived as set themes for composition into the sixteenth century, when Erasmus also recommended them (1963, 60–64). More importantly, Quintilian noted that the indefinite question was always more comprehensive [*amplior*] than the indefinite, and that "we cannot arrive at any conclusion on the special point until we have first discussed the general question" (1921, I 399–401).

Lawyers frequently use Quintilian's strategy, shifting the level of their diction when they move from the *hypothesis*—always the actual issue of the trial—to a more general *thesis.* So of all the features of word choice noteworthy in the epigraph opening this chapter, the deployment of terms at different levels of generality reveals the strategy in Darrow's closing argument. The famous pleader's audience in this case was a single judge, since his two clients, the teenagers Nathan Leopold and Richard Loeb, pleaded guilty to the motiveless murder of a fourteen-year-old acquaintance, Bobby Franks. Darrow wanted the judge to sentence them to life in prison rather than hanging, and presumably he took on this notorious case because he saw it as a chance to argue against capital punishment. Successfully, as it turned out, he based his final appeal on convincing the judge to expand the conception of what was at stake in the trial. It was first, and really only, about the fate of *these boys* (certainly a strategic label for Leopold, aged nineteen, and Loeb, aged eighteen at the time of the murder). But Darrow claims that the judge's decision will progressively also affect *every other boy*. Sentencing his clients to death will "make it harder for *unborn children*" and "easier for *every child*" and even "*every human being.*" Darrow finally envisions "that *all life* is worth saving" (Lief, Caldwell, and Bycel 1998, 208). The chain of terms across the text, increasingly general, could serve a diagram in a General Semantics text: *these boys, every boy, every child, every human being, all life.*

Another famous U.S. trial lawyer, Gerry Spence, won a suit against nuclear industry giant Kerr McGee on behalf of his deceased client, Karen Silkwood, with a summation using the same tactic of switching from the particular to the general claim:

> Now what is this case about? What is the $70 million claim about? I want to talk about it, because my purpose here is to do some changes that has [sic] to do with stopping some things. I don't want to see workers in America cheated out of their lives. I'm going to talk to you about that a lot. It hurts me. It hurts me. I don't want to see people deprived of the truth—the cover-ups. It's ugly. I want to stop it, with your help, the exposing of the public to the hidden dangers, and operating grossly, and negligently, and willfully, and recklessly, and callously. (Lief, Caldwell, and Bycel 1998, 130–31)

Speaking informally to a jury, perhaps even leaning on the railing of their enclosure, Spence ratchets up the issue to include American workers in general and even the entire public put at risk from negligence in the plutonium processing plant where Silkwood worked. These larger groups certainly include his immediate audience. Later in this closing appeal, he is even clearer when he tells the jury, "you're going to have to make some decisions, and they are going to be made not just about Karen Silkwood, and not just about people at that plant, but people involved in this industry and the public that is exposed to this industry" (152). Spence's success in this high-profile case in 1979, shortly after the accident at Three Mile Island, contributed substantially to the stagnation of the nuclear power industry in the United States. It would be impossible to make the kind of far-from-untypical cases made by Darrow and Spence without movement to abstract, generalizing diction. This property of word choice may in fact be favored by such argumentative moves and the inevitable "abstracting" nature of all language.

AD HOC LEVELS OF GENERALITY

Levels of generality have been discussed so far as fixed properties of terms; *every human being* is always a more general term than *every child*. But in any given text, a rhetor can establish a set logic among terms. Some words will be used as category labels, others as words for category members, and overall the terms will stand in hierarchical relation to each other. Writers will move from one level of generality to another and expect their readers to accept the system. For example, in the first week of cleanup in New Orleans after Hurricane Katrina, the *New York Times* ran an article on the front page under the headline "45 Bodies Found in a New Orleans Hospital" with the following opening three paragraphs:

> The bodies of 45 people have been found in a flooded uptown hospital here, officials said Monday, sharply increasing the death toll from Hurricane Katrina and

raising new questions about the breakdown of the evacuation system as the disaster unfolded.

Officials at the hospital, the Memorial Medical Center, said at least some of the victims died while waiting to be removed in the four days after the hurricane struck, with the electricity out and temperatures exceeding 100 degrees.

Steven L. Campanini, a spokesman for the hospital's owner, Tenet Healthcare, said the dead included patients who had died awaiting evacuation as well as people who died before the hurricane struck and whose bodies were in the hospital morgue. (Johnson 2005)

The group at issue here, the forty-five bodies, is placed in relation to other categories in these paragraphs. If the *bodies of 45 people* sharply increase *the death toll from Hurricane Katrina*, then these bodies are a subgroup of the larger category of all those who died as a result of the disaster. The third paragraph, however, cites testimony that the category of *the dead* in the hospital included two subcategories: those who died after the hurricane, and whose deaths could presumably be attributed to it, and those who died before it and whose bodies were already in the morgue. So sketching out the category relations of the groups as they are established in this text, we have the following:

All who died as a result of Hurricane Katrina

↓

the 45 bodies

↙   ↘

died waiting to be evacuated   died before and were in the morgue

Setting out the category relations in this way reveals problems in the *Times'* presentation. The forty-five bodies cannot be a subcategory of those who died as a result of the hurricane, therefore "sharply increasing" its death toll, if some of these "bodies" died before the hurricane and were already in the morgue. And of course it does not follow that, among the ill in a hospital, those who died after the hurricane struck died because they were not evacuated; they might have died if no hurricane had happened. A report appearing in *USA Today* on the same event has the following very different opening:

Forty-five bodies have been recovered from a hospital surrounded by floodwater in New Orleans, state and hospital officials said Monday. However, it was unclear how many of the people who died at the 317-bed Memorial Medical Health Center were victims of Hurricane Katrina or had perished before the storm hit two weeks ago. (2005)

The *USA Today* opening equates the forty-five bodies with those who died in the hospital, and then posits two potential subgroups that cannot be distinguished: victims of the hurricane and those who died before the storm. The *Times* opening, on the other hand, shows in its category confusions the rhetorical pressure to amplify the catastrophe by creating as many victims as possible. As presented, this news item either invites questions or counts on readers not noticing that it contains a "hyponym" that does not fit its category.

Functional Categories

The ancient Greek and Roman grammarians created functional or syntactic word classes that depend on how words work in a sentence; these classes are of course the traditional "parts of speech," and students in antiquity had to parse every word in passages from Homer or Virgil into these categories. Contemporary grammars often list eight such parts: nouns, verbs, adjectives, adverbs, pronouns, conjunctions, prepositions, and interjections; the first four represent the "open" word classes, always growing, while the next three are constitutive and more stable. Contemporary semanticists and grammarians have been anything but content with these traditional sorting bins; structural grammarians, for example, define nouns not as the "name of a person, place, or thing," but as the kind of word that can take a plural or serve as a subject or object in a sentence. Ancient grammarians would actually have easily accommodated such morphological and functional definitions.

The parts of speech have always supported rhetorical analysis, and in one rare attempt, Richard Weaver assigned certain conceptual effects to the functional word classes themselves. His descriptions in *The Ethics of Rhetoric* (1953) reflect postwar language anxieties and the influence of the general semanticists as well as his own preference for arguments from definition. Thus Weaver ranked nouns and verbs in force, since "between them the two divide up the world at a pretty fundamental depth" (135). They express "the two aspects under which we habitually see phenomena, that of determinate things and that of actions or states of being." He was suspicious of adjectives as an apparatus brought in from the outside, resulting in objects slightly "fictionalized" (130).[2] Adverbs, as judgment words, were vehicles of ethos and often "question begging" (134). Weaver even considered the effects of the closed word classes. He had a discriminating sense of conjunctions as providing the "plot" of thought (138), and unlike other style critics of his time, he admired prepositions for their "substantive force," *groundward* in his judgment paling before *toward the ground* (139). Overall, Weaver's evaluative comments on the parts of speech are unconvincing, but his characterization of the "work" performed by the various parts of speech remains intriguing.

TAKING A CENSUS OF PARTS OF SPEECH

Stylistic analysis can begin from simply paying attention to words in the various functional classes. A passage can be decomposed into lists of words under headings for the traditional parts of speech. Such analyses are always more interesting when they are performed on comparable passages—two political speeches on the same issue, two newspaper reports of the same event, two textbook sections covering the same material. The following two passages come from two books written about the desert Southwest, part of the great tradition of epideictic nature writing in the United States: Mary Austin's *The Land of Little Rain* (1903) and John C. Van Dyke's *The Desert* (1901). Both passages concern the same topic of looking at the desert sky at night, and both "argue" for the significance of such contemplation; Van Dyke's passage is longer, but both passages appear as complete paragraphs.

from Austin:

For all the toll the desert takes of a man it gives compensations, deep breaths, deep sleep, and the communion of the stars. It comes upon one with a new force in the pauses of the night that the Chaldeans were a desert-bred people. It is hard to escape the sense of mastery as the stars move in the wide clear heavens to rising[s] and settings unobscured. They look large and near and palpitant; as if they moved on some stately service not needful to declare. Wheeling to their stations in the sky, they make the poor world-fret of no account. Of no account you who lie out there watching, nor the lean coyote that stands off in the scrub from you and howls and howls. (quoted in Bergon 1980, 271–72)

from Van Dyke:

Lying down there in the sands of the desert, alone and at night, with a saddle for your pillow, and your eyes staring upward at the stars, how incomprehensible it all seems! The immensity and the mystery are appalling; and yet how these very features attract the thought and draw the curiosity of man. In the presence of the unattainable and the insurmountable we keep sending a hope, a doubt, a query, up through the realms of air to Saturn's throne. What key have we wherewith to unlock that door? We cannot comprehend a tiny flame of our own invention called electricity, yet we grope at the meaning of the blazing splendor of Arcturus. Around us stretches the great sand-wrapped desert whose mystery no man knows, and not even the Sphinx could reveal; yet beyond it, above it, upward still upward, we seek the mysteries of Orion and the Pleiades. (quoted in Bergon 1980, 279)

Nouns in Austin: toll, desert, man, compensations, breaths, sleep, communion, stars, force, pauses, night, Chaldeans, people, sense, mastery, stars, heavens, rising[s], settings, service, stations, sky, world-fret, account, account, coyote, scrub.

Nouns in Van Dyke: sands, desert, night, saddle, pillow, eyes, stars, immensity, mystery, features, thought, curiosity, man, presence, unattainable, insurmountable [these are used as nouns], hope, doubt, query, realms, air, throne, key, door, flame, invention, electricity, meaning, splendor, Arcturus, desert, mystery, man, Sphinx, mysteries, Orion, Pleiades.

Both authors use words from the lexical field that defines their topic, *desert, stars,* and *night,* and a further sprinkling of concrete nouns that fit the subject (that is, belong to the same field): *sleep, coyote, scrub,* in Austin and *sands, saddle, pillow, eyes* in Van Dyke. Both speak of *man* in the general sense of *humanity,* and both also reach into a vocabulary of abstractions, Austin choosing twice from what might be called a lexical field of "moral" bookkeeping, *toll, compensations,* and *account,* and from words for appointed tasks, *service* and *stations,* and Van Dyke using many more nouns for abstractions representing human mental processes: *thought, curiosity, hope, doubt, query.* Both authors also reach for exotic, learned references, Austin once with *Chaldeans,* and Van Dyke with the *Sphinx,* as well as with *Arcturus, Orion,* the *Pleiades,* specialist names for Austin's nameless *stars.* At one point Austin goes into an official poetic register with *heavens,* but Van Dyke "draws from that well" more often with *realms, throne, key, flame, splendor.* Van Dyke also notably uses abstractions such as *immensity, the unattainable, the insurmountable,* and twice *mystery,* once *mysteries,* as perhaps his most important thematic word. Austin, in contrast, cites the *mastery* suggested by the stars. Van Dyke's most surprising noun is perhaps *electricity,* as a comparative term for a companion mystery. Austin coins the term *world-fret,* which arguably belongs with her moral bookkeeping terms.

> *Verbs in Austin*: takes, gives, comes upon [phrasal verb], were, is, to escape, move, look, moved, to declare, make, lie, stands, howls, howls.
> *Verbs in Van Dyke*: seems, are, attract, draw, keep sending, have, to unlock, cannot comprehend, grope, stretches, knows, could reveal, seek.

Both authors have a minimal verb palette, perhaps surprising given the many observations from style advisors on the importance of verbs. Austin uses OE-derived verbs of generalized actions and motions (*takes, gives, comes upon, move, lie, stand*) and the linking verbs *were* and *is* and *look* (in the sense of *resemble*); only her two infinitives, *to escape* and *to declare,* came into English from Old French. In addition to the linking verbs (*seems, are*), many of Van Dyke's verbs collocate around meanings of motion toward or away from an agent: *attract, draw, keep sending, grope, stretches,* and perhaps *seek.* While he has many nouns referring to human cognition, he makes do with two verbs of related meaning: *cannot comprehend* and *knows.* Both authors stay primarily in the simple present. Only Van Dyke has one progressive (*keep sending*), one negation (*cannot comprehend*), and one verb with a modal auxiliary (*could reveal*).

> *Adjectives in Austin:* deep, deep, new, desert-bred, hard, wide, clear, unobscured, large, near, palpitant, stately, needful, wheeling, poor, no, no, watching, lean.
> *Adjectives in Van Dyke:* lying, alone, your, your, staring, incomprehensible, appalling, what, Saturn's, tiny, our, own, blazing, great, sand-wrapped.

Austin's adjectives concern size and position (*deep, wide, large, near*) and emphasize visibility (*clear, unobscured*). One choice is so unusual that it stands out against the others, *palpitant*, a Latinate choice for *shaking, trembling, pulsating*, but perhaps here also suggesting *touchable*. What negation Austin has occurs in her repeated *nos*. Van Dyke's adjectives noticeably carry the same negative evaluations that his nouns of mystery do: *incomprehensible, appalling*. He also uses adjectives for audience address through the possessives *your, your, our own*.

> *Adverbs in Austin:* out there, off.
> *Adverbs in Van Dyke:* down there, upward, how, how, very, not even, up, upward, still upward.

Adverbs are virtually nonexistent in Austin. In Van Dyke they are orienting place words, and they actually carry the climactic thought of the passage: *upward still upward*.

> *Prepositions in Austin:* for, of, of, upon, with, in, of, of, in, on, to, in of, of, in, from.
> *Prepositions in Van Dyke:* in, of, at, with, for, at, of, in, of, through, of, to, of, at, of, of, around, beyond, above, of.

Counting prepositions amounts to counting prepositional phrases that function as adjectives and adverbs (see below). For the most part, the *of* phrases stand in for the genitive case and denote the relation or possession of one thing by another: *pauses of the night* in Austin or *sands of the desert* in Van Dyke, phrases that could be changed to *the night's pauses* or *the desert's sands*. Avoiding that compression creates the loping rhythm achieved in English with strings of prepositional phrases: *in the sands of the desert, with a saddle for your pillow*. Austin's prepositions are relational and positioning (*in, with, on*). Van Dyke uses prepositions to express his final "unattainability" theme with *beyond* and *above*.

> *Pronouns in Austin:* all, it, it, one, it, they, they, their, they, you, who, that, you.
> *Pronouns in Van Dyke:* your, your, it, all?, these?, we, we, we, our, we, us, whose, it, it, we. [These lists of pronouns include the possessive pronouns, which are also entered as adjectives.]

A distinction between Austin and Van Dyke becomes clear in their choice of pronouns. Austin's choices remain impersonal; the third person *its* and *theys* have the desert and the stars as their referents. In the end, however, she suddenly brings an uncomfortable *you* on stage, intended as the generic *you* or as direct address. Van Dyke, on the other hand, after an opening gesture to the reader with *your*, uses *we* extensively. In context, this *we* refers more to humans in general than to "writer plus reader" united in an inclusive experience. But this difference in the interactive dimension (see below) is crucial in how the experience of the desert night sky is constructed in these two passages.

Conjunctions in Austin: and, that, as, and, and, and, as if, nor, and, and.
Conjunctions in Van Dyke: and, and, and, and yet, and, and, yet, and, wherewith, yet.

Both authors have a limited repertoire of conjunctions, and the differences are again telling. Put back in the passage, Van Dyke's many *and*s reveal his pattern of doubling: *alone and at night; with a saddle for your pillow and your eyes staring upward at the stars; the immensity and the mystery; attract the thought and draw the curiosity; the unattainable and the insurmountable; Orion and the Pleiades.* Austin's *and*s appear in triplets: *deep breaths, deep sleep, and the communion of the stars; large and near and palpitant; stands off...and howls and howls.* Van Dyke's most important logical connective is *yet,* showing that he thinks of things that do not follow but are contradictory. Austin does not foreground a thinking back and forth, but with *as* and *as if* she refers to process and its potential meaning.

What does all this listing add up to? First, the listing does not in itself yield an evaluation of these two passages. Evaluation requires a priori criteria. Given such criteria, these lists could provide evidence supporting or defeating the criteria. For instance, Austin's clutch of "bookkeeping" or "moral ledger" terms may not be apparent on a normal reading, but from them one can infer that the *force* and *mastery* evident in the stars contrast with the unimportance of the human observer who is of "no account"; this insignificance of humans before the universe is an altogether conventional theme (conventional because recurring in texts like these). Van Dyke keeps returning (*yet, and yet*) to reassessments and attempts to understand, another standard theme, but in his case humans come off a bit better. They have names for a star and constellations. The humans who cannot understand the mystery of the heavens in his passage nevertheless keep at it. But which passage is stylistically better? If one criterion is the datedness of the language, Van Dyke's word choice may seem fustier to a twenty-first-century reader. If another is consistency, then Van Dyke's claims of mystery seem undercut by the astronomical names he provides, for if humans do not understand the stars, they have nevertheless been very busy pasting labels on them. And while humans may not understand *electricity,* his imported comparison, they nevertheless were expanding its uses in 1901. If still another criterion is proportion or lack of excess, Van Dyke's final *above, beyond, upward still upward* may sound overdone. These criteria and the evidence provided could lead to an assessment of Van Dyke's style as weaker. But the notion that a passage should not have the usage of its time or that an author cannot play with contradictions or amplify a conclusion seem precarious criteria for judgment in the first place.

Categorizing the words in a passage by part of speech will make it immediately obvious if a text makes much or little use of a particular functional category. More importantly, once these sets of words are separated, the analyst can look for patterns within a set, especially in the sets of nouns, verbs, and adjectives. But the analyst will also need other ways to categorize words within each set—by any principle of selection that seems relevant or by the traditional discriminations according to language of origin, lexical field, register, and the like (the latter methods covered in the following chapter). Nevertheless, this kind of analysis—atomizing and sorting—remains somewhat unsatisfying, since there is so much it cannot detect about exactly how and where the words are used and what their combinations reveal. After all, people do not communicate by handing each other lists of words, and the obsession with individual word choices in some analyses is probably an artifact of the ease of this kind of isolation as a method.

Modern Rhetoricians on Word Choice: Burke and Weaver

Classical and early modern rhetoricians certainly categorized words in a variety of ways, but they were less interested in diagnosis than in prognosis, in offering advice for composing texts. Twentieth-century rhetorical theorists, however, have developed categories of word choice for taking apart rather than for building, and among the most influential has been Kenneth Burke, who considered himself a *logologist*, a student of "vocabularies" or systems of terms that could reveal, in his judgment, social and psychological processes. Burke viewed language *dramatistically*, seeking clusters of terms that could be redescribed as "vocabularies of motive," labeling the *act, agent, scene, agency,* and *purpose* of events. The analyst first identifies keywords related to this "pentad," either by frequency or by a judgment about the word's importance, and then seeks for any recurring terms consistently associated with these key words. With some interpretive freedom, the critic then identifies the unconscious motives or ideological allegiances that these clusters of terms presumably reveal (Foss 1989, 367–70; the resemblance of this method to psychoanalysis by word association is not accidental).[3]

In an essay published in 1965, Burke introduced the further notion of ***terministic screens***, patterns of word choice distinctive of an author or ideology, that have significant consequences for their users: "Even if any given terminology is a *reflection* of reality, by its very nature as a terminology it must also be a *selection* of reality; and to this extent it must function also as a *deflection* of reality" (Burke 1966, 45; Burke is using the figure *homeoteleuton*, see below, p.136). In a *deflection*, Burke elaborated, "any nomenclature necessarily directs the attention into some channels rather than others," and he offered as an example how the same dream would be "filtered" differently by the lexicon of Freudian, Jungian, or Adlerian analysis. Critics usually see a "terministic screen" as a negative, picking up on the notion of something which screens, or prevents accurate seeing. But obviously, as Burke pointed out, a terminology is also a way of seeing and an inevitable requirement of any system of thought. Burke's particular definition, which posits a "reality" that is then subject to varying redescriptions, is perhaps less radical than subsequent constructionists would have it. But the notion of "terministic screens" becomes useful in the case of competing systems of terms that presumably surround the same subject areas.

Burke's provocative remarks about "terministic screens" still call for a methodology. Even Burkean *logologists* require some terministic screen of words about words. In *A Rhetoric of Motives,* Burke produced a three-part categorization of vocabulary into the *positive, dialectical,* and *ultimate* terms, a system that follows the lead of Jeremy Bentham's utilitarian critique of language in the early nineteenth century. The somewhat unfortunately named ***positive*** terms correspond to what others would call concrete terms: "A positive term is most unambiguously itself when it names a visible and tangible thing which can be located in time and place" (1950, 183). Burke considered the terminology of perception basically positive. He next renamed what Bentham had called "fictitious entities" ***dialectical*** terms. These are words for ideas, not things, for principles and doctrines (Burke instances *positivism*), along with "titular" words like *Elizabethan* or *capitalism.* They are *dialectical* because they refer to notions that are often in contention. His final category introduces a new dimension: these are ***ultimate*** terms. This category grows out of Burke's appreciation of how disputes can be resolved.

> The "dialectical" order would leave the competing voices in a jangling relation with one another (a conflict solved *faute de mieux* by "horse trading"); but the "ultimate" order would place these competing voices themselves in a *hierarchy,* or *sequence,* or *evaluative series,* so that in some way, we went by a fixed and reasoned progression from one of these to another, the members of the entire group being arranged *developmentally* with relation to one another. The "ultimate" order of terms would thus differ essentially from the "dialectical" (as we use the term *in this particular connection*) in that there would be a "guiding idea" or "unitary principle" behind the diversity of voices. (1950, 187)

Burke's three categories remain vague, but they can be useful in sorting out the vocabulary of any movement or cultural trend where the same terms reappear from text to text and where patterns in usage determined by an ongoing dispute emerge.[4]

Richard Weaver illustrated another way of looking at ultimate terms when he noted that some carried extreme degrees of positive or negative connotation. In each culture these ultimately positive ***god words***, negative ***devil words,*** or trumping ***charismatic terms*** would be potent rhetorical operators eliciting predictable reactions. For Weaver, analyzing U.S. culture in the late 1940s and 1950s, "god" terms, terms that most people at the time would acknowledge as good, included *science, democracy,* and *progress.* Sixty years later, *science* and *progress* have lost much of their status as uncontroversially eulogistic. It is up to contemporary critics to nominate the reigning set of *god* or *devil* terms that can be used with immediate and predictable effects. Among fragmented publics, the same word may be both a god and devil term.[5]

Summary

Semanticists describe properties in the lexicon of English (and other languages) like their collocation into lexical fields and their extension or "levels of generality." Also, seen in the context of actual usage, language analysts since the ancient grammarians have sorted words into different functional classes or parts of speech. For rhetoricians, these language properties can be connected to argument analysis. Cicero and Quintilian's advice to argue the general over the particular case requires changing the level of abstraction in word choice. On persuasiveness in general depending on this property, Perelman and Olbrechts-Tyteca observed that "though the precise, concrete term makes agreement possible by contributing to presence and favoring univocity," there were also cases where "it is only by the use of an abstract term that the possibility of agreement is kept open" (1969, 148). But they even questioned whether the rhetor's art did not determine the degree of abstraction in the first place (148).

Like the galaxies in a map of the universe, words in the English lexicon cluster in meaning groups or lexical fields. This simple fact determines the predictability of a rhetor's word choices, delimiting both the subject matter of an argument and any ancillary fields brought into use for their effects. The appearance of predictable words can even predispose audiences to the acceptability of a case. Furthermore, languages differ in those areas of meaning elaborated in a lexicon. One can make more precise arguments about responsibilities in extended families in languages other than English.

The functional word classes, or parts of speech, offer perhaps the most mechanical of conscious methods of word analysis. But plucking each word from context and sorting it into one of eight bins offer only a preliminary way of paying attention to word choice. The analyst must then find subgroups or patterns in the choices; these may involve, once again, attention to lexical field and level or generality; the use of another set of descriptors (e.g., *antonyms, meronyms*); or the discovery of ad hoc patterns. The danger in word choice analysis is that, without a priori criteria, the critic will find whatever the critic is looking for. The connection of word choice patterns to argument analysis makes the process somewhat more transparent.

NOTES

1. The Linguistics Research Center of the University of Texas at Austin publishes an online list of broad semantic fields on its website that includes the following overall categories: Physical World, Mankind, Animals, Body Parts & Functions, Food & Drink, Clothing & Adornment, Dwellings & Furniture, Agriculture & Vegetation, Physical Acts & Materials, Motion & Transportation, Possession & Trade, Spatial Relations, Quantity & Number, Time, Sense Perception, Emotion, Mind & Thought, Language & Music, Social Relations, Warfare & Hunting, Law & Judgment, Religion & Beliefs.

2. Another relationship among words is that between **holonyms** and **meronyms**. A holonym labels a whole item in relation to a meronym which labels a part. Thus *chair* is a holonym in relation to *leg, seat, back, arm*, which are meronyms.

3. Essentially the same method of criticism was popularized by Raymond Williams, though in his case key words were derived from a "cluster" of "interrelated terms," assembled first, from which he then selected a term "which seems to contain...deep conflicts of value and belief"

(1983, 22–23). In *Keywords*, Williams offers brief essays on individual terms like *culture, media, status, private,* all abstractions or concept terms (see chapter 6). His essays begin with the uses recorded in the OED and include citations from passages he considered significant as well as alternate terms he judged to overlap in meaning; occasionally, he discusses terms he labels as antithetical to his main entries. Williams did not think that context could sufficiently explain the meaning of a term (22), and he seems to have believed that terms had "their own internal developments and structures" irrespective of their users (23).

4. Sonya Brown (2005) has shown that the same term can at once fulfill all three Burkean roles. In her analysis of the "discourse of weight loss," a virtual industry in contemporary American mass media, Brown describes how the word *fat* functions at the same time as a positive, dialectical, and ultimate term in the Burkean sense. It remains a term with a physical referent that can be scientifically measured, as in the body mass index (BMI). People will go to great lengths to visualize it, the most persuasive being Oprah Winfrey, who celebrated her weight loss by pulling a wagon with 60 pounds of simulated plastic "fat" on stage. *Fat* has also functioned as an ultimate term, an absolute, final term in a hierarchy of bad body conditions, a universally dyslogistic term. In the last twenty years, however, it has lost some of this ultimate status and become a dialectical term with the rise of arguments against extreme thinness and in favor of fuller body types. There is even a web presence for people who celebrate weight. In short, the label *fat* and its negative associations have been resisted in counterarguments. What Brown's analysis shows is that the same term can simultaneously occupy several of Burke's categories in the public play of language around an issue.

5. In 1980, Michael McGee labeled rhetorically potent words and phrases ***ideographs***, "one-term sums of an orientation," a "species of 'God' or 'Ultimate' term" (1999, 429). As the building blocks of ideology, McGee considered general terms like *property, religion, right of privacy, freedom of speech, rule of law,* and *liberty* as unquestionable agents of political consciousness, their usage distinguishing one society or special interest group from another (430). McGee's "ideographs" resemble Raymond Williams' "keywords," and their identification is a tool of political criticism as well as rhetorical analysis: "An ideograph is an ordinary-language term found in political discourse. It is a high-order abstraction representing collective commitment to a particular but equivocal and ill-defined normative goal. It warrants the use of power, excuses behavior and belief which might otherwise be perceived as eccentric or antisocial, and guides behavior and belief…negatively by branding unacceptable behavior" (435). Perelman and Olbrechts-Tyteca would add, however, that words at this level of abstraction cease to invoke unproblematic commitment as soon as specific policies are suggested (1969, 76).

4

LANGUAGE VARIETIES

CLASSICAL RHETORICIANS LISTED criteria for effective language choices based ultimately on audience reception. With alterations in emphasis, the same criteria reappear in manual after manual over the centuries: rhetorically effective language displays *correctness, clarity, forcefulness,* and *appropriateness.* The first quality has to do with language that is well formed grammatically; in inflected languages, words need correct case markers. The second standard, clarity, means that the speaker's or writer's choices are understandable; they convey a comprehensible meaning to the intended audience. The final quality, forcefulness, has to do with finding the memorable or striking expression that will reinforce the rhetor's message. Later sections will consider the standard of forcefulness or effectiveness in more detail. In this chapter, the criterion highlighted is *appropriateness.*

Rhetorical appropriateness is a notion ultimately tied to a culture's norms of propriety, of proper behavior according to circumstances (McKenna 2006). For the limited purposes of this chapter, appropriate language is defined as language that fits the audience, the rhetor, the subject, and the situation. In rhetorical manuals, appropriateness was discussed in terms of three levels of style: the *simple* or *low,* the *middle,* and the *grand* or *high* ([Cicero] 1981, 253–63; Cicero, 1998, 319–21). The simple style was conversational and colloquial, suitable for friendly exchanges and comic accounts; the grand was highly formal and ornate, appropriate for the highest, most serious and intense topics. In between these two was the middle style, which conveyed an unmarked, neutral stance, fitted for straight narration and exposition.

79

The notion of levels of style is still useful, but it intersects with other ways of assessing appropriateness, and the notion of "appropriateness" itself has been expanded and particularized by contemporary writers on the social dimensions of language use. Sociolinguists examine how people adjust their language according to the status, age, or intimacy differences among interlocutors and to their mutual activity or subject matter, as well as to whether the medium of communication is spoken, written, or in some form in between. Normally, people do not speak to small children and to workplace colleagues in the same way, or use the same mode of address in an e-mail message to a friend and in the written analysis of a stock portfolio for a client. Sociolinguists, however, are usually concerned with language patterns in spontaneous discourse, while rhetoricians from antiquity on have been concerned with deliberate choices. From both perspectives, speakers and writers can be described as socially adept when they use language in a way that is appropriate to the situation they find themselves in. But from a rhetorical perspective, speakers and writers can also be described as trying to construct or alter situations, subjects, and status by how they use language.

Low, Middle, and High

As described in the manuals, the "low" style features **informal** or **colloquial language**, appropriate for conversation and for writing that aims to sound conversational. In English, verbs like *get* (e.g., *I get it*) or adverbs like *sure* (*I would sure like to…*) are among the markers of an informal, spoken style. Contractions (*can't, don't, haven't,* etc.) are also common in speech and informal writing. Young people often have strongly marked features in their conversation; they report the speech of their friends to one another with phrases like *So he goes…and I'm like* instead of *He said* and *I said.* Most everyday speech is also loaded with terms from regional and social dialects (see below) that mark informality, but English speakers (American, British, Canadian, etc.) also share a set of widely used terms that experienced language users consider too casual or familiar to appear in most written texts outside of personal letters, e-mail, text messages, or diary entries. Lowest on the formality scale are words that dictionaries label *vulgar* or *obscene.* The set of words and phrases considered too colloquial or vulgar to be spoken in public or to appear in print changes over time and is user-sensitive. When President Obama said during a TV interview that he talked to experts to know "whose ass to kick" in relation to the Gulf Oil Spill of 2010, some commentators found his "tough talking" beneath the dignity of a president and others found it appropriate; however, no one applauded Vice President Biden's accidentally overheard comment that the 2010 Health Care Bill was a "big f…ing deal."

The level of usage that characterizes most written forms of the language, the language used in reputable books, magazines, and newspapers, is referred to in the United States as **Standard Edited American English.** It corresponds to the classical rhetoricians' "middle" level of style, and its signature is not only a certain range of words but also widely accepted conventions of spelling, punctuation, grammatical usage, and sentence structure. This *grapholect* is no one's native language. It must be learned by everyone who uses it.

Who determines what is standard edited usage and what is not? Those whose professions keep them in contact with writing and publishing (such as editors and lexicographers) influence what counts as acceptable usage. Some dictionaries pass judgment on levels of appropriateness. The *American Heritage College Dictionary*, for example, labels as *Informal* any words "that are acceptable in conversation with friends and colleagues" but "unsuitable in the formal prose of an article written for publication in the journal of a learned society" (p. xxiv); *bash* in the sense of "a celebration, party" earns the label *Informal.* This concentration of discriminating power in the hands of publishing professionals may seem undemocratic, but norms of acceptable usage do change over time, typically as the informal and spoken rises into the middle and written.

The upscale variant of Standard Edited English, **formal English**, appears in official documents and scholarly publications (as opposed to publications for general audiences), and in some speeches on highly ceremonial occasions. Formal English corresponds to the rhetorician's "high" or "grand" style. It is characterized by heavy use of polysyllabic words, many of Latin or Greek origin, and by phrases that in other contexts might sound outdated. Sentences are longer and more complex, connectives are elaborate, and the punctuation is likely to be "heavy": that is, the most precise rules for inserting commas are followed, and semicolons and colons are used liberally. Publications in scientific, technical, and medical journals, as well as most legal documents, tend to use formal English in addition to the special features representing their subject matter. In the last thirty years, however, "Plain Language" movements and even Plain Language legislation have attempted to guarantee that technical and legal documents avoid the excesses of formal or highly specialized English.

The notion of levels of style is still a valuable diagnostic criterion in rhetorical analysis. Rough but useful distinctions can be made on the basis of word choice, marking the *informal* or *colloquial* language typical of conversation, the *standard* choices that appear in most mass media publications, and the *formal* style, the language marking important occasions and official documents. The scale from low to high, informal to formal, as the section above on language origins explains, is measured in part by the proportion of Old English versus Latinate diction. But language origin is not an infallible guide to an appropriate level of usage, and analysts must be particularly careful with older texts. What may seem highly formal to twenty-first-century language users may have been the middle standard to eighteenth-century rhetors.

Geographical and Social Varieties of English

In addition to the three widely recognized levels of style that map roughly onto an oral versus written continuum (the informal/colloquial to the standard and formal in print), special language varieties differing in vocabulary, pronunciation, and even grammar have evolved among groups of users who are in frequent communication with each other, because they either live in the same geographical area or belong to the same social group. The study of these spoken variants, generally called *dialects*, is vast and complex and well beyond the scope of this book. The discussion below briefly reviews regional and social dimensions of variability that the rhetorical examination of language might have to take into account.

REGIOLECTS AND SOCIOLECTS

It is now more correct to speak of *Englishes* rather than of English. The main world *Englishes* include British, Australian, Canadian, Irish, Scots, Caribbean, and the English spoken in the United States. Other varieties are spoken in countries where English is one among a set of official languages, including South Africa, India, Pakistan, and Nigeria. Within any area where English is spoken there will be further variants, or *regiolects,* spoken in defined geographical regions. Within the United States itself, local variants (e.g., western, southern, New England) have distinctive lexical items that are amply documented in the *Dictionary of American Regional English.* A New England *johnnycake* (fried or baked cornmeal) is a Southern *hoecake*; a Midwesterner's *pop* is a New Yorker's *soda.* Using regionalisms can be a sign of accommodation or identification with the audience, or a sign marking the speaker's distance. But more than the odd localism, dialect differences are largely matters of what is popularly called *accent,* the way words are pronounced. Presidents Bill Clinton and George W. Bush spoke with the distinctive regional accents of Arkansas and Texas respectively; they could exaggerate or mute these distinctive features to some extent for effect. Both tended to sound more regional when speaking less formally, off-the-cuff.

Groups of people inhabiting the same geographical region may still use different varieties of English if they come from different social, racial, or ethnic groups. These varieties, sometimes referred as *sociolects*, have been documented by sociolinguists, and anyone working with a text using such a variant needs to study it carefully. Perhaps the most extensively examined language variety in the United States, African American Vernacular English (AAVE), has special phonetic and grammatical features (see Dillard 1973; McWhorter 2001). Its earlier forms may overlap with southern and rural speech patterns, but AAVE also varies by region and has changed over time. Other sociolects (or sometimes *ethnolects*) arise among groups living in concentrated communities, as, for example, the English spoken in South Philly versus the English spoken in the Mainline suburbs west of Philadelphia. A general principle accounts for all regiolects and sociolects: people who live together and who are isolated from surrounding groups tend to develop and perpetuate their own form of language. Intensity of interaction can even isolate generations living in the same geographical and social spaces, creating generational dialects. However, pressure from the mass media, a mass form of "living together," works against all these language varieties.

IDIOLECTS

The ways of describing language varieties so far—levels of usage from the colloquial to the formal to dialects—concern language features shared by communities of various sizes and types. But finally, within all of the languages and varieties, spoken or written, each person retains a set of language habits that are unique to that person. This personal pattern of usage is called an *idiolect*. Arguably, if a sizable batch of an individual's speech and writing were submitted to statistical analysis for diagnostic features, and if norms of usage were established for those features, idiosyncratic patterns would emerge. Everyone has favorite words, ways of phrasing things, and tendencies to structure sentences in certain ways; these patterns amount to a profile of frequencies for these features. These individual patterns are presumably so reliable that statisticians have used them to argue for authorship in disputed cases, the most famous being Frederick Mosteller and David Wallace's identification of James Madison as the author of unattributed numbers of the Federalist Papers (Salsburg 2002, 130–31). That there is an irreducible individuality in language use is an enabling premise in literary stylistics; great writers, literary analysts would argue, are worth examining for their unique or even extraordinary linguistic signatures, or, in other words, for their idiolects.

Registers: Occupation, Avocation, Discipline

In addition to levels of usage and geographical/dialectical differences, another dimension of appropriate language use has to do with what linguists and discourse analysts call **register**, a subset of language tied to a particular activity or situation. Registers do not rise to the level of distinctness of dialects; they require special terms and phrases and occasionally distinctive speech patterns, but not alternate grammars. Most adults command several registers or "languages" appropriate for different circumstances. They slip into one special language on the job, another when they discuss sports with friends, another when they are worshipping. Some occupations and professions require highly specialized language practices from their members, to the point that analysts often describe the "language of air traffic controllers" or the "language of naval fighter pilots."[1] Registers also vary in their range of applicability, in the breadth or narrowness of the audiences and situations they are appropriate for, and in their typical mode of transmission. Some are primarily spoken, sometimes requiring special pronunciation (e.g., auctioneers), and others primarily written, requiring unique sentence forms and formatting (e.g., the Emergency Medical Technician repertoire of phrases for filling out forms).

Disciplinary registers include the special lexicon and special ways of talking and writing in a field of learning. Taking a course in a discipline, like astronomy or accounting or rhetoric, requires learning the special vocabulary and verbal mannerisms of that discipline. In the epigraph to this chapter, John McPhee records the experience of being exposed to the specialist lexicon of geology, whose terms sail over his head in the lecture hall (1980, 24). Dictionaries mark words that are appropriate to disciplinary contexts with **subject labels**. In the *American Heritage Dictionary*, for example, *pioneer* has a fourth meaning labeled *Ecology,* "an animal or plant species that establishes itself in a previously barren environment"; *resonance* has a second meaning labeled *Physics,* a third *Acoustics,* a fourth *Linguistics,* a fifth *Medical,* and a sixth *Chemistry*, and there is not much overlap among them. To learn the meaning and proper usage of disciplinary terms is one facet of learning a subject matter. (This text, for instance, is in part an elaborate dictionary of disciplinary terms for rhetorical stylistics.)

While disciplinary registers can be more or less adequately captured in textbooks and glossaries, occupational registers are more difficult to pin down. An occupational register is a fluid subset of the language, but it is nevertheless recognizable because of the repeating who, where, when, and why of its use. The language of law enforcement is a case in point. When the police describe a crime in an official manner, they use a special vocabulary, a "police register." They *conduct an investigation,* they refer to a *suspect* and a *perpetrator.* In the last few years they have adopted a new term, *person of interest*, as a way to designate an individual they wish to question. The police also have their own legally determined taxonomy of crimes: *aggravated assault, armed robbery, vehicular homicide, breaking and entering.* They use the passive voice frequently: *The suspect was apprehended/has been arrested.* Some law enforcement terms have entered wider usage, such as *dui = driving under the influence.* The terms that police officers use when filling out official reports are not, however, the same as their slang, the informal spoken discourse they use with each other.[2]

The medical professions are another occupational area with a highly specialized but constantly changing vocabulary. Here the terms of art come in part from the disciplines mastered by medical professionals: anatomy, neurology, cardiology, etc. Other terms come from the considerable technical apparatus and pharmacological resources that medical professionals rely on (producing, for example, acronyms like *MRI, NSAID, EEG*), and still others derive from the insurance constraints, legal conditions, and even physical settings that medical professionals work in. Fire and rescue personnel and emergency medical technicians (EMTs) also have registers with highly formulaic phrases. The language of medical and rescue personnel has been criticized as impersonal or even evasive, but these special languages can be thought of as linguistic insulation or as verbal robotic arms, necessary for people whose daily work requires them to handle danger, pain, and death.

Other occupations with highly developed registers include information technology, fashion design and merchandising, publishing, stock trading, and finance. The technical terms for specialized objects and activities in these fields can be the residue of many centuries, as in sheepherding or weaving, or they can be deliberately created new words referring to a constant stream of new developments, as in computing or biotechnology. Working in any of these professions can require a period of initiation that is in part an apprenticeship in how to use a special language. Yet even someone who goes to work at an entry-level job in a fast-food restaurant or a record store or a branch bank will also, within a week or two, learn a specialized set of terms and phrases for the common gear and activity of that particular working environment. All that is required to bring about a special register, an insiders' language, is a coherent and persisting environment and a mutual activity.

All occupational, avocational, and disciplinary registers share certain features or tendencies that create problems in accommodation when specialists communicate with outsiders. First, they have a high proportion of technical terms referring to things that most people have no occasion to refer to and making distinctions that most people have no need to make; the vocabularies are *elaborated* in certain areas of meaning.[3] Thus the average person *cooks* dinner, or at most *roasts, fries, boils,* and *bakes,* but chefs who make a living cooking also *braise, sauté, poach, parboil, caramelize, reduce, render, flame,* and so on. Importing these terms into nonspecialist discourse often requires translation.

Second, a specialist's register may use apparently common words in very restricted senses. Paradoxically, these familiar-looking words are among the most difficult for the uninitiated to understand. For example, the following testimonial from a satisfied customer appeared in *Cabela's Hunting, Fishing and Outdoor Gear Catalog* in the blurb for a special camera that can take flash pictures when an animal trips an infrared sensor. It appeared next to two pictures, one of a deer caught in a flash and another of two hunters with a dead buck:

> Your trail camera was invaluable to me in patterning this giant East Texas whitetail. After getting photos of him in July at two different locations I set my stand on a ridge about half way in between. On the first morning with proper rattling conditions, I was able to bring him right under my tree. (*Cabela's* 2003, 345)

This text seems highly accessible, and yet two of its terms are not being used in ways a general reader would understand: *patterning* and *rattling.* It is written by a hunter for hunters, and the special meanings of these two terms in this context are not recorded in dictionaries.[4] Such apparently common words with arcane meanings are among the most misleading and difficult in a special register.[5]

GENRE AND REGISTER

Stable registers, with their co-occurring sets of language features, develop in recurring situations from people in the same types of roles communicating on the same subjects. But registers can also be studied from another perspective, that of types of discourse or texts, or, in other words, of **genres**. In fact, by definition genres are genres because they have consistent language features or registers, and they have these consistent features because they are "gelled" responses to recurring rhetorical situations (Miller 1984). Examples of genres with distinctive registers abound: rental contracts, horoscopes, advice columns, recipes, sports stories—each tends to use a consistent lexicon and predictable sentence patterns. A rhetorical analyst taking a large sample of discourse from any recurring situation will be able to identify consistent register features, though many will involve syntactic and structural elements beyond the word choice features noted so far. Consider as a genre with a distinct register the "species description" found in texts such as bird guides. Here is a sample from Roger Tory Peterson's *Eastern Birds* (4th ed.):

TREE SWALLOW *Iridoprocne bicolor* 5–6" (13–15 cm)

Steely blue-green-black above, *clear white below*. Immature with dusky brown back and incomplete breastband may be confused with Rough-winged swallow (dingy throat) or Bank Swallow (complete breastband). Tree swallow glides in circles, ending each glide with 3 or 4 quick flaps and a short climb.

Voice: Note, *cheet* or *chi-veet*. A liquid twitter. Song, *weet, trit, weet,* repeated with variations.

Range: Alaska, Canada to California, cen.-e. U.S. Winters from s. U.S. to Cen. America.[...] Habitat: Open country near water; marshes, meadows, streams, lakes, wires. Roosts in reeds. Nests in holes in dead trees, snags, birdhouses (1980, 204).

The genre of the "species identification," with its missing articles and its emphasis on descriptive adjectives in predictable categories, is perhaps one influence on what has become a distinct genre on its own: the personal ad in newspapers.

Cheetah with Attitude

SWF, 38, 5'2", 135 lbs, N/S, never married, no kids, Irish-Italian brown-eyed beauty. Enjoys dancing, music, dinner.

Fun and Four-Wheeling

SBM, 20, N/S, 6'1", 190 lbs, muscular, wavy hair, dark brown eyes, loving, caring, outgoing, adventurous, likes four-wheeling. (*The Philadelphia Inquirer*, August 1, 2003, W34–W35)

Genres then, as rhetorical accommodations to recurring situations, determine registers, and hybrid or evolved genres carry traces of the registers of their sources.

Shifting and Mixing Language Varieties

What is the rhetorical payoff for attention to language varieties? The use of a particular level, dialect, or register can indicate a rhetor's awareness of the language appropriate to a subject, situation, and audience. Usually a text stays at an appropriate level or in a particular register: legalese for a legal document, formal academic prose for a scholarly article. Part of the description of its rhetorical effectiveness will then be an assessment of the overall appropriateness of the language to the rhetor's ethos, audience, situation, and genre.

Often, however, and quite deliberately, speakers and writers shift into a different language variety. In a single word, phrase, or sentence they suddenly depart from the prevailing dialect, register, or level and switch to another. Such departures draw attention to themselves by violating the surrounding norm, often with persuasive consequences. Stephen Jay Gould, for example, wrote the following in an article published in *Natural History* on the German poet Goethe's biological theories.

> In particular, Goethe argued for a primacy of imaginative and integrative hypotheses over building toward generality by factual accumulation in the "neutral" mode. (This is a dangerous method, easily leading to dogmatism, unreality, improper respect for the empirical record, and all the speculative excesses less politely known as bullshit.) (1991, 18).

Most of the key words in this passage come from the formal academic level: *primacy, integrative, hypothesis, generality, factual, accumulation, suggestion, explanation.* But ending the parenthesis is a word labeled *obscene* in the *American Heritage Dictionary.* Yet here it appears in a reputable publication.[6] Gould, of course, makes it obvious that he knows he is radically shifting levels by marking his choice as "less politely known." By doing so, he draws attention to the denigrated status of speculation beyond the evidence in the sciences. It is as far down in the value scale as *bullshit* is in the language scale.

Rhetors may also create notable effects with a **register shift**. The following passage comes from a press briefing by then Chairman of the Joint Chiefs of Staff Colin Powell at the beginning of the Persian Gulf War, January 23, 1991. Like most of those speaking in an official role, Powell has multiple audiences: members of the media, his professional peers in the military, the U.S. public, and, in this case somewhat unusually, the enemy on the eve of battle. Powell was providing an overview of what the U.S. Army's tactics would be.

> Let me turn now to the Iraqi Army in the Kuwaiti theater of operations. As the secretary [Secretary of Defense, Dick Cheney] pointed out, this is a large combined-arms army. It has tanks, it has personnel carriers, it has air defense guns, it has very redundant resilient communications between the different operating echelons of the army.
>
> It has stockages of food, ammunition and parts with the army in theater, and they have a very elaborate supply system coming down from the interior of the country to sustain that army. Our strategy to go after this army is very, very simple. First, we're going to cut it off, and then we're going to kill it. (1991, A11)

Powell begins notably in an official, professional military register. He speaks of a *theatre of operations*, he calls the Iraqi army in Kuwait a *combined-arms* force and lists their resources (*tanks, personnel carriers, air defense guns,* not using the more common adjective *anti-aircraft*). This army's *redundant resilient communications* connect its *different operating echelons.* It has *stockages,* not *stocks* or *supplies,* of food, as well as *ammunition* with the *army in theatre.* All these are terms typical of an official military report. The summation in this register in then followed by the succinct statement of strategy: "First we're going to cut it off and then we're going to kill it," rendered in nonspecialist colloquial words from the OE core. The combination of technical assessment and straightforward intention is, as it was no doubt intended to be, a projection of competence and a brutal warning.

While a shift involves the insertion of a word or phrase that comes from another discourse niche, **register mixing** is more extensive. It involves writing part of a text in one language variety and part in another. Register mixes often indicate attempts to reach multiple audiences, and they are common in documents required by law to address several audiences. Money market fund managers, for example, must issue semiannual reports that address both uninitiated shareholders and others with more financial expertise. The following opening paragraphs from such a report illustrate the solution:

> The first six months of 2003 were a good period for both stocks and bonds. Interest rates continued to fall and stock prices rose broadly. In addition, new tax cut legislation was enacted and corporate earnings showed signs of improvement.
>
> American Balanced Fund posted a total return of 10.0% for the six-month period ended June 30. The fund outpaced the Lipper Balanced Fund Index, which had a total return of 8.9%. Stocks, as measured by Standard & Poor's 500 Composite Index, gained 11.8%. Bonds, as measured by the Lehman Brothers Aggregate Bond Index, rose 3.9%. The market indexes are unmanaged. (American Balanced Fund 2003, 1).

The first paragraph here gives the message in very general terms; the second presents the same information again in more detail and in specialist's terms for the more knowledgeable.

LANGUAGE VARIETIES AND HUMOR

A staple source of humor is the unexpected, the violation of a norm or a pattern. A person expects to sit down and confidently backs up; then someone pulls the chair away and—pratfall! Similarly, suddenly pulling away the expected language in a text, the prevailing level or register secured in a genre, produces a linguistic pratfall, a potential source of humor. Laughs may follow when a topic is discussed in an unexpected or inappropriate register, the serious for the trivial or vice versa. Switching to an unpredictable register is the source of chuckles in the following sketch from Woody Allen's *Without Feathers*.

A Brief, Yet Helpful, Guide to Civil Disobedience
In perpetrating a revolution, there are two requirements: someone or something to revolt against and someone to actually show up and do the revolting. Dress is usually casual and both parties may be flexible about time and place but if either faction fails to attend, the whole enterprise is likely to come off badly. In the Chinese Revolution of 1650 neither party showed up and the deposit on the hall was forfeited. (1972, 111).

The humor here (if it takes) comes from recognizing the abrupt switches between levels and registers. The opening phrasing seems to begin a straightforward discussion of a political concept, but by the end of the first sentence, the inappropriate word choice is noticeable. The second sentence uses the register of an etiquette book. The two registers of politics and etiquette then clash in the third sentence, and the rest of the piece continues to interweave these registers, treating revolutions as a matter of correct or incorrect behavior—a compounding that could be taken as a rather trenchant criticism of political posing. Somewhat different is the "register mayhem" of P.J.O'Rourke that produces humor in the following, which originally appeared in *Automobile Magazine*.

There is a select class of motor vehicles with the worst fuel economy in the world. We had seven of them. Our job was to take these splendid gobble wagons and drive like hell.
   In a Rolls-Royce Silver Spirit III, a Dodge Viper, a Ferrari 512TR, a Chevrolet Suburban, a Jaguar XJ12, a Mercedes S600, and a Ford F-150 Lightning pickup truck, we broiled the left lane, we spanked the map. From Ann Arbor across Ontario—that province masquerading as a Mulsanne straight—we wheeled with throttles open. We sped through the alarming cleanliness of Toronto and along the shore of the mare nostrum of hockey and up the St. Lawrence to the froggy delights of Montreal. We skedaddled over rural Quebec and dashed into the wilderness of Maine, where every river, lake, and mountain peak is named after an item of clothing from L.L. Bean. All the while we were staying in swell hostelries and posh country inns, eating meals so rich and toothsome that our waistlines were becoming air bag parodies, smoking fat Havana cigars that cost as much as a pair of shoes and smell the same when lit, and drinking Scotch older than George Stephanopoulos. (O'Rourke 1995, 187–88)

From the special names for car models to the Latin *mare nostrum* (= our sea, the Roman name for the Mediterranean) to the countrified *skedaddle* to the faux British upper-crusty *swell hostelries* and *posh country inns* to the insider's term *Mulsanne straight* from the Le

Mans racing course, the style here careens around the registers the way the cars were driven. This eclectic style, exciting the mind with echoes of different registers, is the signature of frenetic modern humor.[7]

Spoken versus Written Style

In his overview of register in *Stylistics* (1983), G. W. Turner includes *mode of delivery* in speech or writing as a key variable influencing language choice. This issue of spoken versus written language has received considerable attention from psycholinguists, sociolinguists, discourse analysts, and composition specialists, and an impressive body of scholarship is available marking these distinctions. The differences can only be selectively reviewed here. To concentrate on word choice issues, Wallace Chafe and Jane Danielewicz (1987) find less lexical variety in spontaneous speech (both in conversations and in unplanned lectures delivered to small classes) than in written texts. The ratio of different words to total words, which they call the type/token ratio, shows that since writers have time to choose their words, they use a greater variety. Chafe and Danielewicz believe that this difference does not come from differences in context, purpose, or subject matter but is an invariable difference based on the method of text production. They also find that informal hedges, phrases such as *kind of* and *sort of,* are more common in speech and completely absent in the academic discourse in their sample. Speakers also use the all-purpose pronouns *it, that,* and *this,* often in "global references" to large stretches of preceding text. They use frequent contractions and more coined words.

These features do not match the characterization of speech in the rhetorical tradition. There the concern is with *planned* speech, with deliberately prepared and often practiced oral performance, which may even originate from a written text. Prepared rhetorical orators are not searching for words, unless they are doing so deliberately. Hence, prepared speech belongs toward the written end of the speech/writing continuum. Furthermore, a rhetorical education, especially as it is described by Quintilian, aimed to produce fluent extemporaneous speakers who commanded *facilitas,* the ability to speak readily and appositely on any occasion. This *facilitas,* a sign of social astuteness, is far from the conversation studied by discourse analysts.

From the perspective of rhetorical stylistics, a more speech-like or a more written style are options that rhetors can choose in *either* medium. They can even vary between these styles on a single occasion, moving the counter, as it were, along different spots on the continuum, and it is this movement, this perceptible change of styles, that in itself creates effects. Martin Luther King Jr., for example, mixed oral and written features in some of his speeches. The "I Have a Dream" speech represents rehearsed preparation in an orally inflected written style, but a speech like "I've Been to the Mountaintop" shows movement between written planning and spoken spontaneity. Delivered to a group of ministers and supporters to promote the cause of striking sanitation workers, the speech opens with a prepared *fantasia* in the most formal rhetorical tradition: "And you know, if I were standing at the beginning of time, with the possibility of taking a general and panoramic view of the whole of human history up to now, and the Almighty said to me, 'Martin Luther King, which age would you like to live in?'" King then offers a series of visions, saying after each, "But I wouldn't stop there," until he comes to his own era of a global "human rights revolution." This passage then follows:

> I can remember—I can remember when Negroes were just going around as Ralph has said, so often, scratching where they didn't itch, and laughing when they were not tickled. But that day is all over. We mean business now, and we are determined to gain our rightful place in God's world.
>
> And that's all this whole thing is about. We aren't engaged in any negative protest and in any negative arguments with anybody. We are saying that we are determined to be men. We are determined to be people. We are saying that we are God's children. And that we don't have to live like we are forced to live. (1968)

In this section, King turns to a different style displaying the features that Chafe, Danielewicz, and others define as diagnostic of speech. He is redundant without serving emphasis in the repeated "I can remember—I can remember," a digressive move within the speech that marks off this segment from the preceding. He is mindful of someone immediately present and a previous speaker, Ralph Abernathy. He uses proverbial sayings like "scratching where you don't itch" and the formulaic "we mean business." Contractions abound, though not in every place they might occur (e.g., *were not tickled* instead of *weren't tickled* to match *didn't itch*). The clauses, or what Chafe calls "intonational units," are relatively short—certainly shorter than those in the immediately preceding paragraph. King also uses the vague globally referring pronouns summing up previous points: "And *that's* all *this whole thing* is about."

King's variation is typical of successful platform speakers who alternate between more written and prepared versus more spontaneous language features. The *writerly* sections show that the speaker has prepared for the occasion, a mark of respect for the audience and the situation. The more speech-like and hence spontaneous-sounding remarks show that the speaker is moved by the moment, mentally engaged, and responsive to those immediately present.

Familiar Language

If speakers and writers can go off into special language varieties, appealing to narrower and narrower audiences by selecting from special dialects and registers, they can also choose language "without borders," words and phrases appropriate for all kinds of subjects and audiences in all kinds of contexts. A language is, by definition, communal property, so using language effectively sometimes requires using words and phrases virtually owned by everyone. The familiar language singled out now for its rhetorical effects avoids niches; it is language in wide circulation.

PREPARED PHRASES, CLICHÉS, AND IDIOMS

Capable speakers and writers have strings of words that they use frequently, as units, across situations. Language in actual use is predominately, as Paul Hopper describes it, a "vast collection of hand-me-downs" (1998, 159). Such collocations in wide use can be called "stock phrases," "prepared phrases," or even "expected phrases." Like any language element, these prepared phrases have a life span; they come into and fall out of use. They can be identified by their frequency, supported by corpus data, and their appearance across contexts. Any phrase that sounds familiar to a language user without recalling a particular context is likely to be a prepared phrase or, again in Hopper's terms, a "ready-made formula" (173). In the epigraph to this chapter, John McPhee remembers his encounter with terms from the special disciplinary register of geology. But in doing so, he also uses the ubiquitous *it was nothing if not.*

Some prepared phrases are standard adjective-noun pairs: families are *close* or *close-knit*, relationships *intense*, experiences *painful* or *pleasant*, decisions *difficult*. Others are general connectives: *in terms of, taking into account, in consideration of, in lieu of*. A special subset consists of **clichés**, aptly derived from the French term for reused metal type: *She hit the nail on the head, You came in the nick of time, He kicked the bucket*. Often-repeated phrases whose meanings are not the sum of their parts are labeled **idioms**. They are taught deliberately to students of English, since expressions like *putting your best foot forward* may not involve the feet. Another type of familiar language, often originating in ad campaigns, is the **catch phrase**. These flare up into wide use and then subside: "It's the real thing," from Coca-Cola commercials, or "Just say no," a slogan from the antidrug campaign of the 1980s. Political ad campaigns try to craft phrases with the same T-shirt reach as Obama's "Yes we can." These linguistic burrs stick in people's minds and are carried into new contexts. Those who know and use them demonstrate and invoke cultural awareness.

Traditional writing handbooks usually condemn reused language, especially clichés (a term with an ineluctable negative connotation), in passages like the following.

> Students may think they, too, can use trite phrases because they see them used in much newspaper and magazine writing and because they frequently find them in public utterances of speakers who ought to know better. It is true that use of trite expressions and clichés is not a hanging, or even a fining offense, yet the superior student who seriously wants to improve his [sic] writing can readily make great improvement simply by deleting these phrases. (Wilson and Locke 1960, 281–82)

This prissy advice, which violates itself, is wrong on several counts. First, it promotes an aesthetic standard of originality for language choice over a practical standard like clarity or persuasiveness. Second, it sets up this standard as the only one allowed; speakers, for example, who use trite expressions "ought to know better" (a point expressed in a prepared phrase). But depending on the rhetorical situation, a writer's effectiveness with an audience may or may not be served by avoiding familiar phrases. Speakers and writers who aim to produce easily understood pieces for wide audiences and politicians who address large, heterogeneous groups on public occasions would be foolish to avoid prepared or expected language. In fact some of the most admired political language in the United States lopes from one predictable string to another: candidates seek *the road ahead*; events *hang in the balance*; leaders *face challenges*. Even mixed metaphors are tolerable in popular political speeches; Adlai Stevenson, for example, once enjoined his supporters to "make the vale of trouble the door of hope" (Safire 1997, 885).

Familiar language in all its varieties communicates immediately, conveying not only content but also shared values and attitudes. Furthermore, as Perelman and Olbrechts-Tyteca point out in *The New Rhetoric,* commonly used expressions can have considerable power in argument. They note that the cliché in particular is "the result of an agreement as to the way of expressing a fact, a value, a connection between phenomena, or a relationship between people" (1969, 165). The Belgian rhetoricians group it with other linguistic devices for achieving "communion" with an audience:

> The relationship between ordinary language and admitted ideas is not fortuitous: ordinary language is by itself the manifestation of agreement, of a community of thought, by the same right as the received ideas. Ordinary language can help to promote agreement on the ideas. (152–53)

This connection is grounded in the advice of Cicero (1992, I 12), repeated by Quintilian, who observed that "the worst fault in speaking is to adopt a style inconsistent with the idiom of ordinary speech and contrary to the common feeling of mankind" (1921, III 191). The bracketing of *ordinary speech* and *common feeling* is not fortuitous.

Both prepared phrases and clichés are used in the following excerpt from an article on gym shoes that appeared in the center pages of a *Land's End* catalog. The text here, comparable to a magazine feature story, is written for easy readability and a persuasiveness so transparent it does not seem to argue. It first explains how Charles Goodyear created shoes with canvas tops and vulcanized rubber soles in the 1860s. It then continues as follows; bolded italics mark the prepared phrases:

> U.S. Rubber bought Charles Goodyear's business. U.S. Rubber felt that those funny canvas shoes being produced might ***be winners***, but ***something had to be done*** about a name. The term sneakers had ***made its appearance*** by then but it was too generic. They ***wanted something more*** distinctive, ***more their own***.

They wanted to call the shoe a Ped, but another company was already using that term. After three years of vigorous thought, they **narrowed the choice** of a name **down to** two—Ved or Ked. *It boggles the mind*, doesn't it? They ultimately decided on Ked because (again *as the legend goes*) they felt **K** was the strongest letter in the alphabet. So Keds were born. *The rest* as the books love to say *is history*.

By 1897 catalogs were offering the shoe *for a mere* sixty cents, and *in no time at all* it was the preferred gym shoe, selling 25 million pairs in one year. In 1908, Marquis M. Converse who has working hard in Malden, Massachusetts producing rubber overshoes, *came to the* hard *realization* that overshoes would never *set the world on fire* and *turned his attention* to sneakers. In 1917 he introduced the Converse All-Star, the first shoe designed primarily for basketball. (Bell 1990, 64)

The phrases marked in this passage have all been used in many other contexts. They are the workhorses of easy writing and reading, and they are entirely appropriate in an article meant to entertain and mildly inform. If there is a persuasive purpose for this bland epideictic feature writing in a clothing catalog, it is to give a consumer item an aura of historical interest so that someone buying a pair of gym shoes becomes part of a cultural process. Catalog shopping is ennobled.

MAXIMS AND PROVERBS

If word choices and phrases can be familiar, so can whole sentences that express common wisdom or widely accepted notions. These set sentences are maxims or proverbs: *Don't put all your eggs in one basket*; *Nice guys finish last*; *If anything can go wrong, it will*; *When the going gets tough, the tough get going*. A *Washington Post* sportswriter began a feature article on the firing of one-time Indiana University basketball coach Bobby Knight with one of these well-known sayings:

> Whatever happened to spare the rod and spoil the child?
> Fifty years ago, coaches were drill instructors modeled after John Wayne as Sgt. John M. Stryker (Stryker? get it?), the relentless tough Marine training a squad of naive rebellious recruits in "Sands of Iwo Jima." (Garreau 2000, C1)

Since the point of this piece is to show that a past norm about tough coaches has disappeared, this formerly common wisdom is sensibly expressed by recalling a durable proverb: *Spare the rod and spoil the child*. The phrasing is as archaic as the sentiment. Aristotle gave such maxims a special status in his *Rhetoric*, and he knew that the power of well-known proverbs came from their familiarity: "Even hackneyed and commonplace maxims are to be used, if they suit one's purpose: just because they are commonplace, every one seems to agree with them, and therefore they are taken for truth" (Roberts 1984, 137).[8]

ALLUSIONS

In the early 1990s, the Chicago White Sox built a new baseball stadium. A player at the time who had a brief but memorable career with the team was a former football player named Vincent "Bo" Jackson. A magazine ad for the new stadium and the team that appeared at the time featured a picture of Jackson in a White Sox uniform but without shoes, and the only text accompanying the picture said, "If you build it, he will come." Making sense of this clever but cryptic ad required considerable cultural knowledge. Readers had to be familiar with the then recent movie *Field of Dreams*, in which a man, inspired by a mystical voice saying "If you build it, he will come," creates a ballpark in his Iowa cornfield. When he does so, a youthful version of his dead father and players from the 1919 White Sox, including a player known as Shoeless Joe Jackson, banned from the game for supposedly throwing games in the 1919 World Series, come out of the corn to play ball again. Only by recalling the original context of the phrase "If you build it, he will come" in the movie could the ad be decoded: if the White Sox build their stadium, shoeless "Bo" Jackson will be playing in it.

This importation of a phrase from one context into another is an **allusion**. An allusion alludes to or recalls another context, but it does so without naming the other context. The audience is expected to recognize the unnamed source of the imported phrase, and when they do, this original context becomes part of the new use. Allusions are thus examples, in a very precise way, of *intertextuality*, the reliance of one text on language borrowed without citation from another source familiar to the audience.

Allusions have no effect if the reader does not recognize them, and the fact that only certain audience members with the same cultural experiences may recognize an allusion shows that they can be rhetorically potent audience construction devices. Those under thirty will recognize references to recent bands and songs that pass over the heads of their elders, while the many Biblical allusions that saturate older works now go largely unrecognized. When Daniel Webster, in his speech commemorating the Battle of Bunker Hill, referred to the audience as "this cloud of witnesses," he was ennobling them with a phrase out of the New Testament (Hebrews 12:1), and it is likely that they recognized the allusion. But in 1969, when Nixon addressed the nation on his policy in Vietnam, it is questionable how many recognized the Biblical echo to the parable of the Good Samaritan in "Let historians not record that when America was the most powerful nation in the world we passed on the other side of the road" (Luke 10:31; Windt 1983, 135).

Allusions often twist the language borrowed from the other context, and such morphed allusions, often involving puns, are extremely popular in contemporary mass journalism, where playing with movie and song titles occurs frequently. A piece on the actor Nicholas Cage is called "Cage Against the Machine," referring to the band "Rage Against the Machine." A review of a new TV season is called "Catch a Fall Star," playing with the title of the once popular song "Catch a Falling Star," a line taken in turn from a nursery rhyme. The common use of allusions in titles, usually with wordplay, is obviously an attention-getting device. But it also has the effect of audience selection or adaptation. Those who can recognize the allusions to titles and phrases from past or contemporary popular culture are precisely the group being addressed.[9]

Allusions should be distinguished from citations. There is no allusion if the source text or author or some other identifying marker is named. When Obama said, in his inaugural address, "But in the words of Scripture, the time has come to set aside childish things," he was not alluding but making a tethered reference to another text.[10] There is nothing in such a reference for the individual reader or listener to discover. Quotations from or references to other texts have their uses (see chapter 14), but they are not the uses of the allusion.

What is the rhetorical effect of an allusion other than audience construction? Because allusions carry references and associations that the author does not explicitly state, they typically serve evaluation arguments. The following passage comes from the notes accompanying the CD *The Beatles Anthology* 2. The author, Derek Taylor, is both summing up and evaluating the work included in this "volume."

> These were the years of dash and daring. Sweeping out of the final (and wonderfully old-fashioned) 1964 family Christmas Shows into the wider world of 1965, the Beatles would soon find themselves figureheads of a movement far beyond "pop" where a counter-cultural alternative society was made flesh.

The allusion occurs in the last three words, "was made flesh," which come from the Gospel of John 1:14: "And the Word was made flesh and dwelt among us." The Word is John's term for Christ. These three words suggest a more profound importance for the Beatles than the rest of the description states. It could also be that the author is recalling, without stating, John Lennon's controversial claim that the Beatles were more popular than Christ. At any rate, the allusion here, which perhaps reaches a limit of brevity with recognizability, works to import a connotation that serves the evaluation: the Beatles were a profound cultural phenomenon.

Summary

Rhetors inevitably select a socially determined language variety, whether that selection matches or attempts to change their actual rhetorical situation. They pitch to a certain level of formality, filter through a regional or social dialect, and select from the register appropriate to an activity or subject. The dominant level, dialect, and register is clearly one of the key choices a rhetor can make. But effective speakers and writers can also mix or shift levels, dialects, and registers at different points to communicate special emphases and attitudes, often serving their persuasive goals.

Rhetors can also attempt to neutralize differences by choosing the most familiar and general language, imaginatively standardizing the audience by addressing them in an edited standard. This language can feature prepared phrases that "speak" through the material with the following message: "This subject is comprehensible and this argument believable because it is expressed in everyday language and commonly used phrases." Expected, ordinary language can thus co-opt agreement by putting what might be rejected or considered improbable or even offensive into acceptably familiar language.

When rhetorical analysts consider how a text is accommodated to its audience, they can imagine sliding a pointer along several potential scales: informal to formal, common terms to specialized language, marked dialect to constructed standard. Any individual text will present a unique combination and, more importantly, it will shift and mix at critical points of emphasis. Rhetorical stylistics should track the cacophony of language varieties.

NOTES

1. A case in point is the "Language of Naval Fighter Pilots," captured in a glossary compiled by Thomas E. Murray (1986, 121–29). The glossary includes nouns and adjectives like the following used by this highly cohesive group, reflecting their unique situation of landing and taking off from carriers.

> blue-on-blue *adj* Clear blue skies over a clear, blue sea; calm weather
> cruise *n* Tour of duty served by a fighter pilot on an aircraft carrier

However, many of the terms in Murray's list were not unique to naval fighter pilots but were part of the vocabulary of fighter pilots in general, even before the days of jets, showing a high degree of person-to-person transmission of these terms as one generation of pilots trained another. For example, *hop* meaning *combat flight* and *hop out* meaning *to crash* were listed in a 1925 book by Edward Fraser and John Gibbons, *Soldier and Sailor Words and Phrases*. To *jink*, a verb meaning "to flip the steering mechanism of a fighter plane from side to side, causing the plane to roll back and forth" (Murray 123), was recorded in Partridge's 1945 *Dictionary of Slang* and Heflin's 1956 *Air Force Dictionary*. To *punch out*, a verb meaning eject from a plane, was recorded in 1983 in Michael Skinner and George Hall's *USAFE: A Primer of Modern Air Combat in Europe,* and the term *shit-hot*, describing the very best fighter pilots, was listed by Ehud Yonay in his 1983 article on "Top Guns" in naval flight school.

2. The word *slang*, used as a negative label for language that people find inappropriate or offensive, also describes the special language, almost exclusively oral, of small groups that prize social conformity, such as high school cliques and street gangs, and groups that have a consuming occupational life in common, such as emergency room personnel and military units in combat. Such groups often develop a deliberately irreverent and intimate language to name things among themselves in a way that they would not want outsiders to know about. People in illegal occupations, like drug dealers and prostitutes, also have slang terms for their tools and trade that are as outside acceptable usage as are the speakers. The narcotics agents and police who deal with them have a corresponding slang, a language that does not appear in their official reports.

Though slang terms are often short-lived and limited to well-defined groups, they sometimes spread beyond the originating group and have, temporarily, a wider popularity that makes them useful for rhetors. Because it is oral, insider, temporary, and attitude-loaded language, slang evokes its era and social context, and for some stylistic purposes, it is useful for conveying intense, localized, and intimate connotations.

3. The British sociologist Basil Bernstein introduced the distinction between *elaborated* and *restricted codes,* that is, language enriched or impoverished based on social class and educational level. The usage of the term *elaborated* in this text is not meant to suggest the broad social distinctions or "access" to the grounds of one's own socialization that were the focus of Bernstein's attention. Instead, *elaborated* here means that people of any background or level of education can have access to specially adumbrated lexicons in areas of meaning that concern them (for the other sense of *elaborated,* see Bernstein 1972, 162–65).

4. Neither the *American Heritage College Dictionary* nor *Webster's Third International* has a definition of "rattling" that fits this context, and the OED is not much better. It offers an obsolete alternative to the second meaning of the word "to rattle," "To produce an involuntary sound of this kind," as "Of a goat," in use in 1678, and "*To rattle,* in Hunting, a Goat is said when she cries or makes a noise, through desire of copulation." It also lists under the eighth meaning, in a sporting context, "To beat up or chase vigorously." These senses at least involve hunting, but they do not quite account for the apparent use of *rattling* modifying *conditions* in the Cabela's catalog. Nor is *patterning/pattern* defined in any desktop dictionary in a sense that covers the usage cited.

5. In *Writing Science,* Halliday and Martin point to difficulties with the term *rock* for those learning geology. For a geologist *rock* is a general term that can apply to eroded detritus (1993, 178–80). Similarly, scholars in literary criticism and rhetoric use the term *text* to refer to any self-contained piece of discourse, whether written or spoken or sometimes even visual. The common meaning of *text* is not so broad.

6. *Natural History* is a monthly magazine published by the American Museum of Natural History; it is somewhat more sophisticated in its subjects and treatment than a mass media publication, but it is not a scholarly journal.

7. More extreme than O'Rourke is the pyrotechnic language of a postmodern stylist like Mark Leyner in *My Cousin, My Gastroenterologist.* The following sample of Leyner's style uses words that assort to different registers as branching points. The result is a set of associative links characteristic of the thought-disordered speaker:

> I asked the waitress about the soup de jour and she said that it was primordial soup— which is ammonia and methane mixed with ocean water in the presence of lightning. Oh, I'll take a tureen of that embryonic broth, I say, constraint giving way to exuberance—but as soon as she vanishes my spirit immediately sags because the ambience is so malevolent. The bouncers are hassling some youngsters who want drinks—instead of simply carding the kids, they give them radiocarbon tests, using traces of carbon 14 to determine how old they are—and also there's a young wise guy from Texas A&M at a table near mine who asks for freshly ground Rolaids on his fettuccine and two waiters viciously work him over with heavy bludgeon-sized pepper mills, so I get right back into my car and narcissistically comb my thick jet-black hair in the rearview mirror and I check the guidebook. There's an inn nearby—it's called Little Bo Peep's—its habitués

are shepherds. And after a long day of herding, shearing, panpipe playing, muse invoking, and conversing in eclogues, it's Miller time, and Bo Peep's is packed with rustic swains who've left their flocks and sunlit, idealized arcadia behind for the more pungent charms of hard-core social intercourse" (1990, 3–4).

8. Aristotle also included in the category of maxims not only the familiar proverbs passed around in fixed wording for decades or even centuries but also generally worded statements, invented by the rhetor on the spot. He stipulated that these fabricated wise sayings should always concern practical conduct "to be chosen or avoided" (p. 135), and he also thought, somewhat cynically, that invented maxims were useful in arguments because of a perennial failing of human nature:

> One great advantage of Maxims to a speaker is due to the want of intelligence in his hearers, who love to hear him succeed in expressing as a universal truth the opinions which they hold themselves about particular cases.[...] : e.g. if a man happens to have bad neighbors, or bad children, he will agree with any one who tells him "Nothing is more annoying than having neighbors," or, "Nothing is more foolish than to be the parent of children" (Roberts 1984, 139–40).

9. An op-ed writer in 1996 recalled his modest Olympic career in the following:

> I made the Olympic team four years later, and had the thrill of swimming at the Games of Melbourne, Australia. Not the thrill of victory—I didn't win a medal. But not the agony of defeat either. As a reserve on the 800-meter freestyle relay team, I helped qualify the United States for the finals, and then four faster swimmers took over to win a silver medal. (Jecko 1996)

In the 1970s, ABC ran a TV series called *The Wide World of Sports* whose introductory footage featured its coverage of "the thrill of victory and the agony of defeat." The older readership of the *Times* might notice the allusion, but probably not younger readers.

10. Elsewhere in Obama's inaugural address, there is a genuine and somewhat surprising allusion to the lyrics of "Pick Yourself Up," a Fred Astaire and Ginger Rogers song and dance from *Swing Time* (1936): "Starting today, we must pick ourselves up, dust ourselves off, and begin again the work of remaking America." It is possible that Obama's speechwriters and perhaps many in his audience found the phrasing here familiar-sounding but did not know the actual source. The potential for such quasi-familiarity raises another dimension of allusions.

5

TROPES

IN THE VOCABULARY of contemporary literary criticism and cultural studies, the word *trope* has acquired a broad new meaning. It now stands for any recurring feature, term, or image in a text, a genre, or even a culture. This new expanded meaning for *trope* as a widely used and recognized cultural signifier is far from the restricted meaning the term has had in rhetorical stylistics for over two thousand years. In rhetoric, the term *trope* as a label for a group of figures of speech apparently first appears in a Greek treatise (Περι Τροπων) dated to the first century BCE and attributed to Trypho of Alexandria. This manual names the still familiar tropes as well as many other devices identified by the *grammatici* to aid textual parsing (West 1965; Arata 2005). A more influential treatment of the tropes is found in the fourth book of the *Rhetorica ad Herennium* (also first century BCE), where they are grouped (without, however, a category label) as usage "that departs from the ordinary meaning of the words" ([Cicero] 1981, 333). The text lists ten of these "ornaments of words" (*exornationes verborum*): onomatopoeia, antonomasia, metonymy, periphrasis, hyperbaton, hyperbole, synecdoche, catachresis, metaphor, and allegory.[1] Two hundred years later, Quintilian, well versed in the five centuries of rhetorical theory preceding him, once again gave this group the name *trope* on the authority of his predecessors. In his definition, "A trope is a change, with strength, of a word or phrase from its proper signification to another" ("Tropus est verbi vel sermonis a propria significatione in aliam cum virtute mutatio"; 1921, III 301), and he acknowledged endless debates over what devices were or were not correctly classified under this label.[2]

Over the centuries, the set of tropes has been added to and subtracted from in hundreds of rhetorical manuals. Perhaps the greatest work ever written on the tropes, César Du Marsais's

Traité des Tropes (1730), expands the group to nineteen, but defines some as subvarieties of others.[3] In other texts, *onomatopoeia* (words mimicking sounds) and *catachresis* (terms filling a void) are reassigned as devices of word coinage (see chapter 2), while *hyperbaton* and *periphrasis*, at least in English, are described as phrasing alternatives. Of the remaining six devices of the original ten, a core group of four emerged in the pared-down manuals from the sixteenth-century reformers of rhetoric Ramus and Talon: *metaphor, metonymy, synecdoche,* and *irony.* John Smith maintained this selection in the seventeenth century, Vico in the eighteenth, and in the twentieth Kenneth Burke, Hayden White, and others have brought new attention to these four "master tropes." One of them, *metaphor,* has in the second half of the twentieth century assumed an importance eclipsing the other tropes and even all other figures of speech. But all four of the master tropes, as well as certain ancillary devices, deserve attention for their rhetorical functions in delivering a rhetor's chosen arguments and attitudes.

Synecdoche

In 1895, at the Cotton States Exposition, Booker T. Washington told white promoters of the New South about the potential role of African Americans: "Nearly sixteen millions of hands will aid you in pulling the load upward; or they will pull against you the load downward" (Reid 1988, 524). Washington here uses the trope *synecdoche,* referring to people by a part of their bodies, their hands. To Quintilian, a *synecdoche* makes the audience realize "many things from one, the whole from a part, the *genus* from a *species,*" or the reverse, one from many, the part from the whole, the species from the genus (1921, III 311). Famous examples of naming a part to stand for the whole include *All hands on deck,* where certainly the bodies attached to the hands are expected; *This gun for hire,* when not just the gun is for rent; and *The pen is mightier than the sword,* which on its own it certainly is not. Booker T. Washington's traditional substitution of *persons* with *hands* doubled the then estimated population of eight million African Americans, amplifying his point and supporting his argument, but it also cast the owners of those hands, as his critics would point out, in the role of manual laborers.

More common than dramatic part-for-whole replacements like Washington's are those involving singulars and plurals. Indeed, this almost invisible form of synecdoche is in everyday use, and its rhetorical consequences are worth considering. Quintilian himself cited the practice of referring to many individuals by a singular instead of a plural term, as when the historian describes the outcome of a battle by "The Roman won the day" instead of "The Romans [since there were many soldiers in the army] won the day" (III, 313). This use of the singular in effect praises the individual soldier, who yet could be any one of many, so both the member and the group are praised. But this usage can mask differences.

Condensing many individuals into a singular also occurs frequently in social science writing (for both expert and nonexpert audiences), where, for example, welfare mothers are talked about as *the welfare mother* who does or must do something, or children of divorced parents are referred to as *the child of divorce*. Similarly, in medicine persons with AIDS are *the AIDS patient*, nor is it unusual to see *the addict, the alcoholic, the arthritis sufferer*, and so on. These synecdoches promote the idea of the typical member of a category, a conceptual convenience because it is easier to imagine one person undergoing treatment or behaving in a certain way. This usage finds its way into political discourse when statistics are given, as Lyndon Johnson typically gave them, in terms of "the average worker" or "the child born today" (Windt 1983, 88).

Churchill used synecdoche in the epigraph to this chapter when instead of naming the countries that had come under Soviet control he named their famous capitals, the cities more likely to invoke associations in his listeners' minds. A similar and particularly noticeable everyday synecdoche with political consequences is the use of a leader's name for the actions of an entire group or even country. For example, during the 1991 Gulf War, typical usage claimed that *Saddam Hussein invaded Kuwait*, or that *he set fire to its oil wells*, or that *he gassed the Kurds*. Though he personally did none of these things, this wording established him as the source of the decisions to do them and hence as ultimately responsible for them. The same substitutions are used frequently with the names of U.S. presidents: *Kennedy averted the Cuban Missile Crisis, Carter boycotted the 1980 Olympics, Clinton overhauled welfare, Obama passed a health care bill*, etc. The result of such usage can also be an impression, perhaps misleading, of the individual leader's power.

Going in the other direction, substituting the whole for the part, is also a common practice, as in *The FBI is investigating, The CIA reports, The FDA today approved*. Clearly individuals belonging to these agencies perform the actions indicated, but the entire agency becomes the named actor. The use of a term like *the FBI* is not a synecdoche when the whole institution is in fact being talked about, as in *The FBI was founded in 1937*, but it is a synecdoche in sentences like *The FBI stormed the compound*. In between these clear-cut cases are many mixed ones, such as *The FBI released the tapes*. At an even higher level of substitution, an official in a government agency may promote a policy having to do with interstate commerce or regulations for child safety seats in cars. In news reports of these activities, the entire "administration" currently in power may be cited as their source—the whole for the part. Making such substitutions can be a way of spreading praise or blame. Over time, good and bad events attributed to individual administrators or to an entire administration help construct an audience's political attitudes.

Metonymy

While *synecdoche* specifies part/whole or singular/plural substitutions, the category of *metonymy* covers substitutions with terms chosen according to some recoverable, specifiable principle of association. Rhetorical treatises on the figures have always suggested possible categories for these substitutions:

1. *Inventor for the thing invented*: *He was wearing his mackintosh* [a raincoat named after its inventor, Charles Macintosh]. Nowadays this category includes substituting a brand name for the article produced: *He was wearing an Armani.*

2. *Author for work, painter for painting, composer for music, etc.*: *Have you read any Richard Selzer?*; *I saw the Rembrandt at the head of the stairs*; *She plays Mozart extremely well.*

3. *Container for the contained*: *Have another glass!*; *The White House said yesterday that the rumors were untrue.*

4. *Cause for effect/effect for cause*: *Eat a healthy diet.* A potential cause of health, namely *diet,* what one eats, is modified by its presumed effect, *health.* Some manuals, like Melanchthon's *Elementorum Rhetorices* (1542), labeled cause/effect substitutions as the separate trope *metalepsis,* offering as examples *warm wine* because wine brings warmth and *the joyful Gospel* because the Gospel brings joy (La Fontaine 1969, 236).

5. *Location for the thing*: *There was bad news on Wall Street today.* The New York Stock Exchange is located on Wall Street in New York City, but this street has come to stand for financial markets in the United States. Metonymies based on location like *Wall Street* or *Capitol Hill* or *the Pentagon* are so conventional they are rarely noticed. Their argumentative effect is, once again, the creation of a single unified agent or object when multiple, possibly conflicting, entities might be more accurate.[4]

In the epigraph to this chapter, Churchill welcomes *Russia*, the historic and geographical name substituted for the *Soviet Union*, among leading nations and "her flag upon the seas," a conventional metonym for the vessel flying it. Such metonymic substitutions have potential rhetorical dimensions. When the name of the container replaces the contents (*Take a bottle/What an excellent dish/Try a bowl*), the new term acknowledges the necessary physical presence of the container, but it also focuses on the amount consumed. The case of naming a work by its author is also logical, but it has the subtle effect of homogenizing the work of one individual or making it generic, as though there were a standard Rembrandt painting or Mozart composition. Yet since the value of such works rests largely with their originators, these metonymies do pinpoint the locus of value in these objects.

ANTONOMASIA

Of the *Rhetorica ad Herennium's* ten original word-based devices, the *antonomasia* has disappeared from the attention of contemporary analysts, but the practice it names has certainly not disappeared. *Antonomasia* is the device of replacing a proper name with a descriptive label that characterizes while renaming. This device reflects the importance of proper names in classical grammar as well as the presumption that names can signify essence. Arguers were even encouraged to consider the meanings of people's names as a license to make a claim about them: *Rufus* (red) or *Calvus* (bald). If there is an analog to this presumption in contemporary usage, it is in the gender, racial, and ethnic identifiers carried by names in a pluralistic society. A case in point on the effects of renaming comes from the primary campaigns of 2008, when Barack Obama was routinely referred to by his last name and Hilary Clinton by her first. Clinton was presumably referred to by her first name to distinguish her from her husband, but the asymmetry in the naming remained.

Antonomasia is achieved in two ways: either the name itself is morphed, or it is replaced entirely by another term or phrase. Morphing requires some cooperation from the letters or phonemes of the original name: the former Clinton administration official Sandy Berger, arrested for taking documents from the National Archives, was renamed Sandy *Burgler* on talk radio. Replacement requires substitution with descriptive labels, sometimes single terms (*the Schnoz*), but often adjective-noun combinations (*Old Blue Eyes*). These new names, also called *epithets*, are extremely common in sports talk, where players are renamed encomiastically: *The Great One, The Big Hurt, The Big Unit.*

Antonomasia is essentially a metonymy. The new name selects and highlights some feature of the person named, and that selected feature foregrounds the person's value in the immediate context. A case of persuasive renaming appears in a letter to a newspaper printed during the 1840 campaign between Martin Van Buren, renamed *Van Ruin* by his opponents, and William Henry Harrison, known as *Tippecanoe* after a successful military campaign. The writer claims to have switched his allegiance from Van Buren to the folksy Harrison, and he demonstrates his reasons by his tactics of renaming selected from Harrison's campaign themes: "I am going with the log cabin dwelling cider-drinker" (Reid 1988, 286).

Metaphor

The first President Roosevelt warned against "a *sodden* acquiescence in evil" (Reid 1988, 631); Kennedy referred to West Berlin in 1961 as "an *escape hatch* for refugees" (Windt 1983, 25); a movie guru considering the history of heightened sound systems judged that "*Star Wars* was *the can opener*" (Rickey 1999); two scientists titled an article in the *Proceedings of the National Academy of Sciences* "Genome *Rhetoric* and the Emergence of Compositional Bias" (Vetsigian and Goldenfeld 2009, 215). All these phrases exhibit terms inserted into unexpected contexts, and the novelty of these appearances receives support from the absence of these collocations in online corpora.[5] These are instances of *metaphor*, narrowly defined as bringing over a term from an "alien" lexical/semantic field to create a novel pairing that expresses a point trenchantly. These examples satisfy Aristotle's stipulation that metaphors should have a certain novelty and impress an audience with a substantive insight (Roberts 1984, 186; Kirby 1997).

While it is difficult to find commentary on some figures of speech, there are shelves full of books on this ubiquitous trope. Large claims have been made for metaphor: it is the engine of language growth, the signature device of literary works, and, in the theorizing of George Lakoff, Mark Johnson, Giles Fauconnier, Mark Turner, and others, the linguistic source and marker of much of our thinking. The size of these claims depends to some extent on the size of the theorist's definition of metaphor. The rhetorical dimension of metaphor under discussion here is narrower, and the downsized definition provided by Quintilian offers a useful starting point that still leads to an appreciation of metaphor's persuasive power: he defined this trope as a name or word [*nomen aut verbum*] that is transferred [*transfertur*] from a place in which it is "proper" [*proprium*] to another.[6] These transferences are made "where there is no appropriate term or the *transferred* is better." Thus Quintilian grouped in this initial discussion both metaphors that fill a lexical void, called *catachresis* in many later manuals,[7] with metaphors that substitute for available terms (1921, III 303). Quintilian also went further than many current writers on metaphor in assuming that fledgling rhetors could be taught how to create them by mixing and matching animate and inanimate terms, as in his approved example, taken from the *Aeneid,* describing a rushing river as *scorning* a bridge (305–7).[8]

The distinction between metaphor and other tropes is clear in Quintilian's definition and was consistent in all definitions for centuries: a metaphor comes from another "place," from, in contemporary terms, a lexical field other than that of the subject matter at hand. And unlike synecdoche and metonymy, which have logical or circumstantial associations with the term replaced, a metaphor need have no previous or easily categorized link to the words it replaces or joins. Instead it creates new links, allowing the rhetor to illuminate one term (or concept) by features or senses borrowed from another. In doing so, it invokes or epitomizes an analogy; that is its distinctive argumentative work, a point discussed below.

Quintilian did not stress novelty in metaphors, perhaps because he was writing at a time when schoolboys were thoroughly introduced to all the tropes by parsing exercises under a *grammaticus.* Centuries earlier, however, Aristotle did insist on novelty, an emphasis worth highlighting, since so much recent theorizing on metaphor concerns domesticated instances. In the *Rhetoric,* he stressed that "Liveliness is specially conveyed by metaphor, and by the further power of surprising the hearer; because the hearer expected something different, his acquisition of the new idea impresses him all the more. His mind seems to say, 'Yes, to be sure, I never thought of that.'" (Roberts 1984, 192). Thus the "aha" value of a borrowing from another semantic field is a key feature of the rhetorically effective metaphor, as evidence from neuroscience suggests. In an often-cited study published in 1980, Kutas and Hillyard compared the EEGs of subjects reading sentences ending in predictable words with those of subjects reading sentences ending in surprising words (e.g., *He spread the warm bread with socks*). They discovered a consistent spike in brain activity when the anomalous word was encountered (204). From the brain's point of view, consuming language is a matter of playing the averages, and a novel metaphor, an unexpected incorporation, can be a stimulating outlier.

In addition to semantic transfer and newness, the classical definition of metaphor also stressed its basis in comparison or analogy. Here again is the crucial link to argument, since comparison and analogy are sources of premise generation explicitly taught in rhetorical and dialectical manuals. Perelman and Olbrechts-Tyteca (1969, 399ff) thoroughly rehearse the analogical roots of metaphor using Aristotle's example: **A** *Old age : [is to]* **B** *life :: [as]* **A'** *evening : [is to]* **B'** *day* (Roberts, 252; the symbols added do not occur in Aristotle). If in the expression *the old age of life*, **A'** is substituted for **A**, the result is the metaphor *the evening of life*. The substitution of *old age* by *evening* is made possible by a basic analogy between the consecutive stages of someone's life and the consecutive parts of a day. Substituting **B** with **B'** would produce *the old age of day*, an option cited by Aristotle but one that is rarely used because to serve arguments, metaphors typically draw on the more familiar (stages of a single day) to explain the less apparent (life's prolonged stages). The underlying analogy between parts of a day and parts of a life could also license novel combinations like *the mid-afternoon of life* or *the adolescence of day* (and perhaps have), but metaphors typically stay at a level of generality consistent with the underlying analogy.

A richer view of the sources of metaphor, one that can perhaps better account for the constraints on metaphor generation, is available in recent cognitive theories. In explications based on the work of Giles Fauconnier and Mark Turner, a metaphor represents the mental construction of a "blended space" that combines semantic features from a source domain (the metaphor) and a target domain (what it is applied to). On the uptake side, only selected features from one domain can be successfully matched with those from another, assuming that the creator and the consumer of the metaphor share the same conceptual furniture to begin with (see Grady, Oakley, and Coulson 1999).

While the cognitive analysis of metaphors yields intriguing insights, in rhetorical analysis the issue at stake is whether the metaphor successfully serves the rhetor's purposes as novel but comprehensible, analogically illuminating, and charged with appropriate and useful associations. These judgments can only be made by looking at particular uses in situ. A brief example illustrates this approach. During his campaign for the presidency in 1840, William Henry Harrison often emphasized his military career on the frontier; he appealed to veterans of the Indian Wars in his audiences and compared their poor treatment with the benefits received by veterans of the Revolution:

> [W]armth and shelter could always be secured by the soldier of the revolution. In those days, the latch-string of no door was pulled in; when wounded, he was sure to find shelter and very many of those comforts which are so essential to the sick, but which the soldiers in an Indian war cannot procure. (Reid 1988, 291)

Here the "latch-string" refers to the rope through a cabin door; when it dangled outside, anyone could use it to pull up the latch on the inside of the door and enter. It would be hard to imagine a better way of referring to opening a door from the candidate who gloried in his "log cabin" origins. A few sentences later, Harrison makes a campaign promise: "if it should ever be in my power to pay the debt which is due these brave but neglected men, that debt shall first of all be paid. And I am very well satisfied that the government can afford it, *provided the latch-string of the treasury shall ever be more carefully pulled in*" (291; italics in the original). In its first appearance, *latch-string* has a physical referent; in its second appearance, *latch-string* is used metaphorically for access to the treasury— *latchstring : door :: control/access : treasury funds*. There is, however, a significant difference in the point argued, for in the first use, veterans are on the outside, but after Harrison's election, they will be on the inside, controlling the funds by keeping that latchstring pulled in. The Indian War veterans who were once excluded can now exclude. This second metaphoric use gains its power from the first nonmetaphoric use planted in the audience's minds.

Harrison's "latchstring of the treasury" disappeared with his stump speeches, but as potent carriers of analogical arguments and evaluative associations, metaphors may be so successful that they are repeated after their initial use. When they become common, they enter a new category of rhetorical effectiveness. Churchill's *iron curtain* metaphor, displayed in its original context in this chapter's epigraph, or Lyndon Johnson's *war on poverty*, began their rhetorical lives as novel combinations, but their conceptual power transcended their original uses as they were picked up and repeated from mouth to mouth and text to text. In these repetitions they became established terms. Though it is common in critical, scholarly discourse to continue to refer to such usages as metaphors, once they have lost their novelty they cease to be rhetorical metaphors as defined in the tradition. Established coinages like *the iron curtain*, as well as the large residue in the language of what are dismissively called dead metaphors, have to be treated for their far different, even opposite effects, not as striking rhetorical tropes but as familiar language (see above, p. 93).

EXTENDED METAPHOR AND ALLEGORY

A rhetor hitting on one effective metaphorical borrowing can continue to draw terms from the same newly introduced lexical/semantic field of the underlying analogy, thus extending the metaphor. That is what Daniel Webster did in his Bunker Hill dedication speech of 1825 when he turned to General Lafayette and, borrowing from a semantic field new at the time, said, "Heaven saw fit to ordain that the *electric spark* of liberty should be *conducted*, through you, from the New World to the Old" (Reid 1988, 217). And that is what Martin Luther King Jr. did in his "I have a dream" speech: "America has given the Negro people a *bad check*; a *check* which has come back marked '*insufficient funds*.' But we refuse to believe that the *bank* of justice is *bankrupt*. We refuse to believe that there are *insufficient funds* in the great *vaults* of opportunity of this nation. So we have come to *cash* this *check*—a *check* that will give us *upon demand* the riches of freedom and the security of justice" (Safire 1997, 533). Obviously, metaphors extended as fully as King's merge with the tactic, described in chapter 3, of interweaving semantic fields (see pp. 62–3). However, in nonmetaphorical instances of mingled semantic fields, the two or more domains are in use on the same level of reality. In an extended metaphor, one domain is "used," and another is, in a sense, "mentioned."

Extended metaphor becomes *allegory* when the lexical/semantic field of the rhetor's intended subject is absent altogether and the speaker or writer only uses terms from the alternate field. Among the examples of allegory frequently cited in rhetorical manuals is the Prophet Nathan's speech to King David (2 Samuel 12). Nathan tells David the story of the rich man, with ample flocks, who steals the single, beloved lamb of a poor man, and when Nathan succeeds in arousing the king's wrath against the thief, he reveals ("Thou art the man") that the lamb was Bathsheba, the poor man her husband, and the thief the adulterous king himself. Though Erasmus considered the opacity of allegory stimulating,[9] it is a risky strategy for a rhetor who has either to trust the audience to decipher the hidden code or drop the allegory and offer a translation, as Nathan did for David.[10] While untranslated allegories are rare, there are lesser versions delivering half an analogy with some transparency. Early modern rhetorical manuals called these variously *parables, similitudes, apologues,* and *collationes.*

Aside from the synecdoche, metonymy, and metaphor used in the opening quotation from his "Iron Curtain" speech, Winston Churchill also indulged in what could be called, if not a full allegory, than a least an extended similitude or perhaps even a parable. Following an assertion that "special associations" between members of the UN are not harmful (an issue after World War II because of memories of the failed League of Nations after World War I), he launched into the following:

> I spoke earlier, ladies and gentlemen, of the temple of peace. Workmen from all countries must build that temple. If two of the workmen know each other particularly well and are old friends, if their families are intermingled and if they have faith in each other's purpose, hope in each other's future, and charity toward each other's shortcomings, to quote some good words I read the other day, why cannot they work together at the common task as friends and partners? Why can they not share their tools and thus increase each other's working powers? Indeed they must do so, or the temple may not be built, or, being built, it may collapse . . . (Safire 1997, 871)

Churchill's audience would probably have identified the "two friends" as the United States and the United Kingdom. The indirection of this apologue or parable makes the case for their special alliance but also masks it in a way that forestalls the need to refute any objections. Narrative similitudes like Churchill's are still occasionally used in rhetorical discourse. They exemplify Aristotle's advice to use illustrative or fabricated parallel cases as well as factual ones. But pure allegory seems to have disappeared. Once a way to avoid danger, the perils of misinterpretation in an age of 24/7 news coverage have perhaps made it too dangerous.

SIMILE

Similes are traditionally yoked with metaphors, since the simile expresses an explicit comparison and the metaphor an implicit one. To cite Quintilian's very clear distinction: "It is a comparison [*comparatio*] when I say that a man did something *like a lion* [*ut leonem*], it is a metaphor [*translatio*] when I say of him, *He is a lion* [*leo est*]" (1921, III 305). The simile is then not a trope because no substitution is involved, but Quintilian grouped similes with other devices expressing arguments based on analogies and noted their indirect argumentative effects: "Some of these are designed for insertion among our arguments to help our proof, while others are devised to make our pictures yet more vivid" (III, 251; a description intensified by a simile also serves a persuasive case). But Quintilian was of two minds about the familiarity of the material brought in for explicit comparison in a simile. On the one hand, he advised, "we must be especially careful that the subject chosen for our simile is neither obscure nor unfamiliar: for anything that is selected for the purpose of illuminating something else must itself be clearer than that which it is designed to illustrate," but on the other hand, he acknowledged, "the more remote the simile is from the subject to which it is applied, the greater will be the impression of novelty and the unexpected that it produces" (III, 251–53).

Similes are widely used in contemporary argumentative prose, as the following excerpt illustrates. In *The Tragedy of American Compassion* (1995), Marvin Olasky argues that charity was more effective in the nineteenth century than in the twentieth. After a description of the "slum angels" of a hundred years earlier, he writes,

> Coming back to the present, the perspective from 1990 shows that the social revolution of the 1960s has not helped the poor. More women and children are abandoned and impoverished. The poor generally, and homeless individuals specifically, are treated *like zoo animals at feeding time*—some *as carnivores who need cuts of meat thrown into their cages*, and some *as cute-looking pandas who feed on bamboo shoots*. (222; italics added)

The comparison expressed in similes here is quite explicit: the poor are treated *like zoo animals*. There is even an extension of this simile in something of the manner that metaphors are extended: *as carnivores* and *as cute-looking pandas*. Olasky's similes serve his argument well. He wants to persuade readers that the practice of doling out resources impersonally actually demeans welfare recipients. Comparing humans to animals does that. (While comparisons to a select group of animals can be ennobling—e.g., to eagles or lions—a generic comparison to animals is not.) Comparing welfare recipients to *zoo* animals adds the further useful connotations of their captivity and their existence as a spectacle for others. These connotations serve Olasky's point that current practices keep the poor imprisoned in their circumstances and gratify those who want to see a display of social compassion but are not actually interested in long-term benefits for the recipients. The extension of this simile to carnivores or pandas is perhaps less successful, though elsewhere Olasky describes the different treatments of homeless men (the carnivores) and dependent families (the cute pandas). Whether one agrees with his overall claim or not, Olasky's simile delivers his substantive points with some emotive punch.

FULL ANALOGIES

Because of their nature as "semantic shufflers," metaphors, extended metaphors, similes, and allegories express underlying analogies, as explained above. But arguers need not always conceal their full-scale, four-term analogies. Arguments deploying such complete analogies use the stylistic device sometimes known as the *Homeric simile* or the *Ciceronian comparison* (similitude) after the two authors famous for the use of these marked, extended analogies, as in this example from Cicero: "As our bodies can make no use of their members without a mind to direct them, so the state can make no use of its component parts, which may be compared to the sinews, blood and limbs, unless it is directed by law" (*body : mind :: state : laws*; quoted by Quintilian 1921, II 285–97). In a lengthy section, the *Rhetorica ad Herennium* defines this full *similitudo* as "a manner of speech that carries over an element of likeness from one thing to a different thing," and that is used to "embellish or prove or clarify or vivify" ([Cicero] 1981, 377), as in the example it provides:

> Unlike what happens in the palaestra [athletic arena], where he who receives the flaming torch is swifter in the relay race than he who hands it on, the new general who receives command of an army is not superior to the general who retires from its command. For in the one case it is an exhausted runner who hands the torch to a fresh athlete, whereas in this it is an experienced commander who hands over the army to an inexperienced. (377; see also the much longer "detailed parallel" between a man in gorgeous attire who offends a crowd with a rasping voice and repulsive gesture to a man of high station who lacks virtue, 381–83)

The terms of this analogy, refuted in this case, are all named: the runner handing off in a relay race : new runner taking up the torch :: [not] current general in the field : new general taking over. Such complete analogies, explicit in their four terms, can be powerful devices in argument. They do not, however, fit the category of trope, because no substitution of terms is involved. The metaphor as a truncated analogy and the *similitudo* as a full one remain separate devices in all subsequent manuals. The method of presentation is certainly different. Four-term analogies require anything from a full sentence to a full passage, and for that reason they really belong among sentence-level devices. But from the perspective of the type of argument deployed, such full analogies do belong in the same set as the metaphor, the simile, and even the allegory. They can carry the same features of novelty and persuasive clarification in the comparison, weighted with the appropriate connotations.

Irony

The last of the four key tropes is *irony*, and this term, like the word *trope* itself, has contemporary senses well beyond its meaning as a figure of speech. The term and its derivatives (*ironic, ironically*) often label perceptions of unexpected coincidences, surprising juxtapositions, and unintended results, without any language element at all. But narrowly defined, *irony* makes a claim by saying the opposite, with the further stipulation that the speaker uses this mode intentionally and expects the hearer to recognize it. Hence the *primary effect* of irony is communicating to a hearer that the speaker does not mean what he/she is saying but intends the opposite meaning. This *primary effect* should be distinguished from any *secondary effect*, such as supporting the rhetor's argument and/or enhancing the rapport between rhetor and audience.

In the rhetorical tradition, there are at least two figures of speech involving substitutions with "opposites." Quintilian in fact considers *irony* (from the Greek *eironeia* = deception) a genus term for several devices, and among them he distinguishes irony as a trope from irony as a figure (1921, III 399–401). Picking up on this distinction, Renaissance manuals typically listed one device among the "tropes of words" under the label *antiphrasis* and another among "tropes of sentences" as the figure *ironia* (e.g., Susenbrotus 1953, 12, 14).[11] According to Peacham in *The Garden of Eloquence* (1593), "Antiphrasis consisteth in the contrarie sense of a word, and Ironia of a sentence" (35). In other words, the first substitutes a single word with its opposite and the second uses a complete statement to convey a contrary meaning.

Is this a distinction without a difference? Not necessarily. A single-word substitution, an *antiphrasis*, can stand out as contrary to the sense of the rest of the sentence it appears in, as in *He had a beautiful oozing sore on his nose*. Unless audience members are dermatologists, most would assume that *beautiful* has been substituted here for a contrary term like *ugly* or *hideous*. Such an *antiphrasis* only works with terms that have familiar opposites (*beautiful/ugly*). From this sentence alone, no one would assume that *nose* had been substituted for *ear*. A great deal of humor involves such readily perceived antiphrasis in the form of a word or phrase at odds with the rest of its sentence: "A rusted washing machine *decorated* the front porch."[12]

Sentence-level *ironia*, however, is not detectable by a single out-of-place word or phrase and so is harder to construe without extralinguistic cues. Quintilian explains the difference: "the *trope* [*antiphrasis*] is franker in its meaning, and despite the fact that it implies something other than it says, it makes no pretence about it." But "in the figurative form of irony [the sentence-level version, *ironia*] the speaker disguises his entire meaning, the disguise being apparent rather than confessed. For in the *trope* the conflict is purely verbal, while in the *figure* the meaning, and sometimes the whole aspect of our case, conflicts with the language and the tone of voice adopted" (1921, III 401). Since in *ironia* the speaker *pretends* one sense but *intends* the opposite, the listener has to rely on cues to get at the meaning. The sources of detection offered by Quintilian and repeated by others come down to the following (Quintilian 2001, III 457).[13]

1. *From the manner of delivery*: Speakers may use marked changes in pitch, volume, speed, or length of pauses. They may draw out words or add unusual stress, paralinguistic signs (e.g., a laugh), and other physical gestures (e.g., a smirk), all to indicate that they mean the opposite. Whatever device is used to achieve *ironized* pronunciation or presentation, it should contrast with a "normal" manner of delivery.

2. *From the appearance or known character of the speaker*: The established or displayed identity of the speaker (in dress, gender, etc.) may make a particular statement unlikely to impossible, as when a man wearing a tuxedo says, "I'm glad I came dressed for casual Friday." When Stephen Colbert, a Comedy Channel commentator known for his political criticisms, claimed during his remarks at a White House Correspondents' dinner that he admired President Bush, the opposite was inferred. In this case, presumptions about the source made the surface statement highly unlikely.

3. *From the objects of agreement*: *The New Rhetoric* points out that speakers must ground their arguments on "objects of agreement" that they assume their audience shares. These agreements include mutually acknowledged facts and presumptions (beliefs about what usually occurs), as well as values, both concrete and abstract, and principles for ordering values (65–95). If for example, a speaker in the contemporary United States asked, "What did President Harding do today?" the speaker either did not mean it (but meant a comment on the current president) or the speaker is delusional. Flipping a known fact is easy, but basing irony on a shared value is the ironist's greatest risk. In this case, the speaker expresses a judgment at odds with a widely held value and expects the listener to recognize its outrageousness, a difficult feat in a diverse culture. Here's a try: *Crystal meth has been a tremendous cultural benefit.*

4. *From the immediate context*: Given two people standing at a window, looking out at a heavy downpour, if one says, "What a sunny day!" the other is likely to construe the opposite meaning. Here the facts of the case are also involved, but these are "facts" by virtue of the immediate physical situation of the speaker and listener, not the facts as publicly known referred to in #3. This category of immediate, contextual facts is worth distinguishing for its greater reliability.

IRONY IN WRITTEN TEXTS

As clues to irony, the special intonation, the immediate physical context, and the appearance of the person speaking all refer to situations with speakers and listeners immediately present to each other. Written texts that include spoken exchanges (drama, fiction, journalism, feature writing, etc.) can satisfy these cues by simply including the kind of prompts that listeners would supply in real situations; e.g., *"He looked out the window at the pouring rain. Turning to Joan, he said, 'What a sunny day!'"*

But these cues do not translate easily to other written genres, and therefore irony can be difficult to recover from written texts alone, especially from texts that lack pragmatic constraints or obvious application to a particular context. The annals of interpretation are littered with notorious misconstruals, such as readers who thought Swift's *A Modest Proposal* was a serious recommendation to eat the children of the Irish poor. In *A Rhetoric of Irony* (1974), Wayne Booth takes on the difficult case of irony in open-ended literary works. Rhetorical stylistics, however, has to address all the functional communicative genres where irony is allowable. When dealing with written texts, the cues for detecting irony in speaking situations can be adapted as follows.

1. *From the manner of presentation*: Graphic or punctuation features, such as italics or capitalization, can be pressed into service to indicate what would count as an *ironized* pronunciation. In the final sentence of his feature exposé of the '60s celebrity and "Girl of the Year" Baby Jane Holzer, Tom Wolfe describes people watching her and her clique entering a restaurant for breakfast after a night of partying: "One never knows who is in the Brasserie at this hour—but are there any so dead in here that they do not get the point? Girl of the Year? Listen, they will *never* forget" (1999, 214). The italicized *never* communicates the opposite: they will *certainly* forget. And they did.

2. *From the character of the author or source*: This cue can work as well for a written text as it does for a spoken one when the author's identity, status, and reputation are known as well as they are usually known among conversationalists using irony. Part of the ease of construing Tom Wolfe's *never*, cited above, comes from first knowing that he is very likely to use such effects.

3. *From the objects of agreement:* When using irony based on contradicting accepted facts, presumptions, and values, the writer has no choice but to count on the reader's sharing the same facts, presumptions, and values. Such reliance assumes a homogenous, cooperating, similarly endowed audience, a circumstance difficult to guarantee for a written text unless is has a very directed "situation of address" (e.g., a letter to campaign volunteers). Most ironists simply take the plunge, and as a result they often plant the agreements they draw on.

4. *From the context*: The genre of a written text is to some extent a substitute for the speaker and listener's physical context. So a help for detecting contrary meanings in written texts comes from the fact that certain genres are accepted as vehicles for irony. The reader expects statements that are intended to mean the opposite. No one is surprised by a proposition flatly contradicting widely known facts in the infamous *Onion*.

IRONY AND INTENTION

Taking a statement as its opposite, the primary effect of irony, only begins when the hearer/reader notices the mismatch between a word and the rest of its sentence (*antiphrasis*) or between an entire proposition and the how, who, what, and where of saying it (*ironia*). These anomalies also have to be assessed as intentional on the part of the speaker, not as mistakes. Furthermore, the speaker has to intend that the hearer/reader realize this intention. Suppose someone says "You are my friend" but means "You are my enemy." To qualify as *ironia*, the speaker of this sentence would want the hearer to realize that he/she is saying the opposite of what he/she means. If the hearer thinks that this sentence means that the speaker indeed considers the hearer a friend, and the speaker knows that the hearer thinks so, then the speaker is not being ironic. The speaker is lying.

Since rhetorical situations are often more complex than one speaker/one listener, or unified authorial voice/single reader, multiple effects can occur. The speaker lying to one person might also be using irony if there are overhearers who understand the speaker's intended meaning when the addressee does not. Such situations of duped character and knowing audience occur frequently in drama and are labeled dramatic irony, but they are not limited to the theater.[14] Friends dining out together may agree that the food has been horrible, yet one of them may say to the waiter, "The food was delicious." The waiter is presumably duped, but the friends recognize that the speaker has stated the opposite of what he believes and are amused by this duplicitous politeness. The moral is clear: there must always be at least two parties in irony, one using the device and one understanding that the device is being used. Given the potential complexities of rhetorical situations with multiple audiences, the two "in the know" need not be the speaker and the person directly addressed.

Since in all its varieties, irony requires at least two knowing parties to achieve its primary effect (the intention to communicate the opposite has to be noticed), those who wish to remove all construal of authorial intention from interpretation would also have to do away with rhetorical *antiphrasis* and *ironia*. Hence irony stands as a permanent refutation to lack of intentionality. Even the supposed postmodern version of irony, called "ludic irony" by Zoe Williams, does not eliminate imputing intention, although the postmodern translation of any ironic statement, according to Williams, would be, "I'm not saying what you think I'm saying, but I'm not saying its opposite, either. In fact, I'm not saying anything at all" (2003).

If irony (*antiphrasis* and *ironia*) requires imputing intention on the part of the user, what should be done with the following, probably apocryphal, example? In the riots of Muslims following the Danish publication of cartoon images of Mohammed in January 2006, the following sign was allegedly carried by one protester: "Anyone who denies that Islam is a religion of peace deserves to be beheaded." Notions of *peacefulness* and *beheading* are incompatible. If this statement means exactly what it says as the sincere statement of the sign carrier, it is an example of **unintended irony** to unsympathetic viewers. However, by changing the true "author" of the ironic message, the need for intentionality can be preserved. The image on the sign was selected (or fabricated) for a website viewed by non-Muslims. The disseminators of the website intend *their* audience to recognize the opposition (in this case *antiphrasis*) in the statement.

Examples may still come to mind of perceived incompatibilities that seem to amount to unintended irony. They will usually turn out to be lies, subterfuges, blunders, or complications in the rhetor/audience situation. If an analyst still wants to speak up for unintended irony, the response is narrowly definitional: if the *antiphrasis* or *ironia* is not intended, it is not irony. Instead in true irony, a speaker or writer says the opposite and means to.

THE PERSUASIVE EFFECTS OF IRONY

It is one thing to identify the device intended to communicate the opposite; it is another to identify the persuasive effect the rhetor hopes to achieve with the device. Contrary to frequent usage, irony, the device, does not always communicate sarcasm, the effect. The speaker or author's rhetorical goal may be anything from gentle humor, intended to produce a mutual laugh and so establish rapport between speaker and hearer, to corrosive derision meant to insult the audience or reduce a target to a smoking ruin. What is attempted or achieved (the speech act or illocutionary dimension of the utterance) depends, as always, on the variables of the rhetorical situation, and on how the device and its detection contribute to those variables. David Kaufer makes a strong case that the persuasive purpose of irony is typically negative evaluation (1981). Peacham allowed irony to sometimes "reprove by derision" and sometimes to "jest and move mirth" (1593, 36). Whatever the range of these varying effects in particular situations, some general persuasive results of irony can be identified based on the nature of the device.

1. Because successful *ironia* depends on the audience detecting the speaker's intention to say the opposite, it supposes and therefore at the same time constructs agreement over what is the case. In short, the ironic statement may contradict an object of agreement in order to emphasize it. Hence, because it forces the audience to reconstruct the actual message, *ironia* can make the intended message, the object of agreement, more salient.

2. By saying the opposite of what is "self-evidently true" as though it were true, and by counting on the audience to perceive the difference, the ironic statement highlights an incompatibility, an unacceptable contradiction between two views or accounts. As *The New Rhetoric* points out, such incompatibilities are often perceived as "ridiculous," and the standard response to the perception of the ridiculous is laughter, which, depending on the subject matter, can vary from mild to bitter to outraged (Perelman and Olbrechts-Tyteca 1969, 206). The political commentator who says "Both parties

are exhibiting cooperation in the best interests of the country" after an account of persistent partisan snipping produces a bitter, knowing laugh. Hence, especially in political argument, irony serves to ridicule, and ridicule, as Aristotle, repeating Gorgias, describes it, deflates the seriousness, pomposity, or power of an opponent (Roberts 1984, 216–17).

3. Irony serves the projection of ethos. The speaker who uses irony displays certain attributes and attitudes that can range from clever winsomeness to amused distance to offended sensitivity to bitter disgust. A speaker or writer who uses these devices frequently can gain a reputation that compromises their ability to speak nonironically.

4. Because irony requires a certain collusion between the rhetor and at least one audience member, it can create social cohesion between the speaker/writer and the audience or, in cases of multiple address, a segment of the audience: "We who know that it is really raining and wish it were sunny have something in common."

INTOLERABLE IRONY

Another way to get at the secondary or rhetorical effects of saying the opposite is by considering the situations and texts where irony would not be tolerated. For example, irony can never be used in a set of instructions, especially if those instructions involve a difficult or dangerous procedure—e.g., installing electrical equipment. Irony is also not tolerated in any genre of straight news reporting where saying the opposite of what is the case violates the trustworthiness of the source. It is not tolerated in a legally binding contract. It is not tolerated in any major policy statement from any level of government or any institution. It is not tolerated in a scientific research report. In short, in any text which builds on a significant forensic procedure (news, scientific research) or in any situation where there are significant pragmatic consequences (creating or installing something or laying out policies), there can be no irony.

Irony can be, and is, used in the courtroom (in summations to the jury especially) and in policy *debates* preceding policy statements. It can even be used in epideictic situations, such as a funeral eulogy in which a speaker with loving humor describes the deceased as "always punctual" when the listeners know that the departed was habitually late. And of course irony can be endlessly detected in literary texts, since such texts lack pragmatic accountability. But it cannot be used in a software installation manual, knitting instructions, a traffic report, directions for applying to graduate school, responses to airport screeners, a pamphlet on the symptoms of diabetes, military rules of engagement, the text of a UN resolution, a welding inspector's report, contract specifications, recipes, a list of penalties for plagiarism, a consulting physician's letter to a primary care physician, a police incident report, a set of blueprint specifications, etc.

Hyperbole and Litotes

Consider the following three statements made by one person to another while both are standing at a window, looking at a heavy downpour outside.

1. What a sunny day!
2. It's a hurricane out there!
3. I see we're having a bit of a drizzle.

None of these comments would count as an accurate description of the weather that both were observing. The first is, yet again, the familiar example of irony. The speaker's statement is exactly contrary to the case. The other two comments, however, both acknowledge that it is raining, but one overstates the situation and the other understates it. The devices used here are identified in the rhetorical tradition as, respectively, *hyperbole* and *litotes*. (Only *hyperbole* appears in the *Rhetorica ad Herennium's* original list of ten, where it stands for excessive statement in either direction.) *Hyperbole* and *litotes* are slippery devices. They resemble irony in that they require a similar construal of intentional misstatement on the speaker's part. But the subsequent construal can go in several directions. First, the terms can be so inappropriate, so excessive in degree either above or below the mark, that the audience construes the contrary; understatement and overstatement become tools for signaling ironic intention. But in some cases, the rhetor does not mean the opposite, but intends to make a statement salient by the excessive wording. And finally, in rare instances, the exaggerated language is meant "as is," to hit an appropriate level of characterization.

In *litotes*, the speaker requires the listener to reevaluate an expression by judging that the words actually used minimize a subject that the audience does or should estimate differently. Calling the national debt "a week's pay plus change" or the Olympics "a county fair" would qualify as understatements in the face of common perception. These terms are substitutions for more "accurate" descriptions, and for most audiences they would prompt the opposite meaning, that the national debt is considerably more than a week's pay and the Olympics much larger than a county fair.

But *litotes* can be difficult to distinguish from ordinary *meiosis*, the speaker's genuine desire to minimize or downplay a fact, statement, value, issue, etc. This kind of understatement is often used for self-deprecation on the rhetor's part, as when the heavily decorated war hero says "I have a few medals," or someone who has just won on American Idol observes "I did OK." "Sully" Sullenberger, the pilot who landed a stricken airliner on the Hudson River in January 2009, saving all the passengers on board, responded to praise by saying "I was just doing my job." These uses are not ironic, but their effect does depend on the listener recognizing that the wording is inappropriate. *Litotes* therefore demands considerable preexisting agreement on how things should be scaled.

The substitution that comes from overshooting is called **hyperbole**, a term that has passed into common usage, perhaps because the device itself is so common: *If I've told him once I've told him a thousand times = I've told him at least a few times*. The writer uses grandiose words and piles on adjectives in a way intended to be recognized as out of proportion with the subject, like calling getting to work on time a "heroic performance" or backing out of the garage without scraping the door "an astonishing feat of technical driving skill." The rhetorical results may mirror those of irony, from gentle kidding to bitter mocking.

Peacham held the line on nonironic *hyperbole*, defining it as "A sentence or saying surmounting the truth only for the cause of increasing or diminishing, not with purpose to deceive by speaking untruly, but with desire to amplify the greatness or smallness of things by the exceeding similitude." He offers the following example: "Streams of tears gushed out of her eyes, and the greatness of her grief rent her heart in sunder" (1593, 32). This kind of over-the-top exaggeration is not unusual in the early modern manuals, especially those that quote examples from poetry. For twenty-first-century audiences, such exaggeration would more likely be taken as sentence-level irony, as a way of saying "She wasn't bothered at all."

The Amphiboly and Paradox

Irony, again, says one thing but means the reverse. But suppose a statement, as is, can be taken in two ways? Here the device is the **amphiboly**, the phrase that can genuinely be construed as having two meanings. With something like a the famous gestalt switch from faces to vase, the consumer can flip suddenly and completely from one meaning to another. For example, among a well-known set of phrases from job letters that communicate on two levels is the following: "You will be lucky to get this person to work for you." On one reading, the phrase "to get to work for you" means employing or hiring the person. On another reading, the phrase means "to perform a task." The resulting contrary assessments of the candidate are obvious. The intentional amphiboly can be an audience partitioning device. The speaker says one thing to those who get it and another to those who don't.

A *paradox* is something different again. On its face the paradoxical proposition is deliberately self-contradicting: *We need to increase troop levels to decrease them* (the arguments of both Clinton for Somalia in 1993 and Bush for Iraq in 2007). The speaker maintains a contradiction, knowing that the audience will perceive it as such, and then goes on to solve it. Martin Luther, trained in dialectical fisticuffs, maintained in "Concerning Christian Liberty," "A Christian is the most free lord of all, and subject to none; a Christian man is the most dutiful servant of all, and subject to everyone" (1994, 115). He labeled this a contradiction and went on, predictably through dissociations, to defend both claims. Aristotle in effect acknowledged the argumentative force of the paradox when he identified it as a line of reasoning, a presumption to find claims credible *because incredible* (Roberts 1984, 152). A paradox shrunk to two adjoining words is the *oxymoron* (e.g., *living dead, open secret, cowardly hero*), a device oddly more remembered than its double-tongued neighbors.

Paralepsis/Praeteritio: Denying while Saying

Quintilian, as noted above, thought of irony as a category of devices, most of which were *figures* rather than *tropes*. Among this group he includes a device illustrated with the following examples: "Why should I mention his decrees, his acts of plunder, his acquisition whether by cession or force, of certain inheritances?" and "I say nothing of the first wrong inflicted by his lust" (1921, III 403). The common denominator of "saying the opposite" here involves mentioning something in the act of denying the mention of it. The speaker in effect repudiates a "speech act" but delivers the propositional content anyway. This useful strategy endures, though under inconsistent labels, in rhetorical manuals across the centuries. It is listed in the oldest set of figures as *occultatio*, and later labeled *praeteritio* or *paralipsis/paralepsis*, its name in most later manuals (Snoeck Henkemans 2009, 242). It occurs

> when we say that we are passing by, or do not know, or refuse to say that which precisely now we are saying, as follows: Your boyhood, indeed, which you dedicated to intemperance of all kinds, I would discuss, if I thought this the right time. But at present I advisedly leave that aside. This too I pass by, that the tribunes have reported you as irregular in military service. ([Cicero] 1981, 321)

The *ad Herennium* continues to explain, "[I]t is of greater advantage to create a suspicion by Paralipsis [*occultatio*] than to insist directly on a statement that is refutable" (321).

Paralepsis has never been out of fashion. In the following excerpt from her 1976 Democratic Convention keynote, Barbara Jordan manages to accuse her political opponents by listing the problems that she will not dwell on.

> Now that I have this grand distinction, what in the world am I supposed to say? I could easily spend this time praising the accomplishments of this party and attacking the Republicans—but I don't choose to do that. I could list the many problems which Americans have. I could list the problems which cause people to feel cynical, angry, frustrated: problems which include lack of integrity in government; the feeling that the individual no longer counts; the reality of material and spiritual poverty; the feeling that the grand American experiment is failing or has failed. I could recite these problems, and then I could sit down and offer no solutions. But I don't choose to do that either. The citizens of America expect more. They deserve and they want more than a recital of problems. (Linkugel, Allen, and Johannesen 1982, 335)

Embedded in a *dubitatio* ("What...am I supposed to say?"), Jordan attacks with a certain appearance of high-mindedness. Yet her dismissal of problems puts them on the table, and the bulk of her speech offers her own party as the solution.

Paralepsis gains its power from its structural lack of salience. The charges are usually in noun clauses functioning as objects of locutionary verbs (*I am not going to mention X*). The content is thus grammatically and usually prosodically de-emphasized, and yet it is out there. The brevity of the "mention" also means that the terms of the charge can be somewhat vague, so long as suggestive words are dangled before the audience. Perhaps more than any other device, *paralepsis* addresses the conundrum of the visibility of rhetorical figures and their effects. The device is, after all, extremely easy to identify. Anyone can retrospectively notice that a rhetor has listed defamatory topics under a declaration of ignoring them. And yet it seems always fresh and effective.

Classical examples of *paralepsis* come from forensic and political contexts, where the device is invariably used as a tool for damaging opponents. There is, however, a benign version of "saying what is not said," and that is the procedural ground clearing often done in academic arguments. Scholarly rhetors routinely limit their subjects, and they usually do so by listing what they will not go into. However, as in more charged arguments, this device can slip in connections of relevance without burdening the author with their explication.

Grice's Maxims and the Detection of Other Meanings

Pragmaticists and sociolinguists often discuss irony, hyperbole, litotes, and related devices in terms of philosopher Paul Grice's *conversational maxims,* introduced in his essay "Logic and Conversation" (1989). According to Grice, well-formed discourse displays standards of quality, quantity, manner, and relevance, and listeners in turn expect these standards to be met. Speakers who contribute to a conversation in good faith, fulfilling their audience's expectations, observe these four principles or maxims by speaking truthfully (quality), providing neither too little nor too much "information" (quantity), speaking in a way that is typical and acceptable for the exchange (manner), and speaking to the point at issue or staying on topic (relevance). Clearly, a speaker engaging in irony, who says "What a sunny day!" while looking at a downpour, is not matching the "quality" of the statement to the circumstances. Similarly, a speaker who keeps repeating a comment, violating the maxim of manner, will raise suspicions in a listener that the comment should not be taken as stated. The most famous example of repetition triggering a perception of irony occurs in Shakepeare's *Julius Caesar* when Marc Antony, speaking at the funeral of the murdered Caesar, keeps returning to his characterization of the conspirators as "honorable men." Thus repetition in this case undercuts sincerity; if the speaker keeps stating something, listeners assume that there is something defective in the claim and that other, indirect meanings are being signaled.

Grice's maxims clearly overlap with the much older lists of cues for detecting irony and other related figures in the rhetorical manuals. The unusual pronunciation or odd features of delivery that Quintilian pointed out concern *manner*; violations of the maxim of *quality* coincide with the perceived relationship between a statement and the facts of the case and/or the context. Grice's maxims, however, take as their point of departure a universal standard of conversational "politeness" in conveying "information." Hence they are, as stated, less sensitive to unique features like the preexisting reputation of a particular speaker/writer; after all, in some cases it would violate expectations to have the maxims observed. In addition, Grice's maxims focus on detecting an anomaly and stop short of considering what the speaker is trying to accomplish by flouting the maxims. Those further effects belong in the domain of rhetoric.

Analysis: Women Drivers

The hardest cases for detecting intended misstatements (*ironia, hyperbole, litotes*) occur in written pieces coming from sources and appearing in genres where irony is not expected. An example to work through comes from Joe Queenan's review of *Taking the Wheel: Women and the Coming of the Motor Age*, published in *The New York Times Book Review* in 1991. Book reviews do not typically deploy irony, though they may, but most readers of a *Times* book review in the 1990s would consider the cultural history of women drivers a worthy subject. So the context for this piece (genre, place of publication, time period, subject) predicts a straightforward review of a serious work. But the reader is then greeted with the following opening paragraph.

> There is no more scathing indictment of the ferocious sexism rampant in this society than that Americans have had to wait until the 91st year of the 20th century for the first truly comprehensive social history of the female driver. Iconoclastically smashing pernicious cultural and gender stereotypes, Virginia Scharff, who teaches history at the University of New Mexico, argues in "Taking the Wheel" that the political and economic enfranchisement of the American woman is the direct result of her casting off the prim haberdashery of the docile passenger, strapping on her goggles and bonnet, climbing into the driver's seat and putting the pedal to the metal.

Language here is notably askew. First there is the hyperbole of the opening sentence, "no more scathing indictment" and "91st year of the 20th century" and "iconoclastically smashing." Next, there is the notable register shifting within a single sentence from "goggles and bonnet" to "pedal to the metal." In similar fashion, the author complains in the closing paragraph,

> Quibbles? Sure. The author doesn't spend enough time discussing the insidious stereotype of the woman driver qua driver, and she also could have said a bit more

about women and car mechanics, women and the art of getting parking tickets fixed and women and convertibles. Similarly, one would have welcomed a more detailed analysis of women and carburetors, women and glove compartments and perhaps even a chapter entitled "Women and Owner's Manuals: A Feminist, Structuralist, Post-Marxist Deconstruction."

Here again are the signs of hyperbole achieved by piling up ever more arcane topics to be covered. This exaggeration creates "irony the primary effect"; most readers will infer that the author means the opposite, that he could have waited forever for such a work and that there are in fact no further topics he would like to have covered.

Elsewhere in the review, litotes seems to be employed, as in the following: "Ms. Scharff makes a persuasive case that automobiles were essential to the success of the early suffragettes, who might never have won the vote had they been forced to wait for buses. (This is particularly true in places such as New Mexico.)" Here the author "lowballs" the dignity of the subject, creating the absurd image of women protesters, no doubt carrying signs, waiting for a bus.

Directly saying the opposite, *ironia*, also occurs when the author quotes a passage describing how women drivers from respectable families protected soldiers from bootleggers and bad women, and then observes, "And don't think the guys weren't grateful." Of course they were anything but. Again, after noting the book's overall plea that we "have to develop a more pluralistic view of who uses cars, and how, and why," the last line claims, "It is something we all need to get cracking on as soon as possible," by which the reviewer evidently means never. By construing these cues, readers surmise the primary effect; this text does not mean what it says. The secondary effects follow: mocking and flippant ridicule. A straight-up negative review would not achieve the same amused but acidic dismissal.

Are there any extralinguistic cues to confirm the many linguistic ones? As Quintilian and common sense advise, "Consider the source." Does the known character of the author offer any clues? When this review was published in 1991, the author's name may not have warranted an ironic reading, but two decades and several books later, the author, Joe Queenan, has an established reputation as a satirical critic and humorist.

Summary

To Henry Peacham in 1593, a trope was "an artificial alteration of a word, or a sentence, from the proper and natural signification to another not proper, but yet nigh and likely" (1593, 7). One hundred and fifty years later, César Du Marsais also defined a trope as a word "taken in a signification which is not precisely its proper signification" [*sa signification propre*] (1977, 19). The notion of "proper" signification, echoing Quintilian's *proprium*, should be understood as a term's typical or most predictable meaning for language users in a particular time and context. To call this use *literal* and the atypical use *figural* creates two either/or language domains not really licensed in rhetorical treatises. It is "proper," expected, to talk of *soldiers* when referring to an entire army, not of *the soldier*, but this synecdochic substitution is not a radical lunge into an alternate universe of usage. Similarly, if there were no expected meaning, there would be no potential construal of an opposite meaning in irony. Furthermore, the sense of "proper" as common or expected usage also explains how tropes can lose their status. The term *icebreaker*, for example, once "properly" referred to an armored ship capable of heaving its way through surface ice; it was appropriated to refer to any ploy or party planned to introduce strangers and break the social ice. This new meaning of *icebreaker* is now its proper meaning in many contexts.

As substitutions, as alternate choices, tropes have rhetorical work to do. Metonymies and synecdoches, motivated by obvious associations, should lead the audience to think about a subject in a way that helps the rhetor's case. When, for example, Louis XIV's grandson took the throne of Spain, the Sun King allegedly said, "Il n'y a plus de Pyrénées" [There are no longer any Pyrenees]. The mountains had not vanished, but as Du Marsais explains when he cites this example, an obstacle to the alliance of France and Spain had been removed (1977, 19). The king's substitution, which Du Marsais calls a metonymy, denotes the political unification of France and Spain but does so in a way that also expresses its monumental nature. In the same manner, rhetorical metaphors should provoke a supportive analogy that is connotatively demeaning or ennobling in a way that fits the case. The host of fuller similitudes, from allegory to parable to apologue to the full four-part analogy, also serve as vehicles for expressing analogical claims and premises. Finally, the host of devices that deliberately misstate (*antiphrasis, ironia, hyperbole, litotes*) are tropes in the sense of altering "proper" signification, but they must also communicate an attitude that serves the rhetor. For this reason, returning to Peacham's definition quoted above, the altered uses of words and phrases as tropes have to be "nigh and likely," that is recoverable or construable by the audience. Otherwise they lack rhetorical effect.

NOTES

1. Metaphor of course appears in Aristotle much earlier. It is mentioned in the *Topics* (Barnes 1984, I 207, 236, 259), in the *Rhetoric* (Roberts 1984, 187ff), and in the *Poetics* (Roberts 1984, 251ff). In the *Poetics*, Aristotle's definition of metaphor includes devices that would later be classed as synecdoche: "Metaphor consists in giving the thing a name that belongs to something else; the transference being either from genus to species, or from species to genus, or from species to species, or on grounds of analogy" (251; see Kirby 1997).

2. Despite the "interminable disputes" "over the problem of the *genera* and *species* into which *tropes* may be divided, their number and correct classification," Quintilian claims to bypass these disputes by focusing only on the tropes of interest to orators, "contenting myself merely with noting the fact that some tropes are employed to help out our meaning and others to adorn our style,

that some arise from words used properly and others from words used metaphorically [*in tralatis*], and that the changes involved concern not merely individual words, but also our thoughts and the structure of our sentences. In view of these facts, I regard those writers as mistaken who have held that *tropes* necessarily involved the substitution of word for word [*in quibus verbum pro verbo poneretur*]" (1921, III 301). Note that this qualification supports substitution, just not one-for-one substitution.

3. Du Marsais (1977) lists the following as tropes: *catachresis, metonymy, metalepsis, synecdoche, antonomasia, communication, litotes, hyperbole, hypotypose, metaphor, syllepsis, allegory, allusion, irony, euphemism, antiphrasis, periphrasis.* This extended list is produced by fine distinctions. For instance, *hypotyposis*, describing intensely, only makes the list because it typically uses verbs in the present tense which logically should be in the past tense. This usage fits DuMarsais's overall definition, which is the same as Quintilian's, of using a word in a different sense. Also the odd figure "communication" only refers to the habit of addressing another as "we," as when a parent asks a naughty child, "What have we been doing?"

4. Interestingly, Quintilian includes under metonymy a phrase like "the supplies came," an active construction, instead of the passive, "the supplies were brought" (1921, III 315–17). Clearly the supplies could not come on their own.

5. Collocations were searched for in the COCA by entering the relevant pairs: *sodden* with *acquiescence, movie* with *can opener* and *Star* with *can opener, Berlin* with *escape hatch* and *refugee* with *escape hatch, rhetoric* with *genome.* After searches within nine-word strings (the largest tolerance allowed), only *genome* and *rhetoric* produced one instance of co-occurrence, and that involved a comment on *rhetoric* in the traditional sense of a persuasive campaign surrounding the Human *Genome* Project, not the sense used by the authors of the *PNAS* article. A search in the BNC, which allows search by phrases as well as collocations within one word, came up with no instances of *sodden acquiescence, escape hatch for refugees, Star Wars* and *can opener,* or *genome rhetoric.*

6. Both Butler (1921, III 303) and Russell (2001, III 427) in their translations of Quintilian render "nomen aut verbum" as "noun and verb." Since Quintilian's later examples include metaphorical modifiers, this restriction seems unnecessary at this point. Butler also translates "proprium" as "literal"; Russell uses "proper" in quotation marks, a better choice.

7. Another terminological muddle plagues the term *catachresis*. For some catalogers, this term stands not for a borrowing pressed into service where there is no term available but for an excessive or harsh metaphor, probably because the underlying Greek verb, *katakhresthai*, means 'to misuse' (thanks to Steve Dodson for this clarification). An example of an "excessive" metaphor occurs in the following sentence taken from a review of a book on night lighting: "A satellite view of the planet at night reveals swathes and pimples of light, clearly identifying hot spots of human activity—Europe, the United States, India, and Japan" (Hill, 2006, 56). The salient metaphoric borrowing here is of course *pimples of light* to stand for points of light seen from space. The metaphor is based on the analogy *point of light : the night landscape :: a pimple : the skin*, and it suggests infection, even a painful excrescence about to erupt. A reader who guesses that the author's attitude to night lighting is negative on the basis of this metaphor would be right; the author later calls such night lighting by the coined compound *photopollution* and blames it on the "insanities of consumption" (Hill, 2006, 56). Presumably turning off the lights at night will clear up the acne.

8. The full text of Quintilian's twelve-book *Institutio Oratoria* was discovered in 1416 in a heap at the bottom of a tower in the monastery of St. Gallen (Quintilian 2001, I 20). Its effect on early modern rhetoric was galvanizing. Erasmus, Quintilian's most faithful admirer among the sixteenth-century humanists, follows his pedagogical principles in *De Utraque Verborum ac Rerum Copia* [*On Copia of Words and Ideas*] (1512; the first of many editions and printings). Erasmus includes metaphor, without special fanfare, as one of the many methods of "varying" expression listed in Book I. He cites as motives for metaphor, attributed to Quintilian, not only naming per se, but also ornamentation, dignity, vivid presentation, sublimity, and humor (1963, 28). He recommends that students fill their commonplace books with striking examples from the best authors, but adds, "Nothing indeed keeps us from forming metaphors ourselves by reading and by observing the nature of all things, provided only that the metaphor be not harsh, or low, or more exaggerated than is proper, or mixed, or too frequent, especially in the same class" (29).

9. Erasmus observes that allegory can lead to **enigma**, the deliberate writing about one thing in terms of another to the point of obscuring the meaning, but he did not think that such obscurity was necessarily a bad thing: "For things should not be written in such a way that everyone understands everything, but so that they are forced to investigate certain things, and learn" (1963, 30).

10. A case of translated allegory occurs in the speech given by Theodore Roosevelt in 1906 that introduced "the man with the muck rake." This image is in fact taken from one of the greatest allegories in English, Bunyan's *Pilgrim Progress*, as Roosevelt makes explicit:

> In Bunyan's "Pilgrim's Progress" you may recall the description of the Man with the Muck Rake, the man who could look no way but downward, with the muck rake in his hand; who was offered a celestial crown for his muck rake, but who would neither look up nor regard the crown he was offered, but continued to rake to himself the filth of the floor.
>
> In "Pilgrim's Progress" the Man with the Muck Rake is set forth as the example of him whose vision is fixed on carnal instead of spiritual things. Yet he also typifies the man who in this life consistently refuses to see aught that is lofty, and fixes his eyes with solemn intentness only on that which is vile and debasing. (Reid 1988, 628).

Here Roosevelt first gives the borrowed terms—*man, rake, muck, crown, looking up,* and *looking down*—and then in the second paragraph provides the translation into moral terms. Speakers in earlier centuries, like Bunyan himself, might have risked the first paragraph alone. Roosevelt translates.

11. In *The Garden of Eloquence* (Peacham 1593), the tropes of words include most of those already mentioned: *metaphor, onomatopoeia, catachresis, synecdoche, metonymy, antonomasia, metalepsis, antiphrasis.* The tropic sentences comprise the figures *allegoria, aenigma, paroemia, hyperbole, asteismus, ironia, charientismus, sarcasmus, mycterismus, diasyrmus.* Is there a principle behind this group of "tropes of sentences"? The first three are versions of the same thing. An *allegory* is a continuous metaphor, a prolonged talking about one thing in terms of another. Linnaeus uses an extended "allegory" between the marriage bed and the pistils and stamens in a plant. An *aenigma* is a particularly obscure allegory, a useful device in the sixteenth century, when heterodox political opinions could be punished with death. The alchemists used *aenigma*s to reveal and yet conceal their knowledge of chemical manipulations. The *paroemia* is a proverb, familiar as the

medium of religious truth to Peacham and all his readers. The shepherd rejoicing in the return of a lost sheep is the Lord welcoming the repentant soul.

12. Susenbrotus 1953, 12 n. 4, applies *antiphrasis* to words whose presumed etymology suggests a contrary meaning, such as *bellum* [war] from the adjective *bellus* [pleasant, charming]. Ancient grammarians delighted in these anomalous etymologies.

13. In the sixteenth century, Susenbrotus still specifies that this figure "is indicated either by the nature of the situation, by laughter, by one's manner of speaking, or by the personage speaking; the mode of the figure can easily be inferred from the circumstances of the statement" (1953, 15).

14. A great deal has been written about *dramatic irony,* which occurs during observed exchanges, when there are three parties involved. An audience watches characters in a play, and the asymmetries of "speaking the opposite of what is the case" can evolve in at least two ways. 1. Characters speak to each other in ignorance of what the audience, and of course the dramatist, already know. For example, two children talk of what they will do when their father comes home; unknown to them, their father was killed in the previous scene. Or two campers tell each other how glad they are there are no bears around while a bear appears in the background. (This last option is sometimes also called *situational irony*, where the circumstances or context contradict the speakers.) 2. One character tells another things which the speaking character and the audience (and of course the string-pulling dramatist) know to be false; for example, one of the two campers, along with the audience, sees the bear appear over the shoulder of the speaker who is expressing joy at the absence of bears.

6

A turkey is to be killed for our dinner by the electrical
shock, *and roasted by the* electrical jack, *before a fire
kindled by the* electrified bottle: *when the healths of
all the famous electricians in* England, Holland,
France, *and* Germany *are to be drunk in* electrified
bumpers, *under the discharge of guns from the*
electrical battery.

BENJAMIN FRANKLIN, *Letter to Peter Collinson
of the Royal Society (1749)*

FIGURES OF WORD CHOICE

RHETORICIANS WERE INTERESTED in conscious word choice, and the preceding chapter on tropes reviews their most remembered descriptions of such choices. But in other now neglected devices they marked deliberate wordplay of other kinds. For convenience, these devices can be placed in three groups. First are the **schemes of words**, which involve small phonological/orthographical variations to the words themselves, with potentially significant consequences for persuasion. Second are *figures of sound*, exploiting aural similarities among words and creating patterns that audiences might or might not notice. Third is an odd group called *figures of selection*; these make explicit the act of searching for and choosing appropriate wording. Altogether, these devices demonstrate how rhetoricians appreciated the aural/visual embodiment of words and the consequences of deploying words similar in sight and sound or of juxtaposing words with similar meanings. All this attention to deliberately chosen word forms was then justified as expressing the rhetor's argument.

Schemes of Words

AGNOMINATIO

In perhaps his most famous speech, Malcolm X in 1965 challenged leaders of the Civil Rights movement, dedicated to nonviolent protest, with his darker vision of a potential future. He delivered versions of this same speech in several cities, and in the Detroit version, he returned to the same stark alternatives nine times: it was the *ballot* or the *bullet.* This pair of words, closer in sound than appearance, perfectly epitomizes Malcolm X's either/or case and his prediction that one outcome or the other must occur.[1] Writing on the Civil Rights movement over thirty years later, Glenn Loury distinguished "discrimination in *contract,*" in formal transactions subject to legislation, from "discrimination in *contact,*" that is in associations in social life (2002, 95). He argued that "practicing discrimination in contact may be essential to ending discrimination in contract" (97).

To deliver the core of their arguments, both Malcolm X and Loury use a figure of speech identified over two thousand years ago in the *Rhetorica ad Herennium.* This manual recommends that rhetors alter a word by adding, deleting, transposing, or replacing letters to create a pair of "similar words [to] express dissimilar things" ([Cicero] 1981, 303). The result is a *scheme* of words, manipulating letters in words (or, in terms of spoken language, phonemes, which are distinctive features in a language), just as the better-known schemes manipulate words in sentences (see below, p. 223). While tropes involve single-term replacements, schemes of words create patterns, both visual and aural, among nearby words. In his 1599 *Directions for Speech and Style,* John Hoskins calls this device, used so effectively by Malcolm X and Loury, the *agnominatio,* the term preferred here over the alternate label *paronomasia.* Hoskins promotes either visual rearrangements to produce pairs like "Our paradise is a pair of dice," or alterations by letter (or phoneme), producing examples like "Our praying has turned into playing, our fasting into feasting" (1935, 16). Such morphing involves the core of Saussurean linguistics, where phonetic contrasts produce the system of differences distinguishing word from word. But while in linguistics these differences are considered features of a passively received language system, in rhetorical stylistics they are seized on as sites of active manipulation for potential sources of persuasion. So a Christian pastor wanting to emphasize the nature of the *atonement* reprises it as *at-onement.* And the political action group MoveOn.org indicts the U.S. military commander in Iraq in 2007 with a full-page *New York Times* ad headlined "General Petraeus or General Betray Us?"

The *agnominatio* is useful when the arguer wants to pose two—and only two— alternatives. This either/or strategy can be epitomized by two (and apparently the only two) look-alike terms. Their close similarity conveys that these two are competing possibilities, while their slight difference suggests that they need to be distinguished. In addition to loading the language toward constrained alternatives, the *agnominatio* also "implies" that the two terms involved are equal contenders. That implication has been born out by the subsequent history of a famous *agnominatio* used by Francis Galton: *nature* versus *nurture.* A self-conscious coinage by Galton, who called this set a "convenient jingle of words," this pair forces the notion that there are only two possible determiners of a person's physical being and behavior (1874, 12). But it also adds the connotation, based on the close similarity of the words (which vary in their first syllables only), that the represented concepts are balanced alternatives, or even 50/50 possibilities. Given this initial parity, arguers have to make a case for the preponderance of one over the other.

A further argumentative dimension of the *agnominatio* is on display in a piece of accommodated science writing, an attempt to convey a development in psychiatry to the public. *New York Times* health and science writer Jane Brody based a news article on interviews with psychiatrists who study and treat a condition they describe as serious depression in young children. The consequences of such a diagnosis are obvious, for if the syndrome is the same in children and adults, then it can be treated with the same medication. However, children do not manifest the same symptoms of clinical depression as adults do. So child psychiatrists have argued that failure to thrive in infants, reckless and aggressive play in preschoolers, and disruptive and bullying behavior in the early grades are actually signs of depression. One "expert in childhood depression," quoted by Brody, found that 95% of the sixty-nine children she studied "displayed anger and depression through improper behavior at home and at school," and in a perfect epitome of this point, the psychiatrist concluded, "Most of the time, a bad child is really a sad child" (Brody 1997). In this *agnominatio* of *bad* and *sad*, a similar-sounding term with a significantly different meaning displaces its rival. Worried parents may forget the complex profile of symptoms, but they are likely to remember this slogan. The closeness, in this case even the rhyming of the terms, is not decorative. It is part of the argument, the similarity in terms helping to make more plausible the likelihood that one of these states could be confused or misread for the other.

The *agnominatio* draws on the potential confusion presented by nearly identical words and the close attention that can be required to separate them. Psycholinguistic research lends some credibility to this effect. Experiments suggest that words are indeed stored in memory, or are at least accessible in memory, by their sound similarities. In tests, people more readily confuse words differing only in a letter, and they retrieve these words in pairs. Hence arguers draw on a natural parsing mechanism when they play on the confusable closeness of contrasting terms (Fahnestock 2005, 172–74).

Metaplasms: Altering a Single Word

Agnominatio creates pairs of words that must appear near each other in the same text in order to have an argumentative effect. But many of the recommendations for word alteration found in the great early modern style manuals involve shortening or lengthening a single word used on its own. As a result, an *agnominatio* effect occurs when readers or listeners recognize that the form of the word presented is not its typical form. Of course this effect requires some standardization in pronunciation or spelling conventions so that a violation of those conventions can be recognized. Yet even in an era of anarchic word forms, Henry Peacham in the 1577 version of *The Garden of Eloquence* lists fourteen forms of word alteration under the general category *Metaplasmus*. These involve adding, subtracting, or changing letters or syllables in the beginning, middle, or ending of words.[2]

Peacham called these devices "Orthographical Schemes," and he considered them "lawfull only to Poets" who needed to satisfy the metrical demands of a poetic line. He advised against their use in prose genres such as sermons, and he left them out of the greatly expanded and more frequently cited 1593 edition of *The Garden of Eloquence.*

Yet the devices of word alteration that Peacham downplayed still persist in argumentative wordplay, and the regularization of spelling, largely complete in eighteenth-century English, makes such wordplay according to orthographical schemes more noticeable. Take, for instance, the fact that Noah Webster introduced American spelling variants in his 1828 Dictionary: *honor* for *honour, color* for *colour.* For U.S. readers, the British spellings are marked, and for British readers, the American spellings are. When Stephen Jay Gould argued against a particular British school of evolutionary biology in a review article, he consistently referred to its theories as a "programme." This British spelling defamiliarizes their concepts. In other words, a single altered word form can have the effect of an *agnominatio* when the altered word invokes another, usually more familiar, form. For a U.S. audience, *programme* draws attention to itself and suggests a dissociation from a normative *program* (Fahnestock 1993, 178, 327).

Similar wordplay, where one altered word invites two readings, is a staple of the critical idiom of deconstruction, which often "games" single terms into two by the introduction of parentheses. The titles of a pair of articles in a 1999 issue of the *Rhetoric Society Quarterly* include the forms "Copula(tions)," combining grammatical and sexual terms, and "Re(de)-erecting," the latter an *epenthesis* on "Redirecting" (see note 3). Such parenthetical creations of two readings from a single term express deconstructionist assumptions about the instability or multivalency of words by producing, if not an *agnominatio* (two contrasting meanings in two close words), nevertheless two terms with differing meanings from essentially the same set of phonemes.

POLYPTOTON

In inflected languages, words change their form when they change their case. These changes produce visibly different versions of the same words, as, for example, with the five main cases of Latin *homo* (man): *homo, hominis, homini, hominem, homine,* in the singular, and *homines, hominum, hominibus, homines, hominibus,* in the plural. To spread these word forms through a text means to use the same word in different forms and functions. Such persistent reappearances, labeled *polyptoton* in many figure manuals, can in effect argue for the consistency of a term, and hence of a concept or referent, through different syntactic functions. The resources of Latin provide examples of this device in phrases like *saecula saeculorum* (nominative and genitive, *ages of ages* or *for ever and ever*) or *somniavit somnium* (cognate accusative, *he dreamed a dream*) or *amaverunt magno amore* (ablative of means, *they loved with a great love*). The wording of the Nicene Creed, crafted to emphasize the Godhead of Christ, illustrates in its Latin version the epitomizing force of this device in an inflected language: *Deum de Deo, lumen de lumine,*

Deum verum de Deo vero. Early modern writers, trained in these Latin forms, brought them readily into English, though without the case markings: *God from God, light from light, true God from true God* (often translated *God of God*, etc.).

English does not mark most case changes by different word forms, so its resources for inflectional variation are minimal. But English does allow changes that move the same term easily through different parts of speech in the open word classes (noun, verb, adjective, adverb), creating derivational families based on the same root: noun *love/lover*, verb *love*, adjective *loving/loved* (participles), adverb *lovingly*. This migration potential is an easy source of new words (see above, p. 46). It is also a source of support in arguments.

Rhetorical lists of topics in fact recommend fashioning premises from different grammatical forms of the same word (Kennedy 1991, 191). In an early modern dialectical manual like Melanchthon's *Erotemata Dialectices*, intended for Latin users, this resource is called the argument from conjugates or cases, and it is verbally realized by *polyptoton*. Melanchthon offers the following example of such an argument: "Aqua est calida, recte sequitur/Ergo in aqua est calor" [Water is hot, it rightly follows/Therefore heat is in water] (1963b, 670). This reasoning is based on the adjective form for hot, *calida*, justifying the identification of the substance heat, *calor*, as in water that is sensibly hot. This scholastic formalism is the source of the doctrine of *caloric*, the notion that heat is a substance that permeates hot bodies, a notion persisting in western science into the nineteenth century. Melanchthon also calls this example an argument from the concrete to the abstract, the presence of heat to the senses justifying the imputation of an abstract essence of heat in a body.

Arguments deploying *polyptoton* can be subtle but powerful. In his "Farewell Letter," George Washington offered advice to a new nation by reiterating its founding principles. He concluded a section praising the Constitution and recommending adherence to the national government with the following:

> The very idea of the power and the right of the people to establish government presupposes the duty of every individual to obey the established government. (Reid 1988, 195)

The argument here is carried by *to establish/established*, infinitive and past participle forms of the same verb. This repetition epitomizes the connection between the power *to establish* a government and the obligation to obey it, once *established*. The careful placement of these related words perfectly expresses and hence reinforces the point.

> The very idea of the power and the right of the people *to establish government* presupposes the duty of every individual to obey *the established government*.

Both the subject and object phrases, twenty-four and twenty-one syllables long respectively, end with these crucially positioned terms, whose formal and hence conceptual relationship is thus emphasized.

Spreading Concepts through Polyptoton

In a single text, a word can follow a particular path from case to case, starting off as a noun and then becoming a verb or an adjective, or traveling from adjective to noun, and so on. Such in-text changes involve *polyptoton* as an argumentative device, as described above. But what happens in a single text can also happen across time in different texts. Words can enter a language in one part of speech and then travel to other parts as users press them into service in different contexts. This migration from one syntactic class to another is the stylistic signature of the history of an idea, as each distinctive word/concept pair follows a *"polyptotonic"* path in the language, a sign of its expanding semantic territory and usefulness (Fahnestock 1999, 177–94). A standard path, for example, may be from noun to verb: *clone*, according to the *OED*, began life as a term for plants propagated from the parts of other plants; its first form was *clon* in 1903, altered to *clone* in 1905. Fifty years later, *clone* was pressed into service as the gerund *cloning* when a new technique for culturing individual plant cells was developed (Bergmann 1959, 648; for the full history of the term see Mittwoch 2002). In the twenty-first century, the term has shifted meanings under widely used forms as nouns (*clone/cloning*), verb (*to clone*), adjective (*clonal*), and participle (*cloned*).

Etymological Arguments

No single figure of speech quite names the activity that in some instances reverses polyptoton and traces the forms or form of a word back to its roots. Yet a long-identified line of argument depends on disassembling a word into its constituent parts and isolating its "root," the core of meaning irrespective of case or derivation markers. An etymological argument then uses this root to argue for a particular meaning or definition. This tactic is on display in the following passage from philosopher Peter Caws, arguing against the designation of *secular humanism* as a religion in a court decision in the 1980s. Caws's first argument points out that "secular" means nonreligious, so calling secular humanism a religion is something of a contradiction. His second argument recommends looking again at what *religion* means.

> The "-lig-" in "religion" is like the corresponding part of the word "ligament," and it comes from a Latin verb meaning "to bind." Religions characteristically have a binding effect in one or both of two ways: they bind men and women to God or to some transcendent being or state, through worship, or meditation, or faith, or a covenant; or they bind them to one another, in a church, or synagogue, or congregation. To call a set of beliefs [secular humanism] that does neither of these things a religion is to misunderstand the history of ideas. (Caws 1987, B7)

Caws's deft etymology is a classic example of a whole family of arguments that exploit the meanings of roots in compounds to construct definitions favorable to an arguer's position.

Again, such arguments in their stylistic manifestations fall under the broad category of word schemes, since they depend on the audience reseeing or rehearing two versions of the same word: *religion* and *religion*. Caws' argument also uses *polyptoton*, since *bind* appears as a verb and as an adjective, *binding*. His point, that what *binds* has a "*binding* effect," is difficult to refute.

PLOCE

If the *agnominatio* uses similar forms for dissimilar or confusable notions and the *polyptoton* uses similar forms for similar notions, the figure *ploce* epitomizes arguments based on the same form of a word appearing again and again in an argument. *Ploce*, sometimes called *symploce* from the Greek word for *intertwining*, designates the intermittent or unpatterned reappearance of a word, within or across several sentences. It was sometimes classed with the figures of repetition that specified where a word or phrase would reappear (see below, p. 230). *Ploce*, seen from the perspective of this group, was repetition of a word with only one or a few words intervening (Sonnino 1968, 64).[3] A straightforward example can be found in Lyndon Johnson's speech justifying sending troops into the Dominican Republic in 1965 by claiming the agreement of the Organization of American States: "This is and this will be a common action and the common purpose of the democratic forces of the hemisphere. For the danger is also a common danger and the principles are common principles" (Windt 1983, 78). In its four appearances, the adjective *common* links the countries of the Western Hemisphere in *action, purpose, danger,* and *principles*.[4]

When a term is repeated with some frequency in the confines of a short passage, it inevitably acquires a certain force. If this emphasis accrues to Johnson's *common*, how much more does it add hammer-like force to a word already emphasized by its sentence role and position. The possibilities are seen in Churchill's first speech to Parliament in 1940, during the opening months of World War II:

> You ask, what is our aim? I can answer in one word. It is victory. Victory at all costs—victory in spite of all terrors—victory, however long and hard the road may be, for without victory there is no survival" (Safire 1997, 135–36; the section before repeats *war* and the section after *survival* in the same manner)

Here *ploce*, dramatically visible, serves the grand style, completely fitting to the speaker, audience, and situation.

There is no reason, however, to limit *ploce* to neighboring repetition of the same word. A term or phrase can continually, if unobtrusively, reappear over a longer passage, and by its frequency and versatility in different contexts establish itself and the concept it encodes. A case in point is the reappearance of *foreign* twelve times in Washington's Farewell Letter, from its first appearance in the third paragraph to its final appearance near the end (Reid 1988, 186–201; though called an "address," this text appeared originally in newspapers). Washington first used this term when introducing the problem of the young nation's relations with other countries, and he kept this issue in view by its recurrence until the famous extended passage warning against either "inveterate antipathies" or "passionate attachments" for other nations: "Against the insidious wiles of foreign influence (I conjure you to believe me, fellow-citizens) the jealousy of a free people ought to be constantly awake, since history and experience prove that foreign influence is one of the most baneful foes of republican government" (198). Four times after this passage, the term reappears to carry on the theme. Once an analyst has the thread of such repetition to pull on, collocations with the repeated term (in this case the terms modified by *foreign*) and the identification of its synonyms can reveal the spreading influence this concept achieved through *ploce*.

ANTANACLASIS (PUNS)

Polyptoton repeats the same root in different forms of a word. *Ploce* repeats precisely the same word in the same functional category. Between these two stands the *antanaclasis,* which repeats the same orthographic or phonological word but in different functional categories or with different or even contrary meanings. This device is prominent in early modern figure manuals, with their love of wordplay, as in Peacham's example: "In your youth learn some craft, that in thy age thou mayst get thy living without craft" (1593, 57). Here of course the first *craft* means *skill* and the second *guile,* a case of polysemy where the senses have wandered far from the OE root *craeft*. Because English lacks inflections to mark when words fulfill different functions or occupy different parts of speech, it is possible to have identical word forms in different parts of speech, as in Roosevelt's "We have nothing to *fear* [verb] but *fear* [noun] itself." When two words, identical in sight or sound or both, are present in their different senses, the effect is something like that achieved by the *agnominatio*: a momentary confounding and then separation. One step further is the double reading of a term that appears just once, the familiar *pun*, where the two senses must be derived from a single occurrence. So a book critical of then candidate Barack Obama invited reading in two ways with its title *Obama Nation*.

Rhetoricians would not confuse *puns* with the double meanings of *amphibolies* (see above p. 118).[5] Both are defined as single terms having two or more meanings, but puns are often thought of as merely lighthearted or irritating, while the *amphiboly*, introduced by Aristotle in *On Sophistical Refutations*, has had a long life as the fallacy of equivocation. This distinction is based on a difference in intention: arguers using puns intend for the two meanings to be recognized, while arguers using amphibolies do not. The pun's goal is usually humor, though the humor can have a serious point. But the double nature of an amphiboly is not immediately recognized; its different meanings are, in fact, subfusc, and are often addressed to different segments of the audience. The rhetor expects the term to be understood in one sense by one group and in another sense by another. The silent slippages of amphiboly are then not the same as those of elbow-in-the-ribs puns.

In her study of the interdisciplinary recruitment rhetoric of the geneticist Theodosius Dobzhansky, the physicist Erwin Schrödinger, and the biologist E. O. Wilson, Leah Ceccarelli traced the use of amphibolies in polysemous key terms in the scientists' texts that reviewers from different disciplines understood differently. In the case of Wilson's project for a unification and hierarchical ordering of the sciences and humanities outlined in *Consilience*, she noted how critics responded to Wilson's apparently inconsistent use of his key term. Reviewing Wilson's book, Tzvetan Todorov, for example, finally identified two contradictory readings of *consilience*: one a hard, deterministic sense, reducing human behavior ultimately to the laws of physics, and the other a softer sense, acknowledging that human cultural differences were primarily the product of historical contingency and could never be wholly explained by science. Todorov observed, "there is one Wilson who writes, a little cunningly, on two levels. His hard version is the sensational one, designed for the newspapers. His soft version is the prudent one, which enables him to respond to objections by retorting 'But that is exactly what I'm saying!'" (quoted in Ceccarelli 2001, 147).

THE PRESENCE OF THE WORD

Whether through *polyptoton* or *ploce* or *antanaclasis*, the continual reappearance and reassertion of the same term or phrase has undoubted rhetorical force. These devices are a formal mechanism for fulfilling the general rhetorical goal of giving *presence* to certain notions (see below, p. 203). And even if such repetition is not intentional, as seems likely in most cases of dispersed *ploce*, it can still be taken as an index of what has salience for the writer/speaker. Leff and Mohrmann, for example, note that in his "Cooper Union Address" (1860), Lincoln referred to the "fathers," the framers of the Constitution, over thirty-five times and repeated the root "understand," usually in the participle *understanding*, over thirty times, including, strategically, in the last few words of the speech (1993, 179). In these repetitions, Lincoln inevitably foregrounds his argument about a proper understanding of the intent of the framers, and hence about the proper interpretation of the Constitution on the issue of the spread of slavery to the territories.

Analysis by ubiquity, by the number of repetitions or versions of a term, supports the established social science methodology of "content analysis." In texts teaching this method for rhetorical analysis by Roderick P. Hart (1997, 155–75) and Sonja K. Foss (1989, 367–70), key terms are identified as repeated terms. Term repetition lends itself to counting, though in using this method for apparently generating "hard" evidence, some preceding assumption has to be made about what counts as a significant word. After all, interpretive arguments rarely use as evidence the prevalence of definite articles, demonstratives, or prepositions.[6] But the chapter epigraph shows "the presence of the word" deliberately serving Benjamin Franklin's celebration of his Philadelphia group's manipulations of electricity. The phenomenon is as ubiquitous as *ploce*, straight repetition in the passage, can make it, and as versatile as *polyptoton*, its appearance in different functional sentence slots, can demonstrate. At the same time, the variety of terms derived from the same root, *electri-*, captures the state of understanding of the phenomenon in the mid-eighteenth century, available for comparison with its appearances in other eras (Fahnestock 1999, 190–94).

Figures of Sound

While the figures discussed so far (*agnominatia, polyptoton, ploce, antanaclasis*) produce visual and aural families of words, creating linked concepts across a text, sound similarities alone can also create connections among terms with similar argumentative consequences. The figures that create these sound patterns are among the oldest noticed in rhetorical stylistics. In fact, three of the so-called Gorgianic figures, attributed to the fifth-century BCE Sophist Gorgias, whose oral performances entranced Athenians, are prescriptions for sound similarities, including **isocolon**, producing phrases with an equal number of syllables (see below, p. 224), **homeoptoton**, ending successive phrases with words having the same case endings, and **homeoteleuton**, ending successive phrases with like-sounding or rhyming endings (Kennedy 1980, 248 n.3; 1991, 243). Gerry Spence simplified liability law for the jury in the Karen Silkwood trial by repeating the *homeoteleuton* "If the lion gets away, Kerr-McGee has to pay" (Lief, Caldwell, and Bycel 1998, 1440). But perhaps the single most famous example of this figure in contemporary persuasion comes from Johnnie Cochran's summation to the jury in the O. J. Simpson trial, "If it [the glove] doesn't fit, you must acquit."

Two other devices from this category, **assonance** and **consonance**, are frequently cited in studies of poetry, often as part of the aesthetic dimensions of a text. *Assonance* refers to repetitions of vowel and *consonance* of consonant sounds within and among words, and these features are not in fact listed among the figures in early modern manuals. The special case of *alliteration* refers to repetitions in the initial sounds of words that can produce echoes of phonetic similarity throughout a text. In early modern style manuals, this device is known as *paroemion*, another of the Gorgianic figures.[7] Alliteration becomes interesting in argument formation when terms are selected to produce the same opening sound or opening letter for visual alliteration, as in Thomas Jefferson's First Inaugural, "When I contemplate these transcendent objects, and see the honor, the happiness, and the hopes of this beloved country committed to the issue and the auspices of this day" (Safire 1997, 801), or Lyndon Johnson's "So I want to talk to you today about three places where we begin to build the Great Society—in our cities, in our countryside, and in our classrooms" (Windt 1983, 62). And certainly the sound repeated serves this line from Kennedy's 1961 speech on the Berlin crisis with its popping plosives: "Our primary purpose is neither propaganda nor provocation—but preparation" (Windt 1983, 26).

These examples show alliteration at the service of fabricating triplets, where the repeated opening consonant helps the rhetor produce the impression of a coherent set. Often such alliteration works at a greater distance, creating visual or aural links across passages and sometimes across grammatical boundaries.

Figures of Word Selection

The goal of selecting the best word for a particular context motivates most projects of vocabulary building, from Erasmus's system for training schoolboys in copious Latin to the "It Pays to Increase Your Word Power" sections in the *Reader's Digest*. "Right words in their right places," a phrase once used to describe Lincoln's rhetorical skills (quoted in Nichols 1993, 54), will do their work of persuasion unobtrusively. But, paradoxically, among the figures of words were devices that recommended drawing attention to alternative word choices and to selecting among apparently equivalent terms. The third set of devices under consideration here foregrounds these choices and the selection process. These are not the invisible substitutions of tropes or the formal morphing of word schemes. Instead, these devices offer rhetors ways to bring alternative word choices to the audience's attention.

SYNONYMS (*SYNONYMIA*)

Classical and early modern rhetoricians recognized sets of words in a language as *synonyms*, words sharing roughly the same denotation while differing in connotation or suitability for different purposes and contexts. Roget's *Thesaurus* attempts to classify the English lexicon on this principle. Offering a synonym is of course a basic tactic in audience accommodation; the rhetor inserts a presumably equivalent word or phrase as a backup, right after a term that might be unclear to the audience addressed. The basic redundancy in most languages, with many forms coding the same concept, became the principle behind the figure *synonymia* or *interpretatio*. As Quintilian defines this device, the rhetor masses together words with roughly the same meaning, as in the example he cites from Cicero on Cataline: "abiit, excessit, erupit, evasit" ["He went off, he departed, he broke out, he got away" (Quintilian 1921, III 126–27); see below on Congeries, p. 242)]. Such a string of synonyms not only emphasizes a notion but also creates an impression of complete comprehension of a concept by assigning it every possible label.

Synonymia became an end in itself in Latin pedagogy. An early modern grammar school text like Erasmus's *De copia verborum ac rerum* (*On Copia of Words and Things*), which aims to increase facility in Latin composition, prescribes exercises in varying by *synonymia*, substituting words that "express exactly the same thought, so that as far as the meaning goes it makes no difference," though Erasmus, like his classical predecessors, concedes that "scarcely anywhere will you find two words so close in meaning that they do not differ in some respect" (1963, 19–20). Among connotative differences, Erasmus acknowledges that "some words are more becoming than others, more exalted, more polished, more humorous, more emphatic, more sonorous, more suited to composition" (20). In short, the rhetorical doctrine of appropriateness would dictate which single term to select in a particular context.

In a tour de force of synonym substitution, Erasmus offers students two hundred versions of "Your letter delighted me." To ultimately choose the best phrasing for a particular context, difficult for second-language writers like Erasmus's Latin learners, the well-trained student must have a store of synonyms to begin with, garnered from the best authors. Erasmus therefore enjoins students to keep commonplace books with such lists, and he also directs them to categorize words as low, unusual (rare instances from classical authors), poetic, archaic, obsolete, harsh, foreign, obscene, and new. In other words, Erasmus thinks of choices among synonyms along the axes of social formality (low), politeness (obscene, harsh), familiarity in usage (obsolete or foreign), historical change (archaic, new), and genre (poetic). (These categories of usage still appear in dictionaries.) The arguer who uses *synonymia*, a set of synonyms that crosses these boundaries, in effect inserts a concept into several contexts at once.

In addition to "covering" a concept and invoking different contexts, *synonymia*'s greatest persuasive effect is surely emphasis. John Hoskins noted this effect in *Directions for Speech and Style* in the late sixteenth century. He labeled the use of a string of synonyms "Accumulation," grouping it among techniques for achieving amplification. And though he warned, perhaps with Erasmian pedagogy in mind, that anyone using it could sound "like a schoolmaster foaming out synonymies, or words of one meaning," (1935, 24), he nevertheless demonstrated a pileup of synonymous words and phrases for *sedition* that could certainly find its place in a denunciation in the grand style:

> Tumults, mutinies, uproars, desperate conspiracies, wicked confederacies, furious commotions, traitorous rebellions, associations in villainy, distractions from allegiance, bloody garboils, and intestine massacres of the citizens. (24)

Synonyms and Conceptual Drift

There is a significant difference between using a bolus of synonyms all at once (full-fledged *synonymia*) and gradually replacing a term with synonyms in subsequent phrases. Such synonym substitution was recommended in figure manuals as a way to avoid the corresponding fault of *homiologia,* repeating the same term several times, when such repetition was ineffective in itself (Hoskins 1935, 24). But synonym substitution can also have the effect of spreading out a concept so that it gradually "drifts" into alternate senses and connotations across a text. Thus, synonym substitution serves the art of term shifting in an argument, when, for example, a potentially unfavorable term is subsequently replaced with synonyms or partial equivalents with more useful connotations. This process is on view in an editorial in the *Washington Post* from 2007 which announces in a subtitle that its topic is *illegal immigrants*, already a choice that avoids the alternative *illegal aliens*. While *illegal immigrant* continues to appear in this argument against penalizing those who employ or rent to them, it is also replaced from sentence to sentence with *undocumented immigrant, immigrant* (minus modifiers), and once with *newcomer*, synonyms with neutral or even positive connotations ("Next Stop: Underground" 2007). In this way, substitution with apparent synonyms, a practice that can look like mere "elegant variation," can do the work of category and value change in an argument.

Euphemism

Among the types of synonyms available for substitution, modern style advice often pays attention to *euphemism*, the substitution of a polite or mild expression for a crude, offensive, or obscene one. The Orwellian school of style criticism shuns euphemisms as dishonest and assumes a truculent "tell it like it is" standard. According to Orwell himself and his many followers, bureaucratic language is by definition euphemistic to the point of lying. Euphemism can, however, be defended as a response to the need for appropriateness, for tailoring language to the sensibilities of an audience, and not all sensibility is prudishness.

Examples of what would now be called euphemism abound in the many nineteenth-century arguments circulated in the United States among abolitionists. The widely acknowledged sexual exploitation of female slaves by their masters served as a strong argument against slavery, especially among women. But this abuse was typically not stated but instead suggested in phrases deploring "outraged womanhood" (quoted in Martineau 1939, 16) or "the licentious and murderous outrages" upon the "persons" of slaves, as phrased in the Declaration of Sentiments of the American Anti-Slavery Society, 1833 (Reid 1988, 344). Audiences of the time no doubt knew what was meant.

CORRECTIO

In his speech to the Democratic Convention in 2008, vice presidential nominee Joe Biden followed his characterization of voters' economic concerns with the following:

> You know, folks, that's the America that George Bush has left us. And that's the America we'll continue to get if George—excuse me, if John McCain is elected president of the United States of America. Freudian slip. Freudian slip.[8]

Biden's "mistake," which earned a laugh and applause from his audience, voiced one of the arguments of the Democratic campaign, that the Republican nominee would merely continue the policies of his predecessor. The two Republicans were so alike, according to Biden, they were exchangeable, and dislike for one should translate into dislike of the other.

Clearly Biden's mistake was deliberate. It represents a device identified in the *Rhetorica ad Herennium* as **correctio**, when the speaker "retracts what has been said and replaces it with what seems more suitable" (319). Uncharacteristically, the *ad Herennium*, which usually only defines a device briefly and adds a few examples, goes into an elaborate justification for the *correctio*:

> This figure makes an impression upon the hearer, for the idea when expressed by an ordinary word seems rather feebly stated, but after the speaker's own amendment it is made more striking by means of the more appropriate expression. "Then would it not be preferable," some one will say, "especially in writing, to resort to the best and choicest word from the beginning?" Sometimes this is not preferable, when, as the change of word will serve to show, the thought is such that in rendering it by an ordinary word you seem to have expressed it rather feebly, but having come to a choicer word you make the thought more striking. But if you had at once arrived at this word, the grace neither of the thought nor of the word would have been noticed. ([Cicero] 1981, 319–21)

Correctio (also known as *epanorthosis* and *metanoia*) appears consistently in manuals across the centuries, but, as happens with many of the figures, it is often given different specifications. So in the *Orator*, Cicero includes as part of *correctio* a self-censure on the part of the rhetor for carelessness (1988, 135), and Puttenham, fifteen hundred years later, also recommends that the speaker apologize for an incorrect word choice and take it back before replacing it (1593, 215).[9] With or without the apology, the *correctio* plants alternatives in the audience's mind.

The *Rhetorica ad Herennium* points to another version of foregrounded word selection in **dubitatio**, "when the speaker seems to ask which of two or more words he had better use, as follows: "At that time the republic suffered exceedingly from—ought I to say—the folly of the consuls, or their wickedness, or both" ([Cicero] 1981, 329). This device tries to involve the audience in debating the appropriate term choice. One step further, and the speaker claims to be at loss for words, which the audience can imaginatively supply. All these forms of drawing attention to alternative word choices—*correctio*, *dubitatio*, and claiming to be at a loss for words—are still widely used to communicate tendentious clarification and intensification of meaning.

EMPHASIS (*SIGNIFICATIO*)

Another device of word selection well marked in rhetorical manuals has since disappeared as a figure, if not as a useful tactic. This lost device, or rather category of devices, is **significatio**, the use of "leading" words that suggest more than is actually stated.[10] According to the *Rhetorica ad Herennium*, if the rhetor uses this strategy, "the hearer himself [has] to guess what the speaker has not mentioned" ([Cicero] 1981, 403). Almost two hundred years later, Quintilian had a somewhat negative opinion of this device that he cited under its confusing Greek name **emphasis**. He identified three conditions for its use: "(1) if it is unsafe to speak openly, (2) if it is unseemly to do so, (3) when it is employed simply for elegance and gives more pleasure by its freshness and variety than the straight-forward statement would have done" (2001, IV 73). Evidently in the rhetorical schools of Quintilian's day, exercises based on imaginary cases were devised so that students had to speak as though decrees had been laid down by tyrants or passed by the Senate forbidding the mention of the very subjects under discussion on pain of death. In these exercises, Quintilian observes, students would try to speak in ways that could be given alternate interpretations (75). Quintilian thought that his own era did not present such extreme conditions (an observation that may have been his own use of the device), but he agreed there were situations "much more difficult for the speaker to handle, when there are pow-erful personages presenting an obstruction, and the Cause cannot be maintained without blaming them" (75). Such situations can call for suggesting more than is actually said to avoid offending the powerful (75, 77).

What the manual writers mark here as *significatio* or *emphasis*, and sometimes as *enigma*, corresponds to what would now be called *innuendo*, a suggesting without out-right saying. Such cloaking but revealing word choice requires that the audience recog-nize that the selected words are a "front," a substitution for a direct account. Clearly, *emphasis* wanders into the territory of euphemism, allegory, and even irony, but with these differences: there is an adequate surface meaning in the *significatio* that needs no decoding, and danger to the rhetor rather than offense to the audience is avoided. *Significatio* is also an excellent choice when the rhetor wants the benefit of an implication without the trouble of an outright defense. The pressures of a media age make such innu-endo a convenience allowing deniability.

Summary

In the *Gorgias*, Socrates reports hearing a wise man claim that the body (*soma*) is a tomb (*sema*), a definition arguing with an *agnominatio* that defies translation into English (1960, 92n). Perhaps an ancient understanding would maintain that because words are related, so are their referents. No one would agree to that premise today, once it is made explicit. But the pattern-seeking brain necessarily notes aural and visual similarities, and these may predispose a listener or reader to connect words that sound and look alike. When these resemblances epitomize the arguer's point, the style helps make the case.

The rhetorical manuals made fine distinctions among the possibilities here. An *agno-minatio* like Socrates's *soma/sema* plays with the nearness of look-alike words. Their sim-ilarity pairs concepts, and when these concepts are offered as alternatives, their competition or confusion is highlighted. The figure *polyptoton* marks the use of words that share the same root, again creating visual and aural similarities, but the inflections or derivatives of this figure necessarily work differently in a sentence (*differ, differs, difference*). In the figures *agnominatio* and *polyptoton*, similar forms are involved, but in *ploce* and *antanaclasis*, identical forms are involved, with the difference that in *ploce* the same word appears again and again in the same sense and function, and in *antanaclasis*, the same form is repeated in different senses and functions (*We have nothing to fear but fear itself.*) Audiences can often bring their own word knowledge to a text and turn single uses of terms into an *agnominatio* or *antanaclasis*.

Pure sound resemblance is also marked among the figures that distinguish echoes in phrases created by their equal length or by their similar-sounding or even by their rhyming endings. The sound effects of assonance and consonance were ignored unless they created an argument-serving *agnominatio*. In one of the stranger moves recommended in rhetorical stylistics, arguers were invited to draw attention to the very process of word choice. In *synonymia*, a series of terms likely to substitute for one another are offered in a clutch, achieving emphasis and connotative control. In *correctio*, the arguer uses the wrong word and in the repair or the original mistake offers the better choice.

Contemporary analysts are often impatient with the endless lists of odd terms offered in the figure manuals, and the account of the wordplay figures in this chapter actually simplifies the term shifting and definitional overlap found in rhetorical treatises over two thousand years. Arguers, however, still use these devices, and to the extent that the distinctions noted here serve the scrutiny of technique, they are worth retaining.

NOTES

1. Keeping the consonants and changing only the vowels as in *ballot/bullet,* there are in fact other close words possible; one is *billet,* meaning either a lodging for troops or a short, thick piece of wood or metal. But *billet* is not as frequently used as *ballot* and *bullet*; COCA yields 6,305 occurrences of *bullet* in its 350-million-word database, 5,214 of *ballot,* but only 77 of *billet,* so *billet* is not likely to come to mind as an alternative. (COCA is using data post-1990, but it is likely that similar frequencies for these words prevailed in the 1960s.)

2. The examples of metaplasms from Peacham using sixteenth-century spelling conventions, such as they were, are the following (1593, Eii–iii):

Prothesis, adding a letter or syllable to the beginning: beknowne for knowne
Apheresis, taking away a letter or syllable from the beginning: playnts for complaint
Epenthesis, adding a letter or syllable in the middle: steddifast for stedfast
Syncope, taking a letter or syllable away from the middle: prosprous for prosperous
Paragoge, adding a letter or syllable to the end of a word: beforne for before
Apocope, taking away a letter or syllable from the end of a word: Dian for Diana
Antistœchon, a changing of letters in a word: slibbery for slipperye
Metathesis, a transposing of letters in a word: remembre for remember

The remaining six involve changing syllable length (*systole,* long to short; *diastole,* short to long), collapsing two vowels into one (*synalaepha*) or two syllables into one (*synaeresis*), or conversely making two syllables out of one (*diaresis*), and, for a final rarity, dropping a vowel plus the consonant *m* (*ecthlipsis*, for which Peacham can provide no English example).

3. The same term, *ploce*, was sometimes applied to a figure that also went by the name *duplicatio* or *diaphora*, specifying the repetition of the same form with different senses. For Scaliger, "The meaning is inevitably altered on the second appearance of the word" (Sonnino 1968, 103). For Peacham, *ploce* stood for the repetition of a proper name which in its second mention took on the meaning of the quality of the person, for example, "Patrick Kennedy is a Kennedy" (1593, 44). Another example which shows how *ploce* can be used to mask sense differences comes from the following sentence in the English translation of Marx and Engel's *The German Ideology*, "The ideas of the ruling class are in every epoch the ruling ideas" (1970, 64). The adjective *ruling* carries the argument. The claim that ideas of the dominant social class dominate (to express this argument with *polyptoton*) or that those with political or social power control ideology (to paraphrase without word schemes) is best epitomized by the identical modifiers. The two *ruling*'s could of course be said to differ in meaning (the first, "*ruling* class" meaning "having power" and the second in "*ruling* ideas" meaning "prevailing"), but it is precisely this difference that the repetition suppresses in order to make a stronger case for class-based determinism.

4. *Ploce* again, like *polyptoton*, has an older and discredited connection to a particular tactic in classical and early modern arguments. In ancient and early modern medicine, for example, the doctrine of likenesses matched remedies with diseases, a connection epitomized by *ploce*, "Just as evil expels evil and good retains good" (quoted in Boorstin 1985, 344); it is still the principle behind homeopathic medicine: "like cures like."

5. The *Rhetorica ad Herennium* discusses amphibolies [*amphibolia*] among the kinds of things that can be in contention in a written document. The writer accused teachers of dialectic of exaggerating the search for possible double meanings in documents: "In fact these writers are on the lookout for all amphibolies, even for such as yield no sense at all in one of the two interpretations. Accordingly, when some one else speaks, they are his annoying hecklers, and when he writes, they are his boring and also misty interpreters. And when they themselves speak, wishing to do so cautiously and deftly, they prove to be utterly inarticulate. Thus in their fear to utter some ambiguity while speaking, they cannot even pronounce their own names" ([Cicero] 1981, 87). Also, "Chrysippus maintained that every word is by nature ambiguous, while Diodorus Cronus asserted that no word is ambiguous (Gellius 11.12)" (86, note b). A typical sixteenth-century dialectical textbook like Melanchthon's *Erotemata Dialectices* (1547) gives considerable attention to amphibolies.

6. Patterns in the use of the prepositions, determiners, and conjunctions are, however, not without significance in arguments about the identity of anonymous authors where habits with the fixed word classes are considered invariant across subject matter differences and hence diagnostic. All such "insignificant" habits of repetition are could be significant indicators of conceptual assumptions. See Milic 1967.

7. Peacham considered excessive alliteration more appropriate for poetry, where one could get away with a line like "When friendly favor flourished, I found felicitie but now no hope doth helpe my heart in heavinesse so hard" (1593, 50). In prose, he cautioned against excesses like, "This mischievous money, maketh many men, marvellous mad" (50).

8. http://elections,nytimes.com/2008/President/conventions/videos/transcripts/20080827_BIDEN_SPEECH.html. This "Freudian slip" comment matched another *correctio* used by Biden when explaining a delay: "The reason it was initially postponed was that many of us were in

Rome at the president's funeral—excuse me, Freudian slip, I beg your pardon—at the pope's funeral that the president attended" (http://www.slate.com/id/2116667/).

9. There is a kind of opposite to correction where the speaker repeats and affirms a choice: "You obsess (but of course you obsess) until the joy is gone from that thing you'd loved...." (Kephart 2005, 19).

10. *Significatio*, translated as emphasis, is the label used in the *Rhetorica ad Herennium* for an effect that is actually achieved by several different devices: "Emphasis [*Significatio*] is the figure which leaves more to be suspected than has been actually asserted. It is produced through Hyperbole [*exsuperatio*], Ambiguity [*ambiguitas*], Logical Consequence [*consequentia*], Aposiopesis [*abscisio*], and Analogy [*similitudo*]" ([Cicero] 1981, 400–1). Ambiguity as one of the five was produced by a word that can be "taken in two or more senses, but yet is taken in that sense which the speaker intends" (401). The author of the *ad Herennium* thought it was easy to create ambiguities by paying attention to words with double or multiple meanings, but in fact ambiguities can be hard to construct deliberately, since context tends to disambiguate.

Sentences

7

SENTENCE BASICS: PREDICATION

NOW AN AVOIDED subject, grammar was once a routine part of literacy training and a necessary preliminary to rhetorical studies. Indeed the two disciplines, grammar and rhetoric, often overlapped and competed for subject matter, a situation that Quintilian addressed in the *Institutio Oratoria*. Outlining the education of an ideal orator in the first century CE, he gave each discipline its "proper sphere," since the rhetorical study of style depended on knowledge of the allowable options (1921, II 205–7). Notably, for Romans learning Greek and Europeans learning Latin, grammar instruction was not conducted in the student's native language but was an essential part of studying a prestige language.

Today, most English speakers are more likely to have studied the grammar of another language rather than their own. They assume, quite correctly, that an abstract knowledge of English grammar is not necessary for competence in speaking or writing. But anyone who wants to look *at* language critically needs an analytical toolkit for labeling constitutive features beyond individual word choice. Fortunately, most people are intuitively aware of subjects and verbs, the basics of predication that create sentences. Attention to subjects and verbs, the focus of this chapter, overlaps with the word choice issues discussed in part I, and offers a good place to begin to appreciate the contribution of sentence form to rhetorical effects.

Active versus Stative Predication

Traditional English grammar, derived from classical grammars, provides labels for the roles of *subject, verb,* and *direct* and *indirect object,* among other sentence constitutents. Scholars have proposed many other English "grammars" or ways of describing sentence constituents and their relationships, but all systems name the basics of predication, and no available system of grammar (traditional, structural, transformational, construction, etc.) carves up the language without remainder; all create categories, classes, and rules that are then glossed by exceptions. Yet each system offers valuable insights, and one of the most useful has been "case grammar" (see Fillmore 1968; Cook 1989). As an analytical tool popularized by Joseph Williams in *Style: Ten Lessons in Clarity and Grace* (1989), case grammar takes the parts of sentences determined by syntactic rules and relabels them by their functions. So, for example, in many English sentences, the subject names an ***agent***, the doer or source of what is done; the verb names the ***action***, what is done or happens; and the object, if there is one, can name the ***recipient*** or ***goal*** of the action. Certainly not all English sentences have subjects and verbs that are agents and actions, but in what might be thought of as the prototypical English sentence, human agents act on objects in their physical or conceptual world. In such agent-driven sentences, the language has a bias toward causality, toward creating effective actors with the power to influence or bring about results. And while the overall concept of rhetorical agency has been debated (Geisler 2004), a grammatical subject's agency is a function of its sentence role.

The subject/verb choices speakers and writers make are among their most rhetorically important decisions. These choices designate what entities can exist in a textual world and what kinds of actions they can perform or states and qualities they can manifest. Isolating the main sentence constituents, whether in a single critical sentence or across a passage, can therefore be a useful first step in analysis.[1] Here, for example, is the subject/verb/object and also agent/action/recipient structure from the first sentence of Lincoln's Gettysburg Address:

Subject *Agent*	*Verb* *Action*	*Object* *Recipient*	
Four score and seven years ago	**our fathers**	**brought forth** on this continent	**a new nation,**	conceived in liberty, and dedicated to the proposition that all men are created equal.

The label *recipient,* suggesting as it does a preexisting entity, fails to capture the result of the act of creation expressed in this sentence (and alternatives like *goal* or *patient* are not much better). Lincoln made the founding fathers agents with the power to give birth to something that did not exist before. Identifying the main sentence constituents of subject/agent and verb/action in this functional way reveals the dynamics of Lincoln's core idea.

Almost all the sentences in the Gettysburg Address have active verbs and agent/action structure. But in his many speeches touching on the legal issues surrounding the nature of government and civil war, Lincoln often used a different sentence type, one that allows rhetors to define or characterize a subject by connecting it through a linking verb with some other noun or adjective, often called a *predicate complement* in traditional grammar. (A *predicate* is the verb plus all its objects and/or complements.)

Subject	*verb*	*predicate complement (noun)*
A **majority** held in restraint by constitutional checks and limitations and always changing easily with deliberate changes of popular opinions and sentiments	**is**	the only true **sovereign** of the people.

(From Lincoln's First Inaugural. All but one sentence in the paragraph this sentence comes from have the same categorical, linking-verb structure.)

Sentences with linking verbs, like this one from Lincoln, cannot be described with agent/action structure. They express *states of being* rather than *actions* and so allow the defining, categorizing, and qualifying that are indispensable in claims of knowledge and principle. Such categorical claims are the preferred form for logical manipulations (in categorical propositions), and they have been marked in rhetorical stylistics for their uses in argument (see below, p. 235). Thus there are two main predication types in English: active and stative.

Subject Choices

Any noun (or noun phrase or noun clause) can be the subject of a sentence, and any action or state can be attributed to any noun. For purposes of analysis, the following rough taxonomy helps in identifying a rhetor's choices for the important role of sentence subject.

I. HUMANS

Prototypical subjects, often acting as agents, are human beings, and prototypical actions are the kinds of things that humans do: talk, walk, throw, eat. Human grammatical subjects may be **single individuals** referred to by **proper names** (*President Sarkozy, Irene Curie*), or by their **occupations or titles** (*a truck driver, the senator from Maine*). Human agents may also be **named by the action they perform** (*voters, the murderer*), an option that can be a significant rhetorical choice (see *polyptoton*, pp. 130–2).

Subjects can also be **groups** or **collections of people**. These groups can have formal or collective titles (*the Phillies, Congress*), but, with appropriate modifiers, rhetors can create

all kinds of human groups depending on any selected attribute or quality: by place (*residents of our apartment building*), by physical qualities (*people over six feet tall*), by past experience (*those who lived through World War II*), and on and on. Richard Nixon even turned the absence of speech and action into "the silent majority." And certainly an interesting but troublesome human subject created in news reporting is the **anonymous agent**, singular or plural (*an official wishing to remain anonymous*; *sources close to the president*).

Most **personal pronouns** simply carry over human agency when their antecedent is clear (*the queen … she*). But **indefinite pronouns** that have no clear referent can act as stand-ins, as **generic human agents** (*one, everyone, some*, etc.). Many other variants of the generic human agent, singular or plural, are possible with the small set of available human category terms (*a person, every person, individuals, people*).

Animals can be agents too, and they can be treated in all the ways just described for humans: as named individuals (*Flipper, Lassie*), as "occupations" or types (*the race horse, the Pekinese*), as groups (*a flock of birds*), and so on. What becomes interesting with animal agents is whether the actions attributed to them are purely physical or come from the lexicon of human actions: *My dog waited for me at the bus stop.* Humans can certainly wait (an action that includes intention, mental expectancy, and forecasting), but can dogs? Alternatively, because the subject is an animal, one could say that *wait* here simply means *stayed in one place.*[2]

2. RHETORICAL PARTICIPANTS

One type of human grammatical subject deserves the attention of a separate heading. Whenever language is listened to or read, there is a default rhetorical situation with a speaker or writer *and* a listener or reader. These roles can always be made explicit in a text, usually with the pronouns *I, you, we.* Therefore a subject available in any text, unless genre constraints intervene, is the **writer or speaker as *I*** who can self-refer (*I am at a loss for words*) or perform a speech act in a text (*I want to point out here*). The **reader or listener as *you*** can also be made a subject or agent, a practice quite common in advice books and "direct mail" advertising prose: *You should consider remodeling your house every five to ten years.* An interesting choice in this category is the plural pronoun *we.* Depending on the rhetorical situation, *we* can have several meanings, referring sometimes to the speaker plus the speaker's group, sometimes to plural authors, and in each case sometimes including or sometimes excluding all or part of an audience: *We are under no obligation to consider this proposal.* (See Interactive Dimension, pp. 280–5.)

3. THINGS

Anything that has physical existence can become the grammatical subject in a sentence and in some cases an agent: *My computer crashed yesterday. The car swerved off the road. The engine lost power.* Are these very normal-looking sentences instances of **personification**, the figure of speech in which an object is treated as though it were a person? Or have the verbs naming actions in these sentences acquired nonhuman meanings, so that they can be predicated of objects? (See below on *personae fictio*.) In certain contexts, the terms for physical objects become category labels and belong in the following group (*An engine requires maintenance*).

4. ABSTRACTIONS

Abstract nouns name referents that cannot be pointed to easily. Humans and things can be pointed to, but *international trade, voting trends, athletic ability,* and *representative government* cannot be watched, handled, or climbed into the way a red Corvette can be. Yet abstractions are common subjects in linking-verb sentences, they are often agents with active verbs, and they are preferred as subjects in knowledge claims. (See above on Abstract/Concrete language, pp. 64–5.)

Semanticists describe some abstract nouns as the **names of categories or classes of things**. These hypernyms are like umbrellas that sit over many individual instances. Someone who wanted a physical/concrete referent for international trade, for example, could be taken to a dock in San Diego, California, to see ships unloading containers full of resin figurines from China. But to talk about the collective activity of *international trade* at all the ports around the world requires an abstract term. Once created, an abstraction can have considerable rhetorical force, like Eisenhower's "military-industrial complex" or Lyndon Johnson's "Great Society."

Other abstractions name **processes and activities**: *photosynthesis, magnetism, erosion, arbitration*. Again, these terms can stand for many real or potential instances of these actions. They become convenient shorthand, and when they are featured as subjects or agents, that sentence becomes a generalization unless it is carefully qualified. Writers can also create abstractions from actions typically expressed in a verb. To do so they turn the verb into a noun, **a gerund**, by adding *-ing: John jogs →Jogging is John's favorite form of exercise*. This "thing-izing" of a verb turns it into a label for a general activity, process, or event.[3] An **infinitive** construction produces the same transformation, creating an abstract subject from a verb: *To jog is John's favorite form of exercise*.

Still another group of words in this category are **knowledge processing words** like *results, evidence, object, model, system, characteristics, quality, features*. Many of these stand for **mental and textual operations**, like *research, analysis, investigation, assessment, presentation, comparison, distinction, deduction*. Susan MacDonald has demonstrated how these terms, like *data* or *results*, often function as **epistemic agents** in scholarly discourse (1994, 157, 171–75). Most are Latin or Greek borrowings or coinages, a residue from academic treatises that were once exclusively in those languages. As abstractions, they can be tethered to a context and equated with particulars, but more often they work like giant pincers and levers, manipulating a topic. They are indispensable in learned registers.

5. CONCEPTS

For purposes of rhetorical analysis, it is worthwhile separating out a group of abstractions that are such **vague, general, all-encompassing terms** that it is very difficult to pin them down. Yet these are among the most powerful terms in rhetorical discourse: *liberty, beauty, justice, fairness, equality, oppression.* The persuasive power of such terms comes from their vagueness and from the contexts they typically appear in. As the rhetoricians Chaim Perelman and Lucie Olbrechts-Tyteca point out, such terms often appear in propositions that gain widespread agreement *until* an attempt is made to specify and act on what they stand for (1969, 76). Everyone wants *justice*, but perhaps not what some think *justice* means in a particular case.

6. SLOT FILLERS

To create a complete, grammatical sentence, speakers and writers have to fill the subject slot. But English allows "dummy" subjects to fulfill this grammatical requirement while leaving the substantive content for the predicate. Thus sentences can open with a **slot-filling *it***, resulting in idioms like *It was raining* or in *it*-cleft constructions like this sentence from Winston Churchill's speech accepting the reins of government in 1940: *It was the evident will of Parliament and the nation that this should be conceived on the broadest possible basis and that it should include all parties* (Safire 1997, 134–35; *this* refers to *new administration* in the previous sentence and the second *it* refers back to *this* and to *new administration*). Such constructions have stylistic consequences; they empty out the subject slot but foreground the predicate term (in Churchill's sentence *the evident will*). Churchill's *it was* also allowed him to avoid too pronounced an assumption of personal agency.

The second alternative for launching a sentence with a dummy subject uses the **anticipatory *there is*** (*there* + any form of the verb *to be*; e.g., *there will have been*). This choice has an announcing or pointing effect; it also throws attention on the predicate and can be useful for introducing or changing topics. Kennedy used the anticipatory subject repeatedly in his 1963 speech in Berlin, where it has the effect of a verbal pointer singling out groups of potential critics: *There are many people in the world who really don't understand...; there are some who say...; And there are some who say...; And there are even a few who say...*" (Windt 1983, 50).

ANALYZING SUBJECT CHOICES

By observing a rhetor's subject choices from the options listed above, an analyst can detect overall patterns as well as significant shifts for local effects. The brief sample analysis offered here looks at rather stark differences in paired texts. In 1996, *The New Yorker* invited prominent African Americans to comment briefly on the current state of the civil rights movement. Among the responses published were observations from Kwame Ture (formerly Stokely Carmichael) and Julian Bond, whose opening paragraphs follow.

Kwame Ture

(1) The greatest success of the civil-rights movement was raising the level of consciousness about people. (2) Its greatest failure was a lack of organization. (3) When you look at the sixties, the organizations that came to the forefront, like S.N.C.C. and CORE, were incapable of attaching the head and the hands. (4) In the sixties, most of your movement was spontaneous, not organized. (5) This was its greatest weakness. (6) Of course, this weakness can be traced to the fact that those organizations didn't see the need for ideology at that point. (7) Even the Student Nonviolent Coördinating Committee. (8) One of its greatest weaknesses was that it didn't see the need for unifying ideology. (Gates 1996, 61)

Julian Bond

(1) We've lost a great deal of our moral standing. (2) I think we need to try to regain it if we can, (2a) but I think we also have to become more clever politically, in the larger sense. (3) The time hasn't quite come when we can forget group politics altogether, (3a) but we've got to play that politics and larger politics, too. (4) To play only the one is to lock yourself into a little room from which there is no escape. (5) You have your chieftains and your queens, (5a) but that's it. (5) They're presiding over a tiny principality. (Gates 1996, 61)

Writing in response to the same prompt, Ture and Bond produce obviously very different passages. One way to characterize the difference is to compare their choices for the subjects of their sentences, choices that indicate their conceptual perspectives on this issue. In Ture's passage, the subjects in his eight sentences include *success, failure, you* [dependent clause], *organizations, weakness, organizations* [dependent clause], and the phrases *most of your movement* and *one of its greatest weaknesses*; the pronoun that is the subject of sentence (5) refers to the preceding point about spontaneity. With one exception, these subjects are all abstractions; specifically, they are summative qualities identified in afterthought. Ture treats his topic from a distanced perspective, distanced in time and involvement. The only exception appears in the subordinate clause opening the third sentence: *when you look at the sixties*. This *you* is less the rhetorical agent *you*, the addressed reader, and more *you* the generic human observer, the role adopted by Ture himself.

Julian Bond made very different choices. The main clauses of his often compound sentences have the following subjects: *we, I, I, time, we, to play, you, that, they*. Bond himself, as the rhetorical agent *I*, is notably present. His *we*, which also appears as the subject in an additional four dependent clauses, is used less as a rhetorical agent referring to the audience plus the speaker, and more as a pronoun referring to an unspecified group of people who can nevertheless be identified as the civil rights community. The other subjects are abstractions: *time* (in a prepared phrase), the infinitive phrase *to play* (a generic and therefore abstract action), and the two pronouns *that* and *they,* referring to the roles of *chieftains* and *queens.* Thus human agents dominate in Bond's passage, and these human agents are the author and other civil rights activists. Bond writes both about and to this group and in the process *reconstitutes* them, giving them a sense of their continued relevance and correctable involvement in the movement.

Verb Choices

Many writers on style consider verbs the most powerful part of a sentence (Strunk and White 1979), and psycholinguistic research suggests that English speakers do not begin to identify strings of words as *sentences* until a verb is present (Sandell 1977, 91). While subjects tell us what the author's topic is, verbs reveal how the author believes those entities exist or act. Thus, verb choices may be especially good indicators of an arguer's worldview or "mind style" (Leech and Short 1981, 192–93). The English verb system offers several dimensions of verb construction that can have rhetorical consequences, and indeed many of these choices have been marked as figures of speech.

1. TENSE

A story not given much attention when it appeared in the *New York Times* on September 28, 1996, had the following headline and lead sentence:

> *Guerillas Take Afghan Capital as Troops Flee*
> Fundamentalist Islamic rebels captured Kabul today, swarming through the ruined capital, promising to impose strict Islamic rule and hanging a former President in one of their first acts of retribution.

Newspaper openings like this one typically use present tense verbs in the headline for the sake of immediacy (*take* not *took*), while the stories that follow use the simple past (*captured* not *capture*). Obviously, such conventional usage employs past and present tenses not to mark the relation of an event to the speaker's or writer's moment, but to serve the general rhetorical purpose of emphasis.

English has verb forms to mark tense, the time frame of the predication in relation to the time frame of stating it. But the tense used can have less to do with accurate reporting and more to do with conventional usage. For example, the present tense is not as widely used as the simple past. Only in special situations and genres is an action encoded in the present as though it were occurring at the moment of utterance, as in play-by-play sports announcing, *He hits a straight shot to left field!* (see Crystal and Davy 1969, 126–30, for examples of "event broadcasting" on the radio). As the marker of "action at the moment," the present tense also makes the most sense for speech act verbs, verbs that perform an action when they are said or written: for example, from Kennedy's speech on the Cuban Missile Crisis: *"I call upon Chairman Khrushchev to halt and eliminate this clandestine, reckless, and provocative threat to world peace."* Kennedy called upon Khrushchev when he said "I call upon" (Windt 1983, 39).

The present tense is also conventionally used to relate actions or states held to be always in effect, always happening. It is therefore rhetorically important as the tense of shared truths (from Kennedy's 1963 Berlin speech [Windt 1983, 49–50]: *"Freedom has many difficulties and democracy is not perfect"*), of presumptions about human behavior (e.g., *People want the best for their children*), and of the maxims singled out by Aristotle (e.g., *"Nothing is more annoying than having neighbors"* [Roberts 1984, 139]). The present is the tense of choice in science reporting for generalizations about the natural world (*The earth orbits the sun; DNA replication takes place in the nucleus*). It is the tense used when paraphrasing events in literary texts or movies (*Hamlet sees his father's ghost*) and in interpreting the speech acts performed by texts (*The constitution forbids the quartering of troops*). And, oddly enough, the present tense can even characterize the future, when an appropriate adverb to indicate the time shares the sentence: *The president comes tomorrow; The class takes the test next week.* With a suitable conditional clause, the present tense fulfills a prediction: *If you take that, you are dead.*

The newspaper practice of using the present tense in headlines (discussed above) recalls the ancient advice in rhetorical manuals for achieving vividness in narration. Under the figure ***demonstratio*** (translated *ocular demonstration*), the *Rhetorica ad Herennium* recommended that events be described so "that the business seems to be enacted and the subject to pass vividly before the eyes" ([Cicero] 1981, 405). This effect was to be achieved with circumstantial detail and with what came to be called the **vivid** or **historic present**. The tense switch is obvious in the *ad Herennium's* sample narrative recounting the murder of Gracchus: "As soon as Gracchus saw [*prospexit,* past] that the people were wavering…he ordered [past] a convocation of the Assembly. In the meanwhile, this fellow, filled with wicked and criminal designs, bounds [*evolat,* present] out of the temple of Jupiter" (407). Such sudden switching to the present tense for vivid narrative is still widely used, but its effects have to be assessed in context. John Steinbeck, for example, working as a war correspondent in Europe during World War II, filed reports that played with tense changes to create special effects. In passages for October 6, 1943, he used the future tense for his predicted actions, the simple past for predictable correspondent reporting, and the present tense for what he actually saw or experienced: "'The 5th Army advanced two kilometers,' he will write, while the lines of trucks churn the road to deep dust and truck drivers hunch over their wheels. And off to the right the burial squads are scooping slits in the sandy earth" (quoted in Kerrane and Yagoda 1997, 460).

The **progression of tenses** in a text can have great significance as rhetors work to "earn" a tense other than the initial or predictable one. Alan Gross, Art Walzer, and Marie Secor show this process in an analysis of the tense changes in the controversial eulogy for Princess Diana delivered by her brother Charles, Earl Spencer (1999). Spencer began in the opening paragraphs by speaking of his sister in the past tense: "For such was her extraordinary appeal," "Diana was the very essence of compassion, of duty, of style, of beauty," etc. But in the third paragraph Spencer switched to direct address and eventually to the present tense, bringing Diana to life: "There is a temptation to rush to canonize your memory, there is no need to do so. You *stand* tall enough as a human being of unique qualities not to need to be seen as a saint." The authors point out that this tense progression achieves what Perelman and Olbrechts-Tyteca called *presence* for Diana as a living and enduring moral agent (Walzer, Secor, and Gross 1999, 55).

2. ASPECT

In his speech before a Joint Session of Congress several days after 9/11, George Bush began by celebrating the courage and responsiveness of the American people in the many things *we have seen,* a verb phrase used four times in the following sentences (2001). Why did the President use *have seen* instead of the simple past (i.e., *We saw the state of our Union in the endurance of rescuers* versus *We have seen the state of our Union in the endurance of rescuers*)? The difference in these verb forms is a difference in **aspect**, the dimension of verb choice that structures a reported event as ongoing or habitual or complete. The expression of past actions with the auxiliary *have* is not equivalent in **perfective aspect** to their characterization with the simple past. The *have* forms suggest that an action is still occurring or that it is still relevant; the simple past, on the other hand, seems to place a gap between the moment of utterance and the event: *I have jogged every day* versus *I jogged every day.* President Bush's choice of *have seen* makes those things seen continue into the moment of utterance. A choice of *had seen* would have been different again. This construction allows speakers, at the moment of utterance, to project themselves into the past and to describe an event completed at that point in time. It has its own important functions in characterizing events as they were known at some earlier point. Thus, the *had* or past perfect forms often occur in testimony or evidentiary narration.

English also distinguishes (as Latin does not) whether an action was discrete, bounded, and self-contained or ongoing, continuing, and incomplete. To do so, it uses a from of the verb "to be" plus the *–ing* form of a verb, creating the **progressive aspect**, the forms combining with tense markers to depict acts in progress, whether in the past, present, or even the future: *The receiver was catching/is catching/will be catching the ball.* The combined system of verb tense and aspect provides English users with rich options for characterizing the time of an action in relation to the speaker's present and whether that action is completed or ongoing.

3. MOOD

English has a system of verbal *moods,* created by different formal markers, that designate the attitude or intent behind a statement. Grammarians disagree on the full set but generally agree on the basic three: *indicative, imperative,* and *subjunctive* (Greenbaum 1996,

80). The **indicative mood**, by far the most widely used, marks "statements," no matter how intensified (with *do*) or qualified (with modals or adverbs). Speakers use the **imperative mood** to express commands or directives, as in Reagan's famous, "*Chairman Gorbachev, tear down this wall!*" or something closer to invitations, as in the section on future recommendations in Kennedy's Inaugural Address: *Let us never negotiate out of fear. But let us never fear to negotiate* (and six more sentences in a row with the same urging; see Tufte 2006, on five degrees of the imperative, 209–13). The **subjunctive mood** is used to express hypothetical or conditional rather than "actual" events or statements. It is not as well marked in English as it is in other languages, but it appears in conditional clauses like those used by Martin Luther King Jr. to begin a visionary journey through history in his final speech in Memphis: *If I were standing at the beginning of time.…* Notably, King uses the subjunctive *were* in this crucial introductory phrase, and he continues to mark the counterfactual nature of the stages of his journey with *would: I would take my mental flight by Egypt/I would watch God's children/I would move on by Greece/I would go on/I would see,* a total of twenty times (1968).[4]

Some grammarians distinguish other moods, including the **optative**, which expresses wishes: *Would that we could leave the past behind.* The language of prayer seems to be expressed in either wishes or imperatives: *Give us this day our daily bread; Forgive us our trespasses.* Question asking is sometimes called the **interrogative mood**; it requires syntactic rearrangement and/or an appropriate intonation: *What shall we do now?* (see below p. 269). Finally, a possible **exclamatory mood** expresses a host of stronger attitudes, such as amazement or indignation: *This news is outstanding!* Constructions in moods like the subjunctive or optative were more common in speeches from the past.[5]

4. NEGATION

Any action or circumstance can be stated and at the same time canceled by joining a negative adverb with the verb: *They can/cannot, He understands/does not understand, She bought the hat/never bought the hat.* Rhetors often have a choice between a "negative" verb (*The candidate lost the election*) and a negated positive one (*The candidate did not win the election*). Erasmus labeled this alternative *aequipollentia* (Greek *isodynamia*), the adding, taking away, or doubling of a negative to create an equivalent statement: *I accept the condition; I do not reject the condition* (1963, 33–34). Logically, such statements may be equivalent; rhetorically, they are not.

The decision to use a verb and then negate it can be significant. In a section of his speech on 9/11, Bush used a series of negated verbs in the section where he answers the question, "How will we fight this war?" He explains through negatives what the war *will not be like, will not look like,* and what *Americans should not expect.* These choices show his intent to engage prevailing presumptions about war by canceling them out in the case of a war with stateless terror. In his conclusion, he expresses his future resolve again by negations: *I will not forget this wound to our country or those who inflicted it. I will not yield;*

I will not rest; I will not relent in waging this struggle for freedom and security for the American people. These negated future verbs challenge the passing of time.

Another deliberate but often puzzling option is the doubly negated verb. The epigraph to chapter 5, from Winston Churchill's "Iron Curtain" speech, has a striking example: *It is my duty, however—and I am sure you would not wish me not to state the facts as I see them to you—it is my duty to place before you certain facts about the present position in Europe* (Safire 1997, 872). Again, logically, "to not wish me not to state" equals "to wish me to state," but putting this positive version into the sentence instead would change its current suggestion of overcoming the audience's reluctance and bracing them for some bad news.

5. MODALITY

As part of the same speech urging resistance to Soviet aggression, Churchill cited the failure to respond early enough to Hitler: *Up till the year 1933 or even 1935, Germany might have been saved from the awful fate which has overtaken her, and we might all have been spared the miseries Hitler let loose upon mankind* (Safire 1997, 875). Coming in 1946, Churchill's *might have been* (a speculative parallel case) offered an incentive to avoid the *what might be* in the case of the Soviet Union. That small word *might,* a modal auxiliary, constructs a predicate in the realm of possibility. A very significant dimension of verb phrases has to do with whether they are expressed with such modal auxiliaries. An old and small group of English verbs, modals allow rhetors to express their degree of certainty in an attribution or their commitment to its status as real or not. The following pairs show the differences in commitment to an intention—*I will go* versus *I might go*— or to a statement—*It is true* versus *It could be true.* The following are the modals in English: *can, could, may, might, must, should, would, will, shall.* (Various periphrastic verb phrases also modalize, such as *ought to* and *going to.*) The auxiliary *have* expresses differences in tense and aspect, but it can also express modality with an infinitive (*have to go*). The auxiliary *do* can be an intensifier (*They do want new leadership*) or a substitute for a longer verb phrase (*Do you promise? I do*).

Modality marking the degree of confidence or urgency can also be expressed with single adjectives (*the likely suspect*), with adverbs (*probably, perhaps, certainly, maybe*), or with longer phrases (*it seems likely that*). However it is expressed, the modality of an overall claim is a critical dimension in rhetorical argumentation, since rhetorical claims, under Aristotle's distinctions, concern probabilities, not certainties. Rhetoric is the art of making the best possible case, so the modality of a claim should reflect the extent and soundness of the available evidence. This issue is so important in scientific argument that the *hedging* of claims has received considerable attention (Crismore and Vande Kopple 1997; Hyland 1998). Legal procedure codifies three standards of probability, *probable cause* (the standard in indictments), *preponderance of evidence* (the standard in civil trials), and *beyond a reasonable doubt* (the standard in criminal trials), but lawyers arguing cases to any of the three standards are likely to make unqualified claims. Rhetors commonly alter or even elide modal indicators to give an impression of greater certainty to a claim. A useful case for studying the relationship between the degree of evidence and the certainty of the supported claim is the argument made by Colin Powell before the United Nations Security Council (February 6, 2003) on Iraq's continuing violations of UN weapons inspection agreements. The section on biological weapons, for example, compiles testimony from defectors and reconnaissance photos and transfers the certainty of having the evidence to the conclusions from the evidence: "There can be no doubt that Saddam Hussein has biological weapons and the capability to rapidly produce more, many more."[6] Considerable hindsight has questioned the reliability of the sources used to make this case in 2003, but it is worth noting that the level of certainty Powell expresses about his conclusions is in no way unusual coming from a government spokesperson making a case with policy implications based on probable inferences from the available evidence.

6. ACTIVE VERSUS PASSIVE VOICE

The term *voice* is an odd label for a fundamental verb-form decision rhetors can make about the "point of view" on an event. To describe this choice, the concepts of agent, action, and recipient, described above, help to explain what happens when a sentence is expressed in the passive rather than the active "voice." In a passive construction, the grammatical subject no longer names the agent; instead, the recipient becomes the grammatical subject and the agent is pushed into a prepositional phrase or dropped from the sentence. Of the following active and passive versions of a traditional introductory welcome, the number of Google hits shows that the passive form is far more common.

Active:	*Your presence*	*honors*	*us*
	agent	*action performed*	*recipient*
Passive:	*We*	*are honored*	*by your presence*
	recipient	*action received*	*agent*

Only transitive verbs can be used in passive constructions, which are regularly formed according to the following rule.[7]

Any tense/aspect of the verb *to be* (including any modals)	+	– *ed* form of a regular transitive verb or a special past participle form for an irregular transitive verb (e.g., *sung*)

By making the recipient of an action the grammatical subject of a sentence, the passive changes both the meaning and emphasis in a sentence and contributes to larger patterns of coherence. In its most important effect on meaning, a passive construction backgrounds the agent to a prepositional phrase or drops it entirely.

> Active voice: Politicians often deceive the voters.
> Passive voice with agent: The voters are often deceived by politicians
> Passive voice minus agent: The voters are often deceived.

The last of these options, the **agentless passive**, has been called a dishonest construction because it allows an action to be described without attributing it to any source. In some contexts, this deletion means that no one receives blame for an action, as in the classic bureaucratic admission, used by Nixon in one of his Watergate speeches: *Mistakes were made*. There certainly may be occasions where use of the passive is obfuscating or deceptive, but it is hardly the only grammatical construction that can be put to questionable uses.

On dubious aesthetic grounds, agentless passives, and indeed all passive constructions, have also been disparaged as somehow less vivid than the active voice. And there is even a suggestion that the passive is somehow less than "moral," since it seems better to be "active" than "passive." But rhetors can construct energetic sentences with the passive: *Janet was chased down the alley and thrown to the ground*. The passive was also once criticized for presumably requiring more time for mental decoding, making it more difficult to comprehend. But research by psycholinguists has not confirmed that the variable of passive voice affects comprehension time (Scovel 1998, 61–63). The passive voice is evidently neither more difficult to form nor to understand.

Not only are its supposed defects exaggerated, but the passive voice, with or without the agent added, also has definite merits. It would not exist in the language if it did not fulfill certain communicative needs. Some of these needs will be described in later sections (see especially on Emphasis and Topic/Comment organization). For now, it is worth noting that the passive is easily justified when the agent is unknown (*The convoy was fired on from the bushes*), unnecessary (*The mail was delivered late today*), or easily understood from the context, as when a management representative during a strike announces, *All options are being considered*. Furthermore, some verbs are only or predominantly used in passive constructions. Everyone, for example, starts life in the passive voice: *Chandler was born in 2007*.[8]

In Defense of the Passive

Thomas Jefferson produced a first draft of the Declaration of Independence that was then altered by fellow members of the drafting committee (Madison, Adams, Livingston, Franklin) and further revised by the Continental Congress as a whole. One of the most extensive rewordings in the final stage came in the penultimate paragraph. The version presented by the drafting committee is the following (the subjects, verbs, and objects are bolded):

> **We** therefore the representatives of the United States of America in General Congress assembled, **do** in the name, and by the authority of the good people of these states **reject and renounce** all **allegiance** and **subjection** to the kings of Great Britain and all others who may hereafter claim by, through or under them; **we** utterly **dissolve** all **political connection** which may heretofore have subsisted between us and the people or parliament of Great Britain: and finally **we do assert and declare these colonies to be free and independent states**. (Jefferson 1776)

The predications in this first draft are as follows

Agent	action	recipient/goal
We	*do reject and renounce*	*allegiance and subjection*
We	*dissolve*[9]	*political connection*
We	*do assert and declare*	*these colonies to be free and independent states*

The final draft substantially changed this agent/action structure, as well as the overall sentence architecture.

> **We**, therefore, the representatives of the United States of America in General Congress assembled, appealing to the supreme judge of the world for the rectitude of our intentions, **do** in the name, and by the authority of the good people of these colonies, solemnly **publish and declare**, that **these united colonies are,** and of right ought to be free and independent **states**; that **they are absolved** from all allegiance to the British crown, and that **all political connection** between them and the state of Great Britain **is, and ought to be, totally dissolved**;

We	*do publish and declare*	*that*	*colonies*	*are*	*States*
		that	*they*	*are absolved*	
		that	*connection*	*is/ought to be dissolved*	

The drafting committee's original predication gives considerable agency to the representatives in Congress who are capable of the constitutive speech acts of rejecting, renouncing, dissolving, asserting, and declaring. The revised and final version has very different predication. *We* [Congress] appears once as the agent, and performs a different action: *we do publish and declare*. The object/recipient of these speech acts appears in three noun clauses, none of which has agent/action structure. The first, recalling Jefferson's third point, has a linking verb structure, equating the *colonies* to *free and independent states.* The next two, notably, are agentless passives: *they* [the colonies] *are absolved from allegiance* and *all political connection is/ought to be dissolved.* What is the actual agency that absolves the colonies from allegiance or dissolves all political connection? The final form of the Declaration of Independence does not specify, but by implication the result is the outcome of the king's misdeeds and of divinely ordained principles, specified earlier in the document. The representatives (*we*) merely *publish and declare* the inevitable result.

No injunction against the passive appears in any classical or early modern manual. The founding documents of the United States and its political oratory are marked by passages of high and profound seriousness referring to the principles establishing and sustaining the Constitution and the rule of law. These passages are often in the passive, sometimes even in the agentless passive, and they are the stronger for it.

> We hold these truths to be self-evident, that all Men are created equal, that they are endowed by their Creator with certain inalienable rights.
>
> *The Declaration of Independence*
>
> Now we are engaged in a great civil war, testing whether that nation or any nation so conceived and so dedicated can long endure.
>
> *The Gettysburg Address*
>
> The right of citizens of the United States to vote shall not be denied or abridged by the United States or by any State on account of race, color, or previous condition of servitude.
>
> *The Fifteenth Amendment*
>
> I have a dream that one day every valley shall be exalted, every hill and mountain shall be made low, the rough places will be made plain and the crooked places will be made straight, and the glory of the Lord shall be revealed, and all flesh shall see it together.
>
> *Martin Luther King Jr. "I Have a Dream"*

7. SEMANTIC CATEGORIES

In the section above on subject choices, semantic distinctions (humans, things, etc.) were used to create analytical categories. Can the same be done for verbs? Verbs are already conventionally categorized on the basis of whether and what kinds of objects they take or on whether they label actions or states, and some analysts create ad hoc categories for particular cases. In *Stylistics* (2004), Paul Simpson offered a provisional semantic system for categorizing verbs (or verb phrases) by the kind of process encoded: *material, mental, behavioral, verbal, relational, existential* (22–26). Simpson's categories serve literary stylistics and favor the physical and observable actions typically predicated of human agents. Robust semantic categories for the kinds of verbs used in persuasive texts such as political speeches have, evidently, yet to be formulated.

ANALYZING VERB CHOICES

In March 1917, President Woodrow Wilson went before a special session of Congress to ask for a declaration of war on Germany. Since only Congress has the constitutional authority to declare war, Wilson had to persuade that body to act as he desired. His verb choices, revealed especially through his tense shifts, show that in effect he decided for them. Wilson opens his speech, very properly, by acknowledging the situation.

> I <u>have called</u> the Congress into extraordinary session because there are serious, very serious, choices of policy to be made (Reid *1988*, 643).

Here the use of the perfect (*have called*) rightly marks that a past action, calling Congress into session, is still relevant as they all stand there together. With the Congress before him, Wilson, after reviewing the precipitating events of German submarine warfare, then performs the speech act that brought him there.

> I <u>advise</u> that the Congress declare the recent course of the Imperial German Government to be in fact nothing less than war against the government and people of the United States; that it formally accept the status of belligerent...(645).

The main verb in this sentence (*advise*) is in the present tense. The verbs in the noun clauses beginning *that* (*declare, accept*) are actually in the subjunctive, a mood not usually marked in English. Once his proposal is on the table, Wilson next predicts the consequences in a series of sentences all opening *it will involve*. Here the future tense rightly looks ahead to the financial and military commitments necessary when war is declared.

However, after his speech act of advising and his predictions, Wilson's verbs surge ahead of Congress and accomplish what the president can only request. Following a rehearsal of inciting past actions on Germany's part, he assumes the fait accompli:

> We <u>are accepting</u> this challenge of hostile purpose because we know that in such a Government, following such methods, we can never have a friend...
> Just because we <u>fight</u> without rancor and without selfish object, seeking nothing for ourselves but what we shall wish to share with all free peoples...
> We <u>enter</u> this war only where we are clearly forced...(648–649)

Here the present progressive (*We are accepting*) and the simple present (*we fight, we enter*) have the country engaged in a war that Congress had yet to declare. In 1917, Wilson did not have a public or Congress united for war the way Roosevelt did in 1941. Wilson's overall tense/aspect changes serve as a persuasive tactic to force the issue.

Subject/Verb Analysis

The rhetor's choices of subjects and verbs are critical, since these elements of predication convey what the text is "about." Does the rhetor choose predominantly human subjects or are other kinds of entities invoked? What kinds of actions do the subjects perform, what states prevail, and what is the dominant tense or aspect or modality? A great deal of interpretation is an intuitive response to subtle patterns in these features of subject and verb selection.

Linguistic critics examine such issues under the concept of *transitivity* introduced by M. A. K. Halliday in an article that examined the language characterizing Neanderthals versus Cro-Magnons in William Golding's novel *The Inheritors* (1996, 56–86). Halliday combined semantic and syntactic analysis by asking, essentially, how the subject/agent and verb/action choices differed in Golding's portrayal of these two mentalities. He found that Neanderthal language generally lacked transitive verbs, so that things just seemed to happen in their world, outside of human purpose and control as in the following cited examples: *the bushes twitched again; a stick rose upright; the stick began to grow shorter at both ends; it shot out to full length again; the dead tree by Lok's ear acquired a voice* (a sequence that presumably depicts the Neanderthal Lok's perceptions of having an arrow shot at him). By contrast, the Cro-Magnons used transitive verbs with human agents acting on the world. Halliday considered Golding's contrasting characterizations a remarkable success.[10]

THE NORTH POLE

Halliday's method has been put to use by literary stylisticians for the most part, but it can be employed for any text, even, as Roger Fowler has demonstrated, for the kind of mundane news story whose stylistic transparency is in inverse relation to its power in constructing an audience's worldview. The following passage for analysis opens a story by *New York Times* science writer John Noble Wilford.

Ages-Old Icecap at North Pole Is Now Liquid

The North Pole is melting.

The thick ice that has for ages covered the Arctic Ocean at the pole has turned to water, recent visitors there reported yesterday. At least for the time being, an ice-free patch of ocean about a mile wide has opened at the very top of the world, something that has presumably never before been seen by humans and is more evidence that global warming may be real and already affecting climate. (2000)

The grammatical subjects and verbs in this passage are as follows. The predication in dependent clauses is italicized.

Subjects	Verbs	
Icecap	is	(liquid)
North Pole	is melting	
visitors	reported*	
ice	*has turned*	*(to water)*
that	*has covered*	
ice free patch	*has opened*	
something that	*has presumably never before been seen*	
[that]	*is*	*(evidence)*
global warming	*may be*	*(real)*
	[may be] affecting	

(*This pair, appearing at the end of the sentence and providing the source of the evidence, is the actual subject and verb of sentence #2; the opening with the pair *ice/has turned* resides in a noun clause, the direct object of *reported*. This inversion is conventional in news reporting.)

Looking at both subjects and verbs together, the headline and first three sentences repeat essentially the same point. Concentrating on just the verbs, the headline uses a linking verb *(is)* to equate the subject *(icecap)* with a predicate noun *(liquid)*; all the other verbs paired with *ice* in these three sentences are intransitive. The progressive aspect in the second S/V pair, *North Pole is melting*, clashes with the following use of the perfect, *has turned* and *has opened*, choices that describe the process as complete. The potential causal agent, *global warming*, first appears in a relative clause followed first by a modalized linking verb *may be*, and then by the transitive verb, *[may be] affecting*. The synonymous subjects named—*icecap, North Pole*, and *ice that has for ages covered the Arctic Ocean at the pole*—make salient the material thing, the ice, that is changing or has changed phase. The terms *icecap* and *thick ice* are the most physical referents. The *North Pole* is a geographical location (top of the world), but in the popular usage inevitably evoked in a newspaper, it is also a place, home to Santa Claus. An *ice-free patch* is somewhere between a physical referent and an abstract quality, since it is defined negatively.

The work of entity and event construction in these sentences is easier to appreciate thanks to a correction that ran several days later: "A front-page article on Aug. 19 and a brief report on Aug. 20 in The Week in Review about the sighting of open water at the North Pole misstated the normal conditions of the sea ice there. A clear spot has probably opened at the pole before, scientists say, because about ten percent of the Arctic Ocean is clear of ice in a typical summer" (*New York Times*, August 29, 2000). Evidently, the *Times* received complaints about the original phrasing that suggested fixed geographical features rather than meandering ice flows. But to characterize the top of the world as a "solid" place (*icecap, North Pole, thick ice*), though inaccurate, is closer to popular understanding, and the melting of a solid place makes for a more compelling story.

A TREND AT NEW TRIER

News reports like this "melting" story have the cultural power to reinforce or construct fundamental public conceptions, and though they are staged as information, they should be viewed as arguments. In the system of argument types or "stases" described in Cicero's *De Inventione* and the *Rhetorica ad Herennium*, they are first "stasis" conjectural arguments, attempts to convince readers that certain events have happened, or that circumstances and situations exist as characterized. Their routine and even banal nature makes them especially interesting objects of analysis, since they often reveal the acceptable subject/verb or agent/action pairings that fit audience expectations. The following piece is an example of one of these unremarkable arguments, representative in its triviality. It appeared in the mass-circulation magazine *Newsweek*. For purposes of the analysis that follows, the subjects/agents are put in bold and the verbs are put in bold and italics. The pairings in both dependent and independent clauses are marked.

> The school **day** at New Trier High in Winnetka, Ill., ***runs*** from 8:10 a.m. to 3:20 p.m., but not many **students** ***settle for*** that wimpy schedule. The extra "early bird" science and music **classes** at 7 a.m. ***get*** a good turnout, and many **kids** ***study*** well past midnight. So **you** ***can imagine*** the shock when the high-powered **students** ***proposed*** canceling a precious day of classes last month to discuss—easing the cutthroat competition. The **school** ***brought in*** Alfie Kohn, author of "No Contest: The Case Against Competition," and some college-admissions officers to explain why **applicants** ***don't have to be*** superheroes. ***Did* it *help***? "**Kids** ***say*** to me, 'I ***thrive*** under the competition,'" ***says*** **James Conroy**, a New Trier guidance counselor. "**I** ***don't think*** **there** ***are going to be*** dramatic changes."
>
> If **gatekeeping** ***can be*** unfair, even demoralizing, to students excluded from the most challenging courses, **it [gatekeeping]** ***hasn't tamped down*** the runaway ambition of the highest achievers. **Teachers and parents** ***say*** that the increasing **importance** of AP exams—along with early admission programs and expensive SAT tutoring—***has turned*** preparing for college into a four-year nightmare. (1998, 54)

These opening paragraphs have the usual content of an exposé about a supposed trend, a trend that in this case could affect many of the magazine readers' teenage children. Because it is written in news style, it avoids both passive voice and a preponderance of sentences with linking verbs. As a result, it includes some notable agent/action pairs in the form of abstractions teamed with active verbs: e.g., the *day runs* and *classes get a turnout*. The first pairing is perhaps a slightly unconventional twist on the conventional habit of attributing movement to periods of time (*weeks go by*), so *day runs* could be described either as weak personification (an idiomatic usage or a "conceptual" metaphor in Lakoff and Johnson's terms) or as an instance of polysemy where *runs* has an inanimate meaning in addition to its anthropomorphic meaning of what human legs do. The other odd usage, that *classes* (in music and science) *get a turnout*, does endow them with unusual agency, with attractive power; more accurate might be choices like *classes are filled by students* (passive) or *students fill the classes*. (Why extracurricular music classes should signal academic intensity requires explanation.)

The *school brought in* is a predictable metonymy/personification. Someone in the school, perhaps the principal, perhaps the guidance counselor, actually invited the speakers at the prompting of the students and could easily have been named. But *the school* as metonymic stand-in for the students and administrators gives the institution agency and therefore signals the event as official. At one point the *you* of the rhetorical situation comes in, invoking a reader who conveniently imagines how unusual the reported event is, thereby making it newsworthy. Here the writer has constructed a reader who has just the right attitude to be interested in the article.

One abstraction used as a subject is *gatekeeping*. This term seems a somewhat odd summation for actions undertaken voluntarily by students themselves ("early bird" classes and studying past midnight), but it is a word choice that helps the writer make an accusation of *unfairness*. *Gatekeeping* is something done to the students, not by them. At any rate, this *gatekeeping* has not *tamped down the runaway ambition* (a mixing of metaphors?) so it is a rather ineffectual agent.

There is an obvious pattern among the other agents; the young people who are the object of the article's attention are represented by their roles and by generic plural nouns: *students, kids, applicants*. Although the article is written about a visit to a particular high school, and although it does eventually report the observations of the school's guidance counselor, who is an individual with a name, the high-powered, high-achieving students remain an undifferentiated group. They even speak with an undifferentiated voice: "Kids say, 'I thrive.'" (Compare to the normal attribution to James Conroy, "I don't think.") Plurals like *students* and *kids* help to generalize the piece and so attract readers across the nation; these generic human agents could be students in the reader's own school or family. In keeping with these choices of collective human agents, the "teachers and parents" who deal with the students are also generic groups defined by their roles.

The generic plural is, however, also part of the argument. The goal of this piece, as of all such "exposé" pieces, is to convince readers that a trend exists. One overambitious high school student would not be newsworthy. But a trend affecting many students in a typical high school, and so by implication in many high schools, is. Exactly how many students at New Trier were affected by the pressure? One hundred interviewed out of two thousand, 37% of the total student body as sampled in a head count, 88% of respondents to a questionnaire given to the entire senior class? A sociologist would have to present the group as examined in an explicit, replicable way. A logician would demand a verifiable quantifier modifying the subject and a suitable modal with the verb. But a journalist need only suggest multiplicity with the generic plural *students*. This practice represents the usual standard of accountability in the mass media. Such vagueness is perhaps acceptable if the claim, the exposé of a trend, only reinforces beliefs the audience already holds. But such casual cases also plant beliefs and attitudes.

Nominal versus Verbal Style

Sentences, passages, whole texts, and even genres can be distinguished according to whether action verbs or stative linking verbs dominate. This distinction can lead to texts conventionally described as *verbal*, featuring actions depicted in verbs and verbal modifiers (participles, infinitives), or *nominal*, featuring noun phrases sutured together with linking verbs or prepositions (see Wells 1960). The relative proportion of verbal versus nominal constructions separates, at the extremes, texts that convey activities (processes, narratives, explanations) from those that depict states of being (definitions, categorizations, characterizations). Though no entire text would typically use one pattern exclusively, one or the other will dominate, giving the text its primary stylistic character and either helping or hindering it from achieving its function. The venerable *Gray's Anatomy* offers an example of the nominal style with sentences featuring linking verbs to introduce the peripheral nervous system:

> **Peripheral Nerves.**—The peripheral **nerves are** of two types depending on whether their **fibers are** predominately [sic] myelinated or whether **they are** almost exclusively unmyelinated. The **former are** the spinal nerves and their branches, and, with certain exceptions, the cranial nerves. The **latter are** the nerves of the autonomic system. (1959, 935)

The dominance of stative, existential *to be* produces the language of conceptual ordering, of classes and their subclasses. This passage could easily be converted into a tree diagram. Most of the sentences throughout this text have the same magisterial definiteness.[11]

In contrast to the nominal style of the textbook is the following excerpt from Vincent Bugliosi Jr.'s summation before the jury in the trial of the "Manson Family," a drug-addled cult, for a killing spree in 1969 that took the lives of seven people, including the actress Sharon Tate. A prosecutor's jury summation follows the ample advice in rhetorical manuals for constructing the *narratio* in a forensic oration. These rehearsals of the crime typically include a detailed narrative derived from witness testimony and physical evidence. Bugliosi's reconstruction was based on the testimony of one of the cult members turned state's witness, Linda Kasabian. Within the frame of her account, Bugliosi manages to convey how Manson's "agents" acted, as in this expert from the preliminaries to the murders at the Tate mansion.

> She **said** it **took** Tex between a half hour and an hour **to drive** to the Tate residence, and she **guessed** they **arrived** roughly around midnight. Tex **turned** the car around

at the top of the hill, outside the gate of the Tate residence, and **parked** the car next to a telephone pole. And you **will recall** that Linda **testified** that eventually she, Tex, Katie, and Sadie **climbed** over the front gate.

She **said** Tex **got out** of the car, **climbed** the telephone pole, and although she **doesn't remember hearing** Tex **cut** the telephone pole wire, she **did see** a few wires **fall** onto the ground. Tex **got back in** the car, **drove** to the bottom of the hill, and **parked** the car. All four **got out** of the car at that particular point and **started to walk** up the hill. Tex **was carrying** a rope. **Let's pick up** her testimony at this point: "We **climbed** over a fence and then a light **started coming** toward us and Tex **told** us **to get back and sit down**." (Lief, Caldwell, and Bycel 1998, 243; verbs and infinitives in bold)

After sentences with reporting verbs (*she said*), Bugliosi switches to active predications so that jury members "see" the action unfolding. In such accounts, prosecutors have the license to interpolate actions that must have happened in between known events; for example, the perpetrators had to get out of the car at some point. Notably, Bugliosi does not follow strict chronological order, since he mentions the fence-climbing episode twice. The light approaching came from a car driven by a young man who was about to become the first victim.

NOMINALIZATIONS

A complication in distinguishing between nominal and verbal styles comes from the practice of turning verbs into nouns (*polyptoton*). The resulting sentences contain *nominalizations*, a term that performs what it stands for. In a nominalization, a verb becomes a noun with the addition of a suffix (*nominalize → nominalization,* see above, p. 47). This new noun can then find its place in the predicate of a sentence with a linking verb. Any object/recipient of the verb can then slide into various modifiers.

> With active verb: *Irene Curie received the Nobel Prize*
> With nominalization + linking verb: *Irene Curie was the recipient of the Nobel Prize.*

In some cases, a substitution with a related term rather than a nominalization occurs, but the result is the same: an action becomes a state of being or a category.

> With active verb: *Toni Morrison wrote* Beloved.
> With substitution + linking verb: *Toni Morrison is the author of* Beloved.

Nominalizations can also employ other "generic" verbs, as in Al Gore's famous claim: *I took the initiative to create the internet,* which was paraphrased by many with the active-verb sentence *I invented the internet.* As even these few examples suggest, nominalizations are features of a more formal style. Saying that someone *is the recipient of* or *the author of* can sound more impressive than saying he or she *received* or *wrote.*

Personification (*Personae Fictio*)

Writers of rhetorical style manuals paid little attention to the routine patterns of subject/ verb choice outlined above. They did not distinguish nominal from verbal styles, though they were acutely aware of the categorization arguments or narrative modes that featured such styles. But they did focus on atypical predications such as combining nonhuman subjects/agents—an animal, an object, or even an abstraction—with the kinds of action that humans typically can perform. Under a variety of names (*conformatio, attributio, personae fictio, somatopoeia*), classical and early modern style manuals mark this "grammatical" humanizing, making persons out of nonhuman agents by endowing them with intentional actions and even with speech, certainly the most human of actions. Scaliger, under *tractatio*, describes attributing sense "to things without sense" and creating fictive persons such as Fame and the Furies and "things with human properties attributed to them" (quoted in Sonnino 1968, 55). John Hoskins refers to Sir Philip Sidney's giving "meaning and speech to the needle, the cloth, and the silk" (1935, 48), and the most "literary" of the figure manuals, George Puttenham's *The Arte of English Poesie* (1589), notes when "ye wil attribute any humane quality, as reason or speech to dombe creatures or other insensible things, and do study (as one may say) to give them a humane person" (1970, 246). Puttenham also cites under this device the habit, carried over from the ancient Characters, of creating persons out of Avarice, Envy, and Old Age.[12] All these versions are now summed up under the label **personification**, one of a handful of figures still taught.

It would be easy to reclassify the typical personification (*The nation weeps for her lost sons*) as the metaphorical use of a verb. But the emphasis in the manuals was on the combined predication and on the realization, indeed the visualization, of the agent, especially in the case of abstract qualities. So Peacham describes the process in *The Garden of Eloquence*:

> Sometime to Cities, townes, beastes, birdes, trees, stones, weapons, fire, water, lights of the firmament, and such like things he [the Orator] attributeth speech, reason, and affection, and to no other end then to further his purpose and to confirme and make his cause evident, as for example: If an orator having occasion to commend some virtue to his hearers, as truth or such like, he may after he hath sufficiently praised truth, faine it a person, and bring it in bitterly complaining how cruelly she is oppressed and how little esteemed...(1593, 136; Peacham continues the imagined speech of "Truth" for twelve more lines.)

The habit of personifying abstractions, especially virtues and vices, continued in seventeenth- and eighteenth-century prose, where such humanized qualities were often capitalized as though they were proper names. This tendency leaves its trace in texts from the Founders in U.S. history. In the Declaration of Independence, for example, important nouns are capitalized, and some of these are personified abstractions:

> Prudence, indeed, will dictate that Governments long established should not be changed for light and transient Causes; and accordingly all Experience hath shewn, that Mankind are more disposed to suffer, while evils are sufferable, than to right themselves by abolishing the Forms to which they are accustomed...

Contemporary readers, no longer habituated to the personification of moral qualities or virtues like Prudence, may not notice the trace of a *dictating person* in the phrasing, and in the case of "Experience hath shewn" the language is on its way to the unremarkable collocation, "experience shows." What remains in the language in the twentieth and twenty-first centuries is a normalized, unnoticed language of personification for abstractions.

PERSONIFICATION IN SCIENCE

It would be hard to overestimate the importance of personification, the endowing of physical objects and abstractions with human-like agency, in scientific arguments, and most notable is the ancient device of personifying Nature itself. So the seventeenth-century natural philosopher John Ray names *Nature* as the agent behind the admirable accommodations he sees in everything created, such as the simple fact that animals have an even number of feet: "For though a Creature might make a limping shift to hop, suppose with three Feet, yet nothing so conveniently or steddily to walk, or run, or indeed to stand. So that we see, Nature hath made choice of what is most fit, proper, and useful" (1717, 155). Ray compiled his catalog of adaptive miracles as witness to *The Wisdom of God Manifested in the Works of the Creation;* God creates Nature, and Nature then creates everything else. But it is easy to elide the ultimate cause in this series, first as obvious and then as ignored. Ray in fact caught himself in this act of erasure: "I shall now add another Instance of the Wisdom of Nature, or rather the God of Nature, in adapting the Parts of the same Animal one to another, and that is the proportioning the length of the Neck to that of the Legs" (156).[13]

One hundred and fifty years later, Darwin tried to undo the personification of Nature in a passage added to the third edition of *On the Origin of Species*: "it is difficult to avoid personifying the word Nature; but I mean by Nature, only the aggregate action and product of many natural laws, and by laws the sequence of events as ascertained by us" (1861, 85). Darwin's figural problems began with the coinage of his key summarizing term *natural selection,* which he often linked with verbs usually attributed to (that is collocating with) human agents.

It may metaphorically be said that natural selection is daily and hourly scrutinizing, throughout the world, every variation, even the slightest; rejecting that which is bad, preserving and adding up that which is good; silently and insensibly working, whenever and wherever opportunity offers, at the improvement of each organic being in relation to its organic and inorganic conditions of life (2nd ed., 1860, 85)

While marking this usage as figured, Darwin continues to apply the term as an active agent in passages like the following: "Natural selection may modify and adapt the larva of an insect" (86) or "Natural selection will modify the structure of the young" (86–87). This usage drew criticism and Darwin's subsequent apology, added to the third edition:

Several writers have misapprehended or objected to the term Natural Selection. Some have even imagined that natural selection induces variability, whereas it implies only the preservation of such variations as occur and are beneficial to the being under its conditions of life...Others have objected that the term selection implies conscious choice in the animals which become modified; and it has even been urged that as plants have no volition, natural selection is not applicable to them! In the literal sense of the word, no doubt, natural selection is a misnomer; but who ever objected to chemists speaking of elective affinities of the various elements?—and yet an acid cannot strictly be said to elect the base with which it perforce combines. It has been said that I speak of natural selection as an active power or Deity; but who objects to an author speaking of the attraction of gravity as ruling the movements of the planets? (1861, 84–85)

Some of the misreading Darwin complains about may have been stimulated by his own practice of occasionally capitalizing Natural Selection, making it a proper noun. But English afforded Darwin few alternative verbs to combine with his coinage, and without elaborate circumlocution he could never completely remove the tinge of agency from a term he intended only as an abstraction describing the results of a gradual process.

Multiplying Subjects and Verbs

In addition to noticing the anomalous predications that produced personifications, rhetorical style manuals devoted several figures of speech to the sentence dynamics created by multiplying the subjects or verbs in a single predication. Under *membrum*, for example, Peacham describes the sentence with one subject but multiple verb phrases, any one of which could end the construction: *"Thou hast neither profited the commonwealth, done good to thy friends, nor resisted thy enemies."* He advises that such multiple predicates be kept short and without a great difference in "quantity," that is in length (58). Ted Sorensen followed this advice when he wrote John F. Kennedy's Inaugural Address: "Let every nation know, whether it wishes us well or ill, that **we** shall **pay** any price, **bear** any burden, **meet** any hardship, **support** any friend, **oppose** any foe to assure the survival and success of liberty" (Windt 1983, 9).

If in *membrum* several verbs share one subject, in *zeugma* several subjects, and sometimes objects too, share one verb. The following invented example illustrates how this sentence pattern avoids repetition: *The Romans conquered Carthage, the Greeks Troy, the Arabs Byzantium, and the Chinese Tibet.* English is not "comfortable" with this construction, but Greek and Latin would allow the verb to appear at any point in this series, and hyperdescriptive manuals listed the options of placing the verb in the beginning, middle, or end (*prozeugma, mesozeugma,* and *hypozeugma*). Without the ellipsis of *zeugma,* the rhetor would either repeat the same verb each time or use roughly synonymous verbs: *The Romans conquered Carthage, the Greeks destroyed Troy,* etc. This alternative demonstrates the rhetorical consequences of the *zeugma,* which compresses a potential series of clauses into a series of subject/object phrases and so has an equalizing effect on this series. When all the subject/object pairs take the same verb by default, the action must be the same in each case. But a subject/verb combination that might be unremarkable to an audience in one pair, e.g., *the Romans conquered Carthage,* might be unfamiliar on even contestable in another, e.g., *the Chinese conquered Tibet.* (Did they conquer Tibet or simply move in?) The *zeugma* accomplishes the linkage somewhat "under the radar" and homogenizes all the predications so that the actions become comparable, even identical.

If repeating subjects or verbs can be avoided, these basic elements can also be deliberately multiplied so that every subject, in Peacham's account, is joined to a "due verbe" (59). Under the label *hypozeuxis,* Peacham actually describes a megasentence made up of a series of brief, complete clauses. His own example has eighteen predications in a row detailing the consequences of oppression and rebellion, including the following: "ambition shal strive for honor, pride shall disdaine obedience, malice proceede to murder, theft deprive true possessors, idleness neglect labor, impietie scorne religion, and raging tumults violate peace, and turne a happie state into a miserable confusion" (60). President Obama used this same device in his 2008 Inaugural Address to list the nation's economic problems: "Homes have been lost; jobs shed; businesses shuttered. Our health care is too costly; our schools fail too many; and each day brings further evidence that the ways we use energy strengthen our adversaries and threaten our planet." (These examples over four hundred years apart use the same doubled verbs in the final predication.) The distinctive feature of *hypozeuxis* is the "variety with unity" produced by brief subject/verb pairings in a single section. This sentence architecture "piles it on," and it is especially useful for delivering chains of consequences.

Zeugma takes verbs out, *hypozeuxis* puts them in, and still another figure, *syllepsis,* plays with their meaning in a noticeable way, using one verb with two meanings and two corresponding objects. Hence *syllepsis* is really another form of the pun, but it is a pun in the verb only (see above, p. 134). An example endlessly cited comes from Pope: "Great

Anna whom three realms obey/Doth sometimes council take and sometimes tea" (pronounced *tay* in the early eighteenth century). Obviously two meanings of *take* are required to make sense of this line, but the fact that the verb appears once levels the two actions and hence delivers Pope's raillery. There is a probably intentional *syllepsis* in Obama's Inaugural (though the verb takes only one object), "Our schools fail too many." Are the schools not passing enough students on to the next grade or are they not educating them? The cleverness in *syllepsis* comes from forcing the reader to backtrack and reassess the potentially double meaning of the verb that appears just once.

Why the interest in rhetorical stylistics in these jams or elisions of subjects and verbs? One answer has to do with the rhythms produced by strings of truncated phrases. These speed up a text, whether spoken or written, and therefore emphasize the combined content, especially in the case of *membrum* with its multiplied verb phrases. By picking up the pace, these truncated series thus express urgency. Another answer comes from the impression of multiplicity produced, the sheer number of instances that help make a case. While *syllepsis* compresses, *zeugma* and *hypozeuxis* can overwhelm. And the homogenizing of elements with all these figures of predication goes by so quickly that it forestalls criticism. In all these ways the forms of multiple predication can serve the rhetor's persuasive purposes.

Summary

Rhetoric by definition stresses communication with language as its instrument. Choosing sides in dissociations between language as an abstract system and language in use (Saussure's *langue* versus *parole* or Chomsky's i[nternal]-language/competence versus e[xternal]-language/performance), rhetoric stresses *parole* and performance. But in using a language to achieve their ends, speakers and writers observe not only its functional and social norms but its constitutive rules as well, putting well-formed sentences at the service of persuasive messages. Mikhail Bahktin carefully observes the difference: "One does not exchange sentences any more than one exchanges words (in the strict linguistic sense) or phrases. One exchanges utterances that are constructed from language units: words, phrases, and sentences" (1986, 75). For Bakhtin, the fundamental unit of communication is the utterance, which is built from the fundamental unit of language for grammarians and many linguists, the sentence.

Rhetorical stylistics looks at the constitutive options available to a rhetor, and perhaps the most important involve the core predication in a sentence, the subject and verb. This pair determines two basic sentence types: active sentences where a subject is an agent performing the verb, whether transitive (*The Senate approved the measure; The Senate sent the President a tax bill*) or intransitive (*The Senate adjourned*), and stative sentences that categorize or describe the subject (*The Senate is a legislative body*). Whole texts can be characterized by the proportion of active versus stative sentences, producing nominal versus verbal styles, a marker of genre. But rhetorical analysis is best served by scrutiny of individual subject/verb pairings, especially when the evidence of drafts and alternative versions shows that the rhetor has tinkered with these choices.

To facilitate attention to the core predication, this chapter offers a taxonomy of possible grammatical subjects under several broad categories: humans, rhetorical participants, things, abstractions, concepts, or slot fillers. Has the politician decided to give agency to *voters* or *we* or *the American people*, or *the electoral process* or the concept of *liberty*? When are groups constructed as actors or individuals singled out? Does the news feature the president or the administration? This chapter likewise reviews the many dimensions that grammarians use to characterize verbs, including tense, aspect, mood, negation, modality, and voice. The choices and changes in these dimensions across a passage can constrain an argued conclusion into an inevitability.

While the basic options in subject/verb pairings were taught in dialectics and grammar, rhetorical manuals noted bolder choices. They observed over two thousand years ago that using the present rather than the simple past can make an enormous difference in the effect of a narrative on an audience and that yoking verbs for human activities with non-human subjects can animate things and abstractions, producing provocative hybrid predications. They recognized that pairing a single subject with several verbs (*membrum*) or several subjects with a single verb (*zeugma*) could productively elide distinctions in the rhetor's favor. Attention to such anomalies presupposes the default importance of the rhetor's subject and verb choices.

NOTES

1. Following Carroll Arnold, Roderick Hart calls the predication of a sentence the "primary structure" and the added modification the "secondary structure" (1997, 135–37). He produces interesting representations of texts by highlighting the primary structure over the modifiers, in the manner shown here. However, he ignores double predicates and often elevates modifiers to the primary structure.

2. Animal agents are fairly typical in children's books and nature writing, as in this example from a *National Geographic* article on meerkats.

> In the slanting, golden light of a Kalahari evening, Juma, a young male meerkat, stares across the sandy bed of the Nossob River: nothing but the shimmer of hot air and the evening chorus of barking geckos. Six pups, their eyes only recently open, nuzzle at his stomach, hoping to find milk. Juma has been watching over them since dawn, ignoring his own hunger as he scans the sky for eagles and the ridgeline for jackals, snakes, yellow mongooses, and even neighboring meerkats, which would kill the pups if they found their burrow unguarded. (Clutton-Brock 2002, 69)

The naming of the animal, with the suitably African-sounding *Juma*, is the first step in anthropomorphizing. The verb *staring* could be attributed to an animal by an outside observer, but the verbs and objects *watching over them* and the participle *ignoring his own hunger* suggest intentions and hence a humanized agent.

3. A gerund can remain a single word, but because it has the properties of both verbs and nouns, it can also be expanded into a phrase by taking modifiers and/or objects: *Jogging in the streets is John's favorite form of exercise; Cooking gourmet meals is Martin's favorite pastime.* A gerund or gerund phrase can of course fill any role that a single-word noun can fill, not only as a subject (*Driving a school bus is a difficult job*) but also, for example, as a direct object (*My aunt likes singing hymns*) or as the object of a preposition (*He thanked me for adding the pepper*).

4. See Jennifer Riddle Harding's dissertation, "Simple Regrets: Counterfactuals and the Dialogic Mind," available at http://hdl.handle.net/1903/1421.

5. The potential moods of English verbs translate directly into a variety of sentence types: statements, questions, commands, and exclamations. This potential variety is on display in the opening sentences of the series of contributions on "The Future of the American Idea" solicited by the *Atlantic Monthly*:

> The American idea, as I understand it, is to trust people to know their own minds and to act in their own enlightened self-interest, with a necessary respect for others. *John Updike* (2007, 14).
> How heartily sick the world has grown, in the first seven years of the 21st century, of the American idea! *Joyce Carol Oates* (2007, 22).
> Are some things still worth dying for? Is the American idea one of them? [The entire text is in the form of questions.] *David Foster Wallace* (2007, 25).

6. http://www.cnn.com/2003/US/02/05/sprj.irq.powell.transcript/index.html. This text is a transcript of Powell's remarks available on CNN's website. Powell's argument, with separate sections on biological, chemical, and nuclear weapons and contacts between Iraq and Al Qaeda, is quite detailed. Some of its claims are qualified, e.g., "Iraq declared 8,500 liters of anthrax, but UNSCOM estimates that Saddam Hussein could have produced 25,000 liters." In other cases, the certainty of having the evidence seems passed on to the certainty of the content: "Let me take you inside that intelligence file and share with you what we know from eye witness accounts. We have firsthand descriptions of biological weapons factories on wheels and on rails."

7. In standard written English the passive is usually formed with the verb "to be" and occasionally with other linking verbs, e.g., *she becomes/seems/appears easily discouraged by criticism.* In informal discourse, the verb *get/got* can take its place.

> Standard: *The player was covered by mud*
> Informal: *The player got covered by mud.*

The *American Heritage Dictionary* "Usage Note" on the *get/got* passive points out that this informal passive construction actually attributes more agency to the recipient than the standard passive does. They note the meaning distinction between the following two forms: *The fan was arrested by the police* versus *The fan got arrested by the police.* The second version suggests that the fan did something to deserve being arrested, and perhaps, because it provides this nuance, the "got" passive is finding its way into print.

8. Even the most ardent foe of the passive would not ban modifiers like the following: *the deleted passage; the canceled check; Denied access to the voting booth, the citizens…; Hidden in the rafters, the treasure….* Yet all these modifiers, past participles, are in fact remnants of passive constructions: *the passage was deleted; the check was canceled; the voters were denied; the treasure was hidden.* In fact, some passive constructions are difficult to distinguish from sentences with linking verbs. Compare a sentence like *The mail was delivered* to *The man was wrinkled.* Surely no agent is either implicit/understood or "suppressed" in the second sentence.

9. Jefferson's original draft, before the committee's revisions, had a double verb here also, *dissolve & break off*; the doubled verbs are markers of legal language, e.g., *cease and desist*.

10. Using Halliday's method requires either a preestablished or ad hoc categorization of subjects/agents and verbs/actions (or sentence types generally). Halliday divided subjects/agents into three categories, humans, body parts, and inanimate objects, reflecting Golding's usage, and he divided actions into intransitive movement, transitive movement, location/possession, mental process, attribution, and other (1996, 72).

11. The interesting possible exceptions in this passage are the verb phrases "are predominately myelinated" and "are almost exclusively unmyelinated." Rather than linking verbs followed by the contrasting adjectives "myelinated" and "unmyelinated," these phrases could be considered constructions with passive verbs, "are myelinated" and "are unmyelinated." But what then are the agents of the action of myelination or unmyelination? Probable answer from the context: myelin sheaths. These constructions, therefore, can convey the distinguishing characteristics of the peripheral nerves, the attributes that put them in two different classes, or, implicitly, the action of myelination performed by an unnamed agent.

12. The Bible in new vernacular translations offered early modern rhetors copious examples of personified objects, entities, and abstractions: "The land itself vomiteth out her inhabitants (Lev 18:28); "The waters saw thee, O God, the waters saw thee; they were afraid (Ps 77:16); "Sin lieth at the door" (Gen 4:7); "Her sins have reached to heaven" (Rev 18:5); "The heavens declare the glory of God" (Ps 19:1); "The morning stars sang together" (Job 38:7).

13. Here is an entirely unremarkable instance from a 1712 number of the *Spectator* by Joseph Addison.

> Though there is a great deal of pleasure in contemplating the material world, by which I mean that system of bodies into which Nature has so curiously wrought the mass of dead matter, with the several relations which those bodies bear to one another; there is still, methinks, something more wonderful and surprizing in contemplations on the world of life, by which I mean all those animals with which every part of the universe is furnished. (Bredvold, McKillop, and Whitney 1956, 1127; elsewhere in this essay, Addison personifies *Infinite Goodness*. He also uses the terms *Supreme Being* and *Divine Being*, but notably not in positions of agency.)

Rocket-propelled grenades slammed into U.S. military vehicles in two attacks in and around Baghdad on Tuesday, and a massive explosion at a mosque in the town of Fallujah killed at least five Iraqis and injured four others.

Rocket-propelled grenades slammed into U.S. military vehicles in two attacks Tuesday in and around Baghdad after an explosion at a mosque in the town of Fallujah killed 10 Iraqis and injured four others.

8

SENTENCE CONSTRUCTION: MODIFICATION

ON JULY 1, 2003, a reporter for the Associated Press filed a story from Fallujah, Iraq, at 7:25 a.m. ET, that opened with the first sentence quoted above. Periodic revisions to web-posted news stories are not uncommon, and on the same day at noon ET, an updated version filed by the Associated Press began with the second sentence.[1] These two versions differ in details and word order, but most important, they differ in the way the reported events in Baghdad and Fallujah are constructed in relation to each other. How can this difference be described?

The previous chapter focused on subjects and verbs in simple sentences. But "sentences" frequently have more than one subject/verb pairing, so it is better to switch to the term **clause** for the minimum unit featuring a subject and verb.[2] A simple sentence with a single predication is an **independent** clause, and joining two or more of these creates a *compound sentence*. Other types of clauses, called **dependent**, can be added to independent clauses to build up *complex sentences*. The main types of dependent clauses—**adverb, adjective**, and **noun clauses**—are discussed below.[3] Turning an independent clause into a dependent clause shifts it into a different status in a sentence. It becomes part of the modification.

Everything in a sentence that is not predication in an independent clause is modification. To modify is to add specifying detail to basic sentence elements, as in the bolded material in this sentence from the Gettysburg Address (compare above p. 148):

The brave men, living and dead, have consecrated it, **far above our poor power who struggled here,** **to add or detract.**

Clearly modification is not necessary in a well-formed sentence, but English syntax allows subjects and verbs to carry extensive elaboration. And just as subject/verb choices carry the rhetor's argument and implicate a worldview, so do choices in modification. Modifiers are, in fact, strong determiners of a style, since in all but the simplest styles using the briefest independent clauses, most of the words in a sentence will be modifiers that specify, clarify, and amplify the meaning.

Modification can be analyzed in several ways, according to the type of modifier, the extent of the modification, and the placement of the modifiers. This chapter covers types—clauses, phrases, and single words—and the amount of modification. The next chapter will consider the placement of modifiers. In the act of composing, rhetors constantly make small decisions on predication versus modification. Overall, individual rhetors may favor certain patterns in these decisions, but in any one sentence or passage, their choices can be judged in terms of the argument served.

Adverb Clauses

In the first version of the news from Iraq quoted above, a conjunction (*and*) links two independent clauses, each reporting an item no doubt passed on to the press in a daily briefing. This original grammatical choice in effect equates but separates the events; the two clauses are independent and coordinate, and so are the events. In the second version, one of the clauses is subordinated to the other in time: *after an explosion at a mosque in the town of Fallujah killed* 10 *Iraqis and injured four others.* By claiming that the attack on the military vehicles happened *after* the explosions at the mosque, the writer may be reporting the correct chronological sequence (though putting the first event second). But this subordination suggests a causal connection: that the attack on the vehicles happened because of the explosion at the mosque. The second version, therefore, has very different implications.

Adverb clauses, often called **subordinate clauses**, allow rhetors to create a predication, complete with subject and verb, and then to background that predication and tie it to another in a particular way with a *subordinating conjunction*: *because, since, although, unless, while, when, until, after, whereas, if, as, just as,* and dozens more. These conjunctions specify the semantic relation of the subordinate clause to the main clause. The resulting clauses function as adverbial modifiers, and as adverbs, they can come before or after, or even interrupt, the clauses they modify.

Special types of adverb clauses have important functions in argument. Some express the known or projected **result** of the action in the main clause: "Nuclear weapons are so destructive and ballistic missiles are so swift, *that any substantially increased possibility of their use or any sudden change in their deployment may well be regarded as a definite threat to peace*" (from Kennedy, Address on the Cuban Missile Crisis, 1962 [Windt 1983, 43]). Others provide a **purpose** that functions as a premise: "Our arms must be mighty, ready for instant action, *so that no potential aggressor may be tempted to risk his own destruction*" (from Eisenhower, Farewell Address, 1961 [Safire 1997, 409]). Another type, called a **proviso** clause, specifies the circumstances for the action in the main clause: "It is our hope...to convince the Soviet Union that she, too, should let each nation choose its own future, *so long as that choice does not interfere with the choices of others*" (from Kennedy, Commencement Address at American University, 1963 [Windt 1983, 44]).

A common and important type of adverb clause, the **conditional clause**, usually begins with *if*. These clauses have two important uses in arguments. First, they stipulate circumstances, express dependencies, or convey demands with consequences. For example, in the April 3 version of his famous "Ballot or Bullet" speech, Malcolm X made the demands and consequences mutually clear: "*If we don't do something real soon,* I think you'll agree that we're going to be forced to use the ballot or the bullet."[4] Second, *if*-clauses can express **a fortiori arguments**. These constructions argue for the likelihood of one claim based on another claim that is either more or less likely: "*If an adult can't reach the top shelf,* neither can a child." The April 12 version of "The Ballot or the Bullet" uses this form: "*If you can be brave over there* [in Korea], you can be brave right here."[5]

Comparative clauses allow rhetors to introduce standards of reference into an argument. When Nixon justified military forays into Cambodia in a televised speech in 1970, he used a map to illustrate the geographic proximity of "sanctuaries" in Cambodia to South Vietnam. To put the point in terms an American audience could understand, he said: "Some of these, incidentally, are as close to Saigon *as Baltimore is [close] to Washington*" (Windt 1983, 138). Comparative clauses can also deliver arguments from analogy in a single sentence; again taking an example from a Nixon speech: "There is no more justification for wasting money on unnecessary military hardware *than there is for wasting it on unwarranted social programs*" (125).

Adjective Clauses

The most common type of dependent clause is the **adjective clause**, commonly called a **relative clause**, used to modify a noun (or any construction functioning as a noun). An adjective clause typically opens with a **relative pronoun** that refers to the noun modified (as in this sentence): for example, *who, whose, whom, that, which*. For the sake of clarity, an adjective clause usually appears immediately after the term it modifies, as in these antithetical modifiers from Kennedy's Inaugural Address: "If a free society cannot save the many *who are poor,* it cannot save the few *who are rich*" (Windt 1983, 10). Adjective clauses appear in virtually any paragraph of published prose, even in books for children. Only an unusual style avoids modifying nouns with these inserted predications.

Adjective clauses are sometimes further classified on the basis of whether they identify what they modify or merely offer additional and dispensable details. When a relative clause provides necessary clarification, it is called *restrictive* and left unpunctuated in print (*That man who just came in is drunk*). When it contains details treated as peripheral, it is called *nonrestrictive* and set off in commas from the rest of the sentence (*That man, who just came in, is drunk*). This traditional either/or distinction does not really capture the middle option that rhetors actually have, as the following instance illustrates. In the published version of Kennedy's Inaugural Address, the following sentence appears without commas around the adjective clause: "The graves of young Americans *who answered the call to service* surround the globe" (Windt 1983, 11). Since this point follows Kennedy's praise of past generations, answering "the call" defines this group of *young Americans*, who are actually a subset of the young Americans buried in other countries. Had this clause appeared in print set off in commas and thus marked as peripheral, the deaths of these young Americans (*graves* serving as a metonymy for *deaths*) would not necessarily be the result of their service. But in fact Kennedy's point shades off into allowing that any young American buried abroad died in service to the country.

In oral delivery, speakers may distinguish between essential and peripheral modification by not pausing for a restrictive modifier but pausing briefly before and after a nonrestrictive one. The voice may also be lowered slightly for nonrestrictive modifiers. Standard punctuation tries to capture such subtle spoken differences. But in a written text not derived from an oral text, it is the author's punctuation itself that really makes any particular structure restrictive or nonrestrictive, perpetuating the either/or distinction.[6]

Another common type of adjective clause that can modify a noun, and some adjectives as well, is the **complement clause**. These clauses always open with a *that* functioning as a conjunction, not as a relative pronoun. Consider the difference between the following: *The idea that I have is fantastic* versus *The idea that I have a billion dollars is fantastic*. Both the underlined clauses modify *idea*, but in the first, *that* is a relative pronoun referring to *idea* and functioning as the direct object of the clause it appears in (*I have that*), while in the second, *that* is not one of the basic constituents in its clause (subject: *I*, verb: *have*, object: *a billion dollars*).

One of the most famous speeches in American oratory depends again and again on complement clauses: *I have a dream that one day this nation will rise up and live out the true meaning of its creed* (Safire 1997, 535). King's complement clauses specify the content of his vision in the form of separate structures. Notably, King did not use clauses opening with a relative pronoun (*I have a dream that is wonderful...*), nor did he choose *dream* as a verb, which would have allowed him to use the same constructions as noun clauses serving as direct objects: *I dream that one day this nation....* Instead he chose *dream* as his direct object (*I have a dream*), creating a complete sentence first that allows a slight pause after *dream*, highlighting it. He then continues with extensive specifications of that dream in complement clauses. For King, *to dream* and *to have a dream* were not the same thing.

Noun Clauses

Adverb clauses are usually attached before or after an independent clause, while adjective clauses often interrupt an independent clause with qualifying information. A third type of dependent clause is better described as embedded inside another clause. A **noun clause**, as its name reveals, is a complete predication inserted where a single noun or a noun phrase could appear. Though this process sounds unusual, noun clauses are in fact quite common. The following noun clauses (in italics) function in the roles designated in these consecutive sentences taken from Winston Churchill's 1946 "Iron Curtain" speech: "I do not believe *that Soviet Russia desires war* [direct object]. *What they desire* [subject] is the fruits of war and the indefinite expansion of their power and doctrines" (Safire 1997, 874).[7] Noun clauses are also commonly used for indirect speech, for paraphrasing what someone said: The president said *that he would consider the matter* (direct object). Since noun clauses usually function as subjects or objects, they are not really modifiers per se. But the decision to embed an entire dependent clause in one functional slot can be a way of importing elaborating detail.

The Consequences of Clause Types: Kennedy's Options

As this survey of clause types shows, English offers its users various ways to represent the status of predications in relation to each other. Rhetors can leave them as independent clauses or they can "demote" them to dependent clauses, whether adverb, adjective, or noun clauses. These are not trivial decisions. The options and consequences of expressing and relating predications in different types of clauses can be assessed by looking at two sentences from an actual text, once again from Kennedy's speech to the nation on the Cuban Missile Crisis in 1963. Addressing the "captive people of Cuba" on the recently installed Soviet missiles, Kennedy used the following two consecutive independent clauses: "These new weapons are not in your interest. They contribute nothing to your peace and well-being" (Windt 1983, 40). In the form of two independent clauses of roughly equal length, punctuated as separate sentences, Kennedy presents these statements as equivalent in importance. What other options were available?

Kennedy (or his speech writers) could have subordinated one of the clauses as an adverbial modifier of the other. Since their current order could suggest that the second offers a reason for the first (see below, p. 357), that relation could be expressed as follows: *These new weapons are not in your interest because they contribute nothing to your peace and well-being.* The subordination could also have gone the other way: *Because these weapons are not in your interest, they contribute nothing to your peace and well being.* Either way, the resulting construction is a conclusion/premise pair, and the argument has been made explicit. Urged by this reasoning, Cuba would independently assess what was in its self-interest ("your interest") as serving its peace and well-being, rather than, by implication, serving Soviet interests. (Of course, it was also in Cuba's economic and security interests to have the Soviet presence.)

Kennedy could also have made one of the original independent clauses into an adjective clause modifying a term in the other clause. Again, treating the second sentence as more movable could produce *These new weapons, which contribute nothing to your peace and well-being, are not in your interest,* where one of the original sentences now serves as a nonrestrictive clause modifying *weapons.* In this version, one statement serves as an "aside" to the other. The reverse embedding—*These new weapons, which are not in your interest, contribute nothing to your peace and well-being*—yields a similarly "offhand" comment. Trying to make either of the original sentences into a restrictive adjective clause—for example, *These new weapons which are not in your interest*—would not work at all, because such a restrictive specification suggests another group of weapons *that are in your interest* to be distinguished from those which are not.

Finally, with some rewording, Kennedy's two sentences could have been turned into two noun clauses in one sentence: ***That these weapons contribute nothing to your peace and well-being** means **that they are not in your interest.*** The structure here—X means Y—creates a strong cause-effect relationship between the two statements. But given its awkwardness, this alternative can be dropped from consideration.

The actual form that Kennedy chose, which may or may not have been the "best" from a diplomatic or strategic point of view, has a different effect. Standing alone, the first statement (*These new weapons are not in your interest*) is surely a subtle threat. To say that something is not in a nation's interest serves as a *litotes* for unspecified harm. The next separate statement makes a different point, offering a perspective internal to Cuba (its *peace* and *well-being*). In other words, there are two problems here for the Cuban government to consider: external and internal. They occupy, or rather are produced by, the separate sentences. Even the slight alteration of combining these two statements into a single compound sentence with two independent clauses (*These new weapons are not in your interest, and they will not contribute to your peace and well-being*) would obscure the effect of forwarding two separate if related issues for the Cuban government to consider.

Modifying with Phrases

Adlai E. Stevenson, twice the Democratic presidential candidate in the 1950s, made the following concessions in a speech to an American Legion Convention during his 1952 campaign:

Many of the threats to our cherished freedoms in these anxious, troubled times arise, it seems to me, from a healthy apprehension about the Communist menace within our country. Communism is abhorrent. It is strangulation of the individual; it is death for the soul. (Safire 1997, 72)

The predication of the first sentence hardly conveys its meaning: *it seems to me [that] many...arise.* Instead, the modifiers carry the key words: *threats, cherished freedoms, anxious, troubled times* in three prepositional phrases attached (with embedding) to the subject *many,* and *healthy apprehension, Communist menace, our country* in three prepositional phrases attached to the verb *arise.* The second sentence, however, providing a dramatic spoken contrast with the first, contains only basic sentence constituents minus any modification: subject (*communism*), linking verb (*is*), predicate adjective (*abhorrent*). In the final sentence, composed of two independent clauses, the key sentence elements and the modifiers share responsibility as the potent predicate nouns carry heavy identifiers: *strangulation/of the individual, death/for the soul.* Thus, this one short passage displays the alternative options of using the basic predication versus the modification to carry the salient content.

Phrases, like the prepositional phrases favored in Stevenson's first sentence, do the heavy lifting of modification. A phrase (the term preferred here) lacks the subject and verb pair of the clause, but it is inserted or removed as a unit.[8] The easiest way to sort through the available types of phrasal modifiers in English is to distinguish those built on verbs (participial and infinitive phrases) from those built on nouns (appositives, absolute phrases, resumptive and summative modifiers). Phrases built on prepositions belong in a class by themselves.

PHRASES BUILT ON VERBS

Participial Phrases

Suppose a speaker or writer wants to report two actions by the same agent. These two actions could become double verbs attached to the same subject: (1) *John waves a flag and blows a whistle.* But one of these actions could be expressed in a phrase modifying the agent John: (2) *Waving a flag, John blows a whistle* or (3) *Blowing a whistle, John waves a flag.* The differences among these three alternatives are significant. In the first, the two equated actions could be performed consecutively. In the second and third, they are performed simultaneously, but one action becomes the background condition for the other expressed in the main verb. Furthermore, the verb demoted to a participle has become an attribute of the noun, in this case the subject *John.* Choosing to express an action as a participle rather than a verb changes the relation of that action to an agent.

Participles are formed in English either by adding *–ing* to a verb (e.g., *checking, holding,* traditionally the **present participle**)[9] or by adding *–ed* or using the appropriate form of an irregular verb (e.g., *checked, held*, traditionally the **past participle**). Participles can involve auxiliary verbs changing tense and aspect (*being loving; having considered*) or take passive forms (*having been informed*). Also, since participles are formed from verbs, they retain some of the verb's properties; they can, for example, be modified by adverbs (*checking quickly*) or take an object (*checking the schedule*). Add modifiers or objects or more, and the single-word participle becomes **a participial phrase**: *throwing the dog a bone, considering him a success, given another chance*. (Only present participles can take indirect objects or object/complement structures.) Functioning as adjectives, participial phrases usually occur next to the noun they modify (*Wilted by the heat, the lettuce had to be thrown away; The lettuce, wilted by the heat, had to be thrown away*). But participial phrases can sometimes "lose touch" with the noun they modify, causing minor to serious confusion: *Wilted by the heat, the cook threw the lettuce away.*[10]

Participles can contribute significantly to the verbal quality of a passage by increasing the actions referred to. Hence, measuring how "verbal" a style is on the basis of the ratio of tensed verbs to the total number of words can be misleading. Consider the following passage from the opening paragraph of Isaac Newton's 1672 article on the decomposition of white light into colors. Newton is explaining how he first generated a spectrum (his coinage) of colors with a prism:

> And in order thereto *having darkened* my chamber, and *[having] made* a small hole in the window-shuts, to let in a convenient quantity of the Suns [sic] light, I placed my Prisme at his entrance, that it might be thereby refracted to the opposite wall. (Newton 1672, 3076; italics added)

The independent clause in this passage has only one tensed verb, *placed*, in the tight predication *I placed my Prisme*. But the main clause also contains two participial phrases modifying *I* and describing two actions that preceded placing the prism: darkening the room and making a hole in the shutters to admit a stream of sunlight. As verb forms, these participles describe accomplished and still relevant actions (hence the use of *having*), but as adjectives the actions described also become attributes ("accidents" in dialectical terms) of the agent performing the main action. Newton carries these accomplishments into the main predication. As far as the narrative of events is concerned, since these participial phrases come before the main verb, they are in correct order for the sequence of actions Newton performed: he darkened his chamber, made a hole in his shutters, and placed his prism next to the hole. He could have used three tensed verbs in a series of short clauses; he chose instead two participles and one main verb, and the action this verb expresses then becomes the most important. But the net result is not quite a single action. The main clause is therefore somewhat more action-packed than it might seem when a census of verbs reveals just one.

Infinitive Phrases

Another phrase built on a verb is the infinitive phrase (or *to*-infinitival). By itself, the infinitive is an easily recognized structure in English because it always contains *to* followed by the plain form of a verb: *to sing, to impress, to sit down* (phrasal verb). Infinitives also come in perfect (*to have won*), progressive (*to be sailing*), and passive forms (*to be improved*). Given its verbal nature, the infinitive can be modified with adverbs: *to sing sweetly*; *to sing in the shower*.[11] And if the verb in the infinitive is transitive, it can take an object or complement: *to sing a song; to be sending him a letter; to have labeled the fruit organic*. The resulting infinitive phrases are versatile. They can fill any sentence role: *To send a letter* [subject] *requires a stamp*; *Our goal is to win the race* [predicate complement]. Infinitives are often a part of the main verb phrase in a sentence (*She wants to sing light opera*) rather than a modifier of the verb (*She sings light opera to please her grandmother*; the adverbial usage of infinitives can take the insertion of *in order to*). In any of these various roles, heavily used in contemporary English, infinitives pack action into the sentence, just as participles do.

When infinitives are used as modifiers, the usage of interest here, they can function as adjectives: "I announced a decision *to withdraw an additional 150,000 Americans from Vietnam over the next year*" (Nixon; Windt 1983, 137). But they are frequently used as adverbs: "We will harness the sun and the wind and the soil *to fuel our cars and run our factories*" (Obama 2009). In their adverbial roles, infinitives offer rhetors a place to add crucial interpretive details about purposes, motives, and goals.

Again, Newton's scientific prose offers an example of how infinitives, in this case adverbial, add action while modifying. Here is the very first sentence of the same 1672 article on light and color, which took the form of a letter addressed to the Secretary of the Royal Society, Henry Oldenburg.

> Sir, *To perform my late promise to you*, I shall without further ceremony acquaint you, that in the beginning of the Year 1666 (at which time I applied myself to the grinding of Optick glasses of other figures than *Spherical*,) I procured me a Triangular glass-Prisme, *to try therewith the celebrated Phænomena of Colours*. (Newton, 1672, 3075; phrasal italics added)

Newton's sentence brims with activity in the main and dependent clauses (*I shall acquaint, I applied myself, I procured,* and even the gerund, *grinding*). It also opens and closes symmetrically with two infinitive phrases supplying crucial details about the intentions behind his actions. He *shall acquaint* Oldenburg in order *to perform* a promise; he acquired a prism in order *to try* producing colors with it. In this manner, the adverbial infinitive can direct the interpretation of other actions in a sentence.

PHRASES BUILT ON NOUNS

While nouns are easily modified by single words and by phrases built on verbs, they can also be modified by phrases built on a second noun with a clear relationship to the first. The distinct relationship of this new noun to the noun modified becomes the key for sorting through these phrase types and for beginning to appreciate their special rhetorical effects.

> **Appositive:** built on a noun renaming the noun it modifies[12]
> *Botswana, a landlocked African nation*
> **Absolute construction:** built on a noun related to the noun it modifies as a part or feature
> *The driver, his hair invisible under his cap,*
> **Resumptive Modifier:** built by repeating the noun it modifies
> *The letter from the president, a letter without precedent*
> **Summative Modifier:** Built on a noun summarizing or generalizing a preceding clause or phrase
> *The committee voted ten to one, a departure from its usual practices.*

Each of these constructions offers the rhetor special advantages, but one thing they all have in common is that they are more characteristic of written or formal styles than of spoken or informal styles. The fact that these constructions can be found in so many political speeches is merely further evidence of the preparation behind these speeches.

Appositives

An appositive allows rhetors to clarify a noun by inserting another noun, or noun plus modifiers, immediately after it: *William James, a pilot, strongly supports firearms in the cockpit.* The new noun, in turn, can carry any of the modification that a noun usually carries: *William James, a pilot with ten years' experience who flies an international route, supports firearms in the cockpit.* The appositive can rename any noun in a sentence, not just the subject (*She came in her new car, a 1957 Cadillac*). But it has to occur immediately after the noun it renames (or the noun plus its identifying modifiers): *the last citizen to vote, a man with orange hair.* When the modified noun occurs at the end of a sentence, the appositive can function as a dramatic revelation: *He left the meeting without one thing, his conscience.*

In its restricted position, the appositive provides an identifying title, label, or category, allowing the rhetor to control the interpretation of a term. Consider the following alternatives: *Bernard Ebbers, former CEO of Enron; Bernard Ebbers, codefendant in the Enron indictment.* Each choice is factual and verifiable, but each would have a different effect in a developing argument. The appositive also allows a rhetor to retain two characterizations of a subject, but to give one greater prominence (*The chimpanzee, our closest genetic relative; Our closest genetic relative, the chimpanzee*). Furthermore, the "quickness" of the appositive, as well as its typical position immediately after a noun yet subordinated to the main sentence elements, make it something of a "stealth" modifier, inserting an interpretive term almost before the reader/listener is aware of what has happened.

Absolute Phrases

The absolute phrase begins with a noun linked in meaning to another noun in a sentence, usually the subject. This second noun is then further modified in some way, usually by a participial phrase so that the entire construction seems to be a "reduced" clause. The absolute phrase, unlike the appositive, can be placed before or after or even detached from the noun it modifies, as these examples show:

> *Their shouts and laughter filling the hallways*, the fourth graders left
>   school early.
> The swaying, chanting protestors, *the sound of their own voices urging them on*,
>   charged the police.
> John stood at attention, *his arm fixed in a salute*.

Forming these constructions depends on selecting a leading term that can be related to another noun as either a part of it (John as a person plausibly has an arm), or as a manifestation or result of it (fourth graders are a plausible source of shouts and laughter), or as an attribute of it (protestors can be thought of as agents who can make and hear sounds and are capable of being influenced).

What are the special "affordances" of the absolute phrase? It provides ample space for selecting and elaborating on some feature of another noun, and it focuses readers on that feature. This construction also holds its material in a suspended state, coordinated in time or place with a referent in the main clause. And it obviously contributes to the intonational pattern of a sentence. But absolute phrases are more typical of written than spoken language, and they were more common in previous centuries among prose stylists who had been trained in Latin. In contemporary prose, they can seem overly formal, poetic, or even archaic.

Resumptive Modifiers

English allows modifying phrases built on repeated nouns. Resumptive modifiers are actually quite common in political oratory because they facilitate emphasis in the speech stream by allowing the rhetor to return to a key term. Here is the structure from a speech given by Robert Kennedy in South Africa:

For a decade, NUSAS [National Union of South African Students] has stood and worked for the *principles* of the Universal Declaration of Human Rights—*principles* which embody the collective hopes of men of good will around the world. (1966)

The repeated noun, or noun phrase, that anchors such resumptive constructions is rarely the subject. Instead, this structure usually revisits or "rescues" words trapped in unemphatic positions earlier in a sentence. Kennedy, in the above example, retrieved *principles* from a "trough" in a prepositional phrase in the middle of his sentence. He could then both emphasize and modify it.

Summative Modifiers

Instead of repeating a word or selecting a noun with a clear relation to another noun, a writer using a **summative modifier** selects a term that can pick up or sum up the content of all or part of the preceding sentence. Modification is then attached to this newly introduced noun.

> *Congress passed several acts to extend tax relief between 2000 and 2004, a response to the lobbying efforts of tax relief groups.*

This structure has something in common with the absolute phrase, but the summarizing term that heads this phrase is usually more general or abstract than the noun opening the absolute phrase. It also has something in common with the appositive, the structure that renames, but it does not have to be located immediately after the modified noun phrase.

Resumptive and summative phrases, like appositives and absolute constructions, allow an arguer great selective and interpretive power. The resumptive modifier reaches into a string of terms and pulls out one for the emphasis of repetition. The summative modifier imposes an interpretive category for another portion of the sentence, usually the main predication. Meanwhile, the subordinate status of all these noun-dependent structures backgrounds their content. They are less open to challenge, especially if they are not placed in the emphasized ending of a sentence.

Prepositional Phrases

Prepositions are a large class of relational words, most of Old English origin. They appear in phrasal verbs (*set out, set off, set on*), but they occur most often with their own objects: *by the author, in the library, at noon, with the hammer, throughout the world, because of the heat* (two-word preposition), *in spite of the cold* (three-word preposition). Prepositional phrases can do whatever a single-word adjective or adverb can do, modifying any noun, verb, modifier, or larger unit in a clause:

Modifying the subject: The carrots on the table have been cooked.
Modifying the verb: John ran in a circle.
Modifying an adjective: Maria was angry with herself.

Prepositional phrases usually follow immediately after the term they modify, but they can sometimes be placed before it: *Of the three players, one has the winning hand* versus *One of the three players has the winning hand.* A prepositional phrase can also appear before a noun (as a premodifier) if it is hyphenated and in effect turned into a single word: *that under-the-weather feeling; an in-the-loop official.* Prepositional phrases that function as adverbs can move around: *In the spring, she took seven courses* versus *She took seven courses in the spring.*

The relational meanings expressed by prepositions are legion. Working as adverbs, they can provide very precise information about the where of an action (*Casper placed the peg in the hole on the left side of the table under the window in the back room*), or the when (*for the first time, at three o'clock on the afternoon of September 8th*). But many more relations can be expressed, including circumstances, orientation to the speaker, cause, and possession. Prepositions also appear in many idioms, prepared phrases, and figurative constructions. They constitute one of the peskiest parts of English for nonnative speakers, and they even trouble native speakers who attempt new registers.

Single-Word Modifiers

The smallest unit of modification is the single adjective or adverb. As the minimum in modification for clarification, English sentences require most singular nouns to be accompanied by the **determiners,** or **definite articles,** *the* or *a/an.* These particles, traditionally classified as adjectives, perform the crucial function of specifying the status of an object in relation to a rhetorical situation. Consider the difference between *A dog can't go in a restaurant* and *The dog can't go in the restaurant.* The first states a general principle; the second belongs in a specific situation. English allows substitutions for definite articles with **demonstrative adjectives** (*this, that, such*), **quantifiers** (*some, any, all, every, each*) and **possessives** (*my, his, her, our, their*). But altogether, English has a small, ancient, unchanging set of these specifying modifiers. Rhetors can sometimes avoid them by using plurals (*Dogs can't go in restaurants*), but most often they are crucial in building up the world referred to.

While the determiners, demonstratives, quantifiers, and possessives are closed sets, English adjectives and adverbs are large, open classes. Single-word adjectives can modify any noun in a sentence, and single-word adverbs can modify any verb, adjective, or other adverb: *The* **old** *woman* **very quickly** *gave the* **light brown** *dog a* **ham** *bone.* Single-word adjectives typically come immediately before the noun they modify, and single-word adverbs that modify adjectives or other adverbs are also stuck in front: *awfully sincere, excessively angry, very intensely heated.* However, adverbs that modify verbs or whole clauses can move around: *The woman* **quickly** *gave the dog a* bone; **Quickly** *the woman gave the dog a bone; The woman gave the dog a bone* **quickly**.

Single-word adjectives tend to be used to name the essential properties or qualities of the nouns they modify. A *yellow fruit* has the color *yellow* as a distinguishing feature. The prenoun adjective can, in fact, be so fundamental to the identity of a noun that it becomes part of its name: *courthouse, golf club, cell phone* (see above "Compounds," p. 44). The importance of the single adjective shows up when a second is added and constraints in word order have to observed. The more essential/defining the detail, the closer the adjective to the noun. Consider the noun *chef* modified by the adjectives *pastry, Lithuanian,* and *angry.* Native speakers, unwittingly dialecticians, will produce the "natural" order *angry Lithuanian pastry chef,* inevitably placing critical "property" terms closest to the noun and less fixed "accidents" further away.

Single-word adverbs can provide critical information about an action. Critics often complain that adverbs are used when speakers or writers fail to select verbs that convey both the action and the manner of its performance: *John called loudly* versus *John shouted.* But verb + adverb pairings can be defended, and of course the number of single-word adverbs can be multiplied to suggest nuances beyond any single verb's power: *John called loudly, insistently, frantically.*

The single-word adjective and adverb modification available in English includes well-marked comparative and superlative degrees, as in adjective or adverb series like *high, higher, highest* or *often, more often, most often.* The scales these choices express have powerful argumentative potential. A well-placed "degree" adjective or adverb can condense a comparison argument or place an item in an implicit value hierarchy. The language of encomium, for example, often relies on modifiers in the superlative degree, as when Lyndon Johnson praised his assassinated predecessor before a Joint Session of Congress: "The *greatest* leader of our time has been struck down by the *foulest* deed of our time" (Windt 1983, 53; italics added).

AN EPITHETICAL STYLE

Rhetorical style manuals discuss what is in effect the single-word modifier under the figure *epitheton*.[13] In introducing this device, Quintilian noted that poets frequently use expressions like "white teeth" or "liquid wine," but he expected a different standard in oratory, where "an epithet is redundant unless it has some point. Now it will only have point when it adds something to the meaning, as for instance in the following: 'O abominable crime!' 'O hideous lust!'" (1921, III 325). Quintilian went on to give advice about single-word modifiers that has been repeated for centuries: "But the nature of this form of embellishment is such that, while style is bare and inelegant without any epithets at all, it is overloaded when a large number are employed. For then it becomes long-winded and cumbrous, in fact you might compare it to an army with as many camp-followers as soldiers, an army, this is to say, which has doubled its numbers without doubling its strength" (325).

Speakers and writers sometimes ignore this advice and hang a single-word modifier on virtually every noun and an adverb on every verb. The result has been called an *epithetical* style. This pattern of heightened yet predictable descriptive language is typical in genres like the travel ad.

> The perfect eight-day Hawaiian getaway. Journey to Oahu and Maui, two of the most beautiful islands on this all-inclusive, first-class Hawaiian package. Pristine white beaches, crystal waters and friendly people await you...[14]

Multiplying and Embedding Modifiers

The modifying structures available in English—clauses, phrases, and single words—can build up sentences in two ways. First, they can be multiplied. Instead of one prenoun adjective or one participial phrase or relative clause attached to a noun, the writer can add two or three or occasionally even more. These sequences of parallel modifying structures are not uncommon in political oratory.

> ...the torch has been passed to a new generation
> of Americans
>> ↖ born in this century
>> ↖ tempered by war
>> ↖ disciplined by a hard and bitter peace
>> ↖ proud of our ancient heritage
> (Kennedy, Windt 1983, 9)

But modifying structures can also be embedded so that one refers to another. Adjective clauses, for example, can easily nest in each other:

> They [lobbying firms led by former employees of Tom Ridge] are a small part of a booming new lobbying business in Washington that is focused on helping large corporations get a share of the billions of dollars that will be spent by the vast domestic security bureaucracy that Mr. Ridge oversees. (Shenon 2003)

The levels of modification in this sentence can be displayed as follows:

…of a booming new lobbying *business* in Washington

         ↖ that is focused on helping large corporations get a share of the billions of *dollars*

                  ↖ that will be spent by the vast domestic security *bureaucracy*

                        ↖ that Mr. Ridge oversees.

The successive strata here aptly express how lobbying firms might act indirectly, through layers, on the homeland security secretary at the time, Tom Ridge.

Infinitive phrases are also easily multiplied or subordinated to express how one action is performed for the sake of another, as in this line from Eisenhower's "Atoms for Peace" speech:

Clearly it would not be fitting for me

         ↖ to take this *occasion*

                ↖ to present to you a unilateral American report on Bermuda

The two principles of multiplying or embedding modifiers can easily be mixed in the same sentence, as in this visionary encomium from Jefferson's first inaugural address (Safire 1997, 801):

A rising *nation*

    ↖ spread

       ↖ over a wide and fruitful land

    ↖ traversing all the seas [object of the participle]

       ↖ with the rich productions

           ↖ of their industry

    ↖ engaged

       ↖ in commerce

          ↖ with nations

              ↖ who feel power and forget right,

   ↖ advancing rapidly

      ↖ to destinies

         ↖ beyond the reach

              ↖ of mortal eye

Jefferson's sentence attaches four participles, two present and two past in alternating sequence, directly to the *nation* (which is also modified by the prenoun participle *rising*). Each of the four participial phrases has a different amount of internal embedded modification, but each starts off the first level of subordination with a prepositional phrase that gives some added structure.

Amount of Modification

As the section above demonstrates, the type and placement of modifiers can be critical to the meaning and effectiveness of an individual sentence. Other stylistic effects are achieved by cumulative patterns across many sentences or passages. In general, how much modification a passage displays is a revealing indicator of its message and intended impact. Passages, and hence "styles," can be roughly graded by how heavily modified they are.

MINIMAL MODIFICATION

A spare style is one with little modification relative to the basic sentence elements (subjects, verbs, objects or complements). The simplest style of all is found, predictably, in children's primers. The very first sentence children learned in their first McGuffey's Reader was *The dog ran*, followed in the next few lessons with, among others, *The cat is on the mat*, *A man has a pen*, and *Ann can catch Rab*. (Rab is a dog, to be replaced by the immortal *Spot* in the Dick and Jane readers of the 1930s.) The spare style of the primer is not all that far from the preferred style of modernist writers like Hemingway and his many journalist followers. The following excerpt in the modernist manner comes from Bill Buford's firsthand account of British soccer fans rampaging after a match in Italy.

> Directly in front of me—so close I could almost reach out to touch his face—a young **Italian**, a boy really, **had been knocked down**. As he was getting up, an English **supporter pushed the boy** down again, ramming his flat hand against the boy's face. **He fell back** and **his head hit the pavement**, the back of it bouncing slightly.
>
> Two other Manchester United **supporters appeared. One kicked the boy** in the ribs. **It was** a soft **sound**, which surprised me. **You could hear the impact** of the shoe on the fabric of the boy's clothing. **He was kicked** again—this time very hard—and **the sound was still, soft, muted.** The **boy reached down** to protect himself, to guard his ribs, and the other English **supporter then kicked him** in the face. **This was** a soft **sound** as well, but **it was different: you could tell** that it was his face that had been kicked and not his body and not something protected by clothing. **It sounded gritty. The boy tried to get up** and **he was pushed back** down—sloppily, without much force. Another Manchester United **supporter appeared and another and then a third. There were** now **six**, and **they all started kicking the boy** on the ground. **The boy covered his face. I was surprised** that I could tell, from the sound, when someone's shoe missed or when it struck the fingers and not the forehead or the nose. (Kerane and Yagoda 1997, 360–61)

The subjects, verbs, and objects or predicate adjectives or nouns in the independent clauses in this passage are printed in bold to indicate how much of the wording is taken up by these basic sentence constituents. With sickening emphasis, the main clauses relate the violence as the "supporters" repeatedly kick the Italian boy's body and face. Of course action also dominates in the modifying structures, dependent clauses, participial phrases, and even in one absolute construction: *as he was getting up; ramming his flat hand against the boy's face; the back of it bouncing slightly; to guard his ribs; when someone's shoe missed or when it struck the fingers.* Hence the overall style here is predictably highly verbal rather than nominal. Furthermore, the emphasis on sound is an unusual feature of this passage, and its persuasive effect is to heighten the first person accuracy of the narrator as an observer or "experiencer" but not as a participant (and unfortunately not as an intervener) in the attack.

HEAVILY MODIFIED STYLES

The following item appeared on the menu in first class on a trans-Atlantic flight.

Freshly brewed Timothy's Custom Roasted Italian Blend Gourmet Coffee

A string of eight words modifies the single item "coffee." Technically, some of the words in this string modify other words in it; *freshly* modifies *brewed*, *custom* modifies *roasted*, and *Italian* modifies *blend*. But it is the weight and magnificence of all these prenoun modifiers together that establishes the first-class nature of this menu item. In general, on menus, the more adjectives, the more expensive.

Some writers habitually set the modification dial on "high." A heavily modified style is one with a higher number of modifiers in proportion to the main clause elements, as in the eight-to-one modifier to noun ratio for Timothy's coffee. In what genres and for what purposes will a heavily modified style be used? Though there are endless variations depending on the rhetorical situation of a text, in general, heavy modification serves description, and description, in turn, serves various purposes, from straightforward characterization to and including evaluation, and its extremes of praising or condemning.

The following passage comes from a book on baseball by A. Bartlett Giamatti, one-time commissioner of baseball. (Compare this passage visually with the one quoted from Buford above.) In a section excerpted in *Newsweek*, Giamatti wrote a hymn of praise to baseball, a sport he called a "vast, communal poem." To support his encomium, he described the following scene during playoffs in St. Louis. The main sentence elements below are bolded. All the rest is modification.

(1) **The Marriott Pavilion Hotel** in St. Louis **is hard by** the ballpark. (2) **It consists of a pair** of towers linked by a vast lobby and corridors and a ramp, the cavernous space interspersed with plants and some chairs and columns. (3) During the National League Championship Series between St. Louis and San Francisco in 1987, the **lobby was ablaze**—with Cardinal crimson on hats, jackets, sweaters, scarves, ties. (4) Here and there **one glimpsed the orange-and-black** of the House

of Lurie, as a Giant rooter, like some lonely fish, wove its way across a scarlet coral reef. (5) But **such creatures were rare.**

(6) By mid-morning the **lobby is crowded** and **will remain crowded**, except during the game, until about 2 a.m., then to fill up by nine and wait the long day until the game time. (7) **There are** the smiling middle-aged **couples**, festooned in buttons and insignia, this day yet another convention day in a lifetime of conventioneering; the **groups** of teenage boys, in the plumage of scarlet windbreakers, like young birds craning their necks for the nourishment of a glimpse. (8) By a plant or a coffee shop, always **alone**, white hair crisply permed, in electric blue or purple pants suit, holding an autograph book, **is a** grandmotherly **woman**, smiling distractedly, waiting for a hero. (9) **There are** always some single **men** in their forties, in nondescript clothes, hair slightly awry, eyes burning with fatigue and anticipation; **they are** the religiously **obsessed**, drawn by a vision in their heads that will not give them peace. (10) **They stand apart and wait** for hours in this place. (11) Very **different are the middle-aged teenagers**, men in groups, all mid-forties, who shout and drink the day away, some with young women in black leather pants and scarlet T-shirts, their laughter and their manner frenzied. (12) At the back of the lobby, down on a lower level, around a low table, **sit** this morning the **Giants' manager and coaches.** (13) **They are like chiefs** at a gathering of the clan, planning strategy, ignoring the celebrants while absorbing their energy. (1989, 87).

Giamatti vividly catalogs the variety of people, from different age groups and genders, who throng a hotel near the stadium. This variety supports his argument for baseball's wide appeal. It is also his goal to present an image of the scene so that the reader seems to be there, picking up the color, excitement, and devotion, the qualities that support his encomium. Hence the heavy modification delivers detail, most of it concerning the appearance of the fans, some concerning their behavior. The long opening constructions physically place the fans and readers in the hotel panorama. To deliver this excess of description, Giamatti uses prepositional phrases, appositives, participial phrases, adjective clauses, and even an absolute construction—but no adverb clauses that would link his statements to each other as reasons, exceptions, or the like. His argument is indirect.

Analyzing Modification

Patterns in predication and modification can lead to contrasts between passages and writers, as in the rough characterizations of the Buford and Giamatti excerpts above, based on the relative proportion of modification. It is also possible to focus on a single sentence or on a stretch of several to see how the modifiers are working. And finally, in a longer passage, it is possible not merely to note proportions, but to examine what kind of content is distributed into the main sentence elements and what kind into modifying structures, and how any patterns that emerge may serve the argument.

THE UBIQUITOUS SADDAM

Assessing the style of a single sentence to determine how it serves its purpose has to begin with simply identifying its parts, separating the predication from the modification. The following sentence comes from an Associated Press news story on the *Washington Post* website in July 2003:

> Tikrit, Iraq—Attackers gunned down the head of Saddam Hussein's tribe, who recently disavowed the ousted dictator, while he rode in a car in Saddam's hometown of Tikrit, the regional governor said Tuesday.[15]

News leads like this one are highly formulaic. Their purpose is to communicate the essential details of a story (who, what, when, where, why, how) immediately, and, where relevant, the source of the story. Like many such sentences, this one, technically, is backwards. Its true subject is *the regional governor,* its verb is *said,* and the object of this verb is everything that he said, namely the front part of the sentence.

> The regional governor said [that] attackers gunned down the head of Saddam Hussein's tribe […]

The noun clause functioning as the object does, however, contain the important gist of the sentence and the essential details. Its subject is *Attackers,* its verb is *gunned down* (a phrasal verb), and its object is *head.* These elements are essential information; all the rest is modification. The subject is not modified for the simple reason that nothing is known about the perpetrators of the crime; they have in fact been named from the deed. The verb itself also remains unmodified; it is sufficiently strong and colloquial, carrying connotations, no doubt deliberate, of gangland slayings. The object *head,* however, has two modifiers.

> head *of Saddam Hussein's tribe,*
> *who recently disavowed the ousted dictator,*

The prepositional phrase gives the key identifying feature of the victim, the reason this item is considered newsworthy in the first place. The relative adjective clause, *who recently disavowed the ousted dictator,* is punctuated as a nonrestrictive modifier, as dispensable information, but it earns its way into the lead sentence because it suggests, obliquely, a possible answer to the "why" question for the tribal chief's murder at the hands of Saddam loyalists. The final construction is an adverbial subordinate clause modifying the entire kernel clause; it provides the circumstances and location of the event.

> [Attackers gunned down the head]
> *while he rode in a car in Saddam's hometown of Tikrit*

The "where" is conveyed in prepositional phrases within this subordinate clause. All three modifying devices occur after the main elements conveying the agent, action, and recipient. This placement turns them into clarifying detail in a right-branching construction.

In these three modifying structures—prepositional phrase, adjective clause, and adverb clause—the writer has skillfully managed to invoke the presence of Saddam Hussein three times by using well-placed epithets/adjectives, while also choosing the type of structure appropriate to the type of information. The dead man was the leader of *Saddam's* tribe, he was killed in *Saddam's* hometown, and he had recently disavowed the *ousted dictator* (a synonym for Hussein). The repetition of this name inserts this individual event into the large-scale events of the time, the U.S. presence in Iraq after deposing Saddam but, in July 2003, before his capture. In this way, the modification, while factual, "argues for" a particular interpretation of the event reported in terms that would be salient with a U.S. audience. Imagine the difference if it were somehow known that this "tribal head" had been killed for personal motives by a local rival.

"TO THE PEOPLE OF IRELAND"

During the 1916 Easter Rising in Ireland, seven members of the self-proclaimed Provisional Government issued a Proclamation "To the People of Ireland" that opens with the following two paragraphs:

> Irishmen and Irishwomen: In the name of God and of the dead generations from which she receives her old tradition of nationhood, Ireland, through us, summons her children to her flag and strikes for her freedom.
>
> Having organized and trained her manhood through her secret revolutionary organization, the Irish Republican Brotherhood, and through her military organizations, the Irish Volunteers and the Irish Citizen Army, having patiently perfected her discipline, having resolutely waited for the right moment to reveal itself, she now seizes that moment, and supported by her exiled children in America and by gallant allies in Europe, but relying in the first on her own strength, she strikes in full confidence of victory.[16]

Throughout this amazing document, the proportion of modification to predication is lopsided in favor of modification. The single sentence in the second paragraph is a striking example of this imbalance. This sentence opens with a disproportionately large structure which is formed from three parallel participial phrases:

> *having organized and trained her manhood*
> *having patiently perfected her discipline*
> *having resolutely waited*

Furthermore, the first of these participial phrases is disproportionately long in contrast to the other two because it in turn contains two parallel prepositional phrases (*through her secret revolutionary organization; through her military organizations*), and the first of these contains one appositive, the second two. The net effect of this complex, interrupted, and left-heavy initial construction is to hold the reader in suspension for some impending action and hence to place great emphasis on that action when it finally appears in the main predication: *she now seizes.* The placement and amount of this modification is of course not incidental to the meaning. The point of the sentence is that there had been great preparation, perfected patience, and waiting on the part of the rebels before the action announced was taken. The disproportion between this long waiting, the suspended and continued preparation expressed in participles, and the short active verb combined with the personified agent of the country (*she seizes*) is precisely the point of the sentence. If there is one imperfection in the form, it is that the second of the three participial phrases is shorter than the third. It would have been better for the sake of symmetry or end weight if the phrases had each decreased in length so that the shortest occurred just before the reported action. It might also make sense in terms of meaning if the *waiting* preceded the *perfecting of patience.* But the phrasing is as it is.

Summary

When Joe DiMaggio died, the *New York Times* published a front-page obituary that featured the following first sentence:

> Hollywood, Fla, March 8—Joe DiMaggio, the flawless center fielder for the New York Yankees who, along with Babe Ruth and Mickey Mantle, symbolized the team's dynastic success across the 20th century and whose 56-game hitting streak in 1941 made him an instant and indelible American folk hero, died early today at his home here. He was 84 years old. (Durso 1999)

The appositive renames DiMaggio in his defining activity, as a *center fielder*, with the critical qualifiers *flawless* and *for the New York Yankees.* The two relative clauses put his attributes into action: he symbolized his team, and his hitting streak made him a hero. Added to these structures, the two prepositional phrases, *with Babe Ruth and Mickey Mantle* and *across the 20th century*, place DiMaggio with peers as a standard of comparison, scaling his fame in time. All these subject modifiers, placed in a mid-branching construction, postpone the announcement of DiMaggio's death and carry the evaluation argument, the reasons for marking his passing. They deliver details selected from what rhetorical manuals called the topics for persons: the place, age, manner of life, condition of body and mind, family, friends, habits, deeds, and reputation (Cicero 1976, 191–93).

The constructions available for adding modification in English range from the clause to the phrase to the single word. They are sites for amplifying and supporting detail, and each offers persuasive advantages. The single adjective or adverb can appear indissociable from the term it modifies, forestalling refutation. The appositive offers an apparently equivalent, fungible term, and other noun-based modifiers (absolute, resumptive, and summative) propel a feature into attention. The verbal modifiers, participles and infinitives, can turn actions into attributes, less open to questioning. Relative clauses expand details with full predications, and subordinate clauses open with conjunctions that determine the meaning relations between statements, elevating one above the other. Since rhetors can shape the same material into different structures, identifying what structures were chosen at what points, or which tend to be preferred, can offers insights into the rhetorical style of a text.

NOTES

1. The two Associated Press postings appeared on the *Washington Post* and *New York Times* websites respectively: http://www.washingtonpost.com/wp-dyn/articles/A56075-2003Juli .html?nav+hptop_ts. and http://www.nytimes.com/aponline/international/AP-Iraq.html?page wanted=print&position=. Neither is still available. Still another version, which corrects the details but keeps the separate independent clauses, is posted on another site: "Rocket-propelled grenades slammed into U.S. military vehicles in two attacks in and around Baghdad on Tuesday, and an explosion at a mosque in the town of Fallujah killed 10 Iraqis and injured four others." Jim Krane, "New Violence Wracks Iraq: Explosion at Mosque Kills 10 Iraqis" (July 1, 2003, Associated Press) http://www.commondreams.org/headlines03/0701-01.htm.

2. In written texts in English, a sentence can be defined as whatever begins with a capital letter and ends with some concluding punctuation (period, question mark, exclamation mark). The "sentence" of spoken discourse is much more difficult to define. It can be approximated by a prosodic description. Whatever ends with falling intonation is typically a statement, and whatever ends with rising intonation is typically a question.

3. Distinguishing between *sentence* and *clause* here follows standard practice in rhetorical stylistics, beginning in the third book of the *Rhetoric*, where Aristotle described the **period**, akin to our sentence, as a compositional unit made up from **cola**, akin to our clauses (Kennedy 1991, 240–41).Grammarians certainly have many other ways of describing sentences. One system, for example, defines a *nucleus*, essentially the verb, accompanied by various participants such as the causative agent, immediate agent, experiencer, benefactee, content, and place. See Nida et al. 1983.

4. http://www.americanrhetoric.com/speeches/malcolmxballot.htm; accessed 3/20/2005. The American Rhetoric site has since replaced the April 3 version of Malcolm X's "The Ballot or the Bullet" speech with one delivered on April 12 in Detroit. The later version lacks this conditional clause and several that appear just before it, but it uses others: *If they draft you, they send you to Korea and make you face 800 million Chinese* [consequence from a hypothetical circumstance]; *If you—If you go to jail, so what? If you black, you were born in jail. If you black, you were born in jail, in the North as well as the South* [consequence from a hypothetical circumstance—though not hypothetical for Malcolm X, who spent years in jail].

5. http://www.americanrhetoric.com/speeches/malcolmxballot.htm.

6. Some editors and style sheets want restrictive clauses to use *that* and nonrestrictive clauses to use *which*.

> The fish that are bottom feeders collect more toxins in their flesh.
> The fish, which are bottom feeders, collect more toxins in their flesh.

Observing a "that/which" distinction is the mark of a contemporary edited style. It was certainly not the rule in older prose which used *which* to introduce restrictive clauses (like this one).

In current usage, it is also common to dispense with the relative pronoun or the conjunction that marks the relative clause or noun clause.

> The dress *that she borrowed* was ruined. → The dress *she borrowed* was ruined.
> The employee *whom he hired* was an engineer. → The employee *he hired* was an engineer.

In these examples, *that* and *whom* are the direct objects in the relative clause: she borrowed *that (the dress)*; he hired *whom (the employee)*. Since the word the relative pronoun refers to occurs immediately before it, the pronoun can be dropped. If the relative pronoun is the subject of its clause, it cannot be deleted.

> The employee *who came late* was an engineer. ≠ The employee came late was an engineer.

In another common ellipsis, the *that* introducing a noun clause reporting what someone said is dropped without a loss of clarity.

> Leila said *that she is coming tomorrow* →
> Leila said *she is coming tomorrow*.

7. Noun clauses can fill any of the following grammatical slots.

> Subject: *Whether the ship survived the storm* is still uncertain.
> Direct object: No one doubted *that she was the winner*.
> Indirect object: He will give *whoever comes first* a special prize.
> Object of a preposition: He will give the tickets to *whichever contestant wins*.
> Object of an infinitive: He wants to know *how he can become famous*.
> Object of a participle: Calculating *what the car would cost*, George had regrets.
> Object of a gerund: Knowing *that your parents love you* gives children the courage to try new things.
> Complement (Predicate nominative): The prize will be *whatever you want to have from the store*.

8. The term *phrase* is not used here as it is used by many grammarians and discourse analysts who call participial and infinitive phrases *clauses with nonfinite verbs*, that is, verbs without tense. This text maintains a robust distinction between clauses, whether independent or dependent, which have both subjects and verbs with tense, and phrases, which do not have *both* these elements. Another source of confusion may occur for those familiar with transformational/generative grammar, where the term *phrase* refers to any group of noun + modifiers (noun phrase) or verb + modifiers/complements (verb phrase). In this text, the term *phrase* is used for detachable units of modification, corresponding to the sense of *phrase* in traditional grammar and of the *comma* in rhetorical discussions of style.

9. By morphology, there is no way to tell a present partciple, an *–ing* form of a verb, from a gerund, a noun created by adding *–ing* to a verb (see p. 46). Context usually clarifies the difference, but ambiguous sentences like the following can occur: *Racing cars can be dangerous*. The first two

words in this sentence can be read as a gerund, *racing*, plus its object, *cars*. In that case the sentence means that the activity of racing a car is dangerous—presumably to the drivers. But those first two words can also be read as a present participle modifying a noun; there is a certain type of car called a *racing car*. In that case, the sentence means that cars that are racing can be dangerous—presumably to bystanders. Usually the context solves this kind of ambiguity.

Confusion can also occur in sentences with linking verbs: *Hell is waiting in line*. Read one way, this sentence has *hell* as its subject and *is waiting* as its verb in the present progressive tense. It means that, hell is waiting—for you, for someone—in line with other things that are waiting. But read another way, *hell* remains the subject, but the verb is only the linking verb, *is*. The remainder of the sentence is a gerund functioning as a predicate noun, *waiting*, with a modifying prepositional phrase, *in line*.

10. A problem can occur when the participial phrase refers to an element that is not actually in the sentence: **Hoping for a good outcome**, *the meeting began in an atmosphere of expectation*. Hoping is something that humans do, and there is no human in this sentence. Good sense requires a construction like the following: **Hoping for a good outcome**, *the committee members began the meeting in an atmosphere of expectation*. The problem illustrated here is the error of the **dangling modifier**, so called because the modifying participial phrase has nothing to attach to in the sentence. Caveats: Some commentators argue that some apparently dangling modifiers should be looked at as adverbial modifiers of an entire clause, not as adjectival modifiers that have to refer to a single element, so they are not really errors. Besides, these constructions occur so frequently that their commonness "exonerates" them under the license of usage.

11. According to a frequently repeated rule, writers should not "split infinitives." A "split" infinitive has an adverb wedged between the *to* and the verb. *Star Trek* fans will recognize this "error" in the mission statement: "*To boldly go where no man has gone before.*" An editor would put the adverb after the verb: *to go boldly*.

Does this rule make sense? It is of course impossible to split an infinitive when it is one word, so perhaps this "rule" in English came from a mistaken borrowing from classical grammar. However illogical its origins, a preference does persist in some people's minds for always putting the adverb after the verb in an infinitive phrase. Observing this preference is usually the sign of a more formal text. In informal speaking and writing, splitting the infinitive is common.

12. Some grammarians and style commentators do not restrict the notion of apposition to nouns. They label any immediate rephrasing—whether of a noun, verb, adjective, or adverb—an appositive (Tufte 2006). In this text, appositives reprise nouns.

13. Several confusions plague this figure. Quintilian addressed the problem of distinguishing the *epitheton* from *antonomasia* or renaming. Quintilian clarifies that sometimes a modifier can indeed become a substitute name. His example is "he who sacked Numantia and Carthage." Quintilian observes that if the name Scipio is added to this phrase, the phrase becomes an epithet again. Because a modifying phrase could function as an antonomasia, there was a corresponding confusion as to whether it was also a trope. The translators of Quinitilian, Butler (1921, III, 325–27) and Russell (2001, III, 449–51), differ in their labeling.

14. http://www.alohadestinations.com/all-inclusive/.

15. http://www.washingtonpost.com/wp-dyn/A57432-2003Jul1.

16. http://www.iol.ie/~dluby/proclaim.htm.

Between the Chesapeake Capes and the elbow of
Cape Cod the place where the continent ends and
the true sea begins lies from fifty to one hundred
miles from the tide lines. It is not the distance from
the shore, but the depth, that marks the transition
to the true sea; for wherever the gently sloping sea
bottom feels the weight of a hundred fathoms of
water above it, suddenly it begins to fall away in
escarpments and steep palisades, descending
abruptly from twilight into darkness.
RACHEL CARSON, Under the Sea-Wind

9

SENTENCE ARCHITECTURE

TO RICHARD WEAVER, rhetoric was an "art of emphasis," an art of using language so that the words and ideas important to the speaker or writer stood out for the audience (1990, 1048). To Chaim Perelman and Lucie Olbrechts-Tyteca, rhetoric's goal was achieving "presence" for key notions and lines of reasoning while at the same time eliminating potentially distracting or detrimental elements (1969, 116–20). Emphasis and presence are twentieth-century terms for classical rhetoric's insistence on amplification. Successful rhetors fill the audience's attention, and hopefully their convictions, with the desired content, leaving no room for competing thoughts. Stylisticians, pursuing the same issue, call this process foregrounding. Notions of emphasis, presence, and foregrounding apply at the phrase, sentence, and passage levels. The rhetorical stylist works with the options offered in the language for emphasizing some elements over others, for highlighting against a background. If the best possible result occurs, the overall form expresses the content *iconically*. But the beginning of form/content synergy involves emphasis. What are the options for emphasis at the sentence level? How does a speaker or writer bring attention to one word or phrase or clause over others?

Emphasis

The resources for emphasis in spoken language are dramatic. Many have to do with **gestures** of the face and body accompanying speech, the significant hand movement, the direction of gaze, the lowering of eyebrows. Classical rhetoric paid attention to these elements in discussions of delivery, a part of rhetoric that received new attention in the eighteenth century.

Other resources for emphasis occur in the speech stream itself. Every group of words spoken aloud will have a certain **prosody**, a sound contour or a certain music of utterance. Speakers naturally vary the **pitch** of the sounds they produce, making some higher or lower; they vary the **intensity**, making some louder or softer, and the **duration**, prolonging some sounds and hurrying over others. They can also vary **intonation** by, for example, putting glides or slides into vowels and pronouncing them in ways they are not normally uttered. They can **pause** before a significant point, and vary the length of that pause to suggest nuances of reluctance, doubt, anger, embarrassment, and so on. They can add sighs and groans, the catch in the voice, the audible break. In fact, the sound dimension of speech can communicate on its own, irrespective of content. Someone listening to a conversation through a closed door can still, without making out a single word, understand the emotions of the speakers involved. And leaving the word order of a sentence unaltered, a speaker can still achieve different effects by changing the pitch, intensity, or duration of one of the words (using the convention of capitalization to indicate the spoken difference of increased intensity and duration):

Put the ballot IN the box. (By implication, not on, under, next to, etc.)
Put the BALLOT in the box. (By implication, not the instructions, flyers, etc.)
Put the ballot in the BOX. (By implication not in the garbage, on the table, etc.)

A speaker, then, has multiple resources for producing meaningful emphasis. This aspect of spoken language has been described as an evolutionary inheritance, similar to the alarm call systems of other animals that emit bellows, cries, and shrieks to indicate danger. So it is not surprising that sound dynamics are associated with the emotional content of a message. The same sentence can be banal or hysterical, depending on how pitch, intensity, duration, and pauses are manipulated: *The hurricane is coming* versus THEHURRICANEISCOMING!!!

The unconventional use of capitalization, spacing, and exclamation marks in this example reveals the limitations of representing sound differences in print. Discourse analysts and others have developed systems for coding these differences on the page, and one of the most inventive methods comes from Dwight Bolinger, who uses up and down spacing of words to indicate the intonational contour of an utterance (1980, 13–14). In conventionally printed discourse, the writer has fewer options for conveying the emphasis so easily achieved in speech. But even written language, as Walter Ong pointed out (1982), has a residual oral dimension, while written texts also have visual affordances for achieving emphasis unavailable in speech.

Because of the difficulty of mimicking spoken effects in written or printed text, visual conventions have been developed to emphasize words that would be accented in speech. In print, highlighted words can appear in bold, italics, or capital letters, or in odd spacing, or in any combination of these. Extra pauses can be achieved with dashes or inserted spaces. Word processing has made the use of all of these "text image" variants much easier to achieve, and, borrowing from graphic designers, it has made an arsenal of visualizing techniques available for manipulating audience attention: chunking text, varying letter size, changing fonts, using color, adding background and interspersing emoticons, a new symbolic language of accent. These features appear more often in informal prose and in the new genres of e-mail and text messaging. The rich possibilities for artificial visual emphasis cannot be followed in any detail in this chapter. The concentration here will be on the affordances for emphasis irrespective of the visual extras.

EMPHASIS BY POSITION

Conventional printed genres still avoid most of the visual dynamics described above, and writers cannot always control the realization of their texts in print. But they can exploit natural sentence patterns for achieving emphasis. The following options for achieving "natural" emphasis combine patterns of residual intonation and grammatical salience. Altogether they offer rhetors complex trade-offs.

When speakers come to the end of a segment or sentence, they usually drop their voices and linger slightly on the final word, following it with a pause. Linguists would refer more precisely to the *nucleus* or accented syllable in the final tone unit. Indeed, if speakers, or those reading aloud, did not lower their voices at the end of a unit, they would signal to a listener that they were not at the end (Bolinger 1980, 12). When speakers break this convention and raise their voices on a final word, they often signal a question, even if nothing else in the sentence changes. To test this observation, read the following aloud three times, first with lowered pitch on the last word, then with no change, and finally with a raised pitch: *The president came yesterday* (. – ?)

Lowering the voice and then pausing put emphasis on the end of a unit. This principle of oral end focus accords with the general description of information distribution in the sentence. Speakers and writers often use the final spot for information that is new to listeners or readers, the "news" of the sentence, added to what is known (see "Passage Construction" p. 348). This new information typically occupies the place of greatest emphasis in the sentence at the end. The natural process of emphasizing the end as the site of new and communicatively salient information is demonstrated by how questions are normally answered in full sentences. The key word in the answer naturally occurs at the end: *Where are you going? I am going to Rome; When are you going? I'm going in July; Why are you going? I'm going to see the pope.*

Just as the word or phrase that completes a sentence receives the most emphasis in that sentence, so whatever completes a unit within a sentence, whether a clause or a phrase, receives relatively more attention than other elements in that unit. Consider the sentence *Though some are leaving in July, I am staying through the summer.* The word *July* ending the subordinate clause receives some of the lowering and lengthening given to the final word, *summer.* Similarly, the object in a participial or a prepositional phrase receives relatively more attention than the preposition itself or its modifiers (e.g., *in my convertible*). This emphasis on the final element in clauses or phrases increases when they are set off by commas, a visual cue realized as a pause: *Remaining calm in the crisis, the pilot managed a dead-stick landing; The maître d', who previously ruled one of New York's four-star restaurants, could not work with inexperienced waiters.* These slight emphases do not rival the very end as the position of greatest emphasis. For maximum punch, important words or phrases belong at the end.

Next to the ending, the opening of a sentence or unit is a position of emphasis. It comes after the pause between sentences. Beginning words or phrases may receive a slightly elevated pitch in natural speech or in text read aloud. Opening emphasis is indicated by the practice of fronting certain words, phrases, or clauses that would otherwise receive less emphasis buried in the sentence: *I will eventually receive my diploma* versus *Eventually, I will receive my diploma.* Since the opening of the sentence is also traditionally the place for given information, for the sentence topic, speakers and writers will sometimes "front" elements to establish them as topics: *The key, I want it now!*

If the opening and ending of a sentence are positions of relatively greater emphasis, elements in the middle of the sentence are deemphasized. The profile of emphasis in the typical simple sentence therefore follows the pattern below, where numbers indicate the relative level of stress, one the greatest and three the least.

> 2   3   1
>
> *The results from the procedure were inconclusive.*

In this sentence, *the results* and the resolution, *were inconclusive*, receive more emphasis, are more important to the meaning, than the information conveyed in the centrally located prepositional phrase, *from the procedure.* Even if this phrase were moved to the end for greater emphasis (*The results were inconclusive from the procedure*), it would still not have the punch that the concluding verb has in the original version. That is because another dimension of emphasis has entered the picture, the emphasis that naturally falls on words filling major sentence roles.

EMPHASIS BY SENTENCE ROLE

The main constituents of a sentence, the subject, verb, and object, receive more emphasis than secondary sentence elements, all the words, phrases, and clauses that perform adverbial and adjectival functions. Subjects receive this greater attention even when they are not the first item in a sentence, though they then lose the extra emphasis that comes from opening position. It is fortunate for verbs that they often carry the "news" of a sentence and therefore receive emphasis because of their function, since they are often buried mid-sentence. Even in typically muted dependent clauses, the basic sentence elements of subject, verb, and object receive relatively more attention.

EMPHASIS FROM INVERSIONS

The natural positions of emphasis described above follow the standard sentence floor plans in English: *Subject – Verb – Object* or *Subject – Linking Verb – Complement*.[1] As a language that lives by word order, English has predictable and preferred places for sentence constituents and modifiers. In contrast, Latin and Greek signal sentence constituents with inflectional endings, so word order in sentences is much freer. Classical grammarians and rhetoricians paid considerable attention to internal sentence architecture under the headings of several figures of speech. These figures of internal sentence management were then adapted to English in the early modern style manuals. Small variations in word order can shift emphasis and subtly change meaning.

Rhetorical style manuals noted any small switching of two elements under the label **anastrophe**; a larger reordering of constituents was called **hyperbaton**. Oddly, in English the smaller violations can be more noticeable than the larger ones, since English has fairly rigid rules about word order. Single-word modifiers, for example, typically come before the noun and prepositional phrases after: *the thorny, yellow rose in the garden*. But single-word adjectives can be placed after a noun: *the tall cedars* → *the cedars tall; the crooked and homely man* → *the man, crooked and homely*. Positioned after their nouns, these adjectives receive considerably more emphasis and may even suggest a "poetic" or heightened register. Subtle differences can also result from more idiomatic displacements, as in the difference between *the last man in line* versus *the man last in line*; the second version carries the sense of a more adventitious circumstance.

The larger switches of *hyperbaton* involve inverting the typical order of sentence constituents by putting the object or predicate before the subject. In English, it is difficult to switch S-V-O pattern and retain the same meaning (*Dog bites man* versus *Man bites dog*). But it is sometimes possible. For example, since forms of *to be* function like an equals sign, subjects and predicate nouns can be flipped: *Alphonse was the recording secretary* → *The recording secretary was Alphonse*. These versions change emphasis by position, a difference in salience that can only be judged in context. Switching a subject with a predicate adjective, however, produces emphasis by unexpected positioning: *The night was clear and starry* → *Clear and starry was the night*.

Inversions are also possible in the case of sentences with intransitive verbs that have modifiers completing the meaning. These adverbial modifiers can easily be moved to the front of the sentence and the relative positions of the subject and verb switched: *The sound of snoring came from the back of the room* → *From the back of the room came the sound of snoring*. A switch like this is typically made to put the subject in the position of greater emphasis at the end.

By moving sentence elements out of their predictable slots, *anastrophe* and *hyperbaton* often assist the grand style. In his inaugural address, for example, President Obama celebrated earlier generations in a series of sentences beginning with a displaced prepositional phrase: "For us, they packed up their few worldly possessions and traveled across oceans in search of a new life."[2] And of course Lincoln's Second Inaugural includes the often-quoted sentence opening with its prepositional phrases, "With malice toward none, with charity for all" (see above, p. 23).

COMBINING SOURCES OF EMPHASIS

Emphasis is a relative matter. An element in the middle of a sentence that nevertheless ends an interruption and is followed by a comma receives more emphasis than sentence position alone might suggest. Furthermore, surprising words, no matter where they occur, also draw notice. The sources of emphasis also accumulate. If a word or phrase in the opening receives more emphasis, a subject receives more emphasis, and elements in the main clause receive more emphasis, then an element that is in the opening of the main clause and is also the subject receives proportionately more emphasis.

What is true of the overall pattern of emphasis in an individual sentence is also true of the passage or paragraph. A sentence concluding a paragraph receives the greatest emphasis, and a sentence opening a paragraph is also stressed. Anything in the middle sentences of the paragraph receives proportionately less emphasis. And maximum stress in a paragraph falls on the last word or phrase in the last sentence.

How can a word or phrase be deemphasized? By keeping it out of the main clause, out of the main sentence elements, and out of the opening or the ending. The position of least emphasis in a sentence would, then, be something like a phrase in a relative clause or in a series placed in the middle of a sentence: *The king, whose message of concern came last night, was hoping to arrive in time for the funeral.* The modifier *of concern* is likely to pass by unnoticed (except for the special attention here of looking for it). Of course, natural sources of emphasis or de-emphasis mean little if the interest of the reader or listener brings salience to an item, even though that item is buried in a prepositional phrase in a relative clause in the middle of a sentence.

Placement of Modifiers: Branching Left, Right, and in the Middle

Modifiers were discussed in the previous chapter by type (clauses, phrases, single words) and by proportion in heavily versus sparely modified styles. The third feature in modification is critical in sentence architecture: where are the modifiers placed in the sentence? Some modifiers are glued to their appointed place, like appositives after the nouns they rename or adjective clauses kept close to the words they modify. Participial phrases have some degrees of freedom; absolute constructions and adverbial modifiers have even more.

But in terms of position relative to the main predication of a sentence, there are really only three basic options: modifiers can appear before, in the middle, or after.

A sentence that opens with modifying structures and so postpones its subject is said to **branch to the left**: "*In the distance, above the noise of the crowd,* I thought I could hear the sound of guns" (quoted in Kerrane and Yagoda 1997, 349; all the examples in this section come from British journalist John Simpson's account of events in Tiananmen Square in China in 1989). Extensive opening modification asks readers or listeners to hold the provided detail in suspension and wait for the predication, the tie-in. When these opening constructions are adverb clauses (especially conditional clauses), their position before the main clause is essential to the meaning of the sentence: "*When I finally spotted the vehicle,* I could see that it was making its way with speed down the side of the Square" (350). Left-branching modifiers earn their place by controlling the construal of the rest of the sentence.

A sentence that is complete grammatically but continues with modifying clauses or phrases is said to **branch to the right**: "There were hundreds of small groups, *each concentrated around someone who was haranguing or lecturing the others, using the familiar, heavy public gestures of the Chinese*" (348). Sentences may snake along for a considerable time after the main predication. For readers or listeners, the right-branching material is an elaboration, an addendum or a qualification on the meaning delivered in the predication.

Finally, a sentence that inserts material between the subject and verb (like this one) is said to branch **in the middle**: "Even the small children, *brought there with the rest of the family,* stared intently" (348). When the interrupting element modifies the subject restrictively, the structure is less intrusive: "But the tension *that was bonding members of the crowd together* did not have the same effect on the members of our small team" (349). But some inserted constructions interrupt digressively and genuinely delay the subject's linking up with the verb: "A man—*his torso bare*—climbed up the side of the vehicle" (351; dashes punctuate the absolute construction).

English sentences can easily carry modification to the left and the right: "*Just as the third soldier was lifted out of the vehicle, almost fainting,* an articulated bus rushed towards us *stopping, with great skill, so that its rear door opened just beside the group with the soldier*" (p. 351; left and right branching). "*When we reached Changan Avenue, the main east-west thoroughfare,* it was as full of people *as in the days of the great demonstrations—a human river*" (348; left and right branching). "I screamed obscenities at the man—*stupid obscenities, as no one except my colleagues could have understood them*—and threw myself at him, *catching him with his arm up, poised for another blow*" (352; mid and right branching). Across a passage, most speakers and writers will vary branching patterns. Using only one or the other pattern is highly unusual, though writers and speakers certainly have preferences, either in special passages or overall. As it happens, journalist Simpson strongly favors right-branching constructions with modifiers hung on sentences featuring himself as the subject/agent followed by what he saw or experienced. But he uses all the possibilities.

Loose and Periodic Sentences

One of the enduring distinctions in rhetorical stylistics depends on whether a sentence ends with an element from the main predication or with modification. If the first, the sentence is periodic; if the second, it is loose. This distinction begins with Aristotle, who described types of sentences on the basis of how "tight" or how "open" they sounded, a distinction which in turn fed into an overall impression of a *paratactic* or *hypotactic* style when most sentences in a passage ended one way or another. Though some term shifting has gone on over the centuries, the difference in sentence architecture observed here is still an important one when the goal is identifying stylistic features that support the purpose of a text.[3]

PERIODIC SENTENCES

Understanding periodic sentences requires remembering, first, that the position of greatest emphasis in a sentence is the end, and, second, that the main grammatical elements of a clause (subject, verb, object/complement) receive relatively more emphasis than subordinate elements. A periodic sentence is a sentence that completes itself grammatically and/or delivers its meaning, often dramatically, at its end. By definition, a simple sentence stripped of extraneous modification is periodic: "The catalog of ills is long" (Lyndon Johnson; Windt 1983, 62). But the label *periodic* also applies to sentences that branch left or expand in the middle before coming to the main predication.

> *To protect our men who are in Vietnam and to guarantee the continued success of our withdrawal and Vietnamization programs,* I have concluded that the time has come for action. (Richard Nixon; Windt 1983, 137. The left-branching construction is italicized. This sentence concludes with a noun clause and has periodic structure within that noun clause.)

As defined by some stylists, a periodic sentence has a mid-branching interruption between the subject and predicate (Lanham 1983, 56).

> Let us be aware that *while they preach the supremacy of the state, declare its omnipotence over individual man, and predict its eventual domination of all people of the earth*—they are the focus of evil in the modern world. (Reagan; Safire 1997, 493. The mid-branching construction is italicized.)

Speakers or writers may also complete a sentence grammatically and then use a pause or dash to heighten a final revelation.

Now I come to the second of the two marauders, to the second danger which threatens the cottage home and ordinary people—namely tyranny. (Churchill; Safire 1997, 868)

LOOSE SENTENCES

When a sentence completes itself grammatically and then trails off in accumulated detail, neither arousing nor satisfying a compelling need for a concluding point, it is labeled *loose.* Such loose sentences branch to the right with phrases and dependent clauses that clarify and enrich.[4] The following example comes from John McPhee's *The Pine Barrens* (1968) in a section explaining Joseph Wharton's plan to use the Barrens as a water source for Philadelphia.

> Wharton's plan called for thirty-three shallow reservoirs in the pines, *connected by a network of canals to one stupendous reservoir in Camden, from which an aqueduct would go under the Delaware River and into Philadelphia, where the pure waters of New Jersey would emerge from every tap, replacing a water supply that has been described as* "dirty, bacterial soup." (15; italics added for the right-branching modifiers)

Any of the phrases that build on nouns (absolute phrases, resumptive and summative modifiers) are useful devices for creating loose sentences, since these structures can be moved to end position and carry their own modification, as in this further example from *The Pine Barrens.*

> The characteristic color of the water in the streams is the color of tea—*a phenomenon, often called "cedar water," that is familiar in the Adirondacks, as in many other places where tannins and other organic waste from riparian cedar trees combine with iron from the ground water to give the rivers a deep color.* (16; *phenomenon* is a summative term)

Since writers of loose sentences put the main grammatical elements early, the end will never coincide with one of the main sentence elements. Whatever structure actually does conclude the sentence will still receive ending emphasis, but this "last word" will typically be less emphatic than the ending of a periodic sentence. Of course, when the ending is a phrase like "dirty, bacterial soup," readers perk up.

It might seem that the periodic sentence is always the better-crafted sentence, since it exploits the natural emphasis that falls both on main sentence elements and on the last item. But if every sentence in a passage were periodic and other sources of variety were missing, listeners or readers would be pummeled with emphatic points until they lost the sense that any one sentence was more important than any other. On the other hand, a passage that consisted entirely of loose sentences could seem aimless, constantly wandering off in irrelevance as the speaker or writer thought of—oh, yes—one more interesting tidbit to tack on.

A PERIODIC STYLE

Some rhetors do create passages with strings of periodic sentences, as Aristotle observed. The resulting effect can be a passage of emphatic certainty as in the following excerpt from an op-ed piece on the UN peacekeeping mission in the former Yugoslavia.

(1) Sir Michael Rose, the reincarnation of Neville Chamberlain, has just admitted that his U.N. force of 23,000 Europeans is unable to "deter" Bosnian Serbs from destroying cities the Security Council has established as safe havens.

(2) This is tantamount to surrender. (3) A ragtag splinter group of Serbians, with no power but the weaponry and willingness to kill civilians, has rendered the poseurs and pontificators of the United Nations helpless and contemptible.

(4) This proves that as a vehicle for concerted military response to an aggressor or violator of human rights, the U.N. is worthless. (Safire 1994; sentence numbering added)

The first sentence above, setting the context and the immediate "fact" that is the exigence for this argument, is not a periodic sentence. Its subject and verb—*Sir Michael Rose/has admitted*—are completed by a noun clause beginning with *that* and serving as the object. This clause ends with "cities," which is modified by a trailing adjective clause, "[that] the Security Council has established as safe havens." Contrast that structure with the structure of the next three sentences, which are periodic; these, not coincidentally, express Safire's evaluation.

S	V	PA	
(2) This	is	tantamount to surrender	
S	V	O	C
(3) group	has rendered	poseurs and pontificators	helpless and contemptible

S	V	O	[embedded noun clause]		
(4) This	proves	that	S	V	PA
			the U.N.	is	worthless.

Compared to the first sentence, the fourth also ends with a noun clause, but this time the final word of this clause does complete the meaning of both that clause and the sentence. The next several sentences in Safire's argument reiterate and elaborate on the judgment expressed in these three sentences, though not with the same forcefulness. Over the whole editorial, Safire varies his accusatory tone—that is, his emphatic claims and his commentary and support for them—by varying his deployment of periodic sentences. The periodic sentence is an excellent tool in hard-hitting argument.

A LOOSE STYLE

A predominantly loose style is more characteristic of essay writing, particularly when the writer engages in personal reflection or extended narration and description. Such discourse is still argumentative; it still makes a point or promotes an interpretation or worldview. But it may argue indirectly, using the gradual accumulation of meaningful detail. The following excerpt in the loose style opens an article in *Natural History* on tourist attractions in Ghana and provides some grim reminders.

(1) From the tower of what was once the Dutch governor's private bedroom in Elmina Castle, perched over Ghana's coast, I see children playing ball on the beach, brightly painted canoes, tall palm trees blowing in the sea breeze. (2) But the distant ocean horizon provokes grim thoughts of the world beyond, which has swallowed Africa's treasures for the past five hundred years: first gold and spices, then ivory and slaves, and now the continent's forests, cash crops, and minerals. (3) In another corner of the sunlit room, the tour guide tells us about the trapdoor on the floor of the balcony outside, from which the stairs lead down to a courtyard. (4) Below ground is a windowless dungeon, originally built to store gold and spices but later used as a holding pen where captives awaited the European ships that would take them on a journey of no return. (Schildkrout 1996, 36)

The first sentence in this passage concludes with the third of the three objects (I see x, y, z), but the second sentence trails off in a long relative clause modifying "world beyond" and a list of the treasures exported from the continent; thirty-two of the sentence's forty words appear after the sentence is complete grammatically with *thoughts*. In the third sentence, seven words come before and nineteen after the S/V/O (*guide tells us*), and in the fourth sentence, thirty words follow the grammatical core (*below ground is a windowless dungeon*).

The point of this passage is description, both of the sights seen by the author and of the thoughts evoked by what is seen. Since the thoughts are aroused by the sights, the loose sentences aptly express the trailing thoughts in trailing structures. The style here is also typical of descriptive travel prose, whose purpose is often to suggest the provocative richness of the objects and experiences encountered. It is a heavily modified style, and analysis shows that this author prefers to keep her subjects, verbs, and objects tightly together, branching either in long constructions to the left or, more extensively, to the right in digressive associations.

Composition

Rhetorical manuals often included extensive advice on sentence construction well beyond figures like *hyperbaton* or observations on loose versus periodic sentences. The grammarians and teachers of rhetoric also recommended observing certain broad principles of cogency, balance, and euphony in their advice on what was called in ancient stylistics *compositio*. In the sentence construction doctrine under this rubric, especially as it is developed in Hellenistic style manuals, the disposition of elements was critical, and indeed Dionysius of Halicarnassus's treatise (ca. 10 BCE) was known by its Latin title *De Compositione Verborum*, literally "on the composition of words." His approach represented a shift in classical stylistics from concentration on word choice to a concentration on placement: "The function of composition is to put words together in an appropriate order, to assign a suitable connexion to clauses, and to distribute the whole discourse properly into periods" (1910, 73).[5] Throughout his treatise, Dionysius analogizes his approach to the plastic arts (carpentry, shipbuilding, even embroidery), arguing that how materials are put together is far more important than what they are to begin with. Typical of this Hellenistic strain of stylistics, Dionysius aimed at a taxonomy of overall effects in a text built up from choices in smaller units.[6]

A later treatment of the classical doctrine of sentence construction or *compositio* can be found in the lectures on rhetoric left behind by the eighteenth-century Italian jurist Giambattista Vico. Borrowing from Cicero, Vico identified three sentence-level compositional units: the short *caesim* or phrase; the *membratim*, a single predication; and the *circumducte*, a longer, self-contained construction, usually a multiclause sentence that comes to a satisfying point of completion. These three units reprise the Greek terms *comma, colon,* and *periodos* and correspond roughly to the phrase, clause, and multiclause sentence, though certainly the term *sentence* alone does not capture the notion of circling back to completion intended by the words *periodos* or *circumducte*. Vico in fact recommended composing periods in two parts, the *apodosis* and the *protasis*. An opening *apodosis* should contain a concessive or conditional clause and the *protasis* should follow with the point to be maintained. Vico's examples all come from Cicero, but this construction is readily found in oratorical prose over the centuries, as in the following passage from an 1850 speech by Henry Clay on the Missouri Compromise. This *circumducte* is clearly built up from shorter phrases and clauses:

> And without speaking at all as to the causes of the recent war with Mexico, whether they were right or wrong, and abstaining from the expression of any opinion as to the justice or propriety of the war when it commenced, // all must unite in respect to the gallantry of our arms and the glory of our triumph. (Reid 1988, 391; double slash added)

Clay's sentence falls into two parts at the slash, a concessive opening and a certain ending. Vico, however, might not have admired Clay's period, since he preferred, for the sake of rhythm, a *protasis* that was longer than the *apodosis*.

The sentence advice of classical stylistics, carried forward in Latin manuals like Vico's, was transformed into enduring principles of English sentence construction in the late eighteenth century by Hugh Blair.[7] Blair devoted three of his eventually published *Lectures on Rhetoric and Belles Lettres* to the "Structure of Sentences" (XI, XII, XIII). Here, in unprecedented detail, he takes up the management of the English sentence according to four criteria of excellence: 1. Clearness and Precision; 2. Unity; 3. Strength; 4. Harmony (2005, 112). His first and third principles come from the original four virtues of rhetorical style. Clearness and precision mean essentially preventing ambiguity by correctly placing adverbs, mid-sentence insertions and relative clauses (112–15). Strength means giving every word and member "due weight and force," removing redundancies (121), paying attention to connections (122), putting the "capital word or words" in the place where they make the fullest impression, observing a principle of increasing importance as the sentence goes along (127), and avoiding weak words at the end (128). The two remaining principles of good sentence construction, Harmony and Unity, reprise other elements of classical stylistics. Harmony concerns rhythm and the overall correspondence between the thought and "sound" of a sentence, "whether round and smooth, or stately and solemn, or brisk and quick, or interrupted and abrupt" (140). Unity comes from maintaining the "scene" of the sentence so that it produces a single impression; writers, Blair advises, should never switch from person to person, or subject to subject, or crowd into one sentence material that should be divided into two or three (116–18). Unity also requires avoiding parentheses in the middle of sentences, and it demands coming to "a full and perfect close" (119). Blair illustrates his sentence principles with examples from esteemed recent authors, taking apart, sentence by sentence, four numbers of the *Spectator* by Addison and the opening of Swift's *A Proposal for Correcting, Improving, and Ascertaining the English Tongue*. He is surprisingly severe on his dead authors, fearlessly pointing out where his models fail to follow his four principles (McIntosh 1998, xx). Blair's influence on literacy and oratory in the United States, through reprints and abridgements of his lectures as well as through derivative texts, was lasting and profound (2005, xvi–xxiii).

Iconic Form

A little over a month after the 9/11 attacks, the United States was on high alert, with daily news about anthrax-laced letters contaminating government offices and causing the deaths of unsuspecting postal workers and others with no obvious connection to the letters. In this context, in October of 2001, Jennifer Steinhauer filed a story in the *New York Times* on Mayor Rudolph Giuliani's attempts to reestablish normalcy in his city by promoting a local cultural festival. Her story opened with the following sentence:

Yesterday, soon after the United States Capitol closed, and the world learned that more than two dozen people on the Senate majority leader's staff had been exposed to a potent form of anthrax, and Gov. George E. Pataki and other state workers began taking Cipro, and environmental testing began at City Hall, Mayor Rudolph W. Giuliani held a news conference with four large puppets. (B1)

This sentence has a rather unusual form. After the opening adverb of time (*yesterday*), it begins with a large left-branching construction that consists of a series of four subordinate adverb clauses. The subordinating conjunction *after* (modified by *soon*) introduces the first clause (*soon after the United States Capitol closed*), and that same conjunction is understood as the introductory element governing the next three clauses (*and [soon after] the world learned*). The whole long opening tells readers about four overwhelming events, but these events are in a way "suspended," not only because they are in an introductory construction and in dependent clauses, but also because the sentence tells the reader to pay attention to what happens *soon after* them. Furthermore, this opening gives a *series* of subordinate clauses, and a series normally separates its elements with commas and reserves the conjunction before the last item. But this series puts an *and* between each element, giving more weight to each one. To paraphrase: Yesterday, soon after *this* and *this* and *this* and *this*.

The heavy opening subordinate construction is followed by, or even answered by, a rather brief main clause: "*Mayor Rudolph Giuliani held a news conference with four large puppets.*" Because of that lengthy left-branching opening, a great deal of emphasis falls on this short final independent clause, and even more on its incongruous final word, *puppets.*

This sentence exhibits what theorists of style call *syntactic symbolism* (Tufte 2006, 253ff) or iconicity or **iconic form**(Leech and Short 1981; Leff and Sachs 1990). Quite simply, its syntax or *compositio* reinforces or even epitomizes its meaning. The point of this sentence could be paraphrased as follows: in the face of the heavy and unprecedented consequences of the anthrax scare, the mayor focused New Yorkers' attention on lighter things, on "four large puppets." How does the form support this meaning? First it does so by its disproportion. The problems, expressed in the initial four adverb clauses, are onerous and heavy givens; they *preoccupy* most of the sentence. The response to them is only a slight gesture, expressed in the short main clause. But this gesture is the main clause, a clause with an agent who does something. It is also no accident that this sentence was constructed with *four* opening clauses, each a blow in itself, since the mayor responds to these events with *four* puppets. Of course the facts dictated that the mayor had four puppets, but the four opening clauses were at the writer's discretion. Given the number of events in the month following 9/11 and the complexity of the anthrax mystery, any journalist could easily generate more or fewer than four problems. But the four-to-four matching strongly suggests that the author was very deliberate about the design of this sentence.

The order of the four adverb clauses seems to show planning as well. The series starts with closing the U.S. Capitol, moves to problems in the Senate, to the governor of

New York and his staff taking a preventative drug, and finally to testing City Hall for contamination. The series is ordered, then, in terms of the decreasing size of the governmental unit affected. It ends with the unit that Giuliani is responsible for, City Hall. The need to keep this order perhaps excuses the one flaw in this sentence—the greater length of the second item. Ideally, for the sake of prose rhythm reinforcing meaning, the final item should be the longest, creating a pileup before the brief answering main clause.The dramatic contrast in this sentence between the serious events and the news conference with puppets could be a prelude to criticism: how dare the mayor be so frivolous? But in fact the author goes on to interpret Giuliani's attempt at normalcy as modestly heroic.

ABSENCE IN WORDS, PRESENCE IN SYNTAX

The kind of form/meaning synergy demonstrated in the Guiliani sentence contradicts the dogma of the "arbitrariness of the sign." But while motivated form/meaning connections are largely absent at the level of individual words (with exceptions for onomatopoeic or phonaesthetic words), Bolinger and others argue that these connections increase with larger units of discourse: "At the level of sentences, [syntactic] symbolism makes a quantum leap (Bolinger 1980, 20). The preferred term here, *iconic form,* suggests that the text somehow "images" its meaning. In a very literal sense it is, of course, possible for written or printed words to become a picture. The seventeenth-century poet George Herbert wrote verses in line lengths that, when printed on the page, created a visual image of the subject of the poem—an altar, a butterfly. Modern graphic artists are also adept at designing letters, words and text that visually suggest what they are about; for example, tilting the letters in the word *FAST* can suggest speed (see also Lanham 1983, 77–103, on the visual impact of orthography and formatting). But the "image" of the meaning created in the case of iconic form as it is meant here is not precisely visual, since it can also be realized aurally. It is rather a matter of manipulating the syntax in order to place words of importance in positions of emphasis, to provide a reading order that delivers the meaning with maximum effect, and to create a sound pattern that reinforces the content and intended impression as well.[8]

In "Words the Most Like Things," Michael Leff and Andrew Sachs (1990) provide an illuminating analysis of iconic form in passages from Edmund Burke's parliamentary oratory; the prose of rhetorically trained speakers of past generations like Burke richly repays such analysis. For purposes of illustrating iconic form in the sense of an "experienced arrangement," a relatively simple example can be found in the nature writing of Rachel Carson. Though most famous for her polemical *Silent Spring*, Carson had a well-established reputation before that work for her scientifically informed accounts of sea and shore life. Her first book, *Under the Sea-Wind* (1941), is written from the point of view of birds, fish, and eels. Humans appear only as a danger to the animals. The chapter "Migrants of the Spring Sea" opens with the following paragraph, which also appears as the epigraph to this chapter:

(1) Between the Chesapeake Capes and the elbow of Cape Cod the place where the continent ends and the true sea begins lies from fifty to one hundred miles from the tide lines. (2) It is not the distance from the shore, but the depth, that marks the transition to the true sea; for wherever the gently sloping sea bottom feels the weight of a hundred fathoms of water above it, suddenly it begins to fall away in escarpments and steep palisades, descending abruptly from twilight into darkness. (109–10)

The second sentence here breaks into two independent clauses at the semicolon. Its second half postpones the subject and verb with a lengthy subordinate adverb clause: *wherever the gently sloping sea bottom feels the weight of a hundred fathoms of water above it.* (This clause anthropomorphizes the subject, the *sea bottom*, into something that *feels weight.* Carson often resorts to attributing human-like agency to animals and inorganic nature, since she dispenses with human agents.) With this weight of water on it, the sea bottom *suddenly ... begins to fall away.* Fronting the adverb *suddenly* here is somewhat unusual, but putting it first in the main clause makes it just that, *sudden.* So the sentence builds up weight and then suddenly triggers the effect of that weight; the sea bottom begins to fall away. It does not, however, fall straight down, but rather descends in *escarpments* and *palisades.* If these exotic words communicate anything, they should suggest steep cliffs. The process is not over, however, for the sentence ends with a participial phrase expressing the destination: *descending abruptly from twilight into darkness.* In Carson's compound sentence (2) overall, there is an accumulation of verbiage (thirty-seven words) before the word *suddenly* followed by a shorter, "steeper" clause falling away (sixteen words). In addition, the overall word order enacts the destination. The sentence ends where the sea floor does, in *darkness.*

Several paragraphs later, after a description of how mackerel winter on the edge of the continental shelf, Carson runs the process in reverse:

(1) About a hundred miles beyond the place where the mackerel winter, the sea rises out of the deep, dark bed of the open Atlantic and begins its own climb up over the muddy sides of the continental slope. (2) In utter blackness and stillness the sea climbs those hundred miles, rising from the depths of a mile or more until black begins to fade to purple, and purple to deep blue, and blue to azure. (111)

Once again the sea is an agent on the move. The first sentence in this paragraph provides the overall picture; the second sentence enacts that picture. The sea begins where it was left several paragraphs ago, *in utter blackness.* It then climbs a hundred miles (subject, verb, and object of the main clause), and its progress is retold in an ending participial phrase (*rising ...*) and in the figure of speech *gradatio,* sometimes called "the stairs," with its overlapping elements (*black begins to fade to purple, purple to deep blue, blue to azure*). The sentence form here clearly expresses or reinforces the content.

THE DEFAULT FORM/MEANING RELATIONSHIP

The sentences described so far in this section seem to belong to a rather unusual group of constructions deliberately crafted by skillful authors. They illustrate the point that a sentence can be put together so that its syntax expresses or almost "images" its content. But why should form and content only be combined in skillfully constructed occasional sentences? Why isn't the form of a sentence always a part of its meaning? The simple answer: it is. A sentence, as this chapter and the preceding chapters on predication and modification explain, always conveys its content and effect in the arrangement of its elements. This observation is especially the case in English, where word order counts for so much in delivering meaning. For example, just by giving the subject first before an active verb, normal word order in English helps convey the notion that the subject is the origin or source of the action.

Other sources of default iconism have been pointed out. Bolinger noted that when two persons perform an action together, they will both be the side-by-side subjects of a reporting sentence (1980, 20). Leech and Short cite the sequential order of clauses as a reflection of the chronological order of the events narrated and the order of presented details as *psychological form*, the order in which the items occur to the speaker (236–39). And Carey McIntosh describes loose sentences and colloquial wording as expressions of the speaker's "thoughts and feelings in the very act or process of coming to mind" (1998, 25). Furthermore, to the extent that writers can mimic the pace and cadences of speech, they can "image" in a statement the urgency and excitement of the speaker. The issue of how syntax can mirror underlying conceptual structures has also been examined by linguists investigating English and other languages (Haiman 1985).

Form or syntax then is a source of meaning in itself; semantic meaning is another source. In iconic form these two sources of meaning cooperate. Can they also work against each other? Rachel Carson, for example, could have described the profile of the sea off the continental shelf in quite a different sentence:

> To darkness from twilight, down steep palisades and escarpments, falls the sea bottom suddenly when it reaches the weight of a hundred fathoms of water above it in its gentle sloping.

This sentence reverses Carson's original. It opens with the sea's destination and closes with its starting point. It might be tempting to call it a "bad" or "inept" sentence, but it could actually be that the form working "against" the meaning here produces a different and possibly desired effect. Of course, it is always ultimately impossible to judge a single sentence as effective or not out of context. But the point to be made here, counterintuitive though it seems, is that form always contributes a meaning in itself.

Summary

Paying attention to the subject/verb pairings in sentences (chapter 7) and to modifiers in all their forms (chapter 8) leads to an appreciation of the sentence architecture described in this chapter. Referring to the arrangement of parts as the *architecture* of a sentence has precedents in rhetorical stylistics; Casper de Jonge points out, for example, that architectural metaphors were common in ancient composition theory (2008). But the term *architecture* is also misleading, because sentences are not contemplated as visual objects the way buildings are; they are experienced in time. Whether heard or read, they present sequences of parts and accumulating effects; hence analogies to music, also used in antiquity, may be more appropriate.

The sequential arrangement or "composition" of sentences can be appreciated first for positions of relative emphasis. Generally, the final phrase in a sentence is emphatic compared to the other parts, and the beginning is also heightened. Pauses before and after a string of words, as well as pitch changes in openings and endings, create these stresses. Generally, also, the main clause constituents (subject/verb/object or complement) are more salient than the modifiers, unless, of course those modifiers are deployed in more emphatic positions. The typical trajectory of the English sentence (subject/verb/object or subject/linking verb/complement) and its usual places for modification follow positions of emphasis. From these principles of emphasis and position come the variations traditionally noticed in rhetorical stylistics. Rhetors can emphasize elements by displacing them from their expected slots with *hyperbaton* or *anastrophe* (as in the previous sentence), and the two consistently described sentence types, loose and periodic, really have to do with the way sentences are consumed in time. Loose sentences trail away after the completion of their grammatical core, and periodic sentences halt when grammatically complete.

If the placement or sequence of sentence elements reinforces the meaning, the result is *iconic form,* the cooperation of composition and content. Characterizations of iconic form can often seem nothing more than an analyst's ingenious valorization of how a sentence says what it says, and contemporary students find the notion of intended sentence patterning, such as that exhibited by the Steinhauer or Carson sentences described above, far beyond plausibility. The knowledge and care required for such deliberate constructions seem impossible. But writers trained from antiquity through the seventeenth century probably were aware and often did plan sentence form deliberately; having been thoroughly trained in the formal possibilities through parsing and practice, they had appropriate patterns available. Contemporary writers innocent of such training may rely on absorbed models. And even if they are unaware of or cannot rationalize the potential effects of different sentence forms, the default options of sentence construction available in the language, and their own preoccupation with their material and purpose, would favor their using sentence form effectively.

NOTES

1. Structural linguists would want to expand this list of basic sentence floor plans to five or more: S- LV; S-LV- C(PN or PA); S- $V_{intrans}$; S-V_{trans}-O; S-V- O-O (or S-V-IO-DO); S-V-O-C.

2. www.americanrhetoric.com. The sentence and the two that follow cannot, in fact, be rewritten with the prepositional phrases in the conventional place and still make sense. "For us, they packed up their few worldly possessions and traveled across oceans in search of a new life" would become either, "They packed up their few worldly possessions and traveled across oceans in search of a new life *for us*" or perhaps "They packed up their few worldly possessions *for us* and traveled across oceans in search of a new life." It hardly seems plausible that earlier immigrants to the United States took these actions *for us*, as members of Obama's audiences. Therefore, in its repositioning, this prepositional phrase has to be described as something of a global modifier. A later sentence in the address gets into similar trouble. The speechwriter, imitating the apostrophe and addressing different audience segments, begins a series of sentences with the prepositional phrases To *X, To Y*, etc. One of these is "To the Muslim world, we seek a new way forward, based on mutual interest and mutual respect." The phrase should read "With the Muslim world, we seek.…" But this change would have sacrificed the anaphora and the echoes of the grand style.

3. In *Analyzing Prose* (1983), Richard Lanham devotes a chapter to "the periodic style" and "the running style" (53–76). His taxonomy corresponds roughly to the periodic and loose styles described in this chapter. Lanham, however, stresses sentence interruption as the key feature of the periodic style, and he sees the digressiveness of such interruptions as leading back to a loose style (70).

4. In the revival of interest in prose style that occurred in the 1960s and '70s among teachers of composition, the loose sentence was singled out for attention again and renamed *the cumulative sentence*. Francis and BonnieJean Christensen (1977) produced a novel appreciation of this structure, citing example after example from twentieth-century writers, primarily novelists. They argued that the cumulative sentence was especially characteristic of contemporary literate prose and that its patterns could be extended to the level of the passage, in paragraphs that opened with a topic that was then cumulatively modified, much as a main clause was modified by right-branching modifiers.

5. Arrangement is the second of the five canons of rhetoric; the "arrangement," better translated "composition," that Dionysius talks about here is a division *within* the third canon, Style.

6. Dionysius's overall categories of style are the austere, the smooth, and the harmonious. Hermogenes' *On Types of Style* (2009), the most famous of the Hellenistic manuals, defines seven species of effects: clarity, grandeur, beauty, rapidity, character, sincerity, and force. Individual speeches and rhetors would display these features as appropriate in, for example, different sections of a speech. The advice about actual features to achieve these effects are described for Greek: *beauty*, for example, is largely a matter of vowel sounds and *grandeur* a matter of certain rhythms.

7. Blair's advice on style represents a unique late-eighteenth-century amalgam. He continues the Hellenistic tradition of the "characters" of style, though now character also means the character of the writer: "When I entered on the consideration of Style, I observed that words being the copies of our ideas, there must always be a very intimate connection between the manner in which every writer employs words, and his manner of thinking; and that, from the peculiarity of thought and expression which belongs to him, there is a certain Character imprinted on his

Style, which may be denominated his manner; commonly expressed by such general terms, as strong, weak, dry, simple, affected, or the like. These distinctions carry, in general, some reference to an author's manner of thinking, but refer chiefly to his mode of expression" (2005, 197). Thus Blair adds to the older doctrine of "characters" a newer cognitive dimension about language and the mind, as well as the notion of an individual signature in style, the eighteenth century's *Le style c'est l'homme.*

8. In the twentieth century, the importance of "experiencing" sentence architecture was argued into place again by Stanley Fish in an approach to literary texts, particularly to Milton, that he called "affective stylistics." Fish's doctrine builds on what might be called a principle of radical linearity, based on the observation that sentences are "consumed" or experienced as a certain order of words.

> A reader's response to the fifth word in a line or sentence is to a large extent the product of his responses to words one, two, three, and four.... The category of response includes any and all of the activities provoked by a string of words: the projection of syntactical and/or lexical probabilities; their subsequent occurrence or nonoccurrence; attitudes toward persons, or things, or ideas referred to; the reversal or questioning of those attitudes; and much more. (1982, 27)

10

FIGURES OF ARGUMENT

ADVICE ON CONSTRUCTING arguments in classical and early modern rhetorical texts concerned individual "lines of argument," the kinds of reasoning that could be used across cases. The assumption behind this advice was that, while people can argue about any subject, the *types* of supporting arguments available were limited and teach-able. Someone trained in the art of argument as it was taught in the rhetorical tradition would have a repertoire of lines of argument ready to use in different situations. These generic lines were called *topoi* (singular *topos*) in Greek and *loci* (singular *locus*) in Latin, both terms meaning roughly a "place" or resource for finding a supporting premise. Aristotle distinguished twenty-eight in the *Rhetoric* (corresponding to the fuller treatment in his *Topics*) including arguments from opposites, comparisons, correlatives, stipulated definition, and consequences (Kennedy 1991, 190–204). Training people in these generic lines of argumentation is largely missing from current liberal arts curricula, but it was the very substance of the classical and early modern art of rhetorical invention and therefore also the basis of formal education from antiquity through the early nineteenth century.

While the rhetorical tradition separated invention from style in the "big picture" view of the art, many of the lines of argument were linked to "syntax describing" figures of speech called *schemes*. Thus, in rhetorical stylistics, the very form of a statement, its grammatical arrangement, was considered to carry meaning in itself. Those figures of speech associated with particular topics can then be thought of as *figures of argument*. As durable syntactic frames or fixed and predictable structures, they can also be described as *prepared iconic forms*. If the form is filled, the content is shaped by these fixed linguistic grooves of ideation. The following discussion identifies these distinct stylistic devices and their associated lines of reasoning.

Parallelism

In the late eighteenth century, Hugh Blair proposed a "law" for synergy between style and argument: "Where two things are compared or contrasted to each other; where either a resemblance or an opposition is intended to be expressed; some resemblance, in the language and construction, should be preserved" (2005, 128). A "resemblance" in the language is the result of *parallelism*, a formal quality of similarity between two phrases, clauses, or even larger units of discourse. Parallel structure equalizes or coordinates content, and this equalizing can have persuasive consequences as listeners and readers "consume" statements formed into similar units. To understand how parallelism works requires an appreciation of its different but ultimately combinable sources: from comparable length of segments in syllables or words, from similar prosodic or stress patterns, from similar grammatical structure, and from repetition.

IN SYLLABLES (*ISOCOLON*)

In a sequence from his Second Inaugural, Lincoln noted that both North and South prayed to the same God, but that

> The prayers of both could not be answered.
> That of neither has been answered fully.
> The Almighty has his own Purposes. (Reid 1988, 466)

These dissimilar sentences have one thing in common that produces a certain parity and connection: they are roughly the same length—nine, ten, and ten syllables respectively. They are instances of what the figure manuals call **isocolon**, adjacent phrases or clauses of equal syllable length.[1] The manuals advised users that approximate, not absolute, equality in length was good enough to produce the desired result, for "experience and practice will bring such a facility that by a sort of instinct we can produce again a colon of equal length to the one before it" ([Cicero] 1981, 299). By creating sequences of similar length, isocolon can create or reinforce argumentative units. The parallelism in syllable length helps consecutive statements cohere as a set. In the example from Lincoln quoted above, God's final purposes trivialize human petitions. Another example comes from a sentence in George Bush's speech before Congress on September 20, 2001, explaining the motivation of Islamic terrorists: "They stand against us because we stand in their way" (2001). This enthymeme matches five-syllable claims on both sides of the *because*, offering matched force and resistance. And here are sentences in sequence from Dr. Martin Luther King Jr.'s "I Have Been to the Mountaintop" (1968):

The nation is sick. Trouble is in the Land. Confusion all around.

This set exhibits approximate *isocolon* (five, six, and six syllables), and the final element may have been phrased as a fragment to fit the pattern. The sound similarities among these three statements equalize them into a single set expressing the same point. Lyndon Johnson used the same tactic to urge his legislative program in the weeks following Kennedy's assassination: "The need is here. The need is now. I ask your help" (Windt 1983, 55).

IN STRESS PATTERNS

Wĕ dó nŏt wánt tŏ fíght
bŭt wé hăve fóught bĕfóre (Kennedy; Windt 1983, 25)

These two clauses add metrical parallelism to parallelism in syllable length, roughly alternating unstressed and stressed syllables to create the familiar metrical foot known as the *iamb* (~/). Five of these to a line produce iambic pentameter, perhaps the best-known metrical pattern in English poetry. Kennedy's lines have three iambs each, matching reluctance to fight with experience in fighting.

These first two methods, *isocolon* and similar stress patterns, create what might be called sound parallelism, a parallelism that can be effective in written as well as in spoken texts. Sound parallelism based on similar stress patterns is, however, much more noticeable than parallelism based on syllable count, and while in some poetry patterns of length and stress would be followed strictly, in prose they need only be approximated. Too much repetition of identical stress patterns produces the metrical regularity that Aristotle warned against as inappropriate and distracting in rhetorical discourse (Kennedy 1991, 237).

IN GRAMMATICAL STRUCTURE (*PARISON*)

In 1964, after consulting with former Presidents Truman and Eisenhower, President Johnson committed our Nation to work towards a new treaty with the Republic of Panama.
And last summer, after 14 years of negotiation under two Democratic Presidents and two Republican Presidents, we reached and signed an agreement that is fair and beneficial to both countries. (Windt 1983, 249)

These sentences from Jimmy Carter's speech on the Panama Canal Treaty exhibit roughly the same sequence of constituents: an opening adverbial of time is followed by a lengthy adverbial phrase beginning with *after*. Next the subject, verb, and object appear in tight linear order, followed by an ending modifier. Such grammatical parallelism, called *parison* in the style manuals, can sustain some variety (such as the concluding infinitive phrase in one and relative clause in the other). It is also indifferent to syllable count, since a grammatical unit in one sentence can be longer or shorter than the matching grammatical unit in another.

However, the sources of parallelism identified so far can be combined. Clauses or sentences can be parallel in length, prosody, and grammatical constituents all at the same time.

> Those who do nothing are inviting shame as well as violence.
> Those who act boldly are recognizing right as well as reality.
> (Kennedy; Windt 1983, 48)

These consecutive lines are approximately the same length, sixteen and eighteen syllables, and each has five stressed syllables and an overall prosodic similarity without metrical identity. They also share the same grammatical pattern: an opening subject is modified by an adjective clause beginning with *who*, and then a verb in the present progressive takes a double object joined by the conjunction *as well as*. One more source of similarity can be added, the constraint of filling these grammatical slots with words from the same lexical/semantic field. Kennedy's terms in both statements come from what could be called the abstract lexicon of moral action: *shame, right, violence, reality.*

FROM REPETITION

A final form of parallelism combines all the forms described so far: the same syllable length, same order of grammatical constituents, and metrical similarity. All these sources of parallelism, as well as semantic connection, can be achieved by merely repeating most of one clause in another.

> That's the kind of soldiers they are.
> That's the kind of people we are.

These lines occur in a speech by Clinton praising the Marines who defended their comrades in the "Black Hawk Down" incident and justifying a troop buildup to bring the mission to an end: "So let us finish the work we set out to do." (1993; twelve syllables capping two statements of seven syllables each). The qualities of the Marines are transferred to all American citizens by the parallelism from repetition in these statements. Repeating opening or concluding phrases in this way was a much-noticed source of emphasis in the rhetorical tradition (see below on "Strategic Repetition").

USES OF PARALLELISM IN ARGUMENT

Comparison

Parallelism based on grammatical similarity and repetition can produce an impression of coordination, leveling, or similarity between phrases or clauses. Given this coordination, parallel clauses can express comparisons quite effectively. In fact, two adjacent clauses featuring the constraints just mentioned can *epitomize* a comparison.

A verbal epitome is the most succinct and yet complete expression of an argument possible, as in the following:

> Two thousand years ago the proudest boast was "Civis Romanus sum."
> Today in the world of freedom, the proudest boast is "Ich bin ein Berliner."
> (Kennedy; Windt 1983, 50)

These two sentences exhibit strong grammatical parallelism and repeat their subjects exactly. Furthermore, the phrases not repeated come from the same semantic fields: time and "city-zenship." The parallelism (*parison*) makes these statements comparable if not equal, assimilating the new boast to its ancient counterpart and hence epitomizing the comparison. In a theory of figuration that is part of a theory of argument, figures of speech like *parison* are defined as apt or iconic forms for the arguments they express.

INDUCTION

Nothing, of course, stops a rhetor from piling up more than two parallel clauses. The following passage comes from Franklin D. Roosevelt's speech to Congress on December 8, 1941, the day after Pearl Harbor, declaring a state of war between the United States and Japan.

> Yesterday the Japanese government also launched an attack against Malaya.
> Last night Japanese forces attacked Hong Kong.
> Last night Japanese forces attacked Guam.
> Last night Japanese forces attacked the Philippine Islands.
> Last night the Japanese attacked Wake Island.
> And this morning, the Japanese attacked Midway Island.
> Japan has therefore undertaken a surprise offensive extending throughout
> the Pacific area. (Safire 1997, 142; see also Stelzner 1993)

Here Roosevelt has in effect constructed a comparison that involves six items, and his purpose in doing so appears in the final sentence. His "therefore" signals that he offers a conclusion supported by the preceding list, and these individual instances have been united as examples for the conclusion on the basis of their parallel form. So here is the next obvious use of parallelism (with in this case a heavy dose of *anaphora*, see below): it is the iconic form for example sets that support a generalization. The argument form here, supporting a generalization with examples, is classically known as *induction*.[2] In the most direct manner, the six examples of Japanese aggression "add up" to the conclusion. The list strengthens what was already, on the occasion of Roosevelt's speech, an overwhelming case for war. In terms of persuading the immediate audience for the immediate purpose, they were perhaps unnecessary. Nor did they have to take the form of separate statements with so much repetition. Roosevelt could have delivered these multiple examples by writing one sentence with multiple objects:

Within the last twenty-four hours, Japanese forces have attacked Malaya, Hong Kong, Guam, the Philippine Islands, Wake Island, and Midway Island. Roosevelt's particular expression of the case, through repeated parallel predicates, also belies any distinctions that might be made about the targets (the Philippines versus Wake Island, for example) or the nature and size of the attacks. They are instead all equated by virtue of the same presentation, and devoting a separate sentence to each act of war amplifies the extent of the aggression. If Roosevelt were indicting the Japanese in a courtroom, these separate details would amount to the "aggravating circumstances" justifying the severity of the response.

Why does parallel form so effectively deliver the examples that support an induction? A rhetorical rationale is provided by Perelman and Olbrechts-Tyteca in *The New Rhetoric* when they distinguish examples from illustrations. Both examples and illustrations count as particular instances, and they are inevitably expressed in language that is less general than the conclusion. But an illustration usually stands alone and is explained at length; the details provided fix the audience's attention on a single case and give the illustration great force. Examples supporting generalizations, on the other hand, do their work in groups. According to the Belgians,

> …an illustration designed to create presence will sometimes have to be developed with a wealth of concrete and vivid detail, whereas an example should be carefully pruned in order that the mind should not be distracted and depart from the aim the speaker has set himself. (1969, 358)

Perelman and Olbrechts-Tyteca also thought of illustrations as supporting already accepted beliefs and examples as establishing new beliefs. This difference in use is not really plausible; a single illustration can persuade an audience to accept a novel position. But the stylistic distinction remains. Arguers can elaborate or "prune." The ultimate in stylistic pruning of examples reduces them to parallel formulations with or without precise repetition (Fahnestock 2003).

Eduction

Aristotle recognized parallel cola as a rhetorically salient syntactical form in Book III of the *Rhetoric* (Freese 1991, 391); he also used grammatically parallel claims in Book II when offering an inductive argument built from examples (307). However, earlier in Book II, he noted a different type of argument depending on parallel phrasing. In the relevant passage he describes arguments based on *paradeigmata* or *parallel cases*. Aristotle believes these similar cases can be fabricated or based on historical facts, and he offers the following instance of support from factual parallel cases:

> …it is necessary to make preparations against the Great King and not to allow him to subdue Egypt; for Darius did not cross over to Greece until he had obtained

possession of Egypt; but as soon as he had done so, he did. Again, Xerxes did not attack us until he had obtained possession of that country [Egypt], but when he had, he crossed over; consequently, if the present Great King shall do the same, he will cross over, wherefore it must not be allowed. (Freese 1991, 275; the parallelism is in the Greek original)

Here the point is not to support a general conclusion with examples but to predict a new individual occurrence from similar preceding ones. The actions of the current "Great King" of the Persians are predicted from the pattern of his two predecessors, Darius and Xerxes. This argument form is typically termed *eduction* (and sometimes *abduction*) to distinguish it from induction (Black 1967, 169). But this form also requires that the audience appreciate the parallel nature of the instances, and to communicate that nature succinctly and iconically demands parallel phrasing.

The power of clausal parallelism to construct an argument from eduction is seen in the following selection from the opening paragraphs of a newspaper article where the point is to make a third event fit in with two previous cases.

When an explosion ripped through a French airliner flying over the Sahara in 1989, the blast severed the DC-10's front end from the rest of the plane, which stayed aloft for about 20 seconds before plunging into the ground. The black boxes showed that everything on board was normal until a jarring, split-second noise, followed by silence.

Two days later, investigators said the crash was caused by a bomb.

When Pan Am Flight 103 blew up over Lockerbie, Scotland, in December 1988, the nose of the aircraft broke away from the rest of the plane, scattering debris over 80 square miles of Scottish countryside. The black boxes showed everything on board was normal, until a split-second noise, followed by silence.

Within three days, investigators said the probable cause was a bomb.

....

In some ways, the circumstances surrounding the explosion of Trans World Airlines Flight 800 on July 17 are strikingly similar to the bombings of the other two. An explosion caused Flight 800's front end to break away from the rest of the Boeing 747, which continued to fly for about 20 seconds before becoming engulfed in a fireball. Flight 800's black boxes show that everything on board was normal until a split-second sound followed by silence.

Yet two weeks after Flight 800 exploded off the coast of Long Island, Federal officials have not determined the cause of the crash or ever aired their strong, private suspicions that a bomb, possibly hidden in the forward cargo hold, destroyed the craft. (Van Natta 1996)

The sentences opening the first and third paragraphs are parallel: each begins with a "when" clause that fixes the moment of the tragedy, followed by a main clause making a claim about the midair rupture of the fuselage; the final part of each sentence is a trailing modifier, the first in the form of a relative clause (*which stayed aloft*), the second in the form of a participial phrase (*scattering debris*), both bringing the wreckage to the ground. These similar sentence forms argue for the similar nature of the events. The third case, however, does not open in quite the same way, because its status in this set is the subject of the argument. But its main predication and its ending in a trailing modifier match the phrasing of the first two. The strongest case made in this article through parallel wording comes, however, in the last sentence concluding the description for each case. For purposes of seeing this parallelism clearly, here are the three sentences:

Par. 1 *The black boxes showed that everything on board was normal until a jarring, split-second noise, followed by silence.*

Par. 3 *The black boxes showed that everything on board was normal, until a split-second noise, followed by silence.*

Par. 6 *Flight 800's black boxes show that everything on board was normal until a split-second sound followed by silence.*

The author uses the strongest parallelism possible, determined by repetition of the same words, or almost the same, in the same syntactic positions. The text here is presumably a news story on a continuing investigation, but it is clear that the author is using stylistic resources to argue for the case he, or some of his informants, wished to make, one that was in fact abandoned after further investigation (on press coverage of Flight 800, see Durham 1998).

Strategic Repetition

Orators since antiquity have drawn on the power of repetition for emphasis and emotional heightening, and the American oratorical canon is filled with examples of reprised phrasing, from Puritan sermons to the acceptance speeches of both party's candidates in 2008. Figure manuals since antiquity have distinguished patterns of repetition based on where the repeated material appeared.

Repeating the openings of successive clauses (anaphora):
Our policy is based on an historical vision of America's role. **Our policy is** derived from a larger view of global change. **Our policy is** rooted in our moral values, which never change. **Our policy is** reinforced by our material wealth and by our military power. **Our policy is** designed to serve mankind. (Carter; Windt 1983, 247)

Repeating the closings of successive clauses (epistrophe):
In order to end a war **on many fronts**, I initiated a pursuit for peace **on many fronts**.

(Nixon; Safire 1997, 911)

Repeating the closing of one clause in the opening of the next (anadiplosis):

For we can afford all these efforts, and more—but we cannot afford *not* to meet this **challenge**. And the **challenge** is not to us alone. (Kennedy; Windt 1983, 29)

Repeating the opening of a clause in its ending (epanalepsis):

Mankind must put an end to war—or war will put an end to **mankind**.

(John F. Kennedy 1961)

Repeating the same openings and endings in a series of clauses (symploce):

When there is talk of hatred, **let us stand up and talk against it. When there is talk of** violence, **let us stand up and talk against it.** (Clinton 1995)

Repeating a word or phrase immediately, with nothing intervening (epizeuxis):

History shows us, demonstrates that **nothing, nothing** prepares the way for tyranny more than the failure of public officials to keep the streets safe from bullies and marauders. (Goldwater; Safire 1997, 901)

Repeating a word or phrase with one or a few words intervening (diacope):

The people **everywhere**, not just here in Britain, **everywhere**—they kept faith with Princess Diana. (Blair 1997; edited versions omit the second *everywhere*)

Such repetition creates sets of related terms, phrases, clauses, and therefore related meanings in a text, and these sets have persuasive consequences. First, they serve passage construction and arrangement. When listeners hear or readers see that a succession of clauses (or of other text segments) opens with repeated phrasing, they will tend to group those segments in their minds. Opening and ending repetition in places of emphasis (*anaphora* and *epistrophe*) is especially useful to speakers, since they have greater challenges when it comes to imposing structure on the stream of speech. Second, repetition establishes a pattern and so creates expectancy in the listener or reader, who is primed for another instance. Third, the partial repetition created by these devices, especially by *anaphora* and *epistrophe*, produces parallel sentences implicating the argument forms described above, comparison, induction, and eduction. Finally, all these devices, even the immediate repetition of a key term, derive power from their sound effects. They allow the rhetor a patch of incantatory prosody, driving home a point with syncopated insistence.

Antithesis: Argument from Opposites

Any investor who wants to make money from trading in stocks should follow this advice:

Buy low
Sell high

These two statements are equal in length and grammatically parallel. Each begins with an imperative verb (*Buy, Sell*) and ends with an adverb (*low, high*).[3] And most important, each pair deploys "opposite" terms or *antonyms*. There is a figure of speech in this famous phrase, created when two parallel phrases or clauses feature words that an audience would recognize as opposites; it is called an *antithesis*.

In the *Rhetoric,* Aristotle identified the *antithesis* as a particularly effective or urbane kind of phrasing, but he also linked it to a line of reasoning (Kennedy 1991, 243–45; Fahnestock 2000, 174–81). To use Aristotle's example: suppose someone wanted to argue that moderation (or *temperance*) as a behavioral standard is a good thing. Moderation has an opposite, *excess. Moderation,* it could be argued, is a *good thing* because its opposite, *excess* in either direction (too much or too little) has the opposite quality. *Excess is a bad thing.* So if an audience already agrees that "excess is a bad thing," they are also likely to agree that "moderation is a good thing." The arguer has "found" or invented an **argument from opposites**, by using the stylistic form of the antithesis. The figure of speech serves as a template, a prepared iconic form waiting to be filled: if A and A are opposites and B and B are opposites, combining them can yield the antithesis A...B/A...B. The content that Aristotle used in his example does not have much of an argumentative edge 2,500 years later, but the form can be put to more challenging uses.

Understanding how the antithesis can be used depends on recovering, first of all, the ways that words can be "opposed." Classical rhetoricians and modern semanticists distinguish several types of opposition or *antonymy*.[4] One important distinction separates **contraries** from **contradictories**. Contraries are pairs of terms like *hot/cold, wet/dry, rich/poor, up/down.* Such pairs are often thought of as concepts occupying extreme points on a scale with gradable intermediates and perhaps even a midpoint: for example, *lukewarm* between *hot* and *cold, eye level* between *up* and *down*. Contradictory terms, on the other hand, have no such midpoints or mediating possibilities. They represent stark either/or alternatives: *in/out, lost/found, standing still/moving.* It is easy to invent contradictories by simply adding a negative to another term: *here/not here, red/not red, sympathetic/not sympathetic.* Still another type of opposition involves **correlatives** or reciprocal terms, terms that in a sense bring one another into existence: *parent/child, teacher/student,* and, in the example above, *buy/sell.*

A perfect antithesis takes pairs of terms opposed as contraries, contradictories, or correlatives and puts them in parallel phrases. The result epitomizes arguments in which "opposites lying with opposites" reinforce and support each other, as in the following claim from an article in the *Journal of Bacteriology.*

> The experiments presented here suggest to us that ***many poorly translated*** mRNAs (e.g., those with ***weak*** ribosome binding sites) accumulate during ***slow growth in poor media*** and, conversely, ***many frequently translated*** mRNAs (e.g., those with ***strong*** ribosome binding sites) accumulate during ***fast growth in rich media***" (Liang et al. 2000, 3037)

This passage uses parallel phrasing with embedded pairs of opposites: the ***poorly translated*** contrast with the ***frequently translated***. The former accumulate during ***slow growth in poor media*** contrasted with accumulation during ***fast growth*** of the others ***in rich media***. The phrasing here expresses the logic of the single-difference experimental design. If a researcher can design a trial with two contrary features associated with two contrary outcomes, the experimenter has evidence of a causal connection. In fact, the available pattern of this form helped in the design of the experiment to begin with, since being able to make the antithetical claims is the researcher's goal.

The antithesis appears often in arguments when the rhetor wants to draw stark contrasts. For example, in response to criticism for his civil disobedience, Martin Luther King Jr. drew an uncompromising distinction between just and unjust laws in his "Letter from a Birmingham Jail":

> One has not only a legal but a moral responsibility to **obey just** laws. Conversely, one has a moral responsibility to **disobey unjust** laws. I would agree with St. Augustine that "an unjust law is no law at all." Now, what is the difference between the two? How does one determine whether a law is just or unjust? A **just law** is a man-made code that **squares with** the moral law or the law of God. An **unjust law** is a code that is **out of harmony with** the moral law. To put it in the terms of St. Thomas Aquinas: An unjust law is a human law that is not rooted in eternal law and natural law. Any law that **uplifts** human personality is **just**. Any law that **degrades** human personality is **unjust**. (1963)

The terms in bold in this passage are paired as antonyms: *obey...just/disobey...unjust*; *just law...squares with/unjust law...out of harmony with; uplifts...just/degrades...unjust.* And these antonyms, placed in parallel phrases, constitute the opposed claims of antitheses. With this scheme, King opens an unbridgeable gulf between divine moral law and unjust manmade codes.

Antimetabole: Argument from Inversion

> *As an American, I condemn a Republican Fascist just as much as I condemn a Democrat Communist. I condemn a Democrat Fascist just as much as I condemn a Republican Communist.*
> *With skillful manipulating of the press they're able to make the victim look like the criminal and the criminal look like the victim.*

Arguers as different as Senator Margaret Chase Smith in the 1950s and Malcolm X in the 1960s, authors of the two sentences above, nevertheless employed the same rhetorical scheme known as the *antimetabole* (Safire 1997, 668, 671). This figure is also built on parallel phrasing, but now instead of deploying antonyms like the *antithesis*, the speaker or writer retains the same key terms but switches their relative positions in the paired units.

A......B/B......A

Smith switched the positions of the labels *Republican* and *Democrat* to show that the ideological extremes of fascism and communism could be owned or disowned by either party. If party identities are exchangeable in this way, they are negligible; only ideologies remain. Malcolm X's argument uses the *antimetabole* to reverse the positions of reciprocally related terms, *criminal* and *victim*, suggesting the confusion in basic categories that he went on in this speech to attribute to influential whites.

The most famous *antimetabole* in American oratory has yet another form. It is the "corrective" *antimetabole*. One half has a negating term (*not*), so the form says in effect, "It's not A...B, but B...A." The combined statements presume that A and B must be in some relationship:

> *Ask not what your **country** can do for **you**; ask what **you** can do for your **country**.*

Without a negative on one side, the *antimetabole* makes essentially two kinds of arguments, one about identity and one about reciprocal causality or process. For example, Sydney Lamb, author of *Pathways of the Brain*, uses the figure to epitomize the evidence connecting physical aspects of speaking with the sounds produced by humans. Since the relative positions of key terms can be switched, since their order is indifferent, their connection is stronger.

> One very important property, important for the sake of young children learning how to speak as well as for the sake of phoneticians establishing correlations between articulations and acoustic properties, is that these correlations are remarkably strong—for **different articulations** you get **different sounds**, and **different sounds** require **different articulations**. (1999, 21)

Similarly, when the eighteenth-century chemist Antoine Lavoisier wanted to describe equilibrium processes in chemistry he ran his phrases in two directions, switching the positions of three key terms to suggest the reciprocal pathways:

> It is easy with the same apparatus, by means of divers combinations of experiments, to determine the quantity of caloric requisite for converting **solid** substances into liquids, and **liquids** into **elastic aeriform fluids**; and vice versa, what quantity of caloric escapes from **elastic vapours** in changing to **liquids**, and what quantity escapes from liquids during their conversion into **solids**. (Kerr 1952, 14; bold added [These phrases also contain *gradatio* elements; see p. 246])

The *antimetabole,* then, offers an especially strong iconic realization of certain lines of argument featuring identity claims and causal reciprocity. It is unlikely, however, that readers or listeners go through a logical translation of the figure. The form itself epitomizes, or expresses iconically, the connection between the key terms.

Definition as a Figure

The figures described above, *isocolon/parison, antithesis,* and *antimetabole,* are relatively familiar and easily recognized schemes based on syntactic manipulation and strategic semantics. Less well known in the rhetorical tradition is the close tie between other prescribed statement types and certain lines of argument. Since the sentence forms involved here are often unremarkable, their relation to argument forms often escapes notice. But in general, rhetorical stylistics marked various brief sentence forms as useful tools for rhetors.

Among the most important strategies in argumentation is the act of defining, so, not surprisingly, prescriptions for how to define terms and use them in arguments appear throughout traditional rhetoric and dialectic (see Schiappa 2003). For example, Aristotle's list of twenty-eight potential lines of argument (or *topoi*) features definition twice. He recommends either showing that a term has many meanings or stipulating that it has a single meaning (Kennedy 1991, 195–96). Definition is also one of the issues or stases (*quid sit?*) that an entire argument could address: *What is virtue? What is the nature of an ambassador's role?* And issues of definition appear again in the list of potential controversies about written documents: *What does "right to bear arms" mean in the Constitution?* (see the discussion of defining terms in written statutes in Cicero 1976, 321–23).[5]

In rhetoric and dialectic, a definition has a prescribed syntactic form; it must conform to the standard sentence pattern of Subject – Linking Verb – Predicate Noun/Modifier. The term to be defined fills the subject slot and, through a linking verb, it is first placed in a *genus* or larger category (predicate noun) and then distinguished from other members of that genus by the *differentia* (modifiers), the unique features that distinguish it from other members of the genus.

A monarchy is a government headed by a hereditary ruler.
term defined   **genus**   **differentia**

The resulting definition here is called a *categorical proposition*; it is a sentence form that allows inspection of the "set logic" behind the definition.

Taking their cue from Aristotle's *Topics,* dialectical manuals used stylistic manipulation to test for a correctly constructed definition. It had to be convertible; the linking verb in the statement (the *copula*) had to function like an equals sign and allow the subject and predicate to exchange places, resulting in a statement still supportable or acceptable. The sample offered above would be converted into *A government headed by a hereditary ruler is a monarchy.* This conversion requirement produces the stylistic signature of the "emphatic definition," where both directions of the claim are offered:

Venus is the planet second from the sun, and the planet second from the sun is Venus.

This double definition, an *antimetabole* (see above), produces a presumably "irrefutable" identity claim. But more important was the test of conversion itself. A claim that only placed a term in a genus, for example, would not be convertible: *Venus is a planet* and *A planet is Venus.* Arguments from genus, however, had their own special force, as in Lincoln's cogent reasoning from the categorization of slaves as human beings rather than items of property (Weaver 1985, 93–100).

A predication of genus was not singled out in rhetorical stylistics, but from the earliest Latin treatment of style in the *Rhetorica ad Herennium*, *definitio* was listed as a figure of speech, and the examples offered in that treatise display the standard "subject – linking verb – predicate noun/modifier" structure:

Definition [*definitio*] in brief and clear-cut fashion grasps the characteristic qualities of a thing, as follows.... "By an injury is meant doing violence to some one, to his person by assault, or to his sensibilities by insulting language, or to his reputation by some scandal." Again: "That is not economy on your part, but greed, because economy is careful conservation of one's own goods, and greed is wrongful covetousness of the goods of others." ([Cicero] 1954, 316–17).[6]

In the first example offered, the genus of *injury* is "doing violence" and the modifiers cover the species of this genus, violence to a person's body, sensibilities, or reputation. The second example quoted offers a particularly useful "contrast definition" to refute an opponent's term (*economy*) with the speaker's relabeling *(greed)*. Such contrast definitions help an arguer preemptively separate two terms that an audience might confuse, and in some figure manuals these double definitions of one term against another were labeled as the separate device *horismus*.

The stylistic virtue identified in the *definitio* is not, however, its correct logical form but its succinctness and completeness: "Definition is accounted useful for this reason: it sets forth the full meaning and character of a thing so lucidly and briefly that to express it in more words seems superfluous, and to express it in fewer is considered impossible ([Cicero] 1981, 317). The unhedged brevity of the *definitio* survives in later explanations of this figure. In John Hoskins' *Directions for Speech and Style* (ca. 1599), definition "is the shortest and truest exposition of the nature of anything." He refers his readers to Aristotle, Aquinas, and Cicero for exemplary definitions of virtues, vices, and passions, offering the following examples himself: "Fear is an apprehension of future harm./Thrift is a moderate and lawful increase of wealth by careful government of your own estate./

Compliment is performance of affected ceremonies in words, looks, or gesture" (1935, 44). Demonstrating the argument/style connection, Hoskins refers readers to Valerius's *Logic* or the sixth book of Aristotle's *Topics*, but he qualifies, "Your definitions need not be strictly tied to the rules of logic, nor your divisions" (44).

Summary

The epigraph opening this chapter contains sentences from Lyndon Johnson's first major speech to a joint session of Congress, delivered five days after he was sworn in as president following Kennedy's assassination (Windt 1983, 53–55). This speech features several of the syntactic schemes identified since antiquity in rhetorical stylistics. The opening two sentences, for example, constitute an antithesis. Within the framework of grammatically parallel sentences with repetition, a pair of contrary terms, *friend* and *foe*, is matched with a pair of contradictory terms, *seek peace* and *reject the path of peace*. The second half of this antithesis does have a second relative clause, an extension of "foe" status in parallel to its partner. But the core of the antithesis here, pairing opposite terms, succinctly predicts the differences in U.S. posture to perceived allies or enemies. The next sentence offers strongly parallel independent clauses (*parison*), both beginning *those who test*. The key terms matched in these two nine-word clauses do not, however, quite have antonym status: *courage* and *friendship*, *strong* and *honorable*. Here is a case of the form inviting a construal of these paired clauses as antithetical, but the word choice fails the form since it does not match "opposite with opposite."

In the concluding lines quoted, the speech clearly reaches for the formal grandeur of antimetabole with the inverted predications, *the strong can be just* and the *just can be strong*. Johnson's speechwriters might have left those phrases without modification to express the qualities of strength and justice combined against expectation. But they added concluding parallel prepositional phrases that recall the first term in each half of the anitmetabole, *strong/strength* and *just/justice*—an addition deploying the figure *polyptoton* that swings each part back on itself. These additions muddy the figure and the point.

The previous chapter discussed iconic form, the arrangement of sentence elements to epitomize the meaning of a sentence. The syntactic schemes discussed in this chapter can be seen as prepared iconic forms, sentence patterns once deliberately taught in the rhetorical tradition. They structure the content that fills them into fixed lines of argument, and they are always waiting as prompts in the prepared mind.

NOTES

1. Isocolon is always defined and illustrated in the manuals as a feature of adjacent discourse segments. But there is really no reason to limit the effects of equal unit length to adjacent segments. For example, in his speech to Congress following Kennedy's assassination, Lyndon Johnson opened with a sentence eighteen syllables long, "All I have I would have given gladly not to be

standing here today," and a few paragraphs later he produced another eighteen-syllable sentence at the opening of another section, "This Nation will keep its commitments from South Viet-Nam to West Berlin" (Windt 1983, 53). In this manner, a speaker can return to statements of the same length to signal effects such as the initiation of a new discourse segment. On sentence-length effects, see chapter 12.

2. Example sets phrased as a sequence of parallel statements are used to illustrate induction in early modern dialectical treatises. Melanchthon offered an induction based on three types of wine: "*Vinum Creticum calefacit, vinum Italicum calefacit, vinum Rhenanum calefacit, nec ullum dissimile exemplum monstrari potest, ergo omne vinum calefacit*" (1963b, 620). And logical treatises today continue to use such parallelism, though without remarking on the stylistic constraints involved. Here is the example from the fourth edition of the venerable Irving Copi's widely used *Introduction to Logic* where induction is characterized as probable argument and no clause claiming the absence of contrary examples is offered: "All cows are mammals and have lungs/All horses are mammals and have lungs/All men are mammals and have lungs. Therefore probably all mammals have lungs" (1972, 25). In a more recent textbook, Groarke and Tindale still use parallel phrasing for the support: "The group of microchips examined is a representative sample of the chips sent. All of the microchips examined are made to specification. All of the microchips sent are made to specification" (2004, 292).

3. Alternatively, one could almost read those adverbs as though they were objects of the verbs: buy low [undervalued stocks] and sell high [highly or overvalued stocks].

4. Aristotle also distinguished *privatives* as a form of opposition, e.g., blindness versus sight. Contemporary semanticists distinguish absolute and gradable opposites (i.e., contradictories and contraries) as well as directional opposites (north/south, backwards/forwards, left/right) and relational opposites (correlative terms) (Barnes 1984, I 18).

5. In medieval and early modern dialectical manuals, definition is identified as a crucial statement type that comes ultimately from the doctrine of the five predicables, a codification derived from Porphyry's third-century CE introduction (*Isagoge*) to Aristotle's *Topics*. Porphyry's five statement types, so prominent in later dialectical and logical treatises, could concern *species, genus, differentia, property,* and *accident*. See Peter of Spain, *Summulae Logicales* (1990, 17–23); Melanchthon, *Erotemata Dialectices* (1963b, 518).

6. The 1547 *Elementa Rhetorices* of Philipp Melanchthon is particularly interesting for the stylistic analogues of dialectical devices. Figures of definition appear under the heading *Ex definitione*, a category that includes *interpretatio, hyperbole,* and *expolitio*. It [definition] has "the same meaning here [in the section of a rhetorical treatise covering style] as in dialectic"; "For just as in proving many of the firmest arguments are from definition, so in ornamenting [*ornando*] definition is often placed in the open" (1963a, 483, 486; translation mine).

Please do not annoy, torment, pester, plague, molest,
worry, badger, harry, harass, heckle, persecute, irk,
bullyrag, vex, disquiet, grate, beset, bother, tease,
nettle, tantalize, or ruffle the animals

SIGN IN THE SAN DIEGO ZOO

11

SERIES

IN *DESERT SOLITAIRE*, his autobiographical account of a summer as a seasonal ranger in Utah's Arches National Monument (later National Park), Edward Abbey reported how "someone" had placed the following sign on the inside door of a restroom facility:

> Attention: Watch out for rattlesnakes, coral snakes, whip snakes, vinegaroons, centipedes, millipedes, ticks, mites, black widows, cone-nosed kissing bugs, solpugids, tarantulas, horned toads, Gila monsters, red ants, fire ants, Jerusalem crickets, chinch bugs and Giant Hairy Desert Scorpions before being seated. (1968, 35)

Abbey, spiritual godfather of ecoactivism, here uses the syntactic device of an extended series to argue. The very number of items listed on this sign encourages any hapless tourist, about to sit, to look around anxiously and leave as quickly as possible. Furthermore, the precise ordering of items in this series helps to make it effective. The opening item, *rattlesnakes*, the prototypical poisonous snake to Americans, is an immediately recognizable danger to vulnerable humans. Coming first in the list, it instructs readers to interpret the subsequent series as a grouping of "nasty and dangerous things." If Abbey had started with chinch bugs or Jerusalem crickets or the unfamiliar *solpugids* or *vinegaroons*, readers would be uncertain what evaluative frame to adopt for the list, and less certain about what this list was a list of. But when these unknown entities occur in the middle of the list, they become "dangerous things" by virtue of the company they keep. Notice also how Abbey ends the warning. Series are often constructed so that their items increase in some way toward a climax (see below

239

on *incrementum*). Beginning with *rattlesnake* prevents a pure ordering by increasing nastiness, but Abbey nevertheless manages to end with another well-recognized horror, the Great Hairy Desert Scorpion, which also deserves last place as the longest item with four words, all capitalized. Many more examples of lists occur throughout Abbey's text, sometimes to celebrate the variety and beauty in nature (26, 69), and sometimes to defame what threatens it (58). Lengthy series are a consistent element of his style in *Desert Solitaire*.

The opening example from Abbey illustrates several of the features of series that contribute to their potential rhetorical effects: creating categories, ordering items, and closing down or opening up the possibility of more items. Even the length of a series can be an argumentative device, as in the case of Abbey's list of restroom dangers. These features trigger the default assumptions that readers invoke when they encounter a series: that the items have been selected according to some consistent principle, that they are in some deliberate order, and that they represent a complete set. Each of these default assumptions, and the way each can be defeated, will be discussed separately in what follows.

Definition of a Series

A series can be defined as a listing of three or more sentence elements in a row that, as a result, become "residents" of the same grammatical position in a sentence—three or more subjects, verbs, or modifiers.[1]

> *Subjects:* "The Western democracies, the OPEC nations, and the developed communist countries can cooperate through existing international institutions in providing more effective aid." (Carter; Windt 1983, 247)
>
> *Verbs and adjectives:* "But it [the greatest evil] is conceived and ordered (moved, seconded, carried, and minuted) in clean, carpeted, warmed, and well-lighted offices." (Reagan quoting C. S. Lewis; Safire 1997, 493)
>
> *Objects of a preposition:* "This opens up a fine opportunity for us in good will, trade, jobs, exports, and political cooperation." (Carter; Windt 1983, 251)

A series can be composed of any grammatical unit—words, phrases, clauses, etc.—as long as there are more than two of them and as long as they inhabit the same grammatical slot within a longer unit. The items in such a series should be grammatically parallel as well.

> *Predicate nouns modified by prepositional phrases:* "Tonight there is violence in our streets, corruption in our highest offices, aimlessness among our youth, anxiety among our elderly." (Goldwater; Safire 1997, 900)

Series and Categorization

By occupying the same grammatical niche in a sentence, series "tell" readers or listeners that their items have been listed according to some grouping principle, a principle that creates or delivers items in a set. In other words, a series constructs a category. It can offer items from an already recognized grouping: *Do you want a hot dog, a ham sandwich, a slice of pizza, a hamburger, or a turkey wrap?* In the United States, most readers of this series would already recognize that all these items belong in the category "things to eat, usually for lunch." Or a series can introduce a new category, defining it by listing members and sometimes also by announcing the overall category: *Sarah inherited from her aunt a gold ring, a Chippendale chair, and a collection of love letters.* Readers of this series of dissimilar items are explicitly told that they all belong to the category of things Sarah inherited from her aunt. Either invoking the familiar or constructing the new, categorization is the basic conceptual payoff of series construction.[2]

Rhetorical style manuals devoted a surprising amount of attention to series, distinguishing various types as different figures of speech. These figures build series on different principles of categorization, and therefore they have different conceptual and argumentative effects.

> **Partitio**: The items listed can be parts of something, and the entire series can add up to a whole.
> *The midbrain is composed of the mammillary bodies, the pituitary, the thalamus, and the hypothalamus.*
> **Diaeresis**: The items can be types of a kind, or species that belong to a genus.
> *Under metals, Agricola classified earths, stones, salts, and minerals.*
> **Enumeratio**[3]: The items can be features or adjuncts of a subject.
> *He has sparse brown hair, a Southern accent, a mole on his left cheek, and a noticeable limp.*

These three types of series represent the careful distinctions that were routinely made in the early modern verbal arts. The parts into which something was divided were distinguished from the species under a genus or from the miscellaneous features or adjuncts of a subject that were neither. Parts have to add up to a whole, but the species that belong to a genus need not "add up" to a genus. There is always room for a new species, but not for a new "part" in any complete enumeration according to a consistent principle. And the features of an item that can be listed never "add up" to that item the way parts add up to a whole, nor are they species of it. They are simply things that can be noticed or said about a subject, often from different perspectives.

But again, all three of these figures—*partitio, diaeresis,* and *enumeratio*—invoke the same default assumption that by virtue of their occurring together they are members of the same category. Parts (*partitio*) result from division of a whole according to the same principle; species cluster in the same genus; and features or adjuncts, by the nature of the proposition introducing them, necessarily belong to the same thing. This assumption about belonging explains the argumentative power of mere listing, since elements can be inserted into a category simply by being placed in a series. In 2006, Barack Obama inserted himself in the bipartisan group of senators who had forged a compromise bill on immigration policy: "I want to cite Lindsey Graham, Sam Brownback, Mel Martinez, Ken Salazar, myself, Dick Durbin, Joe Lieberman...who've actually had to wake up early to try to hammer this stuff out." Two-thirds of the way in is an inconspicuous position to take in a series, but two *Washington Post* reporters questioned whether Obama belonged in this group at all (Murray and Weisman 2008).

There is only one kind of series that seems to violate the usual assumption about category membership. This noncategorizing series had a special name in rhetorical manuals listing figures of speech.

> *Congeries*: All the items in a series mean roughly the same thing.
> *He was a scoundrel, a rascal, a ruffian, a villain, an outlaw.*

A congeries obviously differs from the typical list, since its terms are not in fact different but are instead synonyms or interchangeable labels, and as such they inhabit a category with one member. The primary effect of a congeries is therefore emphasis and amplification as each item refracts from a slightly different angle the same basic denotation. The list of ways to harass zoo animals quoted as the epigraph to this chapter is a tour de force congeries.[4]

BRACKETING

Since the typical series places three or more members in the same grammatical position and therefore by default in the same group, it follows that series have a certain leveling or *bracketing* effect. What holds for most of the members of the series, or the most dominant, will spread over the members.[5] This effect can have unintended consequences, as in the following example in a letter from a government agency refusing a request for reimbursement: "Over the years NIH [National Institutes of Health] has had a number of requests to provide funds for sitters, housekeepers, dependent's travel, kennel costs, etc." While the bureaucrat who wrote this letter was no doubt factually accurate, he or she nevertheless offended by equating items that, to the recipient, belonged in very different value categories, namely sitters for children and kennel costs for dogs. The potential outrageousness of series bracketing is more dramatically on view in the following from a Maureen Dowd editorial:

Societies built on special privileges—the all-male Saudi rulers, Catholic priesthood and Taliban, and the boys' club running Enron—become far too invested in preserving those privileges. (2002)

Though written during the height of the church sex abuse scandal, linking Catholic clergy so intimately with the Taliban could not fail to offend many U.S. readers, as Dowd no doubt intended.

As the above examples indicate, when series equate items, the evaluative dimension of one or most of the items influences the assessment of the others. Roger Fowler notes this "leveling effect of the list" (1991, 140). It is often invisible unless it is more or less outrageous or is encountered by the wrong readers. Residents of different political orientations would, for example, respond differently to the following answer from Democratic presidential candidate John Kerry, who in the 2004 campaign responded to questions about George Bush's National Guard service during the Vietnam War.

I've never made any judgments about any choice somebody made about avoiding the draft, about going to Canada, going to jail, being a conscientious objector, going into the National Guard." (Pruden 2004)

While Kerry may have intended this series as a neutral listing of options, it was read by some as a negative evaluation about service in the National Guard, a reading reinforced by Kerry's repetition of *going* in the second, third, and fifth items, a repetition that strengthens the grouping of these items.

Series and Order

In addition to inferring that items in a series belong in the same category and share the same evaluative valence, readers can respond to, or construct on their own, some principle of order in a series. In other words, they can infer that the way the items in a series are ordered is precisely the way they should be ordered according to some principle. Rhetorical manuals described two types of series where the ordering of the elements was the rationale for the series' construction. The first is the *incrementum* and the second is the *gradatio*.[6]

Incrementum: Items in a series can be ordered so that they increase or decrease in some way that readers will recognize.

No corporal, sergeant, lieutenant, captain, major, or general could order me to do something that was against my religion.

Here the series is organized according to increasing military rank, and its punch depends on readers recognizing this order.

The hopes of the Allies rose with the Battle of Midway, the invasion of Sicily, the beach-head at Anzio, and the Battle of Tobruk.

The ordering in this series suggests chronological sequence, an implication reinforced by the predication *hopes rose*. *Readers* without independent knowledge of World War II would simply assume that these events occurred in the order listed.

A series can run in either direction, to the greater in amount or importance or to the later in time, or the reverse. In his announcement of his decision not to run for the presidency in 1968, Lyndon Johnson observed, "I am a free man, an American, a public servant, and a member of my party, in that order always and only" (Windt 1983, 105). He meant this series as a list of items in decreasing order of importance on the presumption that the first thing named is the most important. His usage is a *decrementum* (*catabasis*, see note 5). And whether the terms are offered as increasing or decreasing according to some property, the rhetorical principle is the same: the order of the items is significant.

The potential for readers to respond to or create their own order in a series can have consequences beneficial or otherwise for the rhetor. In her widely disseminated speech to the United Nations Fourth World Conference on Women held in China in 1995, Hillary Clinton used series at different points:

- We come together in fields and in factories. In village markets and supermarkets. In living rooms and board rooms...
- There are some who question the reason for this conference. Let them listen to the voices of women in their homes, neighborhoods and workplaces....Let them look at the women gathered here and at Huairou—the homemakers, nurses, teachers, lawyers, policymakers, and women who run their own businesses....
- At this very moment, as we sit here, women around the world are giving birth, raising children, cooking meals, washing clothes, cleaning houses, planting crops, working on assembly lines, running companies, and running countries. (Hillary Clinton 1995)

Each of these series, if read as an *incrementum*, demonstrates the same trajectory from the home to the workplace or political arena. These series therefore implicate a value hierarchy, with the items rising in desirability or importance, an implicit arguing that may not have been appropriate for a global audience representing populations of women for whom living rooms, the office watercooler, and running a company were less relevant images.

ITEM LENGTH AND ORDER

Readers of English also have default assumptions about how a well-formed series should be constructed. If there is no obvious reason to put the items in a certain order, they should be arranged so that the longest item comes last. This ordering by increasing syllable or word length preserves the principle of *end weight*, the preference for constructions to swell as they conclude. Order by length can produce an impression of finality, completeness, and equality among the items in the series.

> A. Joanna preferred simple foods, herb gardens, classical music, and clothing made by her dressmaker.
> B. Joanna preferred simple foods, classical music, clothing made by her dressmaker, and herb gardens.

Because series A follows the preference for putting the longest item last, all its items might seem equal; they are all members of the set of things that Joanna likes. But because series B violates the preference for longest item last, it can suggest some other purpose in the ordering. Perhaps its items are arranged to indicate the least to the most liked or to emphasize the final item. In the example of the *partitio* given above, the fact that the longest item, mammillary bodies, comes first rather than last, violating end weight, suggests that some principle of spatial ordering (top to bottom, outside to inside, front to back) is being followed. There is, at any rate, always a lurking implication of order in a series, though a stylistic preference like *end weight* can work against it.

Series exhibiting these differences occur in Theodore Roosevelt's 1899 lecture in favor of "The Strenuous Life." At one point, Roosevelt uses the heroic efforts of "those who carried the great Civil War to a triumphant conclusion" to justify choosing the harder path: "for in the end the slave was freed, the Union restored, and the mighty American Republic placed once more as a helmeted queen among nations" (Safire 1997, 516). Here the series concludes with its weightiest item in terms of length. A few paragraphs letter he offers another series:

> All honor must be paid to the architects of our material prosperity, to the great captains of industry who have built our factories and our railroads, to the strong men who toil for wealth with brain and hand" (515).

The second item of this series at twenty syllables is longer than the final item at twelve. This series does not observe the principle of end weight. It can either be read as a *congeries*, where all three items really refer to the same group, or to a series with a deliberate order that places "strong men" above "captains of industry."

GRADATIO

Another type of series named in the manuals exaggerates a particular ordering of elements because it repeats or "overlaps" items. This series-figure is called the *gradatio* (or, in some manuals, the *climax*), a name which emphasizes the option of using this device to build up to its final item.

> But also for this very reason, giving all diligence, add to your faith virtue, to virtue knowledge, to knowledge self-control, to self-control perseverance, to perseverance godliness, to godliness brotherly kindness, and to brotherly kindness love (*NKJ* 2 Peter 1:5–6)
>
> [I]t is essential that you should practically bear in mind that towards the payment of debts there must be revenue; that to have revenue there must be taxes; that no taxes can be devised which are not more or less inconvenient and unpleasant. (George Washington; Reid 1988, 196–97)

Without the internal repetition, the series from the New Testament could simply read, "add to your faith, virtue, knowledge, self-control, perseverance, godliness, brotherly kindness and love." What the *gradatio* adds is the implication of a relay across spiritual states or across time, or even a chain of causality. All the qualities are not added to faith at once, but in a sequence which suggests that the acquisition of one leads to the acquisition of the next. The *gradatio* also epitomizes a chain of causes and consequences when Washington observes the inevitable sequence that payment of debts requires revenue, which in turn requires taxes, which in turn means unpleasantness; nothing has changed that sequence since Washington noted it in 1796. The *gradatio* is also the device of choice for epitomizing the conceptual configuration known as *embôitement* or nesting, a containment strategy like a Russian doll where the little doll fits inside the middle-sized doll, the middle-sized doll fits in the big doll, and the big doll fits in the giant-sized doll. (On the argumentative uses of the *incrementum* and the *gradatio,* see Fahnestock 1999, 86–121.)

Series and Conjunctions

Just as default or preferred stylistic practice puts the items of a series in order according to increasing length, so conventional practice puts a conjunction between the final two items in a series. In his inaugural address, for example, Kennedy called for "a struggle against the common enemies of man, tyranny, poverty, disease and war itself" (Windt 1983, 11; the addition of *itself* gave the final item *war* the verbal end weight to match its conceptual weight). In transcribing series into text, style manuals differ over whether a comma should be placed after the item coming just before the conjunction. The usual defense of this comma is that it prevents readers from grouping the final two items (showing again a reading expectation). But with or without that comma, the normal series places a conjunction (*and, or, nor*) before its final item. This default practice can be violated in two ways, and each has special effects.

> *Polysyndeton*: Conjunctions can be placed between each item in the series.
> The forces that tend for evil are great and terrible, but the forces of truth and love and courage and honesty and generosity and sympathy are also stronger than ever before. (T. Roosevelt; Reid 1988, 630)

The effect of this practice is, quite obviously, to emphasize each individual item in the series as well as the very process of series linkage, the progressive adding of yet another and yet another member.

A related practice can occur in a long series where the items are presented in sets of doubles. Both *polysyndeton* and internal doubling are used in the passage from the Book of Acts in the New Testament where the point is to emphasize the number of languages that were understood by those listening to the Apostles on Pentecost:

> And they were amazed and wondered, saying, "Are not all these who are speaking Galileans? And how is it that we hear, each of us in his own native language? Parthians and Medes and Elamites and residents of Mesopotamia, Judea and Cappadocia, Pontus and Asia, Phrygia and Pamphylia, Egypt and the parts of Libya belonging to Cyrene, and visitors from Rome, both Jews and Proselytes, Cretans and Arabians, we hear them telling in our own tongues the mighty works of God. (*NKJ* Acts 2: 6–13; the conjunctions appear in the Greek original with repetitions of *kai* where English has *and*, and the intensified *te kai* with the sense of *both* in the first, third, and final double.)

Obviously, the more languages, the greater the miracle, so sheer quantity has an argumentative purpose here. If doubles add anything to a long series, it is perhaps an impression of randomness that reinforces the impression of quantity. The rising and falling intonation of the doubles also creates a singsong rhythm within the series that invites repetition. A long list is broken up into manageable pairs, but the reader still loses count of the total. Second-order grouping effects also result from this kind of doubling or segmenting within a series.

> *Asyndeton*: Series can be constructed with no conjunctions at all.
> I came, I saw, I conquered. (Julius Caesar; *Veni, vidi, vici*)

This option is one of the few devices mentioned by Aristotle in Book III of the *Rhetoric*: "asyndeta have a special characteristic; many things seem to be said at the same time; for the connective makes many things seem one, so that if it is taken away, clearly the opposite results: one thing will be many. Asyndeton thus creates amplification [*auxesis*]: "'I came; I spoke; I besought' (these things seem many)" (Kennedy 1991, 256; see also Graff 2005). As pointed out above, if *polysyndeton* emphasizes the act of joining, and correspondingly highlights each individual item linked together, then removing all conjunctions emphasizes the accumulation. The items spill out in a rush. Of the many *asyndeta* in the New Testament, the listing of the fruits of the spirit is delivered without connectives, and hence with an impression of unrolling plenitude or copia: "But the fruit of the Spirit is love, joy, peace, longsuffering, kindness, goodness, faithfulness, gentleness, self-control" (*NKJ* Galatians 5:22).

The Overall Length of Series

Is there a default or preferred length for a series? The number of items can often be manipulated, unless the series refers to a set of stipulated size known to the audience (e.g., the four seasons, the seven deadly sins). The minimal series, by definition, has three elements, and many memorable phrases have just three elements, usually ordered by increasing syllable length. To name just two from the Declaration of Independence: "life, liberty, and the pursuit of happiness"; "our lives, our fortunes, and our sacred honor." In his speech to Parliament when he became prime minister in 1940, Winston Churchill pledged his nation's "blood, toil, sweat, and tears" in the coming conflict; yet this quotation is often repeated with just three items, "blood, sweat, and tears" (Safire 1997, 134). Those who shortened Churchill's series actually improved it by removing the one item that did not fit the obvious category of the others. It may be that such triads are preferred in discourse intended to be serious and momentous because they create an impression of stability or finality.

Series can, however, be extended well beyond three items, and their length can be persuasive in itself (as pointed out above in the case of the miracle of Pentecost). A superb example of arguing by length of series occurred in a debate between archaeologists in the late 1980s over when early humans first migrated to the North American continent. A series of articles in *Natural History* forwarded the view that humans came much earlier than the then prevailing belief of about 12,000 years ago (Fahnestock 1989). This proposed earlier date was refuted by Paul S. Martin in an article with the following first paragraph:

During the Pleistocene—the last Ice Age, 1.8 million to 10,000 years ago—elk, moose, musk oxen, mountain goats, buffalo, mountain sheep, Dall's sheep, pronghorns, caribou, white-tailed deer, mule deer, grizzly bears, black bears, wolves, and cougars were not the only large animals living in North America. Mammoths, mastodons, native camels and llamas, native horses, ground sloths, armadillolike glyptodonts, tapirs, giant peccaries, mountain deer, giant beavers, four-pronged antelopes, and various species of woodland musk oxen and other bovids also roamed the continent. In addition to these now-extinct herbivores, the land harbored such predators and scavengers as dire wolves, native American lions, sabertoothed cats, and scavenging birds. (1987, 10)

After naming this overwhelming number of prey animals, Martin makes the point that, as hunters of these animals, the first humans on the scene would have frequented the places they were found. He then follows with another extended list.

Among North American vertebrate paleontologists, some of the sites famous for their late Pleistocene bones are such fresh water and mineral springs as Hot Springs, South Dakota; Boney Springs, Missouri; Saltville, Virginia and Big Bone Lick, Kentucky; certain coastal deposits such as Seminole Field, Florida; numerous alluvial deposits such as Murray Springs, Arizona; various damp caves in the eastern United States, including Big Bone Cave, Tennessee; and an assortment of dry caves and sinkholes in the western United States, notably Gypsum Cave, Nevada, and Natural Trap, Wyoming. In addition, a vast number of bones of large animals have been excavated at Rancho la Brea and various other tar seeps in California. Yet at none of these sites do human remains or artifacts turn up until after 12,000 years ago. (10)

Martin's final statement about the absence of evidence is supported by the number of potential prey species and of hunting sites where fossils could be found, if they were there. Thus the sheer length of Martin's many series argues his case.[7]

Opening Up or Shutting Down

A device in wide use is the little abbreviation *etc.*, standing for the Latin words *et cetera*, "and other things." When a series ends with an *etc.*, the speaker or writer in effect asserts that the series as spoken or on the page is incomplete and that more items of the same sort could be named. Perhaps the listener or reader could fill in items. If not, the cooperative audience member trusts the rhetor that more items in the same category are available. The impression that a series is complete or incomplete depends on all of the features of series construction discussed so far—their category creation, their length, the use or absence of conjunctions, and how they are introduced. Overall, a series can open up or shut down, and either implication can serve the rhetor's argument.

The purpose of some series, like the one in Edward Abbey's stall sign (see above), is to suggest a large and potentially open set. Readers come away with the impression of copiousness, as Thomas Conley has pointed out (1985), and that impression serves the argument. The counter effect is to produce a series that shuts down, that seems complete.

Such a finite series can support the "argument from elimination" found in the oldest arguments in the Western tradition, from the Sophists Gorgias and Antiphon. In his *Encomium on Helen,* for example. Gorgias lists the possible reasons for Helen of Troy running away with Alexander (Paris): fate, force, persuasion, or love (Freeman 1983, 131). If this set of possible motives or causes is complete and Gorgias can exonerate Helen from all four, then she is innocent.

What stylistically makes a series seem closed or open-ended? Open-ended series are more likely to use asyndeton, to use miscellaneous order (not, for example, an order increasing or decreasing in some way), or to be deliberately introduced as incomplete. Series that seem complete are more likely to use the default conjunction before the last item, to follow an obvious order, or to be deliberately introduced as complete. Consider the following two series:

> Berlin and Kay, the widely recognized pioneers of modern color-term theory, assert that the complete set of basic color terms in present-day English is: black, white, red, yellow, green, blue, brown, purple, pink, orange, and gray. (Rossheim 1990, 288–89)
>
> Aristotle talks of sheep, goats, deer, pigs, lions, hyenas, elephants, camels, mice, mules. He describes swallows, pigeons, quails, woodpeckers, eagles, crows, blackbirds, cuckoos. His researches cover tortoises and lizards, crocodiles and vipers, porpoises and whales. He describes every kind of insect. He is particularly informative about marine creatures—fish, crustacea, cephalopods, testacea. (Barnes 1982, 9)

The first of these series is clearly introduced as a complete enumeration. All its items are named using what might be called "small-box-of-crayon" color terms (no puce, magenta, turquoise); these familiar color names reinforce the impression of a coherent set. The series actually also has an internal order—from what the two researchers consider the two basic color terms found in all cultures (black and white), through the names incrementally added as cultures develop a color lexicon—though this order would be invisible to anyone who has not read the full article. On the other hand, Barnes's paragraph on Aristotle features asyndetic lists and multiple doubles, each series covering a phylum and all together reinforcing a claim about the extent and variety of Aristotle's scholarly attention to animals. In each case, the form of the series supports the author's purpose.

Summary

A series fills a sentence slot with three or more items. It is an obtrusive sentence feature with distinct argumentative affordances. First and most salient, series create categories. They can even create a declared category of "things that do not belong together." It is impossible to undo the implication of motivated grouping in a series, even if the motivation is only throwing miscellaneous things together. Once sharing a sentence slot, items in a series affect or even infect each other, as the high or low audience assessment of one item pulls on the others, or vice versa. Thus, subtle "begging the question" can occur in such groupings.

The rhetorical manuals pay extensive attention to series construction under figures of speech specifying the nature of the list: are the items parts of a whole, species of a genus, or features of a subject? This attention to category type occurs because these possibilities represent distinctive lines of argument, also specified in dialectical and rhetorical treatises. One is the topic of *division*: "Whenever we argue from division, or from genera into species or the whole into parts, a complete enumeration of species or parts is made" (Melanchthon 1963b, 672). Similarly, arguments under the topics of *adjuncts* or *circumstances* invite lists of features (690–93).

The precise ordering of the items in a series, noted under the figure *incrementum*, can be important too, reflecting the increase or decrease in some aspect of the items that can vary in degree, such as size, age, or recognized importance. The ordering in the *gradatio*, the series with overlapping items, is also determined, because it fixes the interconnected steps in a causal chain or process. When all else is equal, however, without sequencing of elements, the stylistic principle of end weight usually takes over to order items from the shortest to the longest.

From Aristotle on, rhetorical manuals also emphasized the options of linking items in a series with conjunctions or eliminating all connectives in a series, leaving only baldly juxtaposed items. This attention to conjunctions (*polysyndeton* versus *asyndeton*) is puzzling until it is remembered that one of the most important argumentative effects of series is the impression they convey of completeness or open-endedness. Complete enumerations can serve elimination arguments; if there are only four possible motives or means and three are eliminated, it has to be the remaining one. But opening a series with new items can refute these closed sets, and such open series can be used for other persuasive effects. They hedge against later discoveries and invite the audience to nominate additional members. In surprising ways, then, the nature, order, length, and connectives in a series can argue for the rhetor.

NOTES

1. Doubles do not count as series. Though doubles can have some of the same effects, taking things two at a time rather than three or more at time leads to different consequences. For starters, doubles are always in a binary and hence are potentially in comparison or contrast. Triplets or larger groups cannot be potentially in contrast. Doubles may invite more or less comparison, but they do not require seriation as three or more elements do.

2. Readers may imagine series that are deliberately introduced as a set of items having nothing in common or not belonging to a group. Still, by default those items listed as not belonging together belong to a group of outliers or incompatibles. How far category formation is the result

of an announcement of grouping followed by a list is on display in the following heterogeneous series from Eric Schlosser's contribution to the *Atlantic Monthly*'s "The American Idea": "My idea of America was formed by stories about the Founding Fathers that my grandfather told me when I was a boy, by road trips through the Rockies with my parents, by reading almost everything by Mark Twain, by Emerson, Whitman, and Thoreau, especially Whitman, by Kerouac and John Dos Passos, by Frank Capra films, Coppola films, Jimmy Stewart, and *Billy Jack*, by childhood memories of Bobby Kennedy and Martin Luther King Jr. and their murders, by the war in Vietnam and the protests against it, by Richard Nixon, Spiro Agnew, underground comics, the 1977 New York Yankees, loud music of all kinds, fireworks, hamburgers, and French fries" (2007, 46–48).

3. Over the centuries, the terminology of series figures has become tangled in synonyms labeling slightly different distinctions. The *enumeratio*, as its label implies, also refers to a figure that numbers its items. Speakers often use numbered series to provide structure for a list of recommendations or proposals, as in Johnson's 1964 State of the Union: "First, we must maintain…that margin of military safety and superiority…Second, we must take new steps…toward the control and eventual abolition of arms…Third, we must make increased use of our food…Fourth, we must assure our pre-eminence in the peaceful exploration of outer space…Fifth, we must expand world trade…Sixth, we must continue…our recent progress toward balancing our international accounts" (Windt 1983, 60).

4. An *apparent* congeries would provide a putative list of synonyms but in the process would insert a term not quite the equivalent of the others. There can also be a slight migration across a congeries as a series of near synonyms. When Francis Galton was introducing the probability distribution since known as the normal or Gaussian distribution in *Natural Inheritance*, he acknowledged that it came from Quetelet's "law of error," the notion that in astronomical measurements, there is a tendency for the inaccuracies to cluster in a predictable way about the true value. As Galton goes on to write, "But Errors, Differences, Deviations, Divergencies, Dispersions, and individual Variations, all spring from the same kind of causes" (1889, 55). Here an error in measurement and a variation in some inherited and measurable physical trait are collapsed into the same synonym pool yielding the same distribution upon sampling.

5. *The New Rhetoric* discusses the effects of insertion into the same class as having an effect of "homogenization" or "equalization of values" (Perelman and Olbrechts-Tyteca 1969, 129). Their discussion refers to joining two items into doubles through coordination, but there is no reason not to see the effect of "equalization of values" applying to three or more items in a series.

6. Another terminological muddle attends these terms. Both were sometimes referred to by the term *climax* because both, as the examples show, can carry the notion of reaching an end term. The *incrementum* was also labeled an *anabasis* in Greek with the sense of ascending order and *catabasis* with the sense of descending order.

7. A tour de force use of a lengthy list to make a case for what has been ignored is quoted in Keith Thomas, *Man and the Natural World*: "A recent critic comments on the ideal rural landscape depicted in English poetry of the mid seventeenth century that 'there is virtually no mention of land-clearance, tree-felling, pruning, chopping, digging, hoeing, weeding, branding, gelding, slaughtering, salting, tanning, brewing, boiling, smelting, forging, milling, thatching, fencing and hurdle-making, hedging, road-mending and haulage. Almost everything which anybody *does* in the countryside is taboo'" (1983, 251n).

RHETORICIANSWHOWORKWITHSPOKEN
WRITTENANDWRITTENTOBESPOKENTEXTS
APPRECIATETHEDIFFERENCESINTHESEMODES
ANDTHEDIFFICULTIESOFTRANSCRIPTION
BETWEENTHEMINRESPONSETOTHESE
DIFFICULTIESLINGUISTSWHOSTUDY
THELANGUAGEOFEVERYDAYCONVERSATION
HAVEDEVELOPEDNOTATIONSTOCAPTURETHE
INEVITABLEOVERLAPSINTERRUPTION
SHEMMINGANDTHROATCLEARINGOFSPOKEN
INTERCHANGES

12

PROSODY AND PUNCTUATION

RHETORICIANS WHO WORK with spoken, written, and written-to-be-spoken texts appreciate the differences in these modes and the difficulties of transcription between them. In response to these difficulties, linguists who study the language of everyday conversation have developed notation to capture in text the inevitable overlaps, interruptions, hemming, and throat clearing of spoken interchanges (Levinson 1983). They even record speakers' pauses to the tenth of a second. The problem of accurate transcription also occurs routinely when spoken texts (speeches, press conferences, interviews) reappear in newspapers or online with interpretive punctuation to mark features of the original utterance. Here, for example, is how Special Prosecutor Patrick Fitzgerald's announcement of an indictment was transcribed into text on the *Washington Post's* website:

> A few hours ago, a federal grand jury sitting in the District of Columbia returned a five-count indictment against I. Lewis Libby, also known as Scooter Libby, the vice president's chief of staff.
>
> The grand jury's indictment charges that Mr. Libby committed five crimes. The indictment charges one count of obstruction of justice of the federal grand jury, two counts of perjury and two counts of false statements.[1]

A viewer/listener of a video recording of this statement, also available online, produced the following version by noting with commas the many places where Fitzgerald actually paused.

A few hours ago, a federal grand jury, sitting in the District of Columbia, returned a five-count indictment, against I. Lewis Libby, also known as Scooter Libby, the vice president's chief of staff.

The grand jury's indictment, charges that Mr. Libby, committed five crimes. The indictment charges one count of obstruction of justice, of the federal grand jury, two counts of perjury, and two counts of false statements.[2]

The printed version punctuates according to grammatical units and rules, setting off the introductory phrase and the nonrestrictive participial phrase in the first sentence and marking the separation between the first and second items in the series in the last sentence. The listener's version punctuates according to the pauses introduced by the speaker as he segmented his utterance into breath and phrase units. What is missing in the print version, according to the listener, is a certain tentativeness in Fitzgerald's delivery that listeners might use, along with other clues, to infer his attitude toward his message. The difference between these versions illustrates two competing regimes of punctuation, one to mark the grammatical units in a text and the other to mark performance features in delivery. These competing demands persist in the history and evolution of punctuation marks, revealing much about the two systems of language realization that rhetors work with, the spoken and the written.

Speech and Writing

Written languages based on alphabets or syllabaries are second-order semiotic systems. They record the sounds of a language, and it is the sounds that have meaning. Speech is the primary semiotic system, and writing, for most western languages, is merely its record. Written languages based on ideograms, like Chinese, are independent semiotic systems, separate from the spoken languages, and visual in their method of sign making. The first system of protowriting discovered by Denise Schmandt-Besserat, featuring tokens pressed into clay boluses in ancient Mesopotamia, was certainly based on visual semiosis (2002). But ancient Phoenician used an alphabet, eventually borrowed by the Greeks, that visually represented sounds, both vowels and consonants, and not things.

The nature of writing as a record of speech or as a memory aid for oral performance was clearer in antiquity, when texts were rendered in the minimalist form of *scriptio continua*, sequences of letters without divisions between words, as in the version of the opening sentences of this chapter that serves as the epigraph above and as a visual reminder of the challenges of this practice. Such texts were meant to prompt reading aloud, and though the point has been debated, presumably the act of reading in antiquity was in fact oral performance. A passage in the New Testament (Acts 8:26–31) records the story of the Apostle Philip coming up to the litter of an Ethiopian official reading from Isaiah. Philip asks the Ethiopian if he understands what the prophet means. Clearly he must have been reading aloud for Philip to find this opening for dialogue. Though silent parsing is no doubt as old as writing, it may not have become the default mode of text consumption until the third or fourth century CE (Manguel 1996, 41–53).

Centuries before, Plato complained in the *Phaedrus* about the relatively new technology of writing. He had Socrates criticize writing as inferior to speech because the written text, divorced from its living author and moment, cannot be interrogated by the reader or explain itself (1973, 97). By 90 CE, Quintilian had a better opinion of writing, though he viewed it primarily as a means for perfecting the rhetor's speaking abilities (1921, IV 91–97). One of the social realities downgrading writing in antiquity was its manual difficulty with the materials available. While the higher social classes were certainly trained to write, they typically composed by dictating to scribes, who were often slaves, and the labor of manuscript copying or "publishing" was left entirely to this special indentured class.

The derivative nature of writing and the long dominance of speech, before printing changed the balance, have to be kept in mind to appreciate the persistent oral dimensions of written language. One obvious source of this persistence is the fact that all children in literate cultures learn to speak before they learn to read or write. So it is not surprising that the evidence from neuroscience on brain activity during reading indicates that while the visual cortex is necessarily active, the auditory cortex and even the motor cortex that governs the articulatory muscles are also stimulated. And, amazingly, so are other areas of the motor cortex that correspond to the physical actions encoded in a word (Kandel, Schwartz, and Jessell 2000, 1174–75; LaFuente and Romo 2004, 178–80). Thus, speaking and writing, listening and reading, are never entirely divorced in the brain (Dehaene 2009, 104–19).

However, once these two semiotic systems, an oral and a visual mode of language transmission and consumption, exist as alternatives, they can diverge. Writing can stray from speech and develop features of primary semiosis as a visual medium (distinctive fonts, spacing, emoticons, etc.). Furthermore, reading habits can be developed that deliberately suppress the aural dimensions of language, the internal listening that can go on during silent reading. Eventually, the two systems favor different grammatical features, such as the absolute constructions that are more common in written texts and the mixed constructions that are more typical in speech. Some theorists, like Walter Ong (1982), have even based cognitive and "lifeworld" differences on these distinctions of "orality" versus "literacy."

Prosody

Since writing systems are secondary in origin to spoken language (though capable of developing independent features), it makes sense to ask as a starting point how efficiently text can represent speech. Certain features of oral communication have always been difficult to capture in writing, such as the changes in dynamics from loud to soft, the variations in pitch from high to deep, the manipulations in duration from prolonged to rushed, and the pauses of different lengths (see Emphasis, p. 204). Altogether, these features can be lumped together under the term **prosody**. Together with **paralinguistic features** like facial gestures and body language, these performance qualities were given the attention of an entire canon of rhetoric, that of delivery. Manipulation of voice and movement of face and body can certainly reinforce or even contradict a speaker's meaning and purpose, but these important physical dimensions of communication are beyond the scope of this book. Instead, the focus here will be on some prosodic features of spoken language and their traces in writing.

In antiquity, when oral transmission dominated, so did metered verse. Its regularities enhance both memory and oral performance, and each of the Greek oral poetic genres (epic, lyric, and drama) had its appropriate meter. Aristotle engaged the debate over how metrical prose should be, perhaps in reaction to the influential practice of the orator Gorgias, whose poetic prose was popular in late-fifth-century BCE Athens. Aristotle believed that "speech should have rhythm but not meter; for the latter will be a poem" (Kennedy 1991, 237). He was of course referring to spoken, not written, prose, and by rhythm without meter he seems to have meant that there should be recognizable sound patterns in prose, but not recurring sound patterns that create the predictability of regular meter and potentially divert the listener's attention (237). Aristotle went so far as to recommend a suitable foot for oratory, the *paean*, a unit of one long and three short syllables in a ratio of two counts (for the long syllable) to three (one count each for the short syllables), "for it alone of the rhythms mentioned is not a meter, and thus its presence most escapes notice" (238). He recommended a paean with an emphatic initial foot (/- - -) for the opening of a period, and the opposite with an emphatic final foot (- - -/) for the ending (238). Such rhythmical units are of course easier to construct in an inflected language with mutlisyllabic case or conjugation endings.

The attention to prosody in nonmetrical speech continues in Cicero and Quintilian, but their observations do not translate easily into advice for speakers of English. Classical languages distinguish long versus short syllables as well as accented or unaccented, while English and other Germanic languages distinguish stressed versus unstressed syllables. Anglo-Saxon verse, as in *Beowulf,* did not produce lines of equal syllable length but rather paired lines with equivalent stresses (Crystal 2003, 415). However, in any language, sound patterns can be produced by syllable variation, whether long versus short or stressed versus unstressed. Medieval scribes writing in Latin, for example, followed an elaborate system of fixed patterns in line endings grouped under the notion of *cursus*. According to *cursus* conventions, patterns of syllable length worked as follows for the final two words of a clause: the *cursus planus* (óo/oóo), the *cursus tardus* (óo/oóoo) and the *cursus velox* (óoo/òoóo).[3] English speakers can "hear" these patterns as differences in stress as opposed to differences in quantity; for example, an ending in *cursus planus* would be, "He was *under indictment*." The prosodic effect of this phrasing might explain why such a construction would be preferred to the more succinct "He was indicted." The wordiness that is often relentlessly edited out of contemporary English can in fact produce rhythms that satisfy principles such as "end weight" in phrasing, the preference for ending a unit with longer elements (Wales 2001, 126).

According to Father Craig LaDrière's study of prose rhythm, speakers have a tendency to "replace larger and less symmetrical groupings by regular repetition of a single relatively small pattern" (1943, 454). If this observation holds, speakers will gradually change metrical patterns over the course of a speech. They will, in effect, lapse into syncopation, coming closer to the chanting rhythms typical of liturgical performance. Recordings of Martin Luther King Jr. display this movement from what might be called conversational prosody to something closer to metered syncopation, as do the sermons of some preachers who often command large audiences, like Bishop Eddie Long and T. D. Jakes. Jakes in particular will work himself up from unmetrical conversational prose to powerful rhythmic repetition. It remains an open question whether political speakers outside religious contexts also reveal a tendency to more regular rhythms over the course of a speech.

English prosody does not have to be limited to patterns based on syllable stress or quantity. In his study of the development of English over the last five centuries, Ian Robinson identified four units or levels of prosody using classical rhetoric's distinctions: the foot, the comma, the colon, and the period. While the first concerns words, the latter three correspond to the phrase, clause, and sentence. Robinson correlated certain sound patterns to these units. In feet and commas (the word and phrase level), there were stressed syllables. At a higher level, in the units called cola, there were *beats* or "stressed" stresses, and in the entire period there was an additional sound contour (Robinson 1998, 53). The question of how aware listeners are of "feet" (iambs, trochees, etc.) in prose remains unanswered, though the reality of awareness of stressed versus unstressed syllables (or long versus short) is certainly indicated by the different meanings created by changing the accented syllable (e.g., *íncense* versus *incénse*). In his argument for beats at a level higher than stressed syllables, Robinson observes that speakers in the House of Commons typically use hand gestures to indicate the important words or beats in longer units (1998, 51). Beyond words, phrases, and clauses, the sound patterns across spoken passages are created by complex variations of pitch, duration, loudness, and pausing. These features exceed the transcription resources of ordinary writing and punctuation.

Prosody into Punctuation

Punctuation marks evolved over centuries, from notation on manuscripts to conventions in printing. They began as aids to segment texts in *scriptio continua* into speakable units. The resulting breath units, not surprisingly, correspond to the phrase units in classical rhetoric, always an art of oral performance. The natural breath unit, where the speaker would typically pause, roughly equals the comma or colon, from which shorter units (the foot) or longer units (the period) are derived. In his study of punctuation in English, Wallace Chafe (1988) recaptured this linkage by identifying the units created by punctuation as *intonation units*. Punctuation, however, like other aspects of writing, has departed from its origins. Many have in fact argued that writing produced the grammatical sentence as the unit of language, imposing it on older intonational units of utterance. And the two have been in tension ever since.

In *Pause and Effect* (1993), a work of monumental scholarship on the history of punctuation, M. B. Parkes traces the evolution of these inscribed signs from aids for oral rendering to signals of syntactic structure. Early manuscripts written in continuous script bear marks indicating places to pause for breath. These marks come in three types representing three pause lengths, and indirectly they indicate units of sense as well: a minor pause signals a break even when the sense is incomplete; a second mark is used when the grammatical sense is complete but the rhetor's larger point has yet to be achieved; a final pause indicates when the *periodos* or *sententia* is complete (65). These breath marks, in turn, create discourse segments that roughly correspond to the three syntactic units identified in rhetorical manuals, the *comma, colon,* and *period*, units whose names were eventually used for the marks of punctuation themselves (65).

According to Parkes, "punctuation" marks became an essential component in manuscripts from the sixth through the twelfth centuries. But in a manuscript culture, punctuation frequently differs from copy to copy of the same work. Parkes offers two versions of the same passage from Bede's *Ecclesiastical History of the English People*. Only his English translations are offered here, with the punctuation corresponding to the marks appearing in the original Latin texts.

from an eighth-century copy produced shortly after Bede's death:
Gregory replied my brother you can decide from the character of a thief . how he deserves to be corrected . for there are some who commit theft while having resources and there are others who offend in this matter through poverty . Hence it is necessary . that some be punished with fines . some on the other hand by flogging . and some more severely . others more leniently (69)

from an eleventh-century copy:
Gregory replied; My brother you can decide from the character of a thief .< how he deserves to be corrected; For there are some who commit theft while having resources .< and there are others who offend in this matter through poverty; Hence it is necessary .< that some be punished with fines . some on the other hand by flogging .< and some more severely . others more leniently; (69)

The eighth-century scribe uses only one sign, the *punctus* (.), to mark breath units for oral reading. The eleventh-century scribe, on the other hand, works with three different marks in this passage, the *punctus* (.), *punctus elevatus* (.<) and the *punctus versus* (;). This last, strongest mark indicates major divisions, separating the introductory phrase from the quotation and, within the quotation, creating three main units or periods. Within these periods, the scribe uses the *punctus elevatus*, which does not have a precise current analogue, to create units at a level higher than those created by the comma but lower than those that would be created by the *punctus versus*. Most notable is the segmenting produced in the final "sentence" (beginning at "Hence"), which creates two units with two balanced items each, internally divided by the *punctus*.

some be punished with fines	.	*some by flogging*
	.<	
some more severely	.	*others more leniently*

The resulting pairs correspond to the antithesis created earlier in the passage, also by the stronger *punctus elevatus*:

some commit theft while having resources .<   *others offend through poverty*

In other words, the passage is punctuated to bring out the matching contrasts: that the well-off who steal should be punished with fines, while those who steal through poverty should be flogged. The final contrast between severity and leniency either corresponds directly to the contrast between the well-off and the poor, if flogging is seen as the lesser punishment, or as an *antimetabole*, if flogging is considered more severe. This internal pairing does not come across in the eighth-century manuscript's one-note punctuation, which seems to close with a list of four alternative methods of punishment for any offender. As Parke observes about the eleventh-century excerpt, "The punctuation here is no longer merely a guide to the oral performance of the written word but has already become an essential component of the written medium, which contributes directly to the reader's comprehension of the message of the text" (69).[4]

The textually scrupulous humanists of the fourteenth and fifteenth centuries, with an eye to correct grammatical construal over oral performance, used four punctuation marks to indicate units below the level of the entire sentence. These included (·) a mid-level dot, (ʃ) a virgule with a dot in the middle, (/) a virgule without a dot, and (.<) the *punctus elevatus* (Parkes 1993, 82). The virgules were used to indicate parallel or antimetabolic structures (82). In their manuscript editing, the humanists also introduced the *punctus admirativus* (!), a mark that certainly guides oral realization, as well as the semicolon as a unit between the colon and the *punctus* (84).

PRINTING AND PUNCTUATION

Printing reduced and stabilized punctuation. Though the earliest printed texts reveal marks that are no longer in use (see Rhetorical Question, p. 299), the practice of setting new editions from older editions and the pressure to simplify led to a smaller repertoire of devices. Even this smaller suite of marks was, however, used somewhat differently from current conventions. Until at least the late eighteenth century, units of meaning were created between the comma and the paragraph break that are no longer marked. These units are particularly critical in a project of rhetorical stylistics, since they often mark constituent relations among the argumentative units in a text.

An example of this extra layer of segmentation, common in early modern texts, appears in the dedicatory letter prefacing Peacham's 1593 *Garden of Eloquence*. The opening sentence of this preface continues for thirty-one lines and laps a page before it comes to a full stop, using thirty commas, four colons, and three sets of parentheses along the way. Peacham's highly erratic punctuation, by current standards, allowed him to produce sentences built of subunits like the following:

Finallie, by her [Wisdom] the true felicitie of man is found out and held up, without her it falleth by a sudden, and wofull ruine: by her his honor [sic] is highly advanced, without her it sinketh into shame and reproach, and is utterlie confounded: by her he is indued with a blessed state of life, without her he perisheth in miserie and death. [Peacham Biii recto; punctuation bolded]

Between the initial capital letter and the final period, Peacham uses the colon to mark the three parallel structures with internal contrasts describing what happens with and without Wisdom, signaled with the repeating phases *by her... without her*. The *with* and *without* claims in each unit are separated only by commas, which keep the "voice" from falling too far; it drops instead at the end of the *without* clauses (as anyone will see who tries reading this passage aloud). An editor today would be tempted to put periods for the colons, but Peacham has been able to build a single, many-part unit.

Almost a century later, Isaac Newton, writing to the Secretary of the Royal Society, Henry Oldenburg, about his experiments with prisms, uses a four-mark repertoire in a critical paragraph explaining how he eliminated several possible causes of the oddly oblong spread of colors (or, his coinage, *spectrum*) projected through a prism.

(1) Comparing the length of this coloured *Spectrum* with its breadth, I found it about five times greater; a disproportion so extravagant, that it excited me to a more than ordinary curiosity of examining, from whence it might proceed. (2) I could scarce think, that the various *Thickness* of the glass, or the termination with shadow or darkness, could have any Influence on light to produce such an effect; yet I thought it not amiss, first to examine those circumstances, and so tryed, what would happen by transmitting light through parts of the glass of divers thicknesses, or through holes in the window of divers bignesses, or by setting the Prisme without so, that the light might pass through it, and be refracted before it was terminated by the hole: But I found none of those circumstances material. (3) The fashion of

·the colours was in all these cases the same. (Newton 1672, 3076; punctuation bolded)

Newton's four marks of punctuation are, in decreasing order of pause length, the period, colon, semicolon, and comma. With these four, he can create three levels of structure within a single sentence. Most notable is the first-order division created in the second sentence around the hinge of the colon. The clause *But I found none of those circumstances material* (beginning with a capital that does not, however, follow a period) sums up the results of all the trials reported in the part of the sentence before the colon. Within this long first part before the colon, the text is divided by a semicolon. The first section before the semicolon records his speculations about what could cause the anomalous lengthening of the light refracted through the prism, while the second and much longer part after the semicolon records his various trials to eliminate these possible causes. Within the sections on both sides of the semicolon, commas do the work of segmentation into units, though here, perhaps, Newton could have used a punctuation mark between the comma and the semicolon to point out the parallelism between *by transmitting* (opening a phrase with its own internal parallelism, *through ... or through*) and *by setting.* The entire second sentence then, between the initial capital letter and the final period, functions as a single unit completely dispatching the attempts at some procedural explanation of the elongated spectrum. After this long sentence, Newton concludes with abbreviated force in the following short third sentence, *The fashion of the colours was in all these cases the same.*

A fully functioning four-level system of punctuation allows Newton a more nuanced composition not so much of the grammatical structure of this passage as of its argumentative structure. This kind of "mid-level" management is not possible with contemporary editing practices, which have, for the most part, thrown out the colon as Newton uses it by limiting it to introducing series or brief concluding elements. Contemporary writers have to make do with the comma, semicolon, and period, observing the further restriction that the semicolon can only be used between independent clauses (unless it is separating lengthy items in a series). It is interesting to speculate whether the disappearance of these long, managed periods was the cause or the result of reduced punctuation.

While prose since 1900 usually lacks such structures within sentences, earlier prose features them frequently. In fact, according to Carey McIntosh (1998), these structures are artifacts of writing, and literate English prose became distinctly more "written" than "oral" across the eighteenth century. Later eighteenth-century prose, he argues, features sentences that no one would speak, such as the long, architectural sentences found in the Declaration of Independence. The widely admired prose of Samuel Johnson also offers many examples of sentences that seem assembled into constructions no one would utter spontaneously, as in the following paragraph from *The Idler*, No. 60:

(1) Criticism is a study by which men grow important and formidable at very small expense. (2) The power of invention has been conferred by nature upon few, and the labour of learning those sciences which may, by mere labour, be obtained, is too great to be willingly endured; but every man can exert such judgment as he has upon the works of others; and he whom nature has made weak and idleness keeps ignorant may yet support his vanity by the name of a critic. (3) I hope it will give comfort to great numbers who are passing through the world in obscurity, when I inform them how easily distinction may be obtained. (4) All the other powers of literature are coy and haughty; they must be long courted, and at last are not always gained; but Criticism is a goddess easy of access and forward of advance, who will meet the slow and encourage the timorous; the want of meaning she supplies with words, and the want of spirit she recompenses with malignity. (Bredvold, McKillop, and Whitney 1956, 691)

This passage alternates two shorter (1 and 3) with two longer sentences (2 and 4) of similar construction. Each longer sentence is built around the midpoint fulcrum of an adversative *but*, and the portions on either side, presenting contrasting views, contain considerable parallel phrasing and internal punctuation. A schematic arrangement of sentence 4 brings out the architecture.

```
                                    coy
    All the other powers of literature are     and
                                          haughty

            ;
    they must be long courted,
                and
    at last are not always gained
            ; but
                        easy of access,
    Criticism is a goddess and
                        forward of advance,
                        meet the slow
                who will     and
                        encourage the timorous
                        ;
    the want of meaning she supplies with words,
                and
    the want of spirit she recompenses with malignity.
```

Johnson uses the midpoint to turn from the difficulties of authorship to the easiness of criticism. Unfortunately, where earlier authors or printers might have placed a colon to mark the sentence's hinge at *but,* Johnson works with a three-mark system and must use the same punctuation (the semicolon) to represent two degrees of separation.[5]

In contrast to McIntosh's claim that English prose style became more "written" by the end of the eighteenth century, Wallace Chafe believes that older styles of punctuation persisted into the nineteenth century, resulting in written texts still marked with an "ear" to their oral realization. Illustrating his point is the following passage (not one of his examples) from Charles Darwin's *Voyage of the Beagle,* the second edition of 1845, a date far into the dominance of print culture. It comes from the chapter describing Darwin's first trip ashore on Santiago (which he called "St. Jago") in the Cape Verde islands:

(1) The neighbourhood of Porto Praya, viewed from the sea, wears a desolate aspect. (2) The volcanic fires of a past age, and the scorching heat of a tropical sun, have in most places rendered the soil unfit for vegetation. (3) The country rises in successive steps of table-land, interspersed with some truncate conical hills, and the horizon is bounded by an irregular chain of more lofty mountains. (4a) The scene, as beheld through the hazy atmosphere of this climate, is one of great interest; (4b) if, indeed, a person, fresh from the sea, and who has just walked, for the first time, in a grove of cocoa-nut trees, can be a judge of anything but his own happiness. (2)

Notable in this passage are the punctuation marks that contemporary editors would be tempted to remove. In the second sentence, Darwin commits the "error" of setting off the second half of the double subject from the first half. The two subjects are, however, grammatically parallel constructions of almost equal syllable length (single-word modifier *volcanic/scorching,* head word *fires/heat,* prepositional phrases *of a past age/of a tropical sun*). Darwin's commas create the pauses that bring out this parallelism. But it is sentence 4b that bears the most unusual punctuation, its seven commas inviting a hesitating prosodic realization. Current punctuating conventions would probably retain the commas around *indeed* (as a sentence interrupter) and perhaps around the relative clause: *if, indeed, a person, fresh from the sea, and who has just walked for the first time in a grove of cocoa-nut trees, can be a judge of anything but his own happiness.* This version, still with heavy punctuation by current standards, accounts for four of the commas. But Darwin also paused after *person* and set off *for the first time* with commas. Since he is writing here in the third person about a first-person experience, the commas around *person* produce a coy reference and the similar marks around *for the first time* emphasize this moment in his journey. These are emphases that intonation could create if this sentence were spoken. The prosodic effects in this passage come not only from the heavy punctuation in 4b, but also from the lighter punctuation in the other sentences. The compound sentence 3 only marks with commas the mid-sentence participial phrase (*interspersed with some truncate conical hills*) and bears no punctuation in its second clause (*and the horizon is bounded by an irregular chain of more lofty mountains*). Since sentence 3 is impersonal and 4b is personal, sentence 4a might be designated intermediate, somewhere between the written language of scientific description in sentence 3 (with *truncate conical* hills) and the more intonationally marked, and hence more spoken, personal language of 4b. If Chafe is correct in seeing nineteenth-century punctuation practices as transitional, then writers at this time had the resource of switching between more written versus more utterance-based punctuation choices.

PUNCTUATION AND MEANING

Ignoring an author's punctuation guidelines can sometimes lead to ignoring significant, intentional discourse structure, as happened in the following case. In 1967, Louis Milic published the first quantitative study of style using a computer to parse and count selected features. Milic characterized the style of Jonathan Swift versus that of other writers with special attention to his sentence-initiating transition words. He found that Swift used twice as many coordinating conjunctions (especially *and, but, for*) in this position than did two other eighteenth-century authors, Samuel Johnson and Edward Gibbon. Milic was struck by what he considered a "pseudo-pleonastic" use of connectives in Swift, and he cited the following as a particularly egregious example:

> and therefore if notwithstanding all I have said it shall still be thought necessary to have a bill brought in for repealing Christianity I would humbly offer an amendment that instead of the word Christianity may be put religion in general which I conceive will much better answer all the good ends proposed by the projectors of it. (Milic 1971, 253)

Milic reproduced the sentence in this manner without any punctuation, and he interpreted the four initial conjunctions as a single redundant connective. The only problem is that the actual sentence, as it appeared in the original, quoted in his own footnotes, is as follows:

> And therefore, if, notwithstanding all I have said, it shall still be thought necessary to have a Bill brought in for repealing Christianity: I would humbly offer an Amendment, that instead of the Word *Christianity*, may be put Religion in general; which I conceive, will much better answer all the good Ends proposed in the Projectors of it. (quoted in Milic 1971, 257)

Clearly Swift was using punctuation to create a highly significant grammatical as well as argumentative structure. The correct reading cannot be produced without the commas separating the initial connectives, which, rather than being redundant, indicate the beginnings of successively embedded clauses. Further internal punctuation, such as the commas after *said* and the colon after *Christianity*, are also crucial to the construction of the meaning. A visualization of the linear structure might look like the following:

> *And*
>
> *therefore,*
>
> *if,*…it shall still be thought necessary to have a Bill brought in for repealing Christianity:
>
> ↖
>
> *notwithstanding* all I have said
>
> I would humbly offer an Amendment, that instead of the Word *Christianity* may be put Religion in general; which I conceive, will much better answer all the good Ends proposed by the Projectors of it.

The first conjunction, *And,* can be read as governing the whole construction and setting it in relation as an addition to the preceding sentence (see below, p. 369). The second conjunction, *therefore,* governs everything that follows but applies directly to the main clause (*therefore…I would humbly offer an Amendment*). Between this conjunction and the main clause, an adverb clause beginning with *if* interrupts and is itself interrupted by another adverb clause beginning *notwithstanding.* The punctuation between these opening conjunctions correctly marks the successive levels of embedding.[6]

This entire sentence certainly makes significant processing demands on readers, requiring them to plunge down to a third level of embedding before the main predication. But the commas are there to help the reader manage this parsing feat; they are hardly redundant. And Swift's example is typical of the nuanced use of connectives to manage meaning units by the length of indicated pause. The differing pause lengths marked by comma, semicolon, and colon would probably be observed if this sentence were spoken.[7] Furthermore, in the early eighteenth century, Swift still worked with an active four-level system, like Newton's, in decreasing order of pause length as follows: period, colon, semicolon, comma.

What is the current state of signaling text structure and hence meaning through punctuation? In a study of paragraph length published at the end of the nineteenth century, Edwin Herbert Lewis cited the "well-known fact that the English sentence has decreased in average length at least one-half in three hundred years" (1894, 34). Though no similar study has been done covering the last 100 years, it seems likely that the shrinkage has continued. However, if clause length were measured rather than sentence length, or if spoken rather than printed sentences were also considered, this measured change might disappear. *Clause* length in English may in fact not have changed across the centuries, though certainly how clauses are combined into longer units and how those units are punctuated have changed. If the sentence is defined as what comes between the opening capital letter and the final end punctuation, long multiclause sentences, like those examined above, were certainly more common in the prose of the past than they have been in the last one hundred years. But this change may be a by-product of changing punctuation conventions. A period now does the work once done with different degrees of separation by periods, colons, and semicolons; hence the options for extra levels of *signaled* meaning management have disappeared. As noted above, these changing punctuation conventions make the assessment of changing "sentence" lengths based on how much wording appears between units marked by periods somewhat meaningless. Where older texts would have used a colon or semicolon, modern writers would use periods, making it appear that sentences and hence compositional units have shortened.

Also complicating the meaning/punctuation options in print is the hierarchy of pauses above the level of the period: first the paragraph break, then the extra skipped line between paragraphs, then the section break (often with more white space and an exaggerated capital at the beginning of the next section), then the titled subsection with headings at different levels. All of these formatting devices allow writers to indicate compositional and construal units higher than the sentence. These higher-order units do not have clear parallels in orally performed pause lengths.

Figured Prosody

Rhetorical stylistics, especially in classical manuals, was concerned with pausing and segmenting but not with punctuation per se. It did focus on the units (comma, colon, and period) that require punctuation when they are rendered into print. But classical and early modern rhetoric was more concerned with "high end" oral or prosodic effects. Thus, several of the more dramatic resources of spoken prosody are marked by enduring devices in the figural tradition. In unplanned discourse, speakers use these devices naturally; writers attempt them when punctuation conventions can convey their effects. Among these figures of dramatic prosody is the *aposiopesis*. It occurs, according to the *Rhetorica ad Herennium*, "when something is said and then the rest of what the speaker had begun to say is left unfinished" (1981, 331; the Latin name for this figure in the *ad Herennium* is *praecisio*, and in later texts *reticentia* or *interruptio*). Breaking off and, more generally, omitting something are signaled in writing or print by ellipses or the dash. The examples offered in the *ad Herennium*, however, include not only breaking off in a way that shows that a statement has been left incomplete, but also pointing deliberately to the breaking off: "'The contest between you and me is unequal because, so far as concerns me, the Roman people—I am unwilling to say it, lest by chance some one think me proud" and "You dare to say that, who recently at another's home—I shouldn't dare tell" (331). The *Rhetorica ad Herennium* recommends this figure because "a suspicion, unexpressed, becomes more telling than a detailed explanation would have been" (331).

Brian Vickers cites the *aposiopesis* as a prime example of the polysemous or "polypathous" nature of the figures (1988, 317–18). Breaking off mid-predication signals that the speaker is unable to continue, but the listener has to infer why. Perhaps the speaker has been overcome by emotion, whatever its source (anger, grief, even gratitude). Or perhaps the speaker suddenly decides to avoid saying something scandalous or self-incriminating or boastful or dangerous. The speaker may also have just forgotten what he or she was about to say. This kind of open-ended interpretation is clearly prevented by the figure as fully specified in the *ad Herennium,* since the breaking off is followed by the speaker's drawing attention to it and explaining its significance. In later rhetorical manuals, this "explanation" of the *aposiopesis* disappears. But the figure remains, perhaps because it is one of a handful of dramatic spoken effects that can be visually represented.

Still another device of figural prosody is the *ecphonesis,* the outcry of extreme emotion of any kind, ecstatic to horrific. Naturally realized with a variety of broken sounds, the *ecphonesis* conventionally takes the form of interjections such as *Oh! Ah! Ugh!* or the now archaic *Pshaw!* or *Alas!* In speech, the outcry should be spontaneous, a genuine moment when the speaker is overcome. Such "genuine moments," when scripted into prepared speeches, require considerable acting ability on the orator's part. No doubt Daniel Webster planned the spontaneity of the "But—ah!—Him!" that marked the moment in his Bunker Hill oration when he mentioned the fallen hero, General Joseph Warren; with an emotional crowd he probably pulled it off (Reid 1988, 213).

The prosody of the outcry can also be added to content-bearing words, as in Cicero's famous *O tempora! O mores!* in his first speech against Catiline (see Cicero 1989, 76 for a milder English translation). In writing or print, the *ecphonesis* accomplished in such phrases or sentences can be approximated by the exclamation mark. A poor indicator of the spoken possibilities, the exclamation mark nevertheless still manages to infuse some prosodic drama into a text. When an entire sentence, as opposed to an interjection or a few words, is punctuated as an exclamation, the effect of the spontaneous outcry tends to fade, however, and an expression of amazement or a particular speech act such as a threat or a command takes over. Though some "intensity of the abrupt" may remain in passages bearing exclamation marks, altogether neither the outcry nor the multiple prosodic dynamics of speech can ever be wholly captured by the punctuation conventions of print. Even when the physically present orator is replaced by a square of video clip embedded on a web page, the oral genres—the live political speech, the televised interview, the sound bite from a debate—still have more power over audiences.

Passage Prosody

The prosody of individual sentences, managed by punctuation and the placement of constituents, is only part of the dimension of prosody in texts. More important is the prosody of passages, the "sound" contour and pacing built from the dynamics of sentences in sequence. This subject requires turning to "passage construction," a topic covered in section IV. But passage prosody follows naturally from sentence prosody and so is best taken up here.

Speech without the natural music of human utterance, the "machine speak" of decades ago, is aberrant, and, not surprisingly, speakers and writers usually strive to avoid monotony, that is literally *monos tonos* language, language delivered in *a single tone* or *note*. In writing, the sources of monotony are formal and usually problematic. If all the sentences in a passage are in invariable subject-first order, if they are all about the same length, and if they all make the same kind of flat, declarative statement, listeners or readers will have a difficult time recognizing any single sentence as more salient than any other. Of course this strategy of leveling, when temporary, can serve a purpose.

> Since the early 1990s crime has fallen annually in the U.S., last year by about 7 percent. Many explanations have been put forward for this drop: *more police walk the beat, more people are in prison, the economy has improved, crack use has fallen, alarms and guards are now widespread.* (Holloway 1999, 23; italics added)

The series of italicized independent clauses in this passage are all short and about the same length (varying between five and eight syllables), and they all open with the subject followed immediately by a verb. The local "monotony" in this passage serves the argument by grouping suggested causes for the drop in crime; they are listed quickly and hence somewhat dismissively to prepare for a new suggestion, in this case the highly controversial claim that legalized abortion eliminated potential criminals. However, if this kind of unvarying clause structure had persisted beyond a limited section, readers and listeners would eventually have had trouble keeping their attention fixed.

To avoid monotony, rhetors can vary the openings, the types, and the lengths of their sentences to achieve an effective prosodic profile across a passage. Speakers can add voice dynamics as well as pace and pause variations; writers can add the visual resources of formatting devices (boxes, font change) as well as section divisions. Any competent rhetor will inevitably draw on the available variables in either medium to achieve the highlighting and backgrounding that are essential for managing audience attention. Excellent rhetors will go further and use these sources of variety to reinforce the meanings and effects they want to achieve. Ultimately, rhetors want to create **prosodic units** that are also argument units, whether their texts are heard or read.

To begin with sentence-level changes that accumulate in passages, prosodic variety can be created by breaking the expected subject-first word order in English clauses. This default pattern can be broken when rhetors use left-branching structures to postpone the subject (see above, p. 208). Sentences can open instead with subordinate clauses or phrases that delay the main subject and verb. Or they can shift the main point to the predicate with "There is/are" or "It is" constructions, creating slight anticipations. Or they can invert the predictable S-V order.

Over a series of consecutive clauses, experienced rhetors, especially professional writers and journalists, will habitually vary openings to avoid having too many clauses in a row that begin immediately with the subject and verb, a repetition in pattern that can become monotonous when other sources of variation are absent. In fact, in functional as opposed to oratorical English prose, one-fourth to one-third of sentences or clauses tend to open with a left-branching construction rather than the subject, a generalization that can be tested on any contemporary magazine or newspaper article. Inevitably, by opening some sentences "directly" and some "indirectly," rhetors create troughs and rises and hence a sound pattern across a passage.

The prosodic profile of a passage is also produced by varying sentence types, perhaps by interrupting a string of declaratives with an exclamation or a question. Such switching from claims to questions to orders to wishes is one of the most obvious ways to introduce these dynamics, since the spoken realization of these types differs strongly. The effects of such end punctuation can be seen in those occasional passages where writers risk a series of questions:

> Are some things still worth dying for? Is the American idea one such thing? Are you up for a thought experiment? What if we chose to regard the 2,973 innocents killed in the atrocities of 9/11 not as victims but as democratic martyrs, "sacrifices on the altar of freedom"? In other words, what if we decided that a certain baseline vulnerability to terrorism is part of the price of the American idea? (Wallace 2007, 25)

The author continued to use only questions (fifteen more of various types; see below p. 00) in his short contribution to *The Atlantic Monthly's* collection of commentaries on "The American Idea." The constant uptick to question intonation is difficult to sustain.[8]

VARIETY IN SENTENCE LENGTH

Sentence length is perhaps the most important variable that rhetors manipulate, usually instinctively, to create certain sound units in a text. In fact, of all the sources of variety, sentence length patterns can provide the most telling blueprint of a passage, revealing sections where longer or shorter sentences predominate or alternate. These differences are often significant, and once a profile of sentence length variation is generated, it can be correlated with other rhetorical choices. In order to make the best use of this diagnostic tool, however, sentence length has to be considered from two perspectives: overall average sentence length and the length of individual sentences in sequence.

The average sentence length of a passage (number of words divided by number of sentences) is a preliminary diagnostic tool in indirectly assessing prosodic variations across texts. The word length of sentences is itself linked to their grammatical complexity, since the more clauses and modifying phrases there are, or the more sentence parts are multiplied in series, the longer the sentence. Longer sentences may be more grammatically dense and therefore, presumably, more difficult to understand. Since sentence length is readily counted, some reading theorists and communications experts use various readability formulas based on sentence length and other word features to describe the difficulty of a passage. Readability formulas are literally equations yielding a quantitative assessment of difficulty. Many of them, like the Gunning Fog Index, the Flesch Reading

Ease score, or the more popular Lexile reader measure (based on sentence length and word frequency), are used in decisions about the suitability of textbooks for students of different ages or about the accessibility of government documents intended for the public.[9] Thus, texts can be engineered for certain audiences by manipulating sentence lengths.

But more important than average sentence length for assessing rhetorical style are the actual sentence lengths in sequence. Simply recording these in a row offers a window into the "local management" of an argument. Analysis of the following passage demonstrates these prosodic effects: it comes from Rachel Carson's *Silent Spring* (1962), a book that convinced many Americans about the dangers of pesticide use and helped to launch the environmental movement in the United States. In this paragraph from the chapter "Indiscriminately from the Skies," Carson details the far-reaching effects of airplane spraying against gypsy moths. The length in words is recorded in bold after each sentence.

(1) The contamination of milk and of farm produce in the course of the gypsy moth spraying came as an unpleasant surprise to many people. **24** (2) What happened on the 200-acre Waller farm in northern Westchester County, New York, was revealing. **16** (3) Mrs. Waller had specifically requested Agriculture officials not to spray her property, because it would be impossible to avoid the pastures in spraying the woodlands. **25** (4) She offered to have the land checked for gypsy moths and to have any infestation destroyed by spot spraying. **19** (5) Although she was assured that no farms would be sprayed, her property received two direct sprayings and, in addition, was twice subjected to drifting spray. **25** (6) Milk samples taken from the Wallers' purebred Guernsey cows 48 hours later contained DDT in the amount of 14 parts per million. **22** (7) Forage samples from the fields where the cows had grazed were of course contaminated also. **14** (8) Although the county Health Department was notified, no instructions were given that the milk should not be marketed. **18** (9) This situation is unfortunately typical of the lack of consumer protection that is all too common. **16** (10) Although the Food and Drug Administration permits no residues of pesticides in milk, its restrictions are not only inadequately policed but they apply solely to interstate shipments. **27** (11) State and county officials are under no compulsion to follow the federal pesticides tolerances unless local laws happen to conform—and they seldom do. **24** (Carson 1994, 159–60)

Here is a list of the sentences in sequence by length in words.

(1) **24** (2) **16** (3) **25** (4) **19** (5) **25** (6) **22** (7) **14** (8) **18** (9) **16** (10) **27** (11) **24**

The average sentence length can be calculated from the total number of words in the passage, 230, divided by the number of sentences, 11: 230/11 = 20.9, for an average sentence length of twenty-one words. (Notice that no sentence in the passage is actually twenty-one words long.) Looking at the individual values for the sentences, what is noticeable is how close all the values are to this average value. The distribution runs from a low of fourteen to a high of twenty-seven, but six of the sentences cluster in the mid-twenties. The relative lack of variety in sentence length here has, it could be argued, the interesting effect of making this passage sound factual and evenhanded. Carson passes along the information she obtained—"Here is what happened"—in a steady manner. The one cluster of sentences, seven through nine, that runs shorter than the average (fourteen, eighteen, sixteen) does deal with the most damaging results of this case of spraying, the exposure of consumers to contaminated milk. But even this group expressing danger does not deviate too far from the norm of twenty-one words per sentence. The final sentence does, however have greater emotional punch, and so deserves a second look. It is twenty-four words long overall, but it is actually a compound sentence composed of two independent clauses, the only compound in the passage:

(1) State and county officials are under no compulsion to follow the federal pesticide tolerances unless local laws happen to conform

(2) and they seldom do.

If independent clauses in compound sentences are treated separately, then this sentence of twenty-four words comes apart into two sentences, one of twenty words and one of four. A four-word sentence constitutes a dramatic break from the pattern (the length norm) established in the rest of the paragraph, and this short closing clause, set off dramatically with a dash, does deliver a condemning punch line. The reader's sense of government protections and competence gives way with a snap at the end of this paragraph. As the concluding four-word clause in this paragraph demonstrates, varying sentence length in a passage is an excellent way to achieve a prosodic contour that places emphasis on certain sentences.

Summary

In *Rhetoric and Rhythm in Byzantine Homilies* (forthcoming), Vessela Valiavitcharska documents the extraordinary attention paid to the prosody of persuasive prose in Byzantine rhetorical training. So important, and independent, was this dimension that even in the translation of sermons from Greek to Old Church Slavonic, the translators attempted to keep the same stress patterns, especially in argumentative units like antitheses or parallel clauses. The ancients understood that the cadences produced by stress patterns and the variations in pitch, pace, and pauses across a passage create rhythms in sound that can support an argument. But representing such spoken dynamics in text has always been a challenge. In antiquity, when oral delivery was the norm, written texts existed primarily as aids to and records of performance. Early manuscripts bear marks segmenting the text and indicating breath units. The Greco-Roman school texts recovered in the dry sands of Oxyrhynchus show accent marks and dots added above syllables requiring emphasis (Cribiore 2001, 191).

As writing and print decoupled from speech, so did the purposes and uses of punctuation. The available marks were used less as aids for oral performance and more as boundary markers for meaning units in a text. The punctuation used in manuscripts and early printing often partitions a text according to argumentative units in a way that current practice ignores, requiring vigilance from rhetorical analysts working with older texts. In contrast, the rules in contemporary handbooks prescribe only minimal punctuation to mark grammatical units in sentences. But oral-based punctuation may be making a comeback, thanks in part to e-mail and text messaging. These new media share the spontaneity, turn taking, and informal phrasing of everyday speech. Their users often flaunt the punctuation conventions of print as they adapt and combine traditional marks, especially ellipses and dashes, to new uses.

Building on the basics of prosody drilled into students by the ancient grammarians, rhetoricians taught speech dynamics under the canon of delivery. The figure manuals note only extreme effects, such as breaking off a construction to create a gap rather than a pause, or interrupting the stream of speech with an outcry. But these are still sentence-level effects. Capturing effective prosody often requires switching from the sentence to the passage level, and the prosodic contour of a passage can be roughly assessed by looking at sentence lengths in sequence. Simply listing the lengths of sentences in words can reveal where writers have grouped sentences of similar length or changed precipitously from short to long, long to short. These length differences, tied to differences in pace and pausing, can often be mapped onto argumentative units. But the whole complex subject of prosody in written prose has been neglected, and needs the attention of a new generation of scholars with new techniques of analysis.

NOTES

1. http://www.washingtonpost.com/wp-dyn/content/article/2005/10/28/AR2005102801340.html

2. Thanks to Prof. Jonathan Buehl for the listener's version of Fitzgerald's comments. A video clip of the announcement is available at the *Washington Post* website listed in the previous footnote.

3. These patterns could also be adapted to three words, or even to a single word. In his study of cursus patterns in medieval Latin, Father Craig La Drière derives a single rule: stresses were never allowed to fall on adjacent or final syllables (1943, 454). Words three or four syllables long are common in Latin, so these managed effects were not that difficult. Pontifical scribes strictly adhered to these laws as a way of indicating the authenticity of papal communications.

It is easy to undo the longer prose feet, the paeon and the cursus, into the feet of two or three syllables conventionally used to scan poetry (iamb, oó; trochee, óo; dactyl, óoo; anapest ooó; spondee óó). Furthermore, commentators on English meter frequently distinguish a lesser accent or stress, resulting in a system with three distinctions (as in the *cursus velox* above, òoóo), allowing lines to be scanned in a way that more closely approximates actual pronunciation.

4. Parkes points out that such variations in punctuation were less tolerated in Biblical texts, where marks of varying weight could produce variant reading (1993, 73–76).

5. A classic study of eighteenth-century prose is *The Senecan Amble: A Study in Prose Form from Bacon to Collier* (1951) by George Williamson.

6. Other punctuation later in the sentence controls the precise reference of the two adjective clauses within the main clause. The final relative clause (*which ... will much better answer ...*) is separated by a semicolon because the introductory *which* refers to the entire preceding construction, not to the nearest noun, *Religion*. This clause has within it another modifying clause, *I conceive*; this interrupter is best seen as elliptical, i.e., *which [as] I conceive will much better answer.* ...In a dissimilar but correct manner, the complement clause beginning with *that* (*that instead of the Word ...*) connects to the immediately preceding noun *Amendment* and, in eighteenth-century punctuation conventions, is separated only by a comma from its antecedent.

7. MacIntosh considers Swift a more "oral" writer than figures from the later eighteenth century. I generally agree with his conclusions.

8. An intonation pattern noticed among English speakers (Australia, New Zealand, and the U.S. West Coast) ends declarative sentences with rising intonation, the so-called HRT, high-rising terminal. President Obama was observed to use this pattern in his speeches. Extended over a passage, this phenomenon produces what has recently been called *uptalk* or *upspeak*, an "optimistic" effect. (On the phonetics see Ching 1982.)

9. All of the many readability formulas in existence require counting not only the number of words per sentence (sentence length) but also the number of syllables per word. Calculating the average number of syllables per word can also indicate how Latinate and therefore formal or disciplinary the diction is (see above, p. 34). According to the Gunning Fog Index, any word with three or more syllables counts as a "hard word." The Fog Index measure of reading difficulty is obtained by adding the average sentence length in a passage of 100 words to the number of "hard words" and multiplying by .4 to give the approximate grade level that a reader would have had to reach to find the passage comprehensible.

3

Interactive Dimension

The Salutation of a Pupil to his Teacher
To N—, by divine grace resplendent in Ciceronian
charm, N—, inferior to his devoted learning,
expresses the servitude of a sincere heart
THE PRINCIPLES OF LETTER-WRITING, 1135

13

SPEAKER AND AUDIENCE CONSTRUCTION

THE EPIGRAPH OPENING this chapter comes from a twelfth-century letter-writing manual (Murphy 1971, 14–15). In Europe during the High Middle Ages, the structure and authority of a resurgent church and state were maintained by correspondence, by official letters written up and down the governing hierarchies. A special group of scribes with then-rare literacy skills conducted this correspondence, and they in turn were advised by a burgeoning number of epistolary manuals that adapted the principles of classical rhetoric to the art of letter writing (see Poster and Mitchell 2007). Letters, of course, are written versions of face-to-face address, but the medium requires from the writer special tactics of self-identification and of naming or hailing the intended addressee.[1] The *Ars Dictaminis*, the letter-writing manual, provided models for imitation and paid special attention to the opening salutation, where the parties communicating were identified. This prelude to the content always named both recipient and sender, but the actual order of the names depended on their relative status. Furthermore, individuals' names rarely appeared alone; modification was added to point out their rank and to express the obligations following from it. When the recipient was higher in status, his name and honors preceded the sender's. Here is how the Holy Roman Emperor would be addressed by an archbishop:

> To the renowned, most excellent, most invincible, most eminent conqueror and always august emperor of the Romans, *C—, N—,* archbishop of Pisa, though unworthy, expresses his due obedience in Christ (Murphy 1971, 11)

This salutation follows contemporary practice in memos and letters where the addressee is always named first. But when the sender was higher in rank, his name and position came first, according to the letter-writing manuals.

> N—[fill in the name], by the grace of God bishop of the holy church of Bologna, although unworthy, sends to P—, servant of the church of Holy Mary, greetings and blessings (12)

These very formal salutations of official medieval governance can serve as an extreme case not only of textually identifying the speaker and addressee in a rhetorical exchange, but also of specifying their relationship to each other. These parameters remain in play in all assessments of rhetor/audience interaction, even in that majority of cases where the explicitness of the medieval scribes is missing: *Who is speaking, to whom, in what name, and in what role or authority? And how is this rhetor/audience relationship signaled?*

A central insight of classical rhetoric, beginning with Aristotle, is that the speaking person and the addressed person, the inevitable communicative users *of* language, can be represented *in* language. Furthermore, the rhetor's presented and reputed self, or *ethos*, is a potential persuasive resource, as is the audience's identity, selected and shaped by the rhetor's language. The Aristotelian concept of *pathos*, usually applied only to the emotional state of the audience, can also include any feature of audience. This bedrock rhetorical notion concerning speaker/audience construction has been rediscovered and relabeled many times, often with interesting nuances. Literary critics refer to the *persona* of a poem, the *narrator* of fiction, to focalization and point of view, always emphasizing that textual speakers are not to be confused with the flesh-and-blood author. Pragmaticists who study conversation and speech acts and sociolinguists who investigate the linguistic markers of group identity may be less intent on an essence/performance split. But analysts of differing orientations are likely to agree with the following basic diagram:

Speakers/writers *in the flesh*		*Hearers/readers* *in the flesh*
↘		↗

Spoken or written text

Constructed	→	*Constructed*
Speaker/		*Hearer/*
Writer		*Listener*

A rhetorical perspective on stylistics always considers the presence and projection of the rhetor and audience, both physically and in the language of a text. The stylistic features discussed in this chapter are the visible ones that foreground the presence and nature of the source and the recipients. By default, the absence of these features produces the special rhetor/audience relationship called the objective voice. But their presence does not create, nor does their absence eliminate, the fundamental interactive dimension of all language. Attitudes and bids for alignment are encoded in every language choice, and the rhetor's presence and relation with an audience are the unerasable ground of all discourse. Recent criticism discounts the individual human author as an agent or source of discourse, preferring instead to focus on discourse conventions or the language system itself as "authoring" texts. Rhetorical stylistics can serve either view. Traditional rhetorical theory certainly sees the rhetor as an agent, limited in "available means" by a situation, and offers its advice accordingly. But its emphasis on options amounts to a map of possibilities in a language, an overview of what Foucault called discursive practices without specifying them (1972). Overall, rhetorical stylistics surveys the language choices that are available to speakers and writers when they produce text and that they in turn select, or have selected for them by discourse/genre conventions, in their attempts to influence listeners and readers.

Pronouns

The simplest communication situation possible has one person speaking with another who is physically present. *I* speaks to *you*. This basic situation can be mediated in many ways—by letter, telephone, e-mail, text messaging, and so on. The real-time immediacy of face-to-face interaction may disappear, but the paradigm of a particular *I* to a particular *you* remains. Explicit textual construction of these interactive partners is achieved by the pronoun system of English. Built on the speaking situation, it offers first person to the speaker (singular *I* or plural *we*) and second person to the addressee (singular *you* and plural *you*). The pronoun *we* offers an interesting exception to this polarity, since it can sometimes combine rhetor and audience and sometimes refer to plural authors or exclude the addressees. Unlike the first and second person pronouns, third person pronouns (singular *he, she, it* and plural *they*) isolate their referents from the essential *I/you* of the rhetorical situation. Occasional exceptions to this distancing occur with the third person pronouns (*one, someone, each, everyone, everybody*) that can offer possible points of identification for rhetor or audience member or both.

Whenever there is text, there is an implicit *I* or *we* as a source and an implicit *you* addressed (see above on Rhetorical Agents, p. 150), but the personal pronouns need not appear. So actually using them to draw attention to the speaker or addressee is a choice the rhetor makes, a choice with consequences. Someone enjoying a meal can say to a dining partner *This is great!* or *I love this!* or *You should try this.* The tactical difference between such alternatives was pointed out by the authors of *The New Rhetoric.* Omitting references to the participants emphasizes the object and can anchor the speaker's value judgment in the thing itself. A speaker's self-reference personalizes the evaluation, while addressing the audience directly can turn an evaluation into a recommendation (Perelman and Olbrechts-Tyteca 1969, 161–63). In speaking, then, between people physically present to each other, the use of even an apparently unambiguous referential *I* or *you* can have persuasive effects.

In writing, there are few unproblematic uses of *I* or *you*. Since pronouns are referring words, they have to have something to refer to. Divorced from a particular moment or place, a written *I* or *you* can therefore create the participants who would be physically present in a speaking situation. But the *I* and *you* of written texts, and to some extent of formal speeches as well, can wander far from the straightforward self-references of everyday conversation (*Will you please pass me the ketchup?*) toward identities constructed for the occasion. To take fiction as the extreme case, readers understand that the *I* of a first person narrator does not stand for the actual author but rather for some fictional persona constructed as an intermediate narrator or character in the story. Charlotte Brontë is not Jane Eyre, and Camus's stranger is not Camus. Similarly, any direct address in fictional texts (as in Jane Eyre's famous "Reader, I married him") targets a constructed or fictionalized reader. Wayne Booth's *Rhetoric of Fiction* (1983) provides an enlightening introduction to the layered interactions in fictional texts, and reader response theory in general has produced rich readings of "literary" constructions of authors and readers. These are presumed to be distinct from the author/audience constructions in nonfiction genres. But for purposes of rhetorical stylistics, it is better to see a scale of possibilities, from relatively transparent references to real, physically present interlocutors on one end of the scale to highly constructed fictionalized identities on the other. In between is the practice of putting a name or category into the text for the pronoun to refer to: *We, the people of the United States* (from the preamble to the U.S. Constitution). The various possibilities of rhetor/audience construction certainly involve far more than the pronoun system, but reviewing the options and their effects is a good place to start.

USES OF *I*

Since use of the personal pronoun *I* and its forms—the possessive *my* and *mine* and the object (accusative) form *me*—is an obvious constructive option with consequences, what are the special virtues of the speaker or writer's self-reference in persuasive contexts? Perhaps the most obvious advantage of *I* is its **use in personal testimony**. When an argument deploys personal experience, first person narration with *I* is an inevitable choice. Hence, incorporated witness testimony is often quoted directly to allow the voice of the first person *I* to be heard. *I* can also be used to foreground claims made from a position of authority. When the speaker's position or status is clear to the audience, this **authoritative I** need not be foregrounded; it underwrites every statement. *I* is also sometimes used to direct the audience through the rhetor's text. This **methodological first person** usually features speech act verbs: *I will argue; I concede; I acknowledged,* etc.

All these uses of *I* are on display in a speech that Secretary of State Condoleezza Rice gave in 2006 as the inaugural BBC Today/Chatham House lecture in England. In its opening segment, Rice refers to her alternate identity as a college professor.

I'm delighted to be here to deliver this lecture. As a professor myself, I like to take every opportunity to put on my academic hat, to reflect broadly on the issues of the day.[2]

Of course putting on her academic hat in this situation, with the British foreign secretary on the platform, does not take off her hat as secretary of state. But Rice is certainly attempting an identity-shifting move, labeling the speaking *I* a professor. Later in the speech, reflecting on the changes that Birmingham, England, and Birmingham, Alabama, her hometown, have seen, Rice deploys another identity and the *I* of personal testimony.

> I spent the first 13 years of my life without a white classmate. It was when we moved to Denver, Colorado, that I had my first white classmate. And one Sunday morning in 1963, four little girls, including my good friend Denise McNair, were murdered in church by a terrorist bomb.

In such acts of self-reference throughout the speech (and there are many more), Rice adjusts her identity for her critical audience, the epideictic occasion, and the present though indirectly addressed issue of justifying U.S. Middle East policy. Whenever rhetors enter a rhetorical situation with a salient identity that is likely to dominate the audience's perceptions of them, they may rename themselves and try to specify a different identity from which they speak. When, for example, General Douglas MacArthur, dismissed from command by President Truman, spoke to Congress in 1951, he specified, perhaps disingenuously, "I trust, therefore, that you will do me the justice of receiving that which I have to say as solely expressing the considered viewpoint of a fellow American" (Safire 1997, 402).

USES OF *YOU*

The second person pronoun produces **direct address** when the rhetor deliberately acknowledges the presence of listeners or readers by calling on them in some way or even making some demand on them. In conversation, such direct address can be immediately compelling; in writing, it is a less-pressing invitation, but it is still one of the markers of a more oral and often informal style. This *you* is a feature of advertising prose, junk mail, and advice literature.[3]

The hectoring *you* of direct marketing, which inserts the addressee's name in a flyer and attributes attitudes and needs to *you*, is not, however, the only use of the second person. There is, for example, the **generic *you***, the *you* of "You know" that glances off the actual audience member by positing a *you* that is not necessarily the listener or reader but could be. This *you* is likely to appear in suppositions or conditionals: *If you take stock of yourself.* This *you* could be replaced by *anyone.*

The second person also appears in scenes constructed by the rhetor, who by using *you* invites the audience member to imagine himself or herself in a particular situation. These **scenes starring you** are often real scenarios fictionalized, as in the following excerpt from Tony Blair's speech to a Labour Party Conference shortly after 9/11 and a subsequent trip by Blair to the United States.

> Just two weeks ago, in New York, after the church service I met some of the families of the British victims. It was in many ways a very British occasion. Tea and biscuits. It was raining outside. Around the edge of the room, strangers making small talk, trying to be normal people in an abnormal situation. And as you crossed the room, you felt the longing and sadness; hands clutching photos of sons and daughters, wives and husbands; imploring you to believe them when they said there was still an outside chance of their loved ones being found alive, when you knew in truth that all hope was gone. And then a middle-aged mother looks you in the eyes and tells you her only son has died, and asks you: why? I tell you: you do not feel like the most powerful person in the country at times like that. (Blair 2001)

It was Blair himself who crossed that room, but he chooses to give agency to *you*. This choice could be described as the generic *you*, but it has the effect of substituting the listener for the speaker so that the audience member fills the prime minister's role. The difference between this *you* and that of direct address comes in the immediate juxtaposition of the different referents involved: "I tell *you* [listener/reader]: *you* [constructed identity of the person in the situation] do not feel like the most powerful person in the country at times like that." The most powerful person in the country is of course Blair himself, but he avoids the vainglorious self-reference.

Because of its bid for intimacy, a salient *you* in a painful scene, or a *you* of direct address accompanied by a negative characterization of the addressee, can be a risky choice. This extreme tactic is vividly on display in journalist David Simon's *Homicide*, a nonfiction account of his year with the Homicide Unit of the Baltimore Police Department.

> You are a citizen of a free nation, having lived your adult life in a land of guaranteed civil liberties, and you commit a crime of violence, whereupon you are jacked up, hauled down to a police station and deposited in a claustrophobic anteroom with three chairs, a table and no windows. There you sit for a half hour or so until a police detective—a man you have never met before, a man who can in no way be mistaken for a friend—enters the room with a thin stack of lined notepaper and a ball-point pen. (Simon 1991, 201)

This form of mise-en-scène true crime reenactment continues for pages, the language becoming progressively cruder as Simon recreates how *you,* the foolish criminal, are tricked by interrogators into a confession and plea bargain, waiving your rights to remain silent and have counsel: "Get used to small rooms, bunk, because you are about to be dropkicked into the lost land of pretrial detention. Because it's one thing to be a murdering little asshole from Southeast Baltimore, and it's another to be stupid about it, and with five little words [the confession, "Yeah, he came at me"] you have just elevated yourself to the ranks of the truly witless." (Simon 1991, 205; unlike this section, most of the book is written in standard journalistic third person.)

Since the reader is probably not a "murdering little asshole from Southeast Baltimore," what is the effect of this direct address? First, it creates a degree of discomfort for the reader because of the discrepancy between the reader's actual identity and the reader's constructed and addressed identity in the text. Second, it forces the reader's identification with the criminal suspect, not necessarily for invoking sympathy in Simon's gritty exposé, but for appreciating the drama and high stakes of the situation.

I to *You*: Genres of Fictional Address

The letters of the medieval scribes cited above, though written by a third party, follow the simple form of *I* to *you* communication between determinate partners in an exchange. Beyond this form are letters of introduction or recommendation written from one identifiable person to several possible unknown addressees. But a surprising number of genres are letters in form only; they use the basic epistolary conventions of self-reference and direct address to create mock speaking situations for public display. Among these is the *open letter* addressed to some defined individual or group but really written for a wider audience. Open letters should be distinguished from genuine letters that reach their addressees but are then later collected and disseminated. The Epistles of the New Testament and the correspondence of Cicero fall under this second category, as do the many published collections of letters popular in the seventeenth through nineteenth centuries. Many of these epistolary artists seem to have written with one eye on their real addressee and another on posterity. Still other open letters, ostensibly addressed to an individual or group, are never actually sent to the named recipient. In this category belong all the prefaces addressed by the author to a person of prestige (more common before the nineteenth century) and those op-ed pieces in newspapers addressed to important figures. These open letters display the act of address itself for the actual readers.

The first scientific journal, the *Philosophical Transactions* published by the Royal Society since the late seventeenth century, evolved into open letters from actual correspondence sent to the Society and more immediately to its secretary, Henry Oldenburg. Writers addressing Oldenburg in the beginning years of the journal may indeed have been answering a query from him, but they came to expect or hope that their letters would become public, though they maintained the conventions of direct address to an individual.

Sir,

  To perform my late promise to you, I shall without further ceremony acquaint you, that in the beginning of the Year 1666 (at which time I applied my self to the grinding of Optick glass of other figures than *Spherical,*) I procured me a Triangular glass-Prisme, to try therewith the celebrated *Phænomena of Colours.* (Newton 1672, 3075)

This passage opens Isaac Newton's letter explaining his conclusion that light is a mixture of colored rays. Newton had read the early numbers of the *Transactions* and he knew the required conventions. Research reports published in the British weekly science journal *Nature* are still labeled "Letters" though they now lack all conventions of salutation and address.

  The construction of *I the speaker* and *you the addressee* is more obvious in open letters never sent to their targets. The following "letter" was addressed by novelist John Kenney to Oprah Winfrey, but it was published on the op-ed page of *The New York Times* without epistolary conventions of address and under the title "Pitch Imperfect."

  May I first say how lovely you looked on the latest cover of your marvelous magazine, of which I am a very big fan. What a neat idea, putting yourself on the cover of every issue. You certainly like the color red. (How weird, me too!)

  Let me also say that I do not care for the work of Jonathan Franzen. What "corrections" was he even talking about? And that whole bit where Chip goes to the Ukraine? Hello! I might add that if you were to invite me on your show or pick my novel (which at no point mentions Ukraine or lesbian sex or what was, to my mind, a very cruel, though, in its own way, a very funny depiction of an incontinent elderly Alzheimer patient) for your book club I would say what my parents taught me to say, which is "Yes, Oprah, thank you very much." James Joyce often wrote run-on sentences.

  Did I mention that I recently completed my first novel? It's called "Pass the Gravy, Nana." (Kenney 2005)

The letter conventions of direct address are used here in parody against the effect of Oprah Winfrey's reading club on the sales and hence independence of writers. (Novelist Jonathan Franzen had resisted the selection of his novel *Corrections* and complained that Winfrey promoted sentimental novels for women readers.) A letter actually attempting to persuade Winfrey to change her choices would be quite different. This piece, using antiphrasis and exaggerated colloquialisms, constructs its real audience as "overhearers" who are too sophisticated in their tastes for Oprah's club.

USES OF *WE*

We has long been recognized as having multiple senses in English, making it an especially powerful pronoun in persuasive prose (see Fahnestock and Secor 2004). It can

stand for plural authors and take on all the functions of *I*. The *we* that concludes the Declaration of Independence is the first person plural self-reference of its "authors," that is, its signers: "And for the support of this Declaration, with a firm Reliance on the Protection of divine Providence, we mutually pledge to each other our Lives, our Fortunes, and our sacred Honor." In its **inclusive** sense, *we* unites speaker and listener, writer and reader: "I just went to a great new restaurant. You should try it. We could go together." This inclusive *we* can also place the speaker and listener/reader in some other, larger group, as in the Preamble to the U.S. Constitution: "We, the people of the United States." In its **exclusive** sense, *we* is used by speakers to refer to some group they belong to which the listeners or readers do not belong to. Both these uses are on display in the following opening, also taken from Condoleezza Rice's speech cited above.

> Thank you very much. Well, listening to Jack [Jack Straw, British Foreign Secretary], I'm sure you understand why I value his counsel and his friendship and why the people of the United States are so pleased that we have such a good friend in the Foreign Secretary here in the United Kingdom. The partnership that we forged over this past year, I think is a reflection of our nations' historic alliances, but more than that is a reflection of the values that we share as peoples, because ultimately the work of governments cannot be sustained, particularly democratic governments if there is not a deep bond between their peoples.

The *I* and *you* of the first lines refer to Rice and her immediately present British audience. The first *we* (*we have such a good friend*) refers to "the people of the United States," explicitly named, and therefore excludes the physically present British audience. The second *we* (*we forged*) is also exclusive and most plausibly refers only to Straw and Rice as partners in diplomacy over the preceding year. The final *we*, however, is inclusive (*we share*); it refers to values held in common by U.S. and British citizens, named as *peoples*, a group that the speaker, the U.S. citizens she represents, and her immediate British audience all belong to.

Rice's last inclusive *we* would qualify as a strategy for achieving Kenneth Burke's notion of *identification*, which elevates unity between speaker and audience into the primary source of persuasiveness.

> A is not identical with his colleague, B. But insofar as their interests are joined, A is *identified* with B. Or he may *identify himself* with B even when their interests are not joined, if he assumes that they are, or is persuaded to believe so. (Burke 1950, 21)
>
> Here is perhaps the simplest case of persuasion. You persuade a man only insofar as you can talk his language by speech, gesture, tonality, order, image, attitude, idea, *identifying* your ways with his. (55)

So far as pronoun choices are concerned, the strongest lexicalization of identification is the inclusive *we*, the combining of speaker/writer with listener/reader in a unifying first person plural that can in turn become an agent of various actions or the bearer of various states.

THE OBJECTIVE VOICE

Take away first and second person pronouns and any naming of source or addressee, and the result is a text in the impersonal (literally no person) or so-called *objective* voice. The latter term, currently unpopular, suggests to many a privileged and unjustified epistemological position. But the term *objective voice* can be salvaged as an analytical concept if it is defined operationally as text without the pronouns *I, you, we,* or other naming of the rhetor and audience. Several genres do prohibit or police the use of personal pronouns or the naming of rhetorical participants. In the resulting texts, no one in particular speaks to no one in particular, a situation as impossible as an absolute vacuum but one that can be approximated, like actual vacuums. The speaker is a disembodied and usually institutional source (a law, a dictionary, an instruction manual), and the audience members (readers or listeners) are unspecified overhearers rather than addressees. Of course, the ideological and attitudinal allegiances of the source are inevitably encoded, whether the source is self-referential or not, and awareness of audience is always detectable in the language choices and in what is emphasized or omitted. There is no such thing as a text without an interactional dimension (as this text illustrates). A rhetorical perspective on this interactive dimension prefers to see all texts as *intersubjective,* the cooperative result of mutually, though only provisionally, adopted language.

With a pruned definition, the objective voice emerges as the apt choice for rhetors who believe they are addressing what *The New Rhetoric* calls the "universal audience" (Perelman and Olbrechts-Tyteca 1969, 28–35). A highly debated concept, the universal audience is not a real, demographically identifiable audience. It is rather the individual rhetor's conception of what a correctly prepared and endowed audience would have to agree with. Speakers and writers are often vividly aware of how actual audiences will disagree with them, but they also make claims that they think any rational person, informed as they are informed, would consent to, or, in the formulation that Aristotle gave to this audience in the *Topics,* what all people, or most people, or the wisest and best-informed people would agree with (Barnes 1984, I 167). This conception of the universal audience clearly changes from person to person, group to group, and time to time. A rhetor in 1350 would have a very different sense of what any normal person would agree with compared to a rhetor in 1950. But with this notion of a universal audience as "what any sane person would agree with," the rhetorical definition of facts comes into view. These are statements that the rhetor counts on as believable by anyone. Not surprisingly, when expressed, these statements of fact tend to be phrased in the objective voice, without tethering to the speaker or audience.

The typical news story is delivered in the objective voice operationally defined; that is, without lexicalized rhetorical participants. Though the public widely acknowledges press bias, they still assume that certain categories of reporting—local fires, coverage of sporting events, reports of arrests—recount facts that no one with access to the same sources would disagree with. The test for what counts as a fact in the news can also be seen in what newspapers will bother to correct: usually names, titles, relationships, dates, places, and occasionally the wording of a quotation. *The New Rhetoric* specifies that statements delivered as facts are in effect addressed to the rhetor's conception of universal audience (Perelman and Olbrechts-Tyteca 1969, 67). Facts, in other words, are confirmed in their status when they seem disconnected from the interactive dimension. It goes without saying that a bid for fact status can be made when, paradoxically, sources are not mentioned and spare, unattributed language is used.

Even specifically addressed rhetorical texts move in and out of the "objective" voice, now calling attention to speaker or audience attitudes, now offering a nugget of information without a labeled source or addressee. For example, when Richard Nixon was a candidate in the 1960 presidential election, his half of the first televised debate with Senator John F. Kennedy was marked by a mixture of highly interactive bids to the audience and a litany of statistical facts. The following passage comes from his opening remarks.

> What has happened to you?
> We find that your wages have gone up five times as much in the Eisenhower administration as they did in the Truman administration.
> What about the prices you pay?
> We find that the prices you pay went up five times as much in the Truman administration as they did in the Eisenhower administration.
> What's the net result of this?
> This means that the average family income went up 15 percent in the Eisenhower years as against 2 percent in the Truman years. (Safire 1997, 306)

Following its operational definition as absence of address, only the last statement can be described as in the objective voice. It does not deliver its content from a particular source to a particular addressee as the previous statements do. By contrast, in his opening remarks in the first debate, John F. Kennedy stayed in the objective voice and never addressed the audience directly.

Changing Footing: Managing the Interactive Dimension

A sociologist who studied spoken interactions, "forms of talk," and "everyday" language behavior, Erving Goffman, like many mid-twentieth-century sociolinguists, rediscovered rhetorical principles without, evidently, any awareness of the tradition. In his new theorizing, however, he achieved a unique perspective that is implicit in but is now difficult to extract from canonical rhetorical texts. His central insight in *Forms of Talk* (1981) is the concept of *footing* to describe the relationship between conversational partners: "commonsense notions of hearer and speaker are crude, the first potentially concealing a complex differentiation of participation statuses, and the second, complex questions of production format" (146). Informed by speech act theory, Goffman noted that the relationship between speaker and hearer, that is their "participation status," could change dramatically during the course of a spoken exchange. He illustrated such a change by describing White House journalist Helen Thomas pirouetting before President Nixon at a bill-signing ceremony in response to Nixon's remarks on her appearance. The Thomas/ Nixon relationship changed with his comment and her response.

> A change in footing implies a change in the alignment we take up to ourselves and the others present as expressed in the way we manage the production or reception of an utterance. A change in our footing is another way of talking about a change in our frame for events.... [P]articipants over the course of their speaking constantly change their footing, these changes being a persistent feature of natural talk. (1981, 128)

Goffman concentrated on spoken genres, but his insights can be generalized as well to written texts and certainly to persuasive texts of all kinds. Skillful rhetors alter the footing, the participation status between themselves and audience members over the course of an argument. They may start out with a distanced *I* to *you* but eventually earn a combining *we*. Texts are best seen as constantly changing the footing, the status, the relationship, between the speaker and listener, writer and reader.

PRONOUN ANALYSIS: LINCOLN'S FIRST INAUGURAL

Abraham Lincoln arguably used a varied sequence of pronoun choices to attempt a changed relationship with part of his audience in his First Inaugural Address. Delivered in March of 1861 to a country already divided by the secession of several Southern states, Lincoln nevertheless used his speech to suggest that civil war was not inevitable. His arguments progress from a concessive reiteration of states' rights, and the Constitution's protection of property in slaves, to a defense of the Union and an affirmation that the new president will act if necessary to preserve it. The speech closes, however, with an appeal to Southerners against division, an appeal that begins with this penultimate paragraph.

> In *your* hands, my dissatisfied fellow countrymen, and not in *mine*, is the momentous issue of civil war. The government will not assail *you*. You can have no conflict,

without being yourselves the aggressors. *You* have no oath registered in Heaven to destroy the government, while *I* shall have the most solemn one to "preserve, protect and defend it." (selected pronouns already italicized in the text that Lincoln had printed; Nichols 1993, 67)

The *you* that Lincoln addressed in this passage, named as "my dissatisfied fellow countrymen," were secessionists not in fact physically present; they are *identified with* as "fellow countrymen" though they are distanced by their grievances. Lincoln knew they would be reading his speech in newspapers across the South. Hence the entity invoked by this direct address, though fictionalized for the immediately present audience, was not fictional. The pronouns here accentuate distinct identities for the president and for Southern secessionists, and indeed the final line is an antithesis featuring opposed terms: *you/no oath/to destroy* versus *I/most solemn one* [oath]/*to "preserve, protect and defend."* But after this separation, Lincoln attempted in the version he delivered to repair this footing of antagonism in the final paragraph:

I am loth to close. We are not enemies, but friends. We must not be enemies. Though passion may have strained, it must not break our bonds of affection. The mystic chords of memory, stretching from every battle-field, and patriot grave, to every living heart and hearthstone, all over this broad land, will yet swell the chorus of Union, when again touched, as surely they will be, by the better angels of our nature. (Nichols 1993, 67)

Now the personal pronouns *we* and *our* unite the speaker and his Southern addressees in the text. *We* must not be enemies; *we* share bonds of affection, memories of conflict and loss, and *our* natures have better angels.

But Lincoln did not produce this paragraph in the first version of his speech written over six weeks in January and February of 1861, weeks during which Jefferson Davis was elected president of a confederacy of Southern states. An initial draft of the First Inaugural survives. Indeed, Lincoln had it printed privately, but he continued to work on the speech, inviting comments from selected individuals. In the original version, the speech ends with the second to last paragraph quoted above, followed by these additional lines that continue the antithesis of *I* and *you* and close with an ominous unanswered question:

You can forbear the assault upon it, I cannot shrink from the defense of it. With you, and not with me, is the solemn question of "Shall it be peace or a sword?" (Holzer 2008, 269–70)

These lines sever the president-elect from his Southern audience, reflecting the real political situation. However, Lincoln's prospective secretary of state, William Seward, offered two alternate closing paragraphs. The first, picking up themes used earlier in the speech, verbosely repeats the president's offer to treat all sections of the country equally under the Constitution. The second alternative Seward offered is the one Lincoln followed:

> I close. We are not, we must not be aliens or enemies, but fellow countrymen and brethren. Although passion has strained our bonds of affection too hardly, they must not, I am sure they will not, be broken. The mystic chords which, proceeding from so many battlefields and so many patriot graves, pass through all the hearts and all the hearths in this broad continent of ours, will yet again harmonize in their ancient music when breathed upon by the guardian angel of the nation. (for the version with Lincoln's corrections see Nichols 1993, 86–87)

Lincoln improved on this offered passage in many ways; he shortened and doubled the denial of enmity, added *memory* as the bearer of the *mystic chords*, reduced the sustained metaphor by dropping *harmonize* and *ancient music* and dumped the allegorical figure of the "guardian angel of the nation." But he kept the inclusive pronouns.

DISIDENTIFICATION

Lincoln's revised final paragraph is a paradigmatic instance of what Burke meant by identification attempted through consubstantiation, the sharing of substance, in this case created in part by the inclusive pronoun *we*. However, Burke was surely wrong in thinking that identification, the joining of speaker and audience, was the only persuasive interactive dimension possible. Roughly, there are three: speakers can approach listeners from above, across, or below. Speakers can and do speak down to audiences from positions of authority. They can and do speak up to audiences from positions of inferiority, ingratiating or even intimidating from below (see Hendrickson 1993). They can and do speak to audiences as identified equals. Burkeans might reply that even from initial positions of difference, authors or speakers can construct a temporary footing of equality, of identification. They may. But they can also point up or exaggerate their differences from and *disidentify* before identifying.

Malcolm X disidentified in the opening paragraphs of his speech "The Ballot or the Bullet": "Before we try and explain what is meant by the ballot or the bullet, I would like to clarify something concerning myself. I'm still a Muslim; my religion is still Islam."[4] He then names three Christian ministers in his audience, Adam Clayton Powell, Dr. Martin Luther King, and Reverend Galamison, and claims, "well, I myself am a minister, not a Christian minister, but a Muslim minister." With these opening self-references, he foregrounds the salient difference that would have been in the minds of his audience anyway. Once having named it, he can use it as a means of amplifying the pressure that would bring such dissimilar allies together: "Although I'm still a Muslim, I'm not here tonight to discuss my religion. I'm not here to try and change your religion, I'm not here to argue or discuss anything that we differ about, because it's time for us to submerge our difference and realize that it is best for us to first see that we have the same problem." Their mutual problem, in Malcolm X's view, is "the white man." By initially magnifying the distance between himself and his auditors, Malcolm X increases the importance of an enemy powerful enough to justify overcoming so great a difference.

Figures of Speaker/Audience Construction

The nuances of pronoun use in constructing the interactive dimension represent conventional and typically unmarked linguistic resources. Virtually every normal conversation uses pronouns. But there is much more to the construction and management of the rhetor/audience relationship, and some of the riskier, more dramatic moves were sketched out in the rhetorical tradition. These include devices of salient direct address such as naming and "calling on," methods of simulated audience partitioning or the removal of segments of the audience, and techniques for apportioning speaker and audience roles in asking and answering questions.

Because classical rhetoric had as its paradigm situation a living audience, physically present before a speaker, many of the figures discussed here seem most applicable to that setting. But they all have their analogues in written texts. In either mode of presentation, they have the effect of managing the interaction with the audience in ways that serve the rhetor's goals *in the course of the speech or text*. All of these devices, therefore, flesh out and deliver on Goffman's insight that the footing between rhetor and audience typically changes over the course of a text. Among these are the many figures described in the final section below that mark local effects of attitude inducement.

CALLING ON: APOSTROPHE

Greek and Latin feature a special vocative case for nouns when they are used in direct address, in calling on. English lacks such a case, but rhetors can still signal that they are directly addressing a person or group or even an object. As in all instances of naming (see above on *agnominatio*), the term chosen for the vocative can be an important construction. Julius Caesar, facing a mutinous army, presumably compelled them to allegiance by calling on them as *Quirites*, a name meaning roughly *citizens* and typically used by magistrates addressing civilian assemblies. It was a distancing term. In the past he would have called on his army as *Commilitones*, comrades. They presumably shouted back, "We are *milites*," that is, soldiers, who were again willing to be under his command (van Eemeren and Houtlosser 2002, 131).

The figure *apostrophe* extends the natural resource of calling on those present to calling on persons and even things not present. But the often ignored essence of this figure is not direct address per se but a sudden, abrupt change of address by "calling on" a particular person in the middle of discourse addressed to others or to the whole group. Quintilian defines it in the context of a trial:

> Speech "averted" from the judge [*Aversus quoque a judice sermo*], which is called Apostrophe, is also remarkably effective, whether we (1) turn on the adversary ("What was that sword of your doing, Tubero, on the field of Pharsalus?") or (2) proceed to some kind of invocation ("On you I call, ye hills and groves of Alba") or (3) to an appeal designed to create odium ("O Porcian and Sempronian laws!") (2001, IV 55)

Apostrophe does not require the use of *O* as in the last of Quintilian's examples. The exclamation *O* is an instance of a different figure, *ecphonesis*, a crying out with emotion which need have nothing to do with direct address. The exclamation *O* is, however, often associated with "calling upon" in English, almost as a marker of the vocative.

In its account of apostrophe, the *Ad Herennium* from 80 BCE specified that "calling on" should be reserved for stronger emotional appeals: "Apostrophe [*exclamatio*] is the figure which expresses grief or indignation by means of an address to some man or city or place or object, as follows: 'It is you I now address, Africanus, whose name even in death means splendour and glory to the state'" ([Cicero] 1981, 283). The examples continue to a concluding remark, "If we use Apostrophe in its proper place, sparingly, and when the importance of the subject seems to demand it, we shall instill in the hearer as much indignation as we desire" (285).

In early modern manuals, the notion of calling on a new addressee is caught in the renaming of this device *aversio,* capturing the notion of *turning.* In the *Epitome Troporum ac Schematum*, a widely used textbook from the middle of the sixteenth century, Susenbrotus says that this device "occurs when we turn our address from those to whom we were speaking to another person either present or absent or even already dead" (1953, 65) In short, part of the power of this figure comes from the spectacle, the witnessing by others, of the rhetor's change or narrowing of addressee. Susenbrotus repeats all of Quintilian's examples from speeches, but he also imagines someone "*writing* about the vanity of the world, [who] should subjoin this: 'O earth, how alluring is what you promise, how bitter what you bestow.'" (65) This example, and further examples calling on "sin" and the "serpent," amount to conflating this device, as Susenbrotus admits, with personification. But the apostrophe/*aversio* itself remains an interactional device, recommended for heated discourse, "for it conduces wonderfully to the excitement of the emotions when it is employed with propriety and elegance" (65).

A speech that uses such turning toward and calling on with just such elegance and grace is Daniel Webster's famous epideictic address at the raising of a monument in 1825 to commemorate the Battle of Bunker Hill fifty years after the battle. Present at the ceremony were veterans of the original battle itself and many more veterans of the

Revolutionary War, as well as a "distinguished guest," the Marquis de Lafayette, who had fought with the colonists. Webster calls on the Bunker Hill veterans as "Venerable men, you have come down to us from a former generation," and a lengthy section of praise follows addressed to them as "you" (Reid 1988, 212). The Revolutionary War survivors are also called out and addressed separately: "Veterans, you are the remnant of many a well-fought field," and they too have their turn of attention (214). Finally Lafayette is called on three times as "Sir" and once as "Fortunate, fortunate man!" and he comes in for his own dole of fulsome praise (217–18). The fact that these three sections prefaced by apostrophe and directly addressed are spaced between more general sections demonstrates how a skillful orator like Webster varied his speech through changing his addressee.

PARTITIONING THE AUDIENCE

The apostrophe or *aversio* creates a spectacle for the rest of the audience; they witness the rhetor calling on someone or something, present or absent. A related device recommended in the fourth book of the *Rhetorica ad Herennium* is called *distributio*, "when certain specified roles are assigned among a number of things or persons" ([Cicero] 1981, 346). This rather vague description is illustrated by an imagined passage in which the speaker separates audience members into different roles: "'Whoever of you, men of the jury, loves the good name of the Senate...Whoever of you wishes the equestrian order to be most resplendent...You who have parents...You who have children....'" (346–47). Using this varying direct address, the speaker encourages audience members to think of themselves under different identities: as members of the Senate or the equestrian order, as children of aging parents, as parents themselves. Casting the audience in different roles with different responsibilities can of course be an indispensable tactic in encouraging action according to those perceived roles. But it can also make the audience aware of its own diversity.

The Apostle Paul used his audience's diversity to his advantage when he was brought before the Sanhedrin to hear their charges and to defend himself. Acts 23 records:

> But when Paul perceived that one part were Sadducees and the other Pharisees, he cried out in the council, "Men *and* brethren, I am a Pharisee, the son of a Pharisee; concerning the hope and resurrection of the dead I am being judged!" And when he had said this, a dissension arose between the Pharisees and the Sadducees; and the assembly was divided. For Sadducees say that there is no resurrection—and no angel or spirit; but the Pharisees confess both. (NKJV Acts 23:6–8)

Fortunately for Paul, the Roman soldiers removed him from the ensuing melee. Paul had successfully partitioned his audience, making some aware of themselves as members of one of the groups named and simultaneously as different from another group also present.

This tactic of singling out segments of a larger audience has a benign version in a popular gathering when a speaker asks the veterans, or the moms, or the union members in the audience to stand up and receive a round of applause. It has other potential effects when audience members are asked to vote *yes* or *no* by raising their hands in the presence of the entire assembly, thereby actively placing themselves in one camp or the other. And of course this singling out can have positive or negative effects when audience members can be visibly separated from each other and the speaker can draw the attention of the rest of the audience to them. The result can be public accolades or that public shaming considered by Aristotle one of the strongest emotions in the rhetor's arsenal (Kennedy 1991, 148). Cicero practiced this public shaming dramatically in his speech singling out the Catiline conspirators sitting in the Senate before him (1989, 76).

Segments of an audience thus partitioned can be put on notice in the eyes of others. Delivering a warning to part of the audience, while the rest of the audience watched, was certainly Woodrow Wilson's goal when he spoke to Congress, and in effect to the nation, in 1917 to bring the United States into the war in Europe. With a characteristic gesture, Wilson began by dissociating the people of the enemy nation from their government. But he was especially concerned with the potential enemy within.

> We are, let me say again, the sincere friends of the German people, and shall desire nothing so much as the early reestablishment of intimate relations of mutual advantage between us. . . . We shall, happily, still have an opportunity to prove that friendship in our daily attitude and actions towards the millions of men and women of German birth and native sympathy who live amongst us and share our life, and we shall be proud to prove it towards all who are in fact loyal to their neighbors and to the Government in the hour of test. They are, most of them, as true and loyal Americans as if they had never known any other fealty or allegiance. They will be prompt to stand with us in rebuking and restraining the few who may be of a different mind and purpose. If there should be disloyalty, it will be dealt with with a firm hand of stern repression; but, if it lifts its head at all, it will lift it only here and there and without countenance except from a lawless and malignant few. (Reid 1988, 649)

Unmistakable in Wilson's wording is his separation of German-Americans from *we* and *us*; they live "amongst *us* and share *our* life." And the auxiliary *will* not only marks the future tense but is also an imperative (*will be prompt*) and a warning (*will be dealt with*).

History offers many such examples of audiences physically partitioned by gender, race, ethnicity, or status. Many places of worship still routinely segregate women from men, and audiences at stadium events are economically divided between the bleachers and the skyboxes. The resulting awareness of being categorized, of being in a special group within a larger group, only seems possible in live situations where different subgroups of an audience are physically present to each other. But audience partitioning can also occur routinely in print texts, especially those known to have a wide readership. An awareness on the part of one reader of many other potential readers is like being in the presence of a large audience. So to encounter a positive or negative reference to a group one identifies with in any of the mass media is to experience some of the effects of *distributio,* partitioning of the audience. It can be achieved without the drama of direct address and pointing by simply naming a group in the presence of other groups.

PURGING THE AUDIENCE

Not marked by a separate name among the figures is a device, and indeed an entire strategy, that deserves more attention from rhetorical scholars. In the act of partitioning the audience, the speaker or writer can easily go one step further and purge the partitioned group, ejecting some audience members as not worthy of being addressed. This procedure has of course been done literally many times, when vocal protestors are ejected from conventions or people carrying placards are removed from the galleries of the House or Senate. It can also be done symbolically, in language. Here is how A. M. Rosenthal does it in an editorial written against the legalization of drugs which opens by retelling the heroin death of an affluent young mother, a stockbroker, who was taking drugs procured by her husband, a publisher, while the couple's two children were asleep in the next room.

> Soon somebody wrote a letter to *The Times* explaining how it happened. U.S. anti-drug policies are to blame. The 'demonization' of drugs prevented people from learning how much heroin at what potency was O.K. for holding good jobs without dropping dead. That failure to acknowledge the enduring appeal of drugs is the "larger tragedy."
>
> This was from a professor. He also is a senior fellow at one of those pro-legalization groups supported by tax-free foundation money.
>
> This column is not directed to people like that. They make their reputations and living by being professional legalization pushers; they are gone, goodbye. It is addressed to other people, in academia, or journalism, some lawyers, who simply believe that making drugs legally available would reduce drug crime and save the billions spent on fighting drugs.
>
> They are worth arguing with because they are people of influence. Their activities, writing, their money to pro-drug foundations, help create a casualness, an acceptance, toward drugs that increases their use.
>
> I ask them to rethink the consequences of what they do. (Rosenthal 1995)

Rosenthal could be talking "about" a group that he does not imagine as part of his readership. But the entire section of audience construction quoted here shows that he does imagine *New York Times* readers to include the pro-legalization "pushers" who are beyond persuasion. This group he banishes from the audience. After "witnessing" this purging, those who continue to read *in the role assigned* belong in a different group.

FRANKNESS OF SPEECH: *LICENTIA*

The disparities of power in contemporary Western societies pale before the power disparities in antiquity. Anyone speaking in a way that displeased an absolute ruler risked immediate death, with no recourse to "procedures," appeals, and international press scrutiny. In this atmosphere, "speaking truth to power" was dangerous in the extreme. So it is perhaps surprising that the first-century BCE *Rhetorica ad Herennium* describes a special device for criticizing the powerful.

> It is Frankness of Speech [*Licentia*] when, talking before those to whom we owe reverence or fear, we yet exercise our right to speak out, because we seem justified in reprehending them, or persons dear to them, for some fault. ([Cicero] 1981, 349)

The example that follows comes from a sample address to a jury or assembly: "You wonder, fellow citizens, that every one abandons your interests?…Blame this on yourselves…Bethink yourselves of those whom you have had for defenders…Then remember that thanks to your—to speak aright—indifference, or cowardice rather, all these men have been murdered before your eyes" (349). The "right to speak out" exercised here was the right of a citizen in the assembly or in a trial. In these public settings, the exercise of *licentia* depended on the presence of overhearers or witnesses. In their hearing, a single person or subgroup addressed with frankness could demonstrate innocence or indifference by not responding. In the case of an insult to the entire assembly of thousands of citizens (in Athens) or juries in the hundreds, the sheer size of the audience could protect the offensive speaker from retribution. But the basic tactic described here could be risky.

The *Rhetorica ad Herennium* also recommends an insincere version of this gambit, "when we remonstrate with the hearers as they wish us to remonstrate with them, or when we say 'we fear how the audience may take' something which we know they all will hear with acceptance" ([Cicero] 1981, 353). The rhetor, in other words, prepares the audience for offense but then delivers a compliment: " 'Fellow citizens, you are of too simple and gentle a character; you have too much confidence in every one' " (353).

The rhetorical settings reflected in these examples, democratic Athens or republican Rome, were exceptions in antiquity. In the Book of Kings, when the prophet Nathan blames King David for stealing Bathsheba, he uses an elaborate parable of a rich man stealing a single lamb to arouse the King's ire before he turns the story on David: "Thou art the man." The early modern revival of rhetoric occurred in authoritarian contexts. *Licentia* is replaced by its Greek equivalent *parrhesia*, defined by Peacham in Elizabethan England as "a forme of speech by which the Orator speaking before those whom he feareth, or ought to reverence, & having somewhat to say that may either touch themselves, or those whom they favour, preventeth the displeasure and offence that might be taken, as by craving pardon afore hand, and by shewing the necessitie of free speech in that behalfe, or by some other like forme of humble submission and modest insinuation" (1593, 113). The reference to "free speech" suggests that this device is indeed the descendent of *licentia*, but in his following discussion, Peacham recommends a series of speech acts when saying the unsayable: apologize first, acknowledge your peril, ask for the audience's patience, promise that the message is ultimately for their profit. He does claim that this elaborate method "is the onely forme that boldly delivereth to great dignities and most high degrees of men, the message of justice and equitie, sparing neither magistrates that pervert lawes, nor Princes that do abuse their kingdoms." But he cautions that it is only appropriate to "a man of wisedome and gravitie," and while citing prophets who denounce kings in the Bible, he advises that "their examples in this respect are not to be imitated" (115). In this way, even a device like *licentia* could adapt to realpolitik.

FIGURING SPEECH ACTS

Anyone browsing through an early modern figure manual, from Mosellanus to Scaliger to Hoskins, will find many oddly named devices that have dropped from notice. One example is *asteismus*. Neither a trope involving word substitution nor a scheme arranging syntax, this label marks the discourse move of jesting, trying to make the audience laugh. It joins others that describe local effects, moments of attempted interaction or bids to elicit certain emotions: *lamentatio* to arouse grief in the audience, or *consolatio* to lessen it. Some reflect fine distinctions among kinds of footings: the *obtestatio* is a request or prayer for help, the *querimonia* a request in the form of a complaint that help has been deferred, and the *deprecatio* an outright begging for compassion.[5] Such appeals are always characterized as deliberate choices on the rhetor's part that aim for an appropriate, corresponding response from the audience. They can be grouped roughly into those directly addressed to the audience, or part of it, to lessen the distance between rhetor and audience, and those, paradoxically, that increase the distance in order to achieve other effects. Among the latter are threats in varying degrees (*cataplexis, comminatio, perclusio*), which can be followed by a repairing mollification (*charientismos*).

Because of their association with the emotions, these figures have influenced labeling all figuration a "language of the passions." The essential mistake here is to see the point of these figures, and of all named devices, as tactics of *expression* rather than as tactics of persuasion. Speakers or writers who lament or denounce or beg or threaten do not merely vent personal emotions; they want an appropriate reaction from the audience. Hence these devices belong in the interactive dimension. They represent an attempt to catalog all the bids for a certain rhetor/audience footing that can occur over the course of a text.

To connect figural lore with current language analysis, these devices can be seen as attempts to achieve certain speech acts (illocutions with corresponding perlocutions). But just as there is no definitive catalog of speech acts (unless it is the entire set of "effect" verbs in a language), there is no fixed number of these devices. The listing of these dramatic bids is quite elastic from manual to manual; *The Garden of Eloquence* (1593) contains scores, perhaps because a clergyman like Peacham, writing for clergymen, wanted a comprehensive account of the interactive footings useful in sermons: *ara* (detesting), *eulogia* (blessing), *mempsis* (complaining), *threnos* (lamenting), *euche* (vowing), *obtestatio* (petitioning), *thaumasmus* (marveling), *onedismus* (upbraiding for ingratitude), *protrope* (exhorting), *parænesis* (admonishing), *pæanismus* (rejoicing), *bdelygmia* (detesting) (for these and more see Peacham 1954, 62–84). Furthermore, just as speech acts can be direct or indirect, so these interactional devices can be expressed overtly or they can be implied, "beneath the surface of discourse" (Stubbs 1983, 161–75). Threats, for example, can be explicit or they can take the form of hypothetical speculation or prediction. The overt drama of many of these appeals as recommended in the early modern manuals may be out of fashion. (Peacham, for example, offered the following passage to illustrate *obtestatio* (petitioning): "If innocency may deserve favor, if misery may move to pity, or prayers prevail with men: let your mercy for God's sake relieve misery, and your compassion extend to us that are ready to perish" [71; spelling modernized]). But despite changing tastes in realization, the underlying speech acts of consoling or pitying or beseeching and the like, are still performed.

Asking and Answering Questions

Among the most common speaker/audience interactions are the asking and answering of questions. A normal question (*interrogatio*) is certainly an audience construction device, since it is inevitably addressed and it genuinely invites a response. Hence the simple act of asking a question creates a respondent by default. Ordinary questions represent the speaker's real desire *for* an answer *from* a particular source. Pragmaticists who analyze conversation distinguish such requests for information from requests for services in routine social activities. Speech act theorists identify a host of types under the general heading *request*, and in one of the most common examples of indirection in speech acts, they note that a question like "Can you pass the salt?" is really a mild imperative, not a request for information.

While noting these everyday uses of questions, rhetorical manuals distinguished interrogative forms that are not genuine requests for an answer but that interact with audiences in subtler ways. The following three basic types of tactical questions appear in virtually all the manuals.[6]

> **Erotema:** This term corresponds to what would now be called a *rhetorical question*, understood as a question that requires no answer other than the audience's agreement with the proposition implied. Platform speakers who use questions with large audiences sometimes do intend to elicit an immediate, vocal answer, a roaring

"Yes!" or "No!" But strictly speaking, the rhetorical question is not a question at all, but a statement intoned or punctuated as a question.

Rogatio or *Anthypophora*: This device is a question that rhetors ask but then answer themselves (Quntilian 1921, III, 383). It is useful for managing issue construction and flow of support in arguments and for arranging the subtopics in expository texts.

Aporia: Neither an assertion masquerading as a question nor a question that the rhetor will answer, this figure expresses a doubt, an unresolved point. The asker cannot answer it, or wishes to suggest an answer without specifying, or wants to plant a suspicion.

Other versions of these two main types were noted in some manuals. A pileup of rhetorical questions was identified as a tactic on its own (*pysma*). The effect of such cascades of one rhetorical question after another can be a sustained, emotional rant. Similarly, there were other versions of the *rogatio*. Susenbrotus (under the label *subiectio*) distinguishes three circumstances for self-reply: "First, when we object to ourselves what might be objected by our auditors, and we reply just as if the objection had been made; secondly, when we compel our adversaries to respond [as between prosecution and defense in a courtroom] and we refute them just as though they had responded; third, when we propose various replies, as though deliberating, but then confute them one by one" (1953, 57). These three versions, standard in courtroom oratory, dramatize exchanges that could occur between disputants, but they are all voiced by one side. An even more extreme version of self-reply is offered in the *Rhetorica ad Herennium* as *ratiocinatio* or *aetiologia*, where "we ask ourselves the reason for every statement we make, and seek the meaning of each successive affirmation":

> When our ancestors condemned a woman for one crime, they considered that by that single judgement she was convicted of many transgressions. How so? Judged unchaste, she was also deemed guilty of poisoning. Why? Because, having sold her body to the basest passion, she had to live in fear of many persons. Who are these? Her husband, her parents, and the others involved, as she sees, in the infamy of her dishonour. And what then? Those whom she fears so much she would inevitably destroy. Why inevitably? Because no motive could more easily have led her to this crime than base love and unbridled lust. ([Cicero] 1981, 287; the example continues for as many lines)

It is not hard to appreciate passages structured by *rogatio* as "single-voiced dialogues" and hence as highly interactive. But once moved to longer speeches or written texts, *rogatio* also has text-forming function. By asking and then answering questions, the speaker or writer can foreground the organization of the discourse.[7]

The last of the three major forms, *aporia*, is the voicing aloud of doubts in the form of questions. The examples from antiquity again invoke courtroom settings where the speaker muses over procedures with a puzzled "Where should I begin?" or "How can I answer all these charges?" This device was recommended for those speaking second, following another's obviously persuasive performance, and hence calling for indirection and dissimulation from a temporarily disadvantaged speaker. The doubting, or apparently doubting, speaker enhances an eventual triumph by magnifying the difficulties faced. There is, however, no stipulation that this strategic move should not also be a sincere move, a genuine expression of uncertainty.

The formal features of questions help explain the effects of these different question-asking figures. First of all, questions change the prosodics of a sentence. Though there are special syntactic rules for turning statements into questions (e.g., move the verb or auxiliary to the front), a question can be asked without changing the word order at all simply by raising the voice at the end of a sentence: *He is a PhD* versus *He is a PhD?* The expressed vehemence of questions noted under *erotema* and especially *pysma,* a relentless surge of rhetorical questions, can result in a vocally intense passage. Even in written texts, this raised intonation is brought about for silent readers by the question mark.

A dynamic, challenging speaker, one who means to engage boldly with an audience, will make strategic use of the question form. When Patrick J. Buchanan announced his run for the presidency in 1996, he did so with very direct audience engagement—with direct address (*This campaign is about you* is repeated seven times), with insertion of audience members into roles as workers, parents, and patriots, and with frequent and varied questions, as in the following passage.

> What are we doing to our own people? What is an economy for if not so that workers and their families can enjoy the good life their parents knew, so that incomes rise with every year of hard work, and so that Americans once again enjoy the highest standard of living in the world? Isn't that what an economy is for?
>
> Our American workers are the most productive in the world; our technology is the finest. Yet, the real incomes of American workers have fallen 20 percent in twenty years.
>
> Why are our people not realizing the fruits of their labor?
>
> I will tell you. Because we have a government that is frozen in an ice of its own indifference, a government that does not listen anymore to the forgotten men and women who work in the forges and factories and plants and businesses of this country. (Safire 1997, 981)

The first paragraph exhibits rhetorical questions (*erotema*), questions that are really statements, in this case defining what an economy is for. The later "why" question is a structuring *rogatio*, asked on behalf of all and answered for the audience by the speaker. A single category, *rhetorical question*, will not capture the strategic uses of the question form in persuasion.

ROGATIO AND FORMAL ARGUMENTS

The art of asking and answering questions was not marked only in the local moves grouped under *erotema, rogatio,* and *aporia.* Question formation in itself is of great importance in rhetorical theory. The presence of the *answered question* in an argument ultimately reflects the rhetorical doctrine of forming questions in the first place, the doctrine of issue formation codified in the **stases.** The stases provided a framework for the types of questions that arguments could address. Formulated in works by the second-century BCE rhetorician Hermagoras (no longer extant) but fully treated in Cicero's *De Inventione* (ca. 80 BCE) and Hermogenes' *On Stases* (second century CE; see Nadeau 1964 and Heath 1995), the question sequence derived from stasis theory was still being taught well into the early modern period. The simplest version of the stases lists three questions: *An sit? Quid sit? Quale sit?* Whether it is? (That is, does it exist or did it happen?); What is it?; Of what quality is it?. These three general question were labeled *conjectural, definitional,* and *qualitative stases.* Cicero added a fourth *translative* or juridical stasis—Who shall decide?—asking who has the right to adjudicate a case and what is the proper forum or time for debate.

The formulation of the question at stake in an argument depended on the disputants' contending views, on what claim and counterclaim they were willing to defend. For example, in a trial the prosecution could charge *You stole the urn* and the defendant could maintain *I did not steal the urn.* From that conflict of pleas came the question at issue, *Did he steal the urn?* Juries then, as now, decided whether the affirmative or negative case was more plausible. For disputants locked in this first or conjectural stasis, Cicero offers detailed advice for making or resisting a circumstantial case (1976, 179–213). But it was sometimes possible to change the issue and hence the question being answered. The defendant, for example, could admit to taking the urn, but then move to the definitional stasis and claim that he was borrowing, not stealing. Hence not the occurrence of the act (removal of the urn) but the proper label for that act became the question at issue. Next the defendant might admit the act, concede the definition, but then enter the "qualitative" stasis, attempting to change the evaluation of the act through various mitigating moves: *It was an accident; Another person forced me; I was avoiding a worse act; I was responding to someone else's crime,* etc. A particular question would follow depending on which option the defendant chose; for example, "Did someone else force the defendant to take the urn?"

While the classical doctrine of the stases, of general types of question at issue, is no longer taught in law schools, the determination of the issue, stipulating the precise *question* that needs to be addressed, is standard in legal practice and enshrined in the three-part formula of the legal brief: *issue, resolution, application.* The process of issue or question formation is on display in a ruling of Chief Justice John Roberts when he served as an appeals court judge in the case of *Hedgepeth v. Washington Metropolitan Area Transit Authority*. This case, purporting illegal search and seizure, was brought on behalf of a twelve-year-old girl who was arrested for eating a French fry in a Metro station.

> The question before us, however, is not whether these policies were a bad idea [which his previous language concedes], but whether they violated the Fourth and Fifth Amendments to the Constitution. Like the district court, we conclude that they did not, and accordingly we affirm.[8]

Judge Roberts clearly identified the question at issue, as he had to, though he did not actually use the form of a question to express it. Chief Justice Earl Warren does use question form to set the issue in *Brown v. Board of Education*:

> We come then to the question presented: Does segregation of children in public schools solely on the basis of race, even though the physical facilities and other "tangible" factors may be equal, deprive children of the minority group of equal educational opportunities? We believe that it does.[9]

Aside from such uses in forensic settings, question asking and answering has another path in rhetorical history. Aristotle opened the *Rhetoric* with the memorable observation that rhetoric was the *antistrophos* of dialectic (Freese 1991, 2). Dialectic is essentially an art of arguing over probable matters, and, as defined by Aristotle in the *Topics,* practiced in ancient schools of philosophy, and taken up again in medieval universities, it was conducted in face-to-face exchanges involving the asking and parrying of questions, one side maintaining and the other challenging (Costello 1958, 14–19). In such disputations, the forensic stasis procedure could sometimes run in reverse, a claim inviting corresponding questions. When Martin Luther nailed his ninety-five theses to the church door in Wittenberg, they were phrased as questions that he was ready to defend in disputation by maintaining the affirmative. Formal disputations in the medieval and early modern university began in this manner from questions. In a mock exercise used to entertain James I on a visit to Oxford, selected students were set the question, "Do dogs have syllogisms?" One hapless student had to affirm and the other to deny (Costello 1958, 24).[10] The university disputation, a debate between physically present disputants centered on explicit questions, is the precursor of the single-source scholarly argument.

Summary

From a rhetorical perspective, all language is addressed. It is "spoken" to be "heard," whether the medium of transmission is semaphore signals, a megaphone, scribal scrawl, or printed text. Evolving with our species to facilitate immediate communication for survival, language is used by people to do things to people and to get them to do things. Given its focus on language in use, rhetorical stylistics has always paid attention to the interactive dimension of texts and to how the source of and target for a persuasive message are represented in that message. Though any aspect of language choice can be traced to the nature of the participants, this chapter reviews the salient means for controlling their interaction.

The first method for bringing participants into a text is by referring or naming. Since the source and addressee are always present in any language exchange, they can be brought in explicitly by the personal pronouns (*I, you, we,* etc.) unless genre conventions forbid these references. Participants can also be announced or called upon (apostrophe) by name or by some convenient label. In writing as opposed to speaking, the possibilities for tweaking identities seem more promising; indeed, as Walter Ong memorably argued, "The writer's audience is always a fiction" (1975). But the writer's audience is also to some extent real and the speaker's may be fictionalized, and it is the bids for or changes in identification between rhetor and audience that matter most. In prolonged discourse, rhetors often attempt to change the *footing* or interactive stance between themselves and their audience.

Since persuasive situations often feature one speaker before many listeners, and since writing creates the possibility of many readers, rhetorical manuals noted techniques for managing large and often mixed audiences. Audiences could be partitioned, made aware of their mutual differences, or even purged of some members for the sake of creating an agreeable subgroup, purified from those ejected. Furthermore, a slew of figures of speech cataloged the many speech acts that rhetors could attempt to perform, from condemning to warning to ingratiating to praising and many, many more. Speech acts typically require audience uptake; hence they are part of the interactive dimension of texts.

Finally, question forms create an interaction in spoken or written texts, since they always require an asking rhetor and a potentially answering audience, whether those participants are named or not. Rhetorical manuals, however, distinguished genuine questions, rare in planned rhetorical discourse, from the more common statement in question form that invites agreement (*erotema*), the question that is asked and then answered on behalf of the audience (*rogatio*), or the question that is asked and left unanswered to provoke doubt (*aporia*). In all these ways, rhetors put themselves into their texts to interact with their audiences, calling on them, telling them who they are, asking them questions, acting on them, and trying to elicit a response.

NOTES

1. The use of the term "hailing" will invoke for some Althusser's notion of *interpellation*, the calling upon that produces a person in a certain ideological role or identity (1989, 170–86). Something less is intended here, since it is possible to reject a constructed identity.

2. Rice's speech is available at http://www.state.gov/secretary/rm/2006/63969.htm.

By labeling the bombing of a church in Birmingham, Alabama in 1963 a "terrorist" bombing, Rice was using a word not typically applied to that outrage at the time. But in this word choice, she is of course inserting the actions of those opposing the civil rights movement in the United States into the same category as the terrorists of the late twentieth century. There is an argument in this equivalence: just as it was morally correct to oppose those earlier bombers, it is morally correct to pursue the current ones, who have the same resistance to social change through democratic processes.

3. The English pronoun system is actually impoverished compared to languages that express distinctions of status and affiliation in their pronouns. So, for example, German has a familiar second person singular pronoun, *du*, to be used when addressing friends, family, and inferiors, and a formal second person singular pronoun, *Sie*, to be used when addressing strangers, elders, and people in various positions of authority. When and how these polite pronouns are used has been changing; in their years as a colonial power, the French, for example, would use the familiar *tu* when speaking to Algerians of any age or status and would expect polite *vous* in return. Contemporary speakers of French, German, Spanish, etc., are more likely to use familiar/polite second person pronouns for intimate versus stranger distinctions. But obviously, given such a system, the deliberate misuse of norms of address can add other functions—calling one's child *Sie* can mock his or her demanding behavior, or lapsing into *du* in the middle of a sales pitch can attempt to change footing with a stranger.

4. For the text of "The Ballot or the Bullet," see http://www.edchange.org/multicultural/speeches/malcolm_x_ballot.html; audio versions of this speech differ from the widely circulated text and can be heard online.

5. The inventional theory for criminal cases advised those who had lost on earlier issues (i.e., the conjectural issue), to admit to the crime and plead for mercy. The *deprecatio* is the figural instantiation of this procedural move. It can be a flat-out begging for mercy or something more restrained. Portia's famous speech in *The Merchant of Venice* has the procedural place of the plea for mercy but is delivered as an encomium on mercy.

6. In the *Garden of Eloquence*, Henry Peacham created the grouping "Figures of Consultation," "which by reason of their forme and interrogation seeme to consult and deliberate with the hearers." He praises them for their "great strength and force in an oration," because "they quicken the dulnesse of the hearer, they cause attention, and do urge the hearer to the consideration of the answere, or the expectation thereof" (1593, 104–5). Peacham's category has five figures that, with characteristic elaboration, define the subtleties of questions for constructing audience and speaker interaction.

Interrogatio: Includes genuine questions when the speaker wants an answer, or questions where there is no desire for an answer but "we would make our speech more sharp and vehement" (105). Peacham recommends these "insincere" questions as ways to express emotion.

Erotema: A question used to affirm or deny something strongly.

Pysma: Many questions coming one right after the other, which could not be answered with an affirmation or denial like the preceding *erotema* but would require a prolonged response.

Hypophora: With this device, speakers ask and then immediately answer their own questions.

Aporia: The use of questions to express doubt, especially on matters of procedure such as where to begin or what to say.

Anacenosis: Questions that seem to seek advice from an adversary or consult with a judge over what should be done.

7. Discourse analysts also typically divide questions into Y/N questions, Wh questions, and Tag questions; the wording differs for each type to elicit the appropriate response. (Y/N question: *Is George at home?* Wh question: *Where are my shoes?* Tag question: You don't want that, do you?) The distinction between the *rogatio* and the *erotema* is the distinction between Wh- questions (*rogatio, subiectio*) and Y/N or Tag questions (*erotema*).

8. pacer.cadc.uscourts.gov/docs/common/opinions/200410/03–7149a.pdf.

9. http://www.nationalcenter.org/brown.html.

10. The winning student argued that the king's hunting dogs were capable of enthymemes because, coming to diverging paths, if they could not detect a scent in one direction they would backtrack and follow another. Since enthymemes were truncated syllogisms, he affirmed that dogs have syllogisms; his opponent parried gamely that the king's hounds were exceptional (Costello 1958, 24–26). When the formulation began in a question, that question could be in fact a genuine interrogation to which the answer was not known. The move from the claim questioned to the genuine question is, of course, far from inconsequential in disciplinary inquiry and the advancement of knowledge.

14

INCORPORATING

OTHER VOICES

Just after the election, an old colleague of mine said:
"Come on Tony, now we've won again, can't we drop all
this New Labour and do what we believe in?" I said:
"It's worse than you think. I really do believe in it."

The critics will say: but how can the world be a
community? Nations act in their own self-interest.
Of course they do. But what is the lesson of the
financial markets, climate change, international
terrorism, nuclear proliferation or world trade? It is
that our self-interest and our mutual interests are
today inextricably woven together.

People ask me if I think ideology is dead. My answer
is: in the sense of rigid forms of economic and social
theory, yes. The 20th century killed those ideologies
and their passing causes little regret. But, in the sense
of a governing idea in politics, based on values, no.

So what do we do? Don't overreact some say. We
aren't. We haven't lashed out. No missiles on the first
night just for effect. Don't kill innocent people. We are
not the ones who waged war on the innocent. We seek
the guilty. Look for a diplomatic solution. There is no
diplomacy with Bin Laden or the Taliban regime.

TONY BLAIR, *October 2001*

THE EXCERPTS ABOVE come from a lengthy and wide-ranging speech made by Prime Minister Tony Blair at a political party conference in October 2001.[1] Blair touched on a spectrum of policy issues and addressed his critics at different points, often giving them a voice in his own text so that he could answer them. Blair's techniques of ventriloquism illustrate the many ways that other voices, other speakers and writers, can be brought into a new textual environment. In his actual delivery, these differences were also signaled by intonation; in print, they are approximated by differences in punctuation. In either mode of presentation, Blair's tactics offer a scale of possibilities for representing the speech of others, from the pretended direct quotation of "Come on Tony" to the unassigned and unmarked back-and-forth of the last excerpt.

The notion of an "embedded voice," of another's words carried into a new context, has always been important in rhetorical theory, given its forensic interest in representing witness testimony or documentary evidence and its stylistic interest in imitating other speakers in a speech. Attention to representing speech has also come from literary critics, who have carefully noted methods of presenting spoken exchanges in fiction. The discussion of speech representation in this chapter borrows heavily from the description of such practices in *Style in Fiction* (1981), the work of the literary stylisticians Geoffrey Leech and Michael Short. Insights on speech incorporation might also come from journalists, since they rely heavily on quotations from sources. But apart from a few "rules of thumb," journalists have apparently had little to say about the nuances of speech representation.

Examining the incorporation of other voices can begin by reviewing the standard practices available for placing the spoken word into another text. Contemporary rhetors have a graded set of options, from the most distinct representation of another voice that leaves an unassimilated residue, through various levels of paraphrasing, to a complete replacement of the original with an interpretation of its purpose. This scale of possibilities extends, as Leech and Short pointed out, from direct speech through indirect speech to the narrative report of a speech act.[2]

Direct Speech

For the last five hundred years, punctuation conventions in printing have created the possibility of a visually marked verbatim "transcript" of another's speech. In "direct speech" or direct quotation, the fiction is maintained of moving the exact words of another person from their context of utterance, either spoken or written, into a new context. The incorporated text is typically attributed to a named source and marked off as another's by quotation marks, a punctuation convention only as old as printing. Before this printers' invention, readers (as well as copyists and early printers) relied on changes in verb tense, vocatives of address, and other subtle linguistic cues to make it clear where quotations began and ended (on the *diple* and quotation marks see Crystal 2003, 68, and Parkes 1993, 59). Without either linguistic or orthographic cues, there is no obvious way to tell when another's speech or text begins and ends or whether it is being represented precisely or merely paraphrased. Before clear punctuation conventions, the intertexuality created by embedded voices in manuscripts and early printing had different characteristics. And a new era in such incorporations has arrived, since web-based texts can link to the audio or video recording of an utterance, giving a new a meaning to direct quotation.

The current convention that a speaker's or writer's exact words appear within quotation marks is upheld rigorously as an ideal, but is rarely practiced and is in fact difficult to follow. Direct quotation from written sources may be as easy as copy and paste, but transcribing spoken utterances into text presents many difficulties. Writing and printing offer few resources for representing the prosodics of actual speech—the changes in pitch, intensity, duration, and pause length that inflect meaning so easily in the living voice. And while a writer like Tom Wolfe will go to great lengths to try to represent the sound of speech, orthographic hijinks are not used to approximate sound in most print genres.

Furthermore, even in the days of audio and video recording, from Dictaphone to tape recorder to DVR, there can be surprising differences in direct quotations attributed to the same source. A simple comparison of the same speech event covered in different newspapers can illustrate the problem. When his country was not invited to a meeting of the Commonwealth of Nations in 2003, the president of Zimbabwe, Robert Mugabe, said the following in a televised speech, according to the *New York Times:*

> "If our sovereignty is what we have to lose to be readmitted into the Commonwealth," Mr. Mugabe was quoted as saying on Friday, "we will say goodbye to the Commonwealth. And perhaps the time has now come to say so." (Wines 2003)

And the following according to an Associated Press story in the *Philadelphia Inquirer.*

> "If our sovereignty is to be real, then we will say good-bye to the Commonwealth, [sic; second quotation mark missing] Mugabe said in remarks broadcast on state television. "Perhaps the time has come to say so." (Shaw 2003)

Did Mugabe produce both versions of these comments? If he gave only one, which published version is accurate? Do the versions have different sources? Are the differences in the exact wording significant or not? Both papers did agree, word for word, when quoting Mugabe's claim that Australia's prime minister, John Howard, was "genetically modified because of the criminal ancestry he derives from."

In most genres, direct quotations have to be attributed to a source, even if only to an anonymous source. But how many other elements of the context of utterance are necessary for reconstructing the original source's meaning or intent? Meaning can be lost, for example, when the addressee of an utterance is not specified. During the Democratic primaries in 2003, for example, the candidates' debates, widely televised, were extensively reported in newspapers. When Dick Gephardt debated Howard Dean on the subject of Dean's cutting social services while he was Governor of Vermont, Gephardt concluded his remarks, according to published transcripts, by saying, "You don't just cut the most vulnerable in our society" (Balz 2003). Was this a comment addressed to Dean or a general comment with "you" understood as "generic you"? The second interpretation is probably the most likely, but the *Boston Globe* reported this comment as a specific charge addressed to Dean, "Gephardt contended that Dean 'cut [programs for] the most vulnerable in our society' to balance Vermont's budget" (Healy and Johnson 2003). Though it reproduced the correct string of words, did the *Globe* quote accurately?

Opportunities for misrepresentation despite the presumed accuracy of direct quotation abound. Most obvious is the practice of quoting selectively (sometimes called *quoting out of context*) and of "tendentious recovery," where the inaccuracies in direct quoting clearly serve an editorial purpose. *The Harvard Crimson*, for example, attributed the following comment to Justice Antonin Scalia, "I even take the position that sexual orgies eliminate social tensions and ought to be encouraged," and then published a correction, "In fact, Justice Scalia said, 'I even accept for the sake of argument that sexual orgies eliminate social tensions and ought to be encouraged.'"[3]

In the new journalism of Tom Wolfe, Hunter Thompson, Truman Capote, and Bob Woodward, it is standard practice to represent the speech of real people in real situations by apparently quoting directly as though the reporter were present with a tape recorder when actually all the direct quotations are reconstructions, or, less charitably, fabrications. Such invented direct speech is also standard practice in nonfiction "true event" narratives like Piers Paul Read's *Alive*, Jon Krakauer's *Into Thin Air*, or Sebastian Junger's *The Perfect Storm*. In these prose reenactments of real events, it is considered fair to reconstruct direct speech as the "kind of thing" that might have been said in a situation. In this practice, contemporary nonfiction writers are actually following advice given thousands of years ago in rhetorical manuals (see below on *ethopopoeia*, p. 319).

THE STYLIZATION OF DIRECT SPEECH

Though the aural dimensions of actual speech escape representation in text, writers can attempt certain kinds of recovery. They may, for example, decide to signal a speaker's regional or social dialect or, more rarely, an individual's unique speech habits. Since the accurate transcription of all the clips, diphthongs, and elisions of speech is never possible, what results instead is a conventional approximation or *stylization* of another's speech. When a spoken variant is represented by alternate spellings, the result is called "eye dialect" (Wales 2001, 144).

Speech stylization does occur in contemporary news reporting. For example, in its coverage of the aftermath of Hurricane Katrina, the *New York Times* produced "local color" pieces directly quoting speakers in ways that capture dialect.

> Anne Lambert, who lives in a shotgun house along a remote highway in the unincorporated town of Wilmer, La., has no chain saw, no backhoe or tractor. She has gone at the formidable pile of branches in her yard with rakes and pitchforks.
>
> "Me and him picked up thems we could," said Ms. Lambert, 75, referring to her 88-year-old neighbor, Percy Gill. (Steinhauer and Robertson 2005)

In a similar hurricane story on a family identified in text and photographs as African American (the Jackson-Browns), taken in by a family identified as white (the Delcomyns), the speech of the latter is stylized lightly. "'And I told him if y'all going to be around for a while, you have to get married,' Mr. Delcomyn said." Mrs. Delcomyn's testimony at a church service is also reported: "'I remember as a child being hungry,' she said, crying. 'I remember this one man, he was delivering bread, he stopped and he give us some food.'" The speech of Ms. Jackson and Mr. Brown, while informal, is rendered without dialect features:

> "You feel like you're at home," Ms. Jackson said. "They don't treat us like we're strangers at all, they talk to us like they talk to other family."

"A lot of things we left behind us in our past I hope not to do anymore," Mr. Brown said. "Before the storm hit we were talking about changing our lives. Since the storm hit, it's happening fast" (Wilgoren 2005).

It is of course impossible to know whether the Jackson-Browns used features that a dialectologist would label either Southern or African American. If they did, the *Times* reporters and editors evidently considered any stylized representation of their speech as unacceptable, perhaps because such stylizations have been used in caricatures and race-baiting polemics. Despite pride in and cultivation of a separate dialect on the part of many African Americans, most print media outlets avoid stylizing this dialect when quoting directly.

The issue of racist dialect representation affects the canon of American oratory in the case of the famous "Ar'n't/Aren't/Ain't I a Woman" speech of Sojourner Truth. Given originally to the second Women's Rights Convention in Akron, Ohio, in 1851, the only presumably close to verbatim record of Truth's speech was a version first published by Frances Gage in 1878 in a heavily stylized dialect interrupted by comments from the editor, as the following excerpt shows.

> But what's all dis here talkin' 'bout? Dat man ober dar say dat women needs to be helped into carriages, and lifted ober ditches, and to have de best place every whar. Nobody eber help me into carriages, or ober mud puddles, or gives me any best place [and raising herself to her full hight [*sic*] and her voice to a pitch like rolling thunder, she asked], and ar'n't I a woman? (reprinted in Logan 1995, 24)

If read in the context of late-nineteenth-century practices of representing regional dialects of Yankee New Englanders, Southerners, and Westerners, and of rural voices in general, in contemporary journalism and fiction, this rendition is perhaps not as unusual as it seems in isolation. (The speech of rural Indiana whites was, for example, rendered as stylized dialect in Edward Eggleston's *Hoosier Schoolmaster,* 1871.) But in the judgment of twentieth-century feminist critic Donna Haraway, "That written text represents Truth's speech in the white abolitionist's imagined idiolect of The Slave, the supposedly archetypical black plantation slave of the South" (quoted in Logan 1995, 20). Undoing the stylization, Karlyn Kohrs Campbell revised the speech when she first anthologized it in 1989. Here is her version of the passage quoted above.

> But what's all this here talking about? That man over there says that women need to be helped into carriages, and lifted over ditches, and to have the best place everywhere. Nobody ever helps me into carriages, or over mud puddles or gives me any best place (and raising herself to her full height and her voice to a pitch like rolling thunder, she asked) and aren't I a woman? (reprinted in Logan 1995, 26)

Campbell kept some features of a distinct dialect, but, in much the manner of the *New York Times* characterizing the speech of Southern whites, minimized the differences to a handful of distinctions. Though the acceptable degree may be debatable, some stylization is inevitable whenever attempts are made to capture the dialect or idiolect of a spoken text in a written text.

Indirect Speech

In the opening quotations from Blair's talk, the second excerpt begins to migrate away from direct speech: *The critics will say: but how can the world be a community.* The phrasing after the colon (a mark certainly not "in" Blair's speech) might have been put in quotation marks (another interpretive device), since it is worded as though spoken. However, by the third excerpt, *People ask me if I think ideology is dead*, Blair abandons exact quotation, presumably substituting the phrasing *if I think ideology is dead* for some original remark like *Do you think ideology is dead?* At this point he has moved from direct to indirect speech, perhaps because he is summing up what several people asked. In indirect speech, the exact words of a speaker are paraphrased rather than repeated verbatim. A representation like *He said, "The shoe doesn't fit,"* becomes *He said that the shoe didn't fit.* The reporting verb used in direct speech ("he said") can remain the same, but the content of the utterance becomes a noun clause introduced by *that.* The tense of the verb may also be changed as in this example, from *doesn't fit* to *didn't fit.* However, in some contexts the tense of the verb need not change in the indirect report: *What did he say?/He said that the shoe doesn't fit.*

Indirect speech offers a rhetor more opportunities for interpretive intervention. Readers and listeners usually assume that the words, especially the keywords, quoted indirectly are the same words that would be quoted directly. But they need not be. The shoe comment above, for example, could be rendered in several approximations: *He said that the shoe was not a good fit/He said the shoe was the wrong size/He said that the shoe was uncomfortable.* These are paraphrases substituting roughly synonymous phrases, but they wander farther and farther from the original wording. (A shoe that doesn't fit is plausibly but not necessarily uncomfortable.) The possibilities for rhetors to paraphrase in ways that favor their purposes are obviously greater in the case of indirect speech. Al Gore was widely quoted, indirectly, as stating that he "invented the Internet," a claim cited to his discredit by his critics. According to a transcript of the interview where Gore made the original comment, the direct speech version subsequently paraphrased was, "I took the initiative in creating the internet."[4]

AMBIGUOUS ZONES IN INDIRECT SPEECH

Indirect speech is common in news reports, where it alternates with direct quotations from sources. In one of the special stylistic conventions of newspaper discourse, reporting clauses are usually tacked on to the back of claims that are actually paraphrased from sources. The reader takes in the text and then in the end learns that the whole is attributed indirect speech. Here is a sample of this technique in the opening of an article suggesting improprieties in the conduct of Republican presidential candidate John McCain:

> Early in Senator John McCain's first run for the White House eight years ago, waves of anxiety swept through his small circle of advisers. A female lobbyist had been turning up with him at fund-raisers, visiting his offices, and accompanying him on a client's corporate jet. Convinced the relationship had become romantic, some of his top advisers intervened to protect the candidate from himself—instructing staff members to block the woman's access, privately warning her away and repeatedly confronting him, several people involved in the campaign said on condition of anonymity. (Rutenberg et al., 2008)

The final sentence, and perhaps this entire opening passage, should be mentally rearranged, since what the reader takes to be the main predication (*top advisers intervened*) actually occurs in a noun clause functioning as the direct object of the reporting verb *said*. Such "trailing attributions" could be described as a method of "having it both ways." The content of the paraphrased utterance assumes greater fact status by being taken in first, as an unattributed proposition; in the end, the reader discovers the source, a "save" for the objectivity of the news source. (Citing the source does not necessarily lend credibility to an assertion; an attribution can actually lower the truth status of a claim since what has to be sourced does not have immediate recognition as a fact [on this issue see Perelman and Olbrechts-Tyteca 1969, 67–68]).

The convention of the trailing attribution and the need to provide contextualizing details can sometimes produce anomalies like the following, from a web news item reporting arrests of suspects plotting terrorism in Canada.

> At least 6 of the 17 people in the counterterrorism operation over the weekend regularly attended the same storefront mosque in this middle-class Toronto suburb of modest brick rental townhouses and well-kept lawns, fellow worshipers said Sunday. (DePalma 2006)

It is highly unlikely that the "fellow worshippers" provided the social and economic details about the suburban location of their mosque, or that Yemeni officials gave the political interpretation attributed to them in the following.

> The United States military has decided to release a former driver for Osama bin Laden whose trial became a test case for the Bush administration's system of military commissions for accused terrorists, Yemeni officials said. (Worth 2008)

The same issue of questionable attribution can occur when indirectly reported speech spills over into separate sentences. This crucial source of ambiguity, which Leech and Short labeled *free indirect speech* (325ff), is on display in the first two sentences of the McCain story quoted above. Given its protean qualities and importance in interpretation, this floating indirect speech deserves a closer look in another example. Trying to sift rumors of violence from reality a month after Hurricane Katrina, two *New York Times* reporters presented some results of their interviews with local officials in the following section of a longer article.

> *As the storm winds died down that Monday, small groups that had evacuated from poor neighborhoods as far away as the Lower Ninth Ward passed through the historic French Quarter, heading for shelter at the convention center.*
>
> "Some were pushing little carts with their belongings and holding onto their kids," said Capt. Kevin B. Anderson, the French Quarter's police commander. He said his officers gave food, water and rides. "That also served another purpose," he said. "That when they came through, they didn't cause any problems."
>
> *The jewelry and antique shops in the French Quarter were basically left untouched, though squatters moved into a few of the hotels.* Only a small grocery store and drugstores at the edge of the quarter were hit by looters, he said. From behind the locked doors of the Royal Sonesta hotel on Bourbon Street, Hans Wandfluh, the general manager, said he watched passers-by who seemed to be up to no good. "We heard gunshots fired," Mr. Wandfluh said. "We saw people running with guns."
>
> At dusk on Aug. 29, looters broke windows along Canal Street and swarmed into drugstores, shoe stores and electronics shops, Captain Anderson said. *Some tried, without success, to break into banks, and others sought to take money from A.T.M. machines.* (Dwyer and Drew 2005; italics added).

With the exception of the sentences in italics, everything in these paragraphs is offered as either direct or indirect speech with immediate attribution to named individuals. Such mixing of direct and indirect speech is conventional in journalistic practice, since text offering only direct quotation, the raw material of the interviews, would be less readable. But what can be said about the unassigned sentences represented in italics? The sentence opening the section, before the first direct quotation from Captain Anderson, seems to be in the voice of the reporters, because it occupies a paragraph on its own, immediately after the subtitle and before assigned text begins. However, the sentence opening the second paragraph, also unassigned, contains the kind of information attributed to the captain in the following sentence. It seems more likely to be the captain's report reproduced as indirect speech. (This interpretation would be more secure if the order of the sentences were switched.) The final unattributed sentence (beginning *Some tried*) also seems to belong to Captain Anderson, because it follows his indirectly quoted remarks in the same vein. But attribution becomes more ambiguous as the article continues.

The convention center, without water, air-conditioning, light or any authority figures, was recalled by many as a place of great suffering. Many heard rumors of crime, and saw sinister behavior, but few had firsthand knowledge of violence, which they often said they believed had taken place in another part of the half-mile-long center.

"I saw Coke machines being torn up—each and every one of them was busted on the second floor," said Percy McCormick, a security guard who spent four nights in the convention center and was interviewed in Austin, Tex.

Capt. Jeffrey Winn, the commander of the SWAT team, said its members rushed into the convention center to chase muzzle flashes from weapons to root out groups of men who had taken over some of the halls. *No guns were recovered.*

State officials have said that 10 people died at the Superdome and 24 died around the convention center—4 inside and 20 nearby. *While autopsies have not been completed, so far only one person appears to have died from gunshot wounds at each facility.* (Dwyer and Drew 2005)

The first sentence in this passage does not quote, directly or indirectly, what was said by one individual, but it does summarize the testimony of *many* anonymous speakers (how many?) who *recalled* great suffering. The first part of the second sentence continues the reporters' summary, but its final adjective clause creates a stronger impression of indirect speech (*which they often said*), though assigned to an unspecified "they." Next comes a direct quotation firmly attributed to a fully identified Percy McCormick, followed by two paragraphs of attributed indirect speech: "Capt. Jeffrey Winn...said," "State officials have said..." The difference in verb tenses here (*said* versus *have said*) suggests that the facts attributed to unnamed state officials may come from an official news release. But both of these indirectly quoted assertions are followed by unattributed sentences that contradict the substance of the attributed remarks. In the first case, "No guns were recovered" could be the admission of Captain Winn; in other words, it could be read as a continuation of speech indirectly quoted from him. But the second observation about autopsy results, while also in the position for continued indirect speech, looks like a contradiction assembled from other sources, and therefore, in this article, it is "spoken" by the reporters. What source authorizes these contradictions? The ambiguities of attribution that occur in this article are in no way unusual. And while no crucial difference in interpretation may hang on the distinctions in this case, it could.

Reporting Speech Acts

Beyond direct and indirect quotation, there is still one more important technique used in representing one person's speech or writing in another person's text. This option builds on the fundamentally rhetorical observation put in place by J. L. Austin (1962) that speech is a means of performing actions—that in certain circumstances, saying something amounts to do doing something. The deeds done are "speech acts," the kinds of actions accomplished through speaking such as boasting, promising, denying, praising, arguing, comforting, contradicting, affirming, begging, threatening—actions typically accomplished, as Austin pointed out, with a special set of *performative verbs*. Rather than quoting someone's words, directly or indirectly, a rhetor can instead report the *action* the speaker presumably performed with those words. Using the above shoe example again, the utterance *"The shoe doesn't fit"* could be reported as *He complained about the shoes.* The speaker's actual words are lost in this form of representation. They are replaced by a verb describing the act performed by the utterance, in this case the act of complaining. Reporting another's speech act, as in this example, often involves interpreting the intentions of the speaker, and the opportunities for tendentious representation, or even misrepresentation, are obvious. A speaker may say, for example, "I will come tomorrow," and depending on the oral features of the utterance and on the context (who is speaking to whom and the circumstances), these words could be represented by *He promised to come tomorrow* or *He threatened to come tomorrow* or by other possibilities.

Representing Thoughts

Since unspoken thoughts can be considered "inner speech," all the techniques used to represent actual utterances can apply to the presentation of thoughts in a text. Literary scholars have been especially interested in thought presentation because it is a critical fictional technique. In *Style in Fiction,* Leech and Short make a good case for the tactics of speech representation applying equally to thought (336–42; see also Short, 2007, 230–36). So it is possible to have the following versions of an idea:

> Direct thought: *Lee thought, "I should vacation in Bermuda this year."*
> Indirect thought: *Lee thought that she should vacation in Bermuda in 2002.*
> Report of the "thought act": *Lee considered vacationing in Bermuda in 2002.*

Functional genres, like newspaper reports, do not usually take the liberty of reporting thoughts directly, though they will of course directly quote people reporting their own thoughts: *The President said, "I thought that he should be the first to make the announcement."* However, interpretive journalism, historical works, and forensic arguments often describe thoughts and thought processes indirectly or attribute "thought acts" to agents.

Texts as Speakers and "Text Acts"

Just as speakers and writers can represent the spoken words and thoughts of others in their own speech or writing, they can treat texts in exactly the same way, by quoting directly, quoting indirectly, or representing the "speech act" performed by the text. Consider, for example, how a line from the U.S. Constitution can be represented in other texts:

Direct quotation: *The Constitution says, "Congress shall make no law respecting an establishment of religion or prohibiting the free exercise thereof."*
Indirect quotation: The Constitution says that Congress cannot establish a religion or prohibit worship.
Reporting the speech act of the text: *The Constitution demands/guarantees separation of church and state.*

Texts, then, can be treated like speaking voices, and all the problems and possibilities that accompany the incorporation of another person's speech accompany the incorporation, the "voicing," of one text within another.[5] There are the same opportunities for misrepresentation or misappropriation: direct quoting can become quoting out of context; indirect quoting can wander into inaccurate paraphrase; reporting the "speech act" of another text can mask interpretive license.

A special dimension occurs, however, when rhetors appropriate the content from other texts into their own. Writers and speakers representing the *written* words of another can attribute material either to the author or to the text itself. In older practice, it was common to cite only the author. Erasmus constantly refers to Quintilian, Quintilian in turn to Cicero, taking words from their works, sometimes verbatim, without naming the works. An author's written work was therefore treated as constantly present speech, a text spoken again with every reading.[6]

In interpretive practices that downplay the agency of the author (New Criticism avoiding the "intentional fallacy," deconstruction unmooring texts from contexts, or Foucauldian criticism favoring "discursive practices" over writers), attributions are typically made to texts rather than to authors. This practice in literary criticism of the last fifty years does, however, have a precedent in legal habits of citation that feature the document. And, of course, when the author is unknown or multiple, the text is more often the attributed source, as in the case of the Constitution. Some expressions citing texts, when the author is unknown or unimportant, sound quite normal: *The sign says, "Closed for the summer"* (direct quotation); *The manual says that you can't put this device in water* (indirect quotation); *The instructions warn about giving this to children* (report of a "text" act). The habit of attributing to texts rather than to authors when quoting, paraphrasing, or reporting speech acts can, however, give texts surprising agency in some locutions. In these practices, texts are in effect personified, given all the intentions and powers of the speaking person, though, again, this practice is so routine in some contexts as to be accepted without demur.

Invented Speakers

Ancient orators frequently incorporated the spoken and written words of others into their texts, but the routine practices of quoting, paraphrasing, and attributing speech acts were not highlighted in the rhetorical manuals. The manuals gave more attention to extemporizing the speech of others, perhaps because doing so allowed speakers to create interesting vocal dynamics. The earliest manual, the *Rhetorica ad Herennium,* identifies *sermocinatio,* as "assigning to some person language which as set forth conforms with his character" ([Cicero], 1981, 395), and *conformatio,* as "representing an absent person as present, or in making a mute thing or one lacking form articulate, and attributing to it a definite form and a language or a certain behavior appropriate to its character" (399). These different devices were later grouped under the general label ***prosopopoeia,*** invented speech. This invention of or attribution to other voices could take many forms, as Quintilian explains in his introduction to the whole category of simulating speech:

> Bolder, and needing (as Cicero puts it) stronger lungs, are Impersonations, or *prosopopoeiai* as they are called in Greek. These both vary and animate a speech to a remarkable degree. We use them (1) to display the inner thoughts of our opponents as though they were talking to themselves (but they are credible only if we imagine them saying what it is not absurd for them to have thought!), (2) to introduce conversations between ourselves and others, or of others among themselves, in a credible manner, and (3) to provide appropriate characters for words of advice, reproach, complaint, praise, and pity. We are even allowed in this form of speech to bring down the gods from heaven or raise the dead; cities and nations even acquire a voice. Some confine the term Prosopopoeia to cases where we invent both the person and the words; they prefer imaginary conversations between historical characters to be called Dialogues, which some Latin writers have translated *sermocinatio.* I follow the now established usage in calling them both by the same name, for we cannot of course imagine a speech except as the speech of a person. (2001, IV 51; numbers not in the Latin text)[7]

The practice of incorporating imaginary speech predates theorizing about it. One of the rare speeches preserved from fifth-century BCE Athens is Andocides' defense of himself against charges of impiety in a speech known as "On the Mysteries." As part of his defense, Andocides had to clarify his role in two scandals that had rocked Athens fifteen years earlier, the mutilation of statues of Hermes guarding doorways throughout the city and the profanation of the Eleusinian Mysteries by unsanctioned celebrants. Andocides' speech to the jury contains indirect quotations and reports of others' speech acts. Gaps are also left for the reading of witness testimony, a form of direct quotation. But there are also imagined speeches like the following, in a passage where Andocides stresses that he has remained in Athens to face his trial rather than fleeing the city, as many charged persons often did:

> Thus in my case, when a lot of people were informing me that my enemies were saying I wouldn't stay but would certainly get away into exile—"What would be the point of Andocides' staying for such a serious trial? He can leave here and keep all his possessions; and if he travels to Cyprus, where he's come from, he has plenty of

good land offered to him, and a grant as well. So will he want to risk his own life? For what purpose? Can't he see how things are in Athens?" But in fact, gentlemen, my view is quite the opposite of this. I couldn't bear to live somewhere else and keep all my property while losing my own country, even granting that the situation in Athens is as bad as my opponents say. I'd far rather be a citizen of it than of other cities which may seem to me very prosperous at present. It's because I take that view that I've entrusted my life to you. (Gagarin and MacDowell 1998, 102)

What the editors have set off in quotation marks would of course have only been distinguished in speech by Andocides' manner of presentation; he would certainly have changed his voice at the boundary where he leaves off the supposed speech of his enemies and turns to address the jury directly. "But in fact, gentlemen." The technique of constructing the imagined speech of his opponents here has several potential benefits. It allows Andocides to talk about himself in the third person, putting boasts about his wealth in others' mouths, even the mouths of his opponents. It amplifies greatly the strategy of staying for the trial, and it suggests that his adversaries' real motive was to drive him into exile, not to have him resist the charge. Expanding on the alternative he avoided, the questions in the imagined speech also give it a colloquial inflection, at least in translation, emphasizing that common sense would recommend his taking off for Cyprus, a course he claims not to have pursued out of love of Athens and trust in the Athenian jury.

Later in the speech, Andocides describes his reasons for informing on the real perpetrators of the mutilation of the Hermes. He and many members of his family, including his father, had been thrown into prison as the guilty parties on the testimony of an informer.

Then Charmides, my cousin, who was my age and had been brought up with me in our house since we were boys, said to me: "Andocides, you see how serious the situation is." (Gagarin and McDowell 1998, 116)

Continuing for several lines, Charmides pleads with Andocides to save his family if he knows anything about the real perpetrators. Charmides' speech is a reconstruction plausible to the person and occasion, as Quintilian recommends (though it is not plausible that an extended speech would be exactly recalled), and it is followed by another form of *prosopopoeia* listed by Quintilian almost five hundred years later, the casting of one's own thoughts into quoted speech.

When Charmides said this, gentlemen, and the rest begged me, and every one of them entreated me, I thought to myself: "I must be the unluckiest man in the world! Am I to do nothing while my own relatives are unjustly destroyed, being put to death and having their property confiscated, and are also recorded on monuments as sinners against the gods, when they're not responsible for any of what has happened? And while three hundred other Athenians are going to be put to death unjustly, and the city is in the greatest trouble and mutual suspicion? Or shall I tell the Athenians what was said to me by Euphiletus, the man who actually did it?" (Gargarin and MacDowell 1998, 116; again, modern editors have supplied the quotation marks)

Presenting his thoughts as speech allows Andocides to represent his hesitation, his internal debate over whether to turn someone else in, an action that did not reflect well on him. Dramatizing his self-persuasion, the desire to protect his father and other family members, provides a motive the jury could acknowledge. It is not difficult to see that this same technique of imagining others' speeches is used by Tony Blair in the passages opening this chapter. Particularly apt is the fourth excerpt, imagining a dialogue between Blair and unidentified critics of a war in Afghanistan who raise a series of objections that he answers immediately.

Inventing the speech of others, and presumably delivering it with distinct intonation (hence Quintilian's reference to its animating powers), was reinforced in grammatical and rhetorical training, as evidenced in the composition assignments of the *Progymnasmata*. Among the standard exercises in this series were the *prosopopoeia, ethopopoeia,* and *eidolopoeia*. Distinguished perhaps excessively, the *prosopopoeia* imagines a person speaking, the *ethopopoeia* attributes speech to real persons, while the *eidolopoeia* attributes speech to the dead (Kennedy 2003, 84). Under whatever form, boys from seven to fourteen would at some point in their training be asked to compose speeches in others' voices, such as the characters in the epics or histories they were reading. Aphthonius's version of *the Progymnasmata* includes as an example "What Words Niobe Might Say When Her Children Lie Dead," an exercise in both speaking as a woman and expressing strong emotion (116). The rhetorical curriculum, of which exercises like the *prosopopoeia* were a part, was not designed to train poets or fiction writers. Hence the inclusion of this exercise shows how necessary an ability to "speak as others" was considered in rhetorical training.

DOUBLE VOICING AND HETEROGLOSSIA

So far, the scale of possibilities for incorporating other voices includes quoting directly, paraphrasing, and reporting the acts of the source. Considering only cases where the source's actual words survive, a spectrum of representations is possible: at one extreme is a hyperlink to the audio or video recording of another speaker, and at the other extreme, a snatch of language, even a single word, can be placed into a text without any indication that it comes from or could allude to another source. Attention to practices on the "deep embedding" end of this scale comes from a critic whose insights have been adopted by both literary and rhetorical scholars, Mikhail Bakhtin. Writing under his own name and under various pseudonyms in the Soviet Union from the 1930s through the 1960s, Bakhtin, like Burke, Austin, Weaver, and others in the mid-twentieth century, rediscovered the essential spoken or addressed nature of language. But Bakhtin's particular source of revelation was the language of capacious works of prose fiction, especially the novels of Tolstoy, Dostoevsky, and Dickens. In the broad social canvases of their novels, these artists portrayed the dialects and sociolects, the occupational and situational registers that together make up the language of a culture or an era. The mélange of these languages together turn such novels, according to Bakhtin, into "images" of a national language. "The novel as a whole is a phenomenon multiform in style and variform in speech and voice. In it the investigator is confronted with several heterogeneous stylistic unities, often located on different linguistic levels and subject to different stylistic controls" (1981, 261). Bakhtin pointed out that a novel also typically includes an explicit authorial voice and stylized versions of oral and written genres, as well as the stylistically individualized speech of the characters: "The novel can be defined as a diversity of social speech types (sometimes even diversity of languages) and a diversity of individual voices, artistically organized" (262). This mixture of authorial speech with the speech of narrators, of inserted genres, and of different characters produced altogether what Bahktin called *raznorechie*, translated **heteroglossia.** One finds it, for instance, in the following passage, quoted by Bakhtin, from Dickens's novel *Little Dorrit*.

> The conference was held at four or five o'clock in the afternoon, when all the region of Harley Street, Cavendish Square, was resonant of carriage-wheels and double-knocks. It had reached this point when Mr. Merdle came home *from his daily occupation of causing the British name to be more and more respected in all parts of the civilized globe capable of appreciation of [world-wide] commercial enterprise and gigantic combinations of skill and capital.* For, though nobody knew with the least precision what Mr. Merdle's business was, except that it was to coin money, these were the terms in which everybody defined it on all ceremonious occasions, and which it was the last new polite reading of the parable of the camel and the needle's eye to accept without inquiry. (quoted in 1981, 303; italics added in text)

In his commentary on this passage, Bakhtin points out that the italicized section is a "parodic stylization" of the kind of ceremonial speech one would hear in parliament or at a banquet; the syntax prepares for it and the commentary afterwards identifies it. An ideal reader of such a novel is aware of the many spoken and written genres being invoked (though oddly, Bahktin does not comment on the language of the New Testament echoed at the end of the passage).

Critics have widely adopted and adapted Bakhtin's notion of heteroglossia to other genres, pointing out that it is not only novels that feature such mixtures of styles. Popular journalistic genres (reviews, editorials, letters to the editor) are often heteroglossic hybrids. In the opening quotations from Tony Blair, the fourth excerpt continues, after a snatch of indirect speech (*Don't overact some say*), with an unmarked exchange between Blair and his critics (*Don't kill innocent people. We are not the ones who waged war on the innocent*) that requires readers to assign the consecutive locutions to different points of view.

Bakhtin's *heteroglossia* is in some ways another version of what linguists would call register mixing or the detecting of allusions (see above, pp. 86, 95). However, his insight goes a step further than awareness of mixed registers and their sources. Because he was working with the "artistic" genre of the novel, all the utterances contained within it are inevitably "spoken" by the authorial voice. Hence the language parodied above is spoken both by those who use such ceremonial language *and* by the author (or narrator), who, in an unmarked way, lapses into their language. Hence the text is *double-voiced*, or *dialogic*, and this practice of double voicing is called *dialogism*. Bakhtin's example from Dickens corresponds to the "floating" indirect speech described above,. But this notion of double voicing, of the word spoken simultaneously by two speakers, should really extend to quoted direct speech as well as to indirect speech and free indirect speech marked by register features. After all, a direct quotation is "spoken" by the person or text directly quoting it as well as by the original source. It is, as Bakhtin would say, another's voice "ventriloquized."

Bakhtin also went so far as to claim that heteroglossia and dialogism could be detected in a single word. "For any individual consciousness living in it, language is not an abstract system of normative forms but rather a concrete heteroglot conception of the world. All words have the 'taste' of a profession, a genre, a tendency, a party, a particular work, a particular person, a generation, an age group, the day and hour. Each word tastes of the context or contexts in which is has lived its socially charged life; all words and forms are populated by intentions" (1981, 293). Bakhtin is, of course, placing qualities in words that are really in the perceptions of language users. For those not aware of multiple genres and contexts, a particular word does not bear the accent of other speakers. But for those who are aware, any word, phrase, clause, or passage can richly recall other contexts, speakers, and uses and so impact the persuasion.

MULTIVOICING: THE BLOGGER'S SPECIALTY

Bakhtin's widely cited notion of "double voicing" is unnecessarily limited to two dimensions. There are cases of triple voicing and even further layers of embedding of text that is *spoken by as spoken by as spoken by*, and so on. Nor are the cases of this multiple embedding all that rare. For example, *Harper's Magazine* contains a section early in each issue offering excerpts from other publications. Such quoted passages may in turn contain a quoted passage. In the July 2005 issue, for example, the editors reprinted materials used by the pharmaceutical company Merck Inc. that contained advice to their sales representatives on how to conduct dinners to introduce doctors to the company's drugs. This advice contained imagined "scenarios" between physicians and drug reps:

Physician says: "What a nice restaurant! I hear that the food is wonderful."

Possible rep response: "You're right, it is. I'd only arrange the best for you. I'm sure you feel the same way about your patients. When you decide to prescribe an antihypertensive, what characteristics make one product stand out from another?"

("A Spoonful of Sugar" 2005, 16)

The acts of embedded voicing and address here might be depicted as follows.

At each level, rhetor, audience, and intended speech act change. The drug rep's goal was introducing a product into the conversation. The drug company's manual writers were offering advice to their personnel on sales strategies. The *Harper's* editors, however, were performing quite a different speech act for their readers; presumably their intention was to criticize or mock the drug company and thereby establish solidarity in certain attitudes with their readers.[8] The rhetorical exchange differs from level to level, and each higher level requires construal of the preceding ones.

Blogs perform such acts of multivoicing routinely. Simple blogs that only list links, like the Drudge Report, can be thought of as almost pure revoicing mechanisms. To click on a provocatively worded headline from the Drudge site takes the user to one of any number of other newspaper or news service websites, but the selected text is then read as not solely from that site but as heightened by access through the Drudge site, which has a reputation for discovering sensational breaking news. Similarly, the "Best of the Web" from a *Wall Street Journal* blog may, in the act of selecting a link, constitute a criticism of that link with the implicit added message, "Can you believe this?" Scholars may question whether the multivoicing of the bloggers is really all that unprecedented. The texts of early modern humanists, after all, routinely included passages "revoicing" classical sources, often taken from commonplace books of quoted passages rather than the originals. But the existence of mere lists of links in the case of some blogs does seem to have created unprecedented possibilities for multivoicing and complex rhetorical effects.

Summary

Without the benefit of punctuation, ancient grammarians and rhetoricians still distinguished between *oratio recta* (direct speech) and *oratio obliqua* (indirect speech). Though the words of others are critical sources of evidence, both forms of representation are fictions, since even direct quotation selects from its source and fails to convey the manner of the original's delivery, whether voice dynamics in the case of quoted speech or visual formatting in the case of quoted text. Critics have long noted that direct quotation and paraphrase can be mixed when the indirect quoter retains some of the wording of the original. But the consumer of indirect speech cannot make distinctions between faithfulness *de dicto*, to the wording, or *de re*, to the matter originally referred to: *The dietician says "Don't eat sulfur-containing vegetables"* can become *The dietician said to avoid sulfur-containing vegetables like cauliflower* (Coulmas 1986, 4). The representation of another's speech or thoughts or writing can wander even further when no vestige of the original wording remains but only the speech act intended or accomplished—promise, threat, etc.—is reported (Leech and Short 1981, 323–24). From direct quotation to indirect quotation to the report of a speech act, the chances for interpretive license to serve the rhetor's purposes increase. After all, whether a certain speech act is accomplished by a certain utterance can be a matter of considerable argument, as in the frequent debates over whether a politician's exact words constitute an insult, an apology, and so on.

Speaking in other voices provides prosodic variety in oral performance, and the rhetorical manuals recommend the practice of giving voice to the living, the dead, and even to the inanimate (lands, cities, etc.). So important was this skill that students following the rhetorical exercises of the *Progymnasmata* had to compose extended *prosopopoeia*, practicing their ability to speak as another person. Speechwriters routinely compose "as others," but there is a difference between ghostwriting and foregrounding the representation of another's words in quotation, since the purpose of the revoiced material changes when the audience is aware of its reuse. The possibilities of revoicing have expended dramatically on the internet and through social media, where others' words travel through layers of embedding so that what is "said" can change with each new context.

NOTES

1. Blair 2001.

2. In their original account, Leech and Short identified a scale that included Free Direct Speech (FDS) as a less mediated form of direct speech (DS). The overall scale ran as follows: NRSA [narrative reports of a speech act] – IS [indirect speech] – FIS [free indirect speech] – DS [direct speech] – FDS [free direct speech] (Leech and Short 1981, 324). In FDS, there are excerpts of speech offered without an assignment of speaker or a reporting clause, as in representations of the "voices" of multiple anonymous speakers in a crowd (322). However, in an article reporting on twenty-five years of continued work on speech and thought presentation, conducted in part by corpus analysis, Short reported that the data did not really sustain this category: "Our other main-category conclusion was that the traditional distinction between DS and FDS was not really a distinction between major categories, as had been generally assumed, but effectively a way of marking more minor variation within the (now larger) DS category" (Short 2007, 228). The closest analogue to the fictional and new journalism technique of FDS in functional genres is the *transcript,* which often uses the written conventions of drama, assigning text by naming the speaker before a snatch of speech is provided, usually without quotation marks. The transcript genre can be found in newspaper accounts of presidential news conferences or in magazine or journal interviews offered as verbatim records of the actual speech of the interviewer and inter-

viewee. The published transcript is usually reserved for exchanges with more important subjects, with the implication that the important person's words are less mediated, less controlled by the interviewer.

3. http://www.thecrimson.com/correctionsaspx.

4. http://www.cnn.com/ALLPOLITICS/stories/1999/03/09/president.2000/transcript.gore/.

5. Since Leech and Short's *Style in Fiction* concerned only tactics for dialogue in prose fiction, they did not consider how writing could be represented. However, they eventually included "Writing Presentation" in their model when they began to work with corpus data that included nonfiction genres (Short 2007, 227–28).

6. This older practice of citing the author and not the work, in place before the conventions for punctuating quotations were codified, is also the sign of a unified culture in which canonical texts and their authors are widely familiar.

7. Quintilian seems to be ruling out speech attributed to inanimate objects in this passage; such attributed speech would be covered under personification. The reference to giving speech to cities included in the passage quoted here would actually still involve "persons," since in antiquity cities were usually represented by minor deities, often female.

8. The excerpt from the Merck manual is preceded by the following text in the *Harper's* "voice": "From course materials used to train more than 3,000 sales representatives working for Merck & Co., Inc. between 1999 and 2004. The documents were among the 20,000 pages obtained from Merck by the House Committee on Government Reform for a May 5 hearing on the anti-inflammatory drug Vioxx. Vioxx was withdrawn from the market last September more than four years after a study by Merck first found that it increased the risk of heart attacks. At the time of Vioxx's withdrawal, more than 2 million patients worldwide were taking it" ("A Spoonful of Sugar" 2005, 16). The passage then quoted from the manual is evidently intended to stimulate outrage from readers who discover that a pharmaceutical company creates a sales campaign.

This false-color image from NASA's Mars Exploration Rover Opportunity panoramic camera shows a downward view from the rover as it sits at the edge of "Endurance" crater. The gradual, "blueberry"-strewn slope before the rover contains an exposed dark layer of rock that wraps around the upper section of the crater. Scientists suspect that this rock layer will provide clues about Mars' distant past. This mosaic image comprises images taken from 10 rover positions using 750, 530 and 430 nanometer filters, acquired on sol 131 (June 6, 2004).

NASA, "Mars Rover 'Opportunity' Images"[1]

15

SITUATION AND OCCASION

UNDER THE NOTION of *deixis* (from the Greek word for *pointing*) linguists include those features of language tied to the *context of utterance*, the immediate situation in which a verbal exchange occurs. *Deictic* features bring the participants, the setting, and the time into the actual wording. The epigraph quoted above, a caption to a photo of the Martian surface from a NASA website, performs all these functions and offers a provocative gloss on the discussion of deixis that follows. It contains deictic terms orienting the audience both to the image before their eyes [*this mosaic image*] as well as to details within the image through language that transforms readers into virtual viewers standing on the edge of the crater with the Rover. The caption also locates the scene and the viewer in time, both in Martian (sol 131) and in earth-based (June 6, 2004) terms. It combines those forms of interactive language that orient the listener or reader to a place and time that can be anywhere on a scale from the physically immediate to the imaginary.

Immediate Deixis

In everyday speech, *deictic elements* include all those referring words that identify the people and relevant objects immediately present to the speaker and hearer. Pronouns do the heavy lifting of such "nonce" referring. In a real situation, with people and things physically present, a sentence like *I* am going to give *you this,* with its three pronouns, would be perfectly clear. Expressions referring to time can also be elements of deixis: *Now what's happening? The milk was delivered this morning.* The phrases *now* and *this morning* gain their meaning in relation to the moment of utterance. Similarly, adverbials of place reference the speaker's or addressee's location for clarification: *Put it there. The police are here. The dog is behind you. Look out below.*

Orators have always used deixis in this simple sense to refer to their immediate physical surroundings and to the time of their speaking. But the variety of ways in which place and time can be referenced show the rhetorical dimensions of this category. Lincoln, for example, specified the physical setting and the moment at the dedication ceremony for a cemetery near the town of Gettysburg, Pennsylvania. After opening with a reference to the nation's founding "Four score and seven years ago," a measure of duration only true in 1863, he labels the moment for himself and his audience, "*Now* we are engaged in a great civil war," and he defines their physical place, "We are met *on a great battlefield* of that war" (Reid 1988, 463; italics added). The "portion" that they are dedicating is "this ground." The word "here" is then made salient, as many commentators have pointed out, through its repetition six times in the next three sentences, including the strategic repetition (*epistrophe*) in the endings of consecutive clauses, "The world will little note, nor long remember, what we say *here*, but it can never forget what they did *here*" (463), and with its final use, Lincoln puts the audience in the same place: "that we *here* highly resolve that these dead shall not have died in vain—that this nation, under God, shall have a new birth of freedom—and that government of the people, by the people, for the people shall not perish from the earth" (463). In the final three words, Lincoln changes the scene dramatically. One can only imagine the force of Lincoln's deictic references for his immediately present listeners. To read his speech now is to have the moment and place recreated.

Examples of speakers using their physical setting through deictic references abound, but two worth remembering illustrate the importance of the rhetor's selection of a location for a speech, when selection is possible. Both Kennedy in 1963 and Reagan in 1987 delivered speeches to citizens in a West Berlin divided by a wall from East Berlin. For Kennedy the physical setting was Rudolph-Wilde-Platz, at that time the city hall square, synecdoche for the city itself, which becomes an argument against communism in his speech and a visible symbol of freedom: "I am proud to come to this city," he says to the thousands of Germans massing in the square before him. Kennedy answers those who do not understand the conflict with communism by repeating four times "Let them come to Berlin," the final time in German (Windt 1983, 50).

In 1987 in Berlin, Ronald Reagan faced a welcoming crowd as well as a considerable number of protestors. Reagan delivered his speech on the West Berlin side of the Brandenburg Gate, the main portal through the wall. The setting for his speech was planned so that the televised image of the speaking president could include the wall and this famous feature: "Behind me stands a wall that encircles the free sectors of this city, part of a vast system of barriers that divides the entire continent of Europe." The visible wall becomes a synecdoche, a representation of imposed divisions. It is also the referent for the most memorable line in the speech, a line that apparently was taken out of drafts by his advisors but restored by

Reagan himself. Notably, at this point Reagan also uses an abrupt change of addressee, calling upon the absent leader of the Soviet Union (see above on *apostrophe*, p. 291):

> General Secretary Gorbachev, if you seek peace, if you seek prosperity for the Soviet Union and Eastern Europe, if you seek liberalization: Come here to this gate! Mr. Gorbachev, open this gate! Mr. Gorbachev, tear down this wall! (Reagan 1989, 352)

References to place like Reagan's clearly have persuasive importance, since speakers often go to great lengths to be in a particular setting just to have the opportunity to use physical deixis. Television reporters who cover the president, for example, are often presented standing physically in front of the White House, as though news were shouted from its windows. Clearly there is a presumption that physical immediacy, being on the spot, confers credibility.

Political speakers in a mass media age must also pay special attention to the time frame of their remarks, using careful deictic markers. Here is how President Clinton did so in a televised speech justifying a further deployment of troops to Somalia in 1993:

> <u>Today</u> I want to talk with you about our nation's military involvement in Somalia. <u>A year ago</u>, we all watched with horror as Somali children and their families lay dying by the tens of thousands—dying the slow, agonizing death of starvation, of starvation brought on not only by drought, but also by the anarchy that then prevailed in that country.
>
> <u>This past weekend</u> we all reacted with anger and horror as an armed Somali gang desecrated the bodies of our American soldiers and displayed a captured American pilot—all of them soldiers who were taking part in an international effort to end the starvation of the Somali people themselves. (Clinton 1993)

THEMATIZING DEIXIS

The relatively straightforward deictic references to an immediate physical and temporal situation, on display in the examples offered above, have recently been transformed by discourse analysts into a higher-order principle of the speaker's *deictic center*, credited to Jan Verscheuren (1999) but elaborated by Paul Chilton (2005) and others: "in processing any discourse people 'position' other entities in their 'world' by 'positioning' these entities in relation to themselves along (at least) three axes, space, time and modality. The deictic centre (the Self, that is, *I* or *we*) is the 'origin' of the three dimensions" (Chilton 2005, 58). Social distance (modality), and by extension moral or deontic value, are similarly scaled as near or remote from *I* or *we* (inclusive), *here* and *now*. Deictic terms, then, sometimes metaphoric, reveal the speaker's attitudes to events and to others, invoking schemas of "center/periphery" in hearers' or readers' minds. Thematically interpreted, deictic language choices are understood here as a *sign* of the source's beliefs rather than as an *instrument* put to use.[2]

This mapping of modal or moral judgments onto concepts or images of proximity has a precursor in rhetorical theory. George Campbell based *The Philosophy of Rhetoric* (1776) on late-eighteenth-century theories of the mind, producing, in effect, a "cognitive" rhetoric. Campbell identified seven "circumstances" that can operate on the "passions," that can, in other words, stimulate an audience's receptiveness toward an issue: "probability, plausibility, importance, proximity of time, connexion of place, relation of the actors or sufferers to the hearers or speaker, interest of the hearers or speaker in the consequences" (1963, 81). The first two correspond to Chilton's scale of modality, or the believability of a claim; the last two refer to social dimensions of identification and direct consequences. In between are precisely the same notions of nearness in time and space. Campbell combined the last four (time, space, relationship, and interest) into a single notion of proximity, and he did so using the same terms adopted by contemporary discourse analysts (though with conventional rather than Cartesian imagery): "*Self* is the centre here, which hath a similar power in the ideal world to that of the sun in the material world, in communicating both light and heat to whatever is within the sphere of its activity, and in a greater or less degree according to the nearness or remoteness" (1963, 86). Campbell emphasized immediate physical deixis as a principle:

> With how much indifference, at least with how slight and transient emotion, do we read in newspapers the accounts of the most deplorable accidents in countries distant and unknown! How much, on the contrary, are we alarmed and agitated on being informed that any such accident hath happened in our neighbourhood, and that even though we be totally unacquainted with the persons concerned! (1963 88)

Campbell's account of the proximity functions that engage human interest is meant not merely as description but also as advice for the rhetor who selects from these seven elements to construct or heighten interest in the audience. But the underlying concept is the same in both rhetorical theory and discourse analysis: deixis can aid the construction of persuasive affinities.

IMMEDIATE DEIXIS IN WRITTEN TEXTS

The examples of immediate deixis offered above come from informal or formal speech. What happens to space and time references in written texts, where the actual circumstances of reading are unpredictable? Writing, after all, seems to conquer space and time and to make a message available anywhere a text is read, problematizing any references in the text to specific places and moments. Of course in some instances, a physical and temporal setting can affect how a text is read (e.g., a posted placard), but texts can survive into unprecedented settings. Writers cannot write in idioms of the future, and they usually cannot count on the time frame or physical constants in the reader's setting.

Writers typically solve the problems of immediate deixis with "as if" deixis, another element of the constructed interactive dimension of texts. They can put situations of reading or the enactment of content into their texts. Just as pronouns can invoke factual or fictionalized speakers and addressees, so can deictic references to place and time recreate, or fabricate entirely, physically and temporally defined situations. When these reconstructions work, they work *as if* readers and writer, as hearer and speaker, were standing in the same place at the same time. Many nonfiction genres, such as nature, travel, or feature writing, have as their primary purpose such conjuring of places and moments into existence, usually through the surrogate deixis of detailed descriptions. Examples abound in American nature writing, and samples from that tradition illustrate the options. In some sections of *Walden*, for example, Henry David Thoreau renders the place for readers, though not any particular moment or distinct encounter:

> The scenery of Walden is on a humble scale…It is a clear and deep green well, half a mile long and a mile and three quarters in circumference, and contains about sixty-one and a half acres…The surrounding hills rise abruptly from the water to the height of forty or eighty feet, though on the southeast and the east they attain to about one hundred and one hundred and fifty feet respectively, within a quarter and a third of a mile (1991, 143).

Thoreau the surveyor comes through in this selection of details, and the overall deictic effect is weak without a viewing position specified. Another descriptive alternative realizes a place at a particular moment through the eyes of a writer as a physically present witness who verbally brings the reader into the scene. Edward Abbey vividly recreates time and place as he saw it in *Desert Solitaire,* where such scenes ultimately serve his arguments for wilderness preservation. Abbey narrates his first day as a seasonal ranger in Utah in 1958: "The choice [of the most beautiful place on earth] became apparent to me this morning when I stepped out of a Park Service housetrailer—my caravan—to watch for the first time in my life the sun come up over the hoodoo stone of Arches National Monument" (1971, 2). "The view is open and perfect in all directions except to the west where the ground rises and the skyline is only a few hundred yards away. Looking toward the mountains I can see the dark gorge of the Colorado River five or six miles away" (4). Little, save the *possibility* of verification, separates Abbey's first person descriptions of a real place from fictional scene setting, but that possibility gives the description evidentiary value.

Occasion

Rhetorical theory also gives a meaning to time not quite covered by the linguists' notion of deixis. The key concepts here are *kairos* (Greek) and *occasio* (Latin). *Kairos* is one of two Greek words for time. The other, *khronos*, stands for time in its linear and measured sense of hours, days, months, years; this meaning of time is constructed in Lincoln's use of *now* in relation to *four score and seven years ago* in the Gettysburg Address. Rhetors certainly have choices when it comes to how they will reference linear time—in terms of dates, years, or eras. *Kairos*, on the other hand, refers to time conceived of as a moment, an event; this conception of time is created by Lincoln's reference to the occasion that brought speaker and audience together, the ceremony of dedicating a cemetery. As a concept, *kairos* covers both marking appropriate times and intervening at optimal moments. The closest Latin term for *kairos*, *occasio*, captures this idea and passes it on to its English descendant *occasion*. Occasion is a variable somewhat independent from place and time. The sociolinguist's notion of *situation* comes closest. But an occasion is more formal and is determined by a society in an explicit and self-conscious way. Recurring occasions bring genres into being: the funeral eulogy, the Fourth of July speech, the conference keynote, the French prime minister's New Year's Day address.

The recurring occasion of inaugurating a president of the United States has brought into existence the inaugural address. Yet instances of this genre differ greatly in whether and how the speaker references and hence constructs the particular qualities of the occasion. And, since drawing attention to the occasion is an option, a speaker can simply let it be understood. Here is how Lincoln references the occasion in the opening of his Second Inaugural:

Fellow Countrymen:
At this second appearing to take the oath of the presidential office there is less occasion for an extended address than there was at the first. Then a statement, somewhat in detail, of a course to be pursued seemed fitting and proper. Now, at the expiration of four years...little that is new could be presented. (Reid 1988, 465)

President Clinton constructed the occasion of his second inauguration somewhat differently in his opening words, "At this last presidential inauguration of the 20th century," using linear time as the marker of an era, though he also, like Lincoln, refers to his first inaugural later in the speech with the transitional phrase, "When last we gathered" (Clinton 1997).

A presidential inaugural is part deliberative, setting broad policy goals, and part epideictic, celebrating the inception of a new term. Virtually all epideictic speakers must explicitly refer to the occasion, whether celebratory or sorrowful, that brings about their speeches. Here are Sandra Day O'Connor's opening remarks at the dedication of the National Constitution Center in Philadelphia, on July 4, 2003. "This is an absolutely wonderful occasion. Today we celebrate both our nation's birthday, and also the opening of the National Constitution Center in the great city of Philadelphia" (O'Connor 2003). What Justice O'Connor modestly did not mention was that she was also receiving the Liberty Medal, another element of the occasion.

Occasions are not always recurring or ritually determined. They can also be sui generis, or rather they can be made that way when rhetors highlight this potential element. Here is how Prime Minister Tony Blair draws attention to the uniqueness of an occasion:

> Members of the Dail and Seanad, after all the long and torn history of our two peoples, standing here as the first British prime minister ever to address the joint Houses of the Oireachtes, I feel profoundly both the history in this event, and I feel profoundly the enormity of the honour that you are bestowing upon me. From the bottom of my heart, go raibh mile maith agaibh. (Blair 1998)

No British prime minister could technically have spoken to this Irish parliament before the 1920s, when it came into existence, but Blair creates a much longer perspective of "shared history" and "shared pain" as a setting for the occasion of his appearance. The background for the invitation to Blair was an IRA bombing in Omagh, Northern Ireland, which the government of the Irish Republic strongly condemned, creating a unifying moment for the two governments and new initiatives on the status of Northern Ireland.

Virtually any speech in the canon of oratory studied by communication scholars is a speech in a particular place and moment, to a particular audience, and finally *for a particular occasion*. Justice cannot be done to these texts in interpretation unless all these dimensions are fully explained. Indeed, so important are these factors, they must be plausibly reconstructed *from* language elements when the full "context of utterance" has been lost, as is often the case with texts surviving from antiquity.

CONSTRUCTING SITUATIONS AND OCCASIONS

Using different terms, rhetoricians, linguists, and sociologists have constructed theories about the contextual constraints of time, place, and occasion discussed so far. Most theorizing from linguists treats the occasion or situation as given and considers how language reveals the participants' adjustment to those givens (e.g., casual greetings in chance encounters versus routine verbal exchanges in stores). In rhetorical theory, perhaps the most thorough discussion of contextual givens comes from Lloyd Bitzer, who in two articles, "The Rhetorical Situation" (1968) and "Functional Communication: A Situational Perspective" (1980), laid out the elements of situation, audience, and external constraints to which, in his view, specifically *rhetorical* discourse must respond.[3] As a prototypical example of how such discourse is called forth by situations, Bitzer cited the assassination of John F. Kennedy, which, in his view, virtually demanded responses in news reports, eulogies, and reassurances of government stability from the appropriate sources. A key element for Bitzer in a rhetorical situation is the *exigence*, the compelling external event or circumstance that demands an answer or creates the occasion for a response.

But once again the tactics that are seen as reactive can be turned into proactive choices on the part of rhetors who use language not to respond to occasions and situations but to construct them. Bitzer was answered by Richard Vatz taking the inverted view in "The Myth of the Rhetorical Situation" (1973) that it is rhetoric that creates situations or occasions and not the reverse. Vatz used as his prototypical example the Gulf of Tonkin crisis. This naval encounter could have been downplayed or even ignored, in his view, but the Johnson administration chose, by its subsequent statements and behavior, to create a crisis and hence a rationale for military escalation in Vietnam.

It is easy to split the difference between Bitzer and Vatz. An event like 9/11 hardly seems to be a rhetorical construction, but various political "scandals" can seem like the products of deliberate attention. Many subsequent theorists, including Scott Consigny (1974) and Keith Grant-Davie (1997), have pursued a combined view of the externally determined and at the same time creatively constructed rhetorical situation. Rhetorical art selects from Bitzerian givens with Vatzian art. Or rather, it is often the rhetor's goal to make a case seem Bitzerian, driven by pressing, external circumstances and not by discretionary heightening.

EXIGENCE IN WRITTEN TEXTS

Written texts face a special problem when it comes to their rhetorical situation. Though most print and web-based texts are written for immediate consumption, they can survive their moment and be disseminated in contexts removed from the concerns the writer was responding to. Furthermore, some written genres, notably scholarly articles or scientific reports, do not address narrow, temporary issues, and still other genres in philosophy or religion attempt to address "timeless" ones. So, unlike passing conversations, convened meetings, and politicians' stump speeches, which clearly respond to immediate, external situations, written texts often have to carry their own exigence with them, like a turtle carrying its shell.

As a result, the notion of *exigence*, the term Bitzer introduced for the pressing external occasion that requires a response, has become a term for the rhetor's construction of the occasion, issue, or problem a text will address. When the exigence for communication is not salient in the setting, the rhetor must invoke it in a textual bid, usually in the opening, a bid that answers the audience's unspoken question, "Why are you telling me this?" To use examples from disciplinary discourse, an article in a medical journal on a new type of back surgery begins with the following sentences: "Lumbar disc herniation remains a major national health problem. It has been estimated that up to 80% of the population experiences low-back pain at some time during their lives" (Kambin and Schaffer 1989, 24). These details are selected to give a reason, a niche, for a new ameliorative procedure addressing a persistent health problem; the time is continuing (*remains*) and the place is the United States (*national*). Scholarly articles in many disciplines often have elaborate introductory sections, including a literature review, constructing an exigence worth addressing, and these typically select from a generic set of moves (Swales 1990, 137–43). Once constructed or invoked, exigence establishes a disciplinary occasion that the scholarly argument can then address.[4]

THE BURKEAN SCENE

Another perspective on time, place and occasion as rhetorical constructions comes from the theorizing of Kenneth Burke. In *A Grammar of Motives* (1945), Burke introduced the notion of the pentad, the series of questions that people seek to answer when they try to construct a complete account of an event: *act, scene, agent, agency,* and *purpose* (xv–xx). These terms, which Burke derived from drama, are all featured in traditional rhetorical accounts of forensic invention such as that in Cicero's *De Inventione* (1976, 179–207), and they are of course immediately familiar as a version of the journalist's standard questions answered in the opening of a news story: *who, what, when, where, why,* and *how.* But Burke added several observations on how these terms are used in argumentation. First, in full explanations, audiences expect all the terms filled, all the questions answered. Second, people often select one of the terms as the source or explanatory principle of another, and he called this pairing a *ratio* (1969, 3–9). Finally, audiences also expect a certain "consistency" among the terms, though they are rarely aware of this expectation. So for example, in the *scene-act* ratio, the time and setting (when and where) should "explain" or correspond to the act. Crimes "should" occur in dark and disreputable places, and when they do not, that difference in setting can strike people as significant or paradoxical. Furthermore, Burke observed that different philosophies or regimes of explanation favor different key terms from the pentad. So, for example, explanations of skyrocketing murder rates in U.S. cities have been variously attributed to a class of amoral superpredators (*agent*), to the decayed and collapsed infrastructure of inner cities (*scene*), to the availability of guns (*agency*), to the turf wars of drug gangs (*purpose*), and to the very prevalence of the violence itself as an incentive (*act*).

Burke's *scene* corresponds most closely to the deictic *where* and *when* of situations and occasions. The interactive dimension here concerns how rhetors encourage the audience to locate or place entities and actions. Burke in fact gave *scenic* accounts most of his attention, and he was also well aware of the malleability of scenic explanations in the rhetor's art. He spoke of changing the scene in an explanation as changing the *circumference*: "…one has *a great variety of circumferences* to select as characterizations of a given agent's scene" (1969, 84) The metaphor of *circumference* is an apt one, since it conveys the notion of widening or narrowing the presumed "surroundings" or settings of persons and events. Scene includes time, and Burke observed that a person could be presented (as in an argument of praise) in the context of an era or of centuries, or even from some universal perspective (84). Thus changing the scene, the where and when in which something is placed, can change its characterization and value.

Not surprisingly, other theorists have offered similar notions of rhetorically altering the situation as a way to argue for a certain explanation or evaluation. In *The New Rhetoric,*

Perelman and Olbrechts-Tyteca observe that interpretations vary depending on what they call the "level" on which the interpretation is conducted: "the same process can indeed be described as the action of tightening a bolt, assembling a vehicle, earning a living, or helping the export drive" (1969, 121). Their example dramatically illustrates the concept of changing the circumference and hence the audience's interpretive view of an act. Again, the same basic concept has been described by Norman Fairclough, a discourse analyst, whose focus is on the linguistic means of constructing what he calls "space-times" in texts (2003, 151). He identifies a *local* versus a *global* space-time attributed, in his case study, to different social agents in management textbooks and policy documents (152–54).

Changing the deictic parameters, the scene or setting in which the audience views an event, and therefore the way they evaluate it, is common in persuasive discourse. As noted above, Lincoln begins the Gettysburg Address dedicating "a corner of a battlefield" but ends by dedicating himself and his audience to preserving government of, by, and for the people on the entire earth. The environmental movement, with its *Act locally, think globally* campaign, aims to move people to reconceptualize, change the circumference or level, of trivial, individual acts as consequential for the fate of the planet.

Imaginary Deixis

The linguists' notion of deixis highlights verbal cues to an actual physical and temporal setting. But in rhetorical discourse, the actual setting can be less important than a scene recreated for persuasive purposes. Thus, the forensic speaker reenacts the crime for the jury, or the deliberative orator sketches a vision of an improved city. For these and other persuasive purposes, the verbal construction of real or imaginary places and times was a celebrated stylistic skill exercised in rhetorical training.

The importance of such reconstructions appears in the third book of the *Rhetoric* when Aristotle specifies three features of style that he believes are especially compelling. The first two, antithesis and metaphor, come from the categories of tropes and schemes discussed elsewhere. The third is introduced under two terms in Chapter 10 of Book III. Words, Aristotle explains, are effective "if they set things 'before the eyes' [*pro ommaton poiein*]; for we ought to see what is being done rather than what is going to be done. We ought therefore [summing up the whole discussion in this chapter] to aim at three things—metaphor, antithesis, actuality [*energeia*]" (Freese 1991, 399).

Aristotle's suggestive discussion can be untangled into three strands in the figural tradition. The strand *energeia*, the Greek term, corresponds to language that conveys motion and activity.[5] A second strand involves personification, animating objects so that they move and act. The third strand, the one most pertinent for deixis, comes from concentrating solely on "bringing before the eyes," of visualizing, rendering in words what someone has seen or might see. This last stylistic goal or effect has a long life in the figural tradition under several names: *demonstratio* and *descriptio* in the *Rhetorica ad Herennium*

([Cicero] 1981, 404–5), *enargeia* in Quintilian (1921, II 85; III 245), and the equivalent *hypotyposis* or *evidentia* in later manuals (e.g., Susenbrotus 1953, 83). These various figures all recommend the use of vivid, concrete descriptive language to construct a place, time, and event for the audience.

DEMONSTRATIO AND DESCRIPTIO

The very last stylistic device explained in Book IV of the *Rhetorica ad Herennium* belongs in the family of devices for "bringing before the eyes." Its name in the Latin text is *demonstratio*, and the words defining it recall Aristotle's discussion and were repeated in other manuals for centuries: "It is Ocular Demonstration [Caplan's translation of *demonstratio*] when an event is so described in words that the business seems to be enacted and the subject to pass vividly before our eyes" ([Cicero] 1981, 404–5). The example following this definition is a lurid account of the murder of Gracchus as a prosecutor would deliver it. This kind of visualized narrative was offered in a forensic setting where the defense could refute it by *another* visualization of the same event. Hence, such intensely realized scenes were arguments.

Unlike the advice for other figures, however, the text only sets out a goal—making an event pass vividly before the eyes—but it does not prescribe the linguistic means for achieving such a goal. Effects at the level of "bringing before the eyes" could require a combination of smaller devices such as the use of present tense, of words chosen for their connotative force, and of concise statement to the point of *brachylogia* (brief phrasing) to construct appropriate prosodic effects supporting the iconic representation of actions happening quickly.

Under another label the *Rhetorica ad Herennium* recommends *descriptio*, translated by Caplan as "Vivid Description." It is "the name for the figure which contains a clear, lucid, and impressive exposition of the consequences of an act" ([Cicero] 1981, 356–57). The examples offered contrast such descriptions from opposing sides in a forensic case: one comes from a prosecutor forecasting the dangerous consequences of letting a criminal go, and the other comes from the defense imaging the tragic consequences to the parents and children if a defendant is convicted.

Why was a distinction made between *demonstratio* and *descriptio*? *Descriptio* is defined as visualizing consequences that have yet to occur and may not occur. *Demonstratio* applies to retelling an event that supposedly has occurred. It would have its place in the *narratio* of a courtroom speech but could also be used in an epideictic speech recreating a heroic deed to be praised. The *descriptio* would belong in the peroration, the closing section concentrating appeals to pathos. This distinction between the real and hypothetical scene is maintained in the tradition, though for the consumer of descriptive deictic language, there may be little difference.

In Quintilian "bringing before the eyes" becomes *enargeia*, a quality of language that goes beyond the requirements of clarity and appropriateness and hence is a matter of forcefulness, the fourth quality of a good style.

We must thus count as Ornament the quality of *enargeia*, which I mentioned in giving instructions for Narrative, because vividness [*evidentia*], or, as some say, "representation [*repraesentatio*]," is more than mere perspicuity, since instead of being merely transparent it somehow shows itself off. It is a great virtue to express our subject clearly and in such a way that it seems to be actually seen. A speech does not adequately fulfill its purpose or attain the total domination it should have it if goes no further than the ears, and the judge feels that he is merely being told the story of matters he has to decide, without their being brought and displayed to his mind's eye [*oculis mentis*]. (2001, III 245–47)

Quintilian notes that in his day this quality of *enargeia* had been subdivided into minute varieties; he ignored these to focus on the essential: painting a whole scene in words [*verbis depingitur*], "so vividly that it could not have been any clearer to the spectators" (246), that is to the people physically present. Quintilian selects a passage from Cicero as exemplifying this total experience: "Is there anybody so incapable of forming a mental picture of a scene that, when he reads the following passage from the Verrines, he does not seem not merely to see the actors in the scene, the place itself and their very dress, but even to imagine to himself other details that the orator does not describe?" (247).

DESCRIPTION AND EMOTION

The intense realization of an actual or hypothetical event, as though occurring before the eyes, had a further crucial purpose: rhetoricians believed that such mental images could induce an emotional state in the audience. Aristotle even defined certain emotions by the presence of such visualizations. "Fear may be defined as a pain or disturbance due to a mental picture of some destructive or painful evil in the future" (Roberts 1984, 103). The Greek word for this mental image is *phantasia*.[6] Aristotle further stipulates that fear stems from imaging things plausible and imminent, not a long way off, the notion picked up centuries later by Campbell and Chilton. The opposite of fear, namely confidence, is to Aristotle "the expectation associated with the mental picture [again *phantasia*] of the nearness of what keeps us safe and the absence or remoteness of what is terrible" (106). Shame too is a "mental picture [*phantasia*] of disgrace," of sensing that "eyes are upon us" (108–9). Pity is a bit different. It is "a feeling of pain caused by the sight [*phainomena*] of some evil, destructive or painful, which befalls one who does not deserve it" (113). Here the emphasis is on visualizing what has already happened and hence on *demonstratio* over *descriptio*. Aristotle also recommended the principle of propinquity for rhetors instilling pity in an audience: "Further, since it is when the sufferings of others are close to us that they excite our pity (we cannot remember what disasters happened a hundred centuries ago, nor look forward to what will happen a hundred centuries hereafter, and therefore feel little pity, if any, for such things): it follows that those who heighten the effect of their words with suitable gestures, tones, dress, and dramatic action generally, are especially successful in exciting pity: they thus put the disasters before our eyes [*pro ommaton poiountes*], and make them seem close to us, just coming or just past" (114–15). The unexpressed psychological assumption here, still in force, is that the emotions are reached through the senses, so the best way to create an emotion is to recreate the situation with a deictic immediacy stimulating the senses that would then evoke the emotion.

Visualization as a persuasive tool has one more important place in classical theory: it is one of the sources of the effect that comes to be labeled the *sublime*, defined by the Hellenistic rhetorician Longinus as a power beyond persuasion, an overcoming that sweeps the audience into irresistible agreement (1965, 100). Of the five verbal sources of this power, one is *phantasia*, produced when the rhetor is "carried away by your feelings, you imagine you are actually seeing the subject of your description, and you enable your audience as well to see it" (121).[7] What Longinus recommends here is *phantasia* to the point of hallucination; Milton, for example, uses this device in the *Areopagitica* with "Methinks I see in my mind a noble and puissant nation" in the form of an eagle caring for its young. This conjuring effect is actually routine and somewhat domesticated in written texts, which, having no real space of their own, easily put the author and reader in an "as if" space where they can mutually contemplate a vision. But speakers and their listeners, in a "here and now" physical space, have a more difficult time invoking imaginary sights through *phantasia*, and few orators since the nineteenth century have been bold enough to try this strategy.

EKPHRASIS: THE STAND-ALONE DESCRIPTION

Classical treatments of description highlight its persuasive importance, so, not surprisingly, the verbal construction of real or imaginary places and times was a skill deliberately exercised in rhetorical training. Thus the compositional exercises of the *Progymnasmata* include precisely the kind of practice that would enhance the rhetor's ability to bring objects and scenes "before the eyes" in language. In these exercises, descriptive skills were partitioned according to what was being described, and these separate subjects for description eventually became genres in their own right.

George Kennedy's collection of progymnasmatic textbooks (2003) includes translations of Greek works from the first through the fifth centuries CE, and each includes a separate exercise in description known as an *ekphrasis*. Theon's first-century text sets the parameters of this exercise: "Ecphrasis (*ekphrasis*) is descriptive language, bringing what is portrayed clearly before the sight. There is ecphrasis of persons and events and places and periods of time" (Kennedy 2003, 45). He also offers the following advice on the need for a style compatible with the subject described.

The virtues of the ecphrasis are as follows: most of all, clarity and a vivid impression of all-but-seeing what is described; next, one should not recollect all useless details and should make sure the style reflect[s] the subject, so that if what it described is colorful, the word choice should be colorful, but if it is rough or frightening or something like that, features of the style should not strike a discordant note with the nature of the subject. (Kennedy 2003, 47)

By far the most influential of the progymnasmatic manuals was Apththonius's, which was translated into Latin in the sixteenth century and, as Manfred Kraus has shown, went through an extraordinary number of editions (2008). After the obligatory definition of *ekphrasis* in this manual and a list of subjects for description (which he extends from persons, things, occasions, and places to dumb animals and growing things [Kennedy 2003, 117]), Aphthonius has less to say than Theon on the stylistic features of a good description. But he does do something invaluable in a teaching context. He provides a model for imitation, an extended account of the Shrine of Alexandria (the Serapeum), a structure he may never have seen. Students analyzing this sample description would learn the technique of organizing details by following the course of someone walking through an architectural space. Guided by deictic phrases, the viewer approaches the hill of the shrine, climbs its steps, passes through gates and antechambers and then enters the acropolis. The description of the interior is constructed from the imagined viewpoint of the visitor who looks around from a stationary point in the main courtyard (Kennedy 2003, 118–20; see also Carruthers 1998, 130ff).

Erasmus' early-sixteenth-century teaching manual, *De Copia,* continues to emphasize descriptive skills in a way that is still faithful to Aristotle's original standard of "bringing before the eyes."

The Fifth method of amplification concerns ἐνέργεια [*energeia*] which is translated *Evidentia.* We use this whenever, for the sake of amplifying, adorning, or pleasing, we do not state a thing simply, but set it forth to be viewed as though portrayed in color on a tablet, so that it may seem that we have painted, not narrated, and that the reader has seen, not read. We will be able to do this well if we first conceive a mental picture of the subject with all its attendant circumstances. Then we should so portray it in words and fitting figures that it is as clear and graphic as possible to the reader. (Erasmus 1963, 47)

Erasmus recommended that a place be portrayed "just as if it were in sight, as for example, the appearance of a city, a mountain, a region, a river, a port, a villa, gardens, an amphitheatre, a fountain, a cavern, a temple, a grove" (54). But these descriptions could be of actual places (*topographia*) or fictional ones (*toposthesia* [54]), a distinction impossible to tell from the language alone. Erasmus also recommended descriptions of times (*chronographia*), such as night, dawn, dusk, and of seasons or holidays (spring, harvest, winter).[8] Most important for a specifically rhetorical stylistics, he credits such descriptions with persuasive potential, advising that they be "used in combination whenever we discuss the state of the times, for example, of peace, of war, of sedition, of faction, of monarchy, of democracy, when we show what virtues or vices especially would flourish then" (55). Once isolated from such persuasive contexts, descriptions of places and times became literary genres in their own right. It is not farfetched to understand sixteenth-century works like Campanella's *City of the Sun* or More's *Utopia* as instances of *topothesia*.

First published in 1512, Erasmus's *De Copia*, with its advice that writers describe as though they were "portraying on a tablet," came just at the time when actual portrayals in the form of reliably reproduced, as opposed to one-off, printed woodcuts (and eventually engravings) were becoming more common. From incunabula like the *Peregrinatio in Terram Sanctam* of 1486 featuring a five-foot-long foldout view of Venice or the *Nuremburg Chronicle* of 1493 with its striking mix of text and illustration, verbal descriptions could now be enhanced or even replaced by visual depictions of real or fictitious places or entities. Such visuals offer possibilities for new forms of deixis as viewers orient themselves, with verbal guidance, both to the image before them and to what the image contains. In the words of the epigraph to this chapter, the photo taken by the Mars Rover, "*This* false color image," is in the viewers' immediate physical presence (actually on the computer screen in front of them), while other language choices in the descriptive caption—*downward, before,* and *around the upper section of the crater*—orient viewers imaginatively to a panoramic (360°) view, as though they were standing in the landscape depicted in the image. The cooperative adjustment of verbal style to these new situations and occasions of visualization continues today.

Summary

When disasters occur in the United States—Hurricane Katrina in 2005 or the Gulf oil spill in 2010—presidents are expected to travel to the site and make comments for the press. These visits create opportunities for using *deictic* elements, words that refer to the speaker's immediate physical surroundings, to the people present, and to the moment. Such opportunities for what this chapter calls *immediate deixis*, references to the immediate context, have always been important in rhetorical history as speakers interact with their audience and setting.

Rhetorical theory expands the meaning of physical and temporal situation with the notion of *kairos* or occasion. An occasion is a special circumstance inviting interaction, whether it is a fixed date on the calendar, like the Fourth of July, or a contrived event, like a presidential visit to a widget factory. Occasion, token of the need for communicative relevance, has an analogue in the notion of *exigence*, the immediate problem that rhetorical discourse must address. Exigence may be an external imposition as when political speakers have to respond to high-profile news. But it is often a construction on the part of an arguer who first convinces his audience that a situation is "immediate" and requires the solution of the ensuing argument.

The foil to immediate deixis is *imaginary deixis,* language elements conjuring up an external setting, moment, and participants in an ambient "as if" situation. Imaginary deixis can vary from the static description to the virtual reenactment placing the audience in a space built of words and unrolling a hypothetical scene before their eyes. But speakers and writers need the persuasive skill of transporting their audiences to both real and hypothetical places and times, often to stimulate their emotions at the spectacle. The ability to describe has always been recommended in rhetorical manuals, from Aristotle's promotion of "bringing before the eyes" to figures of speech like *demonstratio* to extended exercises in painting with words. Every description of a person, object, or act in a text, and every reference to an accompanying visual, can be thought of as the creation of an interactive encounter signaled with deictic elements.

NOTES

1. http://nssdc.gsfc.nasa.gov/planetary/mars/mars_exploration_rovers/merb_images.html

2. Chilton's methods in *Analyzing Political Discourse* (2005) include predication analysis and the identification of inferences as well as decoding of the "deictic space." His particular school of critical discourse analysis relies heavily on notions of conceptual metaphor, Gricean pragmatics, and speech act theory, as well as on cognitive linguistics for theories of mental frames.

3. Bitzer's rhetorical theorizing did not include attention to eclectic genres covered in this book. He excluded scientific and literary genres from rhetorical attention.

4. The moves for establishing exigence in a scholarly article include filling a gap in existing scholarship, correcting an error, addressing or solving a point of disagreement, challenging an existing theory, and offering a new theory.

5. Aristotle's high estimation of language that suggests motion receives an odd endorsement from the discovery of "mirror neurons," the neurons in the motor cortex that are activated when a monkey (or human) sees a movement normally activated by that neuron. Presumably the same stimulation effect is produced by words referencing motion, i.e., Aristotle's *energeia.*

6. Kennedy translates *phantasia* as *imagination,* while clarifying in a footnote that the term should be taken literally: "there is an 'appearance' of something bad as going to happen, which the individual 'visualizes'" (1991, 139n).

7. The emotions that Longinus valorizes as stimulated by sublimity are not Aristotle's workhorse emotions: "For some emotions can be found that are mean and not in the least sublime, such as pity, grief, and fear" and "many sublime passages convey no emotion" (1965, 108). The effect instead should be grandeur, dignity, and elevation. When Edmund Burke revives the notion of the sublime in the late eighteenth century, it becomes very much a visual sublime, a set of recommendations not for creating the oratorical emotions that interested Longinus but instead for producing that sense of awe stirred by accounts of powerful storms, by spaces that dissolve into obscurity and darkness, and by the profound spectacle of the heavens. At this point, sublimity is decoupled from functional genres and becomes an end in itself.

8. Erasmus's catalog of subjects for description includes combat, pestilence, famine, portents, eclipses, snow, rain, rivers, thunders, earthquakes, fire, and battle. He mentions descriptions of living things such as the electric ray in Claudian, serpents in Lucan, a parrot in Ovid,

and among countless examples in Pliny, his description of a gnat. He lists in other authors descriptions of paintings, sculptures, "a ship, garments, a panoply, a machine, a chariot, a colossus, a pyramid, or of any other similar things, the description of which should give pleasure" (1963, 50). The largest categories, however, "more suitable for the orator" (51), include *notatio*, descriptions of character like those of Theophrastus, which could include *effictiones*, descriptions of personal appearance (53).

4

Passage Construction

16

COHERENCE

I intend in the present chapter to consider the various manners of connecting the sentences in a discourse, and to make some remarks on this subject, for the assistance of the composer, which are humbly submitted to the judgment of the reader. It will scarcely be doubted by any person of discernment, that as there should always be a natural connexion in the sentiments of a discourse, there should generally be corresponding to this, an artificial connexion in the signs. Without such a connexion the whole will appear a sort of patch-work and not a uniform piece.

GEORGE CAMPBELL, The Philosophy of Rhetoric, 1776

WHEN THE MEANING of a text unfolds easily from sentence to sentence, with little conscious effort on the listener's or reader's part, that text will be described as *coherent*. Each new sentence seems to build on the one before and take its place in the overall structure of the passage. Such *coherence*, described as a property of the text, is really a perception in the minds of listeners and readers. Coherence satisfies the demand for clarity prescribed as one of the four virtues of style in the rhetorical manuals, and later treatises like Campbell's, quoted above, offered advice on one source of coherence through intersentence connections. Rhetors can never guarantee the coherence or complete clarity of their texts. But they can employ techniques that help audiences construct coherence for themselves.

The perception of coherence can break down in two ways. First, listeners or readers may find each individual sentence comprehensible and even connected to the sentences before and after. But after a paragraph or two, especially when the text cannot be pigeonholed into a recognizable genre, they begin to ask themselves, "Where is this going?" "What's the point?" Texts that provoke such questions fail to provide readers with exigence or direction. They lack *global coherence*, an overall plan or purpose.

The second kind of incoherence is a local affair. The reader or listener understands the overall goal but encounters a sequence of sentences that is like a stretch of bad road. Progress halts. With sufficient incentive, the frustrated reader can backtrack and reread or try to bypass the confusion and go on. The frustrated listener has no recourse but to interrupt for clarification, if the situation allows, or if not, to begin to think unfavorably about the speaker.

These two kinds of incoherence, global and local, represent the two reciprocal ways used by reading theorists to describe how a text is constructed into coherence. Readers and listeners do build up meaning from individual sentences encountered in sequence, but they also make sense of individual sentences against an overall pattern that they either learn from the text or invoke based on what kind of piece they think they are reading or hearing and on how such pieces usually develop. These invoked global patterns have been called discourse schemas, story grammars, or genre expectations by various schools of reading theorists, linguists, and literary critics. Rhetoricians address such issues under the *genera dicendi*, the rhetorical genres, and under the canon of arrangement in rhetorical theory.

Solving the first kind of incoherence, overall lack of plan and purpose, also involves what rhetoricians call *exigence*, having a point to make in the first place and finding a way to make that point important and comprehensible to the audience addressed (see above, p. 332). The global issues of purpose are usually solved before any text is produced; indeed, the text usually comes into being because there is a situation calling for it and a niche ready to be filled. Most published texts respond to a perceived need or fill a predictable role and fit a prescribed genre, so they are in effect brought into being by their purpose.

Solving or preventing the second kind of incoherence, the broken series of sentences that snaps the thread of comprehension, is in part an issue of stylistic manipulation, in part an issue of audience awareness. Unfortunately, no single way of accounting for perceived coherence completely explains, or probably ever will explain, an individual reader's or listener's ability to comprehend a passage. But work by linguists, reading theorists, and rhetoricians provides several complementary explanations. This chapter reviews several of these systems of explanation: the use of cohesive ties, given/new or topic/comment organization, schema theory, and interclausal relations.

Signs of Cohesion

Whether there is a "grammar of passages" beyond a "grammar of sentences" has fascinated language theorists for a long time. One milestone in tackling the problem was M. A. K. Halliday and R. Hasan's *Cohesion in English* (1976). The authors distinguished *cohesion* as an observable property in texts from *coherence*, a perception about texts. They focused on clause-to-clause cohesive links and identified the following features connecting a second clause to a preceding one:

Reference:
A second clause can use a pronoun (e.g., *he, she, it, they*), a demonstrative (e.g., *this, that*), or some other phrase that refers to an element in a preceding clause, forging a connection. The grammatical requirement that pronouns agree with their antecedents insures the clarity of this anaphoric (looking back) and occasionally cataphoric (looking ahead) reference.

The McNeills collect and burn a great deal of driftwood, to save coal. In winter, **they** go to the tidal pools of the Ardskenish Peninsula and gather winkles, which **they** can ship to the mainland and sell for two pounds a hundredweight. (McPhee 1976, 165)

Substitution:
This cohesive tie resembles reference, but an element in one clause is not really referred to in a second. Instead, some word or phrase substitutes or stands in for this element, often the predicate in a preceding clause, and cues the listener or reader to retrieve the necessary phrasing.

But none of these developments led to therapeutic progress, and those that might have **done so** went unexploited for decades, even centuries. (Scull 2006, 275)

Ellipsis:
A second clause can use an incomplete construction. Readers or listeners have to fill in the meaning by retrieving content from a preceding clause in order to complete the sense.

I may love street food above all other types of food. I have never figured out just why [**I may love street food above all other types of food**]. (Trillin 2007, 48)

Lexical cohesion:
Linguists identify collocational sets of words or "lexical fields" within a language (see above, p. 62). These sets tend to occur together because they relate to the same area of meaning, and, presumably, their co-occurrence strengthens intersentential ties. The following example mixes terms from two fields, one concerning wine (in bold) and the other a looser field having to do with investigations (in bold italics). This mixture makes sense in an article discussing wine fraud.

Last spring, Jim Elroy took Koch's **magnum** to **Bordeaux** to have it *inspected* at the **winery**. The Petrus staff ultimately *concluded* that the **cork** was the *wrong* length, and that the **cap** and the **label** *appeared* to have been *artificially* aged. (Keefe 2007, 116)

(Halliday and Hasan included a fifth category of cohesive devices, conjunction, covering transition words. These devices will be covered below in the section on "Interclausal Relations.")

The signs of cohesion listed here have the distinct virtue of being easily pointed out. But as Halliday and Hasan admit, they can all be present without insuring that the audience will perceive an unrolling set of clauses as coherent. It is easy to construct a passage with all these cohesive stickers in place which is nevertheless gibberish: *The baseball player signed the ball. It should do so at the game and he did want to.* Fortunately, there are several other ways to capture the cues for constructing coherence.

Given/New or Topic/Comment Patterns

In the early twentieth century, a group of linguists in Prague described a feature of the way sentences in many languages tend to organize information. They noticed that sentences usually begin with "information" already known to readers or listeners—*given* information—and usually conclude with the point the speaker wants to communicate—the *new* information. A typical news item like *Congress passed the farm bill today* assumes that readers are familiar with *Congress* but do not know the *new* information, the *news* about the farm bill passing. This insight into information distribution is essentially rhetorical, rooted in the communicative necessity of patterning sentences according to what the audience knows already and does not know yet. The value of this insight and the passage construction principles that follow from it have been used extensively in contemporary writing texts like Joseph Williams's *Style: Ten Lessons in Clarity and Grace* (3rd ed. 1989) and Martha Kolln's *Rhetorical Grammar* (3rd ed. 1998).

The *given* or known information is also called the *topic* and the *new* information the *comment* on that topic (Clark and Haviland 1977). Once a topic, a local focus, has been set or "given," the rest of a passage can build on this original topic in two different ways. In the first method of topic/comment passage construction, the sentences or clauses following one another maintain the same topic, usually as the grammatical subject, as in the following opening from an article in the popular science magazine *Natural History* by Stephen J. Gould:

> (1) **The Cardiff Giant**, the best American entry for the title of paleontological hoax turned into cultural history, now lies on display in a shed behind a barn at the Farmer's Museum in Cooperstown, New York. (2) **This gypsum man**, more than ten feet tall, was "discovered" by workmen digging a well on a farm near Cardiff, New York, in October 1869. (3) Eagerly embraced by a gullible public, and ardently displayed by its creators at fifty cents a pop, **the Cardiff Giant** caused quite a brouhaha around Syracuse, and then nationally, for the few months of its life between exhumation and exposure. (Gould 1989, 14)

This passage probably strikes most readers as coherent. It manages to give a great deal of information about a famous nineteenth-century hoax, a phony ancient man, without losing readers in the details. In it, Gould has adopted a simple pattern to increase the potential coherence of his passage. The passage topic, *the Cardiff Giant*, is likely to be unknown to readers at first, but the "giant" is pictured on the magazine page, directly to the left of the text, so it is available as visually "given" information for the first sentence. All three sentences in this first paragraph maintain the same topic/subject: (1) *The Cardiff Giant,* (2) *This gypsum man,* (3) *the Cardiff Giant.* Of course these subjects are not "the same" in the sense that exactly the same words are always used, but the same referent is always intended (or so readers assume). Gould chose a synonymous phrase, *this gypsum man* (a renaming or *antonomasia*) as the subject of the second sentence, and the demonstrative *this* directs the reader's identification of *this gypsum man* with the Cardiff Giant of the preceding sentence. Since experienced readers would find maintaining the same topic from sentence to sentence predictable, they would be further disposed to preserve coherence by taking *this gypsum man* as identical to *the Cardiff Giant.* The third sentence returns to the phrasing of the first sentence for its grammatical subject, though it does so only after two opening participial phrases. With this alteration, Gould manages to combine the coherence produced by maintaining the same topic with variety in sentence construction.

While this passage maintains the same topic/subject, each sentence tells the reader something new about that topic. Unpredictable details hang off its simple structural skeleton of repeated topics. When clarity of explanation with unfamiliar material is critical, texts will often observe this pattern, as in sentences 2 through 5 of the following paragraph opening the first chapter of an organic chemistry textbook.

> Organic chemistry is *the study of **the compounds of carbon.*** **The compounds of carbon** constitute the central chemicals of all living things on this planet. **Carbon compounds** include deoxyribonucleic acids (DNAs), the giant molecules that contain the genetic information for all living species. **Carbon compounds** make up the proteins of our blood, muscle, and skin. **They** make up the enzymes that catalyze the reactions that occur in our bodies. Together with oxygen in the air we breathe, **carbon compounds** in our diets furnish the energy that sustains life. (Solomons 1992, 1)

Topic continuity can even be preserved without always making the topic or given information the grammatical subject of the sentence. Left-branching phrases and clauses can also put information in the front of sentences, the tactic Tom Wolfe used in the following passage.[1]

> [Thomas] **Jefferson** created a radically new frame of mind. In a thousand different ways **he** obliterated the symbols and deferential manners that comprise aristocracy's cardiovascular system. Led by **Jefferson,** America became a country in which every sign of aristocratic pretension was systematically uprooted and destroyed. (2007, 62)

The third sentence connects to Jefferson as the passage topic in an opening participial phrase.

There is a second way of building on a given topic drawing again on the principle of the given/new distribution of information in the sentence. Once something new has been communicated about a topic, that new information itself becomes *given*. So it is now available to become a *topic* opening the next sentence. The continuation of Gould's article illustrates this second pattern of topic/comment coherence.

> (3)...**the Cardiff Giant** caused quite a brouhaha around Syracuse, and then nationally, for the few months of its active life between exhumation and exposure.
>   (4) **The Cardiff Giant** was the brainchild of George Hull, a cigar manufacturer (and general rogue) from Binghamton, New York. (5) **He** quarried a large block of gypsum from Fort Dodge, Iowa, and shipped it to Chicago, where two marble cutters fashioned the rough likeness of a naked man. (6) **Hull** made some crude and minimal attempts to give his statue an aged appearance. (7) **He** chipped off the carved hair and beard because experts told him that such items would not petrify. (The paragraph continues with three more sentences opening with *He* or *Hull* as the topic and grammatical subject; Gould 1989, 14)

When Gould begins another paragraph at sentence (4), he keeps the same topic, *the Cardiff Giant*, that he had used in the closing sentence of the preceding paragraph. But sentence (5) begins with *He*. Where did *He* come from? In sentence (4), Gould presented as new information the identity of the creator of the hoax, *George Hull*. His next sentence refers to George Hull as *He*; *He* continues as the topic and grammatical subject of the next five sentences. Gould made the new information or comment of sentence (4) into the topic of sentence (5) preserving the principle that the beginning of a sentence should contain given information; indeed, the reader has just been "given" this information. Gould then goes back to the method of conserving the same topic from sentence to sentence, writing the rest of the paragraph with *Hull* or *he* as the subject of each sentence.

As Gould's two passages illustrate, two basic patterns are available for organizing a series of sentences according to the fundamental expectation that individual sentences begin with given information, the topic, and then add new information, a comment. Since individual sentences feature this internal principle of organization, a series of sentences can either repeat the same topic or use the new information, the comment, from one sentence as the topic of the next. The need to conserve these patterns often explains, and justifies, why a writer uses a passive construction. It can be the best choice for maintaining topic/comment structure. Gould's second sentence (*This gypsum man, more than ten feet tall, was discovered by workmen ...*) uses a passive construction, even with the agent identified, in order to preserve the topic string.

Using the new information from one sentence as the topic of the next can take a passage, and a reader, in surprising directions.

> (1) One of the geological curiosities of the Pine Barrens is that rainwater soaking down through fallen pine needles and other forest litter takes on enough acid to **leach out iron** from the sands below; (2) **the dissolved iron** moves underground

into the streams, where **it** oxidizes on contact with the air and forms **a patch of scum** on the surface that is partly rust brown and partly iridescent blue, and resembles an oil slick left by an outboard motor; (3) drifting over to the edges of the streams, **this iron-oxide film** permeates the sands and gravels of the riverbanks and cements them together into a sandstone composite that has been known for centuries as **bog iron**. (4) From **it ironmasters** of the Pine Barrens made cannonballs by the thousand and sent them by wagon over the sand roads and on to the Continental Army at Valley Forge and elsewhere. (5) **They** brought in seashells for flux, and used charcoal from the pinewoods to fire their forges and furnaces. (6) **They** made **cannon as well as shot**, and (7) **they** ordnanced the War of 1812 as well as the American Revolution. (8) **The twenty-four-pounders** with which **Stephen Decatur** armed his flagship when **he** took his Marines to Algiers, Tunisia, and Tripoli were cast at Hanover Furnace, in the Pine Barrens, in 1814, and (9) **Decatur himself** was there to supervise the casting and to test the product. (McPhee 1968, 26–27: Numbering corresponds to independent clauses; the paragraph continues.)

Readers are unlikely to predict that a paragraph opening with geological curiosities in the Pine Barrens would end on Stephen Decatur's ships in the War of 1812. This journey is made possible by a trail of topic/comment breadcrumbs along the way.

INTERRUPTING THE TOPIC STRING

According to the principle of coherent passage construction based on topic/comment organization, sentences should open with given or established information. Usually that given information comes from a title (the immediate context) for a first sentence and then from an immediately preceding sentence. But listeners and readers may be counted on to have a somewhat larger capacity for what can be considered given information in a particular passage. Consider how the following newspaper article is put together.

Memorial Hall OKd as site for museum

Fairmount Park leaders agreed to talks that would bring the Please Touch Museum to the building.

(1) The Fairmount Park Commission yesterday gave the go-ahead to negotiations that would see the Please Touch Museum move into Memorial Hall, the landmark that now serves as the park's administrative center.

(2) The commission considered two possible future uses for the decaying relic of the 1876 Centennial Exposition: Please Touch and a proposed Civil War museum.

(3) Supporters of the Civil War concept brought passion and history to the table.

(4) But in the end, the group had no funding and no collection.

(5) Please Touch, the children's museum on North 21st Street, has more than $24 million in hand and expects to raise at least $3 million from the sale of its cramped building.

(6) The museum raised the money to construct a new building on Penn's Landing, but that plan fell through when riverfront development plans collapsed last summer. (Salisbury 2003)

This article appeared in the section of the daily paper devoted to "Local News: Philadelphia and its Suburbs." Its writer assumes that readers will recognize both Memorial Hall and Fairmount Park as landmarks in their area, and furthermore, if the headline and subheadline are to make sense, readers should know, or be able to infer, that Memorial Hall is in Fairmount Park. The first sentence of the article picks up on Fairmount Park but identifies its Commission as the agent and topic. The second sentence maintains the Commission as the topic, but delivers the news that two proposals were on the table for the future of Memorial Hall. One of these is a proposed Civil War museum. As a *concept* with *supporters,* this museum becomes the topic of sentence (3), and these supporters continue as the topic of sentence (4).

Sentence (5), however, has as its topic and subject "Please Touch," a term that does not appear in either of the preceding sentences. Its nearest previous appearance comes as new information in sentence (2). If readers are to find the mention of Please Touch comprehensible in sentence (5), they must remember it despite two intervening sentences. This demand on the reader's memory hardly seems outrageous. Recalling Please Touch as previously introduced is also made more likely because it is mentioned in the subheadline and first sentence, and because the second sentence sets up two alternatives; if one is discussed, readers expect attention to the second also. But readers can be made to wait too long and so lose the link to a previously given element.

Schemas and Coherence

If topic/comment patterns were the final answer to cuing coherence, no one would produce an incoherent passage. But there is certainly more to inducing readers or listeners to construct comprehensible passages from a series of sentences. To begin with, following topic/comment patterns cannot actually guarantee the perception of coherence, since the comment sections of sentences may present several candidates for a new topic and the selected topics may wander. Gould, for instance, might have produced the following:

(4) The Cardiff giant was the brainchild of George Hull, a cigar manufacturer (and general rogue) from Binghamton, New York. *(5) Binghamton is the home of a Triple A farm team belonging to the New York Mets. (6) The Mets are certainly struggling this year.*

This kind of unconstrained association from the comment of one sentence to the topic of the next can signal a thought-disordered speaker. Repeating the same topic from sentence to sentence would at least assist coherence, but even with a consistent topic, miscellaneous comments can begin to diffuse clarity.

More important than these misuses of topic/comment connections, however, is the fact that readers can find a sequence coherent even without topic/comment patterns.

(1) I saw a three-story **house**, with a veranda on each story. (2) **It** was gray and wooden and toppling, and (3) **it** reminded me of the Railway Hotel I had seen in Zacapa. (4) But **this one** looked haunted. (5) *Every window* was broken and (6) *an old steam locomotive* was rusting in the weedy front yard. (Theroux 1990, 119)

Most adult readers of English would find this passage coherent. The first clause opens with the author's self-reference as *I*, always an available rhetorical agent, and it introduces as new information the object of his attention, a house. Clauses two through four maintain topic/comment organization with *house* as the topic (*it, it, this one*). The fifth clause, however, repeats nothing from the previous sentence but instead begins with a new topic, *every window*. Why are readers not derailed by this jump? Because they already know— that is, they have available as given information—that houses have windows. They might be confused by the next unprecedented topic, *an old steam locomotive*, but this new item (prefaced by the "introducing" indefinite article *an*) is placed with still another item widely related to houses, a *front yard*.

Any user of English who knows what a house is almost certainly knows what a window is; American speakers would know what a *front yard* is. The banality of this example illustrates the point that along with their knowledge of a language, readers and listeners share an enormous amount of cultural knowledge. Such bundled pieces of information are called *frames* or *schemas/schemata* by psychologists and reading theorists. A schema is like an organized template of background knowledge that a single item fits into, as *window* fits into the schema for *house*. Organized background knowledge can also involve common plotlines called *story grammars* or common event structures called *scripts*. Some schemas are widely shared in a culture, like the knowledge that makes the relation between the following sentences clear.

From the beginning, America has been dedicated to "life, liberty, and the pursuit of happiness." But the signers of the Declaration of Independence assumed that some truths did not have to be proved—that some truths were, to borrow a phrase, self-evident. (Huffington 2007, 39)

Most Americans would recognize that the quotation ending the first sentence comes from the Declaration of Independence mentioned in the second. Other schemas are unique to narrower groups who employ special registers.

Schema theory, like given/new organization, demonstrates once again the rhetorical nature of passage construction. Rhetors creating such leaps make assumptions about their audience's background knowledge. For an audience lacking the appropriate background knowledge, pairs of sentences without other connectives can seem like two disconnected observations. A writer or speaker uncertain about an audience's available knowledge could drop in a sentence that at least created a topic/comment link between the two potentially unrelated items.

> (1) I saw a three-story **house**, with a veranda on each story. (2) **It** was gray and wooden and toppling, and (3) **it** reminded me of the Railway Hotel I had seen in Zacapa. (4) But **this one** looked haunted. (4a) <u>The **house** had many *windows.*</u> (5) *Every window* was broken.

For English users, sentence 4a is absurdly unnecessary; to know what a house is is to know that it has windows. Once invoked, a schema like that for *house* offers a set of available "givens."

A schema-driven sequence of sentences also conforms in a sense to given/new patterning, since each new sentence begins with a "given" available in the reader's memory. An illustration of the connection between schema and given/new patterning comes from the work of two psychologists, Robert P. Abelson and Roger C. Schank (1977), who developed a theory of "scripts" (background information organized narratively) in the course of their research on artificial intelligence. Abelson and Schank used a "restaurant script" in their attempt to get a computer to comprehend a series of sentences. A "mind" that understands what it means to go to a restaurant would find a sequence of sentences like the following comprehensible, despite its lack of topic/comment organization.

> (1) Our group waited an hour to be seated. (2) The waiter brought menus that were mostly in French. (3) The check had to be split on three credit cards.

This passage is coherent to someone familiar with the routine, the "script" followed in a restaurant. Furthermore, another sentence could be inserted coherently into this passage so long as it conformed to the "master" script.

> (1) Our group waited an hour to be seated. (2) The waiter brought menus that were mostly in French. (3) The busboy constantly refilled the water glasses. (4) The check had to be split on three credit cards.

The restaurant script is so well ordered that any rearrangement of this series of sentences (e.g., putting sentence #4 before #2) would violate the reader's sense of coherence.

Story grammars are like scripts in that they represent prepatterned narratives, but they also involve knowledge about motivations and intentions.[2] Take the following sequence of sentences: *(1) Harry was promoted. (2) Maud was elated. (3) The quality control division has a new manager.* Readers could make sense of this sequence by invoking a background narrative: Maud is Harry's wife and she is elated because her husband has been promoted to become the new manager of the quality control division. But the same sequence could be explained by an equally plausible story: Harry was Maud's boss. She disliked him and is elated that he is being promoted out of his position as manager of the quality control division. These possibilities do not exhaust the plausible narratives that readers could invoke to make this passage comprehensible. The background knowledge or story grammar the writer builds on may not be exactly the one the reader uses to understand the passage, so distortions can occur as representations of a passage are built in other minds. But whether the reader invokes the exact schema or an enabling alternative, the passage will only be coherent in so far as it conforms to an already known possible sequence of events. Coherence then, according to this system of explanation, is a matter of conforming to a preexisting schema.

Explaining a reader's perception of coherence solely on the basis of background knowledge has, however, a potentially unfortunate consequence. If a passage could only be understood because of prior knowledge organized in schema and embedded in memory, how would anyone ever learn anything from listening or reading? Everyone would be a prisoner of culturally conditioned schemas and conventional story lines, a view that provides a bleak outlook for education or even for communication.

Fortunately, it is possible to learn from texts, as experience demonstrates every day. Imagine a reader of Paul Theroux's original passage who has only a very rough notion of *houses* as dwelling places. This reader encounters the two sentences in a row that jump from *house* to *window*. The very fact that these sentences are placed one after the other invites the reader to put into place, at least provisionally, the knowledge that would make them comprehensible in sequence. ("Oh," says this innocent reader, "houses must be places that have windows.") The reader or listener in a sense "reads backwards," not drawing on background knowledge to read, but using what is read to construct provisional background knowledge in order to preserve coherence (Fahnestock 1992, 243–46).

Interclause Meaning Relations

Shared schemas and given/new patterning, however, still cannot completely account for how readers or listeners construct coherence. Yet another resource is available, and a key to this resource comes again from this ability to "read backwards" and learn from text. There is another kind of enabling knowledge that readers or listeners can use when they encounter a pair of sentences like the following:

A builder would never repair the foundation of a house and leave the roof leaking.
A doctor would not treat an infected ear and ignore a sore throat.

This pair of sentences does not exhibit topic/comment organization, and each on its own seems to invoke a distinct schema, one on building houses and the other on medicine. But these sentences do exhibit strong grammatical parallelism, and most English users, if asked what transition words might connect these sentences, would supply an answer like *similarly* or *in the same way*. Their answers demonstrate another kind of knowledge available for constructing coherence. Competent language users also know the kinds of meaning or semantic relations that clauses in sequence can have to one another, and one of these relations is **similarity**. This general language knowledge would also come to their rescue with pairs of sentences like the following:

> Philosophers have long debated questions of personal identity regarding whether a given person is the same person across time. Derek Parfit famously argued that people are nothing more than successions of different overlapping selves. (Pronin 2008, 1179)

Most readers would make sense of this pair of sentences by assuming that the second offered an example of a particular philosopher arguing over the issue of personal identity. They would assume that the individual named in the second sentence, *Derek Parfit*, was a member of the group *philosophers* mentioned in the first. In other words, they would assume that the second sentence offered one example from a set of possibilities, and they would make this assumption even if they were encountering a name they had never heard before because giving an example is a predictable function for a clause following a generalization.

Rhetors then can break the given/new contract and exceed an audience's background knowledge if they can call on another kind of knowledge that experienced readers have, namely *discourse knowledge*, a knowledge of the kinds of meaning relations that *can* exist between clauses. These relations are made explicit in the transition words and phrases available in a language. For want of a better term, these meaning relations could be called "logical" relations because they can reflect or direct inferences from sentence to sentence.[3] But they do not conform to the operations and relations identified in formal logic; they represent instead the "informal logic" used in everyday reasoning expressed in natural language.

How many potential meaning relations are there? Halliday and Hasan identify four relations: additive, adversative, causal, and temporal (1976). In contrast, Nida, Louw, Snyman, and Cronje identify two main, four primary, and fourteen subordinate classes of meaningful interclausal relations (1983, 101–4).[4] Even finer distinctions could be made, but the frequently used transition words in a language do suggest a finite set of linkages. The categories of these relations offered in this chapter emphasize the rhetorical dimensions of these devices by offering a rationale for why and when they are used.

INFERRED RELATIONS

While the transition words available in a language reveal the potential set of meaning relations between clauses, the words themselves are not always necessary to signal the relation. The relations can be easily understood, as were those of similarity and exemplification in the examples above. Another readily understood relation connects the sentences opening an article titled "How to Go to Mars":

> Going to Mars would be daunting. The planet never comes closer than 80 million kilometers to ours; a round trip would take years. (Musser and Albert 2000, 44)

Most readers would understand these three sentences in sequence as a claim or "conclusion" followed by two reasons or premises. A paraphrase bringing out these relations could insert the transition words expressing the connections:

> Going to Mars would be daunting [*because*] the planet never comes closer than 80 million kilometers to ours; [*and because*] a round trip [to Mars] would take years.

Notice that the signs of verbal cohesion and given/new ordering are also in place here in addition to the inferable relations, so the coherence cues are strong.

To assert a claim and support it with a reason or premise is the essence of arguing. Because arguing is a common interaction, listeners or readers expect to be given conclusions and premises in certain situations. Because they have that expectation, they do not always need a transition word to tell them that the function of a sentence is to provide a premise. They are prepared to interpret the clause following a claim as a premise. They also expect that premises or reasons can be followed by the claims concluded from them, so rearranging the clauses in the "Mars" example would still make sense.

> Mars never comes closer than 80 million kilometers to our planet, and a round trip [to Mars] would take years. Going to Mars would be daunting.

Most readers could readily insert a *so* or *therefore* before the second sentence. In whichever direction, the conclusion/premise pair identified here matches a common characterization of the Aristotelian enthymeme as a truncated syllogism, the kernel of rhetorical argumentation (see below, p. 374). The order can be flipped and the structure still remain recognizable, though the order is now premise → conclusion, not conclusion → premise.

The reader's or listener's ability to infer the appropriate meaning relations between sentences or clauses is, once again, part of language competence. The stronger the expectation, the less the need for an explicit transition word specifying the relation. Of course, it is not enough to expect a premise or an example to follow a statement. The actual statements offered must also qualify as something that the audience would recognize or count as a premise/reason or example, etc. In the case of the Mars argument, the distance and length of a trip are widely recognized as reasons for its difficulty, and the extremes of distance and time in the Mars case more than justify the characterization "daunting."

In the case of premise/conclusion pairs, some analysts would rightly say that background knowledge or schemas are also operating here, because the listener or reader has to judge whether what is offered as a premise or reason counts as one. But there are really two separate skills involved on the reader/listener's part, both the expectation that a sentence can function as a reason and the cultural or special knowledge to judge whether a particular statement counts as a reason. These two contributions to coherence need to be kept distinct because they work reciprocally. Readers/listeners do assess statements as acceptable premises against their background knowledge, but they also learn possible or acceptable reasons in the first place because they encounter them as statements filling the functional "slot" for premises.

This point about the reciprocal working of background knowledge and discourse knowledge could be made more dramatically away from activities like taking trips, even to Mars, where most adults have well-elaborated schema, to the kinds of reasons or premises that are offered in academic texts on topics that the audience is not already familiar with. For example, a student encountering the protocol for a chemistry experiment may read in a manual, "The pH must be kept between 1 and 2 because sulfides of group IV cations will only precipitate in a highly acidic environment." The student who reads such a sentence is probably not recognizing the application of a familiar reason but is instead learning a new reason, a new fact about a class of compounds that is being applied in the experiment at hand but that could also be applied elsewhere. Fortunately for the student's ability to understand the connection between these two clauses, the claim-premise relationship is made explicit here with *because*. In this way, part of learning from texts involves absorbing how familiar functional slots are filled with new content.

What other relations are so predictable between clauses or sentences in sequence that readers or listeners have an easy time inferring them even without a transition word? Descriptions of actions or states coming after each other are typically understood as reflecting the chronological order of their occurrence. Here are two imperatives from a recipe:

Remove from heat. Stir in eggs.

The order of these clauses indicates the chronological order for performing the actions. Reversing this pair would lead to a different sequence of actions, and in this case a disaster.

In general, readers are prepared to relate a second clause to a first not only as **premises** and **examples** but also as **conclusions, additions, similarities, restatements,** and **chronologically sequenced statements** as predictable. These relations can be forced, reinforced, or emphasized by transition words, but, given the appropriate wording and often the assistance of given/new connections and background schema, these relations can frequently be inferred without the help of transition words.

SIGNALED RELATIONS

Other relations, however, are less expected. Take the following two sentences adapted from an editorial on the effects of toxic chemicals on behavior:

> Human behavior is so easily influenced by toxic chemicals that in the 1980s a new scientific discipline called behavioral toxicology came into existence. We continue to load up our water and food supplies with dangerous chemicals. (Hatherill 1999, 14)

This sequence of statements would puzzle most readers: loading up water and food with "dangerous chemicals" does not follow sensibly from becoming aware of the effects of "toxic chemicals" to the point of founding a new discipline on the subject. The second clause does not restate the first or offer an example or fulfill any other obvious meaning in relation. It is not a conclusion but a *nonclusion*; it violates the usual premise-conclusion pattern. Such flat-out contradictions are not expected in consecutive clauses. Readers will be confused unless they are warned, and indeed, this pair of sentences was actually written with a signposting transition word opening the second clause: "...a new scientific discipline called behavioral toxicology came into existence. **Nonetheless**, we continue to load up our water and food supplies with dangerous chemicals." Suddenly this pair makes sense. The necessary transition word ***nonetheless*** signals a statement that is maintained even though it does not follow from the point made in the preceding sentence. The importance of signposting such ruptures can also be seen in the following example:

> Although such proposals [for reforming English spelling] sound reasonable, they have never been widely accepted. (Miller 1991, 61)

The reasonableness of a proposal is usually grounds for accepting it. Breaking that connection requires a special signal from the speaker or writer, and English does have signals for this "setting aside" of a potential reason: *though, even though,* and *although*. These transition words amount to acknowledging a plausible premise which is then discounted. The speaker or writer using these in effect marks a concession. Conceding is certainly not unheard of, but it is less expected than giving a reason. Because it is the less expected of two alternatives that have to do with supporting statements, because it is, in fact, a kind of "negative" premise, readers and listeners usually need to have this relation made explicit with a transition word.

What other relations are usually signaled? Countering any of the expected relations described above typically requires a signal. So, for example, chronological sequence is readily inferred between statements describing actions or events. Therefore, any consecutive clause which violates a predictable sequence, any **anomalous sequence**, requires some initial time marker so that it can be meaningfully placed in relation to the preceding action or event.

The week Churchill sailed for America the Royal Air Force and Tito's Partisans launched 'Operation Ratweek' designed to cut road and rail routes through Yugoslavia. **Meanwhile** the Red Army was on the Danube pushing southeast. (Dallas 2005, 247)

Another fairly common relation is **restatement**, which can be signaled by transition phrases like *that is* or *in other words*. Rhetors restate when they want to emphasize a point.

> Writing has a conservative influence on language; it works to resist change, not to promote sudden reforms. (Miller 1991, 61)

But instead of making the same point twice, a writer can negate one statement and replace it with another that in effect corrects the first. Such a **replacement** shows an awareness of what the audience might incorrectly think.

> 'Evolution' as a description of Darwin's 'descent with modification' was not borrowed from a previous technical meaning; it was, **rather**, expropriated from the vernacular. (Gould 1977, 35)

Giving an example is also a typical, widely recognized relation, as discussed above. What is the opposite of giving an example? It is making an **exception**, singling out one item in a set as different from the rest.

> All the Kennedys present were very kind to my son. **But** John [Kennedy Jr.] and his lovely bride, Carolyn, were especially so. (McCain 1999, 8)

The list of "Positive and Negative Interclausal Relations" in the appendix to this chapter offers a taxonomy of the potential meaning relations that are part of the English speaker's discourse knowledge. These are organized into pairs combining a more expected "positive" relation with a less expected opposite or "negative" relation.

Combining Sources of Coherence

In passages of prose perceived as coherent, and especially in easy-to-read professional prose, any and sometimes all of the sources of coherence discussed in this chapter will link the sentences in sequence. Cohesive ties, topic/comment organization, reliance on readers' background knowledge, and signposted or inferable relations will all be present. In arguments, explicit or inferable relations are often layered on topic/comment organization, as in this passage from an editorial by a former "Drug Czar":

(1) It is true that the individual initially made the voluntary decision to use drugs. (2) **But** once addicted, it is no longer a simple matter of choice. (3) [**because**] Prolonged drug use changes the brain in long-lasting and fundamental ways that result in truly compulsive, often uncontrollable, drug craving, seeking and use. (4) [**therefore**] Once addicted, it is almost impossible for most people to stop using drugs without treatment. (McCaffrey 1999)

Although three of the sentences here have place holding subjects (*it is true that, it is no longer, it is almost impossible*), the passage nevertheless exhibits many of the sources of cohesion and coherence described in this chapter: ellipsis, lexical repetition, topic/comment organization, and explicit or inferable relations. *Drugs* and *drug, use* and *using* are repeated in three of the four sentences, *addicted* in two; these recurring words and their synonyms (Halliday and Hasan's lexical cohesion) establish the primary lexical field. The need to complete the phrase *once addicted* by mentally filling in *to drugs* establishes the cohesive tie of *ellipsis*.

Does topic/comment organization also play a role in this paragraph? When the ellipses in the second and fourth sentences are filled in (e.g., *But once addicted* [to drugs]), the T/C links across the passage could be described as follows:

$$T_1 \text{ (individual)} \rightarrow C_1 \text{ (decided to use drugs)}$$
$$\swarrow$$
$$T_2 \text{ (once addicted [to drugs])} \rightarrow C_1 \text{ (no longer a matter of choice)}$$
$$\downarrow$$
$$T_2 \text{ (prolonged drug use [=addiction]} \rightarrow C_2 \text{ (changes the brain)}$$
$$\downarrow$$
$$T_2 \text{ (once addicted [to drugs])} \rightarrow C_3 \text{ (impossible to stop without treatment)}$$

The consistent topic from sentences (2) through (4) is *drug addiction*. The comments attached to this dominant topic string are not, however, just a series of miscellaneous details. They are given direction by inferable clause-to-clause relations (provided in bold in the original passage). These relations reveal the structure of the argument, which could be paraphrased as follows: addiction ceases to be a matter of choice because drug use changes the brain and therefore treatment is necessary. The premise for sentences (2) and (4) occurs between them (sentence 3) in the statement about permanent changes to the brain.

In addition to these inferred relations, explicit relations also have a role in establishing sentence-to-sentence coherence in this passage. The second sentence is prefaced by the transition word *but*, which is needed to mark it as "not following" or "not concluding" from the first sentence. In other words, the first sentence concedes (*it is true*) that people begin to abuse drugs voluntarily, but the next sentence denies what would seem to follow: that they can end drug abuse voluntarily.

Because of the repeated topic and the inferable or explicit interclausal relations, there are really no sentence-to sentence "leaps" in this passage that a reader would have to fill in from background knowledge. However, most readers in the United States in the last few decades have heard arguments on this issue; they would probably find the overall point familiar, and they would, in effect, have this familiarity reinforced. In its place in the entire piece, this paragraph serves to give presence to a premise that the author wants to use to argue a further point. Thus, these four sentences coalesce into a single point, and how this "higher" structure is created from a string of sentences, the subject of the next chapter, brings the issue of passage construction firmly into the domain of the rhetorical manuals.

Summary

Some arguers may occasionally intend obscurity, perhaps to demonstrate their sophistication or purge their audience. But rhetorical principles of effective style demand clarity in sentences and coherence in passages. Both require the audience's cooperation, but speakers and writers can make choices that help. Perceptions of coherence come from top down, when the audience understands the overall purpose and genre of a text, and from bottom up, when they can build meaning sentence by sentence. This chapter focuses on smaller-scale sentence-to-sentence (or really clause-to-clause) sources cueing coherence that can be analyzed with the following frames.

1. Cohesive ties, described by the linguists Halliday and Hasan (1976), require the audience to look back to the preceding clause for a pronoun reference or the material to clarify a substitution or fill in an ellipsis.

2. Given/New or Topic/Comment organization builds on the principle that sentences open with material familiar to the audience and add the unfamiliar. A series of sentences can maintain the same topic, or a new sentence can begin with information given in the preceding sentence.

3. Schemas or background knowledge can take the place of "givens" provided in a text. Readers already know (or think they know) why the material in a new sentence is or should be related to content in the preceding one.

4. Meaning relations between clauses can be signaled by transition words. These relations can also be inferred without explicit transition words when they are predictable. But the "negative" meaning relations (the concessions, exceptions, and "nonclusions") typically need posted warnings.

None of these cues or methods guarantee that audiences will find a text coherent. Typically, more than one is present, redundantly connecting sentences in sequence, but even with these links, readers and listeners must still make a significant investment in the act of comprehension. The role of background knowledge in this investment (e.g., schemas, stories, scripts) has been pointed out often. Less appreciated is the role of *discourse knowledge*, which includes an expectation of given/new patterns, especially topic maintenance, and of the kinds of meaning relations that can connect clauses in sequence (covered in the appendix). Most trained audiences, with some exposure to reasoned prose, have the necessary discourse knowledge.

APPENDIX: INTERCLAUSE MEANING RELATIONS

A. **Sequence**: *then, next*

This relation links clauses or sentences in chronological order as in a narrative or set of instructions. Readers assume that the order of the sentences reflects the order of the actions or events or states that the sentences describe (e.g., *I fixed dinner. I watched television.*) If the sequence of sentences were switched, the reader would invert the sequence of actions (*I watched television. I fixed dinner.*) The principle remains: the order of the sentences represents the order of the actions.

A sequence also reflects movement in some consistent time frame. In other words, the events described in a series of sentences will usually be understood to be measurable in the same "kind" of time. Narrative sequences are not usually created out of events that take quite different spans of time: *I watched television. I fixed dinner. I grew four inches.* When there are unexpected jumps in time, time-marking transition words are more likely to be used.

Relation understood:

"The mail plane, a Cessna, showed up. I put the fish in it and flew to Fairbanks, two hundred miles." (McPhee 2007, 86)

Relation marked by a transition word.

"[T]hat year, Mt. Hekla erupted, shaking the entire island [Iceland] and covering it with long spells of darkness followed by a brutally cold winter that melted into spring floods. **Then** came epidemics. **Then**, in 1397, Iceland was transferred from Norwegian to Danish rule." (Kurlansky 1997, 147)

A'. **Anomalous Sequence**: *before, meanwhile*, time adverbials, e.g., *five years later, in the interim.*

If the writer breaks either of the conventions associated with relations of sequence (that the order of sentences reflects the order of events and that the events related in a series of sentences proceed in the same time frame), then the writer should use transition words to help the reader. English is filled with words and phrases that cue readers to unexpected ordering.

Relation marked: Putting a subsequent action or state before a preceding action or state.

> "**Before** Thomas Jefferson sold his personal library of 6,487 volumes to the government in 1815 to 'recommence' the function of the Congressional Library, ... the Library's music collections consisted of only a small number of musical compositions." (Gallo 2006)

Describing actions that are simultaneous, not sequential.

> "The week Churchill sailed for America the Royal Air Force and Tito's Partisans launched 'Operation Ratweek' designed to cut road and rail routes through Yugoslavia. **Meanwhile** the Red Army was on the Danube pushing southeast. (Dallas 2005, 247)

B. *Restatement*: *in other words, that is*

The second of two sentences or clauses in a row can say essentially the same thing as the first, though usually in different words and with different detail. In other words, restatements typically offer more information and alternate wording. Restatements allow the writer or speaker to emphasize, clarify, and repeat to prevent misunderstanding.

Relation understood:

> "Drug use in this country has declined by half since 1979. The number of current [1990s] users has dropped from 25 million in 1979 to 13 million in 1996." (McCaffrey 1999)

Relation marked by a transition word:

> "Epidemiologists say the statistics [on the increase in asthma] may be skewed somewhat by detection bias—**that is**, doctors may now be doing a better job of diagnosing asthma." (Alpert 1999, 20)

B'. *Replacement*: *instead, rather*

The second sentence or clause in a pair can be offered as a substitute for the first, which is being denied or negated (e.g., *He did not fly. He took the train*). In other words, instead of saying roughly the same thing twice, the writer cancels or empties out one statement, which might or might not have been in the reader's mind, and replaces it with another.

Relation understood:

> No one sat down one day and said, "I think I will invent writing." It grew organically out of practical needs. (Miller 1991, 45)

Relation marked by a transition word:

> For Leonardo da Vinci, painting did not mean merely copying the appearance of nature. **Rather**, it involved understanding nature's laws and using them to create a figurative world.... (Grillo 2006, 510)

C. *Exemplification*: *for example, for instance*

A sentence or clause can be related to the immediately preceding one because it gives an example of the "set" introduced in the first. A set is a category that is defined clearly enough so that the reader can recognize whether something belongs in it (is a member of the set) or does not. When a sentence provides an example, its wording is less general or abstract than the wording of the preceding sentence.

Relation understood:

> "The treatment of domestic animals was also lamented [in the eighteenth century]. Tobias Smollett felt compassion for the wretched mules and donkeys in the south of France." (Thomas 1983, 143)

Relation marked by a transition word:

> "The means of creativity have now been democratized. **For example**, anyone with an inexpensive high-definition video camera and a personal computer can create a high-quality, full-length motion picture." (Kurzweil 2007, 15).

C'. *Exception*: *but, except, with the exception of*

If the first of two sentences or clauses establishes a set, the second can exempt a member from that set. In other words, instead of giving an example in a following sentence, the writer gives a non-example, mentioning something that does not belong. Writers may specify exceptions if they believe their readers are likely to include something in a category it does not belong in. Excepting something from a set is also a way of giving it greater presence by making it unique.

Relation marked by a transition word:

> "All the Kennedys present were very kind to my son. **But** John [Kennedy Jr.] and his lovely bride, Carolyn, were especially so." (McCain 1999, 8)

Because readers expect examples rather than exceptions, exceptions usually have to be signaled by transition words. Could the two sentences quoted above be spoken without the transition word in a way that would make the intended relation of exception clear? There is no a rule that says an exception—or any other relation for that matter—must always be marked by a transition word, because there are always special contexts and methods of delivery that can direct readers to make the correct inference.

D. **Premise**: *because, given, for the reason that*

A second sentence or clause can be related to the one before by offering a reason or cause or support for the first. Offering premises amounts to the explicit act of arguing; it is as common in everyday conversation as it is in editorials or legal briefs or academic treatises.

Relation understood:

"Some of them [supporters of the Earth Liberation Front] think that science itself is not worth keeping—it is a facet, they consider, of a civilization rotten to the core." ("To Build Bridges" 2006, 481)

Relation marked by a transition word:

"One hypothesis is that children are breathing more allergens **because** they are spending more time indoors than children did in the past." (Alpert 1999, 20)

English transition words that signal "premise here" also make the clause they mark dependent on the independent supported clause. English does not have a convenient transition word that signals a premise and creates an independent clause at the same time. Writers who want a premise to stand in a clause of its own and be marked at the same time have to resort to more elaborate phrases or even to whole sentences.

"The responses of the Martian ionosphere were similar for these two flares despite their very different peak fluxes. **This is because** the postflare $N_c(h)$ profile for the weaker event (26 April) was measured just 90 s after the peak x-ray flux, whereas for the far stronger event on 15 April the MGS observation was made 20 min into the flare's decay phase." (Mendillo et al. 2006, 1137)

Note: The transition word **if**, sometimes followed by a **then** used in the main clause, often marks a hypothetical premise. An **if ... then** construction can be used to mark the conditions that have to be met if certain circumstances or results are to follow. The conditional nature of this premise has to be marked, and the condition is typically given before the potential result or conclusion. The result or consequence does not have to be signaled with *then*, but it often is, e.g., "**If** project X is going to help, **then** lab and DOE officials will have to bustle it along." (Cho 2008, 1151)

Also, in a Question/Answer structure, the answer, the second clause, often provides the reason for or the explanation of what is asked in the first clause. e.g. "[H]ow on Earth has this radiation resistance evolved? The answer is simple: radiation resistance correlates with resistance to desiccation." (Lovett 2006, 517)

D'. **Concession**: *though, although, even though, granted that*

What is the opposite of giving a reason that supports a claim? It is making a statement not offered in support of a claim, one that the writer deliberately sets aside. Such a statement can be called a "premise without force" or a concession. Some concessions demonstrate the arguer's awareness of the audience's awareness that a contradicting reason is available. But the arguer will set it aside in the act of acknowledging it.

Relation marked by a transition word:

> "**Although** vaccines and other new treatments would be helpful in the long term, some basic means of combating malaria, such as bednets impregnated with insecticide, are available now." ("Malaria Quagmire" 2006)

Again, because readers find premises so much more predictable than concessions, they usually need concessions to be marked by explicit transition words. Concessions that appear as the first clause are *cataphoric* rather than *anaphoric*; they look forward to the next clause, not backwards to the preceding clause.

E. **Conclusion**: *therefore, so, as a result, thus* [U.S. usage; in British usage, *thus* often signals an example]

The premise relation described above inevitably brings into existence the kind of statement that follows from or is "concluded" from it. In other words, if there are supporting statements, there have to be supported statements. If the supporting statement comes before the supported statement, then the relation is one of premise to conclusion. If the supported statement comes before the supporting statement, then the relation is one of conclusion to premise. Relations D and E, then, should be seen as reciprocal.

Relation understood:

> "The problem is that the crab grows, whereas its house does not. Hermit crabs are always on the lookout for new accommodations." (DeWaal 2006, 46)

Relation marked by a transition word:

> "In England, France, Italy, Germany, rare are the parents who urge their children to live out their dreams and rise as far above their station as they possibly can. **As a result**, such dreams, if any, don't last long." (Wolfe 2007, 61)

E'. *Nonclusion*: *nevertheless, nonetheless, but, yet*

If it is possible to have the opposite of a premise in a concession, it is also possible to have the opposite of a conclusion. In this "reverse of a conclusion" relation, the first of a pair of clauses gives a reason from which a predictable conclusion should follow, but the second clause offers a statement that does not follow. This relation can be called a *nonclusion*. The *nonclusion* is another way of breaking up the traditional premise/conclusion pairing. It demonstrates the writer's sensitivity to the pattern of reasoning that readers might find normal. To break that expectation almost always requires an explicit transition word.

Relation marked by a transition word:

"Human behavior is so easily influenced by toxic chemicals that in the 1980s a new scientific discipline called behavioral toxicology came into existence. **Nonetheless,** we continue to load up our water and food supplies with dangerous chemicals." (Hatherhill 1999, 14)

Of course, there was no simple *volte-face*, no dramatic shift from tree-destruction to tree- preservation. **Nevertheless,** the rise of a more sympathetic attitude is unmistakable. (Thomas 1983, 197)

F. *Similarity*: *similarly, likewise, in the same way,*

The second of a pair of sentences can make a point that the author wishes readers to see as parallel or analogous to the first. The similarity between the meanings of the two sentences can be enhanced by parallel structures and repetition between the two.

Relation understood:

"A mechanic would never fix a transmission while leaving pistons cracked. A builder would never repair the foundation of a house and leave the roof leaking. A doctor would not treat an infected ear and ignore a sore throat." (Candaele and McDowell 1999)

Relation marked by a transition word:

"Society has decided that the justice system cannot perform effectively unless the bulk of its adult population is available to serve on juries. **Similarly,** our political process needs to have its voting-age citizens take an active part—even if that activity is just a matter of throwing a lever." (Solomon 1998)

F'. *Contrast*: *in contrast, on the other hand, conversely*

Rather than offering a similar point, a second sentence or clause can state a claim that opposes one or more elements in the previous statement. English offers many words and phrases to mark a contrast between successive sentences, but if the contrast involves a strong pair of antithetical terms (*true/false, hot/cold*), it can be expressed by carefully parallel sentences even without a transition word. The parallelism holds the antithetical words in the same relative position and thus enhances the contrast.

Relation marked by a transition word:

> Garden beans were for the poor and so were pumpkins. White currants, **on the other hand**, were more desirable than black ones... (Thomas 1983, 232)

Relation can be signaled by contrasting adverbials:

> "**Twenty-five years ago**, the main function of guidance counselors was helping students decide on college or jobs. **Today**, they often find themselves having to deal with a range of personal problems before they can even start talking about academics or careers." (Welsh 1999)

G. *Addition*: *and, also, in addition, moreover, furthermore, nor [= and not], not only/ but also*

If a writer sets up a series, the individual elements of that series are connected to each other by addition, whether those elements are single words or entire sentences. They are simply added to one another like beads on a string. Sentences added in a series need not make similar points. Similarity is a stronger relation than addition. Nor do added statements necessarily represent any kind of sequence in their order. They simply represent one more element in a list of items that the writer is providing. If, for instance, the writer mentions several examples in a row, the relationship between the first and second example will be that of addition.

Relation understood:

> "Drug abuse treatment reduces the risk of HIV infection, and interventions to prevent HIV are much less costly than treating AIDS. Treatment tied to vocational services improves the prospects for employment, with 40% to 60% more individuals employed after treatment." (Leshner 1999; the relation between the independent clauses in the first sentence is marked by *and*)

Relation marked by a transition word:

> "Natural history was a historical enterprise in the sense that it generally restricted itself to the descriptions of living things. **Moreover**, until well into the 17th century it was primarily a textual activity." (Harrison 2006, 7)

Note: Writers can set up an enumeration, indicating that they will cover "several" points. The items in that enumeration are then connected additively with transition words like *first, second, third.*

G'. *Alternation*: or, otherwise, either/or, neither/nor

The second of two sentences or clauses can offer a choice that excludes the first rather than adds to it. Alternation is not strictly the opposite or negative of addition. Yet to say "x or y" is quite different in everyday logic from saying "x and y." Careful parallelism in successive sentences can sometimes convey alternation without the help of transition words.

Relation marked by a transition word:

"Do we merely stay in our comfortable nests, concluding that the obligation of these instruments has been discharged when we work at the job of informing the public for a minimum of time? **Or** do we believe that the preservation of the Republic is a seven-day-a-week job, demanding more awareness, better skills, and more perseverance than we have yet contemplated." (Edward R. Murrow, in Safire 1997, 717).

Note: Alternation should not be confused with contrast. In a contrast, both the claims stand, even if they are only hypothetical; one does not cancel the other out, as happens in an alternation. Nor should alternation be confused with replacement, a relation in which one assertion is substituted for another.

Also note that there is a "weaker" use of *or* which expresses added options or chances rather than mutually exclusive alternatives: "So when a skier dies in the avalanche, **or** the celebrity crashes his plane into the ocean, it seems like an even greater violation of the gentleman's agreement we imagine that we have with the world" (Junger 1999).

NOTES

1. The need to put given information or a recognizable topic up front in a sentence can lead to the odd device called *topicalization*—opening with a word or phrase disjointed from the rest of the sentence, just to get it in place first. Imagine continuing the example above with the following: *The party, I need to get there in a limo or not at all.*

2. Story grammars were proposed in the 1970s by Rumelhart, who analogized story structure to sentence structure (see Rumelhart 1980 and Wilensky 1982). The term is used more generally here to refer to typical or recurring plot lines that need not be fictional.

3. The relations involved here differ from the immediate inferences from sentences, sometimes described as relations between sentences, identified by linguists: entailments and presuppositions. In semantic entailment, to say that someone is divorced means that at some point that person was married. (However, to say that a person is not divorced does not necessarily entail that the person is married, though that is what most people would infer from such a statement.) In

syntactic entailment, to say that someone bought an item entails the passive, that the item was bought by that person. Presuppositions refer to the truth claims implicit in a sentence. Thus, to say "The president of Uganda arrived yesterday" presupposes that there is a president of Uganda. Rhetoricians tend to use the term *assumption* for such immediate inferences.

4. The list of relations in Nida et al. is as follows: I. Coordinate/A. Additive: *equivalent, different*; B. Dyadic: alternative, contrastive, comparative; II. Suborinate/A. Qualificational: substance, character; B. Logical (cause-effect, reason-result, means-result, means-purpose, condition-result, basis-inference, concession-result (Nida, Louw, Synman, and Cronje 1983, 102–3).

17

PASSAGE PATTERNS

*Throughout ancient times, men stood convinced that
wealth should properly come out of land. As Cicero put
it, "Of all things from which income is derived, none is
better than agriculture, none more fruitful, none sweeter,
none more fitting for a free man." Well, there may have
been none sweeter nor more fitting for a free man, but
there were plenty that were more fruitful. There was
commerce, for example: A trader, if his ship came in,
could become a millionaire overnight. And industry—
running brick plants, for instance—produced some huge
Roman fortunes. But Cicero's attitude was the norm;
even if a man did make money in an industrial venture,
instead of reinvesting it to make more, he took it out to
put it in land. Spending it on machines to improve his
industrial profits never crossed his mind.*

LIONEL CASSON, *"Godliness and Work"*

THE METHODS FOR cueing sentence-to-sentence coherence, discussed in the previous chapter, offer a starting place for understanding more complex passage construction. After all, when audiences are through listening or reading a text, they do not retain every individual sentence. Instead they pick up the gist and perhaps a salient detail or two. How a string of sentences can condense into one or two remembered points can be illustrated with the paragraph of magazine prose serving as the epigraph to this chapter. This passage displays the sentence-to-sentence linkages typical of professional writing intended for a wide readership. It has multiple cohesive ties and topic/comment patterning through the first four clauses. The connection between the first and second sentences also requires readers to call on their background knowledge and recognize Cicero as a representative man of "ancient times." Most important, however, for building higher-order structures from this sequence of sentences are the interclausal relations, some signaled by transition words and others implicit. These relations are expressed and highlighted in the following version.

(1) Throughout ancient times, men stood convinced that wealth should
properly come out of land.   *Claim*
[**Restatement**] (2) As Cicero put it, "Of all things from which income is
derived, none is better than agriculture, none more fruitful, none sweeter, none
more fitting for a free man."
[**Concession**] (3) Well, there may have been none sweeter nor more fitting for a
free man,

[**Nonclusion**] (3a) **but** there were plenty that were more fruitful.

Nonclusion or contradiction

[**Exemplification**] (4) There was commerce, **for example**:

[**Exemplification—example of the example**] (4a) A trader, if his ship came in, could become a millionaire overnight.

[**Addition**] (5) **And** industry—running brick plants, for instance—produced some huge Roman fortunes.

[**Nonclusion**] (6) **But** Cicero's attitude was the norm; *Nonclusion*

[**Example-Hypothetical**] (6a) [**Embedded concession**] **even if** a man did make money in an industrial venture

(6b) instead of reinvesting it to make more, he

took it out to put it in land.

[**Premise**] (7) Spending it on machines to improve his industrial profits never crossed his mind.

Readers of this paragraph are likely to translate it into three sections, as indicated by the labels to the right. The first two sentences constitute a claim that the ancients believed in land-based wealth. The next three sentences (3a to 5) contradict that belief with evidence of other sources of wealth in antiquity. This evidence is then set aside by a return to the opening assertion of the ancient preference for land as wealth. The main turns are signaled by the strong, sentence-initial adversative *but*.

Throughout ancient times, men [like Cicero] stood convinced that wealth should properly come out of the land.

but there were plenty [of sources of wealth] that were more fruitful.

But Cicero's attitude was the norm.

Within each section created by these main turns, the sentences are related as restatements, supporting examples, and premises. Some of these relations are also signaled with transition words (*and, for example*), but these only reinforce easily inferred relations. The argument, and hence passage construction, here exactly follows the advice of the rhetorical manuals in how to enhance or expand a point. Readers and listeners easily allow restatements, examples, and comparisons (missing here) as embedded enhancement, while keying in on the major turns as indicators of the hierarchical structure of a passage. At a level even higher than that indicated in the right-hand column, the entire paragraph reduces to the single claim: *the ancients thought of wealth in terms of land.*

Compositional Units in the Rhetorical Tradition

Compositional units such as those in the epigraph were described consistently in rhetorical treatises. But they came in different "grain sizes" involving shorter or longer stretches of discourse. Starting top-down at the level of major divisions, the first-century BCE *Rhetorica ad Herennium* ([Cicero] 1981) specified six parts to the persuasive, and especially the forensic, oration: the *exordium, narratio, partitio, confirmatio, refutatio, peroratio*. These parts define an ideal. The length and even order of each section could be varied according to the situation, but each part had its particular work to do: the *exordium* (introduction) to ingratiate the audience, the *narratio* to give the facts of the case with the appropriate spin, the *partitio* to define the issue at stake and the coming points, the *confirmatio* to deliver the arguments in favor of the rhetor's case, the *refutatio* to dispose of the opponents' arguments, and finally the *peroratio* to summarize the argument and strengthen its emotional impact and the audience's involvement.

Since the sections of confirmation and refutation, the meat of the argument, were built on individual lines of support, their content was ultimately defined and illustrated in both rhetorical and dialectical manuals under "invention." In the lists of inventional *topoi*, rhetors would find prompts for thinking up premises using definitions, consequences, comparisons, etc. These individual lines of argument could then be presented stylistically in minimal multiclause units, identified first and most famously by Aristotle as the syllogism and the enthymeme (Kennedy 1991, 33). Or they could be presented in the expanded version of these argument structures, the *epicheireme* (discussed in the next chapter), an all-purpose blueprint for amplifying a single claim-premise pair.

SYLLOGISM AND ENTHYMEME

In the rhetorical tradition, the most important multiclause units delivering individual lines of arguments are the syllogism and the enthymeme. These forms were first identified in Aristotle's logical treatises and his *Rhetoric*, and the literature on both is vast and well beyond consideration here. From the perspective of rhetorical stylistics at issue here, both can be looked at narrowly as linguistic templates, patterns that were in fact prescribed as precisely as many of the figures of speech.

As a three-part structure for inferential reasoning, the syllogism requires, in its ideal form, statements with linking verbs, three carefully positioned recurring terms, and distinct quantifiers, making claims of inclusion, exclusion, and partial overlap. With a focus on the quantifiers and the option of affirming or denying, the resulting statements could take four forms: universal affirmative, universal negative, particular affirmative, particular negative. Textbooks on dialectic designated each of these statement types by a vowel (A, E, I, O respectively). Combined into sets of three statements, these four statement types yielded twenty-four possible syllogisms, and these twenty-four were in turn grouped into sets according to the grammatical position (subject or predicate) of the three critical terms. Students in medieval and early modern universities memorized the formal possibilities with convenient mnemonics of words with three vowels. So, using Melanchthon's examples in the *Erotemata Dialectices* popular in the sixteenth century, the famous *Barbara* stood for a syllogism whose three statements were all universal affirmations:

"Every animal is a substance/Every man is an animal/Therefore every man is a substance." And *Ferio* cued a syllogism with a universal negation, a particular affirmative, and a particular negation: "No law of nature is mutable/The law prohibiting adultery is a law of nature/Therefore the law prohibiting adultery is not mutable" (1963b, 607; author's translation). The strict regulation of these patterns, called *figurae syllogismorum*, has to be appreciated. Students needed enough grammatical competence (usually in Latin) to manipulate the three critical terms into the appropriate subject and predicate positions in comprehensible sentences. The syllogism was therefore as much a stylistic as an argumentative structure.[1]

Reasoning in ordinary arguments is rarely expressed in the stripped-down form of the correctly worded three-part syllogism. The form can, however, often be reconstructed from an arguer's actual phrasing. For example, suffragist Susan B. Anthony defended herself against arrest for attempted voting in 1872 with a speech that included the following passage:

> Webster, Worcester, and Bouvier all define a citizen to be a person in the United States, entitled to vote and hold office.
>
> The only question left to be settled now is: Are women persons? And I hardly believe any of our opponents will have the hardihood to say they are not. Being persons then, women are citizens; and no state has a right to make any law or to enforce any old law, that shall abridge their privileges or immunities. (Safire 1997, 637)

The full three-part syllogism underlying this passage and delivering the definition argument could be paraphrased as follows:

> Citizens are persons in the United States entitled to vote and hold office.
> Women are persons in the United States.
> Therefore women are citizens entitled to vote and hold office.

Of course Anthony did not express her argument in this simplified form. She credits her first premise to three legal authorities. She poses her second premise as a rhetorical question, an *erotema* (*Are women persons?*), which she then answers affirmatively by declaring that not even her opponents could disagree. In other words, she delivers her premises rhetorically, not as disembodied statements but as claims already accepted and endorsed by constitutional authorities and by her adversaries. If Anthony had expressed her argument in the barest form, she would have been forced to choose precise phrasing for her major premise. Was a citizen "a person in the United States entitled to vote and hold office," which would mean that women were not really citizens? Or was any person in the United States (that is, physically resident) a "citizen entitled to vote and hold office"? Both readings raised legal problems, and Anthony's wording is conveniently ambiguous.

Units of argument closer to canonical syllogistic form can carry the appearance of airtight reasoning. They are then a device of emphasis. The following comes from an editorial calling for the death penalty in the case of the convicted terrorist Zacarias Moussaoui.

(1) The death sentence is properly reserved for the most heinous of crimes and least redeeming criminals. (2) But there are few cases more appropriate for this most severe penalty. (3) Here is a criminal [Moussaoui] who admitted to his crime, who expressed no remorse and who yearns to kill more. (4) Justice for the victims of his crime demands the maximum penalty the law allows. (Dinh 2005)

The first sentence here is the major premise, the defining criteria for a death sentence as applicable to heinous crimes and unrepentant criminals. The second and third sentences constitute the minor premise, the identification of Moussaoui and his crimes as fitting the criteria. The final sentence concludes that he therefore deserves the death penalty. Departing from good form, however, this final sentence substitutes the new notion of *justice for the victims* for the strict reiteration that would read, "Therefore his heinous crime and unredeeming criminal nature deserve the death penalty."

If full syllogisms are rare, another structure defined in terms of and presumably derived from syllogisms is common. This typically two-clause structure is the *enthymeme,* defined by Aristotle in terms of the audience:

The enthymeme [is] a kind of syllogism, and deduced from few premises, often from fewer than the regular syllogism; for if any one of these is well known, there is no need to mention it, for the hearer can add it himself. For instance, to prove that Dorieus was the victor in a contest at which the prize was a crown, it is enough to say that he won a victory at the Olympic games; there is no need to add that the prize at the Olympic games is a crown, for everybody knows it. (Freese 1991, 25)

If Aristotle's example were recast as a full syllogism it could be expressed as follows: *The Olympics are games where the prize is a crown; Dorieus has been a victor in the Olympic games; Therefore Doieus has been the victor in games where the prize is a crown.* Unquestionably, for an audience that knows about the prizes in the Olympics (everyone in Aristotle's assessment), the preferred expression of this argument would be the simpler *Dorieus won a crown because he was a victor in the Olympic games.* For purposes of rhetorical stylistics, then, the enthymeme can be defined as a minimum "claim plus premise" unit; the enabling major premise is usually missing. Discussions of the enthymeme often speak of this missing part as "understood" or "supplied" by the audience.[2]

There was however, in antiquity, a competing definition of the enthymeme as a *"sententia* based on contraries" (Quintilian 2001, III 413), and an even more general definition, derived from Isocrates, that the enthymeme is any pithy saying that summarizes an argument (Conley 1984, 171–78). This later definition covers all the "figures of argument" described in chapter ten above as "stylistic cappers," revealing how arguments do indeed ebb and surge around structurally "higher" epitomizing expressions. But the enthymeme as a two-part premise-claim unit does persist in the tradition, and it is, without doubt, a ubiquitous compositional structure. The premise can be signaled with a *because* or some other premise-indicating phrase, or a statement can simply be inferred to function as a premise or a conclusion in relation to another statement, since reasons or conclusions are predictable sentence-to-sentence relations (see above, p. 357).

Enthymemes can also combine in clusters or chains to provide structure for extended passages. Informal logicians have been especially adept at developing diagrams to visualize such structures (e.g., James B. Freeman 1992), structures that are altogether the norm in explicit arguments. A typical example comes from a *New York Times* op-ed piece in which a Harvard government professor laments the decline in enrollments of foreign graduate students in U.S. universities after 9/11.

(1) The costs [of losing foreign graduate students] to the American economy are significant. (2) Educating foreign students is a $13 billion industry. (3) Moreover, the United States does not produce enough home-grown doctoral students in science and engineering to meet our needs. (Nye 2004)

This passage could easily be visualized as a claim followed by two separate premises, one on the loss of revenue and the other on the loss of a needed workforce.

$$(1)$$
$$\nearrow \quad \nwarrow$$
$$(2) \qquad (3)$$

Each premise linked with the claim would constitute its own enthymeme: "The costs [of losing foreign graduate students] to the American economy are significant because educating foreign students is a $13 billion industry" and "The costs [of losing foreign graduate students] to the American economy are significant because the United States does not produce enough home-grown doctoral students in science and engineering." Of course, isolating these arguments reveals some of the problems in Professor Nye's reasoning. He does not, for example, give a time frame for the $13 billion benefit.

Another argument lamenting the loss of foreign graduate students appeared in an edition of *Newsweek* the same week as Professor Nye's op-ed piece. It contains the following passage using a different enthymematic pattern:

(1) The U.S. economy has powered ahead in large part because of the amazing productivity of America's science and technology. (2) Yet that research is now done largely by foreign students. (3) The National Science Board (NSB) documented

this reality last year, finding that 38 percent of doctorate holders in America's science and engineering work force are foreign-born. (Zakaria 2004, 33)

The structure of this argument can be interpreted as a chain of premises and hence of overlapping enthymemes, a multiunit structure called a *sorites* in rhetorical manuals.[3] Sentence (1) claims that the U.S. economy owes its productivity to science and technology. Sentence (2) says that that science and technology research comes "largely" from foreign students, and sentence (3) documents "this reality" by the NSB's statistics on the percentage of the PhD workforce in science and technology who are foreign-born.

(1)

↑

(2)

↑

(3)

Again, problems emerge. Is the economy described in sentence (1) the same as the "research" described in sentence (2)? And are "foreign students" and "foreign-born" PhDs in the work force the same group? Mr. Zakaria's sentence arrangement makes it clear that the information in sentence (3) is meant to support the observation in (2), i.e., "documents this reality." But the compression and category instability here are altogether typical of mass media arguments.

PROGYMNASMATIC PATTERNS

The rhetorical tradition has never been exclusively Aristotelian, with its emphasis on the enthymeme and syllogism. An alternative pedagogy stressed composition in what might be called strategic units of discourse, units that in turn reflected the parts of the full oration, described above. So, for example, since a narrative of the facts of a case was a necessity in most speeches, fledgling rhetors could practice their skills at narration alone, to improve their ability to relate the facts in a forensic case, the deeds of a person to be praised in an epideictic speech, or the circumstances needing remedy in a deliberative speech.

Both the *Rhetorica ad Herennium* and Quinitilian's *Institutio Oratoria* provide evidence for an early tradition of compositional exercises that isolated and practiced the units from which longer discourses could be built (Kennedy 2003, xi). By late antiquity, this exercise sequence, known as the *Progymnasmata*, had been formalized, and its individual exercises became virtual genres in their own right. The most famous of the surviving exercise manuals, the fourth-century CE text by Aphthonius, was recovered and widely used in sixteenth-century Europe (Kennedy 2003, xii). Aphthonius gave clear directions for each exercise and a brief example.

The first exercise in the *progymnasmatic* series required students to retell one of Aesop's fables. The students' ability to narrate would be stretched by the further requirement that they tell the same story backwards or starting in the middle. Another early exercise was the *chreia,* which required the student to take a saying or a deed, or some combination of both, and explain its significance. An example of a mixed *chreia,* interpreting both a speech and an action, used the story of Diogenes' response when he saw a boy behaving badly; he struck the boy's "pedagogue" (the slave entrusted with his training) and said, "Why do you teach him such things?" The ability to expand on an anecdote or pithy saying could be useful in all the argumentative genres, but especially in forensic speeches when the remarks or actions of the defendant were characterized in opposite ways by the two sides arguing the case.

The manuals left little to improvisation in the construction of the *chreia.* Aphthonius prescribed the following sequence of sections: "praise, paraphrase, cause, contrary, comparison, example, testimony of ancients, brief epilogue" (97). The writer opened with a brief encomium *praising,* and conveniently identifying, the author of the saying or performer of the action and then *paraphrased* the saying itself (in words with the correct connotative slant) or retold the action in expanded form. Next followed the *cause,* really an explanation of why the saying was valid or the action significant. Subsequent sections providing the *contrary, comparison, examples,* and *testimony* supported the paraphrase and explanation. In Aphthonius's example, built on Isocrates' saying, "The root of education is bitter but the fruits are sweet," the section offering a *contrary* tells of the losses from fleeing education. The *example* cites Demosthenes, whose labor at self-improvement led to his success, and the *testimony* comes from Hesiod, who observed that the road of virtue is rough. The closing *brief epilogue* thanks the speaker and commends the saying or the action to the audience (98–99).[4] All the *progymnasmatic* exercises came with templates for subsections like those specified for the *chreia.* For some of them, such as the *koinos topos,* an amplification of an evil act, the recommended subroutines were quite complicated: *proemia, contrary, exposition, comparison, digression, rejection of pity, legality, justice, advantage, possibility* (Kennedy 2003, 106–7). Thus, the ancient advice in the world's oldest writing curriculum reinforced the notion that the unit of composition is a several-sentence section, a "chunk" of discourse, that supports a larger discourse purpose. Even if students never used the precise formulas for the individual exercises again, they would learn that the composition of any extended text was a matter of combining smaller, separately formed, and recombinable modules. Composition was an art of *bricolage.*

COMPARISON IN DIFFERENT GRAIN SIZES

One of these modules is worth looking at in more detail to see how a compositional unit could be reduced or expanded. The durable move of making a comparison is defined in the "inventional" side of rhetoric as a line of argument introducing a similarity or dissimilarity, usually for the purpose of characterizing or defining, sometimes for the purpose of evaluating (Melanchthon 1963b, 693–95 on *similia vel paria*). In the progymnasmatic "exercise" tradition, a comparison is a module that can be inserted at any point in a discourse for purposes of support and clarification.

What are the stylistic options for presenting a comparison? Any "grain size" is possible, from a single word or short phrase to an extended passage. All these options are described as different devices in the fourth book of the *Rhetorica ad Herennium*. A comparison condensed into a single word or short phrase is a simile: "I feel like the floor of a taxi" (Egon in *Ghostbusters*). Contrasts or "negating comparisons" tend to stretch into a clause: "Neither can an untrained horse, however well-built by nature, be fit for the services desired of a horse, nor can an uncultivated man, however well-endowed by nature, attain to virtue" ([Cicero] 1981, 379). All the great rhetors of the past have used such brief comparisons, as did Lincoln in his First Inaugural in a section addressed to secessionist-minded Southerners: "Physically speaking, we cannot separate. We cannot remove our respective sections from each other, nor build an impassable wall between them. A husband and wife may be divorced, and go out of the presence, and beyond the reach of each other: but the different parts of our country cannot do this" (Reid 1988, 457). And they have continued in use; Adlai Stevenson on the excesses of anti-communism: "Communism is abhorrent. It is strangulation of the individual; it is death for the soul... Yet, as I have said before, we must take care not to burn down the barn to kill the rats" (Safire 1997, 72).

A comparison can also stretch into a multisentence section. These are the so-called epic similes found in Homer or the "Ciceronian comparisons" found in his orations in the many passages using detailed parallels structured by the connectives *uti... item* or *ita... ut/as... so*. Here is the example from the *Rhetorica ad Herennium*:

> Let us imagine a player on the lyre who has presented himself on the stage, magnificently garbed, clothed in a gold-embroidered robe, with purple mantle interlaced in various colours, wearing a golden crown illumined with large gleaming jewels, and holding a lyre covered with golden ornaments and set off with ivory. Further, he has a personal beauty, presence, and stature that impose dignity. If, when by these means he has roused a great expectation in the public, he should in the silence he has created suddenly give utterance to a rasping voice, and this should be accompanied by a repulsive gesture, he is the more forcibly thrust off in derision and scorn, the richer his adornment and the higher the hopes he has raised. *In the same way*, a man of high station, endowed with great and opulent resources, and abounding in all the gifts of fortune and the emoluments of nature, if he yet lacks virtue and the arts that teach virtue, will so much the more forcibly in derision and scorn be cast from all association with good men, the richer he is in the other advantages, the greater his distinction, and the higher the hopes he has raised. ([Cicero] 1981, 381; italics added)

This example hinges around the connective "in the same way," the pivot for expanded versions of the two sides of the comparison. Such lengthy arguments from similarity were more common in older prose, but they are still in use. The "moral" so far as passage construction is concerned is that, no matter how contracted or expanded, the comparison, and other compositional modules like it, constitutes a unit in the hierarchical structure of a passage.

Paragraphs

In the late nineteenth century, scholars once again became interested in multisentence discourse units under the notion of the *paragraph* as a written and essentially visual unit of discourse. Though the *paragraphos,* the mark on the side of a manuscript to indicate a topic change, is an ancient device (Parkes 1993, 305), the paragraph symbol, and later the practice of indentation, evolved, as did other marks of punctuation, into a term for the unit created for the mark. Neither classical nor early modern rhetoric had any notion of a generic "paragraph" as a unit of discourse, though speakers certainly segmented a speech into units larger than the sentence.

The paragraph as it is now understood was largely a creation of the late-nineteenth-century Scottish psychologist and language theorist Alexander Bain. In his influential *English Composition and Rhetoric* (1866), he identified four "types" of paragraphs which are really genres: *description, narration, exposition, argument.*[5] Bain's types were not descriptive of actual practice so much as they were prescriptions for short writing assignments put to use in the burgeoning writing classrooms of late-nineteenth-century U.S. universities, where his works and those of similar-minded teachers were popular.

Almost one hundred years later, in the 1960s, compositionists initiated several ingenious attempts at paragraph description. One influential effort came from the linguist/rhetorician Alton Becker (1965), who proposed two main types of paragraphs: first, a topic/restriction/illustration pattern that begins with a simple proposition, restates it to clarify, distinguish, or limit the point, and then "illustrates" it with examples or analogies; second, a problem/solution paragraph that first states a problem or effect and then provides a solution or explanation. Actual paragraphs fitting these descriptions are not difficult to find, but these two patterns are far from exhausting potential paragraph species.

A similar perspective on paragraph types was adopted by Walter Nash in *Designs in Prose* (1980). Nash justified his investigation of types with an analogy: "just as graphic design has its basic shapes which are fundamental to the most elaborate compositions, so the rhetoric of expository prose is reducible to a number of primary stratagems, or, as we shall now call them, 'designs'" (9). Nash identified four basic rhetorical designs typically found in paragraphs—*Step, Stack, Chain,* and *Balance*—and he allowed for the possibility of mixed structures.[6] Combining the insights of Becker, Nash, and others produces the following patterns for multisentence and often paragraph-long units readily recognized by readers and listeners:

Sequence structure: Any narration ordered chronologically or any description ordered spatially, provided that it is adequately signposted, will be readily perceived by an audience. Any announced enumeration (e.g., there are three reasons: first, second, third) would also fit under this pattern.

Question/Answer: A paragraph with this structure opens by posing a question and then answering it. This pattern was identified in the rhetorical manuals as the figure *hypophora* (see above, p. 299).

Generalization plus support: This paragraph opens with a general claim and subsequent sentences provide supporting examples or details.

Antithetical structure: Here the speaker develops one point but then contradicts or qualifies it, either devoting the remaining paragraph to the contradiction/ alternative/ contrast. or returning in the conclusion to the opening position. Such a paragraph has, in effect, a hinge in the middle, usually a dramatic adversative which swings it in the opposite direction.

None of the proponents of such paragraph taxonomies ever claimed an exhaustive identification of the possibilities. They recognized that many paragraphs fitting no named pattern were still perceived as coherent and, indeed, all kinds of structures can be improvised so long as readers and listeners find the sentence-to-sentence string coherent. An overall explanation for why coherent discourse is sometimes created in recognizable modules and sometimes not requires a return to the oldest description of types of prose in the rhetorical tradition.

Parataxis and Hypotaxis

An ancient distinction between two kinds of movement or organization in prose style can be found in Book III of Aristotle's *Rhetoric.* There Aristotle distinguishes prose that is, in George Kennedy's translation, "strung on" (*eiromene*) from prose that is "turned down" (*katestrammene*; Kennedy 1991, 239). Aristotle considered the "strung-on" style unpleasant because it did not forecast a destination for listeners. He preferred the "turned down" style because it gave hearers the sense of a coming ending, an impression he considered more "pleasant because opposed to the unlimited and because the hearer always thinks he has hold of something, in that it is always limited by itself, whereas to have nothing to foresee or attain is unpleasant" (240). Aristotle also thought that this preferred style was more easily understood and remembered.

In later Greek stylistics, this difference acquired the labels *parataxis* versus *hypotaxis* and further precise distinctions. In *paratactic* prose, clauses are loosely connected, creating a lopping discourse of *here's another thing and another thing and another thing.* In hypotactic prose, sentences are connected by the interclausal relations described in the preceding chapter. Paratactic prose typically coordinates its consecutive sentences; hypotactic prose subordinates them. Paratactic prose occurs more frequently in narrative and explanation, and hypotactic prose more frequently in explicit arguments.[7] The key difference between these types is sometimes described as an absence of conjunctions in parataxis and their presence in hypotaxis. (For an excellent discussion of these two patterns with contemporary prose examples, see Lanham 1983.)

The ancient difference between parataxis and hypotaxis can also be described using the methods for achieving coherence outlined in the previous chapter. Paratactic prose relies more heavily on topic/comment organization or on background knowledge to cover jumps. Listeners or readers have some sense of the discourse topic, but they cannot predict what will be said about that topic. The following sample passage exhibiting parataxis comes from Clarence Darrow's closing argument in the notorious Leopold and Loeb case in 1920s Chicago (see above, p. 67). Darrow argued before a single judge to save his young clients from the death penalty. In a summation that ebbed and flowed around several themes and strategies, Darrow at one point resumed his complaints about the prosecution.

> I have heard in the last six weeks nothing but the cry for blood. I have heard from the office of the state's attorney only ugly hate. I have heard precedents quoted which would be a disgrace to a savage race. I have seen a court urged almost to the point of threats to hang two boys, in the face of science, in the face of philosophy, in the face of humanity, in the face of experience, in the faces of all the better and more humane thought of the age (Lief, Caldwell, and Bycel 1998, 166)

With opening repetition (*anaphora*) and the consistent topic/subject of the speaker himself, this string of four sentences is certainly coherent. As far as interclausal relations are concerned, however, the sentences are only weakly related to each other as additional items in a catalogue of the offenses that Darrow has experienced during the trial; the most likely transition word that might be placed between each sentence is *and*. In keeping with Aristotle's observation about the open-endedness of paratactic organization, it is not clear from the first sentence where the rest of this paragraph will go, or that it will end up with the series of offenses that closes the final sentence.[8]

A hypotactic passage, in contrast, relies on semantic relations, either "understood" or marked. Darrow switched to this pattern in another part of his summation.

> Why did they kill little Bobby Franks? [**nonpremises**] Not for money, not for spite; not for hate. [**replacement/instead**] They killed him [**premise**] [**comparison embedded**] as they might kill a spider or fly, for the experience. [**Addition**] They killed him [**premise**] because they were made that way. [**premise for the preceding premise**] Because somewhere in the infinite processes that go to the making up of the boy or the man something slipped, and [**consequence/as a result**] those unfortunate lads sit here hated, despised, outcasts, with the community shouting for their blood. (Lief, Caldwell, and Bycel 1998, 173)

This sequence of sentences fulfills one of the standard paragraph models noted above, by asking a key question in any criminal trial—what was the motive?—and then going on to answer. Listeners have clear expectations raised by that opening question and, according to Aristotle, they are more satisfied when they know where a passage is going. Darrow proceeds to replace the predictable motives for murder with two explanations that support his overall "diseased brain" defense. Leopold and Loeb killed because they wanted the experience of killing and because they were "made that way," a claim supported in turn by the further explanation that "something" had "slipped" in their development. Their current desperate state, on trial for their lives, follows inevitably from some hereditary or cosmic determinism. The interclause relations that subordinate one sentence to another in this passage are either clearly signposted or easily inferred.

The loping, additive passage grammar of parataxis and the often explicit, hierarchically related passage structure of hypotaxis provide opposing regimes of prose organization. Rhetors typically alter between the two, now suspending their audience in wandering chains and digressions, now constraining their attention, and agreement, in tightly connected sequences. These two basic patterns can also be combined, as a hypotactic premise-conclusion or claim-support spine opens up for the variable lingering of restatement or comparison or exemplification. The desirability of these mixed structures will be covered in the final chapter under the summum bonum of rhetorical style, amplification.

Metadiscourse: Figures of Discourse Management

As any discourse, overall, is written in sections, whether in the prescribed subroutines of the progymnasmatic exercises or in the six sections of the full oration, another question about passage construction inevitably occurs. How are the transitions between sections handled? This question is not a trivial one of "information management"; it has to do instead with how the audience is guided through a text so that they experience the proper effects in the proper order. Creating an awareness of higher-order structure is an especially acute problem for the speaker facing an audience that cannot "turn back the page." It is often crucial that listeners become aware of the progress of the argument and of the large conceptual blocks building the overall case. It is no wonder that contemporary speakers resort to PowerPoint to display their organization visually.

The manual writers were acutely aware of this problem of building levels of structure in the audience's mind, and they were also conscious of the limits of human attention and memory. The overall plan of the six-part oration, described above, had built into it a section, the *partitio*, that defines the key issue and forecasts the coming parts, on the assumption that listeners will retain these parts longer if they expect them. The *peroratio* also, the last part, was designed to include a recapitulation of the key points in order to mass their persuasive force.

But the issue of higher-order structure was also handled from a stylistic perspective in the form of special devices identified not only to handle organizational problems but also to take persuasive advantage of them. These devices appear in the catalogs of the figures, dispersed in alphabetic lists. But they belong together as Cicero so succinctly grouped them in *De Oratore* by recommending "[a] proposition of what you are about to say, transition from what has been said, and retrogression" (Cicero 1970, 252). The first of these is the forecasting statement, the ***praeparatio***, where the rhetor not only announces the coming sections but also explains ahead of time their purpose and sometimes even their intended effect (Quintilian 1921, III 384). Older works often feature such lengthy formal announcements of coming content. Charles Darwin, for example, sets up the second volume of *The Descent of Man* with a *praeparatio*: "In the following chapters, I shall treat of the secondary sexual characters in animals of all classes, and shall endeavour in each case to apply the principles explained in the present chapter. The lowest classes will detain us for a very short time, but the higher animals, especially birds, must be treated at considerable length" (1871, 242). This passage prepares readers for the material to be covered in several chapters and explains both the sequence of the points Darwin will cover and the relative proportion of attention he will give them. The ascending expectation he creates assists his overall argument, in this case for the role of sexual selection in evolution. Such forecasting moves have by no means disappeared, as the following opening demonstrates:

> This review begins by describing some dramatic examples. After next exploring the depth and underpinnings of differences in how people see themselves versus others, the review closes with the hope that greater insight into these differences may help people understand themselves and each other and thereby may alleviate some aspects of social misunderstanding and conflict. (Pronin 2008, 1177)

Readers of this "preparation" know ahead of time what attitude they should have at the end. Such a disclosure requires a relatively uncommitted audience and a less than controversial subject, both conditions fulfilled in this passage quoted from a research review in *Science*.

The audience's expectations could also be controlled more precisely by ***dinumeratio***, (Cicero 1992, 164) a numbered list of the individual points to come. Peacham defines this device in 1593, under its Greek label *eutrepismus*, as "a forme of speech, which doth not only number the partes before they be said, but also doth also order those partes, and maketh them plaine by a kind of definition, or declaration" (129). Political speakers find this forecasting by number indispensable. A typical example occurs early in Nixon's 1971 State of the Union Address, when he announces, "Tonight I shall present to the Congress six great goals," and each goal then detailed is prefaced by its number: "the second great goal," "the third great goal," and so on (Windt 1983, 151ff). Jimmy Carter took this device as far as it could go when in one of his speeches on energy he listed the ten fundamental principles of his proposed energy policy (240–41). Somewhat different, and much more powerful in argument, is ***expeditio***, the device of setting out numbered options and then eliminating all but the one preferred ([Cicero] 1981, 40).[9] Nixon uses this elimination logic in his speech justifying military action in Cambodia, 1970: "Now confronted with this situation [supplies coming from Cambodia], we have three options. First we can do nothing....Our second choice is to provide massive military assistance to Cambodia itself...Our third choice is to go to the heart of the trouble" (Windt 1983, 138). Almost always, the final option is the preferred option.

Transitio, shepherding the listener or reader from one section to another, appears in the earliest set of figures. The *Rhetorica ad Herennium* defines it as "the figure which briefly recalls what has been said, and likewise briefly sets forth what is to follow next" ([Cicero] 1981, 317–19), hence both summing up and forecasting. The *transitio* can be a substantial multisentence discourse unit that does important interpretive and audience management work. Such devices are especially necessary in long, complex arguments that marshal different strains of evidence of different degrees of strength. Again, Darwin is a master of these moves. To sample once more from *The Descent of Man* (1871), he follows quotations from Huxley with the evaluative directions: "After the foregoing statements made by such high authorities, it would be superfluous on my part to give a number of borrowed details, shewing that the embryo of man closely resembles that of other mammals. It may, however, be added that the human embryo likewise resembles certain low forms when adult in various points of structure. For instance... ." (16).

Figures such as *praeparatio* and *transitio* have been rediscovered by modern discourse analysts and grouped under the useful name of *metadiscourse*, that is, discourse about the discourse. In terms of M. A. K. Halliday's functional linguistics, these devices fulfill the *textual* function of managing text as text (1993, 29). The category *metadiscourse* has been expanded by some discourse analysts to include simple transition words and all the hedges, evaluative phrases, and touches of emphasis by which the rhetor orients the audience to the material (Williams 1989, 93–99). Here the term is reserved for the phrases and sentences and even short paragraphs that show the relations among larger sections of discourse and thereby manage the experience of the text. Beyond the level of analysis into compositional units, at the higher level of imposing overall discourse structure, rhetorical stylistics hands off its jurisdiction to the canon of arrangement within the rhetorical tradition and to the descriptions of genres available in different disciplines.

Summary

How is the thread of sentences, composed and consumed like a strand of spaghetti, turned into a text with foregrounded parts and discrete units? Speakers may use voice dynamics to segment their discourse. Writers can use the visual resources of font and formatting changes. But both speakers and writers have to create higher-order structures in an argument from essentially linear input. Creating and communicating such structures was a focus of attention in rhetoric. Rhetorical manuals are filled with descriptions of multisentence "compositional" modules, built from the bottom up, and they give advice on both local and overall strategies of arrangement, imposed top-down.

To begin with compositional units beyond the clause, certainly the most important in persuasive argumentation are the syllogism and enthymeme, packets of premise and conclusion that "reason" with audiences and that derive their material from the inventional topics. (The expanded version of these units, the epicheireme, is covered in the next chapter.) Less well known are the units of composition prescribed in the rhetorical exercises known as the Progymnasmata. Students wrote by filling templates, and in the process they practiced constructing modules of content (*paraphrase, definition, contrary, testimony,* etc.) that could be endlessly recombined. One such module is the comparison, which can be condensed to a phrase or expanded to a passage. The "descendants" of these exercises, and of the notion of preset formulas for multisentence passages, are the paragraph types that composition teachers from Bain to Becker have promoted.

With or without recognizable compositional units, a wandering string of sentences can also be structured by the basic patterns of parataxis and hypotaxis. In parataxis, sentences in sequence lope along in equal importance; in hypotaxis, they are subordinated to each other in hierarchically arranged structures. Exactly how sentences are related as equal or subordinate requires construal with the interclause relations covered in the previous chapter. Finally, the stream of text can be managed by interrupting directions known as *metadiscourse*. Here once again the rhetorical manuals stepped in with figures of speech prescribing devices of forecasting, transitioning, and summarizing, signposts for how to segment and understand an unfolding discourse that are actually parts of the argument.

NOTES

1. In a pesky distortion of nomenclature, an odd transformation occurred in some later figure manuals turning the *syllogismus* into a figure of amplification. So Peacham defines this device as "a forme of speech by which the Orator amplifieth a matter by coniecture, that is, by expressing some signes or circumstances of a matter, which circumstances be of three sorts, either going before it, annexed with it, or following after it" (1593, 179). He cites the conventional example of Virgil's description of Polyphemus carrying a pine tree as a walking stick and striding through the sea, so that "by this we coniecture what a great bodie he had" (180). Peacham is obviously recalling Quintilian's method of amplifying by inference (see chapter 18); since this method requires a premise-conclusion pairing of sorts, there is some rationale for his labeling.

2. Aristotle's comments on the enthymeme continue in Book I chapter 2 and in Book II chapter 22. Some scholars maintain that enthymemes concern only matters of probability, though Aristotle says in the latter chapter as part of his discussion of the enthymeme, "We should also base our arguments upon probabilities as well as upon certainties" (Roberts 1984, 140).

3. The *sorites* is defined in rhetorical and dialectical manuals as a series of overlapping syllogisms, where the conclusion of one becomes the premise of the next. This structure is identical to

the telescoping arguments identified in informal logic/critical thinking textbooks (Hoskins 1935, 12–13; Melanchthon 1963b, 624–26).

4. The *chreia* became a genre in its own right. One of its descendants is the devotional genre of commentary on the saying or action of a saint. It has an odd descendant in the essay tests like those required on the MCAT in which students are given a quotation and asked to write on it. In reduced form it also has its place when an authority is quoted in an argument and that "saying" has to be harnessed as a premise.

5. Bain actually abandoned this approach in his expanded 1890 edition of *English Composition and Rhetoric*. There he addressed what he called the intellectual and emotional qualities of style (see Lunsford, 1998, 222). Bain was part of a late-nineteenth-century trend that reduced rhetoric to the study of style.

6. Nash defines his paragraph types as follows (1980, 9–19):

The Step: a sequential listing of clauses typical in instructions, descriptions, and narratives. Readers perceive that the sentences are ordered by some chronological or spatial principle.

The Stack: Here the first sentence announces a topic and subsequent sentences diverge or converge. Unknowingly, Nash was reprising Becker's TRI structure, and his examples are argumentative (with premises and conclusions present), not purely expository.

The Chain: This paragraph strings sentences along with only strong topic/comment connections. Nash's description notes the means, but he does not use the language of T/C organization.

The Balance: This kind of paragraph alternates between a thesis and an antithesis. It has a major turn at some point, signaled by an adversative (e.g., *on the other hand, but, yet*), and after a statement of this contrary view, it may or may not return to its opening position. The epigraph to this chapter follows this pattern.

7. In the mid-twentieth-century revival of composition studies, Francis and Bonniejean Christensen (1977) rediscovered the paratactic-versus-hypotactic difference in passage progression. They extrapolated from their empirically derived principles of sentence construction to principles of passage construction: just as the modification within a sentence could be embedded at different levels, so the sentences in a passage could be embedded or subordinated in relation to each other. Here is a sample paragraph that can illustrate a Christensen analysis. It comes from the middle of a short article in *Scientific American* on violent animal rights protestors.

> (1) Many worry that U.S. activists are importing tactics used in 25 years of British violence. (2) Animal-rights terrorism there has caused more than $200 million in property damage over the years and cost millions in policing and security annually, says Colin Blakemore, director of the University of Oxford's Center for Cognitive Neuroscience. (3) Blakemore himself became a target 12 years ago while using kittens in vision research. (4) A razor package injured his secretary, and his three children required 24-hour security after kidnapping threats and bomb scares. (4) Blakemore was beaten, his home was vandalized, and massive demonstrations against him at one point brought out 200 police in riot gear. (4) He still makes no public move without police escort. (Turville-Heitz 2000, 32).

The Christensens would describe this paragraph as a sequence of sentences at different levels of embedding. The first sentence connects U.S. "animal rights" terrorism, discussed in a previous paragraph, to British animal rights violence. The second more particular sentence specifies the scope of the British violence. Sentence 3 then descends to a single target of the British violence (who happens to have just been cited in the comment sentence of the previous section, making for an easy tie-in). The next three sentences, all at a still deeper level of embedding, list specific instances of actions and threats against Blakemore and his family. These details are the factual basis for the argument here characterizing the activities of animal rights terrorists. A diagram of the structure formed from the successive independent clauses would look like the following.

(1) Many worry that U.S. activists are importing tactics used in…British violence
   (2) Animal-rights terrorism there has caused…and cost…says Colin Blakemore…
      (3) Blakemore himself became a target….
         (4) A razor package injured his secretary
         (4) his three children required security
         (4) Blakemore was beaten
         (4) his home was vandalized
         (4) massive demonstrations against him…brought out 200 police
         (4) He still makes no public move without a police escort.

The Christensen diagram reveals the mixed hypotactic and paratactic segments in most functional prose, and this mixture can, in turn, be resolved by the sources of coherence described above.

8. Predictably, the passages in which Darrow recounts Leopold and Loeb's activities during the crime are paratactic. Darrow chooses only those events that show the most inexplicable behavior by the defendants, part of his defense that they had "diseased brains"—e.g., driving around with the body in the car in daylight and stopping for dinner (Lief, Caldwell, and Bycel 1998, 176).

9. Johnson *concludes* his "War on Poverty" State of the Union speech in 1964 with an ambitious "We must advance toward this goal in 1964 in at least 10 different ways, not as partisans but as patriots" (Windt 1983, 60). The numbered specification follows prefacing each point: first second, third…tenth. Nixon sets up five questions to answer in his 1969 address on the Vietnam War (128), but he does not number them.

18

*Thus in rhetoric it is emphasized that the orator
should see what is good in a case, what bad, and he
should augment the good things and the bad
discreetly cover, and he should overwhelm with
amplification of the good things.
[Sic in rhetoricis praecipitur, ut orator videat quid in
causa boni sit, quid mali, bona ornet, et mala
sapienter tegat et amplificatione bonorum obruat.]*
MELANCHTHON,
Erotemata Dialectices, *1547*

AMPLIFICATION

AS MELANCHTHON'S "RHETORIC in a nutshell" makes clear, the need to select and amplify the most persuasive elements in a case drives a specifically *rhetorical* stylistics. To amplify an element means to endow it with stylistic prominence so that it acquires conceptual importance in the discourse and salience in the minds of the audience. The element amplified can be anything from a key word to a factual detail, a telling image to an abstract concept, an individual line of argument to a structural feature of the entire discourse. Deciding, or simply "knowing," what elements will hurt or help with a particular audience, rhetors then have to translate their intentions or instincts into linguistic tactics. How can a potentially damaging element be minimized? How can the importance and benefit of another element be heightened?

Making an element important stylistically is the work of *auxesis* (Greek) or *amplificatio* (Latin). Making an element unimportant stylistically is the work of *meiosis* (Greek) or *diminutio* (Latin). Since any element not amplified is minimized by default, amplification, not surprisingly, always received the greatest attention in the manuals, while advice on its opposite often amounted to "do the opposite." The broad strategy of amplification necessarily includes methods of manipulating sentence structure to put certain words or phrases in positions of emphasis (see above, p. 205). But amplification is a much broader notion than emphasis.

The traditional advice on amplification can be divided into two great strands outlined by Cicero in *De Partitione Oratoria* (1992, 353–55; see also Montefusco 2004). The first groups methods, often particularized under certain figures of speech, for making an element more important through localized devices of heightening. Quintilian offers the best summary of these methods, which range from choosing extreme words to inviting aggrandizing inferences. The second strand concerns amplification in the sense of copiousness, of having more to say. On this tactic, Erasmus produced the greatest single work. Both these strands persist in rhetorical stylistics, from classical treatises to early modern manuals, from eighteenth-century rationalizations of rhetoric to nineteenth- and twentieth-century composition textbooks. In both its senses of heightening and copiousness, amplification offers a fitting summary to a rhetorical stylistics considered at the word, sentence, interactive, and passage levels.

Quintilian's Methods of Amplification

In the eighth book of the *Institutio Oratoria,* Quintilian recommends five strategies for achieving amplification, each with subvarieties. The first method refers to heightening through strategic word choices (1921, III 263). In the sixteenth century, Peacham labeled this single device *auxesis* and defined it aptly as "putting a greater word for a less" (Peacham 1593, 167). In Peacham's examples, a writer enhancing through this method calls a *proud man* a *Lucifer,* a *drunkard* a *swine,* an *angry man, mad,* an *honest man, a Saint,* and *good music, heavenly harmony* (167). As he observes, many of these substitutions are accomplished by tropes: antonomasia in the case of *Lucifer,* metaphor in the case of *swine,* and hyperbole in the case of *heavenly harmony.* The basic tactic behind *auxesis* as an isolated figure of speech might be described as finding a term with associations that push in the direction of the assessment the rhetor wants. Quintilian would approve Peacham's examples, but he also recommends highlighting the very process of word substitution, citing the example of Cicero denouncing Verres: "I have brought before you, judges, not a thief, but a plunderer; not an adulterer, but a ravisher; not a mere committer of sacrilege, but the enemy of all religious observance and all holy things" (1921, III 263).

A second strategy of amplification, or really group of strategies, involves series construction. An item is heightened when it is placed last in a series that builds up to it as an end point, a culmination, the possessor in the highest degree of whatever determines the series in the first place (see chapter 11 on Series). A prosecutor, for example, can list the past crimes of a defendant in such a way that they form not merely a list but an ascending series, each one worse than the preceding, so that the final item, the one at issue in the current indictment, is the worst of all: "He has been arrested for breaking and entering, resisting arrest, armed burglary, and aggravated assault." Imagine the loss of effectiveness, and the corresponding effect of diminishing, if this passage ran the other way: "He has been arrested for aggravated assault, armed burglary, resisting arrest, and breaking and entering."

In a subtler version of this method, the rhetor constructs a series, but then tops it by bringing in an item that is somehow beyond the series. Since series classify, to place an element beyond a series amounts to saying that it escapes classification. As an example of topping, Quintilian cites an often repeated line from Cicero: "It is a sin to bind a Roman citizen, a crime to scourge him, little short of the most unnatural murder to put him to death; what then shall I call his crucifixion?" (III 265). This series of offenses against Roman citizens proceeds in order of increasing offensiveness from binding to scourging to executing. Crucifixion does not even belong in this "normal" series of punishments, itself serialized from sin to crime to little short of murder, and beyond that to something unnameable. Hence its horror is amplified. Yet another version of going beyond or topping a series is a formula like the following that Quintilian provides, quoting Virgil: "Than whom there was not one more fair/Saving Laurentian Turnus." Or to use an example with modern resonance: "He was best pitcher ever—except for Cy Young."

Topping the "topping" strategy, the rhetor enacts amazement before the magnitude of the object contemplated. Having in effect run up against the end of a series that the subject still exceeds, amazement finds itself stunned into repetition: "You beat your mother. What more need I say? You beat your mother" (1921, III 267). The point here is that the element is so great it is incapable of further amplification. Amazement can also be struck dumb, left speechless. But since silence itself is liable to misinterpretation, the rhetor must verbalize speechlessness: "Words fail me." Lyndon Johnson, speaking to Congress for the first time after Kennedy's assassination, marked, opportunistically, the inadequacy of language in the face of the tragedy: "No words are sad enough to express our sense of loss. No words are strong enough to express our determination to continue the forward thrust of America that he began" (Windt 1983, 53). Cicero's famous example also uses this device, "What then shall I call his crucifixion?" Commenting on this passage, Quintilian explains: "[Cicero] had already exhausted his vocabulary of crime, words must necessarily fail him to describe something still worse" (III 265). Words fail because, the audience infers, the element is so extreme—so heinous and egregious, or so rapturous and wonderful—that no one has encountered and found words for it before.

Quintilian's third device of amplification recruits a comparison for the sake of inflating or deflating. Quintilian cites Cicero again, this time castigating Mark Antony for an outrageous display of drunkenness in the Senate: "If this had befallen you at the dinner-table in the midst of your amazing potations, who would not have thought it unseemly? But it occurred at an assembly of the Roman people" (269). In other words, it's bad enough at home, but it's worse in public. The tactic here is obvious and frequently used: the comparison of choice in political invective for last sixty years has been and still is Hitler. Richard Gere used comparison to another figure with the "topping" strategy: "A vicious terrorist is out there. It is not Osama bin Laden, it is AIDS. The biggest threat to our livelihood, our happiness is AIDS."[1]

The fourth tactic of amplification, heightening through reasoning (*ratiocinatio*, a problematic label even to Quinitilian), involves leading the audience to make an inference that results in an amplified assessment of something else: "One thing is magnified in order to effect a corresponding augmentation elsewhere, and it is by reasoning that our hearers are then led on from the first point to the second which we desire to emphasise" (1921, III 271). Quintilian explains how Cicero, in that same vituperation on Antony's drunkenness, comments on Antony's strength and size: "You with such a throat, such flanks, such burly strength in every limb of your prize-fighter's body" (271). These details lead listeners to infer that Antony must have consumed a truly prodigious amount of wine in order for someone with such a strong physique to become as drunk as he was.

This tactic of heightening by directing inferences was considered especially useful in epideictic arguments of praise or blame. Any victory, in sports or war or any other competition, can be amplified by pointing out its difficulty. To enhance the heroism of an army, for example, the skill and size of the opposing army is emphasized. So praise for the tactical brilliance and ferocity of the German army during the Battle of the Bulge, while no doubt well supported, nevertheless has the effect of amplifying the courage and determination of the Allied forces arrayed against them.

ANALYSIS WITH QUINTILIAN'S METHODS

How Quintilian's tactics work in combination can be seen in the following two sentences, which open news stories appearing on the same day in two of the largest-circulation daily newspapers in the United States.

Washington Post:
More than 200,000 allied troops smashed deep into Iraq and Kuwait yesterday, encountering little resistance and capturing thousands of Iraqi soldiers in the most sweeping armored attack since World War II. (Atkinson and Claiborne 1991)
New York Times:
More than 2,000 American air assault troops plunged at least 50 miles into Iraq at first light today in the largest helicopter-borne operation in military history. (Kifner 1991)

These two sentences report on the start of the ground invasion of Iraq during the Gulf War of 1991, and while their content differs, both noticeably use the same structures to present facts of the event. It is unlikely that the writers for these two newspapers saw one another's leads. Yet under the same rhetorical pressures they produced similar sentences, displaying many of the tactics for heightening a subject.

Both sentences begin by taking a large number and "topping it" in an unspecified way to create the impression of a substantial quantity beyond an end point: *more than* 200,000 *troops* and *more than* 2,000 *helicopters*. It is relatively easy to heighten an amount by claiming that it is "more than" the nearest lower rounded number, or, conversely, to diminish it by claiming that it is less than the nearest higher rounded number. Imagine the difference if these sentences had opened "Fewer than 250,000 troops" or "fewer than 2,100 air assault troops." Yet these formulations would be as accurate as the ones provided.

To further establish the evaluative *auxesis*, both sentences end the same way with a comparison, a benchmark so that the size of the force can be placed historically and hence earn its heightening by contrast. For the *Washington Post* the event is "the most sweeping armored attack since World War II," and for the *Times* the helicopter assault is "the largest helicopter-borne operation in military history." Perhaps the possibility of making the latter claim as a superlative (*the largest*) led the *Times* to focus on the helicopter assault in its opening rather than on the ground offensive, though it is also likely that both these benchmarks came from copy provided to media outlets in a military briefing.

Supporting the *auxesis* by suggesting the forcefulness of the attack, and hence by inference the resistance, both writers also use active verbs with dramatic connotations of power and penetration. In the *Post* the "allied troops *smashed* deep into Iraq and Kuwait"; in the *Times,* the "assault troops *plunged* at least 50 miles into Iraq." These are word choices that press in the direction of heightening. And with a conventional use of the trope *synecdoche*, grouping many individuals into a single entity, the grammatical subjects of both sentences (*allied troops* and *air assault troops*), are transformed into unified agents performing the same feats of *plunging* and *smashing* simultaneously, though of course many separate and coordinated actions are needed to achieve a military advance. But a unified agent and action are more powerful.

When further issues of word choice are examined, differences between the two versions begin to show. The more dramatic *Post* opening uses two participial phrases (*encountering* and *capturing*) as attendant but subordinate actions to the main verb *smashed*, making the whole more action-packed. The *Times'* first sentence, on the other hand, extends beyond the main predication with adverbial phrases of time and place (*at least fifty miles into Iraq at first light today*) which are inherently less dramatic and even somewhat *meiotic* or diminishing (*at least fifty miles*), though the somewhat archaic phrase *at first light* (a literal rendering of the Latin phrase for "at dawn," *prima luce*) does bring an ennobling connotation into the mix.

Both writers, however, were under the same rhetorical pressure to convey a sense of the momentous, of great events happening. They do not necessarily have a specific evaluative or deliberative claim to make about the beginning of the ground invasion. The notion of a rhetorical stance toward a subject does not necessitate a specific thesis, but it does require a specific attitude, and, almost inevitably in newspapers, the attitude to be conveyed is that of the amplified importance of whatever is being reported.

Copia and Presence: *Multa de Multis*

Quintilian's fifth and final strategy is one that became an end in itself in early modern style manuals. Quintilian called it amplification through **congeries**: "accumulation of words and sentences identical in meaning may also be regarded under the head of *amplification*" (1921, III 279). In addition to accumulation through repeating or restating, any method of staying on a topic by finding relevant material came to be grouped under the term *copia* or abundance. The subtitle above represents Agricola's version of this virtue, "multa dicimus de multis," literally "we say many things about many things" (1967, 400). Erasmus expanded the meanings of *copia* as a synonym for amplification, and he devoted the most successful pedagogical manual of the sixteenth century to this one summative stylistic norm for effective persuasion. By the end of *De Utraque Verborum ac Rerum Copia* (first edition 1512), after sections pulling together advice dispersed in other rhetorical manuals, Erasmus transformed amplification through accumulation into a great vortex pulling in all the other elements of rhetorical theory.

Copia is a complex construct in humanist language theory. It encompasses the highest standard of eloquence for an orator, a matter of bearing and training as well as linguistic performance. Among its many meanings, it defined a pedagogical method for language instruction.[2] Students learning Latin wrote different versions of the same statement in order to increase their command of vocabulary (through synonyms) and syntax (through alternate phrasing). Erasmus illustrated *copia* in varying by producing 200 versions of the same sentence: *Your letter has delighted me much.* The ability to say essentially the same thing in different forms can assist persuasion in at least two ways: first, with variants to choose from, the rhetor can select the best possible for a particular context; second, the rhetor can retain several of the variants, producing amplification through accumulating restatement, the second strand.

The rationale behind amplification through *copia* differs from that for Quintilian's preceding four tactics. The others amplify by creating salience. This tactic amplifies by creating presence. These effects certainly overlap, but there are also differences. To use an analogy from visual perception, Quintilian's tactics of amplification are like placing something in the center of a visual frame and highlighting it with the maximum in illumination, color saturation, and clarity of focus. This fifth tactic, on the other hand, is like filling the visual frame with one important element to the exclusion of everything else. Nothing else can be seen because the thing emphasized completely fills the visual field.

A reprise of this visual sense of amplification is the concept of *presence*, defined by the twentieth-century rhetorical theorists Chaim Perelman and Lucie Olbrechts-Tyteca (1969) and elevated into a single unifying rhetorical principle by Alan Gross and Ray Dearin (2003, 135–52). The two Belgian originators of the concept stressed the importance of the rhetor's ability to direct the audience's attention to helpful elements and, correspondingly, to make others disappear. Presence is, in the first place, the result of selection. As they explain, "By the very fact of selecting certain elements and presenting them to the audience, their importance and pertinency to the discussion are implied. Indeed such a choice endows these elements with a *presence*, which is an essential factor in argumentation" (1969, 116). Perelman and Olbrechts-Tyteca also base their notion of how presence works on observations from the psychologist Jean Piaget. In his experiments on perception, Piaget demonstrated that when people make assessments against a standard—comparing, for instance, the lengths of different sticks—any item they see more often is overestimated. Perelman and Olbrechts-Tyteca reinforce this point with a Chinese fable about a king who spares an ox on its way to sacrifice and orders a sheep to be slaughtered instead. The king confesses that he did so "because he could see the ox but not the sheep" (116). The conclusion about persuasive strategies is clear:

> Accordingly one of the preoccupations of a speaker is to make present, by verbal magic alone, what is actually absent but what he considers important to his argument or, by making them more present, to enhance the value of some of the elements of which one has actually been made conscious (1969, 117).

ERASMIAN METHODS FOR COPIA

Erasmus' *De Copia* is divided into two parts, the first dealing with word- and sentence-level devices that produce variant expressions by using certain figures of speech. Erasmus recommends *synonymia*, for example, piling up cognate words to express the same notion (1963, 19; see Adamson et al. 2007, 23–26), and *aequipollentia*, making a point by denying its opposite: *He was wide awake; he was not asleep* (33–34). Varying words and phrases according to such devices yields multiple sentences saying the same thing, and such *restatement* is, again, one of the predictable interclausal relations that can produce "filler" in a passage (see above, p. 364). A genre particularly rich in such restatement is the summation to the jury in a trial. Speaking to listeners who are procedurally mute and trapped in a linear stream of aural text, attorneys often repeat and restate their arguments to a degree that seems excessive when their texts are read rather than listened to. An example of a passage amplified through copious restatement comes from a summation by Clara Foltz, one of the first women litigators in the United States, who practiced law in the late nineteenth century. She produced the following as defense attorney in the trial of an arsonist:

> Allow me to say, I have been pleased with much of the speech of the counsel on the other side. He has made of the testimony all there was in it. He has lost no effort in throwing upon it the strongest light in the state's behalf; he has marshaled it with all the skill and ingenuity of a subtle lawyer, a skilled debater, and a practical dialectician; he has spared no pains in the coloring of the testimony to produce the highest effect. When he had finished, you saw the state's case in its most advantageous light and there was indeed nothing more to be said. (Lief, Caldwell, and Bycel 1998, 217)

Erasmus would have admired the many versions of the same thought here. Of course this amplification of her opponent's skill sets up the point obviously waiting in the wings: that despite all this skill, the case itself amounts to little.[3]

The second part of Erasmus's text covers methods of achieving copiousness that draw on *res* rather than *verba,* thus fulfilling the book's title: *On Copia from both words and things.* This confusing distinction between *matter* and *words* simply means that the prompts for expanding offered in Book II are not formal to begin with, as they are in Book I, where they are directed by figures of speech. Instead, expanding through *res* requires the rhetor to search the content of the case; following the methods recommended will still lead to passages with certain predictable stylistic features.

The first of Erasmus's suggested methods of achieving *copia* through *res* could be called *unrolling a generalization,* "as if one should display merchandise first through a lattice-work, or rolled up in carpets, then should unroll the carpets and disclose the merchandise, exposing it completely to sight" (1963, 43). No passage could illustrate this tactic better than the one Erasmus himself provides:

> He lost everything through excess
> This expression, complete in itself, and, as it were, all rolled up, may be developed by enumerating a great many kinds of possessions, and by setting forth various ways of losing property. Whatever had come by inheritance from father or mother, whatever had come by the death of other relatives, whatever had been added from his wife's dowry, which was not at all mean, whatever had accrued from bequests (and considerable had accrued), whatever he had received from the liberality of his prince, whatever private property he had procured, all money, military equipment, clothes, estates, fields, together with farms and herds, in short everything, whether movable or real estate, and finally even his immediate household property, in a short time he so consumed, wasted, and devoured in foulest passion for harlots, in daily banquets, in sumptuous entertainments, nightly drinking bouts, low taverns, delicacies, perfumes, dice, and gaming that what remained to him would not equal a farthing. (1963, 43)

In this method of amplification, as John Genung pointed out four centuries later, the particulars led to the generalization in the first place (1896, 290). The rhetor intent on amplifying by this method uses terms in the resulting passage that feature hyponyms at various levels of specificity, all belonging under a superordinate term in the original generalization and all preferably spread out in multiple clauses.

Erasmus's other recommendations for achieving *copia* through *res* draw on durable elements familiar from rhetorical invention, as well as from individual progymnasmatic exercises and even from Quintilian's original five devices.[4] For example, a rhetor inventing material from the *topoi* of causes and circumstances (place, occasion, instruments, time, etc.) can easily expand the amount of text devoted to an item (1963, 46–47, 57). Another source for expansion inserts a *chreia* commenting on any quotation used or digressing to extol a virtue (56). Still another method, creating a division, means anatomizing a subject that could be referred to as a whole entity. Thus, a dissection into parts, which may seem no more than factual exposition, is yet another device for filling space and keeping the audience's attention fixed on the subject.

Judging by his own copiousness, Erasmus considers some methods of expansion more fruitful than others. Narratives are easy sites for *copia*, since they are elastic depending on the amount of detail provided. The act of setting sail, for example, can be rendered as one event or as scores of smaller events covering planning, preparation, and departure. Likewise, Erasmus recommends multiplying propositions, especially by arguing both the *thesis* and the *hypothesis*, the general and the particular versions of an issue (61–62),[5] or by imagining a more difficult proposition which the arguer then claims not to be arguing for, thus making the one actually supported seem more feasible. If propositions can be multiplied, so can premises, and Erasmus provides an example of seven reasons against Christian kings going to war, and many more reasons that could support a case for a particular king not waging war (64–65). The section devoted to description in *De Copia* is also quite lengthy, and its emphasis on visualization picks up the enduring notion of *energeia* but adapts it to the possibility of using actual visuals, a new awareness in early modern print culture (see above, p. 339). A lengthy discussion follows, with examples and references to passages in famous authors describing things, persons, places, and times.[6]

Erasmus judges the method left for last as the best: "most powerful for proof, and therefore for *copia* [an argument/style connection worth noting], is the force of *exempla*... These are employed either as similes, or *dissimilia*, or contraries; also in comparing the greater to the lesser, the lesser to the greater, or equals to equals" (1963, 67). This recommendation looks initially like Quintilian's *comparatio*, but in early modern rhetorical practice something substantially different is meant in execution. For as Erasmus explains and then goes on to illustrate, "This class embraces the *fabula*, the apologue, the proverb, judgments, the parable, or *collatio*, the imago and analogy, and other similar ones" (67). These are all interpolated set pieces bringing in illustrative material, either factual, drawn from histories or current events, or imaginary, drawn from fables or literary texts or invented for the immediate purpose. Furthermore, "*exempla* are not only varied, but are also enlarged and amplified in handling" (68); they are, in other words, sites of expansion in themselves, and Erasmus provides multiple examples for how such expansion could be accomplished, both for the historical and the fictitious. All the textual baggage that early modern humanists patiently acquired in commonplace books, all the tidbits and stories and great passages from reading, could be imported into a new textual environment for purposes of copious probative illustration.

Lincoln, like many other nineteenth-century orators, was comfortable with the Erasmian *exemplum* as a parable, homely fable, or *collatio* brought in to amplify, clarify, and vivify a line of argument. The "House Divided" speech, for example, delivered in 1858 to the Republican State convention in Illinois, argues for a conspiracy behind the legislation, political strategies, and legal decisions of the preceding few years to make slavery acceptable in all the states. To emphasize this point, Lincoln retells it in terms of seeing all the materials for a house assembled: "when we see these timbers joined together, and see they exactly make the frame of a house or a mill, all the tenons and mortices exactly fitting," it is impossible not to know that "the house was planned ahead of time" (Lincoln 1989, I 431). Similarly, in one of his many speeches made at "Sanitary Fairs" during the Civil War, where money was raised for soldiers and their families, Lincoln in April 1864 gave a trenchant argument contrasting incompatible meanings of *liberty*: "We all declare for liberty, but in using the same *word* we do not all mean the same *thing*. With some the word liberty may mean for each man to do as he pleases with himself, and the product of his labor; while with others the same word may mean for some men to do as they please with other men, and the product of other men's labor" (Lincoln 1989, II 589). After this exercise in argument from antithetical definitions, using phrases anticipating the Second Inaugural, Lincoln launched without preface into the following *collatio*, which might have come from Aesop:

> The shepherd drives the wolf from the sheep's throat, for which the sheep thanks the shepherd as a *liberator*, while the wolf denounces him for the same act as the destroyer of liberty, especially as the sheep was a black one. Plainly the sheep and the wolf are not agreed upon a definition of the word liberty; and precisely the same difference prevails to-day among us human creatures, even in the North, and all professing to love liberty (Lincoln 1989, II 590).

In the paragraph before this passage, in this illustrative fable itself, and then in the discussion which follows it on actions from the people of Maryland that have repudiated the "wolf's dictionary," Lincoln stays on, and hence amplifies, the same point for fully a third of his short speech.

Epicheireme

In rhetoric, as the counterpart to dialectic, the syllogism and enthymeme as minimal units of argument structure were clearly noted. But since the goal in rhetoric is persuading audiences to accept arguments, not merely understand them, the manuals advised that a claim/premise structure should be expanded to give it heft and salience for an audience (see also Whately 1846, 260). In classical rhetorical manuals in the Ciceronian tradition, this amplified unit of argument is called the **epicheireme**.[7] Two versions of this argument form, each in five parts, come down from antiquity. The first is described in Book II of the *Rhetorica ad Herennium* (1981, 107–13). It begins with a statement of the claim to be supported; this statement is followed by a reason, then a "proof of the reason," or reason for the reason. These parts constitute the core of support. They are then followed by a section of embellishment, and finally by a restatement of the original claim. The inclusion of a section of embellishment marks the insertion of amplification as an intensification of the reasoning.

Far from being an ancient oddity, the *epicheireme* is still a satisfying, widely used argumentative unit. A twentieth-century example occurs in Reagan's speech at the Brandenburg Gate in 1987. In response to the occasion of Berlin's 700th anniversary, part of his speech is an encomium on the city and the nation of West Germany including the following passage:

(1) In West Germany and here in Berlin, there took place an economic miracle, the Wirtschaftswunder. (2) Adenauer, Erhard, Reuter, and other leaders understood the practical importance of liberty—that just as truth can flourish only when the journalist is given freedom of speech, so prosperity can come about only when the farmer and businessman enjoy economic freedom. (3) The German leaders reduced tariffs, expanded free trade, lowered taxes. (4) From 1950 to 1960 alone, the standard of living in West Germany and Berlin doubled.

(5) Where four decades ago there was rubble, today in West Berlin there is the greatest industrial output of any city in Germany—busy office blocks, fine homes and apartments, proud avenues, and the spreading lawns of parkland. (6) Where a city's culture seemed to have been destroyed, today there are two great universities, orchestras and an opera, countless theatres, and museums. (7) Where there was want, today there's abundance—food, clothing, automobiles—the wonderful goods of the Ku'damm. (8) From devastation, from utter ruin, you Berliners have, in freedom, rebuilt a city that once again ranks as one of the greatest on earth. (9) The Soviets may have had other plans. (10) But, my friends, there were a few things the Soviets didn't count on—*Berliner Herz, Berliner Humor, ja, und Berliner Schnauze* (Reagan 1989, 350–51)

Analyzing this unit of Reagan's speech as a type of epicheireme yields the following scheme. The first sentence is the claim, obviously a line of argument for the overall epideictic case by praising the economic miracle of Berlin. This miracle has to be grounded not in chance or accident but in the intentions of the German leadership and people given in sentences two and three. The argument so far, and the first three parts of the epicheireme, could be paraphrased as follows: an economic miracle took place in West Germany and Berlin, because the German leaders reduced tariffs, expanded free trade, and lowered taxes, because they understood the practical importance of liberty and economic freedom.

The second paragraph offers the lengthy fourth part of the epicheireme, the embellishment or amplification of the central claim, focusing on West Berlin's revival. The style kicks into grand, using three sentences all opening with the same structure expressing the original state of devastation (*Where four decades ago there was rubble; Where a city's culture seemed to have been destroyed; Where there was want*). Each of these is followed, observing iconic form, by specific and imagistic language describing the new state of abundance and involving lists of features of a thriving city. The purpose of this unit is to hold the audience's attention on the substantiated claim, to intensify it as Reagan praises Berlin to the Berliners.[8] Following these three sentences, sentence eight repeats the claim in a summative way, filling in the fifth slot in the *epicheireme*: "From devastation, from utter ruin, you Berliners have, in freedom, rebuilt a city that once again ranks as one of the greatest on earth." The purpose of this kind of section is to fix the audience's attention on a particular line of argument, achieving all three dimensions of amplification at once: linguistic prominence, psychological salience, and conceptual importance.

A second type of five-part epicheireme appears in Cicero's *De Inventione*, a text that, along with the *ad Herennium*, remained consistently available and influential into the seventeenth century (1976, 111ff; Cicero notes that parts can be deleted from the full form). Cicero's epicheireme essentially expands the syllogism, following each of the premises with supporting embellishment, not unlike Stephen Toulmin's expansion in *The Uses of Argument* (1958). Cicero's own example, interspersed with explanations of the parts, is worth quoting at length because of its importance in the history of science. It offers one of the earliest statements of the argument for Intelligent Design based on the orderly structure of the universe.

Those who think that the syllogism [not Cicero's word; he speaks of *ratiocinatio* and its parts] ought to be divided into five parts say that first one should state the basis of the argument in this way: "Things that are done by design are managed better than those which are governed without design." This they count as the first part. Then they think it should be supported by a variety of reasons and the greatest possible fullness of expression, in the following manner: "The house that is managed in accordance with a reasoned plan, is in every respect better equipped and furnished than one which is governed in a haphazard way with a total lack of design. The army that is commanded by a wise and shrewd general is guided in all ways more advantageously than one which is governed by someone's folly and rashness. The same line of reasoning is applicable to navigation, for the ship which has the services of the most expert pilot makes the most successful voyage." When the major premise [*propositio*] has been proved in this fashion and two parts of the syllogism [*ratiocinationis* = reasonings or arguments] have been completed, in the third part they say you should state as a minor premise what you wish to show, this being in line with the thought of the major premise [*tertia in parte aiunt, quod ostendere velis, id ex vi propositionis oportere adsumere*]; the following will be an example: "Of all things nothing is better governed that the universe." And then in the fourth place they introduce another proof, that is of this minor premise [not in the original], in this way: "For the risings and the settings of the constellations keep a fixed order, and the changes of the seasons not only proceed in the same way by a fixed law but are also adapted to the advantage of all nature, and the alternation of night and day has never through any variations done any harm." All these points are proof that the nature of the world is governed by no ordinary intelligence. In the fifth place they put the conclusion [*complexionem*], which either merely states the necessary deduction from all the parts, as follows: "Therefore the universe is administered by design," or after bringing the major premise and the minor premise [*propositionem et assumptionem*] together in one brief statement adds what follows from them after this fashion: "Therefore if those things are administered better which are governed by design than those which are administered without design, and nothing is governed better than the universe, then the universe is governed by design." This is the way in which they think the argument is expressed in five parts. (Cicero 1976, 100–3)

Diminishing

The two strands of amplification, accumulating and heightening, are answered by two opposite tendencies in rhetorical stylistics. First, copia, staying on a topic, is reversed by brevity, defined by Quintilian as getting a point across "with rapidity and without waste of detail" or as expressing "a great deal in a very few words" (1921, III 257). In an age of sound bites, these effects of efficiency and concision may seem to be the highest stylistic virtues. Indeed, brevity is frequently recommended in contemporary style manuals, while praise for its apparent opposite, prolixity, is unthinkable.[9] Until this century, however, rhetorical manuals recommended *either* copia or brevity as appropriate means, depending on the rhetor's purpose and situation.[10]

Judging where and how much a rhetor amplifies or diminishes requires a real or hypothetical comparison. Comparing summations from prosecution and defense before a jury or opposed speeches in a legislature will inevitably reveal that each side expands the features that help its position and gives cursory treatment to those that hurt it but that nevertheless have to be mentioned. As an example of these differences, the exchanges between candidates in presidential debates are revealing. A candidate with a potentially less popular, previously announced stance will typically gloss over it quickly. The strategic uses of brevity are also worth noting in the advice on the parts of the oration; brevity was recommended for the *narratio*, the opening statement of the case, and for summarizing the case in the peroration. Such brief summaries, whether as a preview or a retrospective, give the rhetor the chance to shape through selection, while the very shortness of the account can enhance an impression of truthfulness. For example, in his 1969 televised address on the Vietnam War, Nixon gave a cursory four-sentence summary of how the United States became involved in Vietnam in the first place (Windt 1983, 129). The predications of his four sentences are *North Vietnam launched, President Eisenhower sent, President Kennedy sent, President Johnson sent*. While accurate, Nixon's brief summary is radically selective. All such summaries of recent events in political speeches are liable to the same criticism of tendentious brevity.

Of course the ultimate opposite of copia is not brevity; it is silence. A rhetor may simply say nothing about an uncomfortable or damaging detail. This strategy for making unhelpful elements disappear only works if the suppressed items are unknown to the audience or are items they can easily overlook. But even when the audience knows and cares, completely ignoring a problem can still succeed when there is no forum for bringing up the silenced material. When rhetors must address audiences with both memory and power, they can always revert to a fourth-stasis defense by declaring the current occasion and forum an inappropriate one for addressing an issue (Cicero 1976, 33). They may even try to declare silence prospectively: "I will have nothing to say about that."

The second form of amplification, heightening, involves giving more attention to an element already included. Its opposite, diminishing, involves cutting back on the attention paid to an included element. The need to diminish an element already "in the field of vision" comes up in any debate or "inquisitorial" setting where the speaker has to answer charges and criticisms. Not surprisingly, the need to diminish occurs in many types of legally mandated communications, such as those from publicly held companies to stockholders or from government agencies to affected citizens. These institutions may have negative news they have to convey—rate hikes, poor performance, new regulations and penalties—yet they want to maintain customer satisfaction, client loyalty, or, in the case of the government, some semblance of a justifying rationale.

The tactics for diminishing reverse the tactics for heightening, as Quintilian noted when he followed his section on amplification with a brief mention of attenuating as "effected by the same method, since there are as many degrees of descent as ascent" (1921, III 279). The rhetor can replace a higher term with a lower, construct a series that declines, place elements "beneath" rather than "topping" with them, make comparisons and invite inferences that diminish rather than enhance. In addition to pointing to these opposite tactics, the figure manuals also particularized advice under individual figures such as *meiosis, extenuatio, minutio,* and *diminutio,* each with slightly different senses. *Meiosis,* the best known of these figures, isolated the tactic of term substitution, "when a less word is put for a greater" (Peacham 1593, 168). *Meiosis* was distinguished from that other figure of understatement, *litotes,* and in fact the difference between these two is substantial. *Litotes* depends for its effects of understating on being noticed; the substitution with a lesser term in *meiosis* should pass unnoticed. Ideally, the audience simply accepts the lesser word choice as the correct or inevitable one and does not construe additional meanings as in the case of *litotes.* If an audience cannot independently assess the appropriateness of a word choice, it is inevitably pushed in the direction of the speaker's assessment; the first term heard "occupies the ground."

Many other tactics for diminishing could be listed here. Putting a term in quotation marks, for example, or using special pronunciation or pauses that amount to spoken quotation marks, can lessen a term even while drawing attention to it. It is disowned by the rhetor. Using a *equipollentia,* a phrasing that negates the opposite (*it was not unpleasant*), also tends to diminish a point, as do anticipatory subjects and nominalizations. There are, furthermore, syntactic methods for burying a damaging item: keeping it out of the openings or endings of clauses or placing it in a dependent clause or phrase below the main predication. Items are also less conspicuous in the middle of a series or buried in the middle of a paragraph.

A brief sample for analysis comes from a pamphlet sent to customers by an electrical utility company, the kind of text that is often thrown away unread. A statement on the inside back cover explains its legal exigence: "This pamphlet is prepared and mailed to each customer on an annual basis in compliance with the Code of Maryland Regulations (COMAR) 20.31.05.03C(2)" (Pepco 1984). The utility is required to tell customers the circumstances under which it can cut off their power and, not surprisingly, this negative message is masked throughout. The pamphlet is euphemistically titled "Maryland Customer Termination Rights," a phrasing that underplays the real source of power, in two senses of that word. On the first page, the announcement of the purpose of the pamphlet also elides agency: "The following is an explanation of your rights and responsibilities in the event your electric utility service becomes subject to termination." This sentence downplays while communicating a threat (*becomes subject to termination = we turn off your electricity*). The customer is also curiously innocent in this pamphlet: "For example, service may be terminated without notice for any of the following reasons:…unauthorized use of service by any method, including diversion of electricity around a meter" (1). "Unauthorized use" is theft, but the phrasing contains no accusation. In later sections concerning turning off service to the elderly or to anyone on life support, the text does speak more directly to *you* about steps for mutual contact. However, most of the choices throughout—the nominalizations, the agentless predications, the legal register—are diminishing choices motivated by a desire to avoid delivering a harsh message in a direct way. If clarity were not the occasional sacrificial victim of these choices, they would be entirely justified.

Amplification and the Sublime

Melanchthon's comment in the epigraph to this chapter not only refers to amplifying the good and burying the bad aspects of a case, it also recommends that the rhetor overwhelm [*obruat*] with amplification. To overwhelm recalls the highest possible rhetorical effect, that of impressing an audience with a sense of the sublime. As defined by Longinus in a treatise usually dated to the first century CE, the sublime (*hypsos*/sublimity) is a state beyond ordinary persuasion: "For the effect of elevated language is, not to persuade the hearers, but to entrance them…The extent to which we can be persuaded is usually under our own control, but these sublime passages exert an irresistible force and mastery, and get the upper hand with every hearer" (1965, 100). The true sublime can also "lift the soul" with a "proud exaltation and a sense of vaunting joy" and leave the audience with the impression that they themselves have produced what they have heard (107).

Longinus divided the sources of sublimity into those innate in the material and those added by art. Material innately sublime included descriptions of the gods and the cosmos; Longinus cites the creation passage in Genesis as an example (110–11). Under artful sources of the sublime, Longinus devoted attention to *amplification*, "when the matters under discussion or the points of an argument allow of many pauses and many fresh starts from section to section, and the grand phrases come rolling out one after another with increasing effect" (116). Though there were "countless forms of amplification" (116), Longinus was aware of the two strands, heightening and accumulation. He emphasized the former as the primary source of sublimity: "sublimity consists in elevation, amplification in quantity" (117). In his judgment, Demosthenes, whose effects he compared to bolts of lightning, epitomized sublimity achieved through heightening, while Cicero, like a wide-spreading conflagration, epitomized amplification through quantity (118). Though reprinted in the sixteenth century, Longinus' text had its greatest influence in the late seventeenth and early eighteenth centuries, when it was translated into French and then English. Its best-known successor is Edmund Burke's *A Philosophical Inquiry into the Nature of Our Ideas of the Sublime and Beautiful* (1756). Burke's treatise, however, redefines the sublime as an aesthetic reaction, triggered largely by visual impressions, or their corresponding word pictures, suggesting vastness, darkness, or obscurity and stimulating fear or awe.

The Last Paragraph of *On the Origin of Species*

Whether or not a particular passage exhibits amplification that could be called sublime is a matter of arguable judgment. Many passages in the Bible, the source text of eloquence in the West, could be cited. Certainly the concluding passage from Lincoln's Second Inaugural, the epigraph to chapter one, would be judged sublime in both conception and style by most readers. Other candidates include the passage in the second chapter of John Stuart Mill's *On Liberty* that argues for the importance of knowing the other side (at least in the opinion of this author), as well as many passages in the speeches of Martin Luther King Jr., especially the conclusion of his "I have a dream" speech. The sample offered for analysis here is the last paragraph of the last chapter of Charles Darwin's *On the Origin of Species*. This passage is often quoted by commentators and critics, an indication that it is both memorable and summative, and M. A. K. Halliday has analyzed both the final paragraph and the preceding one for their style, organization, and intertwined motifs (1993, 86–105). Also, in the best possible situation for stylistic analysis, alternate versions of this last paragraph exist in earlier drafts, both in the first sketch of his theories that Darwin wrote in 1842 and in the fuller essay version written in 1844 and sent to colleagues in case of his death.[11] The analysis of this concluding paragraph offered in the following pages will not only trace its sources of amplification, it will also serve as a summarizing application of the four main sections of this book by identifying tactics at the word, sentence, passage, and interactive levels.

While it is impossible that Darwin would have been aware of all of the features noted in the analysis presented here, he did receive the formal rhetorical training typical for an educated young man of his time, both at his grammar school and at Cambridge. His rhetorical skills are incontestable, and they have been the subject of many studies (see especially John Angus Campbell 1987 and 1990). The *Origin* itself is structured along the lines of the six-part oration, with an *exordium* (Introduction), *narratio* (Historical Sketch added with the third edition), *partitio* (eighth and ninth paragraphs of the Introduction), *confirmatio* (chaps. 1–5), *refutatio* (chaps. 6–13, with 10–13 also functioning as a posteriori arguments), and *peroratio* (chap. 14). Darwin clearly knew that in his conclusion, following the standard advice in rhetorical manuals, he had both to recapitulate his arguments and to give his audience motives for adherence to his claims. He performs these functions in his last chapter. The paragraphs immediately preceding the final paragraph build a case for acceptance, in part by presenting a vision, almost to the point of a *phantasia*, of the future improvement of all of learning: "In the distant future I see open fields for far more important researches" (489). Following detailed speculation on the changing disciplines, and an immediately preceding paragraph that argues for a Creator acting indirectly toward future perfection, Darwin concludes:

It is interesting to contemplate an entangled bank, clothed with many plants of many kinds, with birds singing on the bushes, with various insects flitting about, and with worms crawling through the damp earth, and to reflect that these elaborately constructed forms, so different from each other, and dependent on each other in so complex a manner, have all been produced by laws acting around us. These laws, taken in the largest sense, being Growth with Reproduction; Inheritance which is almost implied by reproduction; Variability from the indirect and direct action of the external conditions of life, and from use and disuse; a Ratio of Increase so high as to lead to a Struggle for Life, and as a consequence to Natural Selection, entailing Divergence of Character and the Extinction of less-improved forms. Thus, from the war of nature, from famine and death, the most exalted object which we are capable of conceiving, namely, the production of the higher animals, directly follows. There is grandeur in this view of life, with its several powers, having been originally breathed by the Creator into a few forms or into one; and that, whilst this planet has gone cycling on according to the fixed law of gravity, from so simple a beginning endless forms most beautiful and most wonderful have been, and are being, evolved. (1860, 490)

This passage remained unchanged through all six published editions of the *Origin* altered by Darwin (1859–1872), with two exceptions. The *entangled bank* became a *tangled* bank in the fifth edition, and, most important, in the second edition of 1860 quoted here, a corrected reprint released within a few months of the first, Darwin added the agent for the perfect passive progressive *having been breathed*, namely *by the Creator.*

Darwin's final paragraph meets Longinus's first qualification for the sublime according to subject matter, since it concerns the very highest concepts that humans can discuss: the origin of life, the Creator, the nature of the universe. The vast, eternal, and ultimate nature of these matters fulfills the Burkean sublime as well. In terms of natural philosophy or science, the passage also reaches to the highest conceptual level in listing the forces identified in nature as laws, that is, as invariant principles of action like gravity. The last sentence carries an analogy transferring this elevation: the planets cycle on *just as* life forms evolve. In a print edition of his father's MSS, Francis Darwin noted that this comparison first appeared in the following form in a notebook from 1837:

> Astronomers might formerly have said that God ordered each planet to move in its particular destiny. But how much more simple and sublime [a] power—let attraction act according to certain law, such are inevitable consequences—let animal[s] be created then by the fixed laws of generation, such will be their successors. (1909, xxviii)

The parallelism in phrasing clearly indicates the intended analogy, and the explicit use of *sublime* suggests Darwin's awareness of the tradition. The scale of these cosmic concepts is matched by the sweep across time recorded in the verbs. The present tense, used in the first through third sentences, reports the laws of nature. In the earlier versions of the last sentence, Darwin switched to the perfect passive and wrote only that *endless forms . . . have been evolved*, but in the final version, he extended the time frame by adding new auxiliaries for a new tense: *endless forms . . . have been, and are being, evolved.*

ON DARWIN'S WORD CHOICES

Among the linguistic tactics that reach for the sublime, Darwin's word choices throughout press and build to amplifying, elevating effects, as Quintilian, Longinus, and Erasmus all recommended. To explain these effects requires recognizing, first of all, that there are three registers mixed in this passage. The first sentence, missing in the 1842 and 1844 versions, features terms in a somewhat conventional or domesticated "poetic" register, the kind found in copybook verses; the bank is *clothed* with many plants, with *birds singing in the bushes* and *insects flitting about*. Though somewhat unpoetic *worms* are *crawling through the damp earth*, the register is still in the familiar if slightly elevated language of sentimental encounters with nature. Notably, terms like *plants, birds, insects,* and *worms,* while descriptive, are also category labels at the same time; that is, these are generic *birds,* not linnets, thrushes, etc. In the second half of the first sentence, which draws conclusions from this scene, the language jumps to an abstract and conceptual register. The birds, insects, and worms are relabeled in Latinate diction as *elaborately constructed forms,* different from and dependent on each other in so *complex a manner*. The diction stays at this abstract, conceptual level in the second sentence (also missing from earlier versions), which lists the laws of nature illustrated by the entangled bank; furthermore, with a glance back to eighteenth-century habits of capitalizing abstractions, each law has its formal title (Variation, Inheritance, etc.), heightening its distinctness and importance.[12]

A third register kicks in in the third sentence. Though Latinate conceptual terms continue (*exalted object, capable of conceiving, production, directly*), the amplified words in this sentence, the words exhibiting *auxesis*, reprise principles of struggle and extinction in the preceding sentence in far more powerful terms persisting from Old and Middle English: *from the war of nature, from famine and death*. This series occurs in quite different forms in the earlier drafts: in 1842, it is "From death, famine, rapine, and the concealed war of nature" (1909, 52)[13] and in 1844, "From death, famine, and the struggle for existence" (Francis Darwin 1909, 254). Darwin's final version with its older words, in the precise order *war, famine* and *death*, recalls the Book of Revelation (6:3–8), as Darwin's original readers were likely to recognize. These are three of the horsemen of the Apocalypse, in their Biblical order, an allusion that takes the style up to the grand.[14] The language continues, dignified and elevated, into the fourth sentence, where the registers combine. Anglo-Saxon verities (*life, breathed, beginning, law, endless, wonderful*) mix with more familiar though ultimately Latin-derived word choices, both those directly borrowed (*forms, originally, Creator, gravity, evolved, cycling, planet* [the last two ultimately from Greek]) and those taken in long ago through French (notably *grandeur* with its elegant long vowels, *view, powers,* and *beautiful*).

ON DARWIN'S SENTENCE ARCHITECTURE

It is not only the word choice, however, it is also the syntax, the phrasing, that elevates the final two sentences that Darwin first drafted seventeen years earlier. Here Longinus is the best guide, since he considered sentence architecture as a source of sublimity. In chapter 22, he recommends *hyperbaton*, "the arrangement of words and ideas out of their normal sequence" (1965, 131), considering such inversions signs of intensity even when the constructions are planned. Demosthenes is his ideal in this device, as in so much else, for his perilously complex constructions, arousing fear in his listeners that the sentence will fall to pieces, until he brings out "the long-awaited phrase just where it is most effective, at the very end" (132). To appreciate how the syntax aids amplification and sublimity in Darwin's final passage requires an overview of the syntax of all four sentences in the final version.

The first and second sentences have straightforward structure. The first dispenses with its main predication quickly before two parallel infinitives (*It is interesting to contemplate... and to reflect ...*), each followed by a lengthy object. The object of *to contemplate* is immediately *an entangled bank* followed by four modifying phrases, and the object of *to reflect* is a noun clause functioning as the object (*that these... have been produced*). Though different grammatically, each of these objects is segmented into four phrases, and each is exactly twenty-nine words long. There is then iconic parity between the evidence resulting from contemplation and its meaning resulting from reflection. (Darwin need not have intended this parity, but as an experienced writer he would have sensed it.) The second sentence is not actually a sentence, because it has a participle (*being*) in place of a tensed verb. It is really an extended list of the *laws* mentioned in the first sentence.

With the third sentence, where the diction also changes, the inversions begin. The predication of this sentence (*object…follows*) is both postponed and interrupted. It is postponed in all the versions behind a left-branching construction beginning with *from* that lists the powerful forces driving natural selection. In the final version alone, however, these forces are segmented into parallel prepositional phrases that feature *isocolon: from the war of nature* (six syllables) and *from famine and death* (five syllables). In the earlier versions, the subject and verb appear immediately after the opening phrase (1842, *we can see*; 1844, *we see*) followed by the object, a large noun clause containing the gist of the sentence. In the final version, Darwin removed this human subject/verb pair entirely and elevated *the most exalted object* into the subject. The verb, instead of occurring immediately after the subject, is postponed by mid-branching constructions: a restrictive modifier, *which we are capable of perceiving*, that picks up the sense of the old subject and verb, and an identifying appositive that persists from the earlier versions, *namely, the production of the higher animals*. Thus the verb, *directly follows* (*has come* in 1842 and *has proceeded* in 1844), paradoxically does not directly follow its subject; the reader waits for the main verb to fall into place until the end, where it receives the greatest emphasis. In "normal" syntax, the prepositional phrases that open the sentence would come at the end and the verb would be lost in the middle: *the production of the higher animals directly follows from the war of nature, from famine and death.* But inverting the syntax and putting the terrible forces first creates an iconic order of cause preceding effect. The lengthy insertion between the subject and verb suspends completion of the meaning. Thus the weight of the opening and interrupting phrases are also suspended until the end when the weight falls on the verbs completing the periodic sentence, and emphasizing that from those forces the higher animals follow.

Between what are now the third and final sentences, the two drafts contain additional clauses (see footnote 11), separated into two sentences in 1842 and sutured into one by a colon in 1844. These sentences (eventually revised and moved to the opening of the penultimate paragraph) extend the theological arguments that concern the final paragraphs in both drafts, by noting how the intricate productions of nature seem to require direct creation. These points are made by a return to Latinate diction, anticipatory subjects, complex syntax, and no immediate tie to the sentences before and after. Fortunately, Darwin excised them.

The final sentence in the final version, perhaps the most memorable in the passage if not in the entire book, is the result of extensive revisions. The main predication that opens it (*There is grandeur*) appeared in the earlier drafts as *There is a simple grandeur*. The modifier *simple* hardly enhances *grandeur*. Even worse, in an earlier draft a sentence in the preceding "paragraph," five sentences before, has a similar opening: *There is much grandeur in looking at every existing organic being* (1909, 51, 253). Competition with this opening would have disastrously compromised the final appearance of this "ultimate" phrasing, and Darwin wisely deleted the earlier sentence.

Beginning with the 1844 version, Darwin hinges the final sentence into two independent parts around a semicolon.[15] The main predication opens the first half (*There is grandeur*), and the main predication closes the second half (*endless forms… have been and are being evolved*). In other words, the whole construction has inverted or chiastic grammatical structure as follows: predication/modifiers, modifiers/predication.[16] The opening unhedged declaration of the grandeur in *this view of life* is elaborated and clarified by a trailing prepositional phrase (*with its several powers*) and a participial phrase (*having been breathed*) that itself contains three further prepositional phrases. The second half has an initial adverbial clause (*whilst this planet has gone cycling on*) containing two embedded prepositional phrases, followed by a prepositional phrase beginning the final clause. In other words, the grammatical chiasmus is carried further, because the modifying structures are themselves inverted by length, short/long, long/short and the short modifiers in both cases are prepositional phrases. The elegance of this pattern is the product of truncation (see again the earlier versions in footnote 11).

The new, streamlined structure prepares for the final clause, which is Darwin's final visionary statement. The first part of the whole sentence, before the semicolon, takes the act of creation, whose agent is the breath of God, and concentrates it into a *few forms or into one*. The second part, after the postponing adverbial *whilst* clause, picks up from this point, that is, *from so simple a beginning*. Though this left-branching prepositional phrase postpones the subject, it launches the timeline of creation forward iconically: *from so simple a beginning, endless forms… have been and are being evolved*. Subject and verb in this final clause are also separated for a slight but dramatic pause by the less conventionally placed postnoun modifiers *most beautiful and most wonderful*. Then, after this interruption and a further pause for the two sets of auxiliaries, the most important word in the sentence, the verb *evolved*, occurs as Longinus would have approved, "just where it is needed, at the very end." Had Darwin written this sentence in conventional order, it would have read as follows: *The most beautiful and wonderful endless forms have been and are being evolved from so simple a beginning*. But he wrote it to ascend.

ON DARWIN'S PASSAGE CONSTRUCTION

Stepping back again to look at the entire passage reveals how its overall construction also supports the ascending trajectory of this paragraph. First, sentence-to-sentence coherence delivers the reader safely to the final sentence. Since the paragraph's content begins anew, without picking up directly from the preceding sentence, it opens with a slot-filling subject and verb, *It is*. The comment of the first sentence, *by laws acting around us*, then becomes the topic of the second sentence, *These laws*. The third sentence drops topic/comment structuring but uses a transition word, *thus*, directing readers to construe the third sentence as a recapitulation rather than a conclusion, since *thus* (especially in British usage) has more the sense of *in this way* than of *therefore*. The fourth sentence constitutes something of a break, a regrouping. It also opens with a placeholder (*There is*) as though beginning anew, but readers can take the phrase *this view of life* as given, a summative reference to the preceding material. The second half of this sentence after the semicolon is connected as an addition to its first half by the explicit transition (*and that*) and by the topic picking up the comment from the first half, *from so simple a beginning.* Hence the reader's linear passage through the four sentences is clearly managed.

At a higher level of passage construction, however, the argument emerges from the sequence of sentences. The first two sentences combine in an enthymeme, claim followed by reason or phenomenon by explanation: the elaborate and interdependent living forms of the entangled bank exist because of natural laws acting around us. The third sentence recapitulates this argument—from these causes, the higher animals directly follow—and it adds the judgment that this production is *the most exalted object which we are capable of conceiving.* Thus the first three sentences constitute a unit, an encapsulation of the book's entire argument. The fourth sentence, after the slight break in continuity, in effect steps to a higher level; this sentence, after all, brings in the Creator and the cycling planet. This sentence looks back on the preceding sentences from a cosmic perspective, and judges creation and its continuity positively. Given this ending in positive evaluation, rhetorical theory suggests another way to describe the overall construction of this passage. The structural pattern here follows the stases, the list of issues that arguments inevitably concern (see above, p. 301). In its four sentences, Darwin's final paragraph in its final version addresses the issues, from "here is what exists in nature" and "here are the laws that have brought it about" to the qualitative stasis that "these results are good" and "they continue."

ON DARWIN'S AMPLIFICATION AND INTERACTION WITH READERS

The evidence from word choice, syntax, and passage construction reviewed so far demonstrates Darwin's strategies of amplification attempting the sublime. What contributions come from the two strands of amplification per se as defined by Erasmus and Quintilian? *Copia* as "saying many things about many things" does not obtrude in this final statement of Darwin's themes, though the extent to which Darwin repeats his vision with elaboration is patent throughout the final pages, and this paragraph in fact sits at the end of a long buildup. Quintilian's tactics of heightening, however, including comparisons, series, and directed inferences, are certainly present. The strategic word choices have been described already. The comparison introduced in the last sentence is an ennobling one: natural selection is compared to the greatest explanatory success in natural philosophy, the "fixed law of gravity" that keeps *this planet... cycling* in orbit. The term *planet* itself, rather than *earth*, reinforces a cosmic perspective, and it gains in elevation from no longer sharing its dependent clause with the earthbound processes of geology.

Darwin also exploits the amplifying potential of series with an extended list of the laws of nature in the second sentence, a list which also reviews topics from the preceding chapters: Growth, Reproduction, Inheritance, Variability, Ratio of Increase, Struggle for Life, Natural Selection, Divergence of Character, Extinction. This nine-item series is long, and length amplifies and delivers on the complexity claimed for the laws of nature in the preceding sentence. The series is also ordered overall by sequence, both of time and of causality, as Variability and Increase create the Struggle, which is the agent of Natural Selection, leading to Divergence or Extinction. However, despite this causal trajectory, the series itself is not strictly linear or smoothed into equal steps. Instead, it is interrupted with modifying phrases that clump the items into stages. Growth is *with* Reproduction and Inheritance is *almost implied by* it. Variability follows from unknown direct and indirect causes (including a Lamarckian *use and disuse*). The next pair is Malthus's contribution: a Ratio of Increase *so high as to lead to* a Struggle for Life, culminating in Darwin's insight, the *consequence* of Natural Selection *entailing* both Divergence of Character and Extinction. *Extinction of less-improved forms* as the last item seems to turn this series into a *decrementum*, but the next sentence will start, in a different register, with the final items of the series, and run it the other way: the war of nature, famine and death, will produce the higher animals.

Keeping with the overall strategy of using series, with their suggestions of order according to degree, there are also amplified quantities and suggestions of "topping" throughout. First, the number of comparative and superlative modifiers used in the final version is worth noting: *so different, so complex, so high, less-improved, higher animals, so simple; the largest sense, the most exalted, most beautiful, most wonderful*. Multiplicity and variety are also stressed in the opening scene of the entangled bank; there are "*many* plants of *many* kinds" (not "*many* kinds of plants"), and the *birds, insects, worms* are all plural, as are the *laws* explaining them. Nature abounds, as it must to produce the raw material for natural selection, and its laws are complex and various, producing the higher *animals*. And these *higher* animals are somewhere far along some series of forms, perhaps pointing to though not mentioning that one higher animal, man. Also multiple are the "several powers" breathed into life by the Creator. In the earlier versions Darwin tried to specify these powers (variously *growth, assimilation, reproduction, sensation*), but he gave up and left only the vague plural. The result of these powers, the final productivity of nature, is amplified to the point of hyperbole in the final reference to *endless forms*. *Endless* is crossed out in the 1844 holograph and then careted in again. These endless forms "top" an implied sequence, since they are *most beautiful* and *most wonderful*, deserving the time-encompassing verbs that follow.

The one anomaly in all this quantity and series building is the phrase that runs the other way: the *powers* of nature were *originally breathed by the Creator into a few forms or into one*. In the 1842 version, the order is reversed and mundane: *originally breathed into matter under one or a few forms* (52); in 1844, the phrase is simplified to *breathed into matter under a few forms*. But in the fair copy of the 1844 text, Darwin penciled in above the line written in the copyist's neat hand, *perhaps into only one.* In the final version, Darwin removed *matter* as the recipient and retained the concentrating order: *into a few forms or into one.* This final phrasing could be a nod to two systems of evolutionary explanation, one tracing back to the multiple originary forms or archetypes of the German *Naturphilosophen,* the other to a single primordial substance, the *Urschleim* or later protoplasm (Richards 1993, 38–39). Whatever the explanation, this potential reduction to a single hypothetical point of creation, to perhaps only one original form, also amplifies as a tour de force sign of omnipotence. For, as explained above, the series climbs again from this single point to *endless forms.*

The amplifying inferences recommended by Quintilian are not only invited from the audience, they are directly elicited and controlled, and these managed inferences determine the overall structure of the passage explained above. As a requirement for this management and its persuasive effects, the passage has an interactive dimension. The audience is deliberately brought into the text to accompany Darwin through this final paragraph and to experience the same revelation he has experienced. They stand with him in the first sentence looking at the entangled bank. For even though a placeholding subject keeps human agents out of the main predication (*it is interesting*), nevertheless the activities recommended as interesting, *to contemplate* and *to reflect,* are mental actions only humans can perform. Furthermore, Darwin and his audience appear together in the unifying pronoun *us,* placed stylistically for greatest emphasis at the end of the first sentence and positioned conceptually in the center of the *laws acting around us.* Author and audience will reappear together in the third sentence as *we,* together conceiving with admiration the production of the higher animals. The sublime, if it works, is an effect on the audience; they have to be brought along.

The entangled bank itself, which Darwin and the audience contemplate in the first sentence, is of course a common image, one any English reader might have seen. It is also an image that recalls the tradition of "ambulatory," "walking around the countryside" natural history that Darwin was building on; it may even allude to the banks with their tangled roots that line the hollow lanes in the greatest work of English nature writing, Gilbert White's 1789 *Natural History of Selborne* (18–19). Of course Darwin's en/tangled bank is not merely mentioned (as if he had written *to contemplate an entangled bank and to reflect*); it is described with some detail to aid the reader's visualization (*plants, birds, insects, worms*). Such envisioning can assist the sublime, though this image itself is not sublime. Once realized through the imaginary deixis of the description, the bank functions in the argument as an exemplum, a hypothetical instance standing in for all the evidence from observations of nature accumulated throughout the *Origin.* Nor is this evidence only seen from a detached view, for, after all, *the earthworms crawling through the damp earth* (subject of an 1881 treatise by Darwin) are not obvious on the surface but require some digging.

Having contemplated together (through fourteen chapters) the entangled evidence of nature, Darwin and his audience note, under his direction, its amplitude and complexity and reflect on the laws that bring it about, laws reprised in the second sentence. After this rehearsal, the third and fourth sentences, with their shifted register and complex syntax, do break away, in one feature, from the traditional advice that linguistic management should be unobtrusive or invisible. For Darwin does not allow his audience to make the final evaluative inferences for themselves. He concludes for them that the *production of the higher animals* is *the most exalted object which we are capable of conceiving,* and, in the summative and majestic final sentence, that *There is grandeur in this view of life* with its *endless forms* that *have been, and are being, evolved.* Instinctively using tactics of amplification—the ascending series, the topping, and the outlying comparison—Halliday wrote of Darwin's final line: "The resounding lexicogrammatical cadence brings the clause, the sentence, the paragraph, the chapter and the book to a crashing conclusion with a momentum to which I can think of no parallel elsewhere in literature—perhaps only Beethoven has produced comparable effects, and that in another medium altogether" (1993, 102). There is indeed *grandeur in this view of life,* and in the powers of language that express it.

Summary

It is always tempting to dissociate stylistic means from the substance of an argument. The place of style *after* invention in rhetorical pedagogy invites this separation, usually to the disparagement of style. But stylistic methods are better seen as the substance, the material in language of argument, since the material of argument is language. Both amplification and diminution are then indissociable effects in argument: the rhetor is always on a rising or falling curve; the slope is always positive or negative.

The techniques identified since antiquity for achieving amplification can give an item stylistic prominence in a text, conceptual importance in an argument, and psychological salience in the mind of a listener or reader. At the same time, techniques of amplification like those described by Quintilian offer a respectable list of how humans quantify, rank, and assess. They order synonyms by degree, line up series to a high point or even beyond, consider the unnamable greater than the namable, value up or down by comparisons, and make a fortiori inferences (the taller the cliff, the stronger the climber). These are the methods of heightening. To amplify by accumulation or quantity is to take advantage of the limitations in human attention and memory. When the audience is looking at *this,* and only *this,* and *this* again, it cannot see *that* for *this.* Pure repetition helps less than the dazzling array of techniques outlined by Erasmus for copious restating and taking up space by adding details, descriptions, propositions, premises, images, comparisons, exempla, parables, and more. A special place for these modules of expansion was offered in the *epicheireme,* the expanded syllogism that comes close to being an all-purpose unit of argumentation. While Amplification is doing all this work, Diminishing runs Quintilian's techniques in reverse or has less, or nothing, to say.

In an ultimate vision of rhetorical effectiveness, audiences are not convinced or persuaded so much as they are overcome and compelled to assent to what they hear or read. They may lapse from agreement later, but at the moment they are swept away by the sublime. Both sublime effects and "ordinary" persuasion can be traced to any of the sources covered in this text, from word choice to sentence and passage construction to interactive dynamic. The analyst identifying such sources in an interpretive argument necessarily anatomizes the text into small-scale features, as the analysis of the last paragraph of *On the Origin of Species* does in this chapter. But of course words, syntax, text, and constructed situation all work together in persuasion, and when they combine to the point that no further improvement seems possible, the result is sublime amplification. No wonder Cicero amplifies amplification in the *De Oratore* as "the highest distinction of eloquence" (1992, 353–55).

NOTES

1. http://sundaytimes.lk/040725/plus/9.html

2. Erasmus explains the pedagogical function of *copia* as follows: "I am not prescribing how one should write and speak, but am pointing out what to do for training, where, as everyone knows, all things ought to be exaggerated. Then I am instructing youth, in whom extravagance of speech does not seem wrong to Quintilian, because with judgment, superfluities are easily restrained, certain of them even, age itself wears away, while on the other hand, you cannot by any method cure meagerness and poverty" (1963, 14).

3. The famous early-twentieth-century trial lawyer Clarence Darrow had an astonishingly repetitive style. In his summation before the judge in the Leopold and Loeb case, he not only used frequent immediate repetition but also brought up the same points and phrases again and again. See Lief, Caldwell, and Bycel 1998, 165–209.

4. Under his ninth method of achieving *copia* in Part II, Erasmus lists *amplification,* by which he means all of Quintilian's five devices. The discussion of Method 9 is virtually a paraphrase of the corresponding section in Quintilian covering *incrementum, comparatio, ratiocinatio,* and *accumulatio* (1963, 58–60).

5. Erasmus offers as an example of the difference between supporting a *thesis* versus a *hypothesis* with arguments first for the general proposition, "Whether any man should marry," and then for the particular proposition, "You ought not to marry her, not at this time" (1963, 62). Erasmus was in fact using a subject that had been set as an exercise for schoolboys from antiquity. Versions remain in St Paul's discussion of marriage and Milton's essay on divorce.

6. Erasmus's separate subjects of description were folded into other catalogs of figures under devices named in *De Copia* in association with the description of things, *hypotyposis* (1963, 47); of persons, *prosopographia* and *notatio* (51); of places, *topographia* and *toposthesia* (54); and of times, *chronographia* (55). Each of these figures pops up in other manuals.

7. The term *epicheireme* has a complicated history of diverse meanings in early texts. See Kennedy 2005, 85, for clarification. Quintilian noted debates about the number of parts in the epicheireme (1921, II 351); he actually favored a three-part epicheireme, emphasizing the syllogistic spine, any element of which could be embellished. In this debate, as in so much else, he was following Cicero, who noted similar disagreements in the *De Inventione* (1976, 101).

8. Praising Berlin to an audience of Berliners matches Aristotle's observation, "for, as Socrates used to say, it is not difficult to praise the Athenians to an Athenian audience," (Roberts 1984, 60).

9. One twentieth-century specialist on style and composition, Nevin Laib (1993), deserves credit for reviving the concept of amplification.

10. In a section of the *Institutio Oratoria* devoted to describing the early education of the rhetor, Quintilian praised Homer as "a model and an inspiration for every department of eloquence. It will be generally admitted that no one has ever surpassed him in the sublimity with which he invests great themes or the propriety with which he handles small. He is at once luxuriant and concise, sprightly and serious, remarkable at once for his fullness and his brevity, and supreme not merely for poetic, but for oratorical power as well" (1921, IV 29).

11. The earlier drafts were published in 1909 by Darwin's son Francis. The monumental Cambridge University Darwin website offers facsimiles of the two original manuscripts (DAR6 and DAR7) as well as Francis Darwin's fair copy of the 1842 "sketch" (DAR113) and a professional copyist's clean version of the much longer 1844 "essay" (DAR217), to which Darwin made further changes. The original drafts of the 1842 and 1844 texts in Darwin's hand contain deleted lines not transcribed by Darwin's son. Of the four sentences of the final paragraph in the published version, sentences 1 and 2 are not in the earlier drafts. The earlier versions of the final sentences as transcribed by Francis Darwin are as follows. Bracketed wording is crossed out in the manuscripts.

1842

From death, famine, rapine, and the concealed war of nature we can see that the highest good, which we can conceive, the creation of the higher animals has directly come. Doubtless it at first transcends our humble powers, to conceive laws capable of creating individual organisms, each characterized by the most exquisite workmanship and widely-extended adaptations. It accords better with [our modesty] the lowness of our faculties to suppose each must require the fiat of a creator, but in the same proportion the existence of such laws should exalt our notion of the power of the omniscient Creator. There is a simple grandeur in the view of life with its powers of growth, assimilation and reproduction, being originally breathed into matter under one or a few forms, and that whilst this our planet has gone circling on according to fixed laws, and land and water, in a cycle of change, have gone on replacing each other, that from so simple an origin, through the process of gradual selection of infinitesimal changes, endless forms most beautiful and most wonderful have been evolved (1909, 52).

1844

From death, famine, and the struggle for existence, we see that the most exalted end which we are capable of conceiving, namely, the creation of the higher animals, has directly proceeded. Doubtless, our first impression is to disbelieve that any secondary law could produce infinitely numerous organic beings, each characterized by the most exquisite workmanship and widely extended adaptations: it first accords better with our faculties to suppose that each required the fiat of a Creator. There is a [simple] grandeur in this view of life with its several powers of growth, reproduction and of sensation, having been originally breathed into matter under a few forms, perhaps into only one [preceding phrase added in pencil above the line in the fair copy]; and that whilst this planet has gone cycling onwards according to the fixed laws of gravity and whilst land and water have gone on replacing each other—that from so simple an origin, through the selection of infinitesimal varieties, endless forms most beautiful and most wonderful have been evolved (1909, 254–55).

12. The laws listed in the second sentence are all Latinate terms in origin, with two exceptions: Growth and Struggle for Life. (*Struggle* first appears in ME but is likely to have an OE origin.)

13. The holograph of the 1842 text shows further second thoughts about this phrasing. Darwin originally wrote only "From death, famine and rapine." He then inserted above it "& the struggle"; he then crossed out "struggle" and wrote "war of nature," and then before the whole he added "concealed" and circled it into place before "war."

14. The fourth horseman, who comes first on a white horse, has a mixed significance in exegetical tradition, either as a conquering Christ or, in a later tradition that makes all four horses evil, as pestilence. As an agent of natural selection, pestilence would be a useful addition to this list, but Darwin's invoking of only the red, black, and pale horses in war, famine, and death is more textually accurate. *Rapine*, which Darwin would have been using in its older sense of *plunder, seizing the resources of another*, might also make sense as an agent of natural selection, but it is not in the Biblical series of the scourges of mankind.

15. The hesitation in calling the overall construction a compound sentence occurs because after the semicolon, the transition phrase in the final version, *and that*, is obviously meant to govern the final clause after the interruption of a dependent clause. In other words, the whole postsemicolon construction could be understood as a noun clause functioning as an object or a complement, as it seems to function in the 1842 version. Alternatively, *and that* could be a conjunction, expected before the second half of a compound sentence.

16. *Chiasmus* is sometimes used as an alternate name for, and hence confused with, the figure *antimetabole,* since both involve inversion. However, *antimetabole* involves the inverted positioning of key words (see above, p. 233), while *chiasmus* involves only the inversion of grammatical structures. (See Fahnestock 1999, 123–25.)

References

Abbey, Edward. 1971. *Desert Solitaire: A Season in the Wilderness*. New York: Ballantine Books.

Abelson, Robert P., and Roger C. Schank. 1977. *Scripts, Plans, Goals, and Understanding: An Inquiry into Human Knowledge Structures*. Hillsdale, NJ: Erlbaum.

Adamson, Sylvia, Gavin Alexander, and Katrin Ettenhuber, eds. 2007. *Renaissance Figures of Speech*. Cambridge: Cambridge University Press.

Agricola, Rodolphus. [1539] 1967. *De Inventione Dialectica*. With Alardus's Commentary. Reprint. Nieuwkoop: DeGraaf.

Allen, Woody. 1972. *Without Feathers*. New York: Random House.

Alpert, Mark. 1999. "The Invisible Epidemic." *Scientific American* (November): 19–20.

American Balanced Fund. 2003. "Semi-annual report for the six months ended June 30, 2003." Pamphlet.

The American Heritage College Dictionary. 3rd ed. 1997. Boston: Houghton Mifflin.

[Anaximenes]. 1984. *Rhetoric to Alexander*. In Jonathan Barnes, ed. *The Complete Works of Aristotle. The Revised Oxford Translation*. Vol. I: 2270–315. Princeton, NJ: Princeton University Press.

Anscombre, Jean-Claude, and Oswald Ducrot. 1983. *L'Argumentation dans la langue*. Bruxelles: Mardaga.

Arata, Luigi. 2005. "The Definition of Metonymy in Ancient Greece." *Style* 39.1: 55–71.

Atkinson, Rick, and William Claiborne. 1991. "Allies Meet Little Resistance, Capture Thousands of POWS." *Washington Post* (February 25): A1.

Austin, J. L. 1975. *How to Do Things With Words*. 2nd ed. Ed. J. O. Urmson and Marina Sbisà. Cambridge, MA: Harvard University Press.

Bacon, Francis. 1952. *The Advancement of Learning*. Great Books, vol. 30. Chicago: Encyclopedia Britannica.

Bain, Alexander. 1866. *English Composition and Rhetoric*. London: Longmans.

Bakhtin, M. M. 1981. *The Dialogic Imagination*. Trans. C. Emerson and M. Holquist. Austin: University of Texas Press.

Bakhtin, M. M. 1986. *Speech Genres and Other Late Essays*. Trans. Vern W. McGee. Austin: University of Texas Press.

Balz, Dan. 2003. "Other Candidates Question Dean's Record, Experience." *Washington Post* (November 25): A3.

Barnes, Jonathan. 1982. *Aristotle*. Oxford: Oxford University Press.

Barnes, Jonathan, ed. 1984. *The Complete Works of Aristotle: The Revised Oxford Translation*. 2 vols. Princeton, NJ: Princeton University Press.

Becker, Alton L. 1965. "A Tagmemic Approach to Paragraph Analysis." *College Composition and Communication* 16.5 (December): 237–42.

Bell, Ethel Paquin. 1990. "A Brief History of the Sneaker." *Land's End* 26.7 (June): 64.

Bergmann, Ludwig. 1959. "A New Technique for Isolating and Cloning Cells of Higher Plants." *Nature* 184: 648–49.

Bergon, Frank, ed. 1980. *The Wilderness Reader*. Reno: University of Nevada Press.

Bernstein, Basil. 1972. "Social Class, Language and Socialization." In *Language and Social Context: Selected Readings*, ed. Pier Paolo Giglioli, 157–78. London: Penguin.

Bitzer, Lloyd. 1968. "The Rhetorical Situation." *Philosophy and Rhetoric* 1.1: 1–14.

Bitzer, Lloyd. 1980. "Functional Communication: A Situational Perspective." In *Rhetoric in Transition: Studies in the Nature and Uses of Rhetoric*, ed. Eugene E. White, 21–38. University Park: Pennsylvania State University Press.

Black, Max. "Induction." *The Encyclopedia of Philosophy*, ed. Paul Edwards. Vol. III. New York: Macmillan and the Free Press, pp. 169–81.

Blair, Hugh. 2005. *Lectures on Rhetoric and Belles Lettres*, ed. Linda Ferreira-Buckley and S. Michael Halloran. Carbondale: Southern Illinois University Press.

Blair, Tony. 1997. "Remarks on the Death of Princess Diana." http://www.history.com/audio/tony-blair-on-the-death-of-princess-diana.

Blair, Tony. 1998. "Address to the Irish Parliament." November 26. http://www.historyplace.com/speeches/blair.htm.

Blair, Tony. 2001. Address at the Labour Party Conference. October 2. http://www.american-rhetoric.com/speeches/tblair10-02-01.htm.

Bolinger, Dwight. 1980. *Language, the Loaded Weapon: The Use and Abuse of Language Today*. London: Longman.

Boorstin, Daniel. 1985. *The Discoverers*. New York: Vintage Books.

Booth, Wayne. 1974. *A Rhetoric of Irony*. Chicago: University of Chicago Press.

Booth, Wayne. 1983. *The Rhetoric of Fiction*. 2nd ed. Chicago: University of Chicago Press.

Bradford, Richard. 1977. *Stylistics*. London: Routledge.

Bredvold, Louis I, Alan D. McKillop, and Lois Whitney. 1956. *Eighteenth Century Poetry and Prose*. New York: Ronald Press.

Broad, William J. 1999. "Evidence Puts Dolphins in New Light, as Killers." *New York Times* (July 6): D1.

Brody, Jane E. 1997. "Invisible World of the Seriously Depressed Child." *New York Times* (December 2): C9.

Brown, Sonya. 2005. "The Rhetoric of Body Formation." PhD diss., University of Wisconsin.

Burke, Kenneth. 1945. *A Grammar of Motives*. Berkeley: University of California Press.

Burke, Kenneth. 1950. *A Rhetoric of Motives*. Berkeley: University of California Press.

Burke, Kenneth. 1966. *Language as Symbolic Action: Essays on Life, Literature and Method*. Berkeley: University of California Press.

Bush, George W. 2001. "Address to a Joint Session of Congress," September 20. http://www.americanrhetoric.com.

Butler, Paul. 2008. *Out of Style:Reanimating Stylisitic Study in Rhetoric and Composition*. Logan: Utah State University Press.

Cabela's. 2003. Master Catalog. Spring Edition 1. Sidney, NE: Cabela's Inc.

Campbell, George. [1776] 1963. *The Philosophy of Rhetoric*, ed. Lloyd F. Bitzer. Carbondale: Southern Illinois University Press.

Campbell, John Angus. 1987. "Charles Darwin: Rhetorician of Science." In *The Rhetoric of the Human Sciences*. ed. J. S. Nelson, A. Megill, and D. N. McCloskey, 69–86. Madison: University of Wisconsin Press.

Campbell, John Angus. 1990. "Scientific Discovery and Rhetorical Invention: The Path to Darwin's *Origin*." In *The Rhetorical Turn: Invention and Persuasion in the Conduct of Inquiry*, ed. H. W. Simons, 55–85. Chicago: University of Chicago Press.

Candaele, Kelly, and John R. McDowell. 1999. "Don't Leave Out Community Colleges." *Los Angeles Times* (June 16).

Carruthers, Mary. 1998. *The Craft of Thought: Meditation, Rhetoric, and the Making of Images*, 400–1200. Cambridge: Cambridge University Press.

Carson, Rachel. [1941] 1991. *Under the Sea Wind*. New York: Penguin.

Carson, Rachel. [1962] 1994. *Silent Spring*. Boston: Houghton Mifflin.

Carter, Ronald, and Walter Nash. 1991. *Seeing through Language: A Guide to Styles of English Writing*. Oxford: Wiley-Blackwell.

Casson, Lionel. 1981. "Godliness & Work." *Science* 81 2(7): 36–43.

Caws, Peter. 1987. "Confused in Alabama." *Washington Post* (March 8): B7.

Ceccarelli, Leah. 2001. *Shaping Science with Rhetoric: The Cases of Dobzhansky, Schrödinger, and Wilson*. Chicago: University of Chicago Press.

Chafe, Wallace, and Jane Danielewicz. 1987. "Properties of Spoken and Written Language." In *Comprehending Oral and Written Language*, ed. Rosalind Horowitz and S. Jay Samuels, 83–113. New York: Academic Press.

Chafe, Wallace. 1988. "Punctuation and the Prosody of Written Language." *Written Communication* 5.4: 395–426.

Chilton, Paul. 2004. *Analyzing Political Discourse: Theory and Practice*. London: Routledge.

Ching, Marvin. 1982. "The Question Intonation in Assertions." *American Speech* 57: 95–107.

Cho, Adrian. 2008. "Does Fermilab have a Future?" *Science* 320: 1148–51.

Christensen, Francis and Bonniejean. 1977. *Notes Toward a New Rhetoric*. New York: Random House.

Cicero. 1942. *De Oratore Book III, De Fato, Paradoxa Stoicorum, De Partitione Oratoria*. Trans. H. Rackham. Cambridge, MA: Harvard University Press.

Cicero. 1970. *On Oratory and Orators*. Trans. J.S. Watson. Carbondale: Southern Illinois University Press.

Cicero. 1976. *De Inventione, De Optimo Genere Oratorum, Topica*. Trans. H. M. Hubbell. Cambridge, MA: Harvard University Press.

Cicero. 1988. *Brutus, Orator*. Trans. H. M. Hubbell. Cambridge, MA: Harvard University Press.

Cicero. 1989. *Selected Political Speeches*. Trans. Michael Grant. London: Penguin.

Cicero. 1992. *De Oratore Books I–III*. Trans. H. Rackham. Cambridge, MA: Harvard University Press.

[Cicero]. 1981. *Rhetorica ad Herennium*. Trans. Harry Caplan. Cambridge, MA: Harvard University Press.

Clark, H. H., and S. E. Haviland. 1977. "Comprehension and the Given-New Contract." In *Discourse Production and Conprehension*. ed. Roy O. Freedle, 1–40. Norwood, NJ: Ablex.

Clinton, Hillary. 1995. "Speech to the United Nations Fourth World Conference on Women, Beijing, China." http://www.americanrhetoric.com/speeches/hillaryclintonbeijingspeech.htm.

Clinton, William Jefferson. 1993. "The Responsibilities of American Leadership." *New York Times* (October 8): A15.

Clinton, William Jefferson. 1995. "Oklahoma City Memorial Prayer Service Address." http://www.americanrhetoric.com/speeches/wjcoklahomabombingspeech.htm.

Clinton, William Jefferson. 1997. "Second Inaugural Address of William J. Clinton." January 20. http://www.yale.edu/lawweb/avalon/presiden/aiaug/clinton2.htm.

Clutton-Brock, Tim. 2002. "Growing from Pup to Patriarch: Juma's Story." *National Geographic* 202.3 (September): 69–72.

Cmiel, Kenneth. 1990. *Democratic Eloquence: The Fight over Popular Speech in Nineteenth-Century America*. New York: William Morrow.

Coatsworth, Elizabeth, and Mabel O'Donnell. 1949. *Runaway Home*. Evanston, IL: Row, Peterson.

Conley, Thomas M. 1984. "The Enthymeme in Perspective." *Quarterly Journal of Speech* 70: 168–87.

Conley, Thomas M. 1985. "The Beauty of Lists: Copia and Argument." *Journal of the American Forensic Association* 22 (Fall): 96–103.

Consigny, Scott. 1974. "Rhetoric and its Situations." *Philosophy and Rhetoric* 7.3: 175–86.

Cook, Walter A., S.J. 1989. *Case Grammar Theory*. Washington, DC: Georgetown University Press.

Copi, Irving M. 1972. *Introduction to Logic*. 4th ed. New York: Macmillan.

Costello, William T., S.J. 1958. *The Scholastic Curriculum at Early Seventeenth-Century Cambridge*. Cambridge, MA: Harvard University Press.

Coulmas, Florian, ed. 1986. *Direct and Indirect Speech*. The Hague: Mouton de Gruyter.

Crismore, Avon, and William J. Vande Kopple. 1997. "Hedges and Readers: Effects on Attitudes and Learning." In *Hedging and Discourse: Approaches to the Analysis of Pragmatic Phenomena in Academic Texts*, ed. R. Markkanen and H. Schröder, 83–114. New York: de Gruyter.

Crystal, David. 1988. *The English Language*. London: Penguin.

Crystal, David. 2003. *The Cambridge Encyclopedia of the English Language*. 2nd ed. Cambridge: Cambridge University Press.

Crystal, David. 2004. *The Stories of English*. Woodstock & New York: Overlook Press.

Crystal, David. 2006. *Words, Words, Words*. Oxford: Oxford University Press.

Crystal, David, and Derek Davy. 1969. *Investigating English Style*. Bloomington and London: Indiana University Press.

Dallas, Gregor. 2005. *1945: The War That Never Ended*. New Haven: Yale University Press.

Darwin, Charles. 1845. *Journal of Researches into the Natural History and Geology of the Countries Visited during the Voyage of the H.M.S. Beagle Round the World*. 2nd ed. London: John Murray.

Darwin, Charles. 1860. *On the Origin of Species by Means of Natural Selection*. 2nd ed, London: John Murray.

Darwin, Charles. 1861. *On the Origin of Species by Means of Natural Selection*. 3rd ed. London: John Murray.

Darwin, Charles. 1871. *The Descent of Man and Selection in Relation to Sex*. London: John Murray.

Darwin, Francis, ed. 1909. *The Foundation of the Origin of Species: Two Essays Written in 1842 and 1844 by Charles Darwin*. Cambridge: Cambridge University Press.

Dehaene, Stanislas. 2009. *Reading in the Brain: The New Science of How We Read*. New York: Penguin Books.

De Jonge, Casper C. 2008. *Between Grammar and Rhetoric. Dionysius of Halicarnassus on Language, Linguistics, and Literature*. Leiden and Boston: Brill.

DePalma, Anthony. 2006. "Canadian Authorities Expect More Arrests." *New York Times* (June 5).

De Waal, Frans B. M. 2006. "How Animals do Business." In *The Best American Science and Nature Writing*, ed. Brian Greene, 46–54. New York: Houghton Mifflin.

Dickson, Barry J. 2001. "Moving On." *Science* 291 (March 9): 1910.

Dillard, J. L. 1973. *Black English*. New York: Vintage.

Dinh, Viet. 2005. "Justice Not Served." *USA Today* (May 4): 19A.

Dionysius of Halicarnassus. 1910. *On Literary Composition*. Trans. W. Rhys Roberts. London: Macmillan.

Dowd, Maureen. 2002. "Father Knows Best." *New York Times* (March 20).

Downs, Douglas and Elizabeth Wardle. 2007. "Teaching about Writing, Righting Misconceptions: (Re)Envisioning 'First-Year Composition' as "Introduction to Writing Studies." College Composition and Communication 58.4: 522–84.

du Marsais, César. 1977. *Traité des tropes*. Paris: Nouveau Commerce.

Durham, Frank D. 1998. "News Frames as Social Narratives." *Journal of Communication* 48: 100–17.

Durso, Joseph. 1999. "Joe DiMaggio, Yankee Clipper, Dies at 84." *New York Times* (March 9): A1.

Dwyer, Jim, and Christopher Drew. 2005. "Fear Exceeded Crime's Reality in New Orleans." *New York Times* (September 29): A1.

Enkvist, Nils Erik, John Spencer, and Michael J. Gregory. 1964. *Linguistics and Style*. Oxford: Oxford University Press.

Erasmus. 1963. *On Copia of Words and Ideas*. Trans. Donald B. King and H. David Rix. Milwaukee, WI: Marquette University Press.

Fahnestock, Jeanne. 1989. "Arguing in Different Forums: The Bering Crossover Controversy." *Science, Technology and Human Values* 14: 26–42.

Fahnestock, Jeanne. 1992. "Connection and Understanding." In *Constructing Rhetorical Education*. ed. Marie Secor and Davida Charney, 235–56. Carbondale: Southern Illinois University Press.

Fahnestock, Jeanne. 1993. "Tactics of Evaluation in Gould and Lewontin's 'The Spandrels of San Marco.'" In *Understanding Scientific Prose*, ed. Jack Selzer, 158–79. Madison: University of Wisconsin Press.

Fahnestock, Jeanne. 1999. *Rhetorical Figures in Science*. New York: Oxford.

Fahnestock, Jeanne. 2000. "Aristotle and Theories of Figuration." In *Rereading Aristotle's Rhetoric*, ed. Alan G. Gross and Arthur E. Walzer, 166–84. Carbondale: Southern Illinois University Press.

Fahnestock, Jeanne. 2003. "Visual and Verbal Parallelism." *Written Communication* 20.2: 123–52.

Fahnestock, Jeanne. 2005. "Rhetoric in the Age of Cognitive Science." In *The Viability of the Rhetorical Tradition*. ed. Richard Graff, Arthur E. Walzer, Janet Atwill, 159–79. Albany: SUNY Press.

Fahnestock, Jeanne, and Marie Secor. 2004. *A Rhetoric of Argument*. 3rd ed. New York: McGraw-Hill.

Fairclough, Norman. 2003. *Analyzing Discourse: Textual Analysis for Social Research*. London: Routledge.

"FDR's Day of Infamy Speech: Crafting a Call to Arms." 2001. *Prologue Magazine* 33.4 (Winter): http://www.archives.gov/publications/prologue/2001/winter/crafting-days-of-infamy-speech.html.

Fehr, Ernest, and Bettina Rockenbach. 2003. "Detrimental Effects of Sanctions on Human Altruism." *Nature* 422 (March 13): 137.

Fillmore, Charles J. 1968. "The Case for Case." In *Universals in Linguistic Theory*, ed. Emmon Bach and Robert T. Harms, 1–88. New York: Holt, Rinehart, and Winston.

Fish, Stanley. 1982. *Is There a Text in this Class?* Cambridge, MA: Harvard University Press.

Fish, Stanley. 2011. *How to Write a Sentence: And How to Read One*. New York: Harper.

Fitzgerald, Patrick. 2005. "Transcript of Special Counsel Fitzgerald's Press Conference." http://www.washingtonpost.com/wp-dyn/content/article/2005/10/28/AR2005102801340.html.

Foss, Sonja K.1989. *Rhetorical Criticism: Exploration and Practice*. Prospect Heights, IL: Waveland Press.

Foucault, Michel. 1972. *The Archaeology of Knowledge and The Discourse on Language*. Trans. A. M. Sheridan Smith. New York: Pantheon Books.

Fowler, Roger. 1996. *Linguistic Criticism*. 2nd ed. New York: Oxford University Press.

Fowler, Roger. 1991. *Language in the News: Discourse and Ideology in the Press*. London: Routledge.

Freeman, Donald. 1981. *Essays in Modern Stylistics*. London: Metheun.

Freeman, James B. 1992. *Thinking Logically: Basic Concepts for Reasoning*. New York: Prentice Hall.

Freeman, Kathleen. 1983. *Ancilla to the Pre-Socratic Philosophers*. Cambridge, MA: Harvard University Press.

Freese, J. H., trans. 1991. *Aristotle: The Art of Rhetoric*. Cambridge, MA: Harvard University Press.

Gagarin, Michael, and Douglas M. MacDowell. Trans. 1998. *Antiphon & Andocides*. Austin: University of Texas Press.

Gallo, Denise. 2006. "Jefferson's Musical Legacy." Library of Congress: Information Bulletin (May). http://www.loc.gov/loc/lcib/0605/jefferson.html.

Galton, Francis. 1874. *English Men of Science: Their Nature and Nurture*. London: Macmillan.

Galton, Francis. 1889. *Natural Inheritance*. London: Macmillan.

Garreau, Joel. 2000. "Tough Love? Tough Luck." *Washington Post* (September 12): C1.

Gates, Henry Louis, Jr. 1996. "After the Revolution." *The New Yorker* (April 29 and May 6): 59–61.

Gaul, Gilbert M., and Mary Pat Flaherty. 2003. "Internet Trafficking in Narcotics Has Surged." *Washington Post* (October 20): A1.

Giamatti, A. Bartlett. 1989. "Giamatti: Talking Baseball." *Newsweek* (November 6): 87.

Geisler, Cheryl. 2004. "How Ought We to Understand the Concept of Rhetorical Agency?" *Rhetoric Society Quarterly* 34.3: 9–17.

Genung, John R. 1896. *The Practical Elements of Rhetoric: With Illustrative Examples*. Boston: Ginn.

Goffman, Erving. 1981. *Forms of Talk*. Philadelphia: University of Pennsylvania Press.

Gould, Stephen Jay. 1989. "The Creation Myths of Cooperstown." Natural History (November): 14–24.

Gould, Stephen Jay. 1991. "More Light on Leaves." *Natural History* (February): 16–22.

Grady, Joseph, Todd Oakley, and Seana Coulson. 1999. "Blending and Metaphor." In *Metaphor in Cognitive Linguistics*, ed. G. Steen and R. Gibbs, 101–24. Philadelphia: John Benjamins.

Gramley, Stephan, and Kurt-Michael Pätzold. 2004. *A Survey of Modern English*. 2nd ed. London: Routledge.

Grant-Davie, Keith. 1997. "Rhetorical Situations and Their Constituents." *Rhetoric Review* 15.2: 264–79

Gray, Henry. 1959. *Anatomy of the Human Body*, ed. Charles Mayo Goss. Philadelphia: Lea and Febiger.

Greenbaum, Sidney. 1996. *The Oxford English Grammar*. Oxford: Oxford University Press.

Grice, H. Paul. 1989. *Studies in the Way of Words*. Cambridge, MA: Harvard University Press.

Grillo, Stefano. 2006. "Leonardo's Vision." *Nature* 443 (October 5): 510.

Groarke, Leo A., and Christopher W. Tindale. 2004. *Good Reasoning Matters! A Constructive Approach to Critical Thinking*. New York: Oxford University Press.

Gross, Alan G., and Ray D. Dearin. 2003. *Chaim Perelman*. Albany: State University of New York Press.

"Guerillas Take Afghan Capital as Troops Flee." 1996. *New York Times* (September 28): A5.

Guzzi, Paul, and Robert Hayes. 1999. "New Fenway Park Is a Good Investment for All." *Boston Globe* (August 18): A13.

Haiman, John, ed. 1985. *Iconicity in Syntax*. Amsterdam: John Benjamins.

Halliday, M. A. K. 1996. "Linguistic Function and Literary Style: An Inquiry into the Language of William Golding's *The Inheritors*." In *The Stylistics Reader: From Roman Jakobson to the Present*, ed. Jean Jaques Weber, 56–86. London: Arnold.

Halliday, M. A. K., and Ruqaiya Hasan. 1976. *Cohesion in English*. London: Longmans.

Halliday, M. A. K., and J. R. Martin. 1993. *Writing Science: Literacy and Discursive Power*. Pittsburgh: University of Pittsburgh Press.

Harding, Jennifer Riddle. 2004. "Simple Regrets: Counterfactuals and the Dialogic Mind." PhD diss., University of Maryland.

Harrison, Peter. 2006. "Reassessing the Butterfield Thesis." *Historically Speaking* (September/October): 7–10.

Hart, Roderick P. 1997. *Modern Rhetorical Criticism*. 2nd ed. Boston: Allyn and Bacon.

Hatherill, Dr. J. Robert. 1999. "Are Today's Teens More Toxic?" *Chicago Tribune* (June 15): A14.

Hayakawa, S. I. 1978. *Language in Thought and Action*. 4th ed. New York: Harcourt Brace Jovanovich.

Healy, Patrick, and Glen Johnson. 2003. "Rivals Launch Attack on Dean at Debate." *Boston Globe* (November 25). Online at http://www.boston.com/news/nation/articles/2003/11/25/rivals _launch_attack_on_dean_at_debate/.

Heath, Malcolm. 1995. *Hermogenes on Issues: Strategies of Argument in Later Greek Rhetoric.* Oxford: Clarendon Press.

Hendrickson, Aletha Staunton. 1993. "The Rhetoric of Intimidation: A Study in the Rhetoric of Institutional Power." PhD diss., University of Maryland.

Hermogenes. 2009. *On Types of Style.* Trans. Cecil Wooten. Chapel Hill: University of North Carolina Press.

Herper, Matthew J. 1999. "Binge and Purge." *Reason* (November): 48–51.

Hill, David. 2006. "The Dark Side of Night Lighting." *Science* 312 (April 7): 56.

Holcomb, Chris, and M. Jimmie Killingsworth. 2010. *Performing Prose: The Study and Practice of Style in Composition.* Carbondale: Southern Illinois University Press.

Holloway, Marguerite. 1999. "The Aborted Crime Wave?" *Scientific American* (December) 281.6: 23–24.

Holzer, Harold. 2008. *Lincoln: President-Elect.* New York: Simon & Schuster.

Hooke, Robert. 1665. *Micrographia.* London: John Martyn.

Hopper, Paul J. 1998. "Emergent Grammar." In *The New Psychology of Language: Cognitive and Functional Approaches to Language Structure*, ed. Michael Tomasello, 155–76. Mahwah, NJ: Lawrence Erlbaum Associates.

Hopper, Paul J. 2007. "Linguistics and Micro-Rhetoric: A Twenty-First Century Encounter." *Journal of English Linguistics* 35.3: 236–52.

Hoskins, John. [ca. 1599] 1935. *Directions for Speech and Style.* Princeton: Princeton University Press.

Howard, Rebecca Moore. 2000. "Sexuality, Textuality: The Cultural Work of Plagiarism." *College English* 62.4: 473–91.

Howell, Wilbur Samuel. 1956. *Logic and Rhetoric in England, 1500–1700.* New York: Russell and Russell.

Huffington, Arianna. 2007. "Pursuit of Happiness." *Atlantic Monthly* 300.4 (November): 39.

Hyland, Kenneth. 1998. *Hedging in Scientific Research Articles.* Amsterdam: Benjamins.

"Inner Circle." 2009. *Family Circle Magazine* (February): 15.

Jasinski, James. 2001. *Sourcebook on Rhetoric: Key Concepts in Contemporary Rhetorical Studies.* Thousand Oaks, CA: Sage.

Jecko, Timothy. 1996. "Swimming in the Media Pool." *New York Times* (July 24): A25.

Jefferson, Thomas. 1776. "Jefferson's 'original Rough draught' of the Declaration of Independence." http://www.princeton.edu/~tjpapers/declaration/declaration.html.

Johnson, George A. 2008. *The Ten Most Beautiful Experiments.* New York: Knopf.

Johnson, Kirk. 2005. "45 Bodies Found in a New Orleans Hospital." *New York Times* (September 13): A1.

Johnstone, Barbara, and Christopher Eisenhart. 2008. *Rhetoric in Detail: Discourse Analysis of Rhetorical Talk and Text.* Amsterdam: John Bejamins.

Junger, Sebastian. 1999. "Risks that Make News." *New York Times* (July 31): A11.

Kambin, P., and J. L. Schaffer. 1989. "Percutaneous Lumbar Discectomy: Review of 100 Patients and Current Practice." *Clinical Orthopedics and Related Research* 238: 24–34.

Kandel, Eric R., James H. Schwartz, and Thomas M. Jessell. 2000. *Principles of Neural Science*. New York: McGraw-Hill.

Kaufer, David S. 1981. "Ironic Evaluations." *Communication Monographs* 48: 25–38.

Keefe, Patrick Radden. 2007. "The Jefferson Bottles." *The New Yorker* (September 3 & 10): 106–17.

Kennedy, George A. 1980. *Classical Rhetoric and Its Christian and Secular Tradition from Ancient to Modern Times*. Chapel Hill: University of North Carolina Press.

Kennedy, George A. Trans. 1991. *Aristotle on Rhetoric: A Theory of Civic Discourse*. New York: Oxford University Press.

Kennedy, George. Trans. 2003. *Progymnasmata: Greek Textbooks of Prose Composition and Rhetoric*. Atlanta: Society of Biblical Literature.

Kennedy, John F. 1961. "Address before the 18th General Assembly of the United Nations." http://www.jfklibrary.org.

Kennedy, Robert. 1966. "Day of Affirmation Address at Cape Town University." http://www.americanrhetoric.com.

Kenney, John. 2005. "Pitch Imperfect." *New York Times* (September 29): A35.

Kephart, Beth. 2005. *Ghosts in the Garden*. Novato, CA: New World Library.

Kerrane, Kevin, and Ben Yagoda. 1997. *The Art of Fact: A Historical Anthology of Literary Journalism*. New York: Simon and Schuster.

Kifner, John. 1991. *New York Times* (February 25): A1.[S1]

King, Martin Luther, Jr. 1963. "Letter from Birmingham Jail." http://www.africa.upenn.edu/Articles_Gen/Letter_Birmingham.html.

King, Martin Luther, Jr. 1968. "I Have Been to the Mountaintop." http://www.americanrhetoric.com.

Kirby, John T. 1997. "Aristotle on Metaphor." *American Journal of Philology* 118.4 (Winter): 517–54.

Kolln, Martha. 1998. *Rhetorical Grammar: Grammatical Choices, Rhetorical Effects*. New York: Longman.

Krakauer, Jon. 1997. *Into Thin Air*. New York: Anchor Books.

Kraus, Manfred. 2008. "Aphthonius and the Progymnasmata in Rhetorical Theory and Practice." In *Sizing up Rhetoric*, ed. David Zarefsky and Elizabeth Benacka, 52–68. Long Grove, IL: Waveland Press.

Kurlansky, Mark. 1997. *Cod: A Biography of the Fish That Changed the World*. New York: Penguin.

Kurzweil, Ray. 2007. "Frontiers." *The Atlantic Monthly* 300.4: 14–15.

Kutas, Marta, and Steven A. Hillyard. 1980. "Reading Senseless Sentences: Brain Potentials Reflect Semantic Incongruity." *Science* 207: 203–5.

Labov, William. 1973. *Language in the Inner City: Studies in the Black English Vernacular*. Philadelphia: University of Pennsylvania Press.

LaDrière, James Craig. 1943. "Prose Rhythm." In *The Dictionary of World Literature*, ed. J. T. Shipley. New York: The Philosophical Library.

LaFontaine, Sister Mary Joan. Trans. 1969. "Melanchthon: Elementorum rhetorices libri duo." PhD diss., University of Michigan.

LaFuente, Victor de, and Ranulfo Romo. 2004. "Language Abilities of the Motor Cortex." *Neuron* 41.2: 178–80.

Laib, Nevin. 1993. *Rhetoric and Style: Strategies for Advanced Writers*. New York: Prentice Hall.

Lakoff, George, and Mark Johnson. 1980. *Metaphors We Live By*. Chicago: University of Chicago Press.

Lamb, Sydney. 1999. *Pathways of the Brain: the Neurocognitive Basis of Language*. Amsterdam: Benjamins.

Lanham, Richard. 1983. *Analyzing Prose*. New York: Scribner's.

Lavoisier, Antoine. 1952. *Elements of Chemistry*. Trans. Robert Kerr. Great Books Series. Vol. 45. Chicago: Encyclopedia Britannica.

Leech, Geoffrey H., and Michael H. Short. 1981. *Style in Fiction: A Linguistic Introduction to English Fictional Prose*. London: Longman.

Leff, Michael C., and Andrew Sachs. 1990. "Words the Most Like Things: Iconicity and the Rhetorical Text." *Western Journal of Speech Communication* 54 (Summer): 252–73.

Leff, Michael C., and Gerald P. Mohrmann. 1993 [1974]. "Lincoln at Cooper Union: A Rhetorical Analysis of the Text." In *Landmark Essays on Rhetorical Criticism*, ed. Thomas R. Benson, 173–88. Davis, CA: Hermagoras Press.

Leshner, Alan I. 1999. "Why Shouldn't Society Treat Substance Abusers?" *Los Angeles Times* (June 11). Online at http://articles.latimes.com/1999/jun/11/local/me-45379.

Levinson, Stephen C. 1983. *Pragmatics*. Cambridge: Cambridge University Press.

Lewis, Edward Herbert. 1894. *The History of the English Paragraph*. Chicago: University of Chicago Press.

Lexington [pseudonym]. 1996. "The Kennedy Mystique." *The Economist* (August 24): 41.

Leyner, Mark. 1990. *My Cousin, My Gastroenterologist*. New York: Vintage.

Liang, S.-T., Y.-C. Xu, P. Dennis, and H. Bremer. 2000. "mRNA Composition and Control of Bacterial Gene Expression." *Journal of Bacteriology* 182.11: 3037–44.

Lief, Michael S., H. Mitchell Caldwell, and Ben Bycel. 1998. *Ladies and Gentlemen of the Jury: Greatest Closing Arguments in Modern Law*. New York: Simon & Schuster.

Lincoln, Abraham. 1989. *Speeches and Writings*. Vol. I. 1832–1858; Vol. II 1859–1865. New York: The Library of America.

Linkugel, Wil A., R. R. Allen, and Richard L. Johannesen. 1982. *Contemporary American Speeches*. 5th ed. Dubuque, IA: Kendall Hunt.

Logan, Shirley Wilson, ed. 1995. *With Pen and Voice: A Critical Anthology of Nineteenth-Century African-American Women*. Carbondale: Southern Illinois University Press.

Longinus. 1965. "On the Sublime." In *Aristotle/ Horace/ Longinus: Classical Literary Criticism*. Trans. T. S. Dorsch. London: Penguin.

Loury, Glenn C. 2002. *The Anatomy of Racial Inequality*. Cambridge, MA: Harvard University Press.

Lovett, Susan T. 2006. "Resurrecting a Broken Genome." *Nature* 443 (October 5): 517–19.

Lexington [pseudonym]. 1996. "The Kennedy Mystique." *The Economist* (August 24): 41.

Lunsford, Andrea A. 1998. "Alexander Bain and the Teaching of Composition in North America." In *Scottish Rhetoric and its Influences*, ed. Lynee Lewis Gaillet. Mahwah, NJ: Lawrence Erlbaum: 219–27.

Luther, Martin. 1994. *Basic Luther*. Springfield, IL: Templegate Publishers.

Lyons, John. 1995. *Linguistic Semantics: An Introduction*. Cambridge: Cambridge University Press.

MacDonald, Susan Peck. 1994. *Professional Academic Writing in the Humanities and Social Sciences*. Carbondale: Southern Illinois University Press.

"Malaria Quagmire [Editorial]." 2006. *Nature* 439 (February 2): 510.

Manguel, Alberto. 1996. *A History of Reading*. New York: Penguin Books.

Martin, Paul S. 1987. "Clovisia the Beautiful!" *Natural History* 96 (October): 10–13.

Martineau, Harriet. 1839. *The Martyr Age in the United States of America*. New York: S.W. Benedict.

Marx, Karl, and Friedrich Engels. 1970. *The German Ideology*, ed. C. J. Arthur. New York: International Publishers.

McCaffrey, Barry R. 1999. "Don't Legalize Those Drugs." *Washington Post* (June 29): A15.

McCain, John. 1999. "That Discourtesy of Death." *The Weekly Standard* (August 2): 8.

McGee, Michael Calvin. 1980/1999. "The 'Ideograph': A Link between Rhetoric and Ideology." In *Contemporary Rhetorical Theory: A Reader*, ed. John Louis Lucaites, Celeste Michelle Condit, and Sally Caudill, 425–40. New York: Guilford Press.

McIntosh, Carey. 1998. *The Evolution of English Prose, 1700–1800: Style, Politeness, and Print Culture*. Cambridge: Cambridge University Press.

McKenna, Stephen. 2006. *Adam Smith: The Rhetoric of Propriety*. Albany: State University of New York Press.

McPhee, John. 1968. *The Pine Barrens*. New York: Farrar, Straus and Giroux.

McPhee, John. 1976. *The John McPhee Reader*. New York: Farrar, Straus and Giroux.

McPhee, John. 1994. *Basin and Range*. New York: Farrar, Straus and Giroux.

McPhee, John. 2007. "My Life List." *The New Yorker* (September 3 & 10): 82–90.

McWhorter, John. 2001. *Word on the Street: Debunking the Myth of "Pure" Standard English*. New York: Basic Books.

Melanchthon, Philip. [1542] 1963a. "Elementorum Rhetorices." In *Corpus Reformatorum, Philippi Melanchthonis opera, quae supersunt omnia*, ed. C. Bretschneider. Vol. 13: 413–506. New York: Johnson.

Melanchthon, Philip. [1547] 1963b. "Erotemata Dialectices." In *Corpus Reformatorum, Philippi Melanchthonis opera, quae supersunt omnia*, ed. C. Bretschneider. Vol. 13: 508–759. New York: Johnson.

Mendillo, Michael, Paul Withers, David Hinson, Henry Rishbeth, and Bodo Reinisch. 2006. "Effects of Solar Flares on the Ionosphere of Mars." *Science* 311 (February 24): 1135–38.

Milic, Louis. 1967. "Winged Words: Varieties of Computer Applications to Literature." *Language Resources and Evaluation* 2.1: 24–31.

Milic, Louis. 1971. "Connectives in Swift's Prose Style." In *Linguistics and Literary Style*. ed. Donald C. Freeman, 243–57. New York: Holt, Rinehart & Winston.

Miller, Carolyn. 1984. "Genre as Social Action." Quarterly Journal of Speech 70.5: 151–67.

Miller, George. 1991. *The Science of Words*. New York: W. H. Freeman.

Mittwoch, Ursula. 2002. "'Clone': The History of a Euphonious Scientific Term." *Medical History* 46: 381–402.

Montefusco, Lucia Calboli. 2004. "Stylistic and Argumentative Function of Rhetorical *Amplificatio*." *Hermes* 132.1: 69–81.

Mueller, Janel M. 1984. *The Native Tongue and the Word: Developments in English Prose Style 1350–1580*. Chicago: University of Chicago Press.

Murphy, James L., ed. 1971 *Three Medieval Rhetorical Arts*. Berkeley: University of California Press.

Murray, Shailagh, and Jonathan Weisman. 2008. "Both Obama and Clinton Embellish Their Roles." *Washington Post* (March 24): A1.

Murray, Thomas E. 1986. "The Language of Naval Fighter Pilots." *American Speech* 61.0032: 121–29.

Musser, George, and Mark Alpert. 2000. "How to Go to Mars." *Scientific American* 282.3 (March): 44–51.

Nadeau, Ray. 1964. "Hermogenes' *On Stases*: A Translation with an Introduction." *Speech Monographs* 31.4: 361–424.

Nash, Walter. 1980. *Designs in Prose*. London: Longman.

Nash, Walter. 1989. *Rhetoric: The Wit of Persuasion*. Oxford: Basil Blackwell.

Newton, Isaac. 1672. "A Letter...Containing His New Theory about Light and Colors." *Philosophical Transactions* No. 80 (February): 3075–87.

"Next stop: Underground [Editorial]." 2007. *Washington Post* (February 7).

Nichols, Marie Hochmuth. 1993. "Lincoln's First Inaugural." In *Landmark Essays on Rhetorical Criticism*, ed. Thomas W. Benson, 51–88. Davis, CA: Hermagoras Press.

Nida, E. A., J. P. Louw, A. H. Snyman, and J. v. W. Cronje. 1983. *Style and Discourse: With Special Reference to the Text of the Greek New Testament*. Goodwood Cape: Bible Society of South Africa.

Nye, Joseph S., Jr. 2004. "You Can't Get Here From There." *New York Times* (November 29): A25.

"Nursing Home Owners Charged in Katrina Deaths." 2005. *USA Today* [Associated Press]. (Updated September 13). Online.

Oates, Joyce Carol. 2007. "The Human Idea." *The Atlantic Monthly* 300.4 (November): 22–23.

Obama, Barack. 2009. "Inaugural Address." http://www.whitehouse.gov/blog/inaugural-address.

O'Connor, Sandra Day. 2003. "Remarks at the National Constitution Center/ Liberty Medal Award Ceremony." July 4. http://www.supremecourtus.gov/publicinfo/speeches/sp_07-04-03.html.

Olasky, Marvin. 1995. *The Tragedy of American Compassion*. Washington, DC: Regnery.

Ong, Walter J. 1975. "The Writer's Audience Is Always a Fiction." *PMLA* 90.1: 9–21.

Ong, Walter J. 1982. *Orality and Literacy: The Technologizing of the Word*. London: Routledge.

Oppenheimer, Stephen. 2007. *The Origins of the British: A Genetic Detective Story*. London: Robinson.

O'Rourke, P. J. 1995. *Age and Guile Beat Youth and Innocence*. New York: Atlantic Monthly Press.

Parkes, M. B. 1993. *Pause and Effect: An Introduction to the History of Punctuation in the West*. Berkeley: University of California Press.

Peacham, Henry. [1593] 1954. *The Garden of Eloquence*. Facsimile reproduction. Gainesville, FL: Scholars' Facsimiles and Reprints.

Pepco [Potomac Electric Power Company]. 1984. *Maryland Customer Termination Rights* [Pamphlet].

Perelman, Chaïm, and Lucie Olbrechts-Tyteca. 1969. *The New Rhetoric: A Treatise on Argumentation*. Trans. John Wilkinson and Purcell Weaver. Notre Dame, IN: University of Notre Dame Press.

Peter of Spain [Pope John XXI]. 1990. *Language in Dispute: An English Translation of Peter of Spain's Tractatus, Called Afterwards Summulae Logicales*. Trans. Francis P. Dineen, S.J. Amsterdam: Benjamins.

Peterson, Roger Tory. 1980. *Eastern Birds*. 4th ed. Boston: Houghton Mifflin.

Plato. 1960. *Gorgias*. Trans. Walter Hamilton. New York: Penguin.

Plato. 1973. *Phaedrus and The Seventh and Eighth Letters.* Trans. Walter Hamilton. New York: Penguin.

Poster, Carol, and Linda C. Mitchell, eds. 2007. *Letter-Writing Manuals and Instruction from Antiquity to the Present: Historical and Bibliographic Studies.* Columbia: University of South Carolina Press.

Powell, Colin. 1991. "Military Briefing: Excerpts from Briefing at Pentagon by Cheney and Powell." *New York Times* (January 24): A11.

Powell, Colin. 2003. "Remarks to the United Nations Security Council" (February 5). http://www.globalsecurity.org/wmd/library/news/iraq/2003/iraq-030205-powell-un-17300pf.htm.

Pronin, Emily. 2008. "How We See Ourselves and How We See Others." *Science* 320 (May 30): 1177–80.

Pruden, Wesley. 2004. "The Kerry Insult of the Guard." *The Washington Times* (September 17).

Puttenham, George. [1589] 1970. *The Arte of English Poesie.* Kent, OH: Kent State University Press.

Queenan, Joe. 1991. "Drive, She Said." *New York Times Book Review* (March 17).

Quintilian. 1921. *Institutio Oratoria.* Trans. H. E. Butler. 4 vols. Cambridge, MA: Harvard University Press.

Quintilian. 2001. *Institutio Oratoria.* Trans. Donald A. Russell. Cambridge, MA: Harvard University Press.

Ramesh, Jairam. 2006. *Making Sense of Chindia: Reflections on China and India.* New Delhi: India Research Press.

Ray, John. 1717. *The Wisdom of God Manifested in the Works of the Creation.* 7th ed. London: Harbin.

Reagan, Ronald. 1989. *Speaking My Mind: Selected Speeches.* New York: Simon and Schuster.

Reid, Ronald F. 1988. *Three Centuries of American Rhetorical Discourse: An Anthology and a Review.* Prospect Heights, IL: Waveland Press.

Rice, Condoleezza. 2006. "Remarks at BBC Today—Chatham House Lecture." http://www.state.gov/secretary/rm/2006/63969.htm.

Richards, Robert J. 1993. *The Meaning of Evolution: The Morphological Construction and Ideological Reconstruction of Darwin's Theory.* Chicago: University of Chicago Press.

Rickey, Carrie. 1999. "A Mighty Force in the History of Moviedom." *The Philadelphia Enquirer* (May 18): F1.

Roberts, W. Rhys. 1984. *The Rhetoric and the Poetics of Aristotle.* New York: Modern Library.

Robinson, Ian. 1998. *The Establishment of Modern English Prose in the Reformation and the Enlightenment.* Cambridge: Cambridge University Press.

Rosch, Eleanor. 1973. "Natural Categories." *Cognitive Psychology* 4: 328–50.

Rosenthal, A. M. 1995. "While the Children Sleep." *New York Times* (September 22): A31.

Rossheim, John. 1990. "The Language of Color." *The World and I* (May): 288–91.

Rumelhart, David E. 1980. "On Evaluating Story Grammars." *Cognitive Science* 4.3 (July–September): 313–16.

Rutenberg, Jim, Marilyn W. Thompson, David D. Kirkpatrick, and Stephen Labaton. 2008. "For McCain, Self-Confidence on Ethics Poses Its Own Risk." *New York Times* (February 21): A1.

Safire, William. 1994. "Robust or Bust." *New York Times* (November 28): A17.

Safire, William. 1997. *Lend Me Your Ears: Great Speeches in History.* New York: W.W. Norton.

Safire, William. 2008. *Safire's Political Dictionary.* New York: Oxford University Press.

Salisbury, Stephan. 2003. "Memorial Hall OKd as Site for Museum." *Philadelphia Inquirer* (April 10): B1.

Salsburg, David. 2002. *The Lady Tasting Tea: How Statistics Revolutionized Science in the Twentieth Century*. New York: Freeman/Owl.

Sandell, Rolf. 1977. *Linguistic Style and Persuasion*. London: Academic Press.

Sapir, Edward. [1921] 1949. *Language: An Introduction to the Study of Speech*. New York: Harcourt Brace Jovanovich.

Schmandt-Besserat, Denise. 2002. "Signs of Life." *Archaeology Odyssey* (January–February): 6–7, 63.

Schiappa, Edward. 2003. *Defining Reality: Definitions and the Politics of Meaning*. Carbondale: Southern Illinois University Press.

Schildkrout, Enid. 1996. "Kingdom of Gold." *Natural History* 105.2 (February): 36.

Schlosser, Eric. 2007. "The Freak Show." *The Atlantic Monthly* (November): 46, 48.

Schoedinger, Andrew B., ed. 1996. *Readings in Medieval Philosophy*. New York: Oxford University Press.

Scovel, Thomas. 1998. *Psycholinguistics*. Oxford: Oxford University Press.

Scull, Andrew. 2006. "Failing the Ailing." *Nature* 443 (September 21): 275–76.

Shaw, Angus. 2003. "Zimbabwe Threatens to Quit Political Unit." [Associated Press] *Philadelphia Inquirer* (November 30): A6.

Shenon, Philip. 2003. "Former Domestic Security Aides Make a Quick Switch to Lobbying." *New York Times* (April 29): A1.

Short, Mick. 2007. "Thought Presentation Twenty-Five Years On." *Style* 41.2: 225–41.

Simon, David. 1991. *Homicide: A Year on the Killing Streets*. New York: Ballantine Books.

Simpson, Paul. 2004. *Stylistics: A Resource Book for Students*. London: Routledge.

Smith, Adam. 1963. *Lectures on Rhetoric and Belles Lettres*. Carbondale: Southern University Press.

Snoeck Henkemans, A. Francisca. 2009. "The Contribution of *Praeteritio* to Arguers' Confrontational Strategic Manoeuvers." In *Examining Argumentation in Context: Fifteen Studies in Strategic Maneuvering*, ed. Frans van Eemeren, 241–55. Amsterdam: John Benjamins.

Solomon, John. 1998. "Vote, or Else." *New York Times* (October 11): C2.

Solomons, T. W. Graham. 1992. *Organic Chemistry*. 5th ed. New York: Wiley.

Sonnino, Lee A. 1968. *A Handbook to Sixteenth-Century Rhetoric*. New York: Barnes & Noble.

"A Spoonful of Sugar." 2005. *Harper's Magazine* 311 (July): 16–17.

Springen, Karen, and Marc Peyser. 1998. "The Rat Race Begins at 14." *Newsweek* (March 30): 54.

Steinhauer, Jennifer. 2001. "In 'Uncharted Territory,' Giuliani Campaigns against Fear." *New York Times* (October 18): B1.

Steinhauer, Jennifer, and Campbell Robertson. 2005. "Areas Isolated After Storm Make Do." *New York Times* (September 15): A1.

Stelzner, Harmann G. 1993. "'War Message,' December 8, 1941: An Approach to Language." In *Landmark Essays on Rhetorical Criticism*, ed. Thomas W. Benson, 105–26. Davis, CA: Hermagoras Press.

Strunk, William, Jr., and E. B. White. 1979. *The Elements of Style*. 3rd ed. New York: Macmillan.

Stubbs, Michael. 1983. *Discourse Analysis: The Sociolinguistic Analysis of Natural Language*. Chicago: University of Chicago Press.

Stubbs, Michael. 2007. "On Texts, Corpora, and Models of Language." In *Text, Discourse and Corpora*, ed. M. Hoey, M. Stubbs, M. Mahlberg, and W. Teubert, 127–61, London: Continuum.

Susenbrotus, Joannes. 1953. "The *Epitome Troporum ac Schematum* of Joannes Susenbrotus: Text, Translation, and Commentary." Trans. Joseph Xavier Brennan. PhD diss., University of Illinois.

Swales, John M. 1990. *Genre Analysis: English in Academic and Research Settings*. Cambridge: Cambridge University Press.

Teachout, Terry. 1999. "Why We're Running Out of Classical Gas." *Washington Post* (July 25): B01.

Theroux, Paul. 1990. *To the Ends of the Earth: The Selected Travels of Paul Theroux*. New York: Ballantine Books.

Thomas, Keith. 1983. *Man and the Natural World: Changing Attitudes in England 1500–1800*. New York: Oxford University Press.

Thoreau, Henry David. [1854] 1991. *Walden; or, Life in the Woods*. New York: Vintage Books.

"To Build Bridges, or to Burn Them [Editorial]." 2006. *Nature* 443 (October 5): 481.

Toulmin, Stephen. 1958. *The Uses of Argument*. Cambridge: Cambridge University Press.

Trillin, Calvin. 2007. "Three Chopsticks." *The New Yorker* (September 3 & 10): 48.

Turner, G. W. 1973. *Stylistics*. London: Penguin.

Turville-Heitz, Meg. 2000. "Violent Opposition." *Scientific American* 282.2 (February): 32.

Tufte, Virginia. 2006. *Artful Sentences: Syntax as Style*. Cheshire, CN: Graphics Press.

Updike, John. 2007. "The Individual." *The Atlantic Monthly* 300.4 (November): 14.

Valiavitcharska, Vessela. Forthcoming. *Rhetoric and Rhythm in Byzantine Homilies*.

van Eemeren, Frans H., Rob Grootendorst, and Francisca Snoeck Henkemans. 1996. *Fundamentals of Argumentation Theory: A Handbook of Historical Backgrounds and Contemporary Developments*. Mahwah, NJ: Lawrence Erlbaum.

van Eemeren, Frans H., and Peter Houtlosser, eds. 2002. *Dialectic and Rhetoric: The Warp and Woof of Argumentation Analysis*. Dordrecht: Kluwer Academic Publishers.

Van Natta, Jr., Don. 1996. "The Fate of Flight 800: Investigators See 'Eerie Similarities.'" *New York Times* (July 31): B5.

Vatz, Richard E. 1973. "The Myth of the Rhetorical Situation." *Philosophy and Rhetoric* 6.3:154–61.

Verdonk, Peter. 2002. *Stylistics*. Oxford: Oxford University Press.

Verrengia, Joseph B., "Chimpanzees Said to Have 'Culture.'" 1999. AP News Service (June 16). Available at http://www.highbeam.com/doc/1P1-23230846.html

Vetsigian, Kalin, and Nigel Goldenfeld. 2009. "Genome Rhetoric and the Emergence of Compositional Bias." *Proceedings of the National Academy of Sciences* 106.1: 215–20.

Vickers, Brian. 1988. *In Defence of Rhetoric*. Oxford: Clarendon Press.

Vico, Giambattista. 1996. *The Art of Rhetoric (Institutiones Oratoriae 1711–1741)*. Trans. Giorgio A. Pinton and Arthur W. Shippee. Amsterdam: Rodopi.

Wales, Katie. 2001. *A Dictionary of Stylistics*. 2nd ed. Harlow: Longman.

Wallace, David Foster. 2007. "Just Asking." *The Atlantic Monthly* 300.4: 25–26.

Walzer, Arthur, Marie Secor, and Alan G. Gross. 1999. "The Uses and Limits of Rhetorical Theory: Campbell, Whately, and Perelman and Olbrechts-Tyteca on the Earl of Spencer's 'Address to Diana.'" *Rhetoric Society Quarterly* 29: 41–62.

Weaver, Richard. [1953] 1985. *The Ethics of Rhetoric*. Davis, CA: Hermagoras Press.

Weaver, Richard. 1990. "Language Is Sermonic." In *The Rhetorical Tradition*. ed. Patricia Bizzell and Bruce Herzberg, 1044–54. Boston: Bedford.

Wells, Rulon. 1960. "Nominal and Verbal Style." In *Style in Language*, ed. Thomas Sebeok, 213–20. Cambridge, MA: MIT and Wiley.

Welsh, Patrick. 1999. "Out of School, Out of Touch." *Washington Post* (June 20): B1.

West, M. L. 1965. "Tryphon *De Tropis*." *Classical Quarterly*, n.s., 15.2: 230–48.

Wharton, Henry Redwood. 1893. *Minor Surgery and Bandaging*. Philadelphia: Lea Brothers.

Whately, Richard. [1846] 1963. *Elements of Rhetoric*. Carbondale: Southern Illinois University Press.

White, Gilbert. [1789] 1993. *The Natural History of Selborne*. Oxford: Oxford University Press.

Wilensky, Robert. 1982. "Story Grammars Revisited." *Journal of Pragmatics* 6(5–6): 423–32.

Wilford, John Noble. 2000. "Ages-Old Icecap at North Pole Is Now Liquid, Scientists Find." *New York Times* (August 19). Online at http://www.nytimes.com/2000/08/19/us/ages-old-icecap-at-north-pole-is-now-liquid-scientists-find.html.

Wilgoren, Jodi. 2003. "A City Family Lands on Its Feet in the Country, but Still Treads Warily." *New York Times* (September 13): A19.

Williams, Joseph. 1975. *Origins of the English Language: A Social and Linguistic History*. New York: Free Press.

Williams, Joseph. 1989. *Style: Ten Lessons in Clarity and Grace*. 3rd ed. Glenview, IL: Scott, Foresman.

Williams, Raymond. 1983. *Keywords: A Vocabulary of Culture and Society*. Rev. ed. New York: Oxford University Press.

Williams, Zoe. 2003. "The Final Irony." *The Guardian* (June 28).

Williamson, George. 1951. *The Senecan Amble: A Study in Prose Form from Bacon to Collier*. Chicago: University of Chicago Press.

Wilson, Harris W., and Louis G. Locke. 1960. *The University Handbook*. New York: Holt, Rinehart and Winston.

Windt, Theodore. 1983. *Presidential Rhetoric: 1961 to the Present*. Dubuque, IA: Kendall Hunt.

Wines, Michael. 2003. "Ostracized by Commonwealth, Zimbabwe Says It May Pull Out." *New York Times* (November 29): A5.

Woodlief, Mark. 1999. Review of Bad Livers, *Industry and Thrift* (Sugar Hill). *CMJ New Music Monthly*. Issue 45 (January): 44.

Wolfe, Tom. [1965] 1999. *The Kandy-Kolored Tangerine-Flake Streamline Baby*. New York: Bantam Books.

Wolfe, Tom. 1982. *The Purple Decades: A Reader*. New York: Farrar, Straus and Giroux.

Wolfe, Tom. 2007. "Pell-Mell." *The Atlantic Monthly* 300.4 (November): 58–62.

Worth, Robert F. 2008. "Bin Laden Driver to Be Sent to Yemen." *New York Times* (November 25).

Yonay, Ehud. 1983. "'Top Guns' in Naval Flight School." *California* 8.5 (May): 94–102, 144–147.

Zakaria, Fareed. 2004. "Rejecting the Next Bill Gates." *Newsweek* 29 (November): 33.

Zarefsky, David. 2006. "Strategic Maneuvering through Persuasive Definitions: Implications for Dialectic and Rhetoric." *Argumentation* 20: 399–416.

INDEX

Abbey, Edward, 239–40, 249

Abelson, Robert P., 354

absolute phrases, 187–8

abstractions, 36, 50, 66, 72, 78, 166–7, 170–1
  abstract diction, 64–6, 365
  as grammatical subjects, 40, 151, 153–4, 167, 175, 177
  level of, 47, 64, 77

acronym, 18, 50, 52, 59, 84

Addison, Joseph, 177, 215

adjective (relative) clauses, 180–2

adverb (subordinate) clauses, 179–80

aequipollentia, 157, 396, 403

Aesop, 378, 399

affordances, 39, 188, 205, 250

a fortiori argument, 6, 180

African American Vernacular English, 30, 82, 310–1

agency, 75, 148, 150, 152, 161, 162, 167, 171–2, 175–7, 218, 282, 316, 404

agents, 149–50
  action structure, 10, 148–9, 159, 161, 166, 198
  created by a suffix, 46
  epistemic, 151
  rhetorical agent versus discourse conventions, 279

agnominatio, 53, 127–9, 130, 133, 134, 141–2, 291

Agricola, 395

allegory, 62, 100, 107–8, 11, 123–5, 141

Allen, Woody, 89

alliteration, 136–7, 143

allusions, 95–6, 99, 124, 321, 408

Althusser, Louis, 303

ambiguity (see also amphiboly), 143, 144, 202, 215
  in indirect speech, 313–4

Amossy, Ruth, 11

amphiboly, 118, 134–5, 143

amplification, 4, 6, 16, 70, 74, 101, 118, 179, 199, 203, 290, 338, 374, 387
  analysis last paragraph Origin of Species, 411–4
  and the sublime, 404–5
  as copia, 394–5
  as heightening vs copiousness, 390–1, 395–6, 405, 414
  Erasmus' methods, 398–9
  Quintilian's methods, 391–4
  through congeries, 394
  through inference, 392–3
  through strategic word choice, 391
  with comparison, 392
  with repetition, 392
  with series, 391–2
  with speechlessness, 392

anacenosis, 305

anadiplosis, 231

analogical word formation, 50–1

analogy, argument from, 105–8, 110–1, 123, 124, 180, 407

anaphora, 221, 227, 230, 231, 383

anastrophe, 207, 208, 220

Andocides, 317–9

Anscombre, Jean-Claude, 11

antanaclasis (see *puns*), 58, 134–6, 142

Anthony, Susan B., 375

antimetabole, 15, 233–7, 259, 417

Antiphon, 250

antiphrasis, 111, 114, 115, 123–6, 284

antithesis, 15, 231–3, 235, 237, 259, 289, 334, 388

antonomasia, 100, 103–4, 124, 125, 202, 349, 391

antonyms, (see also *opposed wording*), 62, 63, 77, 232–3, 237

Aphthonius, 319, 338, 378–9

apodosis, 214

aporia, 299, 300, 301, 303, 304

aposiopesis, 144, 266–7

apostrophe, 221, 291–3, 303, 327

appositives, 5, 184, 187–8, 189, 196, 199, 208, 409

appropriateness/ appropriate language, 66, 79–81, 83–8, 91, 94, 96, 105, 111, 117, 123, 127, 138, 139, 140, 297, 317, 335, 403

argument/ argumentation

    a fortiori argument, 6, 180

    concerning genus, 66–7, 236

    characterizing and evaluating, 38

    eduction, 228–30

    enthymeme, 16, 376–8

    epicheireme, 16, 399–403

    degrees of certainty in and modality markers, 158–9

    figures of, 223–37

    formal argument with *rogatio*, 301–2

    from comparison, 226–7

    from contrast, 37

    from definition (*definitio*), 235–7

    from elimination, 250

    from etymology, 132

    from inversion (with antimetabole), 234

    from opposites, 232

    in figures, 12, 226–7

    induction 227–8

    in narratives of events with *demonstratio*, 335

    in news stories, 17, 166

    in punctuation units, 260–1, 264–5, 272

    levels of generality in argument 66–70

    lines of argument, 15, 223

    over word meaning/ambiguity/ letter versus spirit, 56, 58

prosodic units of, 268–9, 270

syllogisms, 374–6

thesis/hypothesis strategy, 9, 67–8

using antithesis, 231–3

using familiar language, 93

using parallelism 226–30

using *polyptoton/* argument from conjugates 9, 131

using term-shifting through synonyms, 138

with interclausal relations, 357–8, 360, 366–8

with series, 239–40, 242

with stases, 301–2

Aristotle, 9, 16, 58, 94, 99, 108, 116, 118, 134, 155, 158, 210, 212, 225, 235, 236–7, 238, 250, 251, 256, 278, 286, 294, 334, 335, 336, 338, 340, 374, 376, 383, 384, 387, 416

    on metaphor, 104–6, 123

    Rhetoric, 6, 7, 14, 105, 123, 200, 223, 228, 232, 247, 302, 382

    Topics, 123, 223, 235, 237, 238, 286, 302

    On Sophistical Refutations, 134

Arnold, Carroll, 175

Ars Dictaminis, 277

aspect (of verbs), 59, 156, 158, 159, 163, 164, 175, 185

assonance, 34, 136, 142

asteismus, 297

asyndeton, 247–8, 250, 251

Austin, J.L., 10, 314–5, 320

Austin, Mary, 71–4

auxesis, 248, 390, 391, 394, 408

aversio, 292

Bacon, Francis, 53

Bahktin, Mikhail, 174, 319–21

Bain, Alexander, 381

Becker, Alton, 381, 388

Bentham, Jeremy, 76

Bernstein, Basil, 98

Biden, Joseph Jr., 80, 139–40, 143

Bitzer, Lloyd, 331–2

Blair, Hugh, 8, 14, 27, 215, 221–2, 224

    Blair's principles of effective sentences, 215

Blair, Tony, 40, 231, 282, 306, 311, 319, 320–21, 331

Bolinger, Dwight, 204, 217, 219

Bond, Julian, 153–4

Booth, Wayne, 113, 120

bracketing, as evaluation, 242–3

branching modifiers (left, right, middle), 198, 199, 208–10, 211, 213, 216, 221, 268, 349, 409, 410

brevity (see *diminishing*), 96, 120, 236, 402–3, 416

bringing-before-the-eyes (see *demonstratio*), 334, 335, 338, 340

British National Corpus (BNC), 11, 124

Brody, Jane, 129

Buchanan, Patrick J., 300

Buehl, Jonathan, 272

Buford, Bill, 194–5

Bugliosi, Vincent, Jr., 168–9

Burke, Edmund, 217, 340, 405, 407

Burke, Kenneth, 14, 61, 101, 285, 290, 320
    Burkean scene and circumference, 333–4
    identification, 285–6, 290
    pentad, 75, 333
    positive, dialectical, and ultimate terms, 76, 78
    terministic screens, 75

Bush, George W., 48, 82, 112, 118, 139, 156, 157, 224, 243, 312

Butler, Paul, 19

Caesar, Julius, 247, 291

caesim, 214

Campbell, George, 8, 14, 65, 328, 345

Campbell, Karlyn Kohrs, 310–1

Carson, Rachel, 203, 217–9, 220, 270–1

Carter, Jimmy, 63, 102, 225, 230, 240, 385–6

Carter, Ronald, 13

case grammar, 148

catachresis, 49, 100–1, 105, 125
    definition problems, 124

catch phrase, 92

Caws, Peter, 132–3

Ceccarelli, Leah, 135

Chafe, Wallace, 90–1, 258, 263–4

characters of style, 221–2

chiasmus (see *antimetabole*), 410, 417

Chilton, Paul, 327–8, 336, 340

Chomsky, Noam, 174

chreia, 379, 397

Christensen, Francis and Bonniejean, 19, 221, 388–9

chronographia, 338, 415

Churchill, Winston, 100, 192, 103, 107, 108, 133, 147, 152, 158, 182, 248, 360, 364

Cicero, 7, 8, 9, 77, 93, 110, 137, 214, 235, 236, 256, 267, 283, 294, 301, 316, 336, 372, 380, 385, 391, 392, 393, 399, 401, 405, 415
    De Inventione, 58, 166, 301, 33, 401, 405
    De Oratore, 385, 415
    De Partitione Oratoria, 67, 390–1
    Orator, 140
    Topica, 67

circumducte, 214

clarity (as a rhetorical standard), 32, 58, 79, 93, 180, 201, 221, 335, 337, 345–6, 349, 353, 362, 395, 404

clauses
    adjective/relative, 180–2
    adverbial/subordinate, 179–80
    comparative, 180
    complement, 181
    conditional, 180
    consequences of clause types, 182–3
    coordinate, 179
    independent vs dependent, 178
    noun, 182, 201
    proviso, 180
    purpose, 179–80
    restrictive vs nonrestrictive, 181, 200–1
    result, 179

Clay, Henry, 214

cliché, 92–3

climax (see also *gradatio*), 239, 246, 252

Clinton, Bill, 45, 50, 82, 102, 104, 118, 226, 231, 327, 330

Clinton, Hilary, 104, 244–5

clipping, 42, 43, 47, 59

Cmiel, Kenneth, 40

Cochran, Johnnie, 136

codes, elaborated and restricted, 98

cognitive linguistics, 11, 19

cognitive poetics, 19

coherence, between sentences/clauses, 16, 160
    combined sources of, 360–3
    global vs local, 345–6
    inferred meaning relations, 357–9
    interclause transitions, 355–60
    reading backwards to preserve, 355, 358
    rhetorical roots of, 348, 354
    schemas in 352–5
    signaled meaning relations, 359–60
    topic/comment source 348–52

cohesion, signs of, 346–8, 357, 361
    ellipsis, 346
    lexical ties, 347–8

cohesion (*continued*)
  reference ties, 346–7
  substitution, 347
collatio, 108, 398–9
colloquial language, 52, 79–81, 83, 88, 197, 219,
  284, 318
colon/cola, 15, 200, 214, 224, 228, 257–8, 266
comma/commata, 15, 201, 214, 257–8, 266
communication (trope), 124
comparison, argument from, 226–7
comparison, different grain sizes, 380–1
composition (as sentence art), 16, 214–5
  with punctuation 260–4
  compositional units built from sentence
    string, 372–3
  comparison in different grain sizes, 380–1
  enthymeme, 376–8, 387
  syllogism, 374–6
compound words, 44–5
concrete words, 64–6
confirmatio, 374, 406
conformatio, 170, 317
congeries, 137, 242, 245, 252, 370, 382, 394–5
Conley, Thomas, 249
Consigny, Scott, 332
consonance, 136, 142
content analysis, 62, 135
conversions in part of speech, 48–9
Copi, Irving, 238
copia, (see Erasmus, *De Copia*) 16, 247, 402, 403
  definition of, 395
  Erasmian advice on, 396–9, 415
  strand in amplification, 391
  with presence, 394–6
core vocabulary, 14
corpus linguistics/data, 11, 15, 57, 92, 104, 323, 324
Corpus of Contemporary American English
  (COCA), 11, 124, 142
correctio, 139–40, 142, 143
correctness, of language, 79, 144, 259, 287, 360
courtroom speeches (see *forensic*), 116, 299, 300,
  335, 396
criteria for rhetorically effective language, 79 (see
  appropriateness, clarity, correctness, force)
Crystal, David, 23, 40, 49
cursus system, 256–7, 372–3

Danielewicz, Jane, 90–1
Darrow, Clarence, 61, 67–68, 383–4, 389, 415

Darwin, Charles, 16, 360
  Voyage of the Beagle, use of *junk,* 54–6, 263
  Origin of Species, 171–2
  amplification of last paragraph, 405–14,
    416–7
  Descent of Man, passage construction 385–6
Darwin, Francis, 416
Declaration of Independence, 160–2, 171, 248, 261,
  285, 353
decrementum, 244
de dicto vs *de re* (in quotations), 323
definitio, 235–7
definition in argument, 235–7
  contrastive, 399
deixis, 16, 325–9, 339–40, 413
  "as if" deixis, 329, 337
  deictic center, 327
  imaginary, 334–5
  immediate, 325–7, 339
  immediate in written texts, 328–9
  thematized deixis, 327–8
De Jong, J.C., 11
deJonge, Casper, 220
deliberative, genre of rhetorical discourse, 4, 330,
  334, 378, 394
delivery, cannon of, 7, 204, 256, 272
  manner of, 112, 121, 181, 254, 271, 322, 366
demonstratio, 155, 340
  vs *descriptio*, 334–6
Demosthenes, 379, 405, 408
deprecatio, 304
derivational word families, 45–7, 131
de Saussure, Ferdinand, 128
descriptio, 334–5
description, 16, 38, 86, 109, 117, 176, 195, 196, 213,
  218, 230, 264, 329, 335–7, 338–9, 340, 341,
  358, 381, 387, 388, 398, 405, 413, 414
  and emotion, 336–7
  ekphrasis, 337–9
  Erasmian subjects for description, 339, 340–1, 415
diaeresis, 241
dialectical terms, 76, 78
dialectics/dialecticians, 8, 27, 66, 106, 118, 131,
  143, 175, 185, 191, 235, 238, 251, 302, 374, 387,
  396, 399
dialects/ regional and social, 30, 40, 61, 80–3, 86,
  87, 91, 96, 97, 320
  stylization, 309–11
  eye dialect, 309

dialogism (see *heteroglossia*), 321
Dickens, Charles, 320
dictionaries, historical, 59
diminishing, 402–4, 414
dinumeratio, 385–6
Dionysius of Halicarnassus, 214, 221
direct address (see *apostrophe*), 15, 73, 156, 280,
  281–3, 284, 291–2, 293, 295, 300
direct speech/quotation, 307–9, 321, 322
  stylization of, 309–11
discourse analysis, 10, 11, 13, 16, 83, 90, 201, 204,
  305, 327, 328, 334, 340, 386
discourse knowledge, in coherence, 356, 358, 360,
  363
disidentification, 290–1
distributio, 293, 295
Donatus, 7, 10
double voicing (see *heteroglossia*), 318–21
doubling to create new words, 52–3
Dowd, Maureen, 242–3
dubitatio, 120, 140
Ducrot, Oswald, 11
DuMarsais, Cesar, 100–1, 122, 123, 134
duplicatio, 143

ecphonesis, 267, 292
eduction, 228–30
Eggleston, Edward, 310
eidolopoeia, 319
Eisenhart, Christopher, 11
Eisenhower, Dwight, 48, 151, 180, 193
ekphrasis, 337–9
emotion/ passions (see also *pathos*), 52, 77, 204,
  230, 266, 267, 277, 278, 292, 294, 297, 304,
  319, 328, 340, 374, 388
  and description, 336–7,
  figures and emotions, 294, 297
emphasis, 154, 203, 390
  by position, 205–6
  by sentence role, 206–7
  combined sources, 208
  from inversions, 207–8
  with syllogistic form, 376
  with visual word forms 204–5
  with the voice, 204–5
enargeia, 335–6 (see also *hypotyposis*)
encomium (see *epideictic*), 191, 193, 195, 250, 304,
  379, 400
end weight, 199, 245, 246, 251, 257

energeia, 334, 338, 340, 398
English language
  historical layers, 14, 23–29
  range of synonyms, 14, 31
  world Englishes, 30, 82
enigma (*aenigma*), 125, 141
entailment, 370–1
enthymeme, 16, 224, 305, 357, 376–8, 399, 411
enumeration/ *enumeratio*, 241, 250–1, 252, 370, 382
epanalepsis, 231
epenthesis, 130, 142
epicheireme, 16, 399–402, 414, 415
epideictic, genre of rhetorical discourse, 37, 71,
  94, 116, 281, 292, 330, 335, 378, 393, 400
epistrophe, 230, 231, 326
epitheton, 191, 202
epizeuxis, 231
Erasmus, 9, 58, 67, 108, 125, 137, 157, 316, 338, 340,
  391, 394–6
  De Copia, 8, 14, 137–8, 338–9, 395, 397, 415
  methods of amplification, 396–9, 401, 407,
  411, 414
erotema, 289–9, 300, 301, 303, 304, 305, 375,
ethopopoeia, 309, 319
ethos (see also *pronouns, speaker/audience
  construction*), 38, 70, 87, 116, 278
etymological argument, 132–3
etymology, 51, 126, 132
euphemism, 124, 139–41
evidentia, 335, 336, 338
example, in argument, 38, 227–8, 356–9, 365, 366,
  369, 373, 379, 381, 382
  vs illustration, 228, 229, 238
exempla (see *example*), 398, 414
exigence, 212, 331–2, 339, 345, 346, 404
  in written texts, 332–3
  in scholarly articles, 340
exordium, 374, 406
expeditio, 386
expolitio, 238

fable, 378–9
fabrication of new words, 51
facilitas, 90
fact, rhetorical definition of, 286–7
Fagel, Susan, 11
Fairclough, Norman, 334
familiar language, 91–6
fantasia/phantasia, 91, 336–7, 340, 406

Faraday, Michael, 49

Fauconnier, Giles, 105, 106

Federalist Papers, 83

fictional address, 283–4

figurae syllogisorum, 374–5

figures of speech

  and emotions, 294, 297

  as a source of descriptive terminology, 9

  in rhetorical stylistics, 12

  of argument, 223–36 (see *antithesis, antimetabole, definitio, parallelism*)

  of consultation, 304–5

  of discourse management (see *dinumeratio, expeditio, praeparatio, transitio*) 384–7

  of question forms (see *(ant)hypophora, aporia, erotema, interrogatio, rogatio*), 298–302

  of sound, 127, 136–7 (see *isocolon, homeoteleuton, homeoptoton, assonance, consonance, alliteration*)

  of speaker/audience construction, 291–8 (see also *apostrophe, distributio, licentia, partitioning the audience, purging the audience*)

  of speech acts, 297–8

  of word choice, 127, 137–40 (see *synonymia, euphemism, correctio, emphasis, significatio*)

  schemes of words (see *agnominatio, polyptoton, ploce, antanaclasis, metaplasm*), 127–35

  tropes (see *allegory, antonomasia, irony, metaphor, metonymy, synecdoche*), 101–17

Fish, Stanley, 19, 222

Fitzgerald, Patrick, 253–4, 272

fixed expressions, 15

Flotz, Clara, 396

footing, 15, 287–8, 289–90 . 291, 297, 298, 303, 304

force/forcefulness in language, 5, 33, 66, 70, 79, 118, 128, 130, 133, 135, 151, 213, 221, 228, 261, 304, 335, 384, 404

foregrounding, 203, 278, 299

forensic/courtroom, genre of rhetorical discourse, 68, 116, 120, 136, 168–9, 296, 299, 300, 302, 306, 315, 317–8, 319, 334, 333–5, 374, 378, 379, 396, 402

formal language, 29, 34–5, 36, 39, 79, 81, 87, 97, 170, 187, 202, 273, 278

Foss, Sonja K.

Foucault, Michel, 279, 316

Fowler, Roger, 13, 164, 243

Franklin, Benjamin, 127, 135–6, 160

functional classes/categories of words, (see also

parts of speech), 13, 14, 70–7, 134

funeral oration/ obituary (see *epideictic*), 116, 120, 199, 330

Gage, Frances, 310

Galton, Francis, 62, 128, 252

general semantics/ semanticists, 18, 64, 65, 67, 70

generality, level in word choice, 8, 61, 63–4 (see also *abstraction*)

generalization, 151, 155, 227, 228, 356, 382

  in meaning expansion, 55

  unrolling, 397

genre, 10, 11, 14, 15, 16, 17, 42, 43, 48, 87, 100, 113, 130, 138, 150, 154, 168, 175, 192, 195, 205, 256, 267, 279, 280, 286, 288, 303, 307, 308, 315, 320–21, 323, 324, 329, 330, 332, 337, 339, 340, 345, 346, 362, 381, 386, 396

  and irony, 113, 114, 116, 121

  and progymnasmata, 378–9, 388

  and register, 85–6, 88

  of fictional address, 283–4

  of rhetorical discourse, 8, 10, 346 [see *epideictic, deliberative, forensic*]

Genung, John, 397

genus

  argument from, 66–7, 101, 123, 236, 238

  in definition, 235–6

  in series, 241–2, 251

  genus term, 34, 111

Gephardt, Dick, 308

gerund, 46, 132, 151, 176, 186, 201–2

gesture, 112, 203, 237, 256, 257, 285, 336

Giametti, A. Bartlett, 195–6

given/new patterns (see *topic/ comment*), 346, 348–52, 354, 355–8, 362, 363

Goffmann, Erving, 287–8, 291

Gore, Al, 169, 311

Gorgias, 6, 116, 136, 141, 250, 256

  Gorgianic figures, 136

Gould, Stephen Jay, 87, 130, 348–50, 352

gradatio, 218, 234, 243, 246, 251

grammaticus/ grammarian(s), 7, 10, 70, 77, 100, 105, 126, 156, 157, 174, 175, 200, 201, 202, 207, 214, 272, 322

Grant-Davie, Keith, 332

grapholect, 81

Gray's *Anatomy*, 34–5, 168

Grice, Paul, 120

  conversational maxims, 120–1

Groarke, Leo, 238
Gross, Alan, 155, 395

Halliday, M.A.K., 10, 12, 98, 164, 177, 346–7, 356,
    361–2, 386, 405, 414
Haraway, Donna, 310
Harrison, William Henry, 104, 106–7
Hart, Roderick P., 135, 175
Hasan, Ruqaiya, 346, 362
Hayakawa, S.I., 65
hedging, 65, 158
Hermagoras of Temnos, 9, 301
Hermogenes, 221, 301
heteroglossia, 318–21
historic/vivid present, 155
Holcomb, Chris, 19
holonym, 77
homeoptoton, 136
homeoteleuton, 75, 136
Homer, 60, 66, 110, 380, 416
homiologia, 138
homonyms, 31, 40, 58
Hooke, Robert, 53
Hopper, Paul, 11, 92
horismus, 236
Hoskins, John, 128, 138, 170, 236, 237, 297
humor, 111, 115, 116, 122, 125, 134, 138
    and register, 88–90
hyperbaton, 100, 101, 207–8, 214, 220, 408–9
hyperbole, 100, 117–8, 120, 121–2, 123, 124, 125,
    144, 238, 391, 412
hypernym, 63, 67, 151
hyponym, 63, 66, 67, 70, 397
hypophora/anthypophora, 299, 304, 382
hypotaxis/hypotactic style, 16, 210, 382–4, 387,
    389
hypothetical/ conditional premise, 366
hypotyposis, 124, 335, 415
hypozeuxis, 173, 174

I (pronoun choice), 280–1, 283
iconicity/iconic form, 15, 203, 215–9, 220, 223–4,
    335, 400, 408, 409, 410
    default form/meaning relationships, 217, 219
    prepared iconic forms, 15, 223–4, 227, 229, 232,
        235, 237
identification/ disidentification, 82, 283, 290
    Burkean principle of, 285–6, 289, 290, 308, 328
ideographs, 78

idiolect, 83, 310–11
idiom, 39, 57, 92–3, 152, 166, 190, 207, 328
illustration (vs example), 228
incrementum, 240, 243–4, 246, 251, 252, 415
indirect speech/quotation, 182, 307, 311
    ambiguous zones in, 311–14, 321, 322–3
induction, 227–8, 231, 238
infinitive phrases, 186, 202
informal logic/ logicians, 377, 388
intention
    in amphibolies, 134
    in irony, 111, 114–5, 117
    in speech act interpretation, 315
    intentional fallacy, 316
interactive dimension, 15, 277–303
interclausal relations (see also *semantic relations*),
    16, 346–7, 356, 360, 362, 363–71, 372, 382,
    383, 396
    addition/ alternation, 369–70
    conclusion/ nonclusion, 359, 367–8
    example/ exception, 356, 360, 365–6
    premise/ concession, 357–8, 366–7
    positive vs negative, 360, 362
    restatement/ replacement, 360, 364–5
    sequence/ anomalous sequence, 358, 359,
        363–4
    similarity/ contrast, 355–6, 368–9, 370
interpellation, 303
interrogatio, 298, 304, 305
intersubjective voice, 286
intertextuality, 95, 307
intonation, 112, 157, 188, 200, 204, 205, 247,
    263–4, 269, 300, 306, 319
    units of punctuation, 91, 258
invented speakers, 316–9
ironia, 111, 114, 115, 121, 122, 123, 125
irony, 15, 101, 111–7, 118, 119, 120–1, 123, 124, 141
    detecting in spoken and written texts, 112–4
    dramatic/situational, 114, 126
    ironia vs *antiphrasis*, 111–2, 114
    ludic irony, 114
    not tolerated, 116
    persuasive effects, 115–6
    primary vs secondary effects, 111, 114, 116, 122
    requiring intention, 114–5
    unintended irony, 115
isocolon, 12, 136, 224–5, 235, 237–8, 409
Isocrates, 6, 376, 379
it-cleft construction, 152

Jakes, T.D., 257

Jefferson, Thomas, 136, 160–2, 193

Johnson, Lyndon Baines, 34, 102, 107, 133, 136, 151, 191, 210, 223, 225, 237, 244, 332, 389, 392

Johnson, Mark, 105, 166

Johnson, Samuel, 261–3, 264

Johnstone, Barbara, 11

Jordan, Barbara, 119–20

junk, changes in meaning, 54–6, 60

kairos (see *occasion*), 16, 329–30, 339

Kaufer, David, 115

Kennedy, George, 337, 382

Kennedy, John Fitzgerald, 102, 104, 180, 225, 226, 231, 234, 237, 287, 331, 392, 402

    Cuban Missile Crisis, 155, 179, 182–3

    Inaugural address, 157, 172, 180–1, 246

    "Ich bin ein Berliner," 136, 152, 155, 226, 326

Kennedy, Robert, 188–9, 252

Kenney, John, 284

Kerry, John, 243

keywords/ key terms, 36, 75, 78, 135, 311, 333, 390

Killngsworth, M. Jimmie, 19

King, Martin Luther Jr., 17, 51, 90, 91, 107, 252, 257, 290

    I have a dream speech, 33, 90, 107, 162, 181–2, 405

    I have been to the Mountaintop, 90–1, 157, 224–5

    Letter from Birmingham Jail, 233

Kolln, Martha, 19, 348

Koren, Roselyne, 11

Krakauer, Jon, 52, 309

Kraus, Manfred, 338

LaDrière, Father Craig, 257, 272

Lahr, John, 37

Laib, Nevin, 416

Lakoff, George, 105, 166

Lamb, Sidney, 234

language, criteria for rhetorical effectiveness (see *appropriateness, clarity, correctness, forcefulness*)

Lanham, Richard, 221, 383

Larson, Richard A., 19

Lavoisier, Antoine, 234

Leech, Geoffrey, 12, 15, 306–7, 313, 315, 323, 324

Leff, Michael, 18, 135, 216–7

length, of sentences, 237–8, 269–71

level of generality (see also *abstraction*)

    ad hoc levels of generality, 68–9

    in argument, 9, 63–4, 66–8, 77

    in diction, 8, 9, 61, 106

    in Erasmus "unrolling a generalization" 397

levels of style (low/ middle/ grand), 79–81

Lever, Ralph, 29

Lewis, Edwin Herbert, 265

lexical field, 62–3, 77, 104, 107, 108, 226 (See also *semantic field*)

Leyner, Mark 98–9

licentia (frankness of speech), 296–7

Lincoln, Abraham, 17, 40, 43, 137, 236

    Cooper Union Address, 135

    First Inaugural Address, 149, 288–90, 380

    Gettysburg Address, 148–9, 326, 330, 334

    House Divided Speech, 398–9

    Sanitary Fair Address, 399

    Second Inaugural Address, 23, 208, 224, 330, 405

lines of argument (see also *argument, topos/ topoi*), 9, 66, 132, 223, 232, 235, 237, 251, 374, 379, 390, 398, 400, 401

Linguistics Research Center/ University of Texas at Austin, 77

literary stylistics, 12–3, 83

litotes, 117, 120, 121, 122, 123, 124, 183, 403

Long, Bishop Eddie, 257

Longinus, 337, 340, 404–5, 407, 408, 410

loose sentences, 211–2, 219, 220, 382

loose style, 213

loose vs periodic sentences, 15, 210–3, 214, 220, 221

Loury, Glenn, 128

Luther, Martin, 118, 302

MacArthur, Douglas, 281

MacDonald, Susan, 151

Madison, James, 83

Malcolm X, 127–8, 180, 200, 233–4, 290–1, 304

Martin, J. R., 98

maxims, 94, 99, 155

    maxims, Grice's, 120–1

McCain, John, 139, 312–3

McGee, Michael, 78

McIntosh, Carey, 219, 261, 263

McPhee, John, 79, 83, 92, 211

meaning, accumulating senses, 57–8

    loss and migration, 53

meaning change
  borrowing/by metonymy or analogy, 56
  conversion, 56
  expansion through generalizing, 56
  narrowing, 56
  polysemy, 58
meiosis, 117, 390, 394, 403
Melanchthon, Philip
  Elementorum Rhetorices, 8, 103, 238
  Erotemata Dialectices 27, 131, 143, 238, 251, 374,
    379, 390, 404
membratim, 214
membrum, 172–3, 174, 175
meronym, 77
metadiscourse, 384–6, 387
metalepsis, 103, 124, 125
metaphor, 12, 55, 93, 100, 101, 104–7, 124, 125,
    167, 170, 220, 290, 327, 333, 334, 391 (see
    Aristotle on metaphor)
  and analogical arguments, 106, 110–1
  conceptual, 15, 105, 106, 166, 340
  extended metaphor, 107–8, 109
  rhetorical, 15, 105, 123
  vs catachresis, 49
  vs simile, 109
metaplasm, 129–31, 142
metonymy, 54, 55, 56, 100, 102–3, 104, 105, 108,
    123, 124, 125, 167, 181
Milic, Louis, 19, 143, 264–5
Mill, John Stuart, 405
Miller, George, 62
Milton, John, 337
mind style, 154
modification
  amount of, 194–6
  analyzing, 196–9
  branching modifiers, 208–9
  clauses, 179–83
  dangling modifier, 202
  heavy, 195–6
  minimal, 194–5
  multiplying and embedding, 192–3
  phrases, 183–90
  placement of, 208–9
  resumptive modifiers, 188–9
  single words, 190–1
  summative modifiers, 189
Mohrmann, Gerald P., 135
mood (of verbs), 156–7, 163, 175, 176

morphemes, free or bound, 45
Mosteller, Frederick, 83
Mugabe, Robert, 308
multivoicing, 321–2
Murray, Thomas E. 97

narratio, 168, 335, 374, 378, 402, 406
narrative, in argument, 156, 213, 280, 378, 381–2
Nash, Walter, 13, 381, 388
new journalism, quoting practices, 309
newspaper, language choices
  arguability of, 17
  New York Times, 68–9, 121, 128, 129, 154, 164,
    199, 200, 215, 284, 295, 308, 309–10, 313,
    377, 393–4
  USA Today, 69–70
  Washington Post, 94, 139, 197, 200, 242, 253,
    272, 393–5
Newton, Isaac, 185, 186, 260–1, 265, 284
Nixon, Richard, 45, 47, 95, 150, 160, 180, 210,
    252, 287, 288, 385–86, 389, 402
nominal versus verbal style, 168–70, 185
nominalization, 169–70, 403, 404
nonce construction, 42–43 (see *new words*)
nonclusion, 359, 368
notatio, 341

Obama, Barack, 43, 48, 80, 92, 99, 102, 104, 134,
    173, 174, 186, 208, 221, 242, 273
objective voice, 286–7
objects of agreement, 112–3, 115
occasion (see *kairos*), 15, 34, 42, 66, 81, 90, 91,
    227, 280, 281, 318, 329–33, 339, 397, 400, 403
occultatio, 119
O'Connor, Sandra Day, 330
Ohmann, Richard, 19
Olasky, Marvin, 109–110
Oldenburg, Henry, 186, 260, 283
Ong, Walter, 204, 255, 303
onomatopoeia, 51–2, 100, 101, 125, 217
open letter, 283–4
Oppenheimer, Stephen, 24
opposed wording
  contraries, contradictories, correlatives, 232
  privatives, 238
oratio recta vs *oratio oblique* (see *direct* and
    indirect speech), 322
oration, parts of, (see *exordium, confirmatio,*
    narratio, partitio, peroratio, refutatio), 374

O'Rourke, P. J., 89–90, 98
Orwell, George, 18, 29, 139
oxymoron, 119

paean, 256
paradeigmata/ parallel cases, 228
paradox, 118, 119
paragraph structure, 381–2
   antithetical structure, 382
   Bain's types, 381
   generalizations plus support, 383
   Nash's types, 381, 388
   question/answer, 382–4
   sequence, 381–2
paralepsis, 119–20
paralinguistic features, 112, 256
parallelism
   cueing coherence, 356, 368, 370
   from repetition, 226
   in participial phrases, 198
   in series, 240
   in sound, 225
   in stress patterns, 225–6
   in syllables (isocolon), 224–5
   modifiers, 192
   strategic repetition, 230–1
   uses in argument, 226–30
parataxis/ paratactic style, 16, 210, 382–4, 387, 388, 389
parison (see *parallelism*), 225–5, 227, 235, 237
Parkes, M.B., 258, 273, 307
paroemia (see *proverb*), 125–6
paronomasia (see *agnominatio*), 128
parrhesia (see *licentia*), 296–7
participial phrases, 184–5
partitio, 241, 245, 374, 384, 406
partitioning the audience, 293–5
parts of speech (see also *functional categories*) 7, 14, 44, 46, 49, 50, 56, 61, 131, 134
   analysis with, 70–7
passage construction, 16
   compositional units, 373–4
   chains of enthymemes, 376–8
   cued with metadiscourse, 384–6
   epicheireme as passage unit, 399–402
   paragraphs, 381
   progymnasmatic modules, 378–9
passage prosody, 267–9
passive voice, 159–60

agentless 160
defense of passive 160–2
   in preserving topic/comment organization, 350
pathos (see also *emotion, pronouns, speaker/ audience construction*), 278, 335
Peacham, Henry, 115, 118, 122, 123, 126, 134, 142–3, 172, 173, 296–7, 385, 387, 391, 403
   The Garden of Eloquence, 8, 111, 125, 129–30, 170, 260, 298, 304
Perelman Chaim and Lucie Olbrechts-Tyteca, 8, 77, 78, 93, 106, 152, 156, 203, 228, 252, 312, 334, 395–6
   The New Rhetoric/ La Nouvelle Rhetorique, 8, 112, 115, 252, 279, 286, 287
period/*periodos*, 200, 214, 256, 257–61, 265, 266
periodic sentences, 210–1, 220, 409
periodic style, 212–3
periphrasis (circumlocution), 100, 101, 124
peroration/ *peroratio*, 335, 374, 384, 402, 406
personification (*personae fictio*), 150–1, 166–7, 324
   in science, 171–2
persuasive language, 8, 13, 14, 15, 16, 19, 29, 33, 37, 39, 43–4, 48, 51, 52, 53, 66–7
   and footing, 288
   consequences of parallelism, 224
   constructing occasions, 332
   four criteria for effective language, 79
   from historical layers, 33, 37
   from level of abstraction, 77, 152
   from new words, 43, 46, 51, 53
   from predication, 163, 174
   from prosody, 271
   from questions, 301
   from register mixing, 86–7
   from series; 248, 251
   from strategic repetition 230–1
   ideographs, 78
   in arousing emotions, 297, 336–7
   in Burke's terms, 75–6
   in irony, 115–6
   in Weaver's terms, 70, 76
   with copia, 394–5
   with deixis, 327–8, 337–8
   with figured speech acts, 296–8
   with forms of familiar language, 10, 93–6
   with heteroglossia, 321
   with modifiers, 195, 196, 198, 199
   with personal pronouns, 278–86
   with the sublime, 337, 404, 415

with tropes, 12, 104–5, 109, 111
with word forms and selection, 127–8, 137
Peterson, Roger Tory, 86
phrases
    built on nouns, 187–9
    built on verbs, 184–6
    prepositional, 189–90
Piaget, Jean, 395
plain language movement, 81
Plato, 255
    Gorgias, 141
    Phaedrus, 255
    Socrates, 416
ploce, 133–4, 135, 136, 142, 143
polyptoton, 9, 45, 130–2, 133, 134, 135, 136, 141,
    142, 143, 149, 169, 237
    polyptotonic path, 132
polysemy/polysemous words, 58, 134–5, 166,
    266
Powell, Colin, 87–8, 159, 176
praeparatio, 385
praeteritio (see *paralepsis*), 119–20
pragma-dialectics, 11
pragmatics/pragmaticists, 10, 14, 120, 278, 298,
    340
predicables, 238
predication, active vs stative, 148–9
    analysis of, 164–8
prefixes, 45–6
premise/ conclusion pairs (see *enthymeme*), 358,
    359, 368, 384, 387
prepared phrases, 50, 92–3, 97, 154, 190
prepositional phrases, 189–90
presence (as a rhetorical effect), 15, 77, 156, 203,
    362, 365
    and copia, 394–6
    of a word, 135–6
presupposition, 370–1
Priscian, 7, 10
progressive aspect of verbs, 57 . 59, 72, 156, 163,
    186, 202, 226, 406
Progymnasmata/ progymnasmatic genres, 319,
    323, 337–8, 378–9, 384, 387, 397
    chreia, 379, 388
    fable, 378–9
    koinos topos, 379
pronouns, 279–80, 303
    analysis of pronoun choices, 288–90
    familiar vs polite, 304

fictional address, 283–4
managing footing, 287–8
objective voice, 286–7
uses of *I,* 280–1
uses of *I* to *you,* 283–4
uses of *you,* 281–4
uses of *we,* 284–6
Prophyry of Tyre, 27–8, 238
prosody, 15, 255–7
    figured, 266–7
    in passages, 267–9
    monotony, 267–8
    of questions, 300
    oral-based, 272
    prosodic units as arguments, 268
    represented in punctuation, 257–9
prosopopoeia, 317–9, 323
protasis, 214
prototype, 64
proverbs (*paroemia*), 91, 94, 99, 125, 398
punctuation, 257–66
    and meaning, 264–6
    ellipses and dash, 266, 272
    exlamation mark, 267
    four mark system, 259–61, 265
    manuscript and printing, 259–64
    marking argument units, 260–1, 264–5
    oral vs grammatical, 257–9
punctus (*elevatus*/ *versus*/ *admirativus*), 258–9
puns (*antanaclasis*), 58, 95, 135–5, 173
purging the audience, 295–6, 303, 362
Puttenham, George, 140, 170
pysma, 299, 304

Queenan, Joe, 121–2
questions, 298–300 (see *(ant)hypophora, aporia,*
    erotema, interrogatio, rogatio)
    in formal argument/disputation, 301–2
    in the stases, 300–1,
    Peacham's "figures of consultation," 304–5
    Y/N, wh-, and tag questions, 305
Quintilian, 5, 9, 49, 58, 90, 93, 137, 141, 191, 202, 255,
    256, 292, 316, 317, 318, 319, 324, 335–6, 402
    definite vs indefinite questions, 67, 77
    Institutio Oratoria, 7, 14, 125, 147
    methods of amplification, 387, 391–4, 395, 397,
        398, 403, 407, 411, 413, 414, 415, 416
    on tropes, 100, 101, 105, 109, 111, 112, 119, 121,
        122, 123, 124

quotation (see *speech, incorporated*)
  direct, 307–9
  indirect, 311–4

Ramesh, Jairam, 48
Ramus, 101
ratiocinatio, 392, 401, 415
rational distance, 14, 35–6
Ray, John, 171
readability formulas, 269–70, 273
reader response theory, 280
Reagan, Ronald, 45, 50, 157, 210, 240
  Speech at the Brandenburg Gate, 157, 326–7, 400–1
refutatio, 374, 406
regiolect (see also *dialect*), 82
register mixing, 88, 321, 407–8, 412, 414 (see also *heteroglossia*)
register shifts, 14, 87–8, 121
registers, in language use, 14, 39, 44, 52, 61, 72, 74, 83–90, 91, 96
  disciplinary registers, 83–4, 92, 151
  elaborated specialist registers, 85, 190, 353
  genre and register, 85–6, 207, 404
  humor and register, 88–90, 98
  in heteroglossia, 320
  occupational registers, 84–5
repetition
  doubling word forms, 52–3
  in amplification, 392, 415
  in deixis, 326
  in *membrum*, 173
  in modifiers, 188–9, 198
  in parallelism, 224–30
  in *ploce* 133–6
  in prosody, 257, 268
  in series, 243, 246–7
  in similarity relation, 368
  lexical repetition, 361
  of roots, 131
  of sounds, 136, 138, 143
  of tropes, 107, 120
  strategic repetition, 230–7, 383
resumptive modifiers, 188–9
Rhetorica ad Herennium, 7, 49, 58, 100, 103, 110, 117, 128, 140, 143, 144, 155, 166, 236, 266–7, 292, 293, 296, 299, 317, 334, 335, 374, 378, 380, 386, 399, 401
rhetorical question (see also *erotema*), 298–9, 300–1, 375

rhetorical situation (see also *occasion*), 85, 93, 96, 114, 115, 150, 167, 190, 195, 279, 281, 331–2
rhetorical stylistics, 6–9, 10, 12, 14, 16, 36, 58, 66, 84, 90, 97, 100, 113, 128, 136, 142, 149, 174, 200, 210, 220, 223, 235, 236, 237, 260, 266, 279–80, 303, 338, 374, 376, 386, 390–1, 402
rhythm, 73, 174, 214, 215, 217, 221, 247
  cursus, 56–7
  poetic meter vs prose, 256
  tendency to regular rhythm, 257
  Valiavitcharska on, 271–2
Rice, Condoleezza, 280–1
Roberts, John, 302
Robinson, Ian, 257
rogatio (see also *subiectio*), 299, 300, 303, 305
  and formal argument, 301–2
Roget's *Thesaurus*, 62, 137
Roosevelt, Franklin Delano, 17, 48, 134, 163
  December 8, 1941 Speech, 3–6, 19, 227–8
Roosevelt, Theodore, 104, 125, 245, 247
Rumelhart, David, 370

Sachs, Andrew, 217
Sandell, Rolf, 19
Sapir, Edward, 53
Scaliger, 143, 170, 297
Schank, Roger C., 354
schemas, 16, 327, 346, 352–5, 356, 357, 358, 362, 363
schemes, of sentences (see *parallelism, antithesis, antimetabole*), 14, 15, 223–35, 237, 297, 334
schemes, of words (see *agnominatio, ploce, polyptoton*), 15, 47, 53, 61, 127–35, 137, 143
  orthographical schemes (see *metaplasm*), 130
Schlosser, Eric, 251
Schmandt-Besserat, Deniṣe, 254
Scott, Sir Walter, 26
scriptio continua, 254, 257
scripts, in coherence, 353, 354
Searle, John, 10
Secor, Marie, 155
semantic categories, of verbs, 162–3
semantic field, 46, 49, 61, 62–3, 77, 104–5, 107–8, 226, 227 (see also *lexical field*)
semantic relations, 16, 226, 356, 383 (see also *interclausal relations*)
semanticists, 8, 70, 76, 151, 232, 238
semiotic systems, primary and secondary, 254, 255

sentence analysis
    architecture, 203–8
    Blair's principles, 215
    loose versus periodic, 210–3
    modification, 178–96
    predication, 147–64
sentence length, 265, 271, 272, 273
    average and variety, 269–70
    sequence of lengths, 270–1
sentence types
    basic floor plans, 221
    loose vs periodic, 210–3
    sentence vs clause, 200
    simple/ compound/ complex, 178
    stative vs active, 174–5
    varying types, 269
    written vs spoken, 200
sentence variety
    length, 269–70
    openings, 268–9
    types, 269
sententia, 258, 376
series, 15, 216–7, 239–51
    bracketing, 242–3
    categorization, 241
    conjunctions, 246–8
    definition of, 240
    doubles in, 247, 251
    gradatio, 246
    in amplification, 391
    length, 245, 248–9
    open vs shut, 249–50
    order, 243–4
    topping a series, 391–2
sermocinatio, 317
Seward, William, 289–90
Shaugnessy, Mina, 19
Short, Michael, 12, 15, 306–7, 313, 315, 323, 324
significatio, 140–1
silence, 392, 403
simile, 109–10, 111, 398
    Homeric/Ciceronian, 110, 380
similitudo, 110
Simon, David, 282–3
Simpson, John, 209
Simpson, Paul, 162
single-word modifiers, 190–1
    definite articles/determiners, 190
    demonstratives, quantifiers, 191

slang, 97–8
Smith, Adam, 26–7
Smith, John, 101
Smith, Margaret Chase, 233–4
sociolect, 82
sociolinguistics, 10, 14, 80, 82, 90, 120, 278, 287, 330
Socrates, 141, 255, 416
Sorensen, Ted, 172
sorites, 378, 387–8
speaker/audience construction, 95, 96, 277–86, 280, 282, 283, 284, 298, 304
    figures of, 291–8
    universal audience, 286–7
speech acts/speech act theory, 10, 115, 119, 150, 154, 155, 161, 163, 267, 278, 280, 288, 303, 307, 317, 322, 323, 340
    definition of, 314–5
    figuring of, 297–8
    reporting of, 314–5, 316
speech, incorporated into another text
    direct quotation, 307–9
    heteroglossia, 319–21
    indirect quotation and ambiguities, 311–4
    inventing speakers, 316–9
    multivoicing, 321–2
    reporting speech acts, 314
    representing thoughts, 315
    stylized, 309–11
speech versus writing, 254–5
    as registers, 90–1
    transcription problems, 253
Spence, Gerry, 68, 136
Spencer, Charles, 156–7
Standard Edited American English, 80–1
stasis/stases, 166, 235, 301–2, 304, 403, 411
Steinbeck, John, 155
Steinhauer, Jennifer, 215–6, 220
Stelzner, Hermann G., 19
Stevenson, Adlai, 93, 183–4, 380
story grammars, in coherence, 353, 354–5, 370
strategic repetition, 230–1
strategic units of dicourse, 378
Strunk, William Jr. and E.B. White
    Elements of Style, 65–6
style types
    characters of style, 221–2
    epithetical, 191–2
    functional in the rhetorical tradition, 6–9

style types (*continued*)
  minimal vs heavily modified styles, 194–6
  nominal versus verbal, 168–70, 185, 195
  paratactic vs hypotactic, 382–4
  periodic vs loose, 212–4
  postmodern, 98
  spoken versus written, 80, 90–1
stylistics
  affective, 19, 222
  computational, 19, 83
  literary, 12–3, 83, 162
  rhetorical, 6–9, 12, 14–6 (see also *rhetorical stylistics*)
subiectio, 299, 305
subject/verb analysis (see *predication*), 164–8
subject/verb multiplication (see *hypozeuxis, membrum, syllepsis, zeugma*), 172–4
subjects (grammatical), 148–52
  abstractions, 151
  concepts, 152
  humans, 149–50
  rhetorical participants, 150
  slot fillers, 152
  things, 150–1
sublime, the rhetorical, 16, 337, 340
  as amplification, 404–5
  in Darwin, 407, 411–5, 416
suffixes, derivational and inflectional, 46–7
summative modifiers, 189
Susenbrotus, 8, 126, 292, 299
Swift, Jonathan, 24, 29, 113, 215, 264–5, 273
syllepsis, 124, 173, 174
syllogism (twenty-four figures), 374–5
  definition problems, 387
symploce, 133, 231
synecdoche, 100, 101–2, 105, 108, 123, 124, 125, 326, 394
synonyms
  in conceptual drift, 138
  in congeries, 242, 252
  in *synonymia*, 137–8
  rhetorical power, 31–2
  richness in English, 23–4
synonymia, 137–8, 142, 396

taboo deformation, 53
Talon, 101
testimony, personal/witness, 156, 159, 168, 280–1, 306, 309, 314, 317, 318, 379, 387, 396

text "acts," (see *speech acts*) 315–6
Theon, 337–8
thesis/hypothesis strategy, 9, 398, 415
Thomas, Helen, 288
Thoreau, Henry David, 329
thought representation, 315
Tindale, Christopher, 238
Todorov, Tzvetan, 135
topic/comment organization, 16, 160, 346, 348–52, 353–4, 356, 360–2, 372, 383, 388, 410
topicalization, 370
topographia, 338, 415
topos also *topoi*, (see also *argument*), 8, 37, 223, 250, 374, 379, 387, 397
  topics of division and adjuncts/circumstances, 251
  topics for persons, 199
toposthesia, 338, 415
Toulmin, Stephen, 401
tractatio, 170
trailing attributions, 312
transcription/transcript, 253, 257, 307, 308, 309, 323–4
transitio, 386
transition words, in coherence, 347, 356–70
transitions, between discourse sections, 384–5
transitivity analysis, 10
triplets, in phrases, 74, 137, 248, 251
trope (see also *irony, metaphor, metonymy, synecdoche*), 12, 14, 15, 49, 51, 100–7, 110–7, 122–6, 128, 137, 202, 297, 334, 391, 394
  master tropes, 101
  meaning in current criticism, 100
  tropes of words vs tropes of sentences, 111, 125
Truth, Sojourner, 310–1
Truman, Harry, 281
Trypho of Alexandria, 100
Ture, Kwame [Stokely Carmichael], 153
Turner, G.W., 90
Turner, Mark, 105, 106

universal audience, 286–7
upspeak/uptalk, 273
U.S. Constitution, 66, 131, 135, 162, 280, 285, 315, 316
utterance, as basic language unit, 174, 258, 264

Valiavitcharska, Vessela, 271–2
VanBuren, Martin, 104
Van Dyke, John C., 71–4

van Eemeren, Franz, 11
van Leeuwen, Maarten, 11
varieties of English
   familiar language 91–6
   geographical and social, 81–2
   idiolects, 83
   in genres 85–6
   registers 83–5
   regiolects and sociolects, 82
   shifting and mixing varieties, 86–90
   spoken versus written, 90–1
Vatz, Richard, 332
verb choices, 154–62
   active vs passive voice, 159–62
   aspect, 156
   modality, 158–9
   mood, 156–7
   negation, 157–8
   performative, 315
   progression of tenses, 155–6
   semantic categories, 162
Verhagen, Arie, 11
Verscheuren, Jan, 327
Vickers, Brian, 266
Vico, Giambattista, 8, 51, 101, 214–5
vocabulary, American
   influence of Spanish speakers, 30
vocabulary, English language
   American English, 30
   French layer/elegance, 25–7, 33–4, 3, 38
   Latin/Greek layer/formality, 27–9, 34–5, 39
   Old English core/sincerity, 24–5, 32–3, 37, 39, 88
   Scandinavia contribution, 25
   world contact, 29
vulgar/obscene language, 41, 52, 80, 87, 138, 139

Wallace, David Foster, 83
Walzer, Art, 155
Warren, Earl, 302
Washington, Booker T., 101
Washington, George, 131, 133–4, 246
we (inclusive vs exclusive), 285–6
Weaver, Richard, 14, 203, 320
   analysis of parts of speech, 70
   god, devil and charismatic terms, 76
Webster, Daniel, 95, 107, 267, 292–3, 375
Webster, Noah, 59, 130

Whately, Richard, 40–1
Whewell, William, 49
White, Gilbert, 413
White, Hayden, 101
Williams, Joseph, 18, 19, 40, 148, 348
Williams, Raymond, 77–8
Williams, Zoe, 114
Williamson, George, 273
Wilford, John Noble, 164–5
Wilson, E.O., 135
Wilson, Woodrow, 163, 294
Wolfe, Tom, 52, 113, 307, 309, 349, 367
word association tests, 62
word choice/ methods of analysis
   abstract versus concrete diction, 64–5
   content analysis/ clustered words, 62
   functional categories/parts of speech, 70–5
   in Darwin, 407–8
   language of origin 36–9
   levels of generality, 14, 63–4
   lexical field, 14, 62–4
   spoken versus written, 90–1
word formation, sources of, 42–53
   acronyms, 50
   analogy, 50–1
   blends, 47–8
   catachresis, 49
   clipping, 47
   compounds, 44–5
   conversions, 48–9
   doubling, 52–3
   fabrication, 51
   foreign borrowings, 43–4
   onomatopoeia, 51–2
   prefixes and suffixes, 45
   proper names to common nouns, 50
   taboo deformation, 52
word images, 217
WordNet, 64
"writing about writing" movement, 19

you, generic (see also *direct address*), 73, 281, 282, 308

Zarefsky, David, 67
zeugma, 173, 174, 175
Zipf's law, 40

CPSIA information can be obtained at www.ICGtesting.com
Printed in the USA
LVOW10s0216161113

361237LV00004B/10/P